Managerial Economics

IRWIN PUBLICATIONS IN ECONOMICS

Managerial Economics

APPLIED MICROECONOMICS FOR DECISION MAKING

S. Charles Maurice
PROFESSOR OF ECONOMICS

Charles W. Smithson
ASSOCIATE PROFESSOR OF ECONOMICS
BOTH OF TEXAS A&M UNIVERSITY

1985 SECOND EDITION

Homewood, Illinois

ISBN 0-256-02997-0

Library of Congress Catalog Card No. 84–80816

Printed in the United States of America

3 4 5 6 7 8 9 MP 0 2 1 0 9 8 7 6

To Our Former Students

Preface

This text is designed for use by students in undergraduate and introductory graduate courses in managerial economics. In writing this text, we had two fundamental objectives:

1. *We want to present the basic "core" of neoclassical price theory.* In our view, it is imperative that a student have a solid foundation in the basics of microtheory in order to make *sound* managerial decisions. Given this basic objective of providing the core of microtheory, we will concentrate on what we view as the fundamentals and will try to avoid getting bogged down in esoteric issues that have little, if any, bearing on the way managerial decisions ought to be made.

2. *We want to show how the theoretical concepts can actually be implemented by the manager of a firm.* All too often, students leave economics courses with the mistaken view that economics is somehow akin to metaphysics. (Many of our students have been very surprised to find that the solutions we illustrate graphically can be implemented using real-world data to provide the profit-maximizing solution to problems facing firms.) Hence, we want to show how the underlying economic relations can be estimated and how these estimations can be used in conjunction with the theoretical concepts to yield optimizing conditions for a firm.

To summarize, our objective is to show students how economics can actually be USED.

The theoretical concepts used in this text draw heavily from the material in

Economic Analysis.[1] For this, both of us owe Charles E. Ferguson a great debt; he was instrumental in providing a structure for neoclassical microtheory that is reflected in the education of a multitude of students. However, the theory presented in this text is neither a restatement nor a condensation of the theory in that companion text. In this textbook, we have attempted to structure the theoretical discussion so that it will be of maximum use to the student who is interested in managerial decision making. Therefore, we spend much more time looking at the way an optimizing decision—from the point of view of the firm—*should* be made, and very little time on the welfare issues that would be covered in a course in microeconomic theory.

With respect to the empirical discussions, let us make a point here that will be repeated many times through this text: In these discussions, our purpose is simply to demonstrate to students that estimations can be used by managers in applying the theoretical relations. It is not our purpose to teach students how to perform the empirical estimations; rather, we want to show how the results of these estimations can be used—our emphasis is on how to interpret the results, not on how to obtain the estimates.

In our empirical discussions we have tried to indicate various available methods of estimation; but we spend most of our time dealing with regression analysis. There are several reasons for our concentration on statistical regression analysis. First, this technique permits us to use a common "tool" to examine the various functions that we will want to estimate. (We can use the same basic technique to obtain estimates of production, cost, and demand functions.) Second, it is a technique that is widely used in making business decisions. And, given the widespread use of small computers, it appears that this tool will become increasingly more valuable in the near future. We feel that it is essential for students to obtain a background in the manner in which regression should (and should not) be used. Third, limitations on the size of the text precluded a more comprehensive discussion of some of the alternative estimation techniques. Most notable among the techniques that are not covered is linear programming. It was our opinion (and the opinion of many users of the first edition of this text) that the topic is covered in enough other courses that we could dispense with it in this text.

We were gratified by the response of students and of instructors to the first edition of this text. However, as with any first edition, users of the text pointed out to us numerous instances in which the text could be improved. We sincerely believe that this edition represents a major improvement over the first edition.

When we began this revision, we fully expected that our changes would be rather minor. But, as we read the comments of users, we eventually came to the opinion that a major revision was needed. Hence, it turned out that this

---

[1]S. Charles Maurice, Owen R. Phillips, and C. E. Ferguson, *Economic Analysis: Theory and Application,* 4th ed. (Homewood, Ill.: Richard D. Irwin, 1982).

second edition is more than a simple revision. In this edition, we have restructured the order in which the material is presented, expanded many discussions that were too terse, reduced or eliminated some discussions that were not essential to the topic at hand, added some entirely new topics, and added and/or updated many Applications. Our objective was to concentrate on the body of material that the users found most useful and make that material as accessible as possible to students. We hope you will find that we were successful in attaining this objective.

Given the magnitude of the changes made in this edition, permit us to describe some of them. In this way, we can indicate the rationale behind the new material and the altered structure of the text.

Following the introductory chapter, we provide a block of material that we refer to as "The preliminaries." In this block of three chapters, we first provide the usual chapter on supply and demand. This chapter is meant to provide a review (or an overview) of the essentials of supply and demand. Following this, we present a very simple chapter that provides the basic rules for two kinds of optimization—unconstrained and constrained. In the first edition, this material appeared much later in the text. That was clearly a mistake. All of the problems in economics are optimization problems. By introducing the general concept of optimization very early in the text, we are able to show that all of the specific cases of profit maximization or cost minimization encountered in managerial decision making are simply special cases of these general rules of optimization. We conclude this introductory material with a very brief discussion of regression analysis. As noted earlier, our purpose is not to teach students how to do regression; e.g., not how to calculate the parameter estimates. Hence this chapter deals with the basic objective of regression analysis (fitting a scatter of data in the "best" way) and how the resulting estimates can be evaluated for use in managerial decision making.

In contrast to the traditional organization of microeconomics and managerial economics texts (and to the organization of our own first edition) we begin our discussion of the specific theoretical and empirical topics with "Production and cost"(Part 2) rather than "Demand"(Part 3). There are two major reasons for this nontraditional organization.

First, although we had decided to add a chapter dealing with indifference curves and the basics of consumer behavior (a point we will discuss in detail later), our experience has been that students seem to find it easier to understand isoquants than indifference curves. Therefore, by first developing the theory of production, we can essentially build our discussion of indifference curves "on the back of" our discussion of isoquants. (Indeed, in class testing this new edition at Texas A&M, we found that our students had much more success in understanding consumer equilibrium after first being exposed to the cost minimization equilibrium for the firm.

Second, since the empirical analysis of demand requires the consideration of the identification problem—a topic that is somewhat difficult—we felt that it would be better to first expose students to the more "standard" application of regression estimation that is used in the estimation of production and cost functions. Once students have some experience dealing with estimations, it is a little easier to introduce the complication of simultaneous equations.

The chapters that make up our discussion of production and cost (Chapters 5,6,7, and 8) are very similar to those that appeared in the first edition. While we have tried to improve on the discussions and exposition of these topics, the only substantive change is that the discussion of the employment decision that previously appeared in this block of chapters has been deferred. In this edition, we discuss the employment decision in the context of the relevant market structure, so we will discuss the firm's employment decision under both perfect competition and imperfect competition. (Chapters 13 and 15).

As noted above, we have added in our discussion of demand a chapter on consumer behavior and the individual consumer's demand curve. This addition was made in response to the request of many users of this text. Those users who requested this addition felt that a discussion of indifference curves was needed, either to reinforce the essentials of demand theory or to provide an analytical tool that will be used if the student takes additional courses in economics. (Note, however, that this chapter was structured in such a way that it can be skipped if the instructor desires.) In this chapter, we have tried to provide the basics of the theory of consumer behavior, while at the same time making it relevant to the issue at hand—managerial decision making. Thus, our applications are aimed at showing how an understanding of consumer equilibrium can be useful to the manager of a firm. Furthermore, we have included a discussion of advertising in this chapter to illustrate the desired effect of a successful advertising campaign.

In addition to this new chapter, the block of material dealing with demand contains a chapter on market demand (with emphasis on the crucial elasticity concept) and chapters on estimation and forecasting of the demand function. This material was contained in the first edition of this text. However, we believe that the way we have presented it in this edition makes it much more accessible. In particular, econometric forecasting is developed in a way that gives students more of an intuitive understanding of the process, rather than simply a technical or mathematical discussion of the way it is done.

Once the concepts of production, cost, and demand have been developed, we are in a position to look at the profit-maximizing decisions for a firm. Hence, the next two blocks of material provide the "payoff" for the discussions that have preceded them. These discussions use the theoretical and empirical tools developed for production, cost, and demand to provide answers to the three questions that must be answered by the manager of a firm:

1. How much should I produce?
2. What price should I charge?
3. How much of each input should I employ?

These questions are first considered for a firm operating in a perfectly competitive market (Part 4). In the first edition, we considered perfect competition and pure monopoly in a single chapter to describe the benchmark cases. However, we feel that it is easier for students if we differentiate between the perfect competition case (in which the firm has no market power) and cases in which the firm has market power (Part 5).

The theoretical discussion of perfect competition is much like that presented in the first edition. But, we have added a discussion of the firm's employment decision in a competitive market. It is with the implementation of the profit-maximizing decisions that this edition shows the most difference. In the first edition, we provided only a very brief description of the way these decisions could actually be implemented. In this edition, we have turned this discussion into a full chapter. It was our experience that students needed a more complete and more systematic description of the way a firm could use estimates of the production, cost, and demand functions to obtain estimates of the profit-maximizing levels of output and input usage. This new chapter provides that description.

The discussion of the profit-maximizing decisions for a firm with market power again represents a reorganization of the topics that appeared in the first edition. This block of material is made up of four chapters. The first of these provides the theoretical relations for firms operating in a monopoly or a monopolistically competitive market. Except for the addition of the employment decision, this chapter contains basically the same material that was provided in the first edition (albeit reorganized and expanded). This theoretical discussion is followed by a new chapter that provides a more systematic description of the way the profit-maximizing conditions are actually implemented by a firm. (Again, it was our opinion that the brief description in the first edition did not sufficiently explain HOW the profit-maximizing decisions could actually be implemented by a firm.) In the first edition, we had a very complicated chapter that dealt with "alternative pricing policies." As it turned out, this chapter was simply too difficult for many students. We have, therefore, converted most of this material into a new, and we hope more understandable, chapter that sets forth the profit-maximizing conditions under the more realistic conditions of multiple plants, multiple markets, or multiple products. Our objective in this chapter was to demonstrate that the real-world complications do not change the basic optimization conditions; they only make the arithmetic a little more complex. In this vein, we have tried to avoid general algebraic solutions and instead have shown how these complications are dealt with by using some simplified examples. Some of the other material that was contained in this chapter in the first edition was moved to other chapters (e.g., cost-plus pricing was incorporated as an Application on monopolistic competition and limit pricing was moved to the chapter dealing with decision making over time). We felt that the discussion of transfer pricing was sufficiently difficult that it was eliminated in this edition. The final chapter in Part 5 is a new chapter in which we consider oligopolies. While this chapter uses the material contained in the first edition, its stress is somewhat different. In this new chapter, we try to emphasize the mutual interdependence that is inherent in oligopoly then show how firms are induced to behave, given that interdependence. As we note, this interdependence precludes the nice, simple solutions that exist in any of the other market structures and the answer to many questions for an oligopolist is "it depends."

Part 6 analyzes the behavior of a profit-maximizing firm over time. In this material we have substantially expanded the discussion we had in the first edition. In one chapter we look at the general problem of profit-maximization over time in order to get at the essential concept of discounting future flows of incomes (or costs). And we also examine limit pricing—as an example of a pricing strategy that explicitly incorporates the time dimension. In the final chapter we deal specifically with the firm's investment decision. In this discussion we describe the evaluation of investment projects, using both the net-present-value and the internal-rate-of-return approaches. And, we also look at the problem of choosing between competing investment projects.

As in the first edition, the body of the text contains no calculus. Simple algebra and (very little) geometry are all the mathematics necessary for a complete understanding of the material we present. We do, however, provide mathematical footnotes for those students who have had a course or two of calculus. These footnotes should make the text material a little easier for the mathematically inclined student. But, and this is a point we want to emphasize, the footnotes are not necessary to the understanding of the material presented in the text. Indeed, the footnotes can be disregarded entirely without any loss in understanding.

At the end of each chapter (except the first chapter), we provide two types of problems. First, there are several technical problems designed to reinforce the basic material continued in the chapter. The answers to these technical problems are straightforward and can be found in the text material. Second, we provide several analytical problems designed to give the student some practice in decision making. While the answers to some of these analytical problems are straightforward, the answers to others are subject to interpretation. This ambiguity is by design since the solutions to managerial problems frequently are not straightforward.

In writing this text we have benefited greatly from the suggestions of students and colleagues who have used the first edition of *Managerial Economics*. (Many of them are thanked publicly in the following acknowledgments.) We feel that this edition represents a major improvement over the first edition; and these improvements would not have been possible without their input. Nonetheless, we continue to solicit your suggestions for ways in which we can improve this text.

Indeed, we view this text as an ongoing project which has as its goal to demonstrate to students that economics is not some dry and sterile subject, but rather is a discipline that is alive and extremely relevant. As we noted at the outset, our objective is to demonstrate to students that economics can be, and is, used. We feel that this revision represents a step in the right direction toward achieving our goal.

S. Charles Maurice
Charles W. Smithson

We are indebted to many people for the assistance they have provided in the development of this second edition. In particular, we want to acknowledge the comments and suggestions made by

Bruce T. Allen	Michigan State University
Ray Battalio	Texas A&M University
George C. Dery	University of Lowell
Arthur M. Diamond, Jr.	The Ohio State University
Walter D. Fackler	University of Chicago
David E. R. Gay	University of Arkansas
John H. Goddeeris	Michigan State University
Hae-shin Hwang	Texas A&M University
Thomas A. Klaasen	University of New Orleans
Tom K. Lee	University of California, San Diego
Owen Phillips	Texas A&M University
David Schutte	Texas A&M University
Loren C. Scott	Louisiana State University
John Tabb	Old Dominion University
Christopher R. Thomas	University of South Florida
David A. Walker	Georgetown University
W. T. Wilford	University of New Orleans
Daryl Winn	University of Colorado

We also wish to express our appreciation to the entire office staff of the Department of Economics at Texas A&M University, in particular Audrey Abel and Sheryl Thierry. They not only saw to it that this manuscript was prepared but also helped to maintain our sanity in the process.

S. C. M.
C. W. S.

Contents

1

Scope of managerial economics

Most of you probably have already taken one or more courses in economics and may be wondering how managerial economics differs from ''regular'' economics. There is really no substantial difference between ''standard economic theory'' and the theories used in managerial economics. The difference is almost entirely in the way the theories are applied—that is, in the emphasis of the course.

The primary emphasis of a course in microeconomic theory (also called price theory) is on how individual decisions of buyers and sellers lead (or possibly fail to lead) to efficient outcomes for society as a whole. In most price theory courses, the applications generally concern the effects of the actions of private or governmental decision makers on the economy. There is little concern with the way decisions *should be made*; the focus is upon the costs and benefits of the decisions to society as a whole.

On the other hand, managerial economics (or, as it is sometimes called, applied microeconomics) deals with *how decisions should be made by managers to achieve the firm's goals*—in particular, how to achieve profit maximization. These decisions, or their results, may or may not be beneficial from society's viewpoint. Although important, such welfare consequences are of secondary consideration in managerial economics.

Despite the difference in emphasis, a primary concern in a managerial economics course is with learning the fundamentals of microeconomic theory—the basic tools used by economists. Let us emphasize at the beginning that while these theories are relatively simple, they are the same theoretical methods used by "real-world" decision makers. In other words, although the economic theory used in this text is relatively simple, it is sophisticated enough to be used in a great deal of managerial decision making.

In this text, you will use economic theory to analyze important and relevant economic problems. You will learn to analyze decision-making problems similar to those currently being considered by analysts employed by the nation's largest firms. It is not our intention to train you to be a professional economist. This text is designed to help you learn basic economic theory and to allow you to practice using economics in order to become a competent professional decision maker and manager: The basic theoretical tools, the fundamental methods of analysis, and the basic approaches to problem solving used by professional economists and business analysts are those you will learn to use.

The major reason for studying managerial economics is that it is useful. Every manager—in fact, every person—makes economic decisions every day. We will always face problems of scarcities and consequently must make choices. A knowledge of economics helps us make wise choices. Therefore, all students will find managerial economics useful in both their professional and their private lives.

Students who choose business as a career will find economics particularly useful. (Note that people who become doctors, lawyers, or other professionals are in business also.) Economics is extremely useful in business decision making—decision making designed to increase the firm's profit and enable the firm to operate more efficiently. Economics is useful in helping decision makers decide how to adapt to external changes in economic variables. Increasing advertising or undertaking investments involve economic decisions, and an understanding of economic theory helps managers make the right (most profitable) decisions.

A knowledge of economics is useful also to people who work for government agencies or nonprofit institutions. Although the goals of these agencies and institutions do not include profit maximization, they do involve economic efficiency. For example, a government agency may be required to allocate a given budget to attain the maximum benefit—in education, health care, and so forth—permitted by the size of the budget. Or it may be charged with attaining a certain goal at the lowest possible cost. These are economic problems, and managerial economics provides the tools needed to solve these problems. Just as it helps business managers, economics helps these managers of nonprofit organizations adapt to changes in the economic environment in the most efficient manner. So, managerial economics provides useful tools for many people who are employed in nonbusiness positions.

We have barely skimmed the surface, mentioning only a few types of decisions for which economic reasoning is useful. We will consider many such examples throughout the text. You will be able to increase your ability to analyze and solve such decision-making problems through practice. The better your understanding of economic theory and the more you practice applying the theory, the better prepared you will be for carrying out the fundamental tasks of managers.

1.1 WHY FIRMS EXIST

Although economics is useful for people who are not employed by business firms, much of this text will be concerned with the behavior of firms. At the outset, therefore, we should discuss why firms exist. For analytical purposes, economists divide the economy into two sectors—households, which purchase goods and services and sell their inputs, and business firms, which purchase inputs and sell goods and services.

An economy could, of course, function without firms. Some have in the past; some do so today. In the "pioneer era," households were virtually self-sufficient. However, this method of production is inefficient. Society loses the advantage of specialization, and households do not gain from trade.

Over time, households began to specialize in one type of production and to trade their products in the marketplace. This method was more efficient than producing all of the household's goods under a single roof. But large transportation and transaction costs were involved in such exchanges. People discovered that it was more efficient to bring together resources in one place and cooperate in the production of goods and services. This system of production permitted the advantages of specialization and division of labor. And, if there were cost savings associated with producing larger outputs, this cooperative form of organization would produce at a lower cost and drive out other organizational forms of production. Historically, this method of production did develop very rapidly during the 19th century. It is often referred to as the factory system.

But mere cooperation of resources does not necessarily make a firm efficient. To see why, let's look at a very simplified example. Suppose four of us bought a boat and entered the fishing business. We agree to split the profits equally. But, we soon find out that fishing is hard work. We each know that if one of us goofs off a little, we catch fewer fish than if we all fished hard all of the time. But every fish "the loafer" does not catch costs the person doing the loafing only one fourth of the value of that fish, because its value is divided into four parts. Thus, since the cost of goofing off is lower than if each of us received only the value of our own product, we are all induced to goof off more. So, production falls off. The same situation would clearly hold in a factory setting.

Hence, separating the ownership from the operation of the business venture has certain advantages. The owners would contract with workers for a fixed amount of their labor per period in return for a fixed payment per period. The owners would then claim any residual after the output was sold and the workers paid. (They would also suffer the loss if that should result.) The residual claimants (owners) could either personally assume the task of monitoring the workers to make sure they fulfilled their contracts or they could hire monitors, sometimes called managers, to do the job.

Firms of various types arise in an economy because they have been able to organize production more efficiently than other types of institutions could. Generally, we think of the owners of capital as doing the task of contracting with other resources and either hiring managers (monitors) or carrying out this task themselves. While this may be the most prominent form of organization, it is not the only one. In some countries, the labor-managed firm is a frequently used form of organization. Less frequently, we find the consumer-managed firm. But the point is that most production takes place in business firms. These firms are not merely forced onto a helpless society. The institution of business firms exists because this is an efficient form for organizing production. If some more efficient way of organizing production is discovered, that organization will replace the business firm. Until then, economics texts will treat production of goods and services as generally being organized in firms.

1.2 ROLES OF MANAGERS

Making decisions and processing information are the two primary tasks of managers. While we separate these two tasks for analytical purposes, in reality they are inseparable. In order to make intelligent decisions, managers must be able to obtain, process, and use information. Economic theory helps managers know what information should be obtained, how to process the information, and how to use it.

The task of organizing and processing information in conjunction with basic economic theory can take two general forms. The first involves a specific decision that must be made by the manager. The second general form involves using readily available information to carry out a course of action that furthers the goals of the organization.

Examples of the first form of decisions that managers might have to make are (1) whether or not to close down a branch of the firm that has recently been unprofitable, (2) whether or not a store or restaurant should stay open more hours a day, (3) how a government agency can be reorganized to be more efficient, (4) how a hospital can treat more patients without a decrease in patient care, and (5) whether to install an in-house computer rather than pay for outside computing services. All of these and a myriad of other managerial decisions require the use of basic economics. Economic theory helps decision makers know what information is necessary to make the decision and how to process and use that information. In other words, an important purpose of economic theory is to indicate what information will be useful in solving problems and enabling firms to operate more efficiently. After obtaining the desired information managers must then analyze this information and use it in connection with the theoretical and statistical tools available to make the best decision possible under the circumstances.

The second general form of managerial decision making involves using readily available information to carry out a course of action that furthers the goals of the organization. Basic economic theory is extremely useful to managers in this task also. Managers receive useful information every day from many sources. Some of these sources are *The Wall Street Journal*, business magazines such as *Business Week*, local newspapers, television, private newsletters, and conversations with others. Successful managers know how to pick out the useful information from the vast amount of information they receive. They know how to evaluate this information and act on it in order to further the goals of their organizations.

Of course, a manager must know the goals of the organization. As we mentioned above, managerial economics is useful not only to managers in profit-maximizing firms but also to managers in government and in nonprofit organizations. The primary goal of a manufacturing firm would be to maximize profits. The primary goal of a foundation could be to further some cause. A public hospital could have the goal of treating as many patients as possible—subject, of course, to certain standards. A state university could have the goal of educating, above a certain standard, as many students as possible.

We should emphasize, however, that the tasks of managers in practically all of these situations are the same. Each goal involves an optimization problem. The manager attempts either to maximize or minimize some objective function (frequently subject to some constraint). And, for all goals that involve an optimization problem, the same general economic principles apply, a point we will stress in a forthcoming chapter.

1.3 PURPOSE OF ECONOMIC THEORY

Economics might be best described as "a way of thinking about problems"—a logical system for processing and using information. Since this text is in large part concerned with economic theory and its application, we might take time to explain how and why theory is used. No doubt you have heard statements such as "That's OK in theory, but how about the real world?" The fact is that theory is designed to apply to the real world; it allows us to gain insights into problems that would be impossible to solve without a theoretical structure. We can make predictions from theory that will hold in the real world even though the theoretical structure abstracts from many actual characteristics of the world.

The purpose of theory is to make sense out of confusion. The real world is a very complicated place. There are an infinite number of variables that continually change. Theory is concerned with determining which variables are important to the issue at hand and which are not. The theoretical structure allows us to concentrate on a few important forces and ignore the many, many variables that are unimportant. In other words, when using theory we abstract away from the irrelevant.

It is this ability to abstract—to cast aside all factors insignificant to the problem—that allows managers to come to grips with the issue at hand without becoming bogged down in unimportant issues. The ability to abstract and ignore unimportant factors helps managers know what information is useful in making decisions and what is not. As we emphasized above, a major role of managers is obtaining and processing information. Economic theory indicates what information is relevant to the decision at hand and how to use that information.

1.4 PURPOSE OF EMPIRICAL ANALYSES

In this text we will describe several types of empirical (or quantitative) analysis, in particular regression analysis. Why should we be talking about statistical techniques in an *economics* text?

The purpose of these empirical discussions is the same as the purpose of learning economic theory: We need some method of making sense out of the confusion that is inherent in real-world data. But simply collecting data is not enough. The data must somehow be organized in such a fashion that economic theory can be used in making decisions. It is the empirical analyses that provide this necessary organization. Economic theory determines what information should be collected; the empirical analyses provide a structure for organizing this information.

While we will concentrate on regression analysis as a means of organizing real-world data, we do not mean to imply that this is the only method that can be used. We concentrate on regression analysis simply because it is a widely used technique and because space limitations preclude a comprehensive discussion of all of the available empirical techniques. At this point, let us mention something we will stress throughout this text: Our purpose is *not* to teach you how to do statistics. That is a task appropriately left to courses in statistics, business analysis, or econometrics. Rather, our objective is to show how these empirical analyses can be, and are, used in managerial decision making.

1.5 A PREVIEW

Since this text is concerned with using economic theory in conjunction with real-world data to make optimizing (e.g., profit-maximizing) decisions, it might be helpful to look at the kind of decisions a manager is faced with. At this point, we will limit ourselves to some very simplified applications. Subsequent chapters will deal with these topics in more detail.

A decision of primary importance to the manager is the output decision: How much should the firm produce? In a service industry this question might involve the hours of operation.

APPLICATION

Hours of operation for a store

Suppose a store owner is considering keeping the store open an additional four hours a day. What information does the owner need in order to make the decision? The first piece of information necessary is the additional (or incremental) cost of remaining open the additional four hours. These additional costs could be estimated by calculating the added labor required, the additional cost of electricity and gas, perhaps added maintenance and management costs, and any other costs that would not be incurred unless the store stays open the additional hours. Note, as will be obvious later in the text, that the overhead or fixed cost is irrelevant in the decision-making process. The fixed costs must be paid by the store regardless of how many hours the store remains open and therefore can be ignored.

Next, the additional sales revenue that can be expected from remaining open must be estimated. The manager must consider in making this estimation any sales lost during the regular operating hours because of remaining open the additional hours.

If the additional sales expected from staying open longer exceed the expected additional costs, the store should stay open the additional hours. If the added costs exceed the expected additional sales revenue, the store should not extend its hours of operation. The decision is based only on additional (marginal) revenues and additional (marginal) costs.

The preceding application is an example of a maximization problem—maximizing profit. However, the manager is also faced with minimization problems. Most of these problems will deal with cost minimization.

APPLICATION

Breakage in the factory—Should it be eliminated?

The manager of a firm is aware that in the course of day-to-day operation, there is a considerable amount of breakage occuring, such as containers getting crushed on the loading dock of the factory. The breakage is occurring on the conveyer and to some extent because of the way the forklifts are used. The engineering department notes that the conveyer can be modified and the stacking process changed to eliminate the breakage.

Should the manager authorize the modifications and changes to eliminate breakage? Does the manager have enough information to make a decision? First, the engineers and accountants must determine how much the breakage is costing. Next, it is necessary to determine the cost of modifying the conveyer (perhaps capitalized over several years) and the additional daily or weekly costs of eliminating or reducing breakage. Perhaps the forklift operators would need to work slower and the firm would have to hire extra personnel. Or added inspectors might be required. It may well be the case that the cost of eliminating or even reducing the breakage exceeds the saving from the elimination or reduction. In this case no modification should be made.

It is entirely possible that more, not less, breakage is optimal. This would be the case if the cost of additional breakage is less than the expected reduction in cost from the savings in labor and other resources that control breakage. In any case, there is an optimal amount of breakage—and this amount is probably not zero.

To illustrate this important point, suppose the manager obtains the following data for breakage costs and the costs of breakage control for the firm:

(1) Daily cost of breakage control (dollars)	*(2) Average number of containers damaged per day*	*(3) Average daily breakage cost (dollars)*
$ 0	100	$1,000
100	70	700
200	45	450
300	25	250
400	10	100
500	4	40
600	0	0

Column 1 shows amounts the firm might spend daily on breakage control. Column 2 shows the average number of containers damaged per day associated with each level of expenditure. The average expense associated with each damaged container is $10; so column 3 is simply $10 times the corresponding number in column 2 and, therefore, shows the average daily breakage cost associated with each level of expenditure in column 1.

From the table we can see that if the firm spends nothing on damage control, the average daily damage from breakage is 100 units at a cost of $1,000. If the firm increases its expenditure to $100, breakage cost falls to $700, a reduction of $300. Clearly the firm should increase its expense on damage control. Moreover, an additional increase in expenditure to $200 reduces breakage cost by $250. Likewise, you can verify that increases in expenditure from $200 to $300 and from $300 to $400 reduce breakage costs by more than each additional $100 expenditure. But an increase in expenditure from $400 to $500 reduces breakage costs by only $60. Obviously the firm would not make this increase. Thus, the firm would spend $400 daily on reducing damage, with an associated $100 breakage cost. The total cost of this operation is $500. You may, by summing the amounts in columns 1 and 3, verify that the $500 total cost is the lowest total cost possible. Note that the firm could reduce breakage to zero by spending $600, but this method would not give the lowest total cost of the operation.

To summarize, the factory should increase or reduce breakage as long as the added saving is more than the added cost. An engineer might say any amount of breakage is inefficient. An economist would say a positive amount is optimal if the additional cost of a change from that amount exceeds the expected additional saving.

The preceding applications deal with the firm's current decisions. While we will spend the majority of our time dealing with these current (short-run) decisions, we will also consider the decisions the manager must make for the future—the investment decisions.

APPLICATION

Investment—Should the firm purchase a computer?

Suppose a firm has been leasing computer services but is thinking about buying its own computer. Investment decisions of this type involve time, in the sense that the computer would provide services over several time periods, and decisions involving time also involve an interest rate. First, the firm must decide on the time horizon over which the decision to buy or lease is based. Next, the firm must determine the cost of buying a computer now. Finally, the firm must estimate the stream of costs over the relevant time horizon of leasing computer services.

But, these future costs of leasing should not be compared on a dollar-for-dollar basis with the present cost of buying, because a dollar now is worth more than a dollar in some future year. The reason present dollars are worth more than future dollars is that a dollar invested now at some positive interest rate will return more than a dollar in the future, the amount depending upon the rate of interest and the length of investment. For example, if the rate of interest is 10 percent, $10 now will be worth $11 in one year, $12.10 in two years, and so forth. Therefore, the future costs of leasing computer services must be discounted at some relevant rate of interest. That is, $10 to be received in two years is not worth $10 to you today, because you could invest less than $10 at some rate of interest and have $10 in two years. Future incomes and costs must be discounted when compared with present costs and benefits.

Thus, before the decision is made, the discounted stream of costs of leasing services should be compared with the present cost of buying the computer. Other considerations include possible saving from the convenience of having the in-house computer.

From the preceding applications, two points should be emphasized. First, economic theory allows the manager to ignore variables that are unimportant or irrelevant in the decision-making process. One can deduce conclusions, using simple assumptions, while ignoring forces that could have an effect on the outcome but in all likelihood will not. Economic theory gives a formalized structure (or method of analysis) for handling business decisions. When carrying out analysis we should remember that, while everything depends on everything else, most things depend in an essential way upon only a few other things. We usually ignore the general interdependence of everything and concentrate only upon the close interdependence of a few variables. If pressed far enough, the price of beef depends not only on the prices of pork and other meats but also on the prices of butane, color television, and airline tickets. But as a first approximation we ignore the prices of butane, TVs, and so on, because a change in the price of one of these items would have little or no effect on the price of beef. We temporarily hold other things constant and concentrate our attention on a few closely related variables where a change may have a significant impact on the subject variable.

The second major point that should be stressed is that managerial decision making involves marginal analysis in comparing the costs and benefits of a particular activity. Marginal analysis simply means that the decision maker compares incremental or additional changes in the variables. For example, a firm would attempt to increase output if the manager expected the additional revenue from expansion to exceed the additional cost. If the additional or marginal cost is expected to exceed the additional or marginal revenue, output would not be expanded. Managers use this type of analysis to solve many, many similar types of problems. You will receive a considerable amount of practice using this type of analysis throughout this text.

1.6 STRUCTURE OF THE TEXT

This text is divided into six parts. In Part 1 we provide what we refer to as the preliminary material. In addition to an overview of supply and demand, we provide a general discussion of optimization (i.e., maximization or minimization) and a brief discussion of the way to interpret regression results. While all of this material is simple (and may well be a review for many students), an understanding of this material is essential for the subsequent discussions.

Part 2 is concerned with the underpinnings of supply—production and cost. It begins with a consideration of the production process, which may be viewed simply as a method of organizing inputs to produce an output. This subject is more general than the title suggests. Certainly it is clear that managers of manufacturing firms are concerned with organizing inputs to produce an output. But people in service industries or government are also concerned with production processes. Marketing personnel organize inputs—their time, selling aids, travel, and so on—to produce sales. Hospital administrators and educators also use inputs to produce outputs; in these cases, health and education. Doctors, lawyers, and governmental employees also produce an output, even though it may be more difficult to measure than the number of cars or tons of steel produced by a firm. Since much of the theory and methods of processing information apply to these types of managers as well as to manufacturers, the theoretical and empirical discussions will be quite general. The applications will be concerned with all aspects of production processes, not simply manufacturing. Then, the theory of production will be used to derive the cost function facing the organization. An empirical approach to cost will also be provided in Part 2.

Part 3 deals with demand. Although it provides the theoretical basis for demand, the emphasis is on the way the theory of demand is used in decision making. In this vein, we will describe the techniques of demand estimation. The purpose of the material that deals with estimation is not teaching sophisticated statistical methods of estimation; rather, the concern is with teaching you how to have demand estimated and how to interpret these estimations. This part of the book also considers the techniques used in forecasting demand in the future. Again, the emphasis is placed on use and interpretation rather than on statistical methodology.

In essence, Parts 4 and 5 combine the material developed in Parts 2 and 3 in order to show how a manager can make profit-maximizing decisions. Specifically, the objective is to show how the manager of a firm will answer three questions: (1) How much should the firm produce? (2) What price should be charged? (3) What amounts of the inputs should be employed? In Part 4 these questions are answered for a firm in a perfectly competitive industry. In Part 5 the same questions are considered for firms that possess some market power. We present empirical implementations for both structures.

Part 6 provides an overview of the firm's investment decisions. In this discussion we examine how the time dimension affects the firm's decision process and then demonstrate how the basic optimization rules can be applied to the firm's decisions about which investment projects to undertake.

A large part of the text is devoted to the development of the theoretical and empirical techniques and analyses. But much of the book is concerned with applications. No new theoretical material is introduced in the ''Applications'' sections. Spaced throughout each chapter, they are designed to show how the text material is used and to give you practice in using the techniques set forth.

Finally, we should stress that this text does not assume that the student has a mathematical background. All of the analysis uses simple algebraic manipulations. However, for the student with a mathematical background, we provide mathematical expositions in the footnotes. Therefore, the text can be read either excluding or including the footnotes.

Part 1

The preliminaries

2

Supply and demand

Quite possibly the most important tools of economic analysis are the concepts of supply and demand. A thorough knowledge of supply and demand is absolutely essential for sound economic decision making.

In later chapters we will develop the concepts more completely; the purpose of this chapter is to set forth a short overview of supply, demand, and market equilibrium. This overview is meant to be an introduction to, or to most students a review of, these important concepts and how they are used.

The primary importance of supply and demand is the way they determine prices and quantities sold in the market. As we stressed in Chapter 1, managers are extremely interested in forecasting future prices and output, both for the goods and services they sell and for the inputs they use.

A familiarity with the concept of comparative statics, the comparison of market equilibrium conditions before and after certain conditions change, is essential if you want to be able to forecast future market conditions. This technique enables managers to make qualitative forecasts—forecasting the direction of change in price and output—and to know what techniques should be used to forecast the magnitude of the changes. For instance, if you read in *The Wall Street Journal* that Congress is considering a tax cut, comparative statics enables you to forecast whether the price and sales of a product will increase or decrease.

We begin with an analysis of demand, then develop the foundations of supply. Section 2.3 puts these two concepts together to show how they determine the equilibrium price and quantity sold in the market. Then section 2.4 describes comparative statics—how changes in demand and supply affect prices and quantity sold.

2.1 DEMAND

Economists are frequently accused of implying that the only factor that affects the amount of a good or service purchased is its price. This allegation is simply not correct. While economists do stress the importance of price, they recognize that a myriad of factors determines the amount of a good or service consumers will purchase during a given period. But, in order to make analysis manageable, economists concentrate on the more important influencing forces and ignore those that have little or no effect.

In general, economists assume that the quantity of a good or service that individuals are willing and able to purchase during a particular period depends upon five major variables: (1) the price of the good itself, (2) the incomes of the consumers, (3) the prices of related goods and services, (4) the expected price of the good in future periods, and (5) the tastes of the consumers.

As you would expect, consumers are willing and able to buy more of a good the lower the price of the good, when the other variables are held constant. This relation is so important that it is called the law of demand. (If you have doubts about the validity of the law of demand, try to think of specific items you would buy in larger quantities if the price were higher, again holding the other variables constant.) The law of demand holds because, when the price of a good rises, consumers tend to shift from that good to now relatively cheaper goods. Conversely, when the price of a good falls, they tend to purchase more of that good in place of other goods that are now relatively more expensive.

Next let's look at changes in income. Holding the other variables constant, an increase in income can cause the amount of a commodity consumers purchase either to increase or to decrease. If an increase (a decrease) in income causes quantity purchased to increase (decrease), we refer to such a commodity as a "normal" good. That is, in the case of a normal good, income and sales vary directly. There can, however, exist goods for which an increase in income would reduce the quantity purchased—other variables held constant. These types of commodities are referred to as "inferior" goods.

Commodities may be related in consumption in either of two ways: as substitutes or complements. In general, goods are substitutes if one good can be used in the place of the other; an example might be Fords and Chevrolets. If two goods are substitutes, an increase in the price of one good will increase the quantity purchased of the other (holding the price of the good under consideration constant). If the price of Fords rises while the price of Chevrolets remains constant, we would expect consumers to purchase more Chevrolets. A decrease in the price of a substitute good will decrease the quantity purchased of the other good. For example, if the price of beef falls, we would expect the quantity of pork purchased to fall, given a constant price of pork.

Goods are said to be complementary if they are used in conjunction with each other. Examples might be lettuce and salad dressing or automobiles and gasoline. An increase in the price of either complementary good will decrease the quantity purchased of the other good, the price of the other good held constant.

The preceding discussion does not mean that all commodities are either substitutes or complements in consumption. Many commodities are *essentially* independent. For example, we would not expect the price of lettuce to significantly influence the sales of automobiles. Thus, we can treat these commodities as independent and ignore the price of lettuce when evaluating the demand for automobiles.

Expectations of consumers also influence the quantity purchased of a commodity. More specifically, consumers' expectations about the future price of the commodity can change their current purchases. If consumers expect the price to be higher in a future period, sales would probably tend to rise in the current period. On the other hand, expectations of a price decline in the future would cause some purchases to be postponed; thus sales in the current period will fall.

Finally, a change in taste or preferences can change the quantity purchased of a commodity, the other variables held constant. Clearly, taste changes could either increase or decrease sales. Given the difficulty of measuring taste, economists frequently assume that this variable is constant. However, this factor is very important in understanding the effects of advertising, a topic to which we will turn later.

We can write the function describing the quantity that consumers are willing and able to purchase during a particular time period as:

$$Q_{X,t} = f(P_{X,t}, Y_t, P_{R,t}, P^e_{X,t+i}, \mathcal{T})$$

where

$Q_{X,t}$ = the quantity purchased of good X in period t
$P_{X,t}$ = the price of good X in period t
Y_t = the consumers' incomes in period t
$P_{R,t}$ = the price of related goods in period t
$P^e_{X,t+i}$ = the expected price of good X in some future period, $t + i$
$\mathcal{T}$ = the taste patterns of consumers

The effects of changes in the variables that determine the quantity purchased in a market during a particular time period may be summarized as follows, where the symbol Δ means "the change in":[1]

$$\frac{\Delta Q_{X,t}}{\Delta P_{X,t}} < 0$$

[1]Students with a mathematical background will note that we are dealing with partial derivatives of the demand relation. The derivatives evaluate the effect of a change in one variable, holding the other variables constant.

$$\frac{\Delta Q_{X,t}}{\Delta Y_t} \gtrless 0 \quad \text{if the good is} \begin{cases} \text{normal} \\ \text{inferior} \end{cases}$$

$$\frac{\Delta Q_{X,t}}{\Delta P_{R,t}} \gtrless 0 \quad \text{if the goods are} \begin{cases} \text{substitutes} \\ \text{complements} \end{cases}$$

$$\frac{\Delta Q_{X,t}}{\Delta \mathcal{T}} \quad ? \quad \text{(The sign is undeterminant)}$$

$$\frac{\Delta Q_{X,t}}{\Delta P^e_{X,t+i}} > 0$$

Again let us stress that these relations are in the context of all other things equal. An increase in the price of the commodity will lead to a decrease in quantity purchased as long as the other variables—income, the price of related commodities, taste, and price expectations—remain constant.

The demand function

Demand functions show the relation between the quantity demanded by the consumers and the price of the product. These functions are probably the most important tools used by economists. While we emphasized above that many variables determine the quantity consumers wish to purchase in a market, we must emphasize that the price of the commodity is an extremely important, probably the most important, determinant for economic analysis. Let us begin with the following definition of a demand function:

■ **Definition.** A demand function is a list of prices and the corresponding quantities that individuals are willing and able to purchase in some time period. Consumers are willing and able to purchase more of an item the lower its price; that is, quantity demanded per time period varies inversely with price.

At the outset, let us stress that *demand* is a function (or schedule), not a specific quantity. Hence, when we refer to the demand for beef or the demand for automobiles in the United States, we are considering the amounts that consumers are willing and able to purchase at *various* prices. When we talk about demand, we are talking about the entire schedule of quantities and prices. Only when we specify a single price do we consider a single point on the demand schedule and we refer to this point on the schedule as the *quantity demanded*, at that given price.

We generally specify consumer demand in any of three ways: as a schedule, a graph, or a function. A typical market demand schedule is shown in Table 2.1. This table shows the list of prices and the corresponding quantities

Table 2.1
Market demand schedule

Quantity demanded	*Price per unit (dollars)*
2,000	$6
3,000	5
4,000	4
5,000	3
5,500	2
6,000	1

that the consumers demand (i.e., are willing and able to purchase) per period of time. Note again that quantity demanded and price vary inversely in the market.

Quite often it is more convenient to work with the graph of a demand schedule, called a demand curve, rather than with the schedule itself. Figure 2.1 provides the demand curve corresponding to the schedule in Table 2.1. Each price-quantity combination—($6, 2,000), ($5, 3,000), and so on—is plotted; then the six points are connected by the curve labeled DD'. This

Figure 2.1
Market demand curve

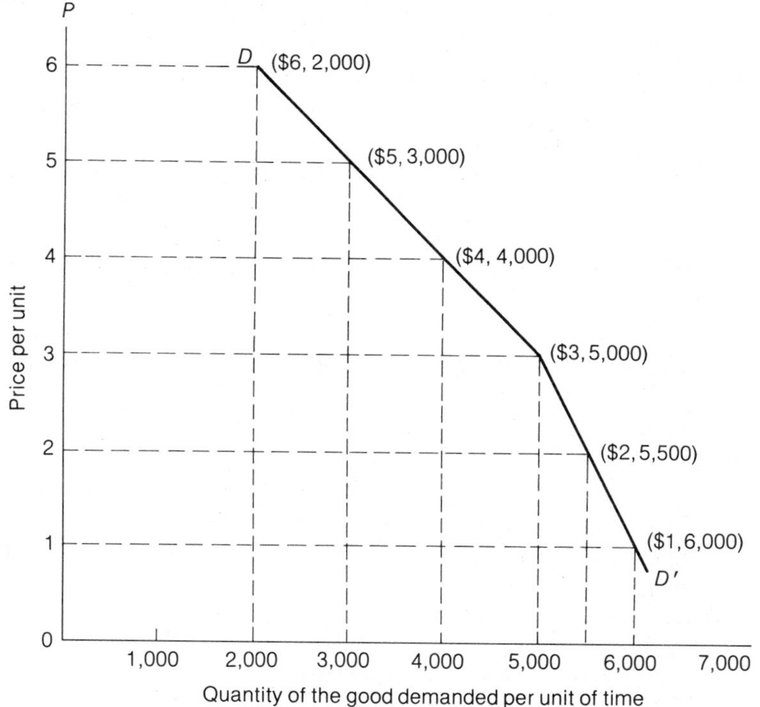

curve indicates the quantity of the good consumers are willing and able to buy per unit of time at every price from \$6 to \$1. Since price and quantity demanded are inversely related, the curve slopes downward.

Indeed, all market demand curves must be drawn downward sloping to conform with the law of demand. Individuals purchase less as price increases. Furthermore, as price increases, some individuals may purchase nothing at all, again causing the quantity demanded at each price to decrease.

Alternatively, we can express demand as a function[2]

$$Q_X = f(P_X)$$

In this function the other variables (income, and so on) are held constant. Quantity demanded is a function of the price of the good, holding constant the other determining variables.

Shifts in demand

From our earlier discussion you know that price is not the sole determinant of the amount of the commodity consumers wish to purchase. Obviously the amount of beef or number of automobiles consumers wish to purchase during a given period depends on other variables, including income, the price of related goods, and so on. In other words, changes in these other variables could change the quantity demanded at each price—they change (shift) the demand function. We refer to these other variables as the *determinants of demand* since they determine where the demand function will be located.

As we emphasized above, when we draw a demand curve like the one in Figure 2.1, we do so under the assumption that other things remain the same. The other things are: (1) consumers' incomes (and the income distribution among consumers), (2) the prices of related goods, (3) price expectations, and (4) tastes. When price falls (rises) and consumers purchase more (less) of a good, other things remaining the same, we say that *quantity demanded* increases (decreases). *Demand* does not increase or decrease when price changes.

Demand is said to increase or decrease only if one or more of the determinants of demand changes. For example, if incomes of consumers increase and they wish to purchase more of a good at each price than they did previously, we say that the demand for the good has increased. That is, consumers demand more at each price in the list of prices. If the change in income causes consumers to demand less of the good than before at each price (i.e., if the good is inferior), then demand decreases.

In this discussion we have been differentiating between (1) changes in quantity demanded, due to a change in the price of the product, and (2) changes (shifts) in demand due to changes in one or more of the determinants

[2]In this functional notation, the inverse relation between price and quantity demand is expressed by the derivative $dQ_X/dP_X < 0$ or $f'(P_X) < 0$.

Figure 2.2
Changes in demand versus changes in quantity demanded

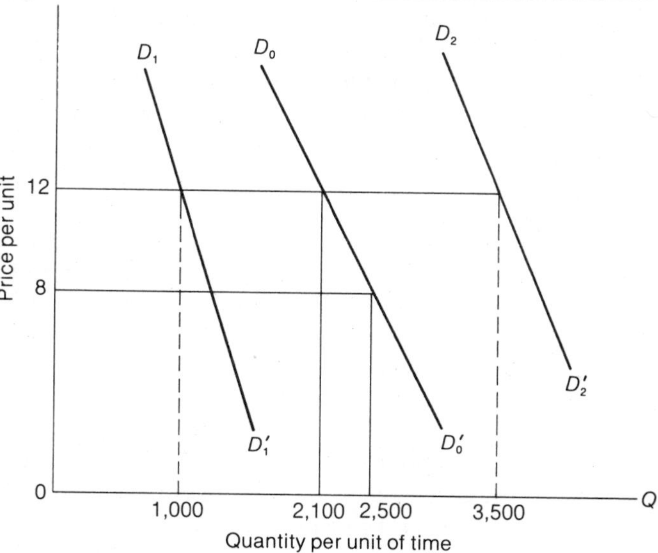

of demand (e.g., income). Figure 2.2 might help to make this difference more clear.

In Figure 2.2 the original demand curve is given by D_0D_0'. Given this demand curve, at a price of \$12, the quantity demanded by the consumers is 2,100 units. If price falls from \$12 to \$8, quantity demanded will increase to 2,500 units. Changes in quantity demanded are caused only by changes in the price of the product itself and changes in quantity demanded are reflected in movements along the existing demand curve.

Now, beginning again with demand curve D_0D_0', let's look at a change in demand. Suppose that income decreases and the good in question is a normal commodity. Consumers will now demand less of the commodity at every price. The demand for the product will decrease as is illustrated by the leftward shift from D_0D_0' to D_1D_1' in Figure 2.2. At every price, quantity demanded is less than before, e.g., at a price of \$12 per unit the quantity demanded is now 1,000 units. In that example, the decrease in the amount consumers are willing and able to purchase, (from 2,500 to 1,000 at a price of \$12 per unit) is the result of a change in demand. Alternatively, an increase in demand would be as illustrated by the rightward shift from D_0D_0' to D_2D_2' in Figure 2.2. In either case, changes in demand are caused by changes in one or more of the determinants of demand (income, prices of related goods, price expectations, and taste). Changes in demand are reflected in shifts of the demand curve, either to the right for an increase in demand or the left for a decrease in demand.

Let's look more specifically at the effects of changes in the various determinants of demand, beginning with income. As we noted earlier, an increase in income causes consumers to demand more of the good at every price, if the good is a normal good. If the good is inferior, consumers will demand less of the good at every price after an increase in income. Thus, an increase in income increases the demand (shifts the curve rightward) for a normal good but decreases the demand (shifts the curve leftward) for an inferior good. Conversely, a decrease in income will decrease (increase) the demand for a normal (an inferior) good.

If goods A and B are substitutes, an increase in the price of good B will cause an increase in the demand for A. For example, if the price of Fords increases by $500, we would expect consumers to demand more Chevrolets at each relevant price. If two goods are substitutes, an increase (decrease) in the price of one will cause the demand for the other to increase (decrease).

On the other hand, if two goods are complements, an increase in the price of one good will decrease the demand for the other. For example, since bread and butter are frequently consumed together, they are probably complements. If the price of butter rises, we would expect consumers to demand less bread at each price, because the good used with bread is now more expensive. If the price of one good rises (falls), we would expect the demand for the other to decrease (increase), if the two goods are complements.

When the price of a good is expected to increase (decrease) in the future, the demand for the good in the current period will increase (decrease). For example, widespread consumer expectations that automobile prices will decline in the future will cause some consumers to postpone purchasing a car and therefore cause a decrease in the current demand for automobiles.

Tastes are extremely difficult to quantify. We can only say that if something causes consumers' tastes to change toward (away from) a particular good, the demand for that good will increase (decrease).

In this section we have developed the following principles:

■ **Principle.** The amount of a product that consumers will purchase depends upon many things, the most important of which are the price of the product, the price of related products, income (and income distribution), tastes, and the price expected in the future.

■ **Principle.** Market demand is a list of prices and the corresponding quantities that consumers are willing and able to purchase per unit of time. Demand can be a schedule or a function. Quantity demanded is determined by and varies inversely with price.

■ **Principle.** An increase in demand means that, at each price, more is demanded; a decrease in demand means that, at each price, less is demanded. Demand changes when one of the determinants of demand changes. These determinants are income, prices of related goods, expected future price, and tastes.

■ **Principle.** When income increases (decreases), the demand for a normal good increases (decreases) and the demand for an inferior good decreases (increases). An increase (decrease) in the price of a substitute good increases (decreases) the demand for the good it is a substitute for. A change in the price of one complement good has exactly the opposite effect on the demand for the other one of the pair. If the price of a good is expected to rise (fall), current demand for the good increases (decreases).

As you will see, demand theory along with demand estimation and forecasting is one of the most important concepts used by business decision makers as well as economists. We shall therefore return to demand later in the text and devote two full chapters to demand theory and two chapters to demand estimation and forecasting.

THE WALL STREET JOURNAL
APPLICATION

Do demand curves really slope downward?

From time to time we hear about products experiencing substantial increases in sales at the same time that the price of the product is increasing. Does this phenomenon imply a contradiction to the law of demand—an upward-sloping demand curve?

A good example of this phenomenon appeared in an article in *The Wall Street Journal*, August 3, 1983,* entitled, "High New-Car Prices Keep Many Looking, Not Buying." From 1979 until the spring of 1983, the U.S. auto industry experienced its most severe slump since the depression of the 1930s. Sales fell by 50 percent over this period. And, during the same period, prices rose substantially (by 50 percent for the more expensive cars.) To get some idea of the increase in real terms, consider that in 1979 the purchase of a new automobile took, on average, 31.2 weeks of salary; by 1983 this purchase took 36.6 weeks of salary. So, from 1979 to the spring of 1983 sales and prices were apparently following the law of demand—sales were falling as price was rising.

But in April of 1983 sales began to increase. During the summer of 1983 sales were running at an annual rate of over 7 million cars, up from an annual rate of 4.6 million during the same period one year before. This increase in sales came in spite of continued increases in automobile prices over the same period. And the *Journal* reported that U.S. manufacturers were planning to increase prices even more. (They subsequently did just that, but sales continued to increase.)

The *Journal* noted that many people did not purchase new cars because of the higher prices (and that the expansion in automobile sales lagged behind the expansions in previous periods of economic recovery). Nonetheless, the fact remained that *sales did increase as prices rose*. Did something happen in the spring of 1983 to repeal the law of demand? To answer the question, we must look at what else was happening.

During the period from the spring of 1983 through the winter of that year, several events were occurring that increased the demand for automobiles. Thus, rather than quantity demanded moving up along a stationary demand curve, sales were responding to an increase in demand. One thing that increased the demand for automobiles was the recovery of the economy (increased GNP and reduced unemployment). The recovery led to increases in consumers' incomes. If, as we would expect, automobiles are normal goods, the increase in income would lead to an increase in demand.

Interest rates had fallen substantially from the previous year. Since most people borrow to purchase a car, the decline in interest rates made it less expensive to finance the new cars and therefore increased demand even more. To see how this would occur, think of the loan as a complementary good to automobiles and the price of the loan as the rate of interest. Thus, the price of a complementary good fell and increased the demand for new cars.

By the spring of 1983, Americans had recognized that the price of gasoline had fallen and, by that time, the experts were not expecting it to rise much, if any, in the near future. Thus the price of another complementary good, gasoline, had fallen, further increasing the demand for automobiles.

The Wall Street Journal noted explicitly that, "One reason the auto makers have been able to raise prices so fast even in a depressed market is the protection they have from their Japanese competitors." The annual imports of Japanese automobiles had been limited by agreement to 1,680,000 units since 1981. As we would expect, this limitation kept the price of Japanese autos higher than it would have been in the absence of the agreement. Since Japanese cars are a good substitute for American cars, the increase in the price of the substitute good would be expected to have increased the demand for automobiles manufactured in the United States.

Thus changes in three of the determinants of demand had increased the demand for U.S. automobiles in 1983: (1) economic recovery and reduced unemployment increased consumer's incomes, (2) reduced interest rates and lower gasoline prices lowered the prices of complements, and (3) limitations on the importation of Japanese cars raised the prices of substitutes. This increase in the demand for U.S. automobiles enabled U.S. firms to increase the prices of their products without decreasing the number of cars sold. Indeed, as we have seen, the number of cars sold actually increased.

Thus, this increase in sales accompanied by an increase in price is not a contradiction to the law of downsloping demand. "Other things" did not remain constant during this period; the changes in the other things actually worked to increase demand.

2.2 SUPPLY

The amount of a good or service offered for sale in a market depends to a greater or lesser extent upon an extremely large number of variables. But, as we did for demand, we ignore all of the relatively unimportant variables in order to concentrate upon those that have the greatest effect upon quantity supplied.

Certainly, the price of the product would affect the quantity offered for sale. The greater the price of the product, the more that would be offered. This relation is attributable to two reactions: (1) A higher price would lead to greater profits for firms already producing and selling the good or service, and thus they would be induced to produce and sell more; (2) The higher price and consequent higher profits would tend to lure new firms into the market and therefore cause more goods to be supplied. (We shall analyze the determinants of a particular firm's output decisions more completely in a later chapter.)

While the price of the good itself is the most important variable affecting the amount of the good offered for sale (we will return to this relation below), several other variables can have an effect. The first of these is the level of available technology. An improvement in the state of technology would lower the costs of producing the good and therefore would, other things remaining the same, increase the quantity offered for sale. (Note, however, that the level or state of technology is difficult if not impossible to quantify.)

Changes in the prices of inputs used to produce the good will also change the quantity supplied at any given price of the good. An increase in the prices that much be paid for the inputs would raise costs and hence decrease the quantity supplied at a given price. Alternatively, a decrease in the prices of inputs would lower costs and increase the quantity offered for sale.

The price of substitute goods in production can affect the quantity of a good offered for sale. For example, if the price of corn increases while the price of wheat remains the same, some farmers may well change from growing wheat to growing corn, and less wheat will be supplied. Or, in the case of manufactured goods, firms can switch resources from the production of one good to the production of a substitute commodity the price of which has risen. Alternatively, it could be the case that commodities are complementary in production. If the price of a complementary commodity increases, the firm should be willing to supply more of the commodity in question.[3] Finally, if firms expect the price of a good they produce and sell to rise in the future relative to the price of other goods, they may withhold the sales of some amount of the good.

From our discussion so far, it should be clear that the quantity of a good that will be offered for sale in a particular time period depends upon many

---

[3]An example of such complementary commodities is found in the mineral extracting industry. Often nickel and copper occur in the same deposit. Therefore, copper ore is a by-product of mining nickel, or vice versa. If the price of nickel rises, the firm would be expected to extract more ore, and so the output of copper would increase.

variables. To summarize the preceding, let us specify a relation describing the amount of a commodity that is offered for sale in a particular time period as

$$Q_{X,t} = g(P_{X,t}, T_t, P_{F,t}, P_{R,t}, P^e_{X,t+i})$$

That is, the quantity of a particular commodity X offered for sale in period t is determined not only by the price of that commodity ($P_{X,t}$) but also by the level of available technology (T_t), the price of the factors of production (inputs) used ($P_{F,t}$), the prices of any commodities related in production ($P_{R,t}$), and the expectations of the producers concerning the future price of the commodity ($P^e_{X,t+i}$). We can summarize the relations between the quantity offered for sale and the various variables as follows. Holding other things constant,[4]

$$\frac{\Delta Q_{X,t}}{\Delta P_{X,t}} > 0$$

$$\frac{\Delta Q_{X,t}}{\Delta T_t} > 0$$

$$\frac{\Delta Q_{X,t}}{\Delta P_{F,t}} < 0$$

$$\frac{\Delta Q_{X,t}}{\Delta P_{R,t}} \begin{matrix} > \\ < \end{matrix} 0 \text{ if the related commodity is a } \begin{Bmatrix} \text{complement} \\ \text{substitute} \end{Bmatrix} \text{ in production}$$

$$\frac{\Delta Q_{X,t}}{\Delta P^e_{X,t+i}} < 0$$

The supply function

While we can analyze the relation between the quantity offered for sale and any of the determinants, economists focus upon the relation between quantity supplied and the product price: As the price of a product increases (decreases), more (less) is supplied by sellers, holding everything else constant. We use the following definition:

■ **Definition.** Supply is a list of prices and the corresponding quantities that a group of suppliers (firms) would be willing and able to offer for sale at each price per period of time.

We can write the supply function as

$$Q_X = g(P_X)$$

or supply can be specified by a schedule or a graph. Consider the market supply schedule for a good shown in Table 2.2. This table shows the minimum price necessary to induce firms to supply, per unit of time, each of the

[4]The student with a background in mathematics will again note that these relations are more properly expressed as partial derivatives.

Table 2.2
Market supply schedule

Quantity supplied (units)	*Prices (dollars)*
7,000	6
6,500	5
6,000	4
5,000	3
4,000	2
3,000	1

six quantities listed. In order to induce the firms to supply greater quantities, price must rise. For example, if price increases from $4 to $5, firms will increase quantity supplied from 6,000 units to 6,500 units.

This schedule shows the minimum price that induces firms to supply each amount in the list. Note that price and quantity supplied are directly related; as price falls firms supply less. While this relation is intuitively appealing, we shall postpone the explanation of why price and quantity vary directly until a

Figure 2.3
Market supply curve

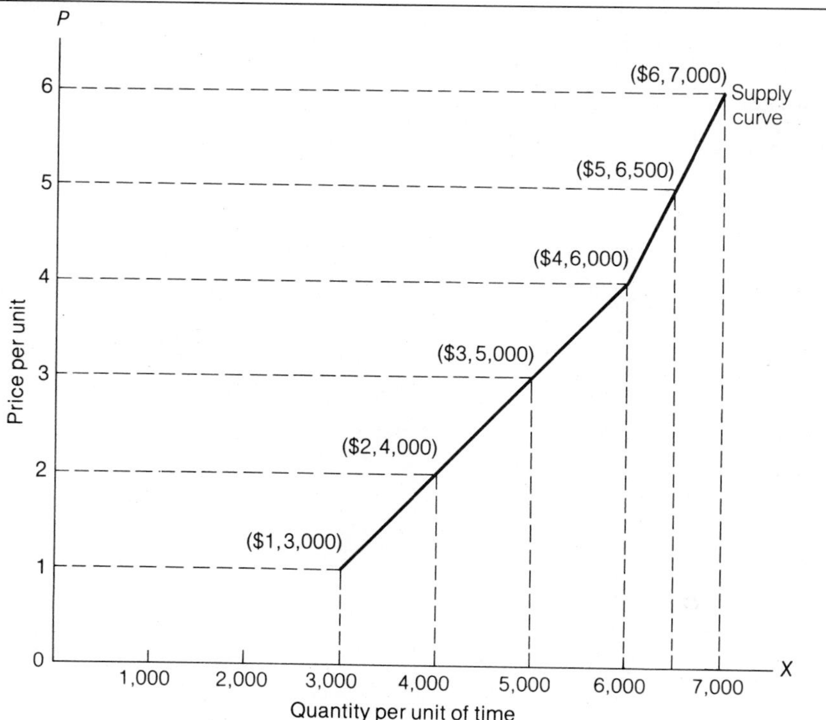

later chapter, after analyzing cost and production. For the present we assume that the supply schedule shows the minimum price necessary to induce producers voluntarily to offer each possible quantity for sale and that an increase in price is required to induce an increase in quantity supplied, other things remaining constant.

Figure 2.3 shows a graph drawn using the schedule in Table 2.2. The price per unit of the product is measured along the vertical axis; quantity supplied per period of time, along the horizontal. All price–quantity combinations in Table 2.2 are plotted; then these points are joined by a line. This line is called a supply curve or simply supply. Since quantity supplied and price are directly related, the resulting supply curve is upward sloping.

Shifts in supply

We should emphasize that a supply schedule is derived or a supply curve drawn under the assumption that the other variables that affect the quantity offered for sale (technology, the prices of inputs, the prices of goods related in production, and price expectations) are held constant. Just as we differentiated between a change in quantity demanded due to a change in price and a shift in demand because of a change in one of the variables held constant when drawing a demand curve, we must make the same distinction with supply. When the price of the commodity in question rises and firms are induced to offer a greater amount for sale, we say that *quantity supplied* increases. If the price of the product falls, quantity supplied decreases. Such

Figure 2.4
Changes in supply versus changes in quantity supplied

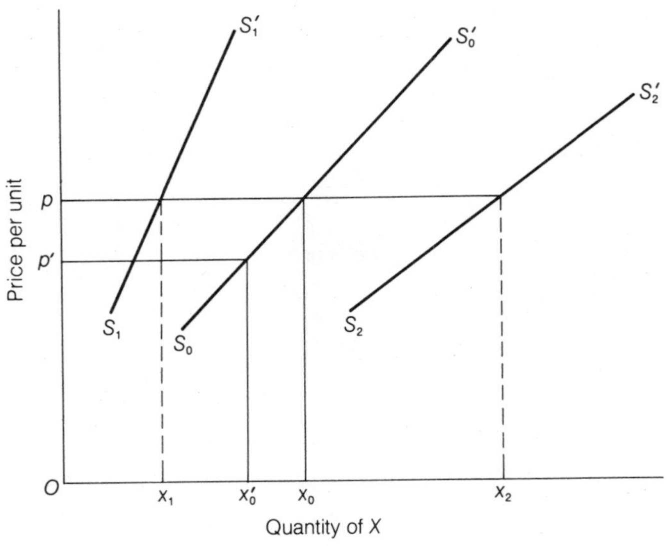

an effect is illustrated in Figure 2.4. Considering the supply curve S_0S_0', if the price falls from p to p', the quantity supplied of X decreases along that supply curve from X_0 to X_0'.

If, however, one or more of the other variables (the determinants of supply) change, firms are induced to offer more or less of the commodity at each price. In this case, we say that supply has shifted. A decrease and increase in supply are illustrated in Figure 2.4 as a shift from S_0S_0' to S_1S_1' and S_2S_2', respectively. (At the original price, p,X_1 units are supplied when supply decreases to S_1S_1' and X_2 units are supplied when supply increases to S_2S_2'.)

Considering the individual determinants, we would expect the following: An increase in the level of available technology should increase supply. Since an increase in the price of the inputs increases the costs of production, an increase in the price of inputs should cause supply to decrease. If the price of a good that is a substitute in production increases, the supply of the commodity in question decreases. If producers expect the price of a good to increase in the future, they will withhold some current production (i.e., increase inventories); thus, supply in the current period will decrease.

The preceding discussion can be summarized as follows:

■ **Principle.** The quantity of a good or service offered for sale in a particular market depends upon the price of the good or service, the state of technology, the prices of inputs, the prices of related goods or services (in production), and the expected future price of the good or service.

■ **Principle.** The supply function or schedule is a list of prices and the corresponding quantities that sellers are willing and able to sell at each price in the list per period of time. A particular supply function is specified holding constant the values of the other variables that affect the quantity offered for sale. Other things held constant, an increase (decrease) in price causes quantity supplied to increase (decrease).

■ **Principle.** If one of the other variables (e.g., the prices of inputs) changes, the entire supply function shifts. That is, supply will increase (decrease) and, at each price, suppliers will supply more (less) to the market.

2.3 MARKET EQUILIBRIUM

The purpose of studying supply and demand is to prepare us to analyze their interaction, the market equilibrium, which determines market price and quantity sold. Let us begin our analysis of the market equilibrium with a hypothetical example. Suppose that in a market for some commodity, the demanders and suppliers have the particular schedules we previously set forth in Tables 2.1 and 2.2. These schedules are combined in Table 2.3. Note that only one price, \$3, clears the market (quantity demanded equals quantity supplied). We will show that market forces will drive the price toward that equilibrium price.

Table 2.3
Market demand and supply

Price	Quantity supplied	Quantity demanded	Excess supply (+) or demand (−)
$6	7,000	2,000	+5,000
5	6,500	3,000	+3,500
4	6,000	4,000	+2,000
3	5,000	5,000	0
2	4,000	5,500	−1,500
1	3,000	6,000	−3,000

Suppose that the price is $5. With this price, 3,000 units are demanded but 6,500 are offered for sale, leading to an excess supply (sometimes called a surplus) of 3,500 units. When there is excess supply, firms cannot sell all they wish at that price and they must reduce price to keep from accumulating surpluses. Indeed, at any price above $3, you can see that there will be an excess supply and price will fall.

Alternatively, let price be $1. Consumers demand 6,000 units, but producers are willing to supply only 3,000, creating an excess demand (a shortage) of 3,000 units. Since their demands are not satisfied, consumers bid the price up. As they continue to bid up the price, quantity demanded decreases and quantity supplied increases until a price of $3 is reached and 5,000 units are sold per period of time.

We can also express the equilibrium solution graphically. In Figure 2.5,

Figure 2.5
Market equilibrium

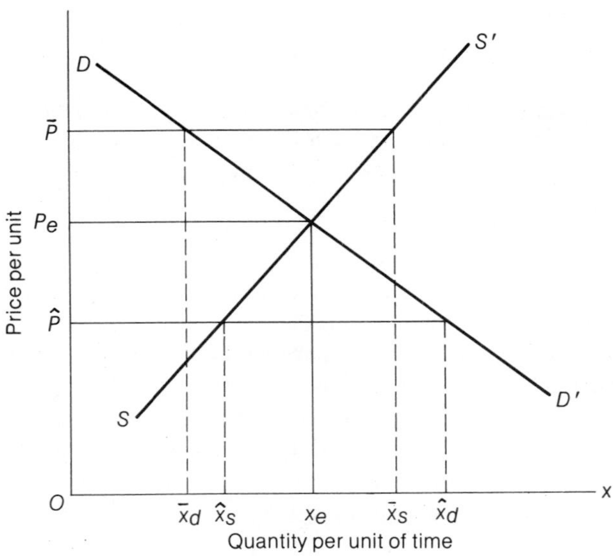

DD' and SS' are the market demand and supply curves. It is clear that p_e and x_e are the market-clearing (equilibrium) price and quantity. Only at a price of p_e does quantity demanded equal quantity supplied.

Suppose that price happens to be $\overline{p}$, which is greater than p_e. At $\overline{p}$ producers supply $\overline{x}_s$ but only $\overline{x}_d$ is demanded. An excess supply of $\overline{x}_d\overline{x}_s$ develops. Thus producers are induced to lower price in order to keep from accumulating unwanted surpluses. At any price above p_e there is an excess supply and producers will lower price.

On the other hand, suppose that price is $\hat{p}$. Demanders are willing and able to purchase $\hat{x}_d$ while suppliers are only willing to offer $\hat{x}_s$ units for sale. There is an excess demand of $\hat{x}_s\hat{x}_d$ in the market. Since their demands are not satisfied, consumers bid the price up. Any price below p_e causes an excess demand, and the shortage causes consumers to bid up the price.

Given no outside influences that prevent price from being bid up or down, an equilibrium price and quantity is attained. This equilibrium price is the price that clears the market; both excess demand and excess supply are zero in equilibrium. Equilibrium is attained in the market because of the following:

■ **Principle.** The equilibrium price is that at which quantity demanded is equal to quantity supplied. When price is above the equilibrium price, quantity supplied exceeds quantity demanded. The resulting excess supply induces sellers to reduce price in order to sell the surplus. If price is below equilibrium, quantity demanded exceeds quantity supplied. The resulting excess demand causes the unsatisfied consumers to bid up price. Since prices below equilibrium are bid up by consumers and prices above equilibrium are lowered by producers, the market will converge to the equilibrium price-quantity combination.

We should note that prices serve two functions. First, prices are a rationing device for the users of the product. If prices rise, they serve to determine who gets the products and therefore perform the service of ensuring that society allocates the product to its highest valued uses.

The second function of prices is the inducement for sellers to supply more or less of the product according to the demands of the consumers. If prices rise, it is because consumers demand more of the good, and producers are induced to supply more. If prices fall, it is a signal that consumers demand less, and producers are induced to supply less of the good.

2.4 COMPARATIVE STATICS

So far, we have examined demand, supply, and the market equilibrium. On a practical basis, managerial decision makers are frequently interested in the effect on price and on sales of changes in the determinants of demand and supply. For example, questions that might be asked include: What will happen to the price of automobiles as the price of energy falls (or rises) or as income rises? What will happen to the quantity of furniture sold as the price of houses rises? What will happen to teachers' salaries as the society becomes older? All of these types of questions are important and interesting for economic decision makers.

And these are precisely the types of questions we are now ready to address. In a general sense all of these questions become: What will be the impact on market price and output (sales) of changes in those determinants that cause a shift in the demand or supply curves? By comparing the market equilibrium positions before and after the changes, we will be able to determine the direction, if not the magnitude, of such effects.

It should be clear from the discussion so far that the price of the commodity in question is the one variable that will not be changed to generate comparative statics results. As we have shown, price adjusts along the prevailing demand and supply curves to eliminate excess demand or excess supply. Thus, price and output are endogenous variables—variables determined by the market equilibrium.

The variables that may be altered to generate comparative statics forecasts are the exogenous variables—those determined outside the market under consideration. Briefly, let us review these determinants. In the case of demand, we include as exogenous variables the incomes of consumers, the prices of those commodities related in consumption to the good in question (i.e., substitutes and complements), taste, and the consumers' expectations about the future price of the commodity. In the case of supply, the exogenous variables include the level of available technology, the prices of inputs used in producing the commodity, the prices of those commodities that are related (in production) to the one in question, and the producers' expectations about the future price of the commodity. In earlier sections we determined how each of these variables will shift the demand curve or the supply curve.

Given that we can identify the effects of the specific determinants of demand and supply, let's proceed to an examination of the effects of shifts in the demand and/or supply curves. In Panel A of Figure 2.6, p_0 and x_0 are the equilibrium price and quantity when demand and supply are D_0D_0' and SS'. Suppose demand decreases to D_1D_1'. At price p_0, quantity supplied exceeds by AB the new quantity demanded; that is, excess supply at p_0 is AB. Faced with this surplus, sellers reduce price until the new equilibrium is reached at p_1 and x_1. Alternatively, suppose that demand increases from D_0D_0' to D_2D_2'. At price p_0, quantity demanded exceeds quantity supplied, and a shortage occurs. The excess demand causes consumers to bid the price up until the new equilibrium at p_2 and x_2 is reached. From this figure, we can see that if supply remains fixed and demand decreases, quantity and price both fall; if demand increases, price and quantity both rise. This direct relation between price and quantity would be expected when we consider that the movements take place along the supply curve, which is positively sloped.

Panel B of Figure 2.6 shows what happens to price and quantity when demand remains constant and supply shifts. Let demand be DD' and supply

Figure 2.6
Changes in equilibrium prices and quantities

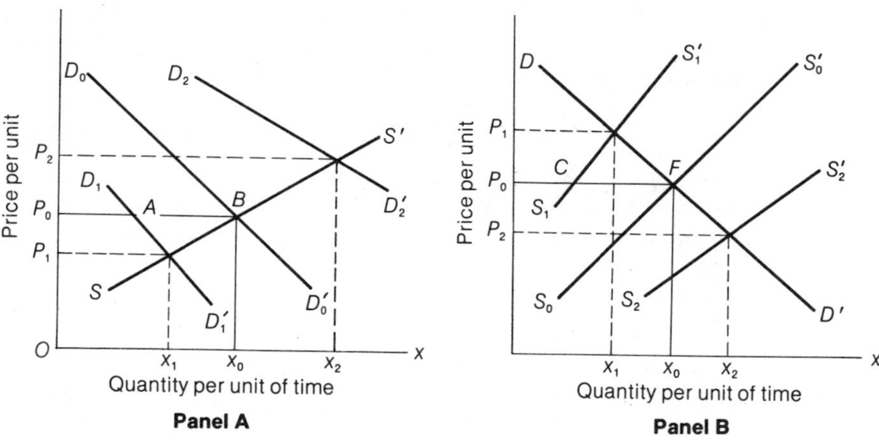

S_0S_0'. The original equilibrium thus occurs at price p_0 and quantity x_0. Now let supply decrease to S_1S_1'. The shortage of CF at p_0 causes consumers to bid up price until equilibrium is reached at the price p_1 and quantity x_1. Alternatively, let supply increase from S_0S_0' to S_2S_2'. The surplus at p_0 causes producers to lower price. Equilibrium occurs at p_2 and x_2. Thus, we see that if demand remains constant and supply decreases, price rises and quantity falls; if supply increases, price falls and quantity increases. This inverse relation is expected since the movement is along a negatively sloped demand curve.

Of course, both demand and supply can change simultaneously. In these cases the resulting changes in equilibrium price and quantity are not so predictable. The total effects frequently depend upon the relative strengths of the shifts in the two curves. In any case, we have established the following principle.

■ **Principle.** When demand increases (decreases), supply remaining constant, both price and equilibrium quantity increase (decrease). When supply increases (decreases), demand remaining constant, price falls (rises) and equilibrium quantity rises (falls).

THE WALL STREET JOURNAL
APPLICATION

An unexpected recovery in housing

From mid-1982 until fall 1983 the housing industry experienced a substantial expansion in sales, an expansion that was expected by very few observers prior to the recovery. Lindey H. Clark, Jr., in his column "Speaking of

Business,'' in *The Wall Street Journal* of August 9, 1983, described the housing situation that had existed in July 1982, just prior to the recovery.*

According to Mr. Clark, in 10 out of the 11 preceding months, housing starts had been below one million. In only seven months over the previous 30 years had housing starts been so low. Indeed, Congress was debating legislation to save the ailing building industry.

Moreover, Mr. Clark noted that, in July 1982, the savings and loan industry was practically ''on the brink of extinction.'' Interest rates had exploded in 1979, and about 500 S & Ls had disappeared. They were carrying portfolios of loans at 10 percent interest rates and were having to borrow at much higher rates.

But in spite of all the adversity, housing began to expand in the late summer of 1982. What happened? Were there changes occurring in the economy that would have permitted people to forecast the housing boom and to profit from their knowledge? As it turned out, there were such changes; and some people did profit from the knowledge.

Writing a year after the expansion began, Mr. Clark cited several of these changes that had begun in mid-1982: (1) In response to monetary policy, interest rates had begun to decline. Since most homes are financed by borrowing, this decrease in interest rates, particularly mortgage rates, reduced the cost of financing a home. (2) The economy was beginning to recover from an extremely severe recession. Since many people had postponed purchasing a home during the recession there was a great deal of pent up demand for housing. (3) Inflation was slowing down appreciably, and people were beginning to believe that the purchasing power of their income was not going to continue to be eroded by increases in the cost of living. (4) The housing recovery was reinforced by declining house prices.

Since we know that supply and demand determine both price and quantity sold in a market, what can we say about the effect of these changes on the demand and supply of housing? Let's translate the changes in the housing market noted by Mr. Clark into shifts in the demand for and supply of housing. In Figure 2.7, let the quantity of housing (possibly new housing) in a particular area be measured along the horizontal axis and the price per unit on the vertical. We denote the original (i.e., 1982) demand and supply for housing as respectively D_0 and S_0. The price and quantity per period prior to the recovery are therefore P_0 and Q_0.

Now we can isolate the effects of the changes mentioned by Clark to see what happened. First consider the decline in interest rates. This change would probably affect both demand and supply. In the case of demand, the decline in interest rates (more specifically mortgage interest rates) made it easier for some people to obtain mortgage loans. We can think of home mortgages as a complementary good for housing. Since most people do not pay cash for a house, they purchase the home and the financing together. As this complementary good, home mortgages, decreases in price or becomes easier to obtain, the demand for housing should increase. We illustrate this effect in

Figure 2.7
Recovery in the housing market

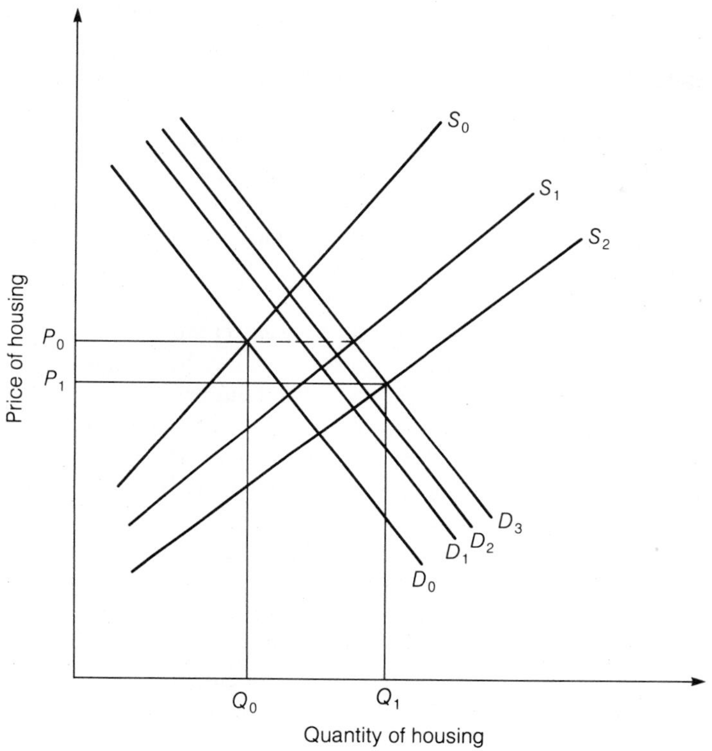

Figure 2.7 as a shift in demand from D_0 to D_1. This shift by itself would have the effect of increasing both the price and the quantity sold of housing. In the case of supply, the decrease in interest rates would lower the price of inputs used in the production (construction) of new houses. Builders find that it is cheaper to borrow funds to finance construction projects and purchase new capital equipment. As the builders' costs of acquiring physical or money capital declined, the price of inputs would fall and supply would be expected to increase. This effect is illustrated as the shift from S_0 to S_1.

We would expect the economic recovery, along with the large reduction in the rate of inflation, to affect demand. The real income of potential purchasers would increase and would result in an increase in the demand for housing. (Considerable evidence indicates that housing is a normal good.) In Figure 2.7 we show the increase in demand resulting from the increase in real income as the shift from D_1 to D_2.

Finally, on the demand side, Clark refers to the "pent up demand for housing." This must mean that potential purchasers put off buying homes when economic conditions were bad, not knowing how long the recession would last. The recovery, if Clark is correct, must have changed people's expectations about future economic conditions. As expectations concerning the future improved, people who had postponed buying houses began to purchase under the expectation of higher real income in the future. We show the effect of improved expectations as the shift from D_2 to D_3.

As we have drawn in Figure 2.7, the effect of shifting demand to D_3 and supply to S_1 would have been to increase the quantity of housing sold, while keeping the price the same. But Clark noted that the increase in housing purchases was due to a fall in housing prices. Unless the shift from S_0 to S_1 was greater than we have shown, something else must have occurred to increase supply even further. This shift could have occurred because of a change in expectations by suppliers.

It is generally recognized that housing is almost always one of the first industries to begin to recover as the economy begins pulling out of a recession. Clark noted this fact in his article. Builders must have recognized this also. As the recovery began they would have changed their expectations about future housing demand. Thus, improved expectations about the future would have increased the supply of housing, shown in Figure 2.7 as the shift from S_1 to S_2.

While many other forces were at work at the time, those we have isolated are probably the most important—improved expectations about the future, reduced interest rates, and higher real income. In our figure, the new equilibrium occurs at the intersection of D_3 and S_2. The quantity of housing sold per period increases to Q_1 and the price falls slightly from P_0 to P_1. All of the forces we have isolated would have had the effect of increasing quantity sold. In Figure 2.7 we showed a small decrease in price; but since both demand and supply increased, price could have remained constant or even risen, depending upon the relative strength of the shifts in supply and demand. We drew our figure so as to be consistent with Clark's discussion of the decline in housing prices.

Of course, for people to make money by watching for changes in economic conditions like those we described in the preceding application, they must be able to predict how these changes will impact the market. As we hope you have seen, this is precisely what comparative statics is designed to do. This ability to use economics to make such predictions is one of the topics we shall emphasize throughout the text. To see how firms make production and investment decisions based upon economic conditions, let's consider another story in *The Wall Street Journal* (August 31, 1983).

THE WALL STREET JOURNAL

APPLICATION

"Chrysler Capacity for Vehicles to Rise 50 Percent"*

In this story, the *Journal* reported that Chrysler, with recent gains in sales and market share, was planning a substantial increase in car and truck production and was planning to increase spending for new products and manufacturing equipment. The vice chairman of Chrysler announced that the company planned to increase capacity by 700,000 cars and trucks over the next year. A recently acquired plant was scheduled to begin production that year and two other plants were scheduled to increase substantially their daily work runs (e.g., from one shift to two).

According to the *WSJ*, the combined actions were designed to increase Chrysler's car and truck production by 50 percent. The company also announced that it was increasing capital spending even more, including increases in the expenses required to engineer and market new models.

This story reveals Chrysler's forecast about future conditions in the U.S. automobile market. As is apparent, Chrysler expected sales of U.S. automobiles to increase; and, given the expenditures planned, Chrysler must have expected price to rise. Looking at the demand and supply curves, it should be clear that the only way this could occur is for the demand for U.S. automobiles to increase.

What could have led the management of the Chrysler Corporation to forecast this increase in demand? It had to be that the determinants of demand had changed in such a manner as to increase the demand for U.S. automobiles. And, as we showed in the first application in this chapter, that is precisely what had happened in 1983.

2.5 SUMMARY

This chapter has established the basic framework for a great deal of economic analysis. We have developed the important tools of demand and supply and the concepts of market equilibrium and comparative statics. We have not, however, fully developed these points. Later chapters will be devoted to the theory of consumer behavior (the underpinning of demand) and the theory of competitive firms and industries (the underpinning of supply). We will also discuss at some length the techniques that can be used for the estimation and forecasting of demand and supply. For now we have the following important definitions and principles.

■ **Definition.** Demand is a list of prices and the quantities that consumers are willing and able to purchase at each price in the list during a particular period of time. The law of demand requires that when price rises (falls), quantity demanded falls (rises). Demand is derived holding constant other variables, such as income, prices of other goods, expectations, and taste. When these variables change, demand shifts. If demand increases (decreases), consumers demand more (less) at each price in the list. When the price of the good itself changes, demand does not change; quantity demanded changes.

■ **Definition.** Supply is a list of prices and the quantities of a good or service that producers are willing and able to sell at each price in the list per period of time. In general, when price rises (falls), quantity supplied increases (decreases). Supply is derived holding constant other variables, such as technology, the prices of inputs, the prices of other goods related in productions, and price expectations. When one or more of these variables change, supply shifts, indicating that firms will supply more or less of the product at each price in the list. When the price of the good itself changes, supply does not change; quantity supplied changes.

■ **Principle.** Equilibrium occurs at the price at which quantity demanded equals quantity supplied. When price is above the equilibrium price, quantity supplied exceeds quantity demanded, and a surplus results. Faced with this surplus, producers will decrease price until equilibrium is reached. If price is below equilibrium, quantity demanded exceeds quantity supplied and a shortage occurs. Unable to purchase all they wish at this low price, consumers will bid up the price until the shortage is eliminated and equilibrium is attained.

■ **Principle.** When supply increases (decreases) and demand remains constant, price falls (rises) and quantity sold rises (falls). When demand increases (decreases) and supply remains constant, price and quantity sold both rise (fall). When both supply and demand shift, some results are indeterminant, depending on the relative strengths of the shifts.

In this chapter we had two purposes. The first was to show you how managers can use economic theory to make qualitative predictions about the effect of exogenous events upon prices and other aspects of their businesses. We have attempted to show what to expect about price and quantity in specific markets when certain variables changed or were expected to change. As we will show in later chapters, the ability to make correct forecasts under difficult conditions separates good (successful) managers from those who are not so good (unsuccessful).

The second purpose was to prepare you for the material we will present in the following chapters. These chapters will show how demand and supply functions are derived from the behavior of consumers and firms and how these functions can be estimated. A thorough understanding of the material set forth in this chapter is essential to developing the ability to use and interpret demand and supply estimations and make accurate forecasts about the future.

TECHNICAL PROBLEMS

1. What happens to demand when the following changes occur?
a. The price of the commodity falls.
b. Income increases and the commodity is normal.
c. Income increases and the commodity is inferior.
d. The price of a substitute good increases.
e. The price of a substitute good decreases.
f. The price of a complement increases.
g. The price of a complement decreases.
h. The price of the good is expected to increase.
i. The price of the good is expected to decrease.

2. What do you expect would be the effect on the demand for Ford automobiles if the following changes occur?
a. Per capita income in the United States increases.
b. General Motors begins giving $400 rebates on all of its cars.
c. The government limits the number of imported automobiles to half the number sold in the previous year.
d. Interest rates rise to an annual rate of 20 percent.
e. The price of gasoline falls 25 percent on average.
f. It is widely publicized in newspapers and TV that Chrysler automobiles are by far the safest automobile built in the world.
g. Several major cities, previously without rapid transit, build citywide subway systems.
h. Ford begins giving rebates on all of its automobiles.
i. Interest paid on all loans other than mortgages is no longer tax deductible.
j. Air fares double.

3. Other things remaining the same, what would happen to the supply of a particular commodity if the following changes occur?
a. The price of the commodity decreases.
b. A technological breakthrough enables the good to be produced at a significantly lower cost.
c. The prices of inputs used to produce the commodity increase.
d. The price of a commodity that is a substitute in production decreases.
e. The managers of firms that produce the good expect the price of the good to rise in the near future.

4. Consider the following simplified demand and supply functions:

$$\text{Demand: } Q = 200 - 2P$$
$$\text{Supply: } Q = 20 + 4P$$

a. What are the equilibrium price and quantity sold?

b. What would be the effect upon price and quantity sold if supply shifts to $Q = 50 + 4P$ and demand remains constant?

c. What would be the effect upon price and quantity sold if demand shifts to $Q = 260 - 2P$ and supply remains $Q = 20 + 4P$?

5. Determine the effect upon equilibrium price and quantity sold if the following changes occur in a particular market:

a. Consumers' income increases and the good is normal.

b. The price of a substitute good (in consumption) increases.

c. The price of a substitute good (in production) increases.

d. The price of a complement good (in consumption) increases.

e. The prices of inputs used to produce the good increase.

f. Consumers expect the price of the good will increase in the near future.

g. It is widely publicized that consumption of the good is hazardous to one's health.

h. Cost-reducing technological change takes place in the industry.

6. What would you expect to happen to the price and quantity sold of orange juice if the following changes occurred?

a. The price of grapefruit juice falls.

b. A major freeze destroys a large number of the orange trees in Florida.

c. Scientists in the agricultural extension service of the University of Florida discover a way to double the number of oranges produced by each orange tree.

d. The American Medical Association announces that orange juice prevents heart attacks.

7. Suppose you own an apartment building. What would you expect to happen to the rents you can charge under the following conditions?

a. A major industry in the city closes down.

b. An urban renewal project destroys a large amount of the rental housing in the city.

c. Interest rates rise 30 percent.

d. Wage rates in the construction industry increase.

e. The economy begins to recover from a serious recession.

f. The population of the city increases.

g. A construction firm builds a large apartment complex in the city.

8. Based upon the application concerning the plans of Chrysler, what did Chrysler expect to happen to sales? To price? To profits? Which of the following events would be consistent with Chrysler's forecast? Explain why (or why not).

a. GNP was expected to rise at an annual rate of over 6 percent.
b. A new contract being negotiated with the UAW was expected to raise wages by 7 percent.
c. GM was implementing a new and expanded rebate program.
d. "Domestics Contents" legislation (i.e., legislation requiring a substantial portion of the parts in foreign cars to be produced in the United States) was probably going to pass in the U.S. Congress.
e. The UAW agreed to relax restrictive work rules.
f. Quotas on imported cars were expected to be increased.
g. Oil prices were expected to increase over the next year.
h. Inflation is expected to remain at about 3.5 percent over the next year.

ANALYTICAL PROBLEMS

1. Several economics faculty members were standing in line in the student union cafeteria for lunch. One was heard to say, "I surely wish the union would raise their food prices." The others agreed. What in the world would motivate such a wish?

2. Suppose you manage a store. How could you tell if the prices you were charging are "too high" or "too low"?

3. Many state universities are increasing their tuition rates. What would you expect to be the effect on admission standards in these state universities? In private universities?

4. In 1983 the price of housing rose 8 percent. Interest rates fell and real per capita income rose. What would you expect to happen to:
a. The demand for owner-occupied housing?
b. The demand for rental housing?
c. The demand for household appliances?

5. Some cities license taxicabs. The cities also fix the rate that taxis may charge. If, after several years, no new licenses are issued, an "unofficial" market for licenses generally arises.
a. Discuss the factors that determine the price of a license.
b. Would an increase in the allowed fare raise or lower the price of a license?
c. Who would benefit and who would lose from an expansion in the number of licenses issued by the city? Explain.

6. Suppose that you are considering investing in an apartment complex in a medium-sized city. There exists a certain demand for apartments in this city. Several conditions are occurring, and you expect these conditions to continue. The city is growing rapidly. Inflation is running at about 12 to 13 percent, but wages in the city are not quite keeping up. The rate of interest has risen to about 16 percent, but, because of the tight money policy undertaken by the Federal Reserve, most authorities expect the interest rate to fall. Some new industries, which will employ a large proportion of white-collar workers, are moving to the city. Finally, the university is undertaking a massive dormitory construction project which is expected to increase the number of dormitory rooms by 50 percent in the next two years. Analyze the effect of each of these influences on the demand for apartments. Show the effects graphically.

7. Some firms experience extreme seasonal fluctuation in the demand for the goods or services produced by their firms. Some examples are air-conditioning repair services, toy retailers, and tax accounting firms.

a. What problems can you think of that would evolve from such seasonal fluctuations in demand?

b. What can managers of such types of firms do to help solve these problems?

c. Would the problems and/or the solutions be different if the extreme fluctuations in demand were not seasonal or regular? An example might be a firm that manufactures a product the demand for which is extremely sensitive to general economic conditions.

8. Consider the market for microcomputers from 1980 through 1983. Some facts that we consider relevant to this market are as follows:

a. Business schools were offering more and more courses in computer programming and use.

b. Techniques were developed by which silicon chips, which are the basis of these machines, could be mass produced at a much lower cost.

c. In 1983 corporate profits were rising substantially.

d. Many new firms began to produce microcomputers.

e. The rate of inflation fell and the economy began recovering from a severe recession.

Using the analysis developed in this chapter, evaluate the impact of these forces on price and quantity sold in the microcomputer market.

As you are probably aware, sales rose dramatically during this period, while prices fell. What does this imply in the context of your evaluation? Assume that prevailing conditions continue. What would your forecast be for prices and sales in this market?

9. This problem anticipates material in later chapters. Suppose you manage a retail store, say, a grocery store, and wish to advertise a particular product. What determines whether or not you reduce the price (and advertise the reduction) concurrently with the ad? What are the benefits and costs of the price reduction?

3

Theory of optimizing behavior

Practically all economic problems and managerial decision-making problems are optimization problems. Firms, consumers, and society as a whole (or its government) base decisions on solutions, explicit or implicit, to maximization or minimization problems. People seek either to maximize the benefits they receive or minimize the costs from the other activities they undertake. In the specific case of a firm, we generally assume that the manager makes decisions in order to maximize profits (or the present value of a stream of profits over time). At the same time, the manager also makes decisions in order to minimize the cost of producing a specific level of output.

Since economics itself is the analysis of decision making, the study of optimization is essential to an understanding of economics. Managerial economics specifically is concerned with how managers make economic decisions, which are essentially optimization decisions.

The optimization process can be divided into two fundamental types of problems: unconstrained optimization and constrained optimization. An example of an unconstrained problem is the manager's decision about how to attain maximum profit. The firm has many choice variables to deal with in its profit-maximizing decision. It must decide how much output to produce, how many inputs to hire, how much advertising to buy, what quality to produce, and much more—all with an eye to making profit.

An example of constrained optimization is the manager's decision about the way a given level of output can be produced at the lowest possible cost.

The firm must choose among many possible input combinations to find the combination that yields the lowest cost, subject to the constraint that the combination must produce some given level of output.

As we shall show, there are many types of maximizing or minimizing decisions, either unconstrained or constrained. But, as you will see, all optimizing decisions follow either one or the other of two simple rules; one for unconstrained decisions and one for constrained decisions. We turn first to the unconstrained decision.

3.1 UNCONSTRAINED OPTIMIZATION

Unconstrained optimization involves choosing a level of some activity (or set of activities) that will maximize the returns from or minimize the costs of the activity. The most simple case of unconstrained optimization is the maximization of an objective function with only one choice variable.

Probably the most frequently encountered example of such a decision in economics is the firm's profit-maximization decision. Most theories of the behavior of the firm are based on the simple assumption that the owners and/or managers try to maximize profits. That is, other things remaining the same, they prefer more profit to less. This assumption does not mean that a manager may not seek other goals. Nonetheless, one who ignores profits or prefers less profit to more would be rather unusual. In any case, a firm generally cannot remain in business very long unless some profits are earned. To be sure, there have been several criticisms of the profit-maximizing assumption; but this assumption is the only one providing a general theory of firms, markets, and resource allocation that is successful both in explaining and predicting firm behavior. In short, the profit-maximization assumption is used, first, because it works well and, second, because it describes to a large extent the way that firms behave.[1]

The basic principles of profit maximizing are really quite simple. A firm will increase any activity so long as the *additional revenue* from the increased activity *exceeds* the *additional cost* of the increase in the activity. The firm will cease to expand the activity if the additional revenue is less than the additional cost.

Suppose, for a more concrete example, that the activity (or choice variable) is the firm's level of output. As the firm increases its output, each additional unit produced and sold adds to the total revenue of the firm. This change in revenue per unit change in output is called *marginal revenue*. As the firm increases its level of output, each unit increase in output also increases the firm's total cost. The additional cost per unit increase in output is called *marginal cost*.

---

[1]In this text, we will concentrate our attention on the profit-maximization objective of the firm. For a discussion of other potential objectives, for example, revenue (sales) maximization, the reader can see the text by W. J. Baumol referenced at the end of this chapter.

Thus, the firm will choose to expand output so long as the added revenue from the expansion (marginal revenue) is greater than the added cost of the expansion (marginal cost). The firm would choose not to increase output if the marginal cost of the increase is greater than the marginal revenue from the increase. Therefore, in order to maximize profit, the firm would select that level of output at which marginal revenue is equal to marginal cost.[2]

We can easily extend the analysis to consider choice variables other than quantity produced and sold. The results are the same. Suppose, for example, that a firm has decided how much to produce and sell but wishes to determine how much to advertise. Each additional (marginal) unit of advertising leads to both increased revenues and increased costs. If the advertising increases the desirability of the product in the minds of consumers, the more the firm advertises, the higher the price it can charge. Thus the marginal benefits to the firm are the higher revenues resulting from the higher price that can be charged. But, the marginal cost is the amount that the firm must pay for the additional unit of advertising.

As long as the marginal revenue derived from an increase in advertising exceeds the marginal cost of the increase, the firm would expand its advertising budget. If, beyond some level, the additional cost is expected to be greater than the increased revenue, the firm would no longer increase its advertising. The optimizing decision is the same as the one for output: The firm would choose the level of advertising at which the marginal revenue derived from the last unit of advertising equals the marginal cost of that unit. The same type of reasoning would apply to a firm's choice of the optimal level of quality or any of its other choice variables. In order to maximize profits, the marginal revenue of the last unit must equal the marginal cost of that unit.

We can generalize the theory of unconstrained maximization quite easily and simply. Suppose any activity (e.g., output in one of the previous examples) adds to benefits but also adds to cost. The positive difference between total benefits and total costs (profit in that preceding example) increases as long as the marginal (incremental) benefit exceeds the marginal (incremental) cost of increasing the activity. The difference between total benefits and total cost decreases if the marginal benefit from increasing the activity is less than marginal cost. Thus, the difference between total benefits and costs is maxi-

[2]The firm attempts to maximize profit (total revenue minus total cost),

$$\pi = R - C,$$

with respect to its level of output, Q. The maximization of profit requires that the derivative of the objective function with respect to output be equal to zero,

$$\frac{d\pi}{dQ} = \frac{dR}{dQ} - \frac{dC}{dQ} = 0$$

Thus, profit will be maximized when marginal revenue $\left(\frac{dR}{dQ}\right)$ is equal to marginal cost $\left(\frac{dC}{dQ}\right)$. Note that this presupposes that marginal cost is rising.

Figure 3.1
Principle of optimization

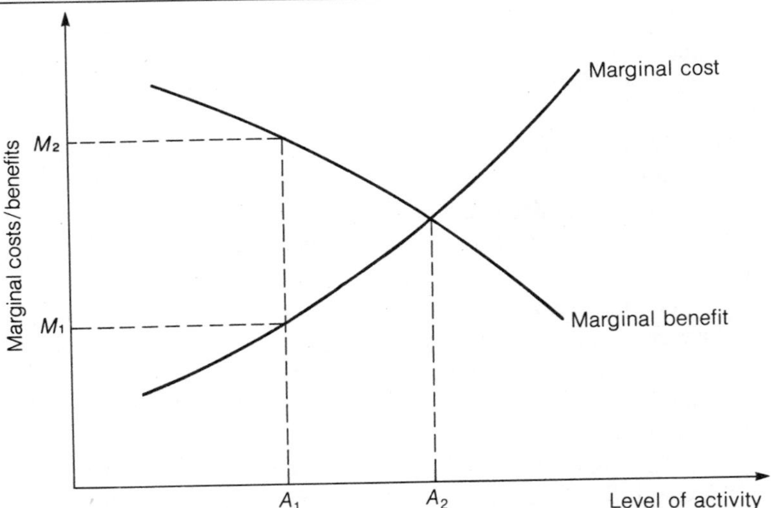

mized at the point at which marginal benefits are equal to marginal costs.[3]

We illustrate the situation graphically in Figure 3.1. The level of some activity is plotted along the horizontal axis. Marginal costs and benefits are plotted along the vertical axis. The positively sloped curve shows the marginal cost of increasing the level of the particular activity by one unit. The negatively sloped curve shows the marginal benefit from increasing the activity by one unit. It should be clear that until the level of the activity is increased to A_2 the marginal benefit from increasing the activity exceeds the marginal cost of the increase. Thus, the decision maker would never choose a level such as A_1, because increasing the activity by one more unit adds slightly more than M_1 to total cost and slightly less than M_2 to total benefits. Since M_2 clearly exceeds M_1, the level of total benefits minus total costs would be increased, and it would be increased until A_2 is reached. Certainly the decision maker would never increase the level of the activity beyond A_2, because beyond this level the marginal cost of an increase always exceeds the marginal

---

[3]We assume that both benefits and costs are determined by the level of activity, A. Thus, the benefit function is

$$B = B(A)$$

and the cost function is

$$C = C(A)$$

Maximizing total benefits minus total cost with respect to the level of activity requires that the derivative of this objective function be equal to zero,

$$\frac{dB}{dA} - \frac{dC}{dA} = 0$$

Thus, the objective function is maximized when marginal benefits are equal to marginal costs.

benefit. Thus we have established the following very important principle:

■ **Principle.** An optimizing decision maker will always choose that level of an activity where the marginal benefit from the activity equals the marginal cost.

As you can see, a firm's profit-maximizing choice of output, advertising, or quality are simply specific applications of this general principle.

The decision concerning how much of any input to hire also follows this principle. Suppose that you manage a firm and are considering hiring one more worker. A firm should hire additional workers as long as each additional worker hired adds more to the firm's revenue than to cost. It would not hire any additional workers if these workers would add more to the firm's cost than to the firm's revenue. Thus, the firm hires workers, or any other factor of production, until the amount an additional worker or other input adds to revenue equals the addition to cost. So, if an additional worker is expected to add $40 a day to the firm's total revenue and the wage rate is less than $40 a day, the worker would be hired. Alternatively, if the wage rate is greater than $40 a day, the worker would not be hired.

The firm's decision concerning how long to hold an asset that is appreciating in value also follows the same optimization principle. Suppose you own a sterile asset—that is, an asset that is not productive.[4] Suppose further that the current price of the asset is $10, but that you expect the price of the asset to increase next year. Should you sell the asset now or wait until the price increases next year? The answer depends upon two factors: How much the price of the asset is expected to increase and the relevant rate of interest.

Suppose that rate of interest is 10 percent. You could, therefore, sell the asset now for $10, invest the $10 at the interest rate, and have $11 next year. In this case you should hold the asset until next year only if the price is expected to be above $11 next year. Alternatively, you should sell the asset if the expected price is less than $11.[5] A firm would hold (rather than use up or sell) any asset only if its value is expected to increase at a rate greater than the relevant rate of interest; otherwise, it would sell the asset and invest the returns.

This result is simply a specific application of the general principle stated above. The marginal return (benefit) from holding an asset is the expected increase in price. The marginal cost of holding the asset is the lost return that could be earned by investing the proceeds from the sale of the asset, which is, of course, the interest rate. Thus, a firm or an individual would maximize the return from an asset by holding the asset until the additional return from

---

[4]A mineral deposit in the ground, such as an oil field or coal deposit, is an example of such a sterile asset that would not be productive until it is exploited.

[5]A sterile asset, as noted, yields no flow of services to the holder. If an asset yields a flow of services, the decision rule would be to hold the asset if the relevant interest return is less than the expected increase in value through price appreciation plus the value of services the asset will yield over the period. Mineral deposits would under normal circumstances be sterile, whereas land might yield a crop or provide recreational services to its owner.

holding the asset (the rate of appreciation in value) equals the additional cost of holding the asset for another period of time (the rate of interest). We shall return to the theory of holding an asset when we discuss investment in a later chapter.

To this point, we have considered only one choice variable. However, precisely the same principle applies when decision makers wish to maximize an objective function with more than one choice variable. As you would expect, the firm attains a maximum of its objective function when the marginal benefit from increasing the level of any activity equals the marginal cost of increasing that activity. The problem is, of course, complicated somewhat with two or more choice variables, because frequently the marginal benefit or return from increasing one activity depends upon the levels of the other activities. The same can be said for the marginal cost. However, this complication does not change the fundamental principle: At the optimum value, the marginal return from each activity equals its marginal cost.

To illustrate this, let us extend our profit maximization problem to include output and advertising as simultaneous decision variables, rather than considering them separately as we did above. Increased advertising, over some range, increases the quantity demanded, and hence the revenue obtained, at each price. Suppose that, at a given level of output and advertising, the marginal revenue from an increase in output equals its marginal cost ($MR_Q = MC_Q$). But suppose that, at these levels of output and advertising, the marginal revenue from an increase in advertising exceeds its marginal cost ($MR_A > MC_A$). The firm should clearly increase its level of advertising in order to increase its profits. (Since additional expenditures on advertising add more to revenue than to cost, additional advertising will lead to higher profits.) But the increase in advertising will change the firm's level of output because increased advertising leads to an increase in demand. When output changes, the marginal revenue and marginal costs associated with output are no longer equal. For instance, with the increase in output, it may be that $MR_Q < MC_Q$, and so the firm would want to decrease output. Then, if output is decreased, the marginal revenue and marginal costs associated with advertising may again change. The point is that the firm will have to adjust both output and advertising until the marginal returns equal the marginal costs in both activities; the firm will have to equate marginal revenues and marginal costs for output and advertising simultaneously.[6]

Another example of unconstrained optimization with several choice variables is the case in which a profit-maximizing firm uses several inputs in the production process. That is, when the level of output depends upon the levels of usage of several inputs. The firm would hire the amount of each input at

[6]Mathematically, this is a case in which revenue and cost are functions of both output and advertising,

$$R = R(Q,A)$$
$$C = C(Q,A)$$

Maximization of profit, $\pi = R - C$, requires that the partial derivatives of the profit function

which the marginal benefit (increased revenue) from each input equals its marginal cost (e.g., the wage rate in the case of labor).[7] The complication exists that the marginal revenue generated by any one input generally depends on the level of usage of the other inputs. Therefore, if for any one input marginal revenue is not equal to marginal cost, the firm will have to adjust (increase or decrease) its usage of that input; and, since this change in the usage of that input will probably change the marginal revenues from the other inputs, their levels of usage must also be adjusted until equilibrium is reached. Again, the complication of multiple choice variables does not change the principle of unconstrained optimization. Each choice variable is set such that $MR = MC$. The only difference is that the several optimization conditions must be satisfied simultaneously.

Thus far we have been looking at unconstrained maximization. Let's next look at unconstrained minimization. While there are not so many examples of unconstrained minimization in business decision making as there are of unconstrained maximization, the main thing we want you to remember is that the basic principle is the same. Let us analyze one example to see how the principle we set out earlier applies to minimization processes.

Suppose that the manager of a store has a problem with shoplifting. The

---

with respect to the choice variables be equal to zero,

$$\frac{\partial \pi}{\partial Q} = \frac{\partial R}{\partial Q} - \frac{\partial C}{\partial Q} = 0$$

$$\frac{\partial \pi}{\partial A} = \frac{\partial R}{\partial A} - \frac{\partial C}{\partial A} = 0$$

Thus, profit is maximized when marginal revenues are equal to marginal costs for both activities.

[7]To formalize this result, consider the inputs: capital (K), labor (L), and land (N). Thus, the production function is

$$Q = Q(K,L,N)$$

It follows that, since $R = P \cdot Q$, the revenue function can be written as

$$R = R(K,L,N)$$

The market prices of the inputs are, respectively, the interest rate (r), the wage rate (w), and the rental rate (n). Thus, the cost function is simply

$$C = rK + wL + nN$$

The firm attempts to maximize profit,

$$\pi = R - C = R(K,L,N) - rK - wL - nN$$

Maximization of this function requires that the partial derivatives with respect to the choice variables, K,L, and N, be equal to zero

$$\frac{\partial \pi}{\partial K} = \frac{\partial R}{\partial K} - r = 0$$

$$\frac{\partial \pi}{\partial L} = \frac{\partial R}{\partial L} - w = 0$$

$$\frac{\partial \pi}{\partial N} = \frac{\partial R}{\partial N} - n = 0$$

Thus, in order to maximize profit, the firm will employ that level of each input at which its marginal revenue product is equal to the factor price (i.e., the marginal cost).

manager wishes to minimize the total cost associated with shoplifting. Note that there are two costs involved in the *total cost* associated with shoplifting. First, there is the cost of losing the merchandise through theft. Second, there is the cost of reducing theft by policing or other security measures.

For any given amount of security measures, there would exist an expected amount of shoplifting. The store could decrease shoplifting by increasing its policing activities and taking additional security measures. However, the added security also imposes a cost. Therefore, the manager would increase store policing and security as long as the marginal cost of the additional security is less than the marginal reduction in the loss from shoplifting resulting from the additional security. This marginal reduction in the loss from theft is the marginal benefit from the added security. If the added security costs more than the resulting reduction in losses from theft, security should not be increased. Thus, the store manager will minimize total cost by employing the amount of security at which the marginal cost of security equals the marginal reduction in the losses through theft.[8]

The principle for unconstrained minimization is precisely the same as for unconstrained maximization. We can see this principle reflected in many cases. High-priced jewelry stores, in which the theft of a single item would involve a great loss, employ more security activities than do shoe stores. Store departments that sell expensive fur or leather coats frequently keep the coats locked to the rack, while the dress or suit departments display the merchandise openly.

THE WALL STREET JOURNAL
APPLICATION

Optimal product quality

An important decision for managers—particularly for managers of manufacturing firms—is deciding how much to spend on improving product quality and on quality control. Some people might say that the firm should pro-

[8] In this instance, total cost is the sum of the costs due to theft, C_T, and the costs of security, C_S. Obviously, the security cost is a function of the amount of security employed, $C_S = C_S(S)$. The costs from theft depend on the level of theft; but the level of theft depends on the amount of security employed. Thus, theft costs can also be expressed as a function of the amount of security employed, $C_T = C_T(S)$. Minimizing total cost,

$$C = C_T(S) + C_S(S)$$

requires that the derivative with respect to the choice variable be equal to zero,

$$\frac{dC}{dS} = \frac{dC_T}{dS} + \frac{dC_S}{dS} = 0$$

That is, $-\frac{dC_T}{dS} = \frac{dC_S}{dS}$. The firm will minimize cost by employing that level of security at which the marginal reduction in theft costs ($-dC_T/dS$) is equal to the marginal cost of security (dC_S/dS).

duce the highest quality product that is possible. But, quality improvement and quality control both cost money. A "perfect" product would not be economically feasible or even desirable in most cases. So what should the firm do?

A good case study of a quality control program was set forth in an article "One Company's Quest for Improved Quality" by John A. Young, President and Chief Executive Officer of the Hewlett-Packard Company, in *The Wall Street Journal*, July 25, 1983.* Mr. Young reported that, a few years before, Hewlett-Packard had decided to analyze in detail the methods and costs of achieving better product quality. To their surprise, they found that 25 percent of all manufacturing assets were being tied up in reacting to quality problems. They also found that production costs and prices were being driven up because of these quality problems. Therefore, Hewlett-Packard was less competitive than would otherwise have been the case.

Clearly, something needed to be done. Major improvements were necessary. The first step taken by Hewlett-Packard was to find out what could be done. A group of managers was sent to Japan to study the quality control procedures of Japanese firms. After the managers returned, a series of improvement and control measures was undertaken.

These measures included an extensive training program, competition and rewards for improved quality, and improved methods for spreading information. The firm set up a computer system to monitor quality and emphasized increased inspection. The company substantially increased the resources devoted to quality improvement and control.

The results were impressive. Within a short time, tangible improvements were becoming evident. For example, the cost of service and repair of desk top computers was reduced 35 percent. For other products, production time fell as much as 30 percent, with product defects declining substantially. These improvements allowed Hewlett-Packard to cut prices on many products. The quality program also permitted the company to cut inventories from 20.2 percent of sales to 15.5 percent within two years. This decrease meant a saving of $200 million that did not have to be tied up in inventories.

So what does this tell us about a quality control plan? It's clearly an example of weighing costs and benefits. Improved product quality has benefits, including reduced repair and services, lower inventory costs, and decreased manufacturing costs. Also, when production costs fall, prices can be reduced in order to increase sales. And the reputation for high quality can stimulate business. In an industry like the microcomputer industry, all of these forces increase revenues. But improved quality also costs something. The measures set up by Hewlett-Packard certainly cost the firm money. The new computers, the added inspectors, and the added expenses for training added to costs.

So how much should a firm spend on quality improvement and control? It could choose almost zero quality control and have a terrible quality performance, or it could spend huge amounts and have almost perfect quality, or it could choose some expenditure in between the two extremes.

Theoretically, the determination of the optimal product quality is quite simple: The firm should try to improve product quality so long as the marginal benefit (revenues) from the additional expenditures exceeds the marginal expense of making the improvements. The firm should not spend more if the marginal return is less than the marginal expenditure. Thus the firm should attempt to attempt to equate the marginal revenue from quality improvement with the marginal cost of attaining the improvement. In this way the firm chooses the optimal—profit maximizing—amount of product quality.

Of course this does not mean that it is always easy to determine the marginal benefit from increases in expenditure. As was pointed out in the story about Hewlett-Packard, a firm may well have to carry out a considerable amount of research to determine to what extent quality improvements will increase revenues. Also the costs of the improvements must be carefully analyzed. Sometimes such research is of a very analytical nature, but at other times a certain amount of intuition and experience is also applied. But no matter how the estimates are made, the basic optimizing principle holds.

3.2 CONSTRAINED OPTIMIZATION

As noted in the introduction to this chapter, economic decisions generally involve one of two types of maximization or minimization decisions. We have already examined the first: maximizing the total benefits or minimizing the total cost of some activity requires choosing the level of the activity at which the marginal benefit equals the marginal cost. The second type of decision involves maximizing the benefits or minimizing the costs of activity subject to some constraint.

Since the concept of constrained optimization is a little more difficult than the concept of unconstrained optimization, let's begin with an example. Suppose that the manager faces the decision of allocating a fixed advertising budget between two media—newspaper ads and radio ads. Hence, the manager is confronted by a problem of constrained maximization: The manager desires to determine the levels of use of the two media that will maximize total revenue subject to the constraint of a limited advertising budget.

In the case of newspaper ads, the marginal benefit of an additional ad is the additional revenues that the ad would be expected to generate. Let's denote this marginal revenue for newspaper ads as MR_N and assume that the marginal revenue (benefit) curve declines as is illustrated in Figure 3.2. (Note that this marginal benefit curve has the same basic shape as that in Figure 3.1.) This assumption implies that additional newspaper ads result in additional sales; but, as more and more ads are taken out, the additions to sales get progressively smaller. The marginal cost of an additional newspaper ad is simply the price of the ad, which we denote as P_N. Similarly, let's denote the (downsloping) marginal revenue for radio ads as MR_R and the marginal cost (price) for radio ads as P_R.

Figure 3.2
A marginal revenue (benefit) curve for advertising

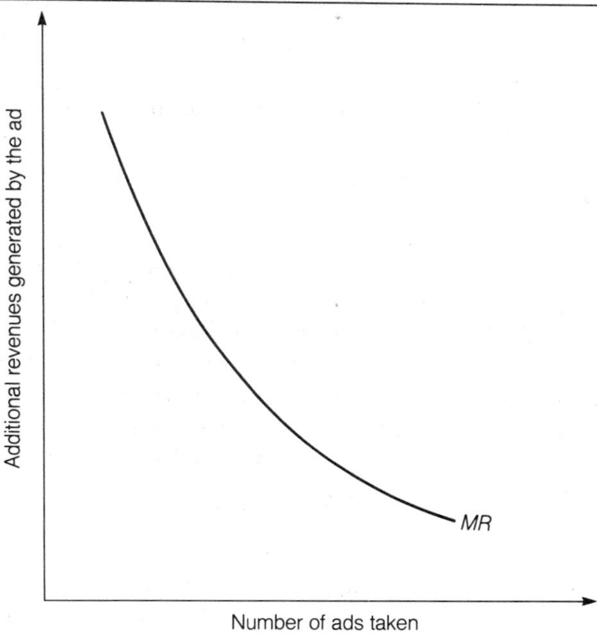

Now, suppose that the original allocation of the advertising budget between newspaper and radio ads is such that

$$\frac{MR_N}{P_N} > \frac{MR_R}{P_R}$$

Is this allocation optimal? Certainly not. The additional revenue per dollar spent on newspaper advertising (MR_N/P_N) is greater than that for radio ads (MR_R/P_R). In this case, the firm could increase revenues—without changing its advertising expenditures—by shifting expenditures from radio ads to newspaper ads. For every dollar increase in newspaper advertising, total revenue increases by MR_N/P_N. For every dollar taken away from radio advertising total revenue falls by MR_R/P_R, clearly a lesser amount. Thus the total effect is an increase in revenue.

As this reallocation continues, more newspaper ads will be purchased; as is shown in Figure 3.2 the marginal revenue from the last ad becomes smaller. Conversely, since fewer radio ads are used, the marginal revenue from the last radio ad gets larger. Hence, as the manager reallocates the advertising budget by shifting expenditures from radio to newspaper ads, MR_N/P_N decreases and MR_R/P_R increases. The manager will continue to reallocate the advertising budget from radio ads to newspaper ads as long as the additional revenue per dollar's worth of newspaper advertising exceeds that of radio advertising.

Only when

$$\frac{MR_N}{P_N} = \frac{MR_R}{R_R}$$

will this reallocation cease.

Alternatively, if the original allocation of the advertising budget had been such that

$$\frac{MR_N}{P_N} < \frac{MR_R}{P_R}$$

the manager would recognize that revenues, and therefore profits, could be increased by shifting expenditures from newspaper ads to radio ads. Again, with decreasing marginal revenue from increased advertising, as shown in Figure 3.2, you can see that as this reallocation occurs, MR_N/P_N will increase and MR_R/P_R will decrease, since MR_N increases with less newspaper advertising while MR_R decreases with more radio advertising. The manager would continue to reallocate expenditures from newspapers to radio until

$$\frac{MR_N}{P_N} = \frac{MR_R}{P_R}$$

Therefore, in order to maximize revenue subject to an expenditure constraint, the manager should select those levels of usage of the two media at which

$$\frac{MR_N}{P_N} = \frac{MR_R}{P_R}$$

If $MR_N/P_N > MR_R/P_R$, revenues could be increased by shifting expenditures from radio ads to newspaper ads. If $MR_N/P_N < MR_R/P_R$, revenues could be increased by shifting expenditures from newspaper ads to radio ads.

Generalizing the results obtained from the preceding example, let's consider two activities, A and B. The objective of the manager is to maximize (or minimize) an objective function determined by these activities, subject to a constraint. If we denote the marginal benefits from activities A and B as MB_A and MB_B and the marginal costs as MC_A and MC_B, the optimal levels for activities A and B are those at which

$$\frac{MB_A}{MC_A} = \frac{MB_B}{MC_B}$$

This condition can be expanded to include more than two activities. If we were to consider activities A,B,C,...,Z, the condition for constrained optimization is[9]

[9]Using mathematics, the principles of constrained optimization can be summarized more explicitly. Consider an objective function involving n choice variables

$$\theta = \theta(X_1, X_2, X_3, \cdots, X_n)$$

The partial derivatives of this objective function, $\partial\theta/\partial X_i$, represent the marginal benefit associated

$$\frac{MB_A}{MC_A} = \frac{MB_B}{MC_B} = \frac{MB_C}{MC_C} = \cdots = \frac{MB_Z}{MC_Z}$$

Hence, we can express the principle of constrained optimization as follows:

■ **Principle.** An objective function is maximized or minimized subject to a constraint if, for all of the variables in the objective function, the ratios of marginal benefit to marginal cost are equal.

To further illustrate this principle let's look at a constrained minimization problem that we will take up in much more detail in Chapter 5. Suppose a firm produces its output using two inputs, capital (K) and labor (L). The manager of the firm desires to produce some given level of output, say, 1,000 units. The problem confronting the manager is the selection of the combination of the inputs, K and L, that will result in the lowest possible cost to the firm: The manager wants to minimize cost, subject to the constraint that the combination selected must yield an output of 1,000 units.

Using the principle set out above, let's see how the manager can solve this problem. In this case, the objective function that is to be minimized is a cost function, which is determined by the levels of usage of the two inputs. That is,

$$C = f(K,L)$$

The question facing the manager is how much of the two inputs to use. Let's look first at capital. The marginal benefit to the firm for using an additional

---

with X_i. Now, consider a constraint function

$$\phi = \phi(X_1, X_2, X_3, \cdots, X_n) = 0$$

In this case, the partial derivatives, $\partial\phi/\partial X_i$, represent the marginal cost of X_i.

To obtain an optimum, we specify the Lagrangian function

$$L = \theta(X_I, X_2, X_3, \cdots, X_n) - \lambda[\phi(X_1, X_2, X_3, \cdots, X_n)]$$

An optimum requires that the partial derivatives of this function all equal zero

$$\frac{\partial L}{\partial X_1} = \frac{\partial \theta}{\partial X_1} - \lambda\frac{\partial \phi}{\partial X_1} = 0$$

$$\frac{\partial L}{\partial X_2} = \frac{\partial \theta}{\partial X_2} - \lambda\frac{\partial \phi}{\partial X_2} = 0$$

$$\vdots$$

$$\frac{\partial L}{\partial X_n} = \frac{\partial \theta}{\partial X_n} - \lambda\frac{\partial \phi}{\partial X_n} = 0$$

Combining these, the condition for an optimum is

$$\frac{\partial\theta/\partial X_1}{\partial\phi/\partial X_1} = \frac{\partial\theta/\partial X_2}{\partial\phi/\partial X_2} = \frac{\partial\theta/\partial X_3}{\partial\phi/\partial X_3} = \cdots = \frac{\partial\theta/\partial X_n}{\partial\phi/\partial X_n}$$

That is, a constrained optimum is attained when the ratio of the marginal benefits and marginal costs are equal for all of the choice variables.

unit of capital is the additional output that would be produced—the marginal product of capital,

$$MB_K = \frac{\Delta Q}{\Delta K} = MP_K,$$

where Δ means "the change in." The marginal cost to the firm of using this additional unit of capital is the price the firm must pay to use this unit of capital. We call this price the rental rate on capital (r); so,

$$MC_K = r$$

Likewise, the marginal benefit for using an additional unit of labor is its marginal product,

$$MB_L = \frac{\Delta Q}{\Delta L} = MP_L,$$

and the marginal cost of using the additional unit of labor is the wage rate (w) that must be paid.

$$MC_L = w$$

Hence, the preceding principle requires that cost will be minimized, subject to the output constraint if the manager selects the levels of usage of capital and labor at which

$$\frac{MP_K}{r} = \frac{MP_L}{w}$$

To see that this is a constrained optimum, suppose that the firm is producing 1,000 units, and is using the levels of labor and capital at which

$$\frac{MP_K}{r} < \frac{MP_L}{w}$$

In this case, the additional output per dollar expenditure for labor exceeds that for capital, and so the firm could reduce cost by releasing some capital and hiring more labor. To see this more clearly, let's use some numerical values. Suppose $MP_K = 20$, $MP_L = 10$, $w = \$2$, and $r = \$6$; therefore

$$\frac{MP_K}{r} = \frac{20}{6} < \frac{10}{2} = \frac{MP_L}{w}$$

Reducing capital by one unit lowers total output by 20 units and total cost by \$6. Since the marginal product of labor is 10, labor would have to be reduced by 2 units in order to hold output constant at 1,000 (i.e., 2 additional units of labor times its marginal product, 10, equals the sacrificed output from the one unit reduction of capital, 20). Since labor costs \$2 a unit, increasing it by 2 units adds \$4 to cost; but, as noted, the reduction in capital saves \$6; total cost is therefore reduced by \$2, while output remains constant. Thus the firm should reduce capital used and add labor.[10] Conversely, if the firm had originally been using levels of capital and labor at which

$$\frac{MP_K}{r} > \frac{MP_L}{w}$$

it should be clear that the firm could reduce total cost by substituting some capital for labor. Only in the case in which $MP_K/r = MP_L/w$, would their exist no reallocation between capital and labor that would reduce cost.[11]

Until now we have concentrated upon problems involving benefits that cost money. Economic decision makers do, however, operate under nonmonetary constraints. An excellent example is a time constraint. Suppose a decision maker has a fixed amount of time available and must decide how to allocate this time among several types of activities, each of which takes time and yields benefits. From the principle of constrained optimization, the decision maker should allocate time so that the marginal benefit per unit of time spent is equal for all activities. To illustrate this point, suppose that the marginal benefit from the last hour spent in activity A exceeds the marginal benefit from the last hour spent on B. The allocator should reduce the time spent in carrying out activity B and increase the time spent on A, because the additional benefit from A outweighs the lost benefit from spending an hour on B.

---

[10]In this numerical example we have deviated a bit from the formal definition of marginal product, which is the additional output forthcoming from one additional unit of the input, holding the usage of all other inputs constant. For simplicity we have assumed that the marginal product of labor remains the same after capital is reduced by one unit. But the approximation is close enough for illustrative purposes if the change in input use is small.

We will also show in Chapter 5 that the equilibrium comes about when the firm substitutes capital for labor or labor for capital, because the marginal product of the input that is increased falls while that of the decreasing input rises.

[11]Alternatively, we can examine the case of maximizing output, subject to a given cost. The objective function is the production function

$$\theta = Q = Q(X_1, X_2, X_3, \cdots, X_n)$$

where X_i represents the levels of input usage. In this case $\partial Q/\partial X_i$ represents the additional output generated by an additional unit of X_i (i.e., the marginal benefit from an increase in X_i). In general, cost can be specified to be a function of the levels of input usage.

$$C = C(X_1, X_2, X_3, \cdots, X_n)$$

In this example, the constraint is that cost be equal to some fixed amount. That is, $C = \overline{C}$; or,

$$\phi = C(X_1, X_2, X_3, \cdots, X_n) - \overline{C}$$

Note that $\partial\phi/\partial X_i = \partial C/\partial X_i$ (i.e., the marginal cost of the input). Using the Lagrangian function, it follows that a constrained maximum occurs when

$$\frac{\partial Q/\partial X_1}{\partial C/\partial X_1} = \frac{\partial Q/\partial X_2}{\partial C/\partial X_2} = \frac{\partial Q/\partial X_3}{\partial C/\partial X_3} = \cdots = \frac{\partial Q/\partial X_n}{\partial C/\partial X_n}$$

That is, constrained output maximizations occurs when the ratio of marginal product (benefit) to marginal cost is equal for all inputs. (Note that, if the input prices are fixed, marginal cost is equal simply to input price.)

The time should be reallocated until the marginal benefit per time period spent on each activity is equal.[12]

Optimization subject to a time constraint is one of the more important problems a decision maker in both the public and private sector must face. Managers have only so much time in the day or week and they have many activities to carry out—probably more activities than they have time to spend on them. Decision makers must decide on their goals—what they wish to optimize—subject to the time constraint. Then they must allocate this scarce time so that the marginal benefit from each activity per unit of time spent is the same for all activities.

APPLICATION

The optimal allocation of study time

Suppose a student has allocated nine hours to study for three examinations coming up the next day. The exams are in statistics, economics, and mathematics. The student's objective is to allocate the study time so as to maximize the total of the scores on the three exams (and therefore maximize the average score). The student's assessment of the grade in each exam for each given amount of study time is shown in the following table.

From the table we can see that were the student to spend no time studying, the grades will be 50 in statistics, 53 in economics, and 65 in mathematics. If one hour is added to study time, it would add 13 points to the statistics grade, 12 points to the economics grade, or 10 points to the mathematics grade. So, the first hour of study would be allocated to statistics, where the return is

[12]Mathematically, the decision maker wishes to maximize an objective (or benefit) function, which is itself a function of the time allocated to activities 1 through n,

$$\theta = \theta(T_1, T_2, T_3, \cdots, T_n)$$

The constraint is that there is a limited amount of time available. That is

$$T_1 + T_2 + T_3 + \cdots + T_n = \overline{T}$$

so the constraint function is

$$\phi = T_1 + T_2 + T_3 + \cdots + T_n - \overline{T}$$

The Lagrangian function is then

$$L = \theta(T_1, T_2, T_3, \cdots, T_n) - \lambda(T_1 + T_2 + T_3 + \cdots + T_n - T)$$

Maximization requires that the partial derivatives of this function be equal to zero. Considering the time spent in activity i,

$$\frac{\partial L}{\partial T_i} = \frac{\partial \theta}{\partial T_i} - \lambda = 0$$

Combining all n of the equilibrium conditions, it follows that the objective function is maximized, subject to the constraint, when

$$\frac{\partial \theta}{\partial T_1} = \frac{\partial \theta}{\partial T_2} = \frac{\partial \theta}{\partial T_3} = \cdots = \frac{\partial \theta}{\partial T_n}$$

That is, a maximum is attained when time is allocated so that the marginal benefit from additional time allocated is the same for all activities.

Study time (hours)	Grade in Statistics	Economics	Mathematics
0	50	53	65
1	63	65	75
2	73	73	80
3	80	78	84
4	85	81	87
5	89	83	89
6	92	84	90

highest. The second hour would be allocated to economics, since it would add 12 points in this subject but only 10 in each of the others. The third and fourth hours should go to statistics and math, since the grade increases are 10 points in each of these subjects, but only 8 in economics. Following the same line of reasoning, the fifth hour would go to economics and the sixth to statistics. The student's nine-hour study time constraint leaves three more hours of study time. The added points from an additional hour of study in each subject at this point are the same—five. Thus the student would allocate one more hour to each course.

Therefore, the optimal allocation of the nine hours would be for the student to spend four hours studying statistics, three hours studying economics, and two studying math. The total expected points would be 243, with an average grade of 81. This is the highest average possible with the nine-hour study constraint. (You can verify this by trying to reallocate the nine hours in different ways.)

Note that this allocation decision is simply a specific application of the principle set forth above for constrained optimization. The marginal cost (in hours) of allocating an additional hour to a particular course is one. The marginal benefit of allocating an additional hour to a particular course is the grade incrase that would result. As we know, the optimization rule is to allocate so that

$$\frac{MB_S}{P_S} = \frac{MB_E}{P_E} = \frac{MB_M}{P_M}$$

Using the above table with the allocation we have proposed, the ratios of marginal benefits to marginal costs for the last hour spent in each course are

$$\frac{5}{1} = \frac{5}{1} = \frac{5}{1}$$

The marginal benefit for the last unit of expenditure in time is the same for all three subjects, and the nine-hour constraint is met. Thus the student maximizes the total, and hence the average, grade possible, given the constraint.

3.3 SUMMARY

This chapter has set forth some of the fundamental tools of analysis that will be used throughout this text. The great majority of economic problems involve a decision maker who is attempting either to maximize the total benefits from various activities or to minimize the costs. These decisions always involve marginal analysis and follow either of two fundamental principles.

■ **Principle.** To maximize or minimize an unconstrained objective function that itself is a function of certain activities or variables, each activity is carried out until the marginal return (marginal benefit) from an increase in the activity equals the marginal cost of the increase.

■ **Principle.** To maximize or minimize an objective function subject to a constraint imposed by another function, the ratios of the marginal benefit to marginal cost must be equal for all activities.

As you will see, if you follow these simple rules, most economic analysis will be clear and straightforward. These two rules, although simple, are very useful tools for making economic decisions and are extremely useful to managers when making decisions. Let us emphasize once more that *marginal changes* are the key factors in optimization decisions.

TECHNICAL PROBLEMS

1. A toy manufacturer is experiencing quality problems along its assembly line. The marketing division estimates that each defective toy that leaves the plant costs the firm $10, on average, for replacement or repair. The engineering department recommends hiring quality inspectors to sample for defective toys. In this way many quality problems can be caught and prevented before shipping. After visiting other companies, a management team derives the following schedule showing the approximate number of defective toys that would be produced for several levels of inspection.

Number of inspectors	*Average number of defective toys (per day)*
0	92
1	62
2	42
3	27
4	17
5	10
6	5

The daily wage of people qualified to be inspectors is $70.

a. How many inspectors should the firm hire?

b. What would your answer be if the wage rate is $90?

c. What if the average cost of a defective toy is $5 and the wage rate of inspectors is $70?

2. A mining firm believes that it can increase labor productivity and, therefore, net revenue by reducing air pollution in the mine. It estimates that the marginal cost function for reducing pollution by installing additional capital equipment is

$$MC = 40P$$

where P represents a reduction of one unit of pollution. It also feels that for every unit of pollution reduction the marginal increase in net revenue (MR) is

$$MR = \$1{,}000 - 10P.$$

How much pollution reduction should the firm undertake?

3. A firm has the options of advertising on TV, radio, and in newspapers. It has a weekly advertising budget of $2,300 and wishes to maximize the number of units sold. Its estimates of the *increase* in weekly sales from ads in each of the three media are given in the table below.

	Increase in units sold		
Number of ads	*TV*	*Radio*	*Newspaper*
1	40	15	20
2	30	13	15
3	22	10	12
4	18	9	10
5	14	6	8
6	10	4	6
7	7	3	5
8	4	2	3
9	2	1	2
10	1	0	1

The prices of each type of ad are as follows:

TV	$300 each
Radio	$100 each
Newspaper	$200 each

a. How should the firm allocate its advertising budget among the three media?

b. Show that the allocation you suggest satisfies the condition for constrained optimization.

c. If the advertising budget is reduced to $1,100, how many ads will be purchased in each of the media?

4. A large shipping firm has established a minimum standard of truck maintenance and repair that the management believes is necessary. It uses a combination of skilled mechanics and unskilled labor to perform the maintenance. The director of the maintenance division believes that any of the following combinations of unskilled and skilled labor would achieve this minimum requirement.

Combination	Skilled mechanics	Unskilled labor
A	2	30
B	5	22
C	8	15
D	12	8

From the table, we see that if less unskilled labor is used, more skilled mechanics must be added, and vice versa. Clearly the two are substitutable.

Assume the going wage of skilled mechanics is \$180 a day and the wage of unskilled labor is \$40 a day.

a. Which combination results in the minimum cost for performing the required maintenance?

b. If the combination you found is indeed optimal and the marginal product of a skilled mechanic is 90, what would the marginal product of unskilled labor be?

c. If the price of unskilled labor rises to \$80 per day, what combination will the firm choose?

5. Suppose that, in this "new tech" world in which we live, someone came up with a machine with which we could measure the increase in an individual's happiness as he or she consumed more of a product. Using this machine on one of our friends who consumes only beer and sandwiches, we found that her additional happiness function—let's call it a marginal happiness function—for beer was

$$MH_B = 25 - 2B$$

That is, the first beer gave her 23 extra units of happiness, the second gave her 21 extra units, the third 19, and so on. Likewise, her additional happiness function for sandwiches was

$$MH_S = 36 - 4S$$

If the price of beer is \$1.50 per bottle, the price of sandwiches is \$2.00 each, and if our friend has a daily budget of \$15.50, how much of each of these commodities would we expect her to consume each day?

ANALYTICAL PROBLEMS

1. Explain how the value of a businessperson's time would affect the decision whether to drive or to fly on a business trip. What other factors would affect the decision? What is the full cost of the trip?

2. In an article in *The Wall Street Journal*, of January 5, 1984—"Fast-Food Firms' New Items Undergo Exhaustive Testing"—John Koten reported that before switching to Pepsi from Coke in 1983, Burger King Corporation spent more than two years examining data from the soft-drink industry and doing its own market research. Burger King went so far as to send employees on "undercover missions" to Jack-in-the-Box franchises to clock how much time was wasted informing customers who asked for Coke that the chain serves Pepsi instead.

What information was Burger King looking for? Why was it collecting this information? What other information would be relevant other than time wasted?

3. We know that consumers engage in price search—shopping for lower prices for the products they wish to purchase.
   a. How, in general, would a consumer determine how much time to spend in price search?
   b. For what kinds of goods would we expect to see consumers engaging in more price search?
   c. How might the manager of a firm be able to use the existence of this price searching to increase the firm's profit?

4. An article in *The Wall Street Journal* of November 3, 1983, presented some results from a survey by the Association of National Advertisers. Of the 138 national marketers surveyed, 92 claimed that at least half of their new products were profitable. This clearly represented a lot of successes but there were also a lot of failures. From the results of the survey the *WSJ* concluded that to improve the odds of finding a successful new product, a firm should spend more time studying markets and less time designing new products. Many of the companies surveyed recommended that more resources be devoted to searching for promising markets rather than on developing and testing new products.

Suppose the "new product" division of a firm is allocated a specific budget for its activities. Within this budget, the firm can spend on product development and/or market research. Discuss how the manager of the new-products division could obtain the necessary data and make the decision regarding the allocation of this limited budget between product development and market research.

SUGGESTED ADDITIONAL REFERENCES

Allen, R. D. G. *Mathematical Analysis for Economists*. New York: St. Martin's Press, 1938.

Baumol, W. J. *Business Behavior, Value, and Growth*. New York: Harcourt Brace Jovanovich, 1967.

Chiang, A. C. *Fundamental Methods of Mathematical Economics*. New York: McGraw-Hill, 1974.

4

Basic estimation techniques

In order for managers of firms to be able to use the various techniques that will be described in this text, it is necessary that they be able to obtain estimates of the functions we will describe—production functions, cost functions, and demand functions. While there do exist alternative estimating techniques—some of which we will describe—these estimates are often obtained from *regression analysis*.

In this chapter, we will describe to you the *basics* of regression analysis: how a regression line is fitted, how tests of hypotheses are conducted, and how the estimates can be used in managerial decision making. Throughout this discussion and the applications of regression analysis that will appear later in this text, please keep in mind that we are not so interested in your knowing the way the various statistics are calculated as we are in your knowing the way these estimates can be employed. We are primarily concerned with familiarizing you with the interpretation of statistical results rather than with the estimating techniques themselves. We want you to be able to *use* the results of estimations in making managerial decisions.

4.1 FITTING A REGRESSION LINE

Regression analysis is simply a statistical technique used to ascertain the relation between one variable (called the dependent or endogenous variable) and one or more other variables (called the independent or exogenous variables). Let's consider a simple, two-variable case. Suppose you believe that there exists a linear relation between Y and X. That is, you hypothesize the linear relation

$$Y = a + bX$$

Put most simply, the objective of regression analysis is to provide estimates of the parameters a and b.

To obtain such estimates, an analyst would first collect data on the values of Y and X. The data could be collected over time for a given firm (or a given industry, etc.) or the data could be collected from many different firms, industries, and so forth, at a given point in time. (The former is called time-series data while the later is called cross-section data.) Notwithstanding the manner in which the data were collected, the result would be a scatter of data points through which a regression line would be fit.

To see how this would be done, let's consider a simplified example. Suppose that you wanted to examine the relation between advertising expenditures and sales. Suppose further that you had a cross-section data set available on the sales and corresponding advertising expenditures for six firms:

Table 4.1

Firm	*Sales ($000)*	*Advertising expenditures*
1	40	$ 6,000
2	40	10,000
3	60	15,000
4	50	14,000
5	20	3,000
6	30	7,000

A regression line is nothing more than a method of organizing the data into a simplified form in order to obtain an estimate of the relation between the dependent variable (sales) and the independent variable (advertising). To illustrate, the six observations on quantity sold and advertising expenditures presented in Table 4.1 are plotted in Figure 4.1. Note that there seems to be a positive relation between advertising expenditures (the independent variable) and sales (the dependent variable). The higher the level of advertising, the greater are sales. We have drawn a regression line through the scatter of data points that seems to "fit" the data rather well.

But this line is only one of the many possible lines that fit the data. The objective of regression analysis is to determine the straight line that "best fits" this scatter of data points. Regression analysis is designed to determine this best-fitting line statistically.

In our hypothetical example we want to obtain an *estimate* of the relation between advertising expenditures (A) and sales (S). For simplicity, we assume that this relation is linear; so, we want to obtain an estimate of the relation

$$S = a + bA,$$

Figure 4.1
A regression line

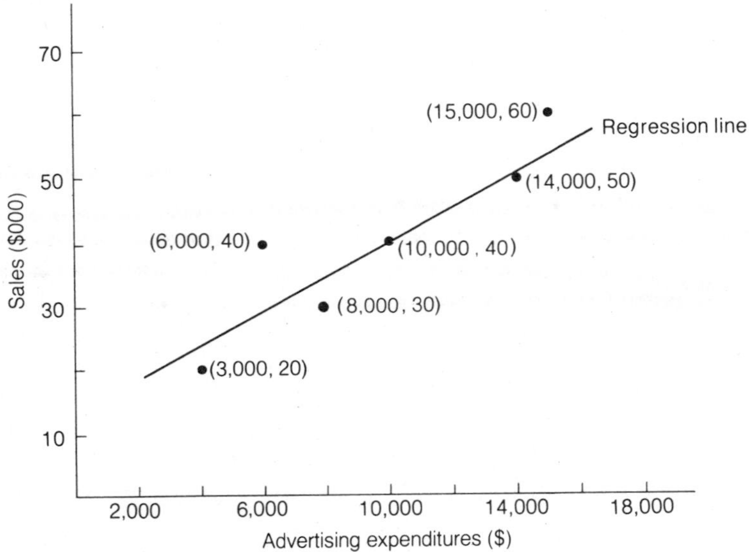

where the parameter a measures expected sales with no advertising and the parameter b represents the additional sales that would be generated by an additional $1 expenditure on advertising. In terms of the discussion in Chapter 3, b provides a measure of the marginal addition to sales generated by an additional unit (dollar's worth) of advertising, i.e., $b = \Delta S/\Delta A$. Hence, our objective is to obtain estimates of a and b. We will denote these estimates as $\hat{a}$ and $\hat{b}$ respectively.

Once we have these estimates, we can use them in making managerial decisions. For example, given the estimate of b in conjunction with the optimization techniques described in Chapter 3, we can determine the optimal level of advertising. Or, we might use the estimated regression line (regression equation) to provide forecasts of future sales.

In Figure 4.2 we have reproduced our data scatter on the more general X and Y axes. Through the data scatter we have put a representative regression line, $\hat{Y} = \hat{a} + \hat{b}X$. The vertical distance of a data point from the regression line is called the error. A representative error is shown in Figure 4.2 as the distance e_i. Regression analysis selects the straight line, $\hat{Y} = \hat{a} + \hat{b}X$, that minimizes the sum of the squared errors (Σe_i^2).[1]

[1]Alternatively, we can denote the error as the difference between the actual value of the dependent variable, Y_i, and the value that would be predicted from the regression line, $\hat{Y}_i = \hat{a} + \hat{b}X_i$. Thus, regression analysis means that the values $\hat{a}$ and $\hat{b}$ are selected in order to minimize

$$\Sigma(Y_i - \hat{Y}_i)^2 = \Sigma(Y_i - \hat{a} - \hat{b}X_i)^2$$

Figure 4.2
Fitting a regression line

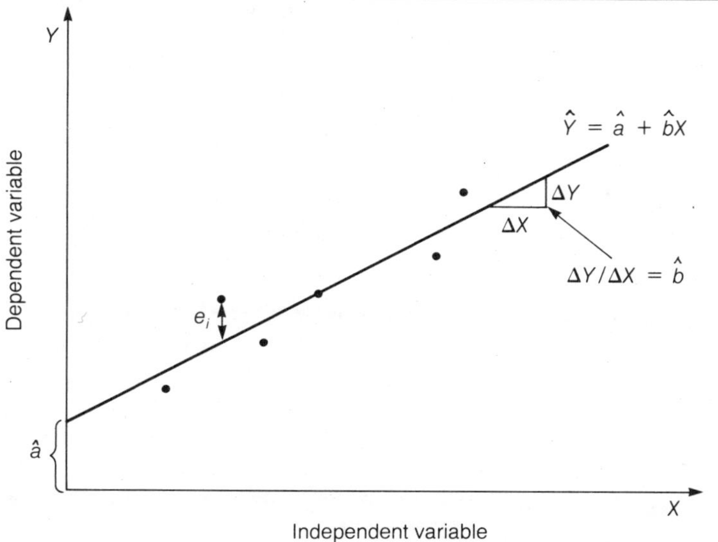

Therefore, regression analysis is simply a technique that employs available data to provide an estimate of the relation between the independent and dependent variables. Given the existing data on Y and X, regression analysis is a way of calculating values for $\hat{a}$ and $\hat{b}$ so that regression equation

$$\hat{Y} = \hat{a} + \hat{b}X$$

best fits the data. The criterion for selecting the line that best fits is the minimization of the sum of the squared errors. (Since regression analysis uses this criterion, it is often referred to as least squares analysis.)

4.2 TESTS FOR SIGNIFICANCE

The output of any regression computer program will provide the analyst with estimates of the parameters (i.e., $\hat{a}$ and $\hat{b}$). However, the question remains whether or not these estimates are "statistically significant." A regression program might provide a positive estimate for $\hat{b}$. But, the *estimate* $\hat{b}$ is a random variable. Since $\hat{b}$ is calculated on the basis of the available data, $\hat{b}$ has a variance which is itself dependent on the variance of the data in the sample. Notwithstanding the positive estimate of $\hat{b}$, the *true* value of b may be zero; and, if $b = 0$, there is no relation between X and Y. (For our example in the preceding section, this would mean that advertising does not alter sales.)

Thus, we normally test for *statistical significance* of the estimated parameters. In other words, if the estimated value of $\hat{b}$ is too close to zero, it could be

Figure 4.3
Possible distributions for $\hat{b}$

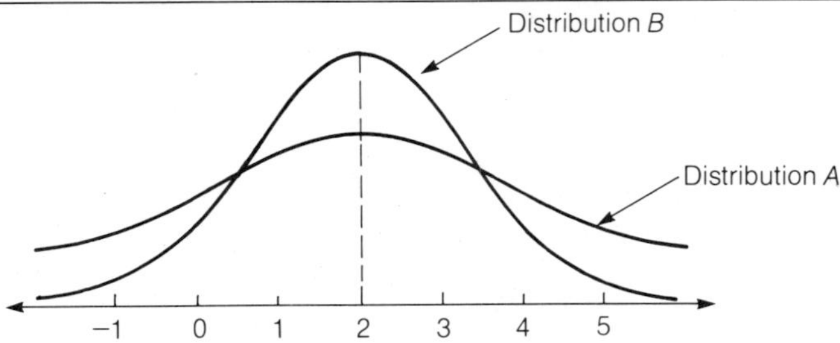

that the positive estimate occurred purely by chance. On the other hand, if the estimate of $\hat{b}$ is sufficiently large, we would say that there is a positive relation between X and Y because there is a very small probability of obtaining that large an estimate of b when in reality there is no relation between the variables. The problem is determining the value below which the estimate is "too close" to zero and that above which it is "sufficiently large."

We normally test for statistical significance of the estimated parameters, using what is referred to as a *t*-test. To see what a *t*-test means, let's continue to look at our estimate of b. As noted above, the estimate $\hat{b}$ is a random variable. Thus, $\hat{b}$ has a variance associated with it and this variance measures the dispersion of the possible values of $\hat{b}$ about its mean. In Figure 4.3 we have illustrated two possible distributions for our estimate of $\hat{b}$. Both of these distributions have the same mean value (2.0), so the estimated value of $\hat{b}$ is 2.0 in both cases. But, the variance of $\hat{b}$ in distribution A is much larger than the variance illustrated as distribution B. (The dispersion about the mean is larger in distribution A.)

In which case is it more likely that b is *really* positive—really greater than zero? Another way of asking this question is to say: In which case is it less likely that the true value of b is zero? As you can see from Figure 4.3, the probability that $\hat{b}$ is equal to zero is much less for distribution B than for distribution A. In either of the two cases illustrated, the estimated value for $\hat{b}$ is 2.0. In both cases, the estimated values indicate that the true value of b is positive. But, if the distribution of $\hat{b}$ is that illustrated as distribution B, we are more sure that b is *really* positive than we would be if the distribution of $\hat{b}$ is as illustrated as distribution A. Clearly then, the variance of our estimate of $\hat{b}$ will play a large part in the determination of statistical significance.

To generalize this somewhat, let's try the following: Let's define a measure of the variance of $\hat{b}$ as its "standard error,"[2] and denote this standard error as $S_{\hat{b}}$. As the variance of $\hat{b}$ gets larger, $S_{\hat{b}}$ gets larger. (For example, in Figure 4.3, the value for $S_{\hat{b}}$ for distribution A would be much larger than that for distribution B.) Now, let's form the ratio:

[2]More correctly, the standard error is the square root of estimated variance.

$$\frac{\hat{b}}{S_{\hat{b}}}$$

In terms of this ratio, when would we be more sure that the true value of b actually is larger than (significantly different from) zero? Clearly, the larger is this ratio, the more sure we are that the true value of b is greater than zero. Note that if we had estimated $\hat{b}$ to be negative (for example if we were estimating the relation between profits and shoplifting), we would be more sure that b was really negative if the preceding ratio had a larger (negative) magnitude. Hence, in general terms, we could say that we are more sure that the true value of b is significantly different from zero if *the absolute value* of $\hat{b}/S_{\hat{b}}$ is sufficiently large.

But, how large is large enough? For this purpose, we use the t-test alluded to earlier. The ratio we defined above is called a t-statistic,

$$t = \frac{\hat{b}}{S_{\hat{b}}}$$

Using the calculated value of t, we can test the hypothesis that the true value of b equals zero in order to find out if b is significantly different from zero. If the calculated value of t is larger than some "critical value," we can say that the true value of b is significantly different from (greater than or less than) zero.

In regression analysis, it is often said that something is significant at a 90 percent, 95 percent, or 99 percent confidence level. Thus, if we say that sales and advertising expenditures are significantly related at the 95 percent confidence level, we mean that the calculated value of $\hat{b}$ is far enough from zero that there is only a 5 percent probability that the true value of b is zero.

We obtain the critical value of t from the t-table, provided at the end of this book along with explanatory text. The critical value of t is defined by the risk level (the level of confidence) and the appropriate degrees of freedom. The t-statistic will have $n - k$ degrees of freedom, where n is the number of observations in the sample and k is the number of parameters estimated. (In our advertising example, we have $6 - 2 = 4$ degrees of freedom since we had six observations and estimated two parameters, a and b.) As noted above, the risk level may be described simply as the probability of finding the parameter to be statistically significant, when in fact it is not. The appropriate risk level is determined by the analyst on the basis of the "cost" of making an error. For example, if you will lose your job if you make a mistake, you will probably want to use a low risk level (a high confidence level).

As noted above, if the absolute value of the calculated t-coefficient is greater than the critical value of t (obtained from the table), we can say that the estimated parameter is statistically significant. If it is smaller, we say there is no statistically significant relation.

In all of the preceding discussion we have been concerned with tests to determine if the parameters are significantly positive or negative. That is, we have been trying to determine if the estimates are significantly different from *zero*. The *t*-test we have outlined can be generalized to determine if an estimated parameter is significantly different from any value—e.g., significantly different from one. We will return to this in Chapter 6.

4.3 EVALUATION OF THE REGRESSION EQUATION

Two other statistics are frequently employed to evaluate the overall acceptability of a regression equation. Let us provide a very brief look at the way we can interpret these statistics.

The first of these statistics is called the coefficient of determination, normally denoted as R^2. This statistic reflects the percentage of the total variation in (dispersion of) the dependent variable (about its mean) that is explained by the regression equation. In terms of the example we used earlier, it is the percent of the variation in sales that is explained by variation in advertising expenditures. Therefore, the value of R^2 can range from 0 (the regression equation explains none of the variation) to 1 (the regression equation explains all of the variation).

If the value of R^2 is high, we say there is high correlation between the dependent and independent variables; if it is low, there is low correlation. For example, in Figure 4.4, Panel A, the observations in our data scatter all lie very close to the regression line. Since the deviations from the line are small, the correlation between X and Y is high and the value of R^2 will approach 1. (At the extreme, if all of the observations were on the line, R^2 would be equal to 1.) In Panel B the observations are scattered widely about the regression line. The correlation between X and Y in this case is much less; so the value of

Figure 4.4
High and low correlation

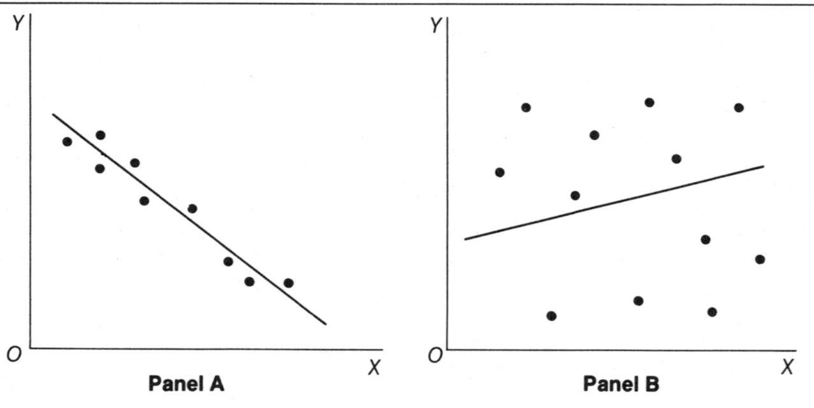

R^2 is closer to zero. (We might note that high correlation between two variables or a statistically significant regression coefficient does not necessarily mean the variation in the dependent variable is caused by variation in the independent. Variations in the two may be caused by something else.)

Although the R^2 is a widely used statistic, it is subjective in the sense of how much explained variation—explained by the regression equation—is enough. An alternative is the F-statistic. In very general terms, this statistic provides a measure of the ratio of explained variation (in the dependent variable) to unexplained variation. To test whether the overall equation is significant, this statistic is compared to a critical F-value obtained from an F-table (at the end of this book). The critical F-value is identified by two degrees of freedom and the confidence level. The first of the degrees of freedom is $k - 1$ (i.e., the number of independent variables) and the second is $n - k$. If the value for the F-statistic exceeds the critical F-value, we can say that the regression equation is statistically significant at the specified confidence level.

4.4 MULTIPLE REGRESSION

Thus far we have dealt with simple regressions involving a linear relation between only two variables—one dependent variable and one independent variable. Frequently we use two or more independent variables. Again we are interested in obtaining the equation for the line that gives us the best fit.

Linear equations

Continuing to use a linear specification, a typical, multiple regression equation would be

$$Y = a + b_1X_1 + b_2X_2 + b_3X_3$$

In this equation, Y is the dependent variable, a is the intercept term, X_1, X_2, and X_3 are the independent variables, and b_1, b_2, and b_3 the coefficients for the independent variables.

As in simple regression, the coefficients b_1, b_2, and b_3 measure the degree of variation in the dependent variable associated with variation in each independent variable. That is, $b_i = \Delta Y/\Delta X_i$. These coefficients are estimated in the computer program, as is the coefficient of determination, R^2 (which, as above, measures the proportion of variation in the dependent variable associated with variation in the independent variables), and the value of the F-statistic (the F-ratio). The significance of the coefficients and of the regression equation can be determined by t-tests and F-tests. Indeed, the only real complication introduced by multiple regression is that we will have more t-tests to perform. Although (as many of you know from courses in statistics) the *calculation* of the parameter estimates gets much more difficult as additional independent variables are added, the manner in which they are *interpreted* does not change.

All of the statistics you will need in order to analyze a regression—the coefficient estimates, the standard errors, R^2, and F—are automatically calculated and printed by all of the many available regression programs. For example, a computer program for the multiple regression noted above might present results in the following format:

```
DEPENDENT VARIABLE:  Y                    F-RATIO:  ...

OBSERVATIONS:  ...                        R-SQUARE:  ...

                        PARAMETER              STANDARD
 VARIABLE               ESTIMATE                ERROR

INTERCEPT                  ...                   ...
X1                         ...                   ...
X2                         ...                   ...
X3                         ...                   ...
```

Indeed it is this format that we will use to provide you with regression output in the remainder of this text.

As we have mentioned before, our objective is not that you understand how these statistics are calculated. Rather, we want you to know how to set up a regression and interpret the results. In this vein, let us provide you with an example to illustrate the topics we have discussed.

APPLICATION

A simple consumption function

Suppose we wish to examine the relation between households' consumption expenditures and two independent variables—family income and the number of children in the household. We could specify a linear relation

$$C = a + bY + cN$$

where C is monthly consumption expenditures, Y is monthly income, and N is the number of children. Since we expect income and consumption to be positively related, we expect b to be positive. Likewise, we should expect c to be positive. Furthermore, we would also expect a to be positive since it reflects something like minimum subsistence expenditures for a family with no children.

In order to estimate a, b, and c we could obtain data from a sample of families. Suppose that such data were obtained from 30 families and used in an available regression program. We provide below the output from the estimation of our simple consumption function:

DEPENDENT VARIABLE: C		F-RATIO: 141.391
OBSERVATIONS: 30		R-SQUARE: 0.8347
VARIABLE	PARAMETER ESTIMATE	STANDARD ERROR
INTERCEPT	443.7286	124.8189
Y	0.80572	0.06776
N	132.5073	66.9560

As we expected, our estimates of a, b, and c are all positive. Looking at the estimates, this regression equation suggests that the "minimum monthly subsistence" expenditures for a family with no children is \$443.73. Each child is estimated to add \$132.51 to monthly subsistence expenditures. (Minimum monthly subsistence expenditures for a family with one child is estimated to be \$443.73 + 132.51 = \$576.24. For a family with two children this figure is \$443.73 + (2 × 132.51) = \$708.75.) The estimate of b indicates that households will spend 81 cents of each additional dollar received on consumption expenditures (and, presumably, save the remaining 19 cents).

However, we need to determine if these estimates are statistically significant. That is, are a, b, and c "really" positive? As we have explained, this entails a t-test.

First, let's obtain the critical value of t. Since we have 30 observations and have estimated 3 parameters, the degrees of freedom are $n - k = 30 - 3 = 27$. Let's use a 5 percent risk level (a 95 percent confidence level). From the table at the end of the book, the critical value of t is 2.052.

Next, we calculate the t-values for $\hat{a}$, $\hat{b}$, and $\hat{c}$ as the ratio of the estimated parameter to its standard error,

$$t_{\hat{a}} = \frac{\hat{a}}{S_{\hat{a}}} = \frac{443.7286}{124.8189} = 3.555$$

$$t_{\hat{b}} = \frac{\hat{b}}{S_{\hat{b}}} = \frac{0.80572}{0.06776} = 11.891$$

$$t_{\hat{c}} = \frac{\hat{c}}{S_{\hat{c}}} = \frac{132.5073}{66.9560} = 1.979$$

Comparing the calculated t-values with the critical t, we see that the absolute values of $t_{\hat{a}}$ and $t_{\hat{b}}$ exceed the critical value; so, we can say that the estimates of a and b are statistically significant—in this case both are significantly positive. However, the calculated value of $t_{\hat{c}}$ is less than the critical value $(1.979 < 2.052)$. In this estimation, the parameter c is not indicated to be significantly positive at a 95 percent confidence level. (Although, as you can confirm, it is significant at a 90 percent confidence level.) The upshot is that we are less sure about the impact of the number of children on monthly consumption expenditures.

We can also consider the overall equation. From the value of R^2, we can see that 83.47 percent of the total variation in consumption is explained by the regression equation, i.e., by variation in Y and N. To test for significance of the entire equation, it is necessary to use the F-statistic F-. To obtain the critical F-value, note that we have $k - 1 = 3 - 1 = 2$ and $n - k = 30 - 3 = 27$ degrees of freedom. From the F-table at the end of the book, the critical F-value for $F_{2,27}$ at a 5 percent risk level is 3.35. Since our F-statistic exceeds this value, we can say that our regression equation is statistically significant.

Nonlinear equations

So far, we have considered only linear equations, for example,

$$Y = a + bX + cZ$$

However, as will describe in subsequent chapters, there will be times when economic theory requires that we use a nonlinear specification. In this context, we will use two types of nonlinear equations.

The first of these nonlinear equations involves nonlinearity in the variables. More specifically, we will want to estimate an equation of the form

$$Y = a + bX + cX^2$$

This equation is clearly not linear; but it presents no real problem in estimation. Indeed, the simplest way to look at this kind of estimation is to define $Z = X^2$. This nonlinear equation then becomes a linear, multiple regression equation

$$Y = a + bX + cX^2 = a + bX + cZ$$

The other kind of nonlinear equation we will use is a little more difficult to work with. This second kind of nonlinearity is referred to as nonlinearity in the parameters. The form we will employ in this text is

$$Y = aX^bZ^c$$

This functional form is particularly useful because of the interpretation of the parameters b and c:

$$b = \frac{\text{Percentage change in } Y}{\text{Percentage change in } X}$$

$$= \frac{\Delta Y/Y}{\Delta X/X}$$

$$= \left(\frac{\Delta Y}{\Delta X}\right) \cdot \left(\frac{X}{Y}\right)$$

$$c = \frac{\text{Percentage change in } Y}{\text{Percentage change in } Z}$$

$$= \left(\frac{\Delta Y}{\Delta Z}\right) \cdot \left(\frac{Z}{Y}\right)$$

As you should remember from your course in the principles of economics, these parameters measure elasticities—a concept we will discuss in later chapters. Hence, using this form for our equation permits us to estimate elasticities directly—the parameter estimates are elasticity estimates.[3]

But, the problem we face is how to estimate such a function. While it is clearly not linear, it is linear in its logarithms. That is, taking the logarithm of the function $Y = aX^bZ^c$, we obtain

$$\log Y = (\log a) + b(\log X) + c(\log Z)$$

So, if we define

$$\begin{aligned} Y' &= \log Y \\ X' &= \log X \\ Z' &= \log Z \\ a' &= \log a \end{aligned}$$

we once again have a linear, multiple regression equation

$$Y' = a' + bX' + cZ'$$

Once estimates have been obtained, significance tests and evaluation of the equation are done precisely as we have described earlier. The only difference

[3]If $Y = aX^bZ^c$, then

$$\frac{\partial Y}{\partial X} = baX^{b-1}Z^c = b\frac{Y}{X}$$

$$\frac{\partial Y}{\partial Z} = caX^bZ^{c-1} = c\frac{Y}{Z}$$

and

$$\left(\frac{\partial Y}{\partial X}\right)\left(\frac{X}{Y}\right) = \left(b\frac{Y}{X}\right)\left(\frac{X}{Y}\right) = b$$

$$\left(\frac{\partial Y}{\partial Z}\right)\left(\frac{Z}{Y}\right) = \left(c\frac{Y}{Z}\right)\left(\frac{Z}{Y}\right) = c$$

is that the intercept estimate provided by the computer output is not $\hat{a}$; rather it is log $\hat{a}$.

APPLICATION

A log-linear regression

To illustrate a log-linear regression, let's look ahead to an equation we will describe in detail in Chapter 6. Suppose an analyst specified output to be a function of the firm's levels of usage of capital and labor

$$Q = f(K,L)$$

and wanted to use a log-linear specification,

$$Q = aK^bL^c$$

The analyst collected a cross-section data set made up of data from 32 firms. Using these data, the analyst estimated the equation.

$$\log Q = (\log a) + b(\log K) + c(\log L)$$

The resulting computer output was as follows:

```
DEPENDENT VARIABLE: LOGQ        F-RATIO: 160.621

OBSERVATIONS: 32                R-SQUARE: 0.9172

                  PARAMETER          STANDARD
 VARIABLE         ESTIMATE            ERROR

INTERCEPT          -0.693             0.106
LOGK                0.578             0.216
LOGL                0.423             0.186
```

From these results, the analyst knows that

$$\hat{a}' = \log \hat{a} = -0.693$$
$$\hat{b} = 0.578$$
$$\hat{c} = 0.423$$

As noted earlier, and will be stressed in Chapter 6, $\hat{b}$ and $\hat{c}$ are estimates of elasticities. (Specifically, $\hat{b}$ is the estimate of the elasticity of output with respect to capital usage—the output elasticity of capital. Likewise, $\hat{c}$ is an estimate of the output elasticity of labor.)

Tests for significance are performed in precisely the same way as for a "normal" equation: Since there are 32 − 3 = 29 degrees of freedom, the critical value of t at a 95 percent confidence level is 2.045. The calculated t values are

$$t_{\hat{a}'} = \frac{-0.693}{0.106} = -6.538$$

$$t_{\hat{b}} = \frac{0.578}{0.216} = 2.676$$

$$t_{\hat{c}} = \frac{0.423}{0.186} = 2.274$$

And, since the absolute values for all of these exceed the critical value, all of the estimates are statistically significant.

The R^2 value indicates that 91.72 percent of the variation in output is explained by the regression equation. And, given that the critical value for F at a 95 percent confidence level is 3.33 (2 and 29 degrees freedom), the analyst knows that the equation is statistically significant.

In order to find the value of $\hat{a}$, it would be necessary to take the antilog of $\hat{a}'$,[4]

$$\text{Antilog}(-0.693) = 0.5$$

Using this value, the estimated function could be written as

$$Q = 0.5K^{0.578}L^{0.423}$$

4.5 REGRESSION IN MANAGERIAL DECISION MAKING

From this very brief overview of regression analysis, we hope that you have been able to see that this technique will be very useful in obtaining measures of those marginal benefits and marginal costs that we discussed in Chapter 3. While we will have more to say about the specific applications of regression in later chapters, at this point we want you simply to understand that it is actually used in managerial decision making.

As Robert F. Soergel (General Marketing Manager, E. L. Weingard Division, Emerson Electric Company)[5] put it, "regression analysis can be extremely helpful, and it's not as difficult as its name suggests." Regression analysis is simply a tool to provide the input necessary for the manager to make the decisions necessary to maximize profits, or as Mr. Soergel observed, "the computer is a tool, not a master." We will use this tool to find estimates of the various functions we will describe later in the text. It's not

---

[4]In this text we will use natural logarithms, i.e., $\log_e$. Hence

$$\text{Antilog}(-0.693) = e^{-0.693}$$

[5]"Probing the Past for the Future," *Sales and Marketing Management*, March 14, 1983.

that hard, and we would agree with Mr. Soergel's conclusion of "the best part: it's not expensive."

The statistical analyses (or, if you wish, econometrics) that we are going to use in this book are really very simple. Our two major objectives are also simple:

1. We want you to be able to set up a regression equation that could subsequently be estimated using one of the readily available regression packages.
2. We want you to be able to use the output of a regression to examine those economic issues that are of interest to the manager of an enterprise.

Hence, in terms of the field of study known as econometrics, we will concentrate our attention on helping you to avoid what are called *specification errors*. In simple terms, this means that we will show you how to set up an estimation equation that is appropriate for the use to which it is to be put. Specification errors—such as excluding important explanatory variables or using an inappropriate form for the equation—are very serious; they can result in the estimates being *biased*.[6]

Later in this text, we will introduce you to another problem in econometrics that we feel is particularly relevant for managerial economics—the so-called *identification problem*. This problem, like specification errors, is very serious, since it could also lead to biased estimates of the coefficients of a regression equation.

4.6 SOME ADDITIONAL PROBLEMS

In addition to specification errors and the identification problem, there are other problems that can be encountered in regression analysis. These prob-

[6] We say that an estimate is unbiased if the expected value of the estimate is equal to the actual value of the parameter being estimated. Defining $\hat{b}$ to be an estimate of b, this means

$$E(\hat{b}) = b$$

The estimate $\hat{b}$ is a random variable with some distribution. Graphically, this definition requires that the mean of the distribution of $\hat{b}$ is at the true value of b.

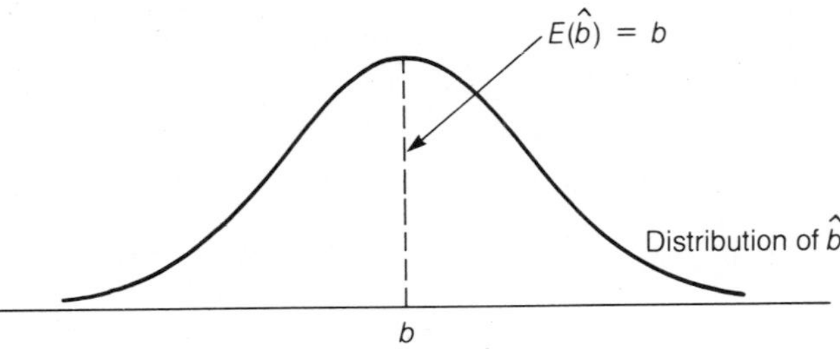

Clearly, it is important that our estimates be unbiased.

lems are normally discussed in a course in econometrics, and they are much more difficult than the material we want to cover in this text. So, let us simply mention these problems very briefly. (If you are interested in pursuing these topics, you can find much more complete descriptions in the references at the end of this chapter.)

Multicollinearity

When using regression analysis, we assume that the explanatory (right-hand side) variables are linearly independent of one another. If this assumption is violated, we have the problem of multicollinearity. Under normal circumstances, multicollinearity will result in the estimated standard errors being larger than their true values. This means, then, that if multicollinearity exists, finding statistical significance will be more difficult. More specifically, if moderate multicollinearity is present, the estimate of the coefficient, $\hat{b}$, will be unbiased; but the estimated standard error, $S_{\hat{b}}$, will be increased. Thus, the *t*-coefficient, $t = \hat{b}/S_{\hat{b}}$, will be reduced and it will be more difficult to find statistical significance.

Multicollinearity is not unusual. The question is what to do about it. As a general rule, the answer is *nothing*. To illustrate, consider the following function that denotes some "true" relation,

$$Y = a + bX + cZ$$

If X and Z are not lunearly independent—if X and Z are collinear—the standard errors of the estimates for $\hat{b}$ and $\hat{c}$ will be increased. Shouldn't we just drop one? Not in the normal instance. If Z is an important explanatory variable, the exclusion of Z would be a *specification error* and would result in biased estimates of the coefficients—a much more severe problem.

Heteroscedasticity

The problem of heteroscedasticity is encountered when the variance of the error term is not constant. It can be encountered when there exists some relation between the error term and one or more of the explanatory variables—for example, when there exists a positive relation between X and the errors (i.e., large errors are associated with large values of X).

In such a case, the estimated parameters are still unbiased, but the standard errors of the coefficients are biased; so the calculated *t*-coefficients are unreliable. This problem, most normally encountered in cross-section studies, can sometimes be corrected by performing a transformation on the data or equation. Otherwise, it becomes necessary to employ a technique called weighted least squares estimation.

Autocorrelation

The problem of autocorrelation, associated with time series data, occurs when the errors are not independent over time. For example, it could be the case that a high error in one period tends to promote a high error in the following period. Such a phenomenon is sometimes called *tracking*.

With autocorrelation (sometimes referred to as serial correlation) the estimated parameters are unbiased, but the standard errors are again biased, resulting in unreliability of the calculated t-coefficients. Tests for determining if autocorrelation is present (most notably the Durbin-Watson test) are included in most of the available regression packages. Furthermore, most packages also include techniques for estimating an equation in the presence of autocorrelation.

TECHNICAL PROBLEMS

1. Define endogenous and exogenous variables.

2. Contrast time series and cross-section data sets.

3. Following is the computer output obtained from a regression used to estimate the equation $Y = a + bX$.

```
DEPENDENT VARIABLE:  Y              F-RATIO:  141.391

OBSERVATIONS:  25                   R-SQUARE:  0.8347

                    PARAMETER             STANDARD
 VARIABLE           ESTIMATE                ERROR

INTERCEPT            443.72                124.82
X                    0.80572               0.06776
```

a. How many degrees of freedom remain?
b. What is the critical value for t at a 95 percent confidence level?
c. Test to see if the estimates of a and b are statistically significant.
d. What does the R^2 statistic tell us?
e. What are the appropriate degrees of freedom for the F-statistic?
f. What is the critical value for the F-statistic at a 95 percent confidence level? Is the regression equation statistically significant?

4. What does an analyst mean when he or she states that a regression coefficient is statistically significant at a 95 percent confidence level?

5. An analyst wanted to determine the relation between a firm's sales and its advertising levels in newspapers and on radio. That is, the function presupposed was

$$S = f(N,R)$$

If the relation was specified as

$$S = a + bN + cR$$

a. Interpret the parameters a, b, and c. (E.g., what does the parameter b measure?)

Alternatively, if the relation was specified as

$$S = aN^bR^c$$

b. Interpret the parameters a, b, and c.

c. How could this nonlinear function be estimated?

6. If the "true" relation was

$$Y = a + bX + cZ$$

but the analyst estimated

$$Y = a + bX$$

What might be the result on the parameter estimates?

ANALYTICAL PROBLEMS

1. In "least squares" regression, we minimize Σe_i^2. Why don't we just minimize the errors, i.e., Σe_i?

2. If an analyst uses a model of the form,

$$Y = a + bX + cX^2$$

doesn't the problem of multicollinearity exist?

3. In general, under what circumstances would a log-linear form,

$$Y = aX^bZ^c$$

be preferred to a linear form,

$$Y = a + bX + cZ?$$

4. We made a distinction between specification errors and the additional problems that might be encountered in a regression (multicollinearity, heteroscedasticity, and autocorrelation). Distinguish between the two with respect to the impact on the parameter estimates.

SUGGESTED ADDITIONAL REFERENCES

Kelejian, Harry H., and Wallace E. Oates. *Introduction to Econometrics*. New York: Harper & Row, 1974.

Kmenta, Jan. *Elements of Econometrics*. New York: Macmillan, 1971.

Rao, Potluri, and Roger LeRoy Miller. *Applied Econometrics*. Belmont, Calif.: Wadsworth, 1971.

Wonnacott, Ronald J., and Thomas H. Wonnacott. *Econometrics*. New York: John Wiley & Sons, 1979.

Part 2

Production and cost

5

Theory of production

The theory of production is essential to understanding managerial economics. Production theory forms the foundation for the theory of supply, which, as we have seen, is one of the basic concepts in the determination of prices. Moreover, production decisions are an important part of managerial decision making.

Managers make essentially four types of production decisions: (1) They decide whether or not to actually produce some output or to shut down; (2) They choose how much output to produce; (3) They choose what input combination to use; (4) They decide what type of technology to use in producing the output.

This chapter is concerned primarily with the manager's choice of the input combination and choice of technology. Analysis of the shut-down and output decisions is postponed until later chapters.

We shall see that production involves the transformation of inputs—such as capital equipment, labor, and land—into output—goods or services. In this production process, the manager is concerned with *efficiency* in the use of these inputs. And, this objective of efficiency will provide us with some basic rules about the manner in which firms should utilize inputs to produce goods and services.

You will see that basic production theory is simply an application of the constrained optimization we told you about in Chapter 3. The firm attempts either to minimize the cost of producing a given level of output or to maximize the output attainable with a given level of cost. It will become clear that both optimization problems lead to the same rule for the allocation of inputs and choice of the technology. And this rule is applicable to a wide range of resource allocation problems.

We begin with a general discussion of what is meant by a production function. In this chapter we limit our attention to firms that produce a single product. We will take up the issue of multiproduct firms later. We then consider production in the short run, when only one input may be varied. Next we consider production and the optimal combination of inputs when two or more of the inputs are variable. To conclude our discussion, we consider the effect of an increase in all inputs on total output, and we consider the effect of changes in input prices on relative input usage.

5.1 PRODUCTION FUNCTIONS

A production function is the link between input usage and an attainable level of output. That is, the production function formally describes the relation between physical rates of output and physical rates of input usage. With a given state of technology, the attainable quantity of output depends upon the quantities of the various inputs employed in production.

■ **Definition.** A production function is a schedule (or table, or mathematical equation) showing the *maximum* amount of output that can be produced from any specified set of inputs, given the existing technology or "state of the art." In short, the production function is a catalog of output possibilities.

Many different inputs are normally used in production. So, in the most general case, we can define maximum output, Q, to be a function of the level of usage of the various inputs, X. That is

$$Q = f(X_1, X_2, \cdots, X_n)$$

But in our discussion we will generally restrict our attention to the simpler case of one output produced using either one input or two inputs. As examples of the two inputs, we will normally use capital and labor. Hence the production function we will usually be concerned with is

$$Q = f(K,L)$$

However, we must stress that the principles we will develop apply to situations with more than two inputs and, as well, to inputs other than capital and labor.

Let us emphasize that the production function shows the *maximum output* attainable from specified levels of input usage. For example, suppose the production function indicates that combining 10 units of capital and 40 units of labor (however measured) yields 100 units of output per period. Clearly, 10 units of capital and 40 units of labor could produce less than 100 units of output if they are used inefficiently, but they can produce no more. If we want more output we must increase labor or capital, or both.

When analyzing the process of production, it is convenient to introduce an important distinction: *the classification of inputs as fixed or variable*. A *fixed* input is defined as one for which the level of usage cannot readily be changed. To be sure, no input is ever absolutely fixed, no matter how short the period of time under consideration. However, while all inputs are in fact variable, it can well be the case that the cost of immediate variation in the use of a particular input is so great as to make it irrelevant for the particular decision at hand. For example, buildings, major pieces of machinery, and managerial personnel are inputs that generally cannot be rapidly augmented or diminished. A *variable* input, on the other hand, is one for which the level of usage may be changed quite readily in response to desired changes in output. Many types of labor services as well as certain raw and processed materials could be in this category.

Given the preceding classification of inputs, economists introduce a distinction between *short* and *long runs*. The short run refers to that period of time in which the level of usage of one or more of the inputs is fixed. Therefore, in the short run, changes in output must be accomplished exclusively by changes in the use of the variable inputs. Thus, if producers wish to expand output in the short run, they must usually do so by using more hours of labor (a variable service) and other variable inputs, with the existing plant and equipment. Similarly, if they wish to reduce output in the short run, they may discharge only certain inputs. They cannot immediately "discharge" a building or a blast furnace (even though its use may fall to zero).[1] In the context of our simplified production function, we might consider capital to be the fixed input and write the resulting short-run production function as

$$Q = f(\overline{K}, L)$$

where the bar over capital means that it is fixed. Furthermore, since capital is fixed, output depends only on the level of usage of labor; so we could write the short-run production function as simply

$$Q = f(L)$$

On the other hand, the long run is defined as that period of time (or planning horizon) in which all inputs are variable. The long run, in other words, refers to that time in the future when output changes can be accomplished in the manner most advantageous to the producers. For example, in the short run a producer may be able to expand output by operating the existing plant for more hours per day. In the long run, it may be more economical to install additional productive facilities and return to the normal workday.

---

[1]Alternatively, we can say that, in the short run, the firm can vary its output, but it cannot change its capacity. As will be shown, in the long run the firm can vary both output and capacity. We could consider a time period so short that all inputs are fixed. In this case, sometimes referred to as the very short run, output as well as capacity is fixed.

5.2 PRODUCTION IN THE SHORT RUN

To clarify analysis we first introduce some simplifying assumptions in order to cut through the complexities of dealing with hundreds of different inputs. Thus our attention is focused upon the essential principles of production. More specifically, we first assume that there is only one variable input, which can be combined in different proportions with fixed inputs to produce various quantities of output. We let the variable input be labor (the number of workers), but the analysis applies to any type of input. Note that these assumptions also imply that inputs may be combined in various proportions to produce the commodity in question.

Total, average, and marginal products

We now develop three important concepts in production theory—total product, average product, and marginal product. Assume that a firm with fixed plant and equipment can vary its output only by varying the number of workers employed. The relation between the amount of output produced (Q) and the number of workers employed (L) is shown in columns 1 and 2 in Table 5.1. These columns define a production function of the form $Q = f(L)$ for 1 through 10 units of labor, the only variable input.

Total output is the maximum output attainable from each number of workers working with the given plant. In our example, total output rises up to a point (nine workers) and then declines.

Average and marginal products are obtained from the production function and may be viewed merely as different ways of looking at the same information. The average product of labor is the total product divided by the number of workers

$$AP_L = Q/L$$

Table 5.1
Total, average, and marginal products of labor

(1) Number of workers (L)	(2) Total output per unit of time (Q)	(3) Average product ($AP_L = Q/L$)	(4) Marginal product ($MP_L = \Delta Q/\Delta L$)
1	10	10	10
2	25	12.5	15
3	45	15	20
4	60	15	15
5	70	14	10
6	78	13	8
7	84	12	6
8	88	11	4
9	90	10	2
10	88	8.8	−2

In our example, average product first rises, reaches a maximum at 15, then declines thereafter. The marginal product of labor is defined to be the additional output attributable to using one additional worker with a fixed plant (or with the use of all other inputs fixed). That is,

$$MP_L = \Delta Q/\Delta L,$$

where Δ means "the change in." Assuming no output can be produced with zero labor, the first worker hired adds 10 units of output, the second adds 15 units (that is, increases output from 10 to 25), and so on. Note that increasing the amount of labor from 9 to 10 actually decreases output from 90 to 88 units. Thus the marginal product of the 10th worker is negative. In our example, marginal product first increases as the amount of labor is increased, then decreases, and finally becomes negative.

We might emphasize that we speak of the marginal product of labor, not of the marginal product of a particular laborer. We assume all workers are the same, in the sense that if we reduce the number of workers from eight to seven, total product falls from 88 to 84 regardless of which of the eight workers is released. Thus, the order of hiring makes no difference; a third worker adds 20 units no matter who is hired.

Look at the relation between average and marginal products. When average product is rising (falling) marginal product is greater (less) than average. When average reaches its maximum, average and marginal products are equal. This result is not a peculiarity of this particular table; it occurs for any production function in which the average product peaks.[2] An example might help to illustrate this point. If you have taken two tests on which you have grades of 70 and 80, your average grade is 75. If your third test grade is higher than 75, the marginal addition is above the average; so your average rises. Conversely, if your third grade was less than 75—if the marginal grade was below the average—your average would fall. This relation holds for all marginal and average schedules. In production theory, if each additional worker adds more than the preceding worker, average product rises; if each additional worker adds less than the preceding worker, average product falls.

■ **Definition.** The average product of an input is total product divided by the amount of the input used. Thus, average product is the output-input ratio for each level of output and the corresponding level of input usage. The marginal product of an input is the change in total product attributable to

[2]For the student with a mathematical background, these relations are easy to demonstrate. Differentiating the average product function yields

$$\frac{dAP_L}{dL} = \frac{d(Q/L)}{dL} = \frac{L(dQ/dL) - Q}{L^2} = \frac{1}{L}\left[\frac{dQ}{dL} - \frac{Q}{L}\right] = \frac{1}{L}(MP_L - AP_L)$$

If average product is rising, $dAP_L/dL > 0$; so $MP_L > AP_L$. Likewise, if average product is falling $dAP_L/dL < 0$ and $MP_L < AP_L$. Finally, when average product is at its maximum, $dAP/dL = 0$; so, $MP_L = AP_L$.

the addition of one unit of the variable input to the production process, the fixed inputs remaining constant.

The short-run production function set forth in Table 5.1 also incorporates a very common assumption in production theory. Marginal product first increases and then decreases, with marginal product becoming negative after a point. These relations mean that total product at first increases at an increasing rate, then increases at a decreasing rate, and finally decreases. Let us turn to a graphical exposition to illustrate this point and those we have made earlier.

In Figure 5.1 we present graphically a total product curve that embodies the characteristics presented in Table 5.1. In order to draw this figure, we add the assumption that both output and the variable input are continuously divisible. This assumption, which sacrifices little realism while providing a great deal of analytical convenience, will be used in the remainder of this section.

In the figure, X_0 is the maximum amount of output which can be produced when L_0 workers are combined with the fixed (and ingredient) inputs. Likewise, L_1 workers can produce a maximum output of X_1, and so on.

The total product curve reflects the following assumptions:

1. No output can be produced with zero workers,
2. Output first increases at an increasing rate. In Figure 5.1 this occurs until L_0 workers are employed. Over this range, marginal product is increasing,

Figure 5.1
Shape of total product curve

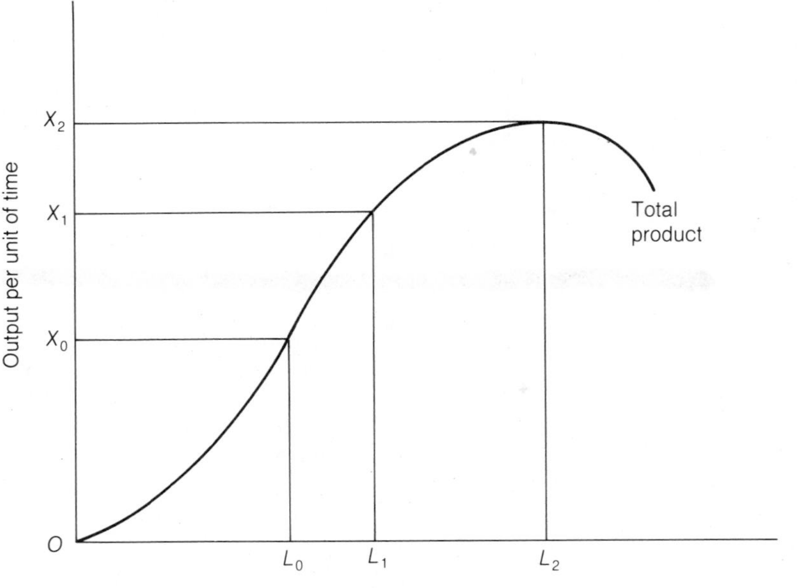

3. Total product then increases but at a decreasing rate, i.e., between L_0 and L_2. Over this range marginal product is decreasing,
4. Finally a point will be reached beyond which output will decline, indicating a negative marginal product. In Figure 5.1 this occurs for employment levels greater than L_2.

The corresponding average and marginal product curves are shown in Figure 5.2. Note that both curves first rise, reach a maximum, then decline. Note further that marginal product attains a maximum (at L_0) at a lower input level than the level at which average product attains its maximum (at L_1). While the average product is always positive, marginal product is zero at L_2 units of labor and is negative thereafter. Beyond L_2 the firm is using so much labor (relative to the fixed inputs) that output actually falls with the addition of more units of labor. One way of looking at this is that so much labor is being used that additional workers simply get in each other's way and therefore reduce the total output that can be produced.

Note again that when marginal product is greater than average product, the average product is increasing. When marginal product is less than average product, the average must be falling. Of course, when average product is at its maximum, i.e., neither rising nor falling, marginal product equals average product. The reason for this was discussed previously.

The concepts of average and marginal product will become quite important later, when we analyze how firms decide how much of an input to hire—one

Figure 5.2
Shape of marginal and average product curves

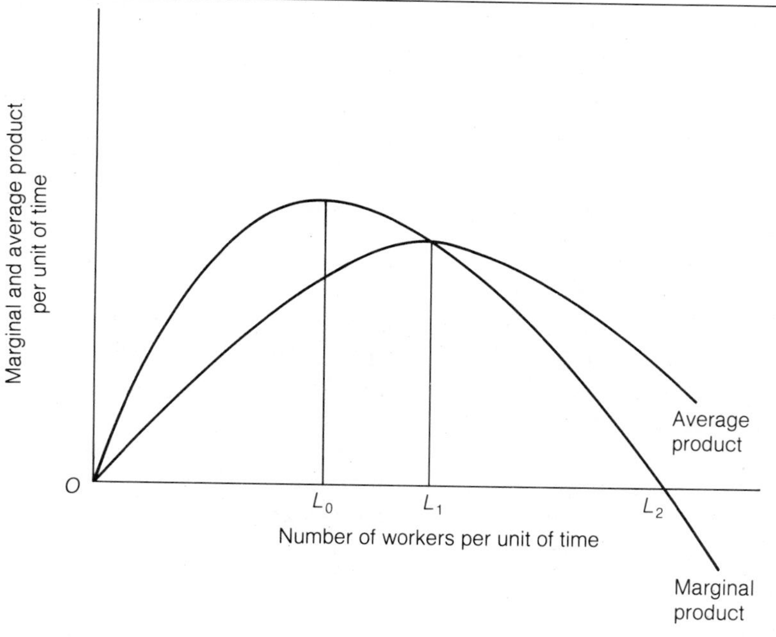

of the four production decisions a firm must make. While we have called the variable input in our analysis labor, we should emphasize that similar relations hold for any variable input—capital, land, management, and so on.

Law of diminishing marginal physical product

The slope of the marginal product curve in Figure 5.2 illustrates an important principle, the law of diminishing marginal physical product. As the number of units of the variable input increases, other inputs held constant, there exists a point beyond which the marginal product of the variable input declines. When the amount of the variable input is small relative to the fixed inputs, more intensive utilization of fixed inputs by variable inputs may increase the marginal output of the variable input as this input is increased. Nonetheless, a point is reached beyond which an increase in the use of the variable input yields progressively less additional output. Each additional unit has, on average, fewer units of the fixed inputs with which to work.

■ **Principle.** (The law of diminishing marginal physical product.) As the amount of a variable input is increased, the amount of other (fixed) inputs held constant, a point is reached beyond which marginal product declines.

This is a simple statement concerning physical relations that have been observed in the real economic world. While it is not susceptible of mathematical proof or refutation, it is of some worth to note that a contrary observation has never been recorded. That is why it is called a law.

5.3 PRODUCTION IN THE LONG RUN

We will now consider the more general case of production with two or more variable inputs. In order to be able to draw graphs, we use only two inputs, but all of the results hold for more than two. You could assume either that these two inputs are the only variable inputs or that one of our two inputs represents some combination of several other variable inputs.

Production isoquants

When analyzing production with more than one variable input, we cannot simply use sets of average and marginal product curves like those discussed above, because these curves were derived holding the use of all other inputs constant (fixed) and letting the use of only one input vary. If we were to change the level of use of the fixed input, the total, average, and marginal product curves would shift. In the case of two variable inputs, changing the use of one input would probably cause a shift in the marginal and average product curves of the other input. For example, an increase in capital would quite possibly result in an increase in the marginal product of labor over a wide range of labor use.

The upshot of the preceding is that, if both labor and capital are variable, each factor has an infinite number of product curves, one for every level of usage of the other factor. Therefore, another tool of analysis is necessary when there is more than one variable factor. This tool is the *production isoquant*, which can be defined as follows:

■ **Definition.** An isoquant is a curve (a locus of points) showing all possible combinations of inputs physically capable of producing a given level of output.

Figure 5.3 illustrates two such isoquants. Isoquant I indicates the combinations of capital and labor that will yield 100 units of output. As is shown, the firm can produce 100 units of output by using 10 units of capital and 75 of labor, or 50 units of capital and 15 of labor, or by using any other combination of capital and labor specified by isoquant I. Similarly, isoquant II shows the various combinations of capital and labor that can be used to produce 200 units of output. However, each capital-labor combination can be on only one isoquant. That is, isoquants can not intersect. Isoquants I and II are only two of an infinite number of isoquants that could be drawn.

A group of isoquants is called an isoquant map. In an isoquant map, all isoquants lying above and to the right of a given isoquant indicate higher levels of output. Thus in Figure 5.3 isoquant II indicates a higher level of output than is indicated by isoquant I.

Figure 5.3
Typical isoquants

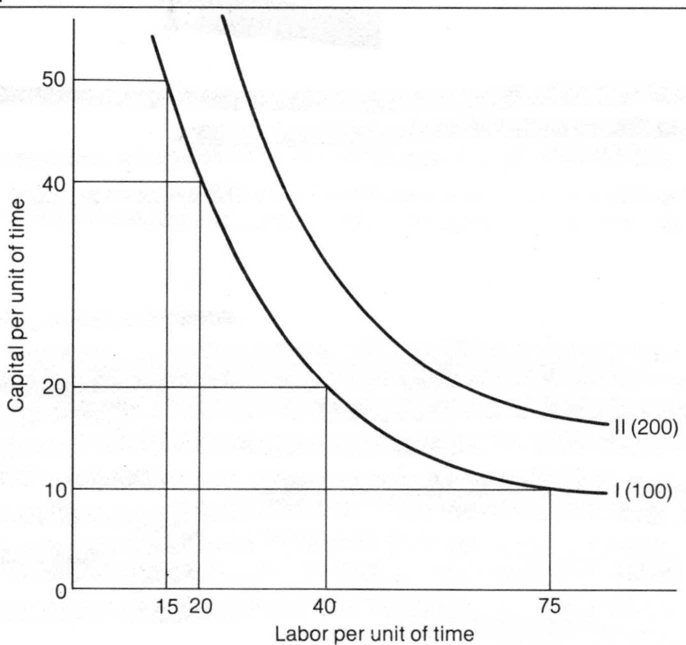

We should also note that combinations other than those on a given isoquant can be used to produce the given level of output; but such combinations would not reflect the ''maximum-amount-of-output'' concept we introduced in our definition of a production function. In Figure 5.3 it is clear that 100 units of output *could* be produced using *more than* 10 units of capital and *more than* 75 units of labor. However, such production would ''waste'' inputs. In contrast, it is impossible to produce 100 units of output using less than 10 units of capital with 75 units of labor, or vice versa. For any combination along an isoquant, if the usage level of either input is reduced and the other is held constant, output must decline.

Marginal rate of technical substitution

As depicted in Figure 5.3, isoquants slope downward over the relevant range of production. This negative slope indicates that if the firm decreases the amount of capital employed, more labor must be added in order to keep the rate of output constant. Or, if labor use is decreased, capital usage must be increased to keep output constant. Thus, the two inputs can be substituted for one another to maintain a constant level of output.

Great theoretical and practical importance is attached to the rate at which one input must be substituted for another in order to keep output constant. This rate at which one input is substituted for another along an isoquant is called the *marginal rate of technical substitution* (*MRTS*), and is defined as

$$MRTS = -\frac{\Delta K}{\Delta L}$$

The minus sign is added in order to make *MRTS* a positive number, since $\Delta K/\Delta L$, the slope of the isoquant, is negative.

Over the relevant range of production the marginal rate of technical substitution diminishes. That is, as more and more labor is substituted for capital while holding output constant, the absolute value of $\Delta K/\Delta L$ decreases. This can be seen in Figure 5.3. If capital is reduced from 50 to 40 (a decrease of 10 units) labor must be increased by only 5 units (from 15 to 20) in order to keep the level of output at 100 units. That is, when capital is plentiful relative to labor, the firm can discharge 10 units of capital but must substitute only 5 units of labor in order to keep output at 100. The marginal rate of technical substitution in this case is $-\Delta K/\Delta L = -(-10)/5 = 2$, meaning that for every unit of labor added two units of capital can be discharged in order to keep the level of output constant. However, consider a combination where capital is more scarce and labor more plentiful. For example, if capital is decreased from 20 to 10 (again a decrease of 10 units) labor must be increased by 35 units (from 40 to 75) to keep output at 100 units. In this case *MRTS* is 10/35, indicating that for each unit of labor added capital can be reduced by slightly more than one quarter of a unit.

Thus, as capital decreases and labor increases along an isoquant, the amount of capital that can be discharged for each unit of labor added declines. Or, put another way, the amount of labor that must be added for each unit of capital eliminated, holding output constant, must increase. This relation is seen in Figure 5.3. The slope of the isoquant reflects the rate at which labor can be substituted for capital. It is easy to see that the isoquant becomes less and less steep as you move downward along the isoquant. Thus *MRTS* declines along an isoquant.

Relation of *MRTS* to marginal products[3]

For very small movements along an isoquant, the marginal rate of technical substitution equals the ratio of the marginal products of the two inputs. Let us demonstrate how this comes about.

The level of output, Q, depends upon the use of the two inputs, L and K. Since Q is constant along an isoquant, ΔQ must equal zero for any change in L and K that would remain on an isoquant. Suppose that, at a point on the isoquant, the marginal product of capital (MP_K) is 3 and the marginal product of labor (MP_L) is 6. Then, if we add one unit of labor, output would increase by 6 units. How much capital must be discharged to keep Q at the original level? Capital must decrease enough to offset the increase in output generated by the increase in labor. Since the marginal product of capital is 3, two units of capital must be discharged. In this case the $MRTS = -\Delta K/\Delta L = -(-2)/1 = 2$, which is exactly equal to $MP_L/MP_K = 6/3 = 2$.

Or, if we were to decrease capital by one unit, output would fall by 3. Labor must increase by ½ of a unit to offset the decline of 3 units of output and keep output constant, since $MP_L = 6$. In this case the $MRTS = -\Delta K/\Delta L = -(-1)/1/2 = 2$, which is again equal to MP_L/MP_K.

In more general terms, we can say that, when L and K are allowed to vary slightly, the change in Q resulting from the change in the two inputs is the marginal product of L times the amount of change in L plus the marginal product of K times its change. Put in equation form

$$\Delta Q = (MP_L)(\Delta L) + (MP_K)(\Delta K)$$

In order that we remain on a given isoquant it is necessary to set ΔQ equal to zero. Then, solving for the marginal rate of technical substitution, we have

[3]For the student with a mathematical background, we can summarize this relation rather quickly. Define the two-input production function as

$$Q = Q(K,L)$$

Taking the total differential and holding output constant to remain on a particular isoquant,

$$dQ = Q_K dK + Q_L dL = 0$$

Therefore,

$$MRTS = -\frac{dK}{dL} = \frac{Q_L}{Q_K} = \frac{MP_L}{MP_K}$$

$$MRTS = -\frac{\Delta K}{\Delta L} = \frac{MP_L}{MP_K}$$

Using the preceding relation, the reason for diminishing *MRTS* is easily explained. As additional units of labor are substituted for capital, the marginal product of labor diminishes. Two forces are working to diminish labor's marginal product: (1) less capital causes a downward shift of the marginal product of labor curve, and (2) more units of the variable input (labor) cause a downward movement along the marginal product curve. Thus, as labor is substituted for capital the marginal product of labor must decline. For analogous reasons the marginal product of capital increases as less capital and more labor is used. The same two forces are present in this case: a movement along a marginal product curve and a shift in the location of the curve. In this situation, however, both forces work to increase the marginal product of capital. Thus, as labor is substituted for capital the marginal product of capital increases. Combining these two conditions, as labor is substituted for capital, MP_L decreases and MP_K increases; so $MP/_L\ MP_K$ will decrease.[4]

5.4 THE OPTIMAL COMBINATION OF INPUTS

We have shown that any desired level of output can be produced by a number of different combinations of inputs. But, as we noted in the introduction to this chapter, one of the four production decisions a manager must make is which input combination to use. What is the "optimal" input combination?

As you might have guessed, this decision is an application of the constrained optimization rule we discussed in Chapter 3. The firm can choose among many different input combinations to produce a given level of output. Or, faced with specified input prices, it can choose among many combinations of inputs that would lead to given level of cost, i.e., expenditure. Thus we can think of the firm as making either of two input choice decisions:

1. Choose the input combination that yields the maximum level of output possible with a given level of expenditure.
2. Choose the input combination that leads to the lowest cost of producing a given level of output.

Thus, the firm minimizes cost, subject to an output constraint, or maximizes output, subject to a cost constraint.

As we saw in Chapter 3, the solution to any constrained maximization or minimization problem is choosing the level of each activity whereby the marginal benefits from each activity per dollar cost of the activity are equal:

[4]Note that we have really violated our assumption about marginal product somewhat. The marginal product of an input is defined as the change in output per unit change in the input, the use of other inputs held constant. In this case we allow the usage of both inputs to change; thus the marginal product is really an approximation. But we are speaking only of slight or very small changes in use. Thus violation of the assumption is small and the approximation approaches the true variation for small changes.

$$\frac{MB_A}{P_A} = \frac{MB_B}{P_B}$$

Since the activity here is the level of usage of the input, the relevant marginal benefit is marginal product. The additional cost of each unit of input is the price of the input in question. Applying the preceding rule, the firm chooses the input combination for which the marginal product divided by input price is the same for all inputs used. This means that for our two-input case a firm attains the highest level of output for any given level of cost or the lowest possible cost of producing any given level of output when

$$\frac{MP_L}{w} = \frac{MP_K}{r}$$

where w and r are respectively the prices of labor and capital. Thus the marginal rate of technical substitution (MP_L/MP_K) equals the ratio of input prices (w/r). To reinforce this conclusion, let us develop this concept graphically.

Input prices and isocosts

In determining the optimal input combination, producers must pay attention to relative input prices if they are to minimize the cost of producing a given output or maximize output for a given level of cost. Input prices are determined by supply and demand in the input markets. For producers who are not "monopsonists" or "oligopsonists" (that is, the sole purchaser of, or one of a few purchasers of, an input), input prices are given by the market. We concentrate upon a producer who is a competitor in the input market facing given, market-determined input prices; so we treat the input prices as constant.

If we continue to denote the quantities of capital and labor by K and L and their respective prices by r and w, the total cost, C, is $C = rK + wL$. Total cost (total expenditure) is simply the sum of the cost of K units of capital at r dollars per unit and of L units of labor at w dollars per unit.

Let's look at a specific example. Suppose capital costs \$1,000 a month per unit ($r = \$1{,}000$) and labor receives a wage of \$2,500 a month per unit ($w = \$2{,}500$). Then our total cost function is

$$C = 1{,}000K + 2{,}500L$$

Now suppose that the firm decides a total of \$15,000 a month is to be spent for inputs. At this cost, the equation becomes $\$15{,}000 = \$1{,}000K + \$2{,}500L$. Solving this equation for K, we can see the combinations of K and L that can be chosen: $K = 15 - 2.5L$. Similarly, if \$20,000 is to be spent on inputs, the firm can purchase combinations that adhere to the relation: $K = 20 - 2.5L$. More generally, if a fixed amount $\bar{C}$ is to be spent, the firm can choose among the combinations given by

$$K = \frac{\overline{C}}{r} - \frac{w}{r}L$$

This equation is illustrated in Figure 5.4. If \$15,000 is spent for inputs and no labor is purchased, 15 units of capital may be bought. If \$20,000 is spent for inputs and no labor is purchased, 20 units of capital may be bought. More generally, if $\overline{C}$ is to be spent and r is the unit cost, the maximum amount of capital that can be purchased is $\overline{C}/r$ units; $\overline{C}/r$ is, therefore, the vertical intercept of the line. If one unit of labor is purchased at \$2,500, two and one half units of capital must be sacrificed; if two units of labor are bought, five units of capital must be sacrificed; and so on. Thus, as the purchase of labor is increased, the purchase of capital must decrease if cost is held constant. For each additional unit of labor purchased, w/r units of capital must be foregone. In Figure 5.4, $w/r = 2.5$. Attaching a negative sign, this ratio is the slope of the line. This slope shows the market rate of trade-off between the two inputs.

The lines in Figure 5.4 are called *isocost curves* because they show the various combinations of inputs that may be purchased for a given level of expenditure. It is obvious from the figure that an increase in cost, holding input prices constant, leads to a parallel upward shift in the isocost curve. Thus the isocost curve for $C = \$20{,}000$ lies above the curve for $C = \$15{,}000$. There would exist an infinite number of isocost curves, each relating to a different level of cost.

Figure 5.4
Isocost curves for $r = \$1{,}000$ and $w = \$2{,}500$

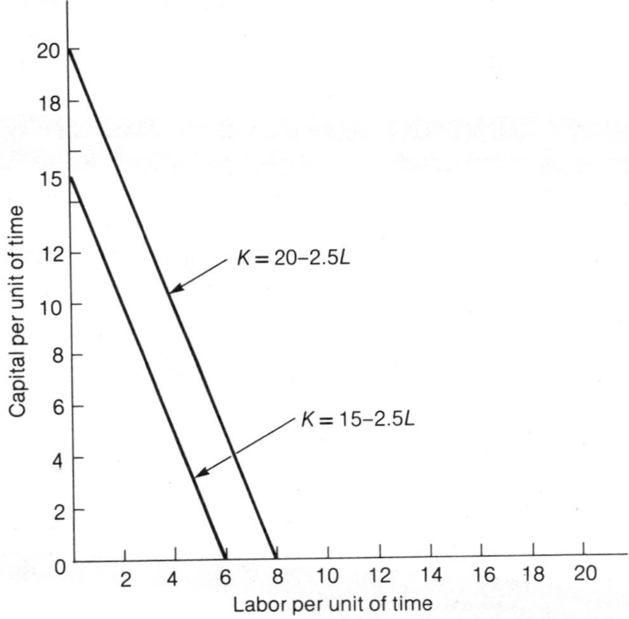

■ **Relation.** At fixed input prices, r and w for capital and labor, a fixed outlay $\overline{C}$ will purchase any combination of capital and labor given by the following linear equation:

$$K = \frac{\overline{C}}{r} - \frac{w}{r}L$$

This is the equation for an isocost curve, whose intercept ($\overline{C}/r$) is the amount of capital that may be purchased if no labor is bought and whose slope is the negative of the input-price ratio (w/r).

If the relative input prices change, the slope of the isocost curve must change. If w rises relative to r, the isocost becomes steeper. If w falls relative to r, the isocost becomes less steep.

Production of a given output at minimum cost[5]

Whatever output a firm chooses to produce, the manager wishes to produce it at the lowest possible cost. To accomplish this objective, production must be organized in the most efficient way.

Suppose that at given input prices r and w a firm wishes to produce the output indicated by isoquant I in Figure 5.5. Isocost curves KL, $K'L'$, and $K''L''$ are three of the infinite number of isocost curves from which the producer can choose at the given input prices. Obviously, the firm will choose the lowest level of expenditures that enables output level I to be produced. In Figure 5.5 output level I will be produced at the cost represented by isocost curve $K'L'$. Any resource expenditure below that, for example that represented by KL, is not feasible since it is impossible to produce output I with these resource combinations. Any resource combinations above that represented by $K'L'$ are rejected because the firm wishes to produce the desired

[5]Using mathematics, this relation can be presented quickly as follows. The firm wants to minimize cost, $rK + wL$, subject to the constraint that output is at some specified level, $Q(K,L) = \overline{Q}$. For such a problem, it is necessary to minimize the Langrangian function

$$\mathcal{L} = rK + wL + \lambda[\overline{Q} - Q(K,L)]$$

Minimization with respect to the usage of capital and labor requires that the partial derivatives be equal to zero:

$$\frac{\partial \mathcal{L}}{\partial K} = r - \lambda Q_K = 0$$

$$\frac{\partial \mathcal{L}}{\partial L} = w - \lambda Q_L = 0$$

Combining these two conditions, it follows that the necessary condition for minimizing cost for a given output is

$$\frac{r}{w} = \frac{Q_K}{Q_L}$$

The ratio of input prices must equal the ratio of marginal products (i.e., the marginal rate of technical substitution).

Figure 5.5
Optimal input combination to minimize cost, subject to a given level of output

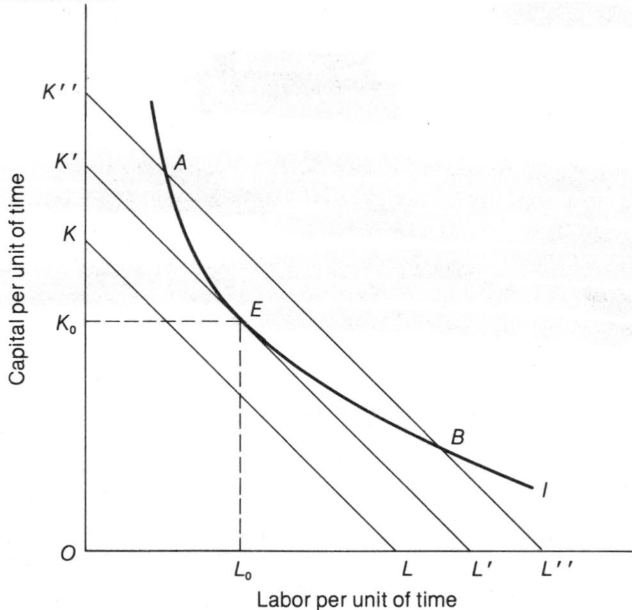

output at least cost. If combinations A or B are chosen, at the cost represented by $K''L''$, the producer can reduce costs by moving along I to point E. Point E shows the optimal resource combination, using K_0 units of capital and L_0 units of labor.

Equilibrium is reached when the isoquant representing the chosen output is just *tangent* to an isocost curve. At this tangency the slopes of the two curves are equal. That is

$$\frac{MP_L}{MP_K} = \frac{w}{r}$$

or

$$\frac{MP_L}{w} = \frac{MP_K}{r}$$

Put another way, least-cost production requires that the marginal rate of technical substitution of capital for labor be equal to the ratio of the price of labor to the price of capital. The market input-price ratio tells the producer the rate at which one input can be substituted for another in purchasing. The marginal rate of technical substitution shows the rate at which the producer can substitute between the inputs in production. If the two are not equal, a firm can always achieve a lower cost by moving in the direction of equality.

■ **Principle.** To minimize the cost (expenditure) necessary to produce a given level of output with given input prices, the producer must combine inputs in such quantities that the marginal rate of technical substitution of capital for labor is equal to the input-price ratio (the price of labor to the price of capital).

We can analyze the equilibrium condition in another way similar to that used in Chapter 3. Assume that the equilibrium condition did not hold or, specifically, that we are at point B in Figure 5.5. At point B,

$$\frac{MP_L}{MP_K} < \frac{w}{r}$$

Rearranging,

$$\frac{MP_L}{w} < \frac{MP_K}{r}$$

In this case the marginal product of an additional dollar's worth of labor is less than the marginal product of an additional dollar's worth of capital. The firm could reduce its use of labor by \$1, expand its use of capital by *less* than \$1, and remain at the same level of output—but with a reduced cost. It could continue to do this so long as the above inequality holds. Eventually MP_L/w would become equal to MP_K/r, since MP_L rises with decreased use of labor and increased use of capital, and MP_K falls with increased capital and decreased labor. By the same reasoning it is easy to see that firms substitute labor for capital until the equality holds if the inequality is reversed, such as is the case at point A.

Production of maximum output with a given level of cost.[6]

The most realistic way of examining the optimization problem is to assume, as above, that firms choose a level of output and then choose the input combination that permits production of that output at least cost. As an alternative we could assume that firms can spend only a fixed amount on production and wish to attain the highest level of production consistent with that amount

[6] Mathematically, this situation is quite similar to that presented in the preceding subsection. In this case, the firm wants to maximize output, $Q(K,L)$, subject to a given level of expenditures, $\overline{C} = rK + wL$. Again, we form the Lagrangian function

$$\mathcal{L} = Q(K,L) + \lambda(\overline{C} - rK - wL)$$

Maximization requires that the partial derivatives with respect to the choice variables, capital and labor, be zero,

$$\frac{\partial \mathcal{L}}{\partial K} = Q_K - \lambda r = 0$$

$$\frac{\partial \mathcal{L}}{\partial L} = Q_L - \lambda w = 0$$

Combining these necessary conditions, we obtain precisely the same result as in cost minimization,

$$\frac{Q_K}{Q_L} = \frac{r}{w}$$

Figure 5.6
Output maximization for a given level of cost

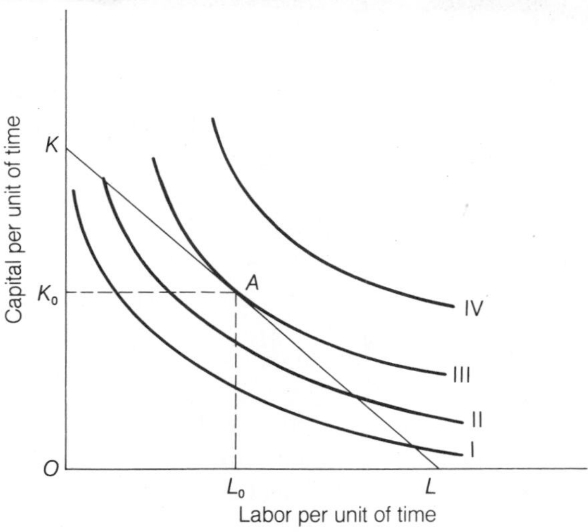

of expenditure. Not too surprisingly, the results turn out the same as before.

This situation is shown in Figure 5.6. The isocost line *KL* shows every possible combination of the two inputs that can be purchased at the given level of cost and input prices. Four of the infinite number of possible isoquants are shown. Clearly, at the given level of cost, output level IV is unattainable. And, neither output level I nor level II would be chosen, since higher levels of output are possible with the given level of expenditures. The highest level of output attainable with the given level of cost is produced by using L_0 labor and K_0 capital. At point *A*, the highest attainable isoquant, isoquant III, is just tangent to the given isocost. Thus, in the case of constrained output maximization, the marginal rate of technical substitution of capital for labor equals the input-price ratio (the price of labor to the price of capital).

■ **Principle.** In order either to maximize output, subject to a given cost, or to minimize cost, subject to a given output, the manager must employ inputs in such amounts as to equate the marginal rate of technical substitution and the input-price ratio.

THE WALL STREET JOURNAL

APPLICATION

An airline reduces costs

1982 and 1983 were generally disastrous years for the major U.S. airlines. Continental declared bankruptcy in the fall of 1983. Eastern was struggling to continue. Braniff had gone bankrupt a few years before. Most of the major carriers were foundering in a sea of red ink. Deregulation, begun in 1979, had brought on a series of price wars and an increase in competition from many smaller regional airlines.

But one major airline was an exception. Northwest Airlines showed a substantial profit in 1982 and 1983 and continued to expand, while the other major carriers were reducing their flights. Writing in *The Wall Street Journal*, Harlan S. Bryne explained the reasons for the success of Northwest while the other airlines were having so much trouble, "At Northwest Airlines, Emphasis on Keeping Costs Low Pays Off," October 31, 1983*.

Byrne noted that many of the troubled airlines had grown fat under regulation. Protected from fare competition, they had little incentive to clamp down on costs—increases in costs could simply be passed along to consumers in the form of fare increases. In contrast, Northwest continued to operate as though competition were fierce. Once the regulations ended and fares began to fall, Northwest was in a superior position compared to its rivals.

At the end of 1982, Northwest was the only debt-free major airline. For all other major airlines, long-term debt was almost $3 billion above total equity. For many airlines, this debt constituted a serious drain on resources during a depressed period.

And this was not the only advantage Northwest enjoyed. Northwest's labor costs were the lowest of any of the 11 major lines—24.2 percent of operating costs, compared with the industry average of 35.2 percent. Cost per available seat mile (passenger carrying capacity) for Northwest was 13 percent below the average. Revenue ton mileage per employee, an indicator of efficiency, was 66 percent above that of major rivals. Operating revenue per employee was 27 percent higher. And overhead costs for Northwest were 2 percent of costs, compared with 5 percent for major competitors. Table 5.2 summarizes Northwest's position relative to its competition.

So by almost any criterion, Northwest was in an enviable situation in

Table 5.2

	Northwest	*10 major U.S.-based airlines*
Debt	0	$10.4 billion
Revenue ton miles per employee (1982)	$164,000	$98,000
Operating revenue per employee (1982)	$136,000	$107,000
Maintenance (percent of operating revenue, 1982)	8	9
Labor cost (percent of operating revenue)	24	35
Cost per available seat mile	$0.07	$0.08

regard to its competition. The question is, what enabled Northwest to attain this position?

One reason was that, as we mentioned, Northwest cut its debt while other lines were substantially increasing theirs, enabling Northwest to escape the high interest payments made by other airlines. Another reason is that Northwest didn't take part in the plane-buying spree during the period of regulation. Its purchases were more evenly spaced.

Another of Northwest's cost-reducing measures was its labor policy during regulation. According to the *Journal*, Northwest was much more willing to take strikes than were other carriers. The company took advantage of mutual aid, an airline agreement during the period of regulation under which a struck airline received compensation from other lines for the extra traffic diverted to them because of a strike. Thus Northwest entered the period of deregulation with lower labor costs.

During the recession of 1981–82, Northwest purchased no new airplanes. Instead, they added enough new seats to their existing planes to give the equivalent of 14 new planes. (The *Journal* noted that the cost was only about 10 percent of what the new planes would have cost.) Only in 1983 did the company begin purchasing new planes to replace older models. According to an executive of Northwest, "Most airlines seem to buy a lot of planes just as earnings are peaking, only to be burdened with taking deliveries as earnings get near the bottom of a downturn." Northwest avoided this problem by purchasing planes at a more steady pace.

Northwest used a standard engine for planes made by different manufacturers—one for wide bodies, one for narrow bodies—enabling the company to reduce its costs for spare parts. At Northwest spare parts cost to aircraft cost was 10 percent; at many major competitors, this figure was as high as 20 percent.

According to the *Journal*, the reason for Northwest's turnaround from a depressed airline to a profitable one was its consistent cost-saving measures. While its profits declined after deregulation, it did not suffer the staggering losses of many of its major competitors.

The expansion path

In Figure 5.5 we illustrated one optimizing point for a firm. This point shows the optimal (least cost) combination of inputs for a given level of output. However, as you might expect, there exists an optimal combination for every level of output the firm might choose to produce. And, the proportions in which the inputs are combined need not be the same for all levels of output. To examine several optimizing points at once, we use the *expansion path*.

The expansion path shows the way in which factor proportions change

Figure 5.7
Expansion path

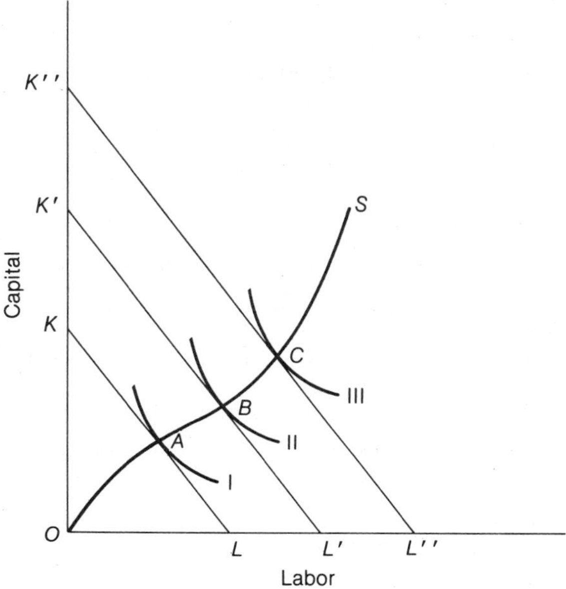

when output changes, with the factor-price ratio held constant. In Figure 5.7 the curves I, II, and III are isoquants depicting a representative production function. The isocosts *KL*, *K′L′*, and *K″L″* represent the minimum costs of producing each of the three output levels, since they are tangent to the respective isoquants. Note that, since the factor-price ratio does not change, these isocosts are parallel.

Look at the three optimum points, *A*, *B*, and *C*. Since at each of these: (1) factor prices remain constant, and (2) the marginal rate of technical substitution is equal to the factor-price ratio, it follows that the marginal rates of technical substitution are equal at *A*, *B*, and *C*. Therefore, the expansion path, *OS*, is a locus of points along which the marginal rate of technical substitution is constant and equal to the input-price ratio. But it is a curve with a special feature: It is the locus along which output will expand when factor prices are constant. We may accordingly formulate a definition.[7]

[7]We should note that thus far in our discussion of the expansion path we have assumed that as the firm expands output, it increases its usage of all inputs. This need not be the case however. It is possible that as a firm expands, it actually decreases the usage of one or more—though not all—inputs over the relevant range. For example, in the two-input case, a firm may increase output by using more capital and less labor. In this case, labor would be called an *inferior input*. An input is said to be inferior if, over a range, increased output causes less of the input to be used. In such cases, the expansion path curves backward if the quantity of the inferior input is plotted along the horizontal axis, or curves downward if the quantity of the inferior input is plotted along the vertical. Since this phenomenon is not of particular theoretical importance, we will not consider it further in our analysis.

■ **Definition.** The expansion path is the curve along which the firm expands (or contracts) output when factor prices remain constant. The expansion path indicates how factor proportions change when output (or expenditure) changes, input prices remaining constant. Since it is made up of points of efficient (least cost) input combinations, the expansion path is the locus of efficient combinations of the inputs. On the expansion path, the marginal rate of technical substitution is constant, since the factor-price ratio is constant.

As we shall see in Chapter 7 the expansion path gives the firm its cost structure. That is, the expansion path shows the optimal (least cost) combination of inputs to be used to produce each level of output. The sum of the quantities of each input used times the respective input price gives the minimum cost of producing every level of output. This in turn permits us to relate cost to the level of output produced.

THE WALL STREET JOURNAL
APPLICATION

The allocation of managerial resources

As we have shown, the expansion path provides the optimal usage of two (or more) resources for each level of output. We can use this concept to analyze how a single resource should be allocated between two (or more) tasks as the level of output changes. An extremely important example is the decision of a manager concerning how to change the allocation of his or her time (or resources) between various duties as the firm expands.

The problem was summarized succinctly in the opening paragraph of the article by Stanford L. Jacobs, "Owners See Need to Delegate Authority as Concerns Grow" in *The Wall Street Journal*,* July 18, 1983: "The trouble usually starts when the company has survived the start-up phase and is safely on its way. It has outgrown the hands-on, one-man management structure that worked in the early stages. The owner must redefine his role in the company if it is to continue to grow."

The article pointed out examples of successful owner/managers who, as their firms grew, increasingly delegated day-to-day details to subordinates, concentrating more and more of their own time on long-range planning and worrying about finances and capital outlays. For many managers this delegation was a difficult task. They had become used to being involved in daily decisions and solving immediate problems. There are no immediately apparent results from long-range planning, and most people like to see immediate results.

But, according to the *Journal*, if managers are involved in operational details, they don't have time for the job of being the chief executive. A prominent business consultant pointed out in the article that the head of a company is its primary asset and should, therefore, provide a broad vision of the enterprise, planning its future, looking for new opportunities to exploit and problems to avoid. He compared an owner who spends too much time on details with a talented surgeon who sterilized instruments and straightened up the operating room because of dissatisfaction with the way subordinates did it.

So we see that managers must not only allocate other resources in the production process but also allocate their own resources among the various tasks that must be performed. Solving this second problem may well be as important as solving the first, or perhaps more important. And there are no concrete rules as to the optimal allocation of a manager's time among these tasks. The allocation may even depend upon the personality of the manager and the nature of the firm. But we can say that the allocation decision must involve a comparison of marginal productivities among the various managerial functions. If a manager believes that his or her marginal productivity is greater in one function than in another, then more time should spent on that task and less on the other. Of course, these types of productivity estimations are difficult to make, since, as the *Journal* emphasized, many of the most important tasks involve payoffs far into the future while those of less importance show immediate results, particularly for growing concerns. But, difficult or not, this is an allocation decision that good managers have to make.

Changes in relative prices

We have derived the expansion path under only one set of input prices. But, it should be clear that changes in relative input prices change the expansion path and hence the cost structure. For example, consider first the expansion path OS shown in Figure 5.8. The relative price of capital and labor is given by the slope of KL, $K'L'$, and $K''L''$. The tangencies of these isocosts to isoquants I, II, and III indicate the optimal quantities of capital and labor used to produce each of these three levels of output, and OS, of course, gives the optimal combination for every other level of output over the range.

Next let the price of labor increase relative to the price of capital. Since the ratio w/r increases, the slope of the isocost curves must become steeper. These new isocosts are shown as ZF, $Z'F'$, and $Z''F''$. Now the tangency on each isoquant occurs at a lower amount of labor and a greater amount of capital. These new optimal combinations indicate that the firm substitutes capital for labor to produce each level of output when the price of labor rises relative to the price of capital. This is called the *substitution effect* from a change in input prices. The new expansion path, OR, now gives the new optimal combinations of inputs for each level of output.

If input prices change again, the firm would substitute once more. The direction of substitution depends upon the direction of the relative change in

Figure 5.8
Expansion paths with changed input prices

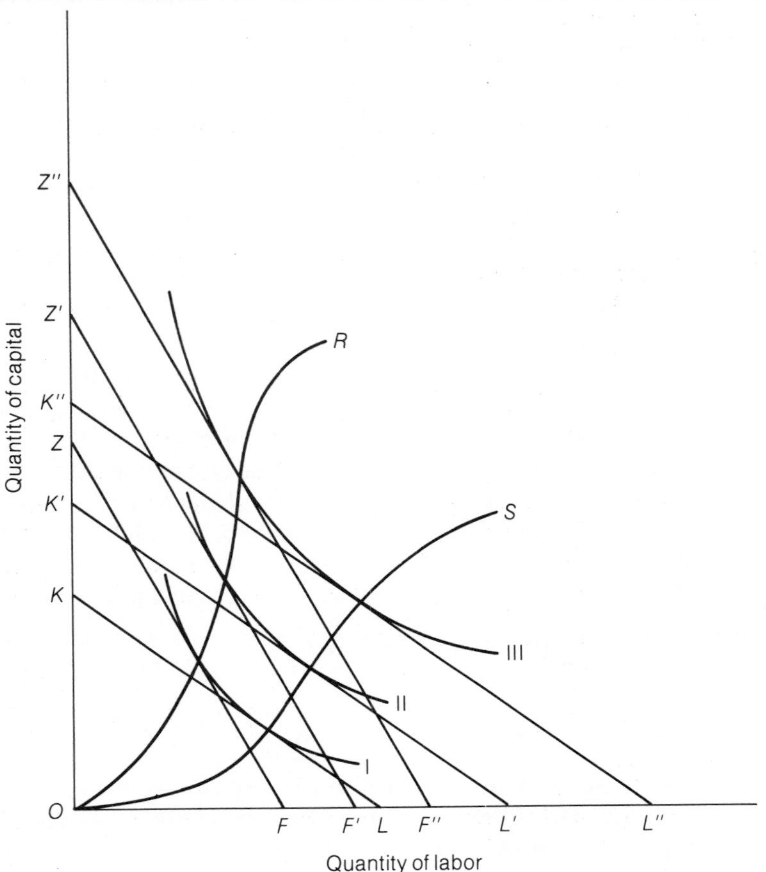

input prices. If the price of labor rises relative to the price of capital, the firm substitutes capital for labor at each level of output. If the price of capital rises relative to the price of labor, the firm substitutes labor for capital. Firms will always substitute away from the input that becomes relatively more expensive and toward the input that becomes relatively less expensive. These relations can be summarized in the following:

■ **Definition.** The expansion path shows the optimal or least cost combinations of inputs used to produce each relevant level of output. At each point on the expansion path the *MRTS* equals the input-price ratio. If the input-price ratio changes, firms substitute toward the input that becomes relatively less expensive and away from the input that becomes relatively more expensive. In the case of labor and capital, if w/r increases (decreases), K/L increases (decreases).

Thus far, the analysis has concentrated upon production under variable proportions. But, as mentioned at the beginning of this chapter, a production function could possibly be characterized by production under fixed proportions. For example, if two units of labor and five of capital are necessary to produce 100 units of output, 200 units of output require four of labor and ten of capital, 300 units require six of labor and fifteen of capital, and so on. If labor is limited to two units, no matter how much capital is added beyond five units, only 100 units of output can be produced. In this case the capital to labor ratio, K/L, is always 5/2, regardless of the level of output.

All fixed proportions production functions are characterized by a constant K/L ratio at every output level. Since an expansion path indicates the K/L ratio at each level of output and since K/L remains constant under fixed proportions production, the expansion path in such cases is a straight line from the origin. This means that if labor remains at a given level while capital is increased, no more output can be produced. Neither can an increase in labor increase output if capital remains fixed. It therefore follows that no matter what the ratio of input prices is, the firm uses the same combination of inputs to produce each given level of output. It follows that there is not a substitution effect from a change in relative prices under fixed proportions production.

5.5 RETURNS TO SCALE

Let us now consider the effect of a proportional increase in all inputs on the level of output produced. For example, if we were to double the firm's usage of all inputs, output would increase. But, the question is: By how much? To address this question, we need the concept of returns to scale.

Consider a k percent increase in the usage of all inputs. If output increases by exactly k percent, we say that the production function exhibits *constant returns to scale*. If, however, output increases by more than k percent, we say that the production function exhibits *increasing returns to scale*. Alternatively, if output increases by less than k percent, we say that the production function is characterized by *decreasing returns to scale*.

These relations can be illustrated, using Figure 5.9. We begin with an arbitrary level of usage of capital and labor at K_0 and L_0. This combination of capital and labor produces some level of output, Q_0. For purposes of illustration, let us define Q_0 to be 100 units. Now, we double our level of input usage to $2K_0$ and $2L_0$. Output will increase to Q_1. The question is the magnitude of the increase. Input usage has increased by 100 percent. Has output increased by 100 percent, more than 100 percent, or less than 100 percent? If Q_1 is equal to 200, output would have exactly doubled in response to the doubling of input usage; so constant returns to scale are indicated. If Q_1 is greater than 200 units (say, 215), increasing returns to scale are indicated. If Q_1 is less than 200 units (say, 180), the production function exhibits decreasing returns to scale.

Figure 5.9
Returns to scale

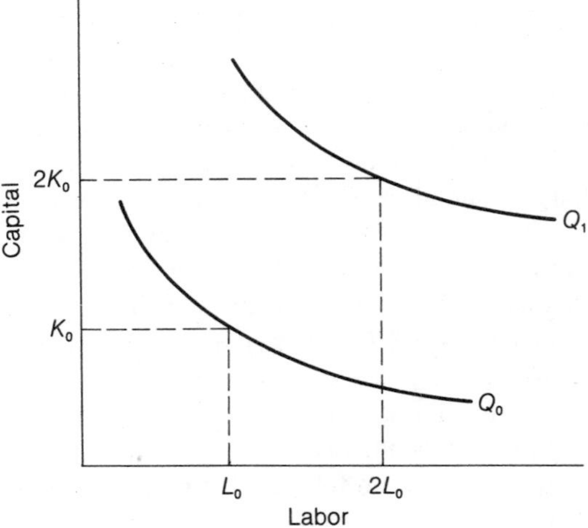

We can define returns to scale more analytically by first writing the production function in functional form as

$$Q = f(L,K)$$

Suppose we increase the inputs by a constant proportion (say, λ) and observe the proportionate change (z) in output. We have

$$zQ = f(\lambda L,\lambda K)$$

Again remember that λ and z represent proportionate increases in the scale of operation and level of output, respectively.

We have noted, in the case of constant returns to scale, if inputs are increased by a given percent, output rises by the same percent, that is, $z = \lambda$. More generally, if all inputs are increased by a factor of λ and output goes up by a factor of z, then a firm experiences:

1. Increasing returns to scale if $z > \lambda$. (Output goes up proportionately more than the increase in input usage.)
2. Constant returns to scale if $\lambda = z$. (Output goes up by the same proportion as the increase in input usage.)
3. Decreasing returns to scale if $\lambda > z$. (Output goes up proportionately less than the increase in input usage.)

Do not deduce from this discussion of returns to scale that with variable-proportions production functions, firms actually expand output by increasing their usage of every input in exactly the same proportion. As we have seen above, the very concept of variable proportions means that they do not necessarily expand in the same proportions. The expansion path may twist and turn in many directions. Nonetheless, the concept of returns to scale will be important for the development of the theory of long-run cost in Chapter 7.

5.6 SUMMARY

This chapter has set forth the basic theory of production and the optimal combination of inputs under a given set of input prices. The basic concepts upon which production theory is based are given in the following definitions:

■ **Definition.** A production function is a schedule, table, or equation showing the maximum output that can be obtained from any given combination of inputs.

■ **Definition.** An isoquant is the locus of points showing combinations of inputs physically capable of producing a given level of output. The slope of the isoquant, the marginal rate of technical substitution, shows the rate at which one input can be substituted for another while maintaining the same level of output.

■ **Definition.** An isocost line shows all combinations of inputs that can be purchased at some given level of expenditure. The slope of the isocost line, the ratio of input prices, shows the rate at which the market allows inputs to be substituted.

The optimal combination of inputs is determined by the following:

■ **Relation.** The firm minimizes the cost of producing any given level of output or maximizes the output that can be produced at any given level of cost when the marginal rate of technical substitution equals the ratio of input prices. This requires that for all inputs used, the ratios of the marginal products to the prices of the inputs are equal.

TECHNICAL PROBLEMS

1. Fill in the blanks in the following table.

Usage of the variable input	*Total product*	*Average product*	*Marginal product*
1		20	
2			34
3	81		
4		26	
5			21
6	138		
7		21	
8			5
9	153		
10		15	

2. Below are hypothetical data for a manufacturer possessing a fixed plant who produces a commodity that requires only one variable input. Total product is given. Compute and graph the average and marginal product curves.

Usage of the variable input	*Total product*	*Average product*	*Marginal product*
1	100		
2	250		
3	410		
4	560		
5	700		
6	830		
7	945		
8	1,050		
9	1,146		
10	1,234		
11	1,314		
12	1,384		
13	1,444		
14	1,494		
15	1,534		
16	1,564		
17	1,584		
18	1,594		

After completing the table and graph, answer the following questions:

a. When marginal product is increasing, what is happening to average product?

b. Does average product begin to fall as soon as marginal product does? That is, which occurs first, the point of diminishing marginal or average returns?

c. When average product is at its maximum, is marginal product less than, equal to, or greater than average product?

d. Does total product increase at a decreasing rate: (1) when average product is rising? (2) When marginal product is rising? (3) when average product begins to fall? (4) when marginal passes its maximum value?

3. You are an efficiency expert hired by a manufacturing firm that uses two inputs, labor (*L*) and capital (*K*). The firm produces and sells a given output. You have the following information

$$P_L = \$2,\ P_K = \$30,\ MP_L = 4,\ MP_K = 40$$

a. Is the firm operating efficiently? Explain.

b. Should it increase or decrease the quantity of labor relative to capital or the quantity of capital relative to labor to produce the given output? Explain your answer.

4. A firm can produce a certain amount of a good, using three combinations

of labor and capital. Labor costs $2 per unit, capital $4 per unit. The three methods are:

	A	B	C
Labor (units)	5	6	2
Capital (units)	7	5	9

a. Which method should be chosen?

b. If the price of labor rises to $4 while the price of capital falls to $3, which method should be chosen?

c. Under the second price structure (part b) the labor is done by you and you hire capital at $3; now which method should be chosen? Why? Can you even answer this? What information would need?

5. An expansion path can be derived under the assumption either that firms attempt to produce each output at minimum cost or that they attempt to gain maximum output at each level of cost. The paths are identical in both cases. Explain.

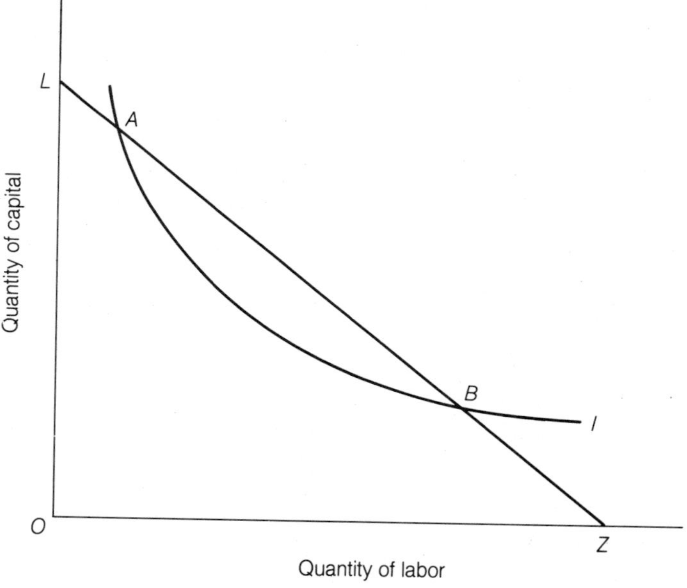

6. In the graph above, *LZ* is the isocost and I is an isoquant. Explain precisely why combinations *A* and *B* are not efficient. Explain in terms of the relation of the ratio of the marginal products to the ratio of the input prices. Explain, in these terms, why the direction of substitution in each case, labor for capital or capital for labor, is optimal. Using the ratio of input prices given by *LZ*, find and label the least cost combination of labor and capital that can produce the output designated by I. In the above terms, explain why this combination is optimal.

7. Explain precisely why *MP* exceeds (is less than) *AP* when *AP* is rising (falling).
8. In the graph below, the isoquants I, II, and III are associated respectively with 1,000, 2,000, and 3,000 units of output. The price of capital is $2 a unit and the price of labor is $1 a unit.

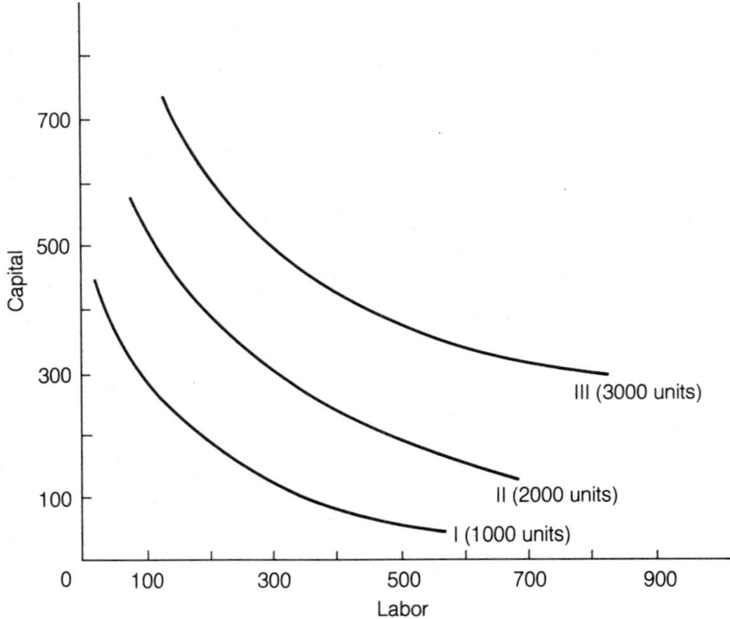

a. Construct the expansion path.
b. How many units of each input are used to produce each level of output efficiently?
c. What is the minimum cost of producing each level of output?
d. Answer each question under the assumption that the price of labor is now $2 a unit and the price of capital is $1 a unit.

ANALYTICAL PROBLEMS

1. Explain why the marginal product of any input might become negative. That is, why would additional units of the input cause output to fall. (Do not answer that the firm hires inferior inputs. Assume all units of the input are alike.)
2. Over the past two decades, more and more firms have begun using computers. (We might say that the computer-labor ratio has risen.) Provide the economic rationale for this trend.
3. Suppose we select three isoquants which describe a firm's technology.

Each represents a doubling in output from the one below; e.g., they represent output levels of 100, 200, and 400 units as they move outward. In relative terms, explain what the distance between the isoquants would be if the firm experienced:

a. Constant returns to scale.

b. Increasing returns to scale.

c. Decreasing returns to scale.

4. Explain the following statement: "It is possible for a producer to be technically efficient and not economically efficient, but it is impossible for a producer to be economically efficient without being technically efficient."

5. In the application concerning Northwest Airlines, the author of *The Wall Street Journal* article noted that many airlines had grown fat during the period of price regulation. Protected from fare competition, they had little incentive to clamp down on costs. What does this mean in terms of our theory of cost minimization? Why would some airline, like Northwest, be more efficient than others? Why did price deregulation force the airliners to operate more efficiently?

6. Along the same line as problem 5, what would you look for in a manufacturing firm if you were hired to improve the firm's efficiency? What about a government bureaucracy; for example, the Bureau of the Census, or the Department of Education? What about a university?

7. If you were the owner/manager of a small, but rapidly growing firm, how could you tell whether or not you were allocating your time efficiently?

8. What types of changes do you believe will occur because of the recent rapid expansion of desk top computers and their dramatic fall in price?

6

Quantitative analyses of production

In the preceding chapter we provided you with the theoretical foundations of production theory. We now need to provide some methodologies that can be used to implement the theory. In this chapter, we will use the theoretical discussion to develop some quantitative models that both adhere to the basic characteristics of the production relation and permit an empirical investigation of the properties of specific production relations, using real-world data.

While there exist several other ways to consider empirical production functions—notably linear programming—in this chapter, we will illustrate the quantitative analysis of the production relation, using regression analysis. We will be particularly concerned with the estimation of the marginal products of the inputs, the output elasticities, and a measure of returns to scale. Furthermore, we will show you how to use these estimates to determine whether or not a firm or an industry is using inputs efficiently.

In this chapter, we will concentrate on production in the long run (i.e., all inputs are variable). The properties of the short-run production function will be reflected in the short-run cost function, which will be described theoretically in Chapter 7 and empirically in Chapter 8.

We will begin our discussion with a description of a widely accepted technique for the estimation of production functions. Using this technique, we will demonstrate the methodologies for estimating marginal products, output elasticities, and a measure of returns to scale. Then we will discuss a technique for determining whether a firm or industry is using its inputs efficiently or if particular inputs are being over- or underutilized.

6.1 ESTIMATION OF PRODUCTION FUNCTIONS

Let us set forth a methodology for actually obtaining estimates of production functions. We use the techniques of regression—developed in Chapter 4—to estimate the relation between output and the levels of usage of inputs. We will continue to consider the case of two inputs—capital and labor. The technique can, however, be used to consider several inputs.

Let's begin with the general production function we employed in Chapter 5,

$$Q = f(K,L)$$

In order to estimate this function, it is first necessary to express the production relation in *explicit* functional form. Given our discussion of regression techniques, the form that might first come to mind is a simple linear form. For example, we could specify output as

$$Q = \alpha K + \beta L$$

There are, however, some major problems with this linear functional form:

First, in this form, it is not necessary to use positive amounts of both of the inputs in order to produce output. For instance, let K equal zero. Output would then be equal to βL, which is positive if L is positive. Therefore, production could take place without using any capital. (The same is true for labor.)

Second, with this formulation, the isoquants are straight lines. While they still slope downward, they are not concave from above. Hence, we do not have the diminishing marginal rate of technical substitution (*MRTS*).

Third, given the linear isoquants, the marginal products are constant. Consider, for example, the marginal product of labor that would exist in this linear specification,

$$MP_L = \Delta Q/\Delta L = \beta$$

Holding capital usage constant, the marginal product of labor is constant. Hence, the law of diminishing marginal physical product is violated.

These three problems indicate that the linear form does not adhere to the necessary theoretical characteristics of a production function. Therefore, these problems effectively eliminate the simple linear specification as an appropriate form to use for estimating a production function.

Given the problems with the linear specification, it is necessary to choose a more complex functional form, i.e., a nonlinear specification. As we described in Chapter 4, a tractable nonlinear form is a log-linear specification. Let us use this specification and define our production function to be

$$Q = AK^{\alpha}L^{\beta}$$

This form of an empirical production relation was developed in the 1920s by Charles W. Cobb and Paul H. Douglas and is now commonly referred to as the *Cobb-Douglas production function*.

Note first that, in this functional form, both inputs are required in order to produce output. If either capital or labor usage equals zero, output equals zero. That is, $f(K,0) = f(0,L) = 0$. Furthermore, this form exhibits the required concave isoquants; so, the MRTS will diminish as required by the theory of production.

Also, with a Cobb-Douglas production function, the marginal products of capital and labor are, respectively,[1]

$$MP_K = \alpha(Q/K) \text{ and } MP_L = \beta(Q/L)$$

These marginal products are not constant but vary with the level of usage of the inputs. Recall from Chapter 5 that the marginal products must be positive. In the context of this production function, that requirement implies that α and β be positive. Further, the law of diminishing marginal product requires, in this specification, that α and β be less than one. Hence, in order that the properties of the Cobb-Douglas specification conform to the properties of the production relation discussed in Chapter 5, it is required that

$$0<\alpha<1$$

and

$$0<\beta<1$$

If these requirements are satisfied, we can say that the properties of the Cobb-Douglas specification conform to the theoretical properties described in Chapter 5.[2]

---

[1]For the student with a background in mathematics, let us summarize the properties of a Cobb-Douglas production function,

$$Q = AK^{\alpha}L^{\beta}$$

First, the marginal products are

$$Q_K = \alpha AK^{(\alpha-1)}L^{\beta} = \alpha\frac{Q}{K}$$

$$Q_L = \beta AK^{\alpha}L^{(\beta-1)} = \beta\frac{Q}{L}$$

Since the marginal products must be positive, both α and β must be positive. The law of diminishing marginal product requires that the second derivatives be negative (i.e., Q_{KK} and Q_{LL} must be negative). In this specification,

$$Q_{KK} = \alpha(\alpha - 1)AK^{(\alpha-2)}L^{\beta}$$
$$Q_{LL} = \beta(\beta - 1)AK^{\alpha}L^{(\beta-2)}$$

Thus, both α and β must be less than one. Combining these, in order that a Cobb-Douglas production function adhere to the properties described in Chapter 5,

$$0 < \alpha,\ \beta < 1$$

[2]The Cobb-Douglas production function has an additional property: It is a homothetic production function. A homothetic production function has a straight-line expansion path, i.e., changes in the level of output will have no effect on relative input usage (the ratio of labor to capital usage in the two-input case).

In a Cobb-Douglas production function, the coefficients α and β measure, respectively, the output elasticities of capital and labor,[3]

$$E_K = \alpha$$
$$E_L = \beta$$

Using these coefficients, we can evaluate the impact of changes in capital or labor usage on output.

In the preceding chapter we introduced the concept of returns to scale. To summarize that discussion, we will denote the percentage increase in input usage as k and the corresponding percentage increase in output as ℓ. Then, we can determine returns to scale by the following:

$$\text{If } \begin{Bmatrix} \ell > k \\ \ell = k \\ \ell < k \end{Bmatrix} \text{ the production function exhibits } \begin{Bmatrix} \text{increasing} \\ \text{constant} \\ \text{decreasing} \end{Bmatrix} \text{ returns to scale.}$$

In a more quantitative manner, we can consider the question of returns to scale by consideration of a measure called *the function coefficient*. Basically, this measure is an elasticity reflecting the percentage change in output in response to a given percentage change in the level of usage of all inputs. We define the function coefficient, $\mathscr{E}$, as

$$\mathscr{E} = \frac{\text{Percentage change in output}}{\text{Percentage change in input usage}}$$

From the preceding, it follows that, if there exist constant returns to scale, $\mathscr{E} = 1$. If the production function exhibits increasing returns to scale, $\mathscr{E} > 1$. Likewise, if there exist decreasing returns to scale, $\mathscr{E} < 1$. This function coefficient can be decomposed further. Since the increase in output is attributable to increases in the levels of usage of the individual inputs, we can write it in terms of the inputs themselves. For example, in our two-input case,

$$\mathscr{E} = \frac{\text{Percentage change in output}}{\text{Percentage change in } K} + \frac{\text{Percentage change in output}}{\text{Percentage change in } L}$$

Hence, the function coefficient is equal to

$$\mathscr{E} = E_K + E_L$$

---

[3]The output elasticity of capital is

$$E_K = \frac{\partial Q}{\partial K} \cdot \frac{K}{Q} = Q_K \cdot \frac{K}{Q}$$

Using the Cobb-Douglas specification,

$$E_K = \left(\alpha \frac{Q}{K}\right) \cdot \frac{K}{Q} = \alpha$$

Likewise, the output elasticity of labor (E_L) will equal β.

That is, the function coefficient is equal to the sum of the output elasticities.[4]

Therefore, in the case of our two-input, Cobb-Douglas production function, the function coefficient is simply

$$\mathscr{E} = \alpha + \beta$$

If $\alpha + \beta$ is greater than one, we know that the production function exhibits increasing returns to scale. Conversely, if $\alpha + \beta$ is less than one, there exist decreasing returns to scale.

However, as always, we must consider the question of statistical significance. It is not sufficient that the sum of the estimates of α and β is greater (less) than one. Rather, we must determine whether this sum is *significantly* greater (less) than one. If the sum is not significantly greater (less) than one, we cannot reject the existence of constant returns to scale. As was the case with the tests of significance of individual coefficients described in Chapter 4, this will require that we perform a t-test.

In the tests of the significance of an individual estimated coefficient that we described in Chapter 4 we determined whether the estimate is significantly different from *zero*. For example, looking at $\hat{\alpha}$, we calculated a t-statistic that we wrote as

$$t_{\hat{\alpha}} = \frac{\hat{\alpha}}{S_{\hat{\alpha}}}$$

where $S_{\hat{\alpha}}$ is the standard error of $\hat{\alpha}$. Since we were testing "different from zero," the more correct way of writing this t value is

---

[4]Using mathematics, we can demonstrate this relation more explicitly. Consider the production function

$$Q = Q(K,L)$$

If we increase the usage of both inputs by the same proportion λ,

$$Q = Q(\lambda K, \lambda L)$$

the function coefficient is by definition

$$\mathscr{E} = \frac{dQ/Q}{d\lambda/\lambda}$$

Now, let us take the total differential of the production function

$$dQ = Q_K dK + Q_L dL$$

We can rewrite this as

$$dQ = Q_K K \frac{dK}{K} + Q_L \frac{dL}{L}$$

Since all inputs are increased by the same proportion, $dK/K = dL/L = d\lambda/\lambda$ and

$$dQ = \frac{d\lambda}{\lambda}(Q_K K + Q_L L)$$

Using the expression derived, the function coefficient is then

$$\mathscr{E} = \frac{dQ/Q}{d\lambda/\lambda} = Q_K(K/Q) + Q_L(L/Q) = E_K + E_L$$

where E_K and E_L are the output elasticities of K and L.

$$t_{\hat{\alpha}} = \frac{\hat{\alpha} - 0}{S_{\hat{\alpha}}}$$

The zero is the value we are testing "different from." Then, we compare (the absolute value of) this calculated t-value with the critical value of t from the t-table at the end of the book.

However, in this case, we must determine whether the sum, $\alpha + \beta$, is significantly different from *one*. In this case, our t-statistic becomes

$$t_{\hat{\alpha}+\hat{\beta}} = \frac{(\hat{\alpha} + \hat{\beta}) - 1}{S_{\hat{\alpha}+\hat{\beta}}}$$

where the value 1 indicates what we are testing "different from" and $S_{\hat{\alpha}+\hat{\beta}}$ is the estimated standard error of the sum of the estimated coefficients (parameters). After calculating this statistic, we would compare it with a critical t-value in precisely the manner described in Chapter 4. Again note that, since this calculated t-statistic can be negative (if $\hat{\alpha} + \hat{\beta} < 1$), we compare the *absolute value* of the calculated t with the critical t obtained from the table.

The only problem involved in performing this test is that of obtaining the estimated standard error of $\hat{\alpha} + \hat{\beta}$. The available regression packages will provide the user with variances and covariances of the regression coefficients, $\hat{\alpha}$ and $\hat{\beta}$, in a variance-covariance matrix.[5] Let us denote the variances of $\hat{\alpha}$ and $\hat{\beta}$ as $\text{Var}(\hat{\alpha})$ and $\text{Var}(\hat{\beta})$ and the covariance between $\hat{\alpha}$ and $\hat{\beta}$ as $\text{Cov}(\hat{\alpha},\hat{\beta})$. As you may remember from your statistics course, $\text{Var}(\hat{\alpha} + \hat{\beta}) = \text{Var}(\hat{\alpha}) + \text{Var}(\hat{\beta}) + 2\,\text{Cov}(\hat{\alpha},\hat{\beta})$; so, the estimated standard error of $\hat{\alpha} + \hat{\beta}$ is

$$S_{\hat{\alpha}+\hat{\beta}} = \sqrt{\text{Var}(\hat{\alpha}) + \text{Var}(\hat{\beta}) + 2\text{Cov}(\hat{\alpha},\hat{\beta})}$$

It follows then that the Cobb-Douglas form will enable us to estimate the following:

1. Marginal products of the inputs.
2. Output elasticities.
3. Returns to scale.

As we noted in Chapter 4, in order to estimate this Cobb-Douglas production function, is necessary to convert it into logarithms. Thus, the equation that will actually be estimated is

$$\log Q = \log A + \alpha \log K + \beta \log L$$

To see how such an estimation can be used, let us now turn to an example.

APPLICATION

Production in U.S. electric utility firms

To illustrate the way production functions are estimated, we shall use an estimation of a production function for electric utility firms in the United

---

[5]As with any other variance measure, the variance of the regression coefficient provides a measure of the dispersion of the variable about its mean. The covariance of the regression coefficients provides information about the joint distribution—that is, the relation between the two regression coefficients.

States. We use this estimation for two reasons. First, the methodology used is illustrative of the technique described above.

Second, the results have interesting implications. The fact that governments allow electric utilities to operate as monopolies is predicated on the existence of increasing returns to scale. If the firms exhibit substantial increasing returns to scale, they are referred to as "natural monopolies" (a subject to which we will return to in a later chapter). Therefore, an important question relating to electric utilities is whether or not increasing returns to scale actually exist. Recently, the existence of increasing returns to scale in this industry has been questioned. While we will not replicate the more complicated studies, we can use our Cobb-Douglas production function to illustrate the manner in which you may test for increasing returns to scale.

To simplify the problem, let's continue to consider only two inputs—capital and labor. We will employ a Cobb-Douglas specification; so our production function will be

$$Q = AK^{\alpha}L^{\beta}$$

In order to estimate this production function we will require data for output, capital input, and labor input. A sample of 20 privately owned electric utility firms was selected. The data collected for each firm were:

Output: Total generation and transmission of electric power, expressed in million kilowatt-hours.

Capital: Stock of physical capital held by the firm, expressed in million dollars.

Labor: Total number of employees, expressed in thousand workers.

The resulting data are as follows.

Firm	*Q*	*K*	*L*
1	4.612	321.502	1.019
2	8.297	544.031	2.118
3	1.820	156.803	0.448
4	5.849	250.441	1.265
5	3.145	247.983	0.603
6	1.381	82.867	0.665
7	5.422	366.062	0.962
8	7.115	485.406	1.435
9	3.052	99.115	0.829
10	4.394	292.016	1.501
11	0.248	21.002	0.145
12	9.699	556.138	2.391
13	14.271	667.397	2.697
14	17.743	998.106	3.625
15	14.956	598.809	3.085
16	3.108	118.349	0.714
17	9.416	423.213	1.733
18	6.857	468.897	1.406
19	9.745	514.037	2.442
20	4.442	236.043	1.497

In order to estimate our production function, we first convert it to logarithms,

$$\log Q = \log A + \alpha \log K + \beta \log L$$

We then used an available regression program to estimate this equation, using the preceding data. The computer output we obtained is reproduced below. Note that in this regression "run" we also requested the variances and covariances for the regression coefficients. On our printout, these values appear in the matrix following the estimates of the coefficients.

```
DEPENDENT VARIABLE:  LOGQ        F-RATIO:  241.261

OBSERVATIONS:  20                R-SQUARE:  0.9660

                  PARAMETER                STANDARD
 VARIABLE         ESTIMATE                   ERROR

INTERCEPT         -1.5416                  0.6560
LOGK               0.53296                 0.12071
LOGL               0.65384                 0.14248

         VARIANCE-COVARIANCE MATRIX FOR
               ESTIMATED COEFFICIENTS

                 INTERCEPT          LOGK          LOGL

INTERCEPT         0.43029        -0.07900       0.08476
LOGK             -0.07900         0.01457      -0.01575
LOGL              0.08476        -0.01575       0.02030
```

We first note that the values for the F ratio and R^2 are both quite acceptable. (As you can confirm, the critical value for F at a 95 percent confidence level is 3.59; so the equation is significant.) From the printout, we know that the estimated values for the parameters are

$$\begin{aligned} \log\hat{A} &= -1.5416 \\ \hat{\alpha} &= 0.53296 \\ \hat{\beta} &= 0.65384 \end{aligned}$$

Taking the antilog of $\log\hat{A}$ (as described in Chapter 4), the estimated value of A is 0.214; so, the estimated Cobb-Douglas production function could be written as

$$\hat{Q} = (0.214)\, K^{0.53296}\, L^{0.65384}$$

The standard errors for the estimated parameters are also provided (e.g., $S_{\hat{\alpha}} = 0.12071$ and $S_{\hat{\beta}} = 0.14248$). From the variance-covariance matrix for the estimated coefficients, we can see that $\text{Var}(\hat{\alpha}) = 0.01457$. [This has to be the case, since $\text{Var}(\hat{\alpha}) = (S_{\hat{\alpha}})^2$, i.e., $0.01457 = (0.12071)^2$.] Likewise, $\text{Var}(\hat{\beta}) = 0.02030$. Finally, $\text{Cov}(\hat{\alpha},\hat{\beta}) = -0.01575$.

Before using these estimates, we need to make sure that they conform to the properties of a production function we discussed in Chapter 5. As we noted earlier, these properties are guaranteed if

$$0<\alpha<1$$

and

$$0<\beta<1$$

The estimates themselves suggest that these properties are satisfied. That is,

$$0 < 0.53296 < 1 \qquad \text{and} \qquad 0 < 0.65384 < 1.$$

But, to determine if these conditions are really satisfied, we must perform t-tests for these estimated coefficients. With 20 observations and 3 estimated coefficients we have $20 - 3 = 17$ degrees of freedom. Thus, from the t-table at the end of this text, the critical value of t for a 95 percent confidence level is 2.110.

We first need to see if $\hat{\alpha}$ and $\hat{\beta}$ are significantly greater than zero. This requires that we calculate the t-values:

$$t_{\hat{\alpha}} = \frac{\hat{\alpha}}{S_{\hat{\alpha}}} = \frac{0.53296}{0.12071} = 4.415$$

$$t_{\hat{\beta}} = \frac{\hat{\beta}}{S_{\hat{\beta}}} = \frac{0.65384}{0.14248} = 4.589$$

Since both of these exceed the critical value, we can say that $\hat{\alpha}$ and $\hat{\beta}$ are both significantly greater than zero.

Next, to test for decreasing marginal products, we must determine if $\hat{\alpha}$ and $\hat{\beta}$ are significantly less than one.[6] Using the method described in our discussion of the estimation of returns to scale, this test requires that we calculate the following t values:

$$t_{\hat{\alpha}} = \frac{\hat{\alpha} - 1}{S_{\hat{\alpha}}} = \frac{0.53296 - 1}{0.12071} = -3.869$$

$$t_{\hat{\beta}} = \frac{\hat{\beta} - 1}{S_{\hat{\beta}}} = \frac{0.65384 - 1}{0.14248} = -2.430$$

[6]We should note that, throughout this text, we employ what are referred to as "two-tailed" t-tests. In this case, a single-tail test would be more appropriate; but such a distinction could confuse our primary objective. The interested reader should see the references listed at the end of Chapter 4.

Since the *absolute values* of both of these calculated t-statistics exceed the critical t, we can say that both $\hat{\alpha}$ and $\hat{\beta}$ are significantly less than one. Thus, our estimated function does indeed satisfy the properties of a production function.

Before continuing, remember that the coefficients $\hat{\alpha}$ and $\hat{\beta}$ are the estimates of the output elasticities of capital and labor. Thus, our estimates indicate that a 10 percent increase in capital usage will lead to a 5.3 percent increase in output. That is,

$$E_K = \frac{\text{Percentage change in output}}{\text{Percentage change in capital usage}}$$

so,

$$\begin{aligned} \text{Percentage change in output} &= (\text{Percentage change in capital usage}) \times (E_K) \\ &= 10 \times 0.53296 \\ &= 5.3296 \text{ percent} \end{aligned}$$

Likewise, our estimates indicate that a 10 percent increase in labor usage would result in a 6.5 percent increase in output.

We now turn to the question of the existence of increasing returns to scale. As we showed earlier, the function coefficient is equal to the sum of the output elasticities

$$\begin{aligned} \mathscr{E} &= E_K + E_L \\ &= \alpha + \beta \end{aligned}$$

If $\mathscr{E}$ is greater than one, we would say that there exist increasing returns to scale. In our case, the estimate of the function coefficient is

$$\begin{aligned} \hat{\mathscr{E}} &= \hat{\alpha} + \hat{\beta} \\ &= 0.53296 + 0.65384 \\ &= 1.1868 \end{aligned}$$

While this estimate *suggests* that increasing returns to scale do exist, we must determine whether this estimate is *significantly* greater than one. As we showed earlier, this requires an additional t-test, where the calculated t is

$$t_{\hat{\alpha}+\hat{\beta}} = \frac{(\hat{\alpha} + \hat{\beta}) - 1}{S_{\hat{\alpha}+\hat{\beta}}}$$

The standard error of $\hat{\alpha} + \hat{\beta}$ is

$$S_{\hat{\alpha}+\hat{\beta}} = \sqrt{\text{Var}(\hat{\alpha}) + \text{Var}(\hat{\beta}) + 2\text{Cov}(\hat{\alpha},\hat{\beta})}$$

Using the estimates from the variance-covariance matrix provided,

$$\begin{aligned} S_{\hat{\alpha}+\hat{\beta}} &= \sqrt{0.01457 + 0.02030 + 2(-0.01575)} \\ &= \sqrt{0.00337} \\ &= 0.05805 \end{aligned}$$

It follows that the calculated t-statistic will be

$$t_{\hat{\alpha}+\hat{\beta}} = \frac{1.1868 - 1}{0.05805} = 3.2179$$

Since this value exceeds the critical t-value (2.110), we can say that $\hat{\alpha} + \hat{\beta}$ is significantly greater than one. Thus, for this sample, the data indicate that increasing returns to scale do exist.

6.2 THE EFFICIENCY CRITERION[7]

An additional use can be made of the estimates of a production function—the determination of whether or not the firm or industry is using the optimal combination of inputs. As we showed in Chapter 5, regardless of whether the firm is minimizing cost for a given output or maximizing output for a given expenditure, the optimality condition is

$$MP_L/MP_K = w/r$$

If

$$MP_L/MP_K < w/r$$

the firm is overutilizing labor—using too much labor relative to capital. Likewise, if

$$MP_L/MP_K > w/r$$

the firm is overutilizing capital.

The optimal level of use of its inputs is an important consideration for the firm; so the relation between the marginal rate of technical substitution and the input-price ratio is one that should be estimated. In this section, we will provide a methodology by which such an estimation may be accomplished.

In the context of the Cobb-Douglas production function, we know that

$$MP_L = \beta(Q/L)$$

and

$$MP_K = \alpha(Q/K)$$

Therefore, the marginal rate of technical substitution is

$$\frac{MP_L}{MP_K} = \frac{\beta}{\alpha} \cdot \frac{K}{L}$$

and we can write the optimally condition as

$$\frac{\beta}{\alpha} \cdot \frac{K}{L} = \frac{w}{r}$$

---

[7]The empirical test outlined in this section is considerably more complicated than other tests we describe in this text. However, this section can be skipped with no loss in continuity.

or

$$\frac{\beta}{\alpha} \cdot \frac{K}{L} - \frac{w}{r} = 0$$

Then, multiplying by α, the efficiency criterion becomes

$$\beta\frac{K}{L} - \alpha\frac{w}{r} = 0$$

In this form,

$$\beta\frac{K}{L} - \alpha\frac{w}{r} < 0$$

implies that the firm is overutilizing labor, since this inequality implies that $(MP_L/MP_K) < (w/r)$. Likewise,

$$\beta\frac{K}{L} - \alpha\frac{w}{r} > 0$$

implies that the firm is overutilizing capital.

To observe this relation empirically, we obtain estimates of α and β from the estimation of the production function. We can then obtain the values of K,L,w, and r that are relevant for the particular firm under consideration. Using these values, we can calculate the value for the expression presented above, which we will denote as ψ. That is,

$$\psi = \hat{\beta}(K/L) - \hat{\alpha}(w/r)$$

It is virtually impossible that the calculated value of ψ will be equal to zero. Instead, the question is whether or not the calculated ψ is *significantly* different from zero. The answer to this question will require yet another t-test. As in the preceding t-tests, it is necessary to form this calculated t value by dividing the estimate by its own standard error. In this case, the t-statistic would be

$$t = \frac{\psi}{S_\psi}$$

The problem is, as you might expect, obtaining an estimate of the standard error for ψ. Using more advanced statistical techniques, it can be shown that the estimated variance of ψ can be calculated as[8]

---

[8]In the most general terms, let us define ψ to be simply a function of the estimated parameters α and β,

$$\psi = f(\alpha,\beta)$$

Then, the asymptotic variance of ψ is

$$\text{Var}(\psi) = \left(\frac{\partial\psi}{\partial\alpha}\right)^2 \text{Var}(\alpha) + \left(\frac{\partial\psi}{\partial\beta}\right)^2 \text{Var}(\beta)$$
$$+2\left(\frac{\partial\psi}{\partial\alpha}\right)\left(\frac{\partial\psi}{\partial\beta}\right)\text{Cov}(\alpha,\beta)$$

Note that, in our calculations, we treat the values of K,L,w, and r as constants.

$$\text{Var}(\psi) = \left(\frac{K}{L}\right)^2 \text{Var}(\beta) + \left(\frac{w}{r}\right)^2 \text{Var}(\alpha) - 2\left(\frac{K}{L}\right)\left(\frac{w}{r}\right)\text{Cov}(\alpha,\beta)$$

The estimated standard error of ψ is then

$$S_\psi = \sqrt{\text{Var}(\psi)}$$

Given this value, the t-value for ψ may be calculated, and, if the absolute value of the calculated t exceeds the critical value of t, we can say that ψ is significantly different from zero. We illustrate this technique with an application.

APPLICATION

Input efficiency in the U.S. electric utility industry

Another question of considerable interest in the context of electric utilities, and of course for other firms, is whether or not the firms are efficiently utilizing inputs. It has been argued that, as a result of the regulation imposed on electric utilities, such firms would overutilize capital. From the preceding discussion, this would imply that

$$MP_L/MP_K > w/r$$

or, in the context of a Cobb-Douglas production function,

$$\beta\frac{K}{L} - \alpha\frac{w}{r} > 0$$

Let us use the sample of 20 firms provided in the preceding example to examine this question.

As you can verify, we already have everything we need to calculate the marginal products. We still need data on the input prices for labor, w, and capital, r. For the 20 firms in our sample these data are in the table that follows.[9]

[9]In this example, the input price for labor, w, was obtained simply by dividing total salaries and wages by the number of employees, giving us the average annual payment per worker expressed in thousand dollars. Calculation of the input price for capital is somewhat more complicated. In general, the user price of capital can be expressed as

$$r = q_K(i + \delta)$$

where q_K is the unit acquisition cost of the capital stock, i is the real rate of interest, and δ is the rate of depreciation (assuming that the relative prices of different capital goods do not change). In our case, capital is measured in dollars; so, the unit acquisition cost is by definition equal to one. However, it is necessary to account for differences in the price level at the time of acquisition by using a price index. The real rate of interest was estimated using a rational expectations approach. Finally, a straight-line rate of depreciation was employed.

Firm	r	w
1	0.06903	8.5368
2	0.06903	9.9282
3	0.06754	10.1116
4	0.07919	10.2522
5	0.06481	11.1194
6	0.06598	9.6992
7	0.06754	10.0613
8	0.06565	10.9087
9	0.10555	10.1954
10	0.06572	11.2585
11	0.07919	10.8759
12	0.06903	9.8758
13	0.06789	10.9051
14	0.06903	7.4775
15	0.06572	7.8062
16	0.07919	9.2689
17	0.06565	8.3906
18	0.06565	9.8826
19	0.06860	9.8235
20	0.08206	12.9352

We could examine the cost minimization condition for any of the 20 firms. But, since the question posed is whether the industry is overutilizing capital, let's evaluate the cost-minimization condition at the mean values for this sample of firms. Using the preceding data and that presented in the earlier application, we calculated the mean values of K, L, w, and r as:

$$\begin{aligned}\overline{K} &= 372.411\\ \overline{L} &= 1.529\\ \overline{w} &= 9.966\\ \overline{r} &= 0.072\end{aligned}$$

Using these means and the estimates of α and β from the preceding application, we calculated our variable ψ,

$$\begin{aligned}\hat{\psi} &= \hat{\beta}\cdot\left(\frac{\overline{K}}{\overline{L}}\right) - \hat{\alpha}\cdot\left(\frac{\overline{w}}{\overline{r}}\right)\\ &= 0.65384\cdot\left(\frac{372.411}{1.529}\right) - 0.53296\cdot\left(\frac{9.966}{0.072}\right)\\ &= 85.482\end{aligned}$$

As hypothesized, $\hat{\psi} > 0$. It would *appear* that the firms are overutilizing capital. However, we must determine whether this overcapitalization is statistically significant.

As we have demonstrated, the test for significance of ψ involves a t-test, in which we calculate the t-value

$$t = \frac{\hat{\psi}}{S_{\hat{\psi}}}$$

and compare it to our critical t-value. Remember from the preceding example that the critical t in this case is 2.110. It is first necessary to calculate the variance of $\hat{\psi}$:

$$\begin{aligned} \text{Var}(\hat{\psi}) &= \left(\frac{\overline{K}}{\overline{L}}\right)^2 \text{Var}(\hat{\beta}) + \left(\frac{\overline{w}}{\overline{r}}\right)^2 \text{Var}(\hat{\alpha}) \\ &\quad -2\left(\frac{\overline{K}}{\overline{L}}\right)\left(\frac{\overline{w}}{\overline{r}}\right)\text{Cov}(\hat{\alpha},\hat{\beta}) \\ &= (243.565)^2(0.02030) + (138.417)^2(0.01457) \\ &\quad -2(243.565)(138.417)(-0.01575) \\ &= 2{,}545.401 \end{aligned}$$

Then, the standard error of $\hat{\psi}$ is

$$S_{\hat{\psi}} = \sqrt{\text{Var}(\psi)} = 50.452$$

It follows then that the t-value is

$$\begin{aligned} t &= \frac{85.482}{50.452} \\ &= 1.694 \end{aligned}$$

Comparing this calculated t-value with the critical value, we see that ψ is not statistically significant (at the 95% confidence level). Thus, for this sample, the hypothesized overcapitalization cannot be confirmed empirically. That is, since ψ is not significantly different from zero, this data set does not indicate that there exists any significant overutilization of capital. We can not reject the hypothesis that the firms in this sample are using the optimal amounts of capital and labor.

TECHNICAL PROBLEMS

1. Consider the linear production function

$$Q = \alpha K + \beta L$$

Examine the marginal rate of technical substitution and explain why this functional form does not adhere to the theoretical properties of a production function.

2. We estimated a Cobb-Douglas production function

$$Q = AK^{\alpha}L^{\beta}$$

Following is the resulting computer output

DEPENDENT VARIABLE: LOGQ		F-RATIO:
OBSERVATIONS: 30		R-SQUARE:
VARIABLE	PARAMETER ESTIMATE	STANDARD ERROR
INTERCEPT	−3.0	0.5
LOGK	0.60	0.15
LOGL	0.55	0.20

VARIANCE-COVARIANCE MATRIX FOR ESTIMATED COEFFICIENTS

	INTERCEPT	LOGK	LOGL
INTERCEPT	0.25	−0.03	0.10
LOGK	−0.03	0.023	−0.02
LOGL	0.10	−0.02	0.04

The values for output and input usage (all in thousand units) for the firm under consideration are

$$Q = 100.0$$
$$K = 150.0$$
$$L = 1.0$$

a. Determine if these estimates indicate:
(1) Positive marginal products.
(2) Diminishing marginal products.

b. Calculate the marginal products for capital and labor. (Use the values provided for Q, K, and L.)

c. Suppose capital usage increases by 10 percent. By what percentage would output be expected to increase? What would be expected to happen to output if labor usage increased by 5 percent?

d. Determine whether these estimates indicate increasing, constant, or decreasing returns to scale. (Make sure you test for statistical significance.)

3. Use the estimates presented in Question 2 and let the values of the input prices for the firm under consideration be

$$r = 0.5$$
$$w = 50.0$$

Determine whether or not the firm is using the optimal combination of capital and labor.

ANALYTICAL PROBLEMS

1. Suppose the firm you manage is faced with an investment decision. It can either expand its existing plant or build another plant of the same size. Under what conditions would one or the other of these options be preferred? How would you go about obtaining the necessary data to make the decision?
2. Recently, it has been argued by many persons that the major oil companies are investing "too much" of their resources in such things as coal, rather than in the exploration and development of new petroleum sources. Using the techniques provided in this chapter, outline a methodology by which this proposition can be examined.

SUGGESTED ADDITIONAL REFERENCES

Intriligator, M. D. *Economic Models, Techniques, and Applications*. Englewood Cliffs, N.J.: Prentice-Hall, 1978.

Miller, R. L. *Intermediate Microeconomics: Theory, Issues, and Applications*. New York: McGraw-Hill, 1978.

Theil, H. *Introduction to Econometrics*. Englewood Cliffs, N.J.: Prentice-Hall, 1978.

7

Theory of cost

This chapter sets forth the fundamentals of the theory of cost. This theory is important in managerial decision making because it provides the foundation for two important production decisions made by managers: whether or not to shut down, and how much to produce. As such, the theory of cost provides the framework for the theory of supply.

We will develop the theory of cost from the underlying theory of production. Recall from Chapter 5 that production theory shows how to determine the least-cost method of producing a given output with a specific set of input prices. Therefore, just as cost theory will provide the foundation of supply, production theory provides the foundation for the theory of cost. That is, the production function and input prices determine the cost of producing any specific level of output.

After discussing a few important concepts, we set forth the theory of cost in the short run, when the level of usage of some inputs is fixed. In this case some costs are fixed also. We then analyze cost in the long run, when all inputs are variable.

7.1 SOME BASIC CONCEPTS

Fixed and variable costs

Recall from Chapter 5 that we divide production into the short run and the long run. Since cost is derived from production, we make the same distinction in the theory of cost. In the long run, all inputs are variable; hence all costs are variable. As we shall see, we treat cost in the long run as the firm's planning horizon.

In the short run some inputs are fixed. Since these inputs have to be paid regardless of the level of output produced, these payments to the fixed factors of production remain constant no matter what output is produced. This payment is called fixed cost. An example would be monthly payments on a loan outstanding on the firm's plant. These payments must be made even if the firm ceases production during a given period.

The payments to variable factors of production are called variable costs. Producing more output requires more inputs. Thus, variable cost increases as the level of output increases. Examples of variable cost would be many types of labor, ingredient inputs or raw material, and some types of capital.

Explicit and implicit costs

When most people think of cost, they think only of the explicit cost—the actual payment by firms to labor, capital, and other factors of production. Whether these costs are fixed or variable, they are straightforward; they are the amounts that firms must pay to owners of the resources in order to bid these resources away from alternative uses.

Producers also incur some costs referred to as implicit costs and in a complete analysis of costs they must take implicit costs into consideration. Managerial decision makers should do the same. To aid in analyzing the nature of implicit costs, consider two firms that produce a particular good and are in every way identical, with one exception. Both use identical amounts of the same resources to produce identical amounts of the good. The owner of one firm rents the building in which the good is produced. The owner of the other firm inherited the building the firm uses and therefore pays no rent. Whose costs are higher? For decision-making purposes, the costs for both are the same even though the second firm makes lower payments to outside factors of production. The reason the costs are the same is that using the building to produce goods costs the second firm the amount of income that could have been earned had it been leased at the prevailing rent. Since these two buildings are the same, presumably the market rentals would be the same. In other words, a part of the cost incurred by the second firm is the (implicit) payment from firm owners to themselves as the owners of a resource (the building). Thus, one implicit cost would include what firm owners could make from selling or leasing the capital they own if they were not using it in their firms.

Another implicit cost would include the value of the firm owner's time that is used to manage the business. Presumably, if the owner of a firm were not managing the business or working for the firm in another way, he or she could obtain a job with some other firm, possibly as a manager. The salary that could be earned in this alternative occupation is an implicit cost that should be considered as part of the total cost of production. These implicit costs are just as real as explicit costs.

■ **Definition.** The implicit costs incurred by firms in producing a specific commodity consist of the amounts that could be earned in the best alternative use of the owner/manager's time and of any other of their resources currently used to produce the commodity in question. Implicit costs must be added to explicit costs in order to obtain total costs.

With this definition in mind, we can turn to the analysis of short-run and long-run costs.

7.2 COST IN THE SHORT RUN

As we noted above, in the short run the levels of use of some inputs are fixed, and costs associated with these fixed inputs must be paid regardless of the level of output produced.[1] Other costs vary with the level of output. The sum of these costs—fixed and variable, explicit and implicit—is short-run total cost.

■ **Definition.** Total fixed cost is the sum of the short-run explicit fixed costs and the implicit cost incurred by a firm owner. Total variable cost is the sum of the amounts spent for each of the variable inputs used. Total cost in the short run is the sum of total variable and total fixed cost.

Short-run total cost

A short-run total cost curve (*SRTC*) is illustrated in Figure 7.1. This curve indicates the firm's total cost of production for each level of output when the input of one or more of the firm's resources is fixed.

Note that at zero output, cost is positive; in this case, total fixed cost is F, the amount that must be paid to the fixed inputs regardless of output. Total variable cost is the difference between total cost (*SRTC*) and total fixed cost (F). In Figure 7.1 the total cost (C) of producing Q units of output is F plus the distance FC, indicating total variable cost.

Clearly, variable cost and, therefore, total cost must increase as output is increased. Also, from the graph, we can see that variable cost first increases at a decreasing rate (the slope of *SRTC* decreases) then increases at an increasing rate (the slope of *SRTC* increases). This is the "typically assumed" cost structure and, as we shall see, follows from our assumptions about the short-run production function.

---

[1]As was noted in Chapter 5, it is not quite precise to say that the inputs of some resources cannot be changed. Certainly the firm could scrap a very expensive piece of capital equipment, buy another one twice as large, and have it installed before lunch, if it is willing to pay the price. In fact, the firm can probably change any input rather rapidly, given, once more, its willingness to pay. It is frequently helpful in analyzing problems to assume that some inputs are fixed for a period of time. Moreover, it does not deviate too much from reality to make this assumption since firm owners often consider certain resources as fixed over a period of time. You should not be overly concerned about the time factor in the short and long run. The fixity of resources is the important element.

Figure 7.1
Short-run costs

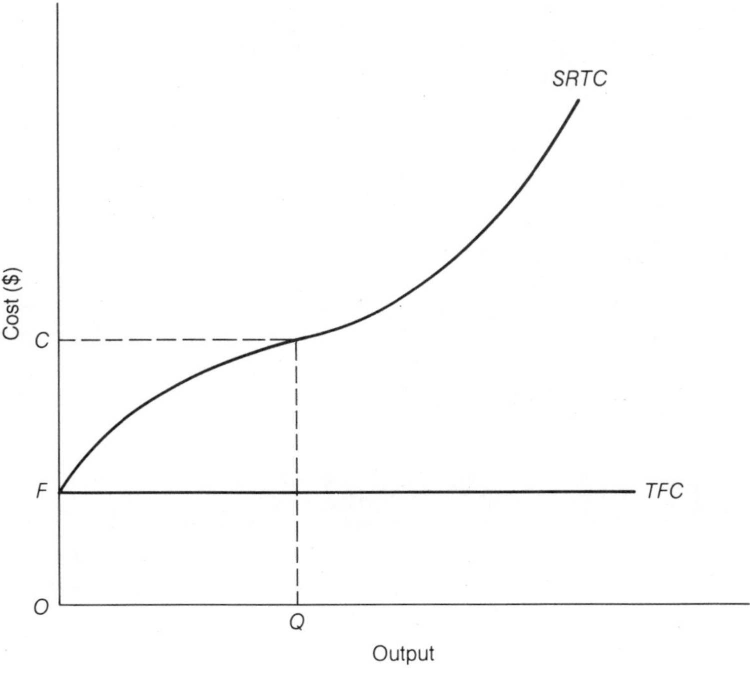

Average and marginal cost

You can obtain a better understanding of the firm's cost structure by analyzing the behavior of short-run average and marginal costs. First, let's consider average fixed cost (*AFC*).

■ **Definition.** Average fixed cost is total fixed cost divided by output

$$AFC = TFC/Q$$

Note that average fixed cost is a constant amount divided by output. Average fixed cost is relatively high at very low output levels. However, since the denominator increases as output increases, *AFC* decreases continuously as output increases, approaching zero as output becomes very large.

Next, consider average variable cost (*AVC*).

■ **Definition.** Average variable cost is total variable cost divided by output

$$AVC = TVC/Q$$

In Figure 7.2, *AVC* is a typical average variable cost curve. The shape of this curve is consistent with the shape of the total variable cost curve shown in

Figure 7.2
Short-run average and marginal cost curves

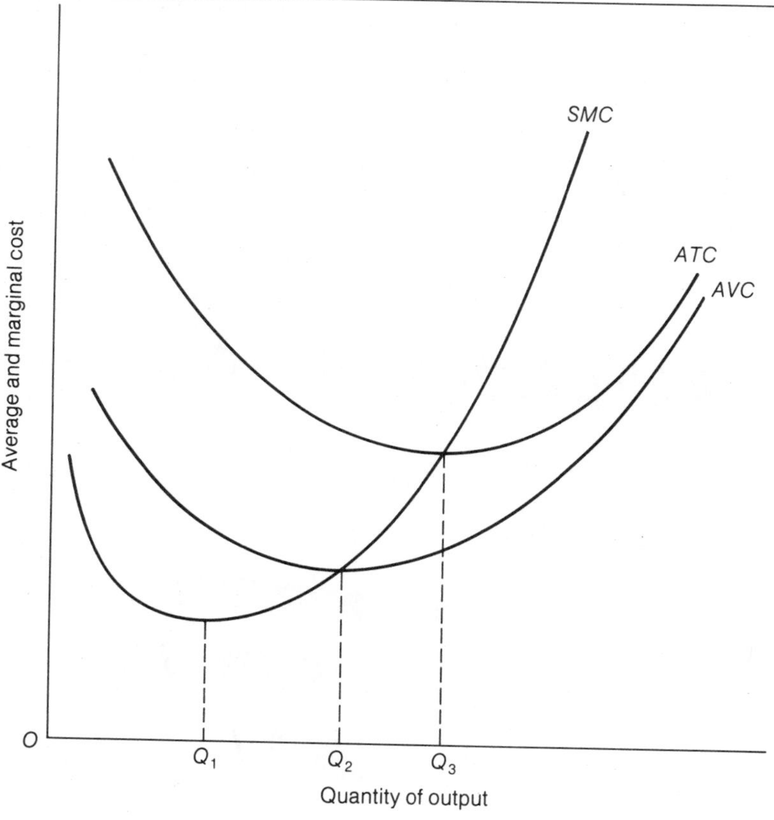

Figure 7.1. Average variable cost first declines, reaches a minimum point (at output Q_2), then increases thereafter.

Next consider average total cost (*ATC*).

■ **Definition.** Average total cost is short-run total cost divided by output,

$$ATC = SRTC/Q$$

It is, therefore, the sum of average fixed cost and average variable cost,

$$ATC = AFC + AVC$$

Average total cost as illustrated by ATC in Figure 7.2 has the same general shape as the average variable cost curve. It first declines, reaches a minimum (at Q_3 units of output), then rises thereafter. The minimum point on *ATC* is reached as a larger output than that at which *AVC* attains its minimum. This result can be easily shown. We know that

$$ATC = AFC + AVC$$

and that average fixed cost declines over the entire range of output. Thus, *ATC* declines at first because both *AFC* and *AVC* are falling. Even, when *AVC* begins to rise after Q_2, the decrease in *AFC* continues to drive down *ATC* as output increases. However, an output is finally reached, at Q_3, at which the increase in *AVC* overcomes the decrease in *AFC*, and *ATC* begins to rise.[2]

Since $ATC = AFC + AVC$, the vertical distance between average total cost and average variable cost is average fixed cost. Since *AFC* declines over the entire range of output, *AVC* becomes closer and closer to *ATC* as output increases.

Finally, let's consider short-run marginal cost (*SMC*).

■ **Definition.** Short-run marginal cost is the change in short-run total cost attributable to a one-unit change in output; or

$$SMC = \frac{\Delta SRTC}{\Delta Q}$$

And, since $SRTC = TFC + TVC$,

$$SMC = \frac{\Delta TFC}{\Delta Q} + \frac{\Delta TVC}{\Delta Q}$$

$$= 0 + \frac{\Delta TVC}{\Delta Q}$$

$$= \frac{\Delta TVC}{\Delta Q}$$

Short-run marginal cost refers to the change in cost resulting from a change in output when the use of the variable inputs changes. As illustrated in Figure 7.2, marginal cost first declines, reaches a minimum at Q_1 (note that minimum marginal cost is attained at a level of output below that at which *AVC* and *ATC* attain their minimum), then rises thereafter.

Marginal cost crosses *AVC* and *ATC* at their respective minimum points. This result follows from the definitions of the cost curves. If marginal cost is below average variable cost, each additional unit of output adds less to total cost than the average variable cost. Thus average variable cost must fall.

---

[2]For the mathematically inclined student this result is easily derived. Minimum average total cost is attained where

$$\frac{d(ATC)}{dQ} = \frac{d(AFC)}{dQ} + \frac{d(\text{AVC})}{dQ} = 0$$

Since $\frac{d(AFC)}{dQ} = \frac{-TFC}{Q^2}$, this term must be negative; thus $d(AVC)/dQ$ is positive (*AVC* is rising) when *ATC* is at its minimum.

When *SMC* is above *AVC*, each additional unit of output adds more to total cost than *AVC*. Thus, in this case, *AVC* must rise.[3]

So, when *MC* is less than *AVC*, average variable cost is falling. When *MC* is greater than *AVC*, average variable cost is rising. Thus *MC* must equal *AVC* at the minimum point on *AVC*. Exactly the same reasoning would apply to show that *MC* crosses *ATC* at the minimum point on the latter curve.

The properties of the average and marginal cost curves, as described in this section, are illustrated by the set of short-run cost curves shown in Figure 7.2. The curves indicate the following:

■ **Relation.** (1) *AFC* declines continuously, approaching both axes asymptomatically (as shown by the decreasing distance between *ATC* and *AVC*). (2) *AVC* first declines, reaches a minimum at Q_2, and rises thereafter. When *AVC* is at its minimum, *MC* equals *AVC*. (3) *ATC* first declines, reaches a minimum at Q_3, and rises thereafter. When *ATC* is at its minimum, *MC* equals *ATC*. (4) *MC* first declines, reaches a minimum at Q_1, and rises thereafter. *MC* equals both *AVC* and *ATC* when these curves are at their minimum values. Furthermore, *MC* lies below both *AVC* and *ATC* over the range in which these curves decline; *MC* lies above them when they are rising.

Table 7.1 illustrates numerically the characteristics of the cost curves we have thus far analyzed graphically. As seen in this table, average fixed cost decreases over the entire range of output. Both average variable and average total cost first decrease, then increase, with average variable cost attaining a minimum at a lower output than that at which average total reaches its mini-

---

[3]A precise derivation of this relation can be developed mathematically. Marginal cost is

$$MC = \frac{d(TC)}{dQ}$$

That is, marginal cost is the slope of the total cost function. Average cost (either variable or total), defined as

$$AC = \frac{TC}{Q}$$

attains a minimum when

$$\frac{dAC}{dQ} = \frac{(dTC/dQ)Q - TC}{Q^2} = 0$$

Rewriting this condition as

$$\frac{1}{Q}\left(\frac{dTC}{dQ} - \frac{TC}{Q}\right) = 0$$

it follows that, when average cost is at its minimum, average and marginal cost are equal. It is easy to see that $\frac{dAC}{dQ} > 0$ (average cost is increasing) when $MC > AC$, and $\frac{dAC}{dQ} < 0$ (average cost is decreasing) when $MC < AC$.

Table 7.1
Short-run cost schedules

(1) Output	(2) Total cost	(3) Fixed cost	(4) Variable cost	(5) Average fixed cost	(6) Average variable cost	(7) Average total cost	(8) Marginal cost (per unit)
100	$ 6,000	$4,000	$ 2,000	$40.00	$20.00	$60.00	$ 20.00
200	7,000	4,000	3,000	20.00	15.00	35.00	10.00
300	7,500	4,000	3,500	13.33	11.67	25.00	5.00
400	9,000	4,000	5,000	10.00	12.50	22.50	15.00
500	11,000	4,000	7,000	8.00	14.00	22.00	20.00
600	14,000	4,000	10,000	6.67	16.67	23.33	30.00
700	18,000	4,000	14,000	5.71	20.00	25.71	40.00
800	24,000	4,000	20,000	5.00	25.00	30.00	60.00
900	34,000	4,000	30,000	4.44	33.33	37.77	100.00
1,000	50,000	4,000	46,000	4.00	46.00	50.00	160.00

mum. Marginal cost per 100 units is the incremental increase in total cost and variable cost. Marginal cost (per unit) is below average variable and average total cost when each is falling and is greater than each when *AVC* and *ATC* are rising.

Relation between short-run costs and production

To see the relation between production and cost in the short run, let's return to the very simplified production function discussed in Chapter 5. In this case there is only one variable input, which we will call labor. Columns 1 and 2 of Table 7.2 show the points on the production function for three and four units of labor, which can produce respectively 32 and 40 units of output. The average and marginal products are shown in columns 3 and 4. (Since we do not have total output for two workers, we cannot compute the marginal product of three workers.)

Assume the wage rate is $100 per worker. Thus, hiring three workers to produce 32 units of output gives a total variable cost of $300, shown in column 5. Similarly, producing 40 units of output with four workers costs $400. Clearly, the average variable cost at an output of 40 units is $TVC/Q =$ $400/40 = $10.

Table 7.2
Derivation of cost from production

(1) Labor	(2) Output	(3) Average product	(4) Marginal product	(5) Total variable cost	(6) Average variable cost	(7) Marginal cost
3	32	10.67	—	$300	$ 9.38	—
4	40	10	8	400	10.00	$12.50

But we can write total variable cost as the price per worker, \$100, times the number of workers, four. We can also write total output, Q, as the average product, 10, times the number of workers, four. Thus, we can define average variable cost as

$$AVC = \frac{\$100 \times 4}{10 \times 4} = \frac{\$100}{10} = \frac{w}{AP} = \$10$$

We can show a similar relation between marginal cost and marginal product. The marginal cost of adding an additional worker to produce an additional 8 units of output is $\Delta TVC/\Delta Q = \$100/8 = \$12.50$. Note that the change in variable cost from producing the additional 8 units of output is the cost of hiring the additional unit of labor, \$100. The additional output is simply the marginal product of the additional worker, 8. Thus we can write marginal cost as

$$MC = \frac{w}{MP} = \frac{\$100}{8} = \$12.50$$

Thus we see that when only one input is variable in the short run, the following relations must hold:

$$AVC = \frac{w}{AP} \qquad MC = \frac{w}{MP}$$

From these relations, we can determine the shapes of the average variable cost and marginal cost curves. When average product is increasing, average variable cost is decreasing. When average product is decreasing, AVC is increasing. Therefore, since average product first increases, reaches a maximum, then decreases, average variable cost first decreases, reaches its minimum (when average product attains its maximum), then increases. The shape of the average product curve leads to a U-shaped AVC curve.

From the second relation, as marginal product rises, marginal cost falls; when marginal product declines, marginal cost rises. Marginal cost attains its minimum point when marginal product attains its maximum.

The same type of reasoning can be expanded to consider a firm operating in the short run with several variable inputs. The average products of some inputs may be increasing while others are decreasing. But with some inputs fixed, the decreasing average products must begin to outweigh those that are rising, and average variable cost must begin to increase. Eventually all average products must decline since the usage of some inputs is fixed. By the same reasoning, a similar situation holds for the relation between marginal product and marginal cost when several inputs are used. Eventually declining marginal products must cause marginal cost to rise.

The relations may be generalized to several variable inputs. Suppose there are n variable inputs. Let $X_1, X_2, X_3, \cdots X_n$ denote the quantities of these inputs used and $w_1, w_2, w_3, \cdots w_n$ the prices of the inputs. Thus

$$AVC = \frac{w_1X_1 + w_2X_2 + w_3X_3 + \cdots + w_nX_n}{Q}$$

$$= \frac{w_1X_1}{Q} + \frac{w_2X_2}{Q} + \frac{w_3X_3}{Q} + \cdots + \frac{w_nX_n}{Q} = \sum_{i=1}^{n} \frac{w_i}{AP_i},$$

where AP_i is the average product of the i-th input. Again the falling average products of the inputs must, after a point, cause *AVC* to rise.

Under the same conditions, marginal cost can be written as

$$MC = \frac{w_1\Delta X_1 + w_2\Delta X_2 + w_3\Delta X_3 + \cdots + w_n\Delta X_n}{\Delta Q}$$

$$= \frac{w_1\Delta X_1}{\Delta Q} + \frac{w_2\Delta X_2}{\Delta Q} + \frac{w_3\Delta X_3}{\Delta Q} + \cdots + \frac{w_n\Delta X_n}{\Delta Q} = \sum_{i=1}^{n} \frac{w_i}{MP_i}$$

As was the case for *AVC,* the declining marginal products of the inputs must, after a point, cause marginal cost to a increase.

APPLICATION

Irrelevance of fixed cost

Marginal cost is by far the *most important* cost function for decision-making purposes. And, fixed cost is the *least important.* As you will recall, we emphasized in Chapter 3 that decision making involves comparing the marginal benefits from a particular activity with its marginal costs. This is frequently called benefit–cost analysis.

To see the irrelevance of fixed costs for this type of analysis, consider the following hypothetical example. The manager of a restaurant which is open from 6:00 A.M. to 10:00 P.M. is considering keeping the restaurant open 24 hours a day. Under the current 16-hour-per-day operation, the restaurant averages $1,700 a day in revenues with total costs of $1,600 a day. Of this, $240 a day is fixed cost—interest payments on capital.

Based upon market surveys, the manager believes that keeping the restaurant open the additional eight hours would increase average daily total revenue to $2,150 and average daily cost to $2,000. Thus the marginal revenue from remaining open all night is expected to be $450; the expected marginal cost is $400. Should the restaurant be opened the additional eight hours? Certainly. The marginal revenue exceeds the marginal cost; so $50 a day, on average, would be added to profit.

Note that in making the decision the manager considers only *marginal cost.* Fixed cost should not be considered. To see this, suppose that the manager had allocated a proportion of fixed cost to the additional eight hours. If this were done, 1/3 of the fixed cost, $80, would be added to the cost of staying open the extra time. Thus the manager would compute the total cost of remaining open the additional time as \$400 + \$80 = \$480. Since this amount exceeds the additional revenues that would be generated, the decision would be to remain closed at night. But, as we have seen, staying open adds \$50 a day to profit. Taking fixed cost into consideration would have led to an incorrect decision. Marginal changes are all that matter when making such types of decisions.

To illustrate the point further, we might consider why airlines sometimes put on flights that cause losses to occur when all costs are considered, or why trucking companies sometimes make seemingly unprofitable hauls. The reason is that the marginal benefit exceeds the marginal cost. It may be that a particular flight has so little passenger and freight demand that the total cost of the flight exceeds the total revenue when the cost of the plane is spread over this extra flight. But if the plane would be idle otherwise, the real cost of the additional flight is the added labor and fuel costs, the added wear and tear on capital, and any other costs that would not be encountered if the flight was not made. In other words, only the marginal costs matter. If these marginal costs are expected to be less than the expected additional revenues from making the additional flight, the trip will be made. Exactly the same rationale applies to the decision of trucking companies about additional hauls.

Employees who manage departments or divisions of firms frequently use the same line of reasoning. Say you manage a department in a large department store. How do you convince your store manager that you need more advertising? You know more advertising will increase sales and therefore your revenues. Convince the manager that the additional returns from the additional sales will exceed the additional cost of increased advertising. Use the same argument when you wish more sales help or more of any resource, like floor space, that will increase sales. Managers of offices or branches of plants can use much of the same type of argument.

The point is, therefore, when making decisions about changes, only marginal cost should be considered. Fixed cost is irrelevant.

7.3 LONG-RUN COSTS: THE PLANNING HORIZON

Recall from Chapter 5 that the long run is not some date in the future. The long run simply means that all inputs are variable to the firm. Therefore, one of the first decisions to be made by the owner and/or manager is the scale of operation, that is, the size of the firm. To make this decision the manager must know the cost of producing each relevant level of output. We will learn how to determine these long-run costs.

Derivation of cost schedules from a production function

Let us assume for analytical purposes that the firm's levels of usage of the inputs will not affect the price that must be paid for the inputs. Further, assume that the production function has been evaluated for each level of output in the feasible range. Using the methods described in Chapter 5, the manager can derive an expansion path.

As an example, let's assume that the firm uses only two inputs, labor and capital, that cost \$5 and \$10 per unit, respectively. The characteristics of a derived expansion path are given in columns 1 through 3 of Table 7.3. Column 1 gives seven output levels and columns 2 and 3 give the optimal combinations of labor and capital for each output level, at the prevailing input prices. That is, these combinations make up seven points on the expansion path.

Column 4 shows the total cost of producing each level of output. For example, the least-cost method of producing 300 units of output requires 20 units of labor and 10 of capital. At \$5 and \$10, respectively, the total cost is \$200. It should be emphasized that column 4 is a least-cost schedule for various rates of production. Obviously, the firm could pay more to produce any output, but it could not produce that output at a cost lower than the one given.

Average cost is shown in column 5. Average cost, the total cost of producing a given level of output divided by that output, is the number in column 4 divided by the corresponding number in column 1. Column 5 reflects an important assumed characteristic of long-run average cost: average cost first declines, reaches a minimum, then rises, just as was the case for the short run.

Long-run marginal cost, the change in total cost divided by the change in output, is provided in column 6. For example, increasing output from 100 to 200 units raises total cost from \$120 to \$140. Therefore, \$20 divided by the change in output, 100 units, gives a per-unit marginal cost of 20 cents. Note that marginal cost first decreases then increases, as was the case in the short run.

Let us now summarize the situation graphically. In Figure 7.3, we continue to assume that output is produced using two inputs, K and L. The known and fixed input prices give the constant input-price ratio, represented by the slope

TABLE 7.3
Derivation of long-run cost schedules

(1)	(2)	(3)	(4)	(5)	(6)
	Least-cost usage of		*Total cost at \$5 per unit of labor, \$10 per unit of capital*		
Output	*Labor (units)*	*Capital (units)*		*Average cost*	*Marginal cost (per unit)*
100	10	7	\$120	\$1.20	\$1.20
200	12	8	140	0.70	0.20
300	20	10	200	0.67	0.60
400	30	15	300	0.75	1.00
500	40	22	420	0.84	1.20
600	52	30	560	0.93	1.40
700	60	42	720	1.03	1.60

Figure 7.3
The expansion path and long-run cost

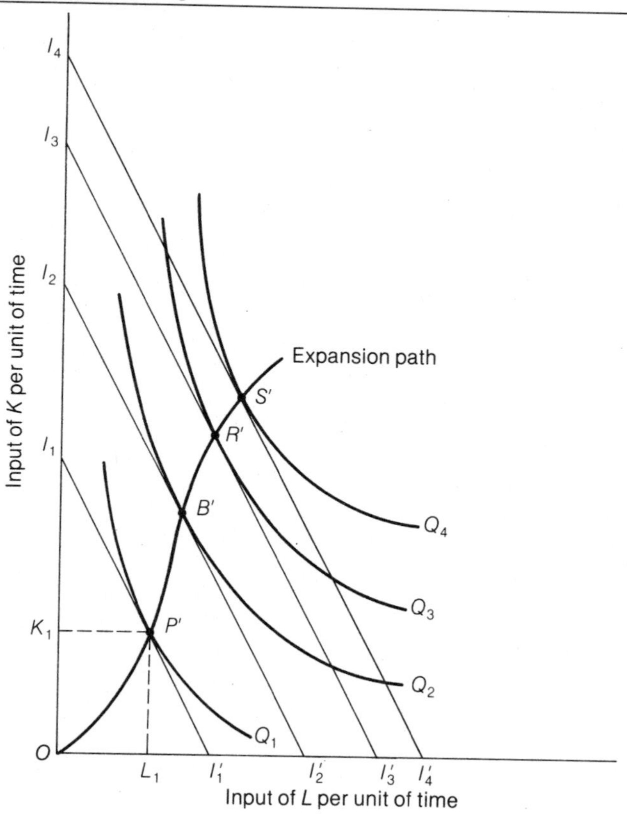

of the isocost curves $I_1I'_1$, $I_2I'_2$, and so on. Next, the known production function gives us the isoquant map, partially represented by Q_1,Q_2, and so forth, in Figure 7.3.

As we know from Chapter 5, when all inputs are variable (that is, in the long run), the manager will choose input combinations that minimize the cost of producing each level of output. In Figure 7.3 these combinations give us the expansion path $OP'B'R'S'$. Given the factor-price ratio and the production function, the expansion path shows the combinations of inputs that enable the firm to produce each level of output at the least possible cost.

Now let us relate this expansion path to a long-run total cost (*LRTC*) curve. Figure 7.4 shows graphically the "least cost curve" associated with the expansion path in Figure 7.3. This least cost curve *is* the long-run total cost curve. Points P,B,R, and S are associated with points P',B',R', and S' on the expansion path. For example, in Figure 7.3 the least cost combination of inputs that can produce Q_1 is K_1 units of capital and L_1 units of labor. Thus in

Figure 7.4
Long-run total cost curve

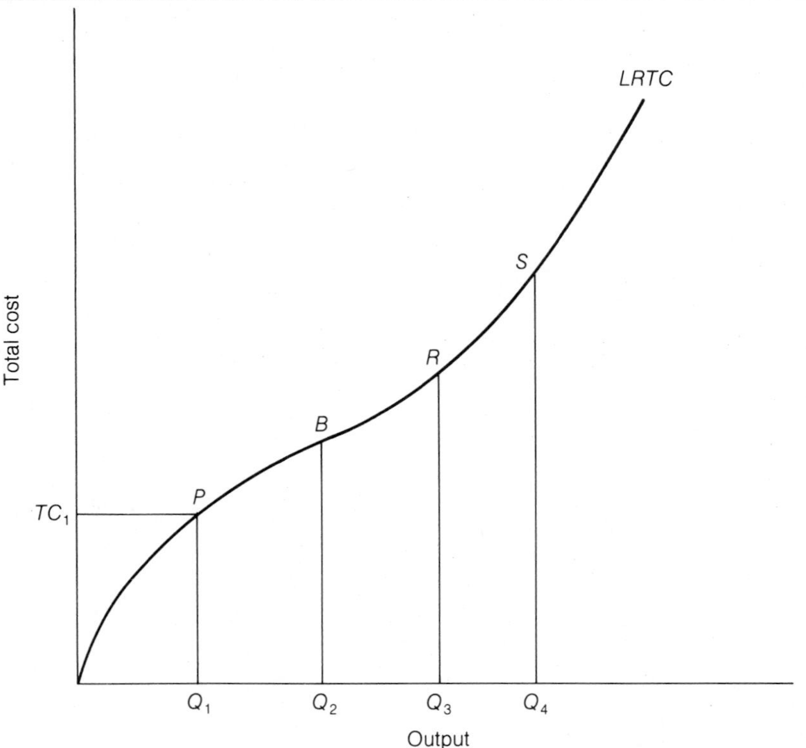

Figure 7.4 the lowest attainable cost of producing Q_1 units of output is TC_1, which is the price of capital times K_1 plus the price of labor times L_1. Every other point on LRTC is derived in the same way.

It is important to note that in the long run the firm may use different amounts and combinations of inputs to produce different levels of output. Nothing is fixed except the set of technological possibilities (the state of the art) and the prices at which the firm can purchase inputs. Thus, completely different production processes may be used to achieve minimum cost at (say) Q_1 and Q_2 units of output. This "planning horizon" in which nothing is fixed except factor prices and technology is called the long run, and the associated curve that shows the minimum cost of producing each level of output is called the long-run total cost curve.

■ **Definition.** Long-run total cost is the least cost at which each quantity of output can be produced when no input is fixed in quantity or rate of use.

The shape of the long-run total cost (*LRTC*) curve depends exclusively on the production function and the prevailing factor prices. The schedule in Table 7.3 and the curve in Figure 7.4 reflect two of the commonly assumed characteristics of long-run total costs. First, costs and output are directly related; that is, the *LRTC* curve has a positive slope. It costs more to produce more, which is just another way of saying that resources are scarce or that one never gets something for nothing.

The second characteristic is that costs first increase at a decreasing rate (until point *B* in Figure 7.4), then increase at an increasing rate thereafter. This shape indicates that long-run marginal cost first decreases then increases. We assume that all implicit costs of production are included in the *LRTC* curve. Since no costs are fixed in the long run, the long-run cost curve begins at the origin rather than at some positive cost as was the case for the short-run total cost curve.[4]

Long-run average and marginal costs

We turn now to average and marginal cost in the long run. Long-run average and marginal costs are defined just as they are in the short run.

■ **Definitions.** Long-run average cost is the total cost of producing a particular output divided by that quantity

$$LRAC = LRTC/Q$$

Long-run marginal cost is the addition to total cost attributable to an additional unit of output when all inputs are optimally adjusted,

$$LRMC = \Delta LRTC/\Delta Q$$

It is therefore the change in total cost per unit of output as the firm moves along the long-run total cost curve (or the expansion path).

Figure 7.5 illustrates typical long-run average and marginal cost curves. They have essentially the same shape as they did in the short run. Long-run average cost first declines, reaches a minimum (at Q_2 in Figure 7.5), then increases. Long-run marginal cost first declines, reaches minimum at a lower output than that associated with minimum average cost (Q_1 in Figure 7.5), then increases thereafter.

---

[4]Note that since the cost curve begins at the origin and not at some positive value on the vertical axis, we tacitly assume that the firm owner can readily vary the amount of time and other resources he or she ''invests'' in the business. That is to say, the implicit costs are as readily variable as the explicit costs when one is considering the long run, or planning horizon. It is only in the short run that implicit costs may be fixed.

Figure 7.5
Long-run average and marginal cost curves

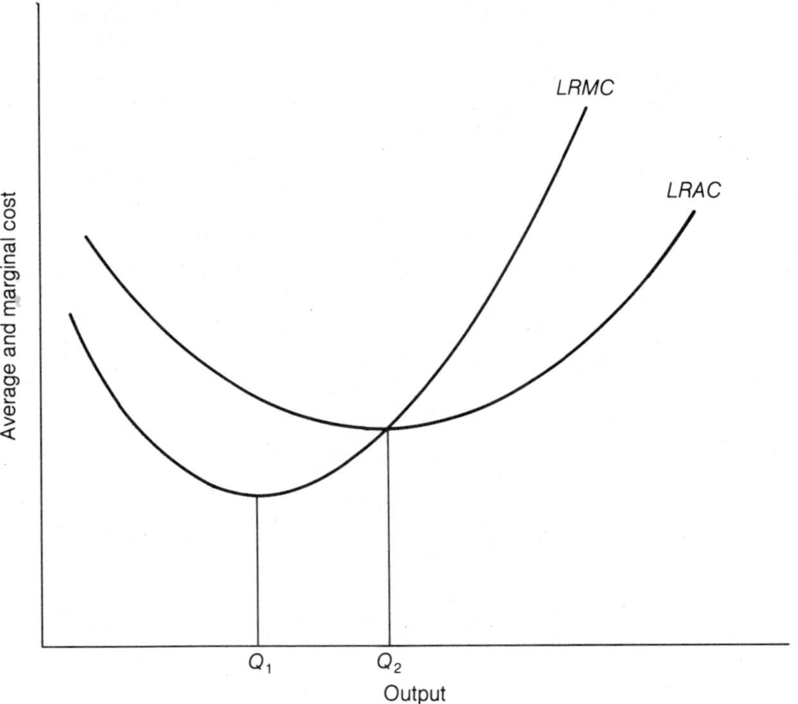

Marginal cost crosses the average cost curve at the minimum of average cost (as it did in the short run). The reasoning is the same as that given for short-run average and marginal cost curves. When marginal cost is less than average cost, each additional unit produced adds less than average cost to total cost; so average cost must decrease. When marginal cost is greater than average cost, each additional unit of the good produced adds more than average cost to total cost; so average cost must be increasing over this range of output. Thus marginal cost must be equal to average cost when average cost is at its minimum.

We can summarize with the following:

■ **Relation.** (1) *LRTC* rises continuously, first at a decreasing rate then at an increasing rate. (2) *LRAC* first declines, reaches a minimum, then rises. When *LRAC* is at its minimum, *LRMC* equals *LRAC*. (3) *LRMC* first declines, reaches a minimum, and then increases. *LRMC* lies below *LRAC* over the range in which *LRAC* declines; it lies above *LRAC* when *LRAC* is rising.

Economies and diseconomies of scale

Thus far we have concentrated exclusively upon describing the generally assumed shapes of the long-run cost curves. But we have not yet analyzed the economic forces behind these shapes. These forces are economies and diseconomies of scale.

Recall from Chapter 5 our discussion of increasing and decreasing returns to scale: When all inputs are increased in the same proportion and output increases in a smaller proportion, the result was referred to as decreasing returns to scale. Alternatively, when all inputs are increased in the same proportion and output increases in a greater proportion, we referred to that as increasing returns to scale.

In the preceding section, we told you about the relation between the short-run production function and short-run cost curves. As you have probably guessed, there also exists a specific relation between returns to scale (a production concept) and the shape of the long-run cost curves. With constant input prices, increasing returns to scale require that the average cost curve decline. This case is referred to as *economies of scale*. Over the range of decreasing returns to scale, the long-run average cost curve is rising and we say that the cost function is characterized by *diseconomies of scale*.

A simplified example might help to demonstrate this point. Suppose there exist increasing returns to scale. Doubling output requires less than twice as much of each input; so the increase in cost is less than double (again assuming constant input prices) and average cost falls. Conversely, in the range of decreasing returns to scale, doubling output requires more than twice as much of each input. In this case, cost will more than double; so average cost will rise. (This example assumes fixed proportions, but it should be noted that the relation holds in the case of variable proportions when inputs are not increased in the same proportion.)

In any case, increasing returns to scale lead to economies of scale which in turn cause long-run average cost to decline. As the size of plant and the scale of operation become larger, certain economies of scale are usually realized. That is, after adjusting all inputs optimally, the unit cost of production is reduced as the firm produces more output.

Adam Smith gave one reason for this phenomenon: specialization and division of labor. When the number of workers is expanded, with a fixed stock of capital equipment, the opportunities for specialization and division of labor are rapidly exhausted. The marginal product curve rises, to be sure; but not for long. It very quickly reaches its maximum and declines. But, in the long run, when workers and equipment are expanded together, very substantial gains may be reaped by division of jobs and the specialization of workers in one job or another.

Proficiency is also gained by concentration of effort. If a plant is very small and employs only a small number of workers, each worker will usually have to perform several different jobs in the production process. In doing so he or she is likely to have to move about the plant, change tools, and so on. Not only are workers not highly specialized but a part of their work time is consumed in moving about and changing tools. Thus, important savings may be realized by expanding the scale of operation. A larger plant with a larger work force may permit each worker to specialize in one job, gaining proficiency and decreasing or eliminating time-consuming interchanges of location and equipment. There naturally will be corresponding reductions in the unit cost of production.

Technological factors constitute a second force contributing to economies of scale. If several different machines, each with a different rate of output, are required in a production process, the operation may have to be quite sizable to permit proper "meshing" of equipment. Suppose only two types of machines are required, one that produces and one that packages the product. If the first machine can produce 30,000 units per day and the second can package 45,000 units per day, output will have to be 90,000 units per day in order to utilize fully the capacity of each type of machine.

Another technological element is the fact that the cost of purchasing and installing larger machines is usually proportionately less than the cost of smaller machines. For example, a printing press that can run 200,000 papers per day does not cost 10 times as much as one that can run 20,000 per day—nor does it require 10 times as much building space, 10 times as many people to work it, and so forth. Again, expanding size tends to reduce the unit cost of production.

A final technological element is perhaps the most important of all: as the scale of operation expands there is usually a qualitative, as well as a quantitative, change in equipment. Consider ditchdigging. The smallest scale of operation is one laborer and one shovel. But as the scale expands beyond a certain point the firm does not simply continue to add workers and shovels. Shovels and most workers are replaced by a modern ditchdigging machine. In like manner, expansion of scale normally permits the introduction of various types of automation devices, all of which tend to reduce the unit cost of production.

Thus two broad forces, (1) specialization and division of labor and (2) technological factors, enable producers to reduce unit cost by expanding the scale of operation.[5] These forces give rise to the negatively sloped portion of the long-run average cost curve.

But why should the long-run average cost curve ever rise? After all possible economies of scale have been realized, why doesn't the curve become horizontal?

---

[5]This discussion of economies of scale has concentrated upon physical and technological forces. There are financial reasons for economies of scale as well. Large-scale purchasing of raw and processed materials may enable the buyer to obtain more favorable prices (quantity discounts). The same is frequently true of advertising. As another example, financing of large-scale businesses is normally easier and less expensive: a nationally known business has access to organized security markets, so it may place its bonds and stocks on a more favorable basis. Bank loans also usually come easier and at lower interest rates to large, well-known corporations.

The rising portion of LRAC is usually attributed to decreasing returns to scale, causing diseconomies of scale, which generally implies limitations to efficient management. Managing any business entails controlling and coordinating a wide variety of activities—production, transportation, finance, sales, and so on. To perform these managerial functions efficiently, the manager must have accurate information; otherwise the essential decision making is done in ignorance.

As the scale of plant expands beyond a certain point, top management necessarily has to delegate responsibility and authority to lower echelon employees. Contact with the daily routine of operation tends to be lost, and efficiency of operation declines. Red tape and paperwork expand; management is generally not as efficient. Thus, the cost of the managerial function increases, as does the unit cost of production.

It is very difficult to determine just when diseconomies of scale set in and when they become strong enough to outweigh the economies of scale. In businesses where economies of scale are negligible, diseconomies may soon become of paramount importance, causing LRAC to turn up at a relatively small volume of output. Panel A of Figure 7.6 shows a long-run average cost curve for a firm of this type. In other cases, economies of scale are extremely important. Even after the efficiency of management begins to decline, technological economies of scale may offset the diseconomies over a wide range of output. Thus the LRAC curve may not turn upward until a very large volume of output is attained. This case (typified by the so-called natural monopolies) is illustrated in Panel B of Figure 7.6.

In many actual situations, however, neither of these extremes describes the behavior of LRAC. A very modest scale of operation may enable a firm to capture all of the economies of scale and diseconomies may not be incurred until the volume of output is very great. In this case, LRAC would have a long horizontal section as shown in Panel C of Figure 7.6. Some economists and business executives feel that this type of LRAC curve describes many produc-

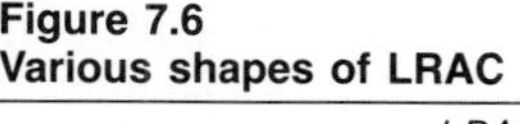

Figure 7.6
Various shapes of LRAC

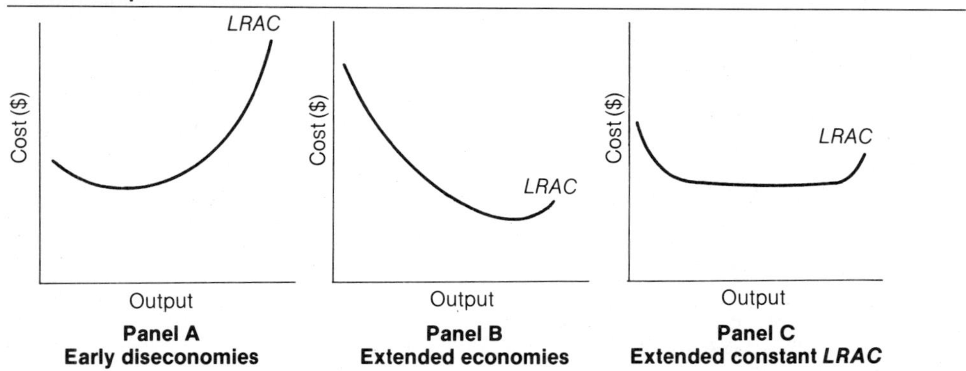

Panel A
Early diseconomies

Panel B
Extended economies

Panel C
Extended constant *LRAC*

tion processes in the American economy. For analytical purposes, however, we will assume a "representative" LRAC, such as that illustrated earlier in Figure 7.5.

THE WALL STREET JOURNAL

APPLICATION

Are diseconomies of scale a real problem?

We have discussed why expanding firms *could* encounter diseconomies of scale as they grow. But, you may be thinking that there are a lot of giant firms in the world, and they seem to be doing all right. And you would be correct. But this is not to say that growth doesn't involve problems. Many firms that have become large and successful have had to find ways to overcome the diseconomies that come with size.

Let's look at a general trend in American business. Federick C. Klein, in an article in *The Wall Street Journal* pointed out the declining role of very large companies in the U.S. employment picture.* The proportion of people working for firms employing 500 or more workers peaked in 1967 and declined steadily until 1979, the last year for which data were available. Moreover, total employment by U.S. companies that employed 100,000 or more remained constant from 1970 to 1980, while the U.S. work force increased 24 percent. A 1979 study by a MIT research group found that between 1969 and 1976, 66 percent of the net new jobs created came in firms employing 20 or fewer workers, and more than 80 percent from firms employing 100 or fewer. The same research group found that the number of "dying" establishments was significantly greater for acquired firms than for those remaining independent. Thus there appears to be some evidence of diseconomies for large firms that purchase smaller firms.

Klein pointed out that the blame for the laggard performance of many large corporations is focused on their structured and entrenched ways of doing things. He noted that a growing body of opinion has it that the "economies of scale" made possible by bigness often are more than nullified by organization rigidities and bottlenecks. Larry E. Greiner, a professor of business at the University of Southern California, is quoted: "More companies seem to be showing concern that their neat organizational charts don't always reflect reality and certainly don't, in themselves, overcome the tensions between autonomy and control that get worse with size."

The article went on to say that big-corporation management can't always work their wills on large and cumbersome work forces. As Richard C. Edwards, an economics professor at the University of Massachusetts, said, "Big companies tend to react slower to marketplace changes than small ones, and bounce back from adversity slower."

One corporation that was trying to "think small" was the Minnesota Mining and Manufacturing Co. (3M). The top personel officer at 3M said, "We are keenly aware of the problems of large size. We make a conscious effort to keep our units as small as possible because we think it keeps them flexible and vital. When one gets too large, we break it apart. We like to say that our success in recent years amounts to multiplication by division."

Even though 3M employed some 87,000 workers, its average manufacturing plant employed only 270 people. Many product management groups consisted of only five people. Despite the declining role of many of the largest firms, 3M's earnings grew almost fourfold during the 1970s, while its work force increased 40 percent. Thus it appears that 3M had successfully overcome the problems brought about by large size by breaking its huge production facility into many smaller, more manageable divisions.

Another corporate giant was, in 1984, attempting to overcome the problems of diseconomies of scale in a somewhat different manner. During 1984, General Motors made plans to reorganize its entire corporate structure. According to an article in *The Wall Street Journal*, GM was planning to consolidate its five U.S. sales divisions into one small car division and one large car division.[†] The five sales divisions would remain only as marketing organizations. Chevrolet and Pontiac would sell only the cars manufactured by the small car division while Buick, Oldsmobile, and Cadillac would sell only large cars.

According to GM sources, the idea was to restore more realistic profit centers. The various divisions, originally intended to be self-sufficient, had evolved into a hodgepodge of staff and manufacturing responsibilities that contributed more cost than profit to the bottom line. The reorganization was intended to eliminate thousands of white collar jobs through attrition. GM officials said that they could do away with the diffusion of responsibility that existed by forming two groups that would be responsible for their own cars from start to finish. They also hoped to eliminate duplication of effort and streamline communication.

The point is that GM had grown so large that the management structure had become unwieldy; and serious diseconomies had been encountered. The reorganization was a way to eliminate or at least reduce some of these problems.

Obviously, a firm does not have to be nearly as large as 3M or General Motors to experience managerial diseconomies of scale when expanding. One example of a smaller company that encountered problems with rapid expansion is Nutri/System Inc., a franchiser of weight loss centers throughout the country. According to *The Wall Street Journal*,[‡] when Nutri/System went public in January 1981, it quickly became a "Wall Street star." Revenues and earnings doubled in both 1981 and 1982 and "there seemed to be no end in sight to its growth". Profit had risen from \$3.8 million in 1980 to \$18.1 million in 1982. But expansion brought problems.

The company made several acquisitions that turned bad, and revenues and profits from the weight loss centers decreased sharply. During 1983 Nutri/

System stock fell from $48.18 to $11.25. Several franchises, upset over the high prices being charged for food, were suing the company to allow them to purchase food from alternative sources.

As the *Journal* pointed out, "Like many rapidly growing companies, Nutri/System yielded to the temptation to pursue even faster growth through acquisitions." During its period of rapid growth, Nutri/System purchased an executive placement service, a cosmetics firm, and a chain of figure salons. The purchases were based upon the owner's belief that "once you know how to handle one business of the service nature and sales nature, you can handle any type business in that field."

But the placement service quickly began to lose money. Several of the major executives left the firm. Also, Nutri/System's management didn't know the cosmetics business, and the people they hired to run it didn't work out. They soon sold the firm back to the original owners. Furthermore, the techniques that succeeded for Nutri/System didn't work well for the figure salons. Many of the unprofitable salons had to be dropped.

---

*"Some Fight Ills of Bigness by Keeping Employment Units Small," *The Wall Street Journal*, February 5, 1982. Reprinted by permission of *The Wall Street Journal*.

†"GM Revamp Seeks to Solve Corporate Ills that Persist Despite Rebound in Finances," by Jim Koten, *The Wall Street Journal*, January 12, 1984. Reprinted by permission of *The Wall Street Journal*.

‡Virginia Inman, "How Nutri/System Developed Indigestion from Its Acquisitions", *The Wall Street Journal*, October 14, 1983. Reprinted by permission of *The Wall Street Journal*.

7.4 RELATIONS BETWEEN SHORT-RUN AND LONG-RUN COSTS

We can summarize our discussion of cost thus far by noting that firms *plan* in the long run and *operate* in the short run. Indeed, we call the long run the firm's planning horizon. The long-run cost function gives the most efficient (the least cost) method of producing any given level of output, because all inputs are variable. But once a particular firm size is chosen and the firm begins producing, the firm is in the short run. Plant and equipment have already been constructed. Now if the firm wishes to change its level of output, it can't vary the usage of all inputs. Some inputs, the plant and so forth, are fixed to the firm. Thus the firm cannot vary all inputs optimally and therefore cannot produce this new level of output at the lowest possible cost.

Such a situation is shown in Figure 7.7; LRTC is the firm's long-run total cost curve. Suppose that, when making its plans, the firm had decided that it wanted to produce Q_0 units of output per period. It chooses the optimal combination of inputs to produce this output at the lowest possible cost, which is shown as TC_0 in the figure. Since it would not wish to vary any of its inputs so long as it continues to produce Q_0, the short-run cost of producing Q_0 is the same as the long-run cost.

Figure 7.7
Long-run and short-run total cost curves

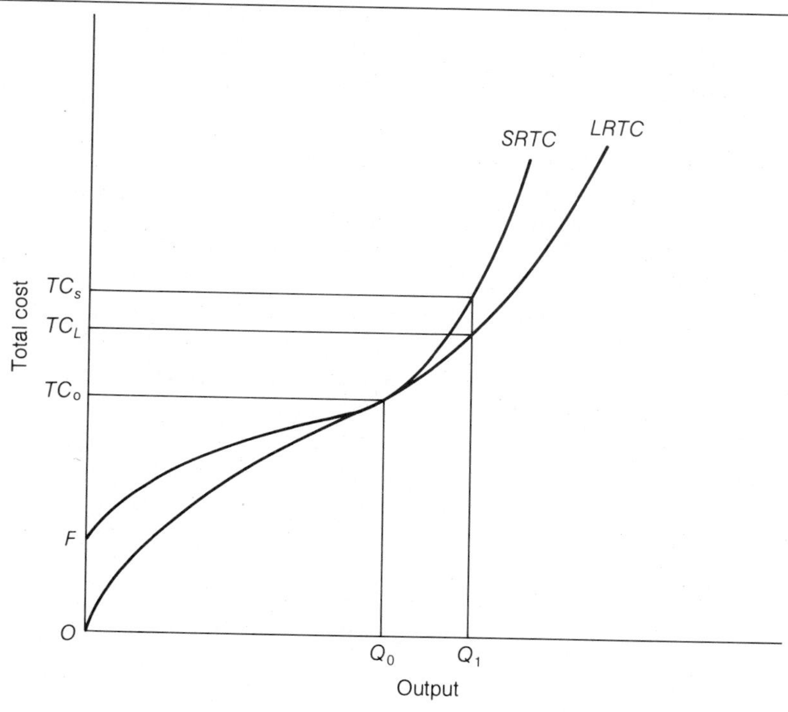

Thus, the short-run total cost curve, SRTC, is tangent to LRTC at Q_0. But, since some inputs are fixed in the short run, if the firm wishes to vary its output in the short run, it cannot produce the new output at the lowest possible cost. At any output other than Q_0, the short-run input combination is less efficient—would result in a higher cost—than the combination that would be chosen if all inputs were variable.

Suppose, for example, that the firm wants to increase its output from Q_0 to Q_1. If all inputs were variable, it could produce this new output at TC_L. But, if plant and some other inputs are fixed, *SRTC* gives the cost of producing Q_1. This cost is TC_s, which is clearly greater that TC_L. The fixed cost is F and the variable cost is $TC_s - F$. Clearly, from Figure 7.7, *SRTC* is greater than *LRTC* at any output other than Q_0. Only at output Q_0 are the two curves equal.

The relation between *LRTC* and *SRTC* will, of course, determine the relation between the long-run and short-run average cost curves. Given the total cost curves in Figure 7.7, short-run average cost will be equal to long-run average cost only at an output of Q_0. (Since $LRAC = LRTC/Q$ and $ATC = SRTC/Q$, *LRAC* can only be equal to *ATC* when *LRTC* is equal to *SRTC*.) At any other level of output, short-run average cost is greater than long-run average cost because *SRTC* is greater than *LRTC*.

Figure 7.8 shows the typical relation between short- and long-run average and marginal cost curves. In this figure, *LRAC* and *LRMC* are the long-run average and marginal cost curves. Three short-run situations are indicated by the three sets of curves: $SRAC_1$, MC_1; $SRAC_2$, MC_2; and $SRAC_3$, MC_3.

Let's look at $SRAC_1$ and MC_1. These are the short-run curves for the plant size designed to produce output Q_s optimally. Since the short-run total cost curve would be tangent to the long-run total cost curve at this output, the two average cost curves are also tangent at this output. Since marginal cost, $\Delta C/\Delta Q$, is given by the slope of the total cost curve, long-run marginal cost equals short-run marginal cost at the output given by the point of tangency, Q_s. Finally, short-run marginal cost crosses short-run average cost at the latter's minimum point. Note that because Q_s is on the decreasing portion of *LRAC*, $SRAC_1$ must be decreasing also at the point of tangency.

$SRAC_3$ and MC_3 show another short-run situation—a different plant size. Here tangency occurs at Q_L on the increasing part of *LRAC*. Thus $SRAC_3$ is increasing at this point also. Again the two marginal curves are equal at Q_L, and MC_3 crosses $SRAC_3$ at the minimum point on the latter.

Finally, $SRAC_2$ is the short-run average cost curve corresponding to the output level—plant size—at which long-run average cost is at its minimum. At output level Q_m the two average cost curves are tangent. The two marginal cost curves, MC_2 and *LRMC*, are also equal at this output. And, since both average cost curves attain their minimum at Q_m, the two marginal cost curves

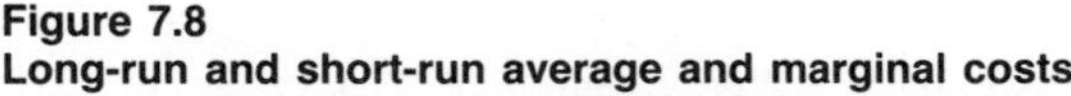

Figure 7.8
Long-run and short-run average and marginal costs

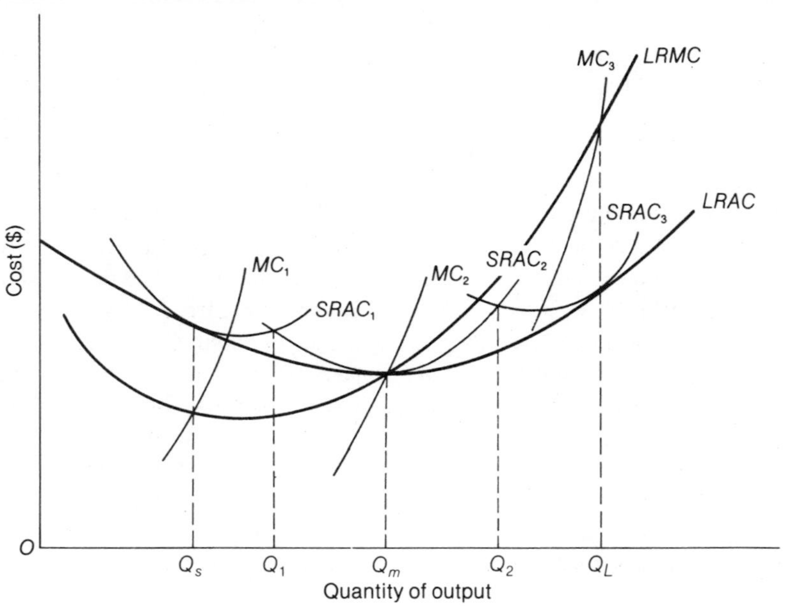

must intersect the two average cost curves. Thus all four curves are equal at output Q_m. That is, at Q_m, $LRAC = SRAC_2 = MC_2 = LRMC$.

If the firm is limited to producing only with one of the three short-run cost structures shown in Figure 7.8, it would choose the cost structure—plant size—given by $SRAC_1$ to produce outputs from zero to Q_1, because the average cost, and hence the total cost, of producing each output over this range is lower under this cost specification. If it wishes to produce any output between Q_1 and Q_2, it would choose the plant size given by $SRAC_2$. This average cost curve lies below either of the other two for any output over this range. It would choose the cost structure shown by $SRAC_3$ for any level of output greater than Q_2.

But typically the firm is not limited to three sizes—large, medium, or small. In the long run it can build the plant whose size leads to lowest average cost. The long-run average cost curve is a planning device, because this curve shows the least cost of producing each possible output. Managers therefore are normally faced with a choice among a wide variety of plant sizes.

The long-run planning curve, *LRAC*, is a locus of points representing the lowest possible unit cost of producing the corresponding output. The manager determines the desired size of plant by reference to this curve, selecting the short-run plant that yields the lowest unit cost of producing the volume of output desired.

■ **Relations.** (1) *LRMC* intersects *LRAC* when the latter is at its minimum point. There exists some short-run plant size for which the minimum *SRAC* coincides with minimum *LRAC*. (2) At each output where a particular *SRAC* is tangent to *LRAC*, the relevant *SRMC* equals *LRMC*. At outputs below (above) the tangency output, the relevant *SRMC* is less (greater) than *LRMC*. (3) For all *SRAC* curves, the point of tangency with *LRAC* is at an output less (greater) than the output of minimum *SRAC* if the tangency is at an output less (greater) than that associated with minimum *LRAC*.

7.5 SUMMARY

The physical conditions of production and resource prices jointly establish the cost of production. If the set of technological possibilities changes, the cost curves change. Or if the prices of some factors of production change, the firm's cost curves change. Therefore, it should be emphasized that cost curves are generally drawn under the assumptions of constant factor prices and a constant technology.

We have distinguished between cost in the short run and in the long run. Except for one output level, cost is always higher in the short run than in the long run for every short-run situation.

While the cost of production is important to business firms and to the economy as a whole, it is only half the story. Cost gives one aspect of economic activity; it is the obligation to pay out funds. The other aspect is revenue or demand. To the individual manager, revenue constitutes the flow of funds from which the obligation may be met.

Thus both demand and cost must be taken into consideration. We will turn to an analysis of demand after considering empirical estimation of cost in the next chapter.

TECHNICAL PROBLEMS

1. Return to Problem 2 at the end of Chapter 5. Total product is given, and you have computed average and marginal product. You are now given the following information:

a. Total fixed cost (total price of fixed inputs) is $220 per period.

b. Units of the variable input cost $100 per unit per period.

Using this information, complete the following table:

Units of variable input	Product			Cost			Average cost			Marginal cost
	Total	Average	Marginal	Fixed	Variable	Total	Fixed	Variable	Total	
1	100									
2	250									
3	410									
4	560									
5	700									
6	830									
7	945									
8	1,050									
9	1,146									
10	1,234									
11	1,314									
12	1,384									
13	1,444									
14	1,494									
15	1,534									
16	1,564									
17	1,584									
18	1,594									

c. Graph the total cost curves on one sheet and the average and marginal curves on another.

d. By reference to table and graph, answer the following questions.

(1) When marginal product is increasing, what is happening to:

(i) Marginal cost?

(ii) Average variable cost?

(2) When marginal cost first begins to fall, does average variable cost begin to rise?

(3) What is the relation between marginal cost and average variable cost when marginal and average product are equal?

(4) What is happening to average variable cost while average product is increasing?
(5) What is average variable cost when average product is at its maximum? What happens to average variable cost after this point?
(6) What happens to marginal cost after the point where it equals average variable cost?
   (i) How does it compare with average variable cost thereafter?
   (ii) What is happening to marginal product thereafter?
   (iii) How does marginal product compare with average product thereafter?
(7) What happens to total fixed cost as output is increased?
(8) What happens to average fixed cost as:
   (i) Marginal product increases?
   (ii) Marginal cost decreases?
   (iii) Marginal product decreases?
   (iv) Marginal cost increases?
   (v) Average variable cost increases?
(9) How long does average fixed cost decrease?
(10) What happens to average total cost as:
   (i) Marginal product increases?
   (ii) Marginal cost decreases?
   (iii) Average product increases?
   (iv) Average variable cost decreases?
(11) Does average variable cost increase:
   (i) As soon as the point of diminishing marginal returns is passed?
   (ii) As soon as the point of diminishing average returns is passed?
(12) When does average cost increase? Answer this in terms of:
   (i) The relation of average cost to marginal cost.
   (ii) The relation between the increase in average variable cost and the decrease in average fixed cost.

2. Suppose that, if labor costs $10 per unit and capital costs $5 per unit, the least cost combinations of capital and labor are as follows:

Output	*Labor*	*Capital*
100	5	10
200	6	12
300	8	14
400	10	20
500	13	28
600	18	38
700	24	54

a. Prepare a table showing long-run total cost, long-run average cost, and long-run marginal cost.
b. Graph these cost functions.
c. At approximately what output does long-run average cost attain its minimum?
d. Over what range of output do economies of scale exist? Over what range are diseconomies of scale indicated?

3. Assume that labor—the only variable input of a firm—has the average and marginal product curves shown in the following figure. Labor's wage is $2 per unit.

a. When the firm attains minimum average variable cost, how many units of labor is it using?
b. What level of output is associated with minimum average variable cost?
c. What is the average variable cost of producing this output?
d. Suppose the firm is using 100 units of labor. What is marginal cost? What is average variable cost?

4. Explain why long-run average cost first falls, then rises. Why does short-run average variable cost first fall, then rise?

5. Explain why short-run marginal cost increases at a greater rate than long-run marginal cost beyond the point at which they are equal.

6. Fill in the blanks in the table on the facing page.

	Total cost	Fixed cost	Variable cost	Average fixed cost	Average variable cost	Average total cost	Marginal cost
1	$	$100	$ 900	$	$	$	$
2					850		
3							700
4					800		
5						900	
6							1,500
7			7,900				
8						1,300	
9	14,000						

7. Explain why short-run average cost can never be less than long-run average cost.
8. Suppose you run a business located on a commercial lot, which you own. Last year revenue exceeded cost by $250,000. The lot next to yours is approximately the same size as yours and rents for $60,000 a year. What is your profit for the year?
9. Suppose average variable cost is constant over a range of output. What is marginal cost over this range? What is happening to average total cost over this range?
10. Economists frequently say that the firm plans in the long run and operates in the short run. Explain.

ANALYTICAL PROBLEMS

1. Explain why it would cost John McEnroe or Chris Evert Lloyd more to leave the professional tennis tour and open a tennis shop than it would for the coach of a university tennis team to open a tennis shop.
2. You are the adviser to the president of a university. A wealthy alumnus buys, then gives a plot of land to the university to use as an athletic field. The president says that, as far as the land is concerned, it does not cost the university anything to use the land as an athletic field. What do you say?
3. We frequently hear several terms used by businesspersons. What do they mean in economic terminology?
   a. Spreading the overhead.
   b. A break-even level of production.
   c. The efficiency of mass production.
4. How much does it cost you to keep money in a checking rather than a savings account? If there is this cost, why do people keep money in a checking account? What would cause people to keep less in a savings account and more in checking?

5. Suppose that you manage a business and have to make business trips of two to four days at least once a month. What factors determine the total cost of a trip? What factors would you consider when deciding whether your salespeople should travel by automobile or airplane? Are these necessarily the same factors that determine the cost of your own travel?
6. Recently a large number of steel manufacturers have closed down or disposed of a large number of steel mills. What factors must they have considered in making this decision?
7. This question anticipates material in the next chapter, but it should be worthwhile to think about it now.
   a. Why would managers want to have estimates of costs?
   b. What costs would be the most important?
   c. How would you go about having costs estimated?
   d. What might be some of the problems you would encounter?
8. Based upon the Application concerning the 3M company, what would have caused the diseconomies of scale had 3M decided upon a more centralized operation instead of breaking into small units?
9. From the same Application, what factors seem to have led GM to carry out the reorganization plans that were described? If you were a GM dealer, how would you expect this reorganization to affect your business? (We might note that, at the time the decision was made, many dealers were upset.)
10. Fixed costs are very real in the sense that the firm must pay them. Then why do we say that managers should totally ignore fixed cost when making decisions?
11. In line with Problem 10, suppose you have gone to school two years. In two more years you can obtain your degree, but someone offers you a well-paying job now. What factors would you consider when making the choice whether or not to leave school and take the job? How would the fact that you have already put in two years toward your degree affect your decision?

8

Quantitative analyses of cost

In Chapter 7 we provided the theoretical basis for the analysis of cost. We hope you have seen that an understanding of the cost function is essential to the manager, both for the pricing decision and for the investment decision. Knowledge of the cost function, coupled with knowledge of the demand function (obtained by using the analyses we will provide in Chapters 9–12), will allow the manager to make the decisions that will maximize profit for the firm.

In this chapter we will set forth some methodologies by which the theoretical analyses of cost can actually be implemented. Although we will describe an engineering cost function approach, we will concentrate our attention primarily on regression analysis. However, again keep in mind what we stressed in Chapter 4—our purpose is not to teach you actually how to perform estimations; rather, we want you to be able to use, interpret, and evaluate the estimates made by others.

8.1 REGRESSION ANALYSES OF COST—SOME GENERAL CONSIDERATIONS

If we can assume that firms have been operating efficiently, that is, minimizing cost, we can use the techniques of regression analysis to obtain an estimate of the cost function. As we demonstrated in Chapter 7, cost is defined to be a function of output. That is,

$$C = f(Q)$$

Or, more generally, we can say that total cost is determined by the level of output and a set of additional characteristics, X, including such things as the prices of the inputs:

$$C = f(Q;X)$$

It follows then that our basic task is to estimate the relation between cost and the level of output.

Short-run versus long-run estimation

Before we describe the estimation procedures, we should note that there exist several methodological differences between short-run and long-run cost estimation, and the differences are substantial. Indeed, even the objectives of the two types of estimations are quite different.

In the case of estimates of short-run cost functions, the resulting estimates would be used in the firm's pricing decision. More specifically, such estimates would be used to determine the marginal cost associated with producing additional units of output.

Conversely, since we have already defined the long run to be the firm's planning horizon, it follows that estimates of the long-run cost function would be used in the firm's investment decisions. More specifically, a primary objective of long-run cost estimation is to determine the extent of economies and diseconomies of scale, in order that the manager can select the optimal plant size.

With this basic difference in the objectives of short- and long-run estimation in mind, let us turn now to some more specific differences. We begin with a consideration of short-run cost estimation.

To estimate a short-run cost function, the data must be such that the usage level of one (or more) of the inputs is fixed. (In the context of the simple, two-input production function we employed in Chapter 5, this restriction could be interpreted to mean that the firm's capital stock is fixed while labor usage is allowed to vary.) The most widely accepted method for obtaining such a data set is to use time-series data for a specific firm. That is, the analyst could collect cost and output data for a firm over a period sufficiently short that the firm's level of usage of one (or more) of its inputs is fixed. For instance, the analyst might collect monthly observations over a two-year period in which the firm did not change its basic plant (i.e., capital stock). Thus, the analyst could obtain 24 observations on cost and output. With such a time-series data set, there exists a potential data problem. While output is expressed in physical units, cost is expressed in nominal dollars. Hence the nominal cost data would include the effect of inflation. That is, over time, inflation would cause reported costs to rise, even if output remained constant. Such a situation is depicted in Figure 8.1. As you can see in this figure, estimation based upon such a data set would indicate that the cost function has

Figure 8.1
Problem of inflation

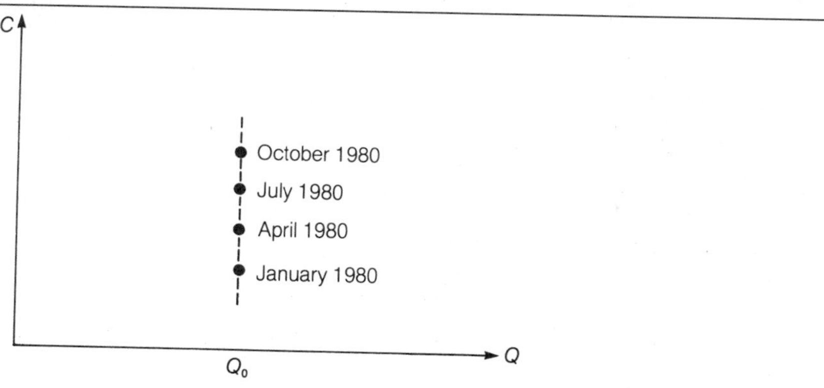

an extremely large positive slope—even if the slope of the true cost function is zero or negative. Hence, it is necessary to eliminate the effects of inflation. As we will demonstrate below, such an elimination can be accomplished by deflating the cost data by an appropriate price index.

In the case of long-run cost estimation, the analyst would want to have a data set in which the usage level of all inputs is variable. While it might be possible to obtain such a data set from time-series observations on an individual firm, the most generally used method is to collect a cross-section data set. That is, observations are collected from several different firms at a given point in time. In this kind of a data set, the objective is to include firms that use different levels of the inputs and produce different levels of output. The primary difficulty encountered in such data sets is that it is possible—particularly if the firms are separated geographically—that the input prices paid by the various firms in the data set are different. For example, consider the following hypothetical situation: Suppose that two firms produce the same level of output using the same amounts of capital and labor. However, the input prices for Firm 1 are twice those facing Firm 2. This situation is depicted graphically in Figure 8.2. As was the situation in the short-run problem, estimation using such a data set would indicate that the cost function is rising steeply, even if the true cost function (i.e., abstracting from different input prices) does not exhibit such a relation. Hence, it will be necessary to eliminate the effect of the input price differences.

While it is theoretically possible to use some sort of an index for input price differences (similar to the price index approach used in short-run estimation), the calculation of such an index may not be practical. Instead, the approach normally used in long-run cost estimation is to adjust for different input prices in the regression equation itself. In the context of the two-input production process we have been considering, such an adjustment would imply that the cost function to be estimated is

$$C = f(Q,w,r)$$

Figure 8.2
Problem of differing input prices

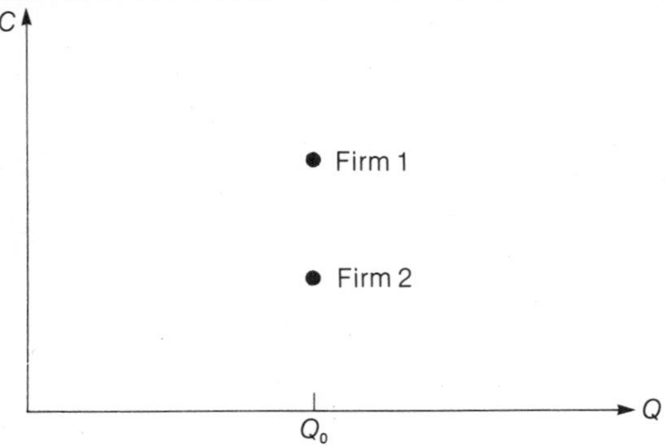

where w and r are, respectively, the prices of labor and capital. That is, in order to estimate the long-run cost function (using cross-section data), it may be necessary to include, as independent variables, not only output but also the prices of the inputs.

Data problems

A potentially troublesome problem can also result from the difference between the accounting definition of cost and the economic definition of cost. As we stressed in Chapter 7, the economist's definition of cost is based on opportunity cost. However, since accounting data are of necessity based on expenditures, opportunity cost may not be reflected in the firm's accounting records. Let's use an example to illustrate this problem. Suppose a firm owns its own machinery. The opportunity cost of this equipment is the income that could be derived if the machinery were leased to another firm. However, this cost would not be reflected in the accounting data.

In a two-input setting, total cost may be defined as

$$C = wL + rK$$

The wage rate should reflect the opportunity cost of labor to the firm; so, expenditures on labor, wL (including any additional compensation not paid as wages), would reflect opportunity cost. The problem is the calculation of the firm's opportunity cost of capital. We need to calculate the cost of capital, r, in such a way that it reflects the *user cost* of capital. User cost must include not only the acquisition cost of a unit of capital but also (1) the return forgone by using the capital rather than renting it, (2) the depreciation charges resulting from the use of the capital, and (3) any capital gains or losses associated with holding the particular type of capital. Likewise, the measurement of the capital stock, K, must be such that it reflects the stock actually owned by the firm. For example, you might want the capital variable to reflect the fact that a given piece of capital has depreciated physically or embodies less technology than a new piece of capital. While these problems are difficult, they are not insurmountable. The main thing we want you to remember is that such opportunity cost data would be expected to differ greatly from the reported cost figures in accounting data.

An additional data problem relates to the matching of output and cost data. Using accounting data, it is often difficult to relate cost to the corresponding output. For example, it could be the case that a firm enters a constant depreciation charge, while in fact the machinery depreciates more rapidly in earlier periods than in later periods (or vice versa).

8.2 ESTIMATION OF A SHORT-RUN COST FUNCTION

We need first to specify an estimable short-run cost function. As we have already noted, cost would be defined to be a function of output,

$$C = f(Q)$$

As with our estimation of the production function, it is necessary to convert this general function into an explicit functional form. And, in selecting the functional form to be employed, we want to be sure that our empirical cost function conforms to the properties and relations described in Chapter 7.

To this end, let's look again at the short-run cost function we developed in Chapter 7. (Recall that these cost functions embody the characteristics of production theory which we discussed in Chapter 5.) In Figure 8.3, we illustrate again the total variable cost, average variable cost, and marginal cost curves. We want our empirical cost function to reflect the properties shown in these graphs.

Since the shape of any one of these three curves will uniquely identify the shape of the remaining two, let's begin with the average variable cost curve. We know that this curve should be U-shaped. What does this imply about the functional form of the average variable cost function? Let's first consider the simplest possible form—a linear specification,

$$AVC = a + bQ$$

Figure 8.3
Representative cost curves

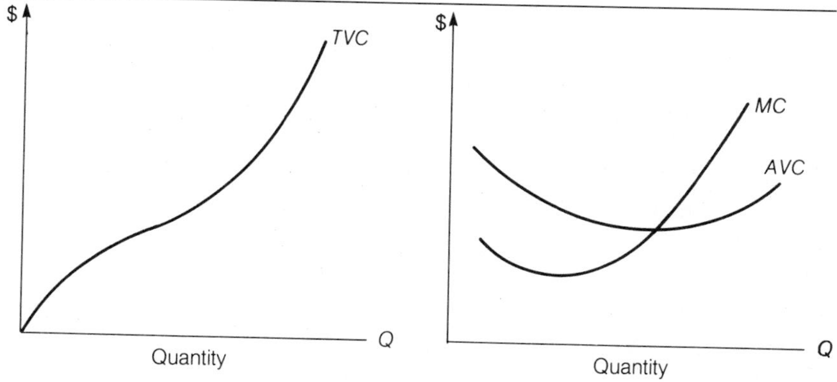

Since the intercept of the average variable cost curve on the vertical axis would be positive, it is necessary that $a > 0$. If b is positive, this function is an upward-sloping straight line. Likewise, if b is negative, this function is a downward-sloping straight line; and, if b is zero, it is a horizontal line. Therefore, under no circumstances could this function exhibit the desired U-shape. That is, this simple linear specification would be inappropriate. Since the simplest form won't work, let's turn next to a slightly more complex specification,

$$AVC = a + bQ + cQ^2$$

Again, we know that a must be positive. If b is negative and c is positive, the following relations would hold: At low levels of output, the negative coefficient b could dominate, in the sense that

$$|bQ| > |cQ^2|$$

and the average variable cost curve would slope downward. However, as output increases, Q^2 gets much larger than Q and the positive coefficient c would dominate, thus

$$|bQ| < |cQ^2|$$

and the average variable cost curve would be upward sloping. Hence, if $a > 0$, $b < 0$, and $c > 0$, the specification we proposed could indeed result in a U-shaped average variable cost curve.[1]

Given our specification for average variable cost,

$$AVC = a + bQ + cQ^2,$$

what can we say about the specification of the total and marginal cost functions? Specification of total cost is straightforward. Since $AVC = TVC/Q$, it follows that

$$\begin{aligned} TVC &= AVC \cdot Q \\ &= (a + bQ + cQ^2) \cdot Q \\ &= aQ + bQ^2 + cQ^3 \end{aligned}$$

[1]Using mathematics, this can be demonstrated somewhat more explicitly. The slope of the average variable cost function is

$$\frac{\partial AVC}{\partial Q} = b + 2cQ$$

Average variable cost will attain a minimum at the point at which this derivative is equal to zero (i.e., $Q = -b/2c$). However, to guarantee a minimum, the second derivative must be positive. That is

$$\frac{\partial^2 AVC}{\partial Q^2} = 2c > 0$$

so, c must be positive. Therefore, if the slope of the average variable cost curve is ever to be negative, it is necessary that b be negative.

Marginal cost is slightly more difficult to derive. However, after some manipulation, it can be shown that[2]

$$MC = a + 2bQ + 3cQ^2$$

Note again that, if $a > 0$, $b < 0$, and $c > 0$, the marginal cost curve will also be U-shaped. Notice that all three of these functions employ the same three parameters, a, b, and c.

It follows that, since all three functions contain the same parameters, it is necessary only to estimate any one of the three functions in order to obtain estimates of all three. For example, if we were to estimate the total variable cost function, we would obtain estimates of the parameters a, b, and c. Then, using the preceding specifications, the marginal and average variable cost functions can be generated.

As to the estimation itself, ordinary least squares estimation of the total (or average) variable cost function is usually sufficient. Once the estimates of a, b, and c are obtained, it is necessary to determine whether the parameter estimates are of the hypothesized signs and statistically significant. The tests for significance are again accomplished using t-tests.[3] (We will return to this procedure in an Application to follow.)

Using the estimates of a total or average variable cost function, we can also obtain an estimate of the output at which average cost is a minimum. Remem-

---

[2]By definition

$$MC = \frac{\partial TVC}{\partial Q} = \frac{\partial(aQ + bQ^2 + cQ^3)}{\partial Q} = a + 2bQ + 3cQ^2$$

[3]We should note a potential difficulty. Suppose that the data for average variable cost are clustered around the minimum point of the average variable cost curve, as in the following figure.

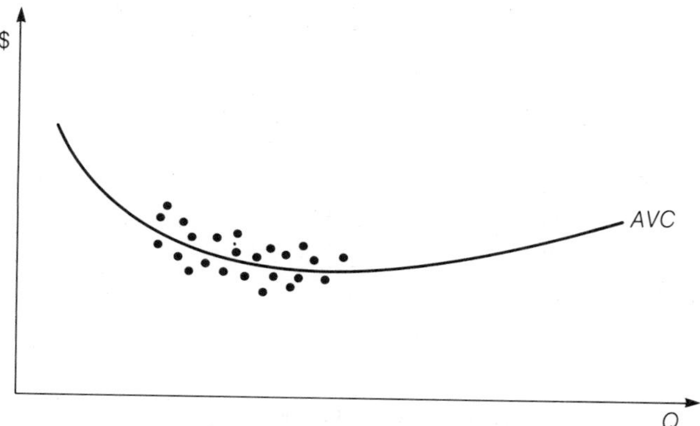

If we estimate the average variable cost function, using these data points, the result would be that, while $\hat{a}$ would be positive and $\hat{b}$ would be negative, the coefficient $\hat{c}$ would not be statistically significant. That is, the t-test would indicate that c is not statistically different from zero. Does this result mean that the average cost curve is not U-shaped, since c must be treated as equal to zero? Not necessarily. The problem is that since we do not have observations for the larger levels of output, our estimation simply cannot tell us whether or not average cost is rising over that range of output.

ber that when average variable cost is at its minimum, average variable cost and marginal cost are equal. Thus we can define the minimum of average variable cost as that output at which

$$AVC = MC$$

Using the specifications of average variable cost and marginal cost that we presented above, we can write this condition as

$$a + bQ + cQ^2 = a + 2bQ + 3cQ^2$$

or

$$bQ + 2cQ^2 = 0$$

Solving for Q, the level of output at which average cost is minimized is[4]

$$Q = -b/2c$$

APPLICATION

A short-run cost function

Suppose we knew that the capital stock of a particular firm had remained unchanged from the fourth quarter of 1981 through the fourth quarter of 1983. We could then collect quarterly observations on cost and output over this period and use the resulting data set to estimate a short-run cost function.

Data on output and average variable cost were collected from this firm over this period. These data are as follows:

Quarter	*Output (000 units)*	*Average variable cost*
1981IV	30	$72
1982I	10	75
1982II	15	55
1982III	25	56
1982IV	40	94
1983I	20	65
1983II	35	89
1983III	45	118
1983IV	50	134

At this point, we must recognize the problem we told you about in Section 8.1. While output is measured in physical units, average variable cost is measured in nominal (i.e., current) dollars. Hence, the reported cost data are subject to the effects of inflation. That is, over the period considered, reported

[4]In this, you can see how an insignificant estimate of the parameter c leads to problems. (See footnote 3.)

costs have increased due to the effects of inflation. We wish to eliminate the influence of inflation. The most common method for accomplishing this is to "deflate" the nominal costs. Such a deflation involves the use of a price index. In order to convert nominal cost into a constant dollar cost, we divide the nominal cost by the appropriate price index for that period. For purposes of illustration, we will use the price index for personal consumption expenditures. Following are the values for this index for the period under consideration. These values were obtained from the *Survey of Current Business* (U.S. Department of Commerce).

Quarter	*Price index for personal consumption expenditures (1972 = 1.0)*
1981IV	1.992
1982I	2.017
1982II	2.036
1982III	2.069
1982IV	2.090
1983I	2.101
1983II	2.129
1983III	2.147
1983IV	2.161

For example, to obtain the constant dollar average variable cost for the 30,000 units produced in the fourth quarter of 1981, we would divide $72 by 1.992 to obtain $36.14. Doing the same thing for each of the cost figures, we obtain the following data set:

Quarter	*Output (000 units)*	*Deflated average variable cost*
1981IV	30	$36
1982I	10	37
1982II	15	27
1982III	25	27
1982IV	40	45
1983I	20	31
1983II	35	42
1983III	45	55
1983IV	50	62

Given these transformed data, we can now proceed to the estimation of the cost function. As we have shown, it is sufficient to estimate any one of the three cost curves. In this example, we have elected to estimate the average variable cost function. Remember that the form of this function is

$$AVC = a + bQ + cQ^2$$

The computer printout obtained from the estimation of this equation is reproduced below. (Note that, in the printout, $Q2$ stands for the variable Q^2.)

```
DEPENDENT VARIABLE:  AVC          F-RATIO:  51.404

OBSERVATIONS:  9                  R-SQUARE:  0.9449

                  PARAMETER            STANDARD
 VARIABLE         ESTIMATE              ERROR

INTERCEPT           44.35               6.17
Q                   -1.44               0.46
Q2                   0.04               0.008
```

We first must determine whether the signs of the estimated coefficients are as hypothesized. Recall that the theoretical analysis requires $a > 0$, $b < 0$, $c > 0$. Inspection of the regression output indicates that our estimated coefficients do conform to this sign pattern. However, we must also ensure that these coefficients are statistically significant. As always, this determination of significance is made using a t-test. In this example, since there are nine observations and three estimated parameters, we have $9 - 3 = 6$ degrees of freedom; thus, from the table at the back of the book, the critical value of t (at a 95 percent confidence level) is 2.447. Calculation of the test statistics for the individual coefficients yields

$$t_{\hat{a}} = 7.19$$
$$t_{\hat{b}} = -3.13$$
$$t_{\hat{c}} = 5.0$$

Clearly, the absolute values for these calculated t statistics all exceed the critical value of t. Hence, all of the coefficients are of the hypothesized sign and are statistically significant. Thus, our estimates will yield a short-run cost function with the shape of those described in Chapter 7.

A primary objective of short-run cost estimation is to obtain an estimate of the marginal cost function. Suppose that the firm desires to produce 27,000 units of output. What is the marginal cost associated with this level of output? As we have shown, the marginal cost function associated with the average cost function above is

$$MC = a + 2bQ + 3cQ^2$$

Using our estimates of $\hat{a}$, $\hat{b}$, and $\hat{c}$, our estimated marginal cost function is

$$\begin{aligned} MC &= 44.35 + 2(-1.44)Q + 3(0.04)Q^2 \\ &= 44.35 - 2.88Q + 0.12Q^2 \end{aligned}$$

And, the marginal cost associated with 27,000 units of output is, therefore,

$$\begin{aligned} MC &= 44.35 - 2.88(27) + 0.12(27)^2 \\ &= 44.35 - 77.76 + 87.48 \\ &= \$54.07 \end{aligned}$$

Average variable cost for this level of output is

$$\begin{aligned} AVC &= 44.35 - 1.44(27) + 0.04(27)^2 \\ &= 44.35 - 38.88 + 29.16 \\ &= \$34.63 \end{aligned}$$

Then, total variable cost for 27,000 units of output is

$$\begin{aligned} TVC &= AVC \times Q \\ &= 34.63 \times 27{,}000 \\ &= \$935{,}010 \end{aligned}$$

Finally, we can calculate the output level at which average variable cost is minimized. As we have shown, this output is

$$Q = -b/2c$$

In our examples, this becomes

$$Q = \frac{1.44}{2 \times 0.04} = 18$$

That is, average variable cost reaches its minimum at an output level of 18,000 units.

8.3 ESTIMATION OF A LONG-RUN COST FUNCTION

Earlier we argued that the general form for the long-run cost function in a two-input setting is

$$C = f(Q, w, r)$$

That is, using cross-section data, we must include as independent variables the prices of the inputs. Hence, it is necessary to specify an estimable cost function that includes the input prices.

At first glance, it would appear that the solution would be simply to add the input prices as additional explanatory variables in the cost function developed above. That is, total cost would be

$$TC = aQ + bQ^2 + cQ^3 + dw + er$$

However, such a function fails to satisfy a basic characteristic of cost functions. A total cost function can be written as

$$TC = wL + rK$$

If we double both of the input prices, holding output constant, input usage will not change; but total cost will double. That is,

$$\begin{aligned} TC' &= (2w)L + (2r)K \\ &= 2(wL + rK) \\ &= 2TC \end{aligned}$$

The cost function suggested above does not satisfy this requirement. For a given output, if we were to double the input prices,

$$\begin{aligned} TC' &= aQ + bQ^2 + cQ^3 + d(2w) + e(2r) \\ &= aQ + bQ^2 + cQ^3 + dw + er + (dw + er) \\ &= TC + dw + er \end{aligned}$$

Clearly, TC' is not equal to $2TC$.

Therefore, we must consider an alternative form for estimating the long-run cost function. The most commonly employed form is a log-linear specification. With this type of specification, the total cost function would be expressed as

$$TC = \alpha Q^{\beta} w^{\gamma} r^{\delta}$$

Using this functional form let's see what happens if we double input prices while holding output constant:

$$\begin{aligned} TC' &= \alpha Q^{\beta}(2w)^{\gamma}(2r)^{\delta} \\ &= (2^{\gamma+\delta})(\alpha Q^{\beta} w^{\gamma} r^{\delta}) \\ &= 2^{(\gamma+\delta)} TC \end{aligned}$$

It follows then that, if $\gamma + \delta = 1$, doubling input prices will indeed double the total cost of producing a given level of output—the required characteristic of a cost function. Hence, it is necessary to *impose* this condition on the log-linear cost function we proposed. We do so by defining δ as $1 - \gamma$; so

$$TC = \alpha Q^{\beta} w^{\gamma} r^{1-\gamma}$$

or

$$TC = \alpha Q^{\beta}(w/r)^{\gamma} r$$

At this point, we encounter an estimation problem. If we convert the preceding equation to logarithms in order to estimate it, we have

$$\log TC = \log \alpha + \beta \log Q + \gamma \log \left(\frac{w}{r}\right) + 1 \log r$$

While we can estimate the parameters $\log \alpha$, β, and γ, this formulation requires that the coefficient for $\log r$ be *precisely* equal to one. If we were to estimate this equation, such a value cannot be guaranteed; so, we must impose this value. This is done simply by moving $\log r$ to the left-hand side of the equation

$$\log TC - \log r = \log \alpha + \beta \log Q + \gamma \log (w/r)$$

In this way, the coefficient on log r is forced to be equal to one. Finally, using the rules of logarithms, we can rewrite this equation as

$$\log \left[\frac{TC}{r} \right] = \log \alpha + \beta \log Q + \gamma \log (w/r)$$

It is this equation that we will actually estimate in order to obtain an estimate of the long-run cost function.

Once we have this function estimated, what can we do with it? As we have noted earlier, the primary use of the long-run cost function is in the firm's investment decision; so a primary objective of long-run cost estimation is to determine the extent of economies of scale. The coefficient β indicates the elasticity of cost with respect to output.[5] (At this point you might note the similarity of this log-linear cost function to the Cobb-Douglas production function we introduced in Chapter 6.) That is, the coefficient β is interpreted as

$$\beta = \frac{\text{Percentage change in cost}}{\text{Percentage change in output}}$$

Note that, when $\beta > 1$, cost is increasing more than proportionately to output (e.g., if the percentage change in output is 25 percent and the percentage change in cost is 50 percent, β would be equal to 2); therefore long-run average cost would be increasing. Hence if $\beta > 1$, the estimates would indicate diseconomies of scale. Conversely, if $\beta < 1$, economies of scale would be indicated. Furthermore, note that the magnitude of the estimate of β will indicate the "strength" of the economies or diseconomies of scale. The statistical significance of β can be tested in the manner outlined in Chapter 6.

APPLICATION

Costs in the U.S. electric utility industry

In order to illustrate the techniques of long-run cost estimation, let's return to the data for the electric utility firms that we first presented in Chapter 6.

---

[5]Using the general definition of elasticity, the elasticity of cost with respect to output is

$$E_{C,Q} = \frac{\partial C}{\partial Q} \cdot \frac{Q}{C}$$

Then, using the log-linear specification of the cost function

$$\frac{\partial C}{\partial Q} = \beta \alpha Q^{\beta-1} w^{\gamma} r^{\delta} = \beta \frac{C}{Q}$$

so,

$$E_{C,Q} = \beta \cdot \frac{C}{Q} \cdot \frac{Q}{C} = \beta$$

Again, in order to keep our example simple, we limit our attention to two inputs—capital and labor.

In Chapter 6 we reported data for output, capital usage, labor usage, the price of capital, and the price of labor for 20 firms. However, for long-run cost estimation, the required data are total cost, output, and the input prices. Thus, we need to calculate total cost. As we have noted, total cost is

$$C = rK + wL$$

So, using the data we presented in Chapter 6, you could calculate total cost. After making these calculations, the data set to be employed is shown in the table below.

Firm	C	Q	r	w
1	30.8923	4.612	0.06903	8.5368
2	58.5825	8.297	0.06903	9.9282
3	15.1205	1.820	0.06754	10.1116
4	32.8014	5.849	0.07919	10.2522
5	22.7768	3.145	0.06481	11.1194
6	11.9176	1.381	0.06598	9.6992
7	34.4028	5.422	0.06754	10.0613
8	47.5209	7.115	0.06565	10.9087
9	18.9136	3.052	0.10555	10.1954
10	36.0902	4.394	0.06572	11.2585
11	3.2401	0.248	0.07919	10.8759
12	62.0032	9.699	0.06903	9.8758
13	74.7206	14.271	0.06789	10.9051
14	96.0053	17.743	0.06903	7.4775
15	63.4357	14.956	0.06572	7.8062
16	15.9901	3.108	0.07919	9.2689
17	42.3249	9.416	0.06565	8.3906
18	44.6781	6.857	0.06565	9.8826
19	59.2520	9.745	0.06860	9.8235
20	38.7337	4.442	0.08206	12.9352

The function to be estimated is

$$\log (TC/r) = \log \alpha + \beta \log Q + \gamma \log (w/r)$$

Following is the computer output obtained from this estimation:[6]

[6]A user of the first edition of this text pointed out a troublesome point in this estimation: In the log-linear specification, both γ and δ would be expected to be between 0 and 1. In this estimation, $\hat{\gamma}$ was estimated to be $1.05435 > 1$. However, the estimate of $\hat{\gamma}$ is not significantly greater than (different from) one. The t statistic in this case is

$$t = \frac{1.05435 - 1}{0.20939} = 0.260$$

Clearly $0.260 < 2.110$. So, albeit troublesome, these estimates do not conflict with the required theoretical properties.

DEPENDENT VAR: LOG(TC/R) F-RATIO: 324.328

OBSERVATIONS: 20 R-SQUARE: 0.9745

VARIABLE	PARAMETER ESTIMATE	STANDARD ERROR
INTERCEPT	-0.41600	1.03943
LOGQ	0.83830	0.03315
LOG(W/R)	1.05435	0.20939

As we have shown, the coefficient β is of primary importance since it indicates the existence of economies or diseconomies of scale. In our estimation $\beta < 1$, so economies of scale are indicated. However, it is necessary to determine if this coefficient is statistically significant. Using the methodology described in Chapter 6 the appropriate test statistic is

$$\begin{aligned} t_{\hat{\beta}} &= \frac{\hat{\beta} - 1}{S_{\hat{\beta}}} \\ &= \frac{0.083830 - 1}{0.03315} \\ &= -4.87783 \end{aligned}$$

We then compare the absolute value of this test statistic with the critical t-value. In this example, since we have $20 - 3 = 17$ degrees of freedom, the critical value of t (at a 95 percent confidence level) is 2.110. Since 4.87783 exceeds 2.110, it follows that $\hat{\beta}$ is statistically significant and that there is indeed evidence of economies of scale.[7]

Before we conclude this section, let us note a limitation of the technique illustrated in the preceding example and suggest a possible extension. As shown, this methodology is capable of indicating either economies or diseconomies of scale, but not both. That is, this technique could indicate either a rising or a falling long-run average cost curve; but, it would not, in its present form, provide an estimate of a U-shaped long-run average cost function. Since one objective of any long-run analysis is to determine the plant size at

[7]Note that these results are consistent with the results from the estimation of the production function we presented in Chapter 6—both indicate the existence of increasing returns to, or economies of, scale. However, such a result is to be expected. Since the cost function is itself derived from a production function, both should reflect the same characteristics. If the production function indicates increasing returns to scale, the cost should, under fairly normal circumstances, show economies of scale.

which long-run average cost is at a minimum, an estimate of a U-shaped average cost curve is definitely desired.

One possible way to handle this limitation is to segment the available data. To illustrate this procedure, let us suppose that the true long-run average cost curve is as illustrated by *LAC* in Figure 8.4. What the manager of the firm wants to know is the smallest plant size for which long-run average cost is a minimum (Q^*). Suppose that the analyst has data relating to outputs between Q_1 and Q_3. If the analyst were to estimate the cost function described above using all of these data points, it is quite likely that the result would be an estimated long-run average cost function similar to that shown by $\hat{LAC}$ in Figure 8.4. Alternatively, the analyst could obtain three estimates of the cost function. In the first, we would want to use data relating to outputs between Q_1 and Q^*. The second estimate would use data between Q^* and Q_2, and the third, data between Q_2 and Q_3. Combining these estimates, the analyst would then obtain an estimate of the long-run average cost curve that would look something like that illustrated in Figure 8.5. From such an estimation, the analyst could obtain an estimate of the minimum optimal plant size, Q^*.

Obviously, the problem is determining the proper manner of segmenting the data. If you knew beforehand the proper data to include in each of the individual estimations, such estimation would be redundant. That is, if you knew the value of Q^*, why estimate it? Thus, the segmenting of the data must be made on the basis of estimation results. That is, in reality, numerous estimates must be made using alternative data segmentations. Then, the most appropriate manner of segmenting the data would be the one that provides the "best" estimations. One criterion that could be used would be to employ that segmentation of the data that maximizes the R^2 values for the individual estimated cost functions.

Figure 8.4
Long-run average cost

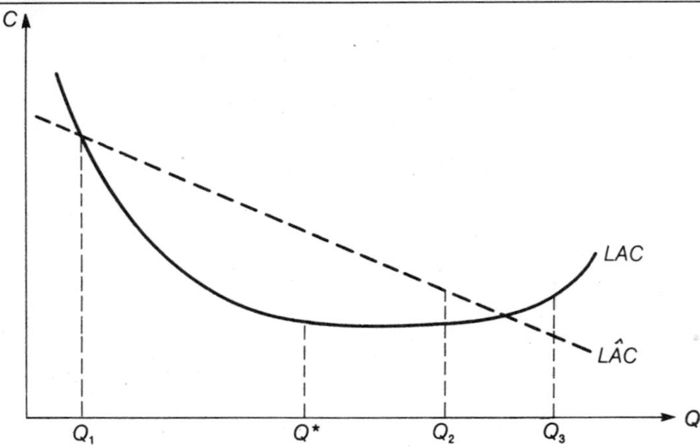

Figure 8.5
Estimate of long-run average cost

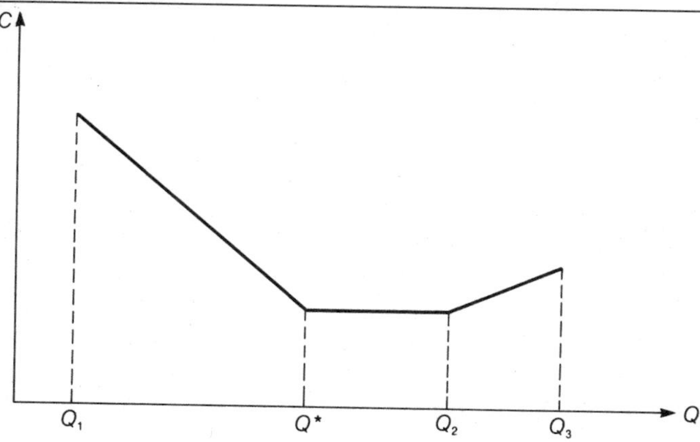

8.4 AN ALTERNATIVE APPROACH— THE ENGINEERING TECHNIQUE

Given the problems associated with the regression methodologies described in the preceding sections, several alternative approaches to the analysis of cost have been suggested. In this section, we will briefly describe the most widely used alternative approach—the engineering technique.

The engineering approach to cost analysis represents an attempt to avoid a problem we mentioned earlier—accounting costs may not reflect opportunity costs. In this approach, the analyst begins with what we might call an engineering production function. That is, a function that determines the optimal input combinations for producing any given level of production is identified. Then, given these *technologically efficient* input levels, cost can be obtained by multiplying each level of input usage by the current price of the input and summing over the inputs. This methodology should be more clear in an example to follow.

The engineering technique has several obvious advantages: (1) Since it avoids the difficulties encountered when we attempt to obtain a measure of cost from accounting data, it reduces the probability of errors from measurement. (2) Using such an approach, the analyst can eliminate many extraneous factors that might tend to complicate the problem without increasing precision. (3) This approach fits well with our theoretical analysis, since it involves current technology and current input prices.

APPLICATION

An engineering cost function in petroleum refining

An industry in which the engineering technique is apparently widely used is petroleum refining. If a firm is considering the construction of a new refinery, it needs some estimates for the investment (fixed) and operating (variable) costs associated with the proposed refinery. Since the refinery does not exist at the time these evaluations must be made, the firm must resort to the engineering technique. In this application, we present a simplified example of the manner in which these estimates are obtained.*

At the outset, note that petroleum refineries are designed to handle a specific type and quantity of crude oil. In this example, let's assume that the refinery is designed to process 30,000 barrels per day (bpd) of a particular crude oil or mix of crude oils. The first process used in refining the crude oils is atmospheric distillation. On the basis of physical evaluation of the specific crude oils to be processed, the engineers estimate that this process will result in 8,000 bpd of finished products (e.g., gasoline and fuel oils) and 22,000 bpd of materials that require further processing. Part of the materials requiring further processing (18,000 bpd) can be processed via vacuum distillation to yield final products. The remainder (4,000 bpd) must be sent through a hydro-desulfurizer. As a result of this process, the engineers estimate an output of 561 pounds per day of sulfur, 1,000 bpd of finished products, and 2,900 bpd of materials that require still further processing. These 2,900 bpd are processed in a catalytic reformer to yield 2,700 bpd of finished products. The complete processing flow is described in Figure 8.6.

Given this knowledge of the production process, the firm knows what types of capital are required and the necessary capacities for each (e.g., this refinery will require a catalytic reformer with a capacity of 2,900 bpd). The firm can then use available industry sources to obtain the cost of such capital

Figure 8.6
An engineering production flow

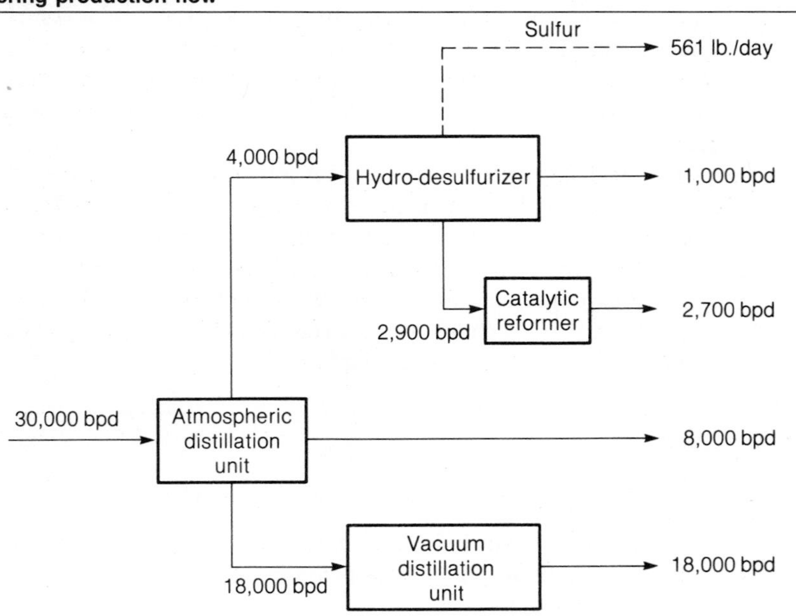

equipment. In this way, the firm will be able to obtain estimates of the capital costs associated with this proposed refinery. These capital costs are summarized below:

Item	*Required capacity (bpd)*	*Cost**
Atmospheric distillation unit	30,000	$1,900,000
Vacuum distillation unit	18,000	1,200,000
Hydro-desulfurizer	4,000	625,000
Catalytic reformer	2,900	1,800,000
		$5,525,000

*All costs are as of 1973.

Thus, total fixed costs are $5,525,000.

The next task is to obtain an estimate of the variable costs associated with this refinery. These are normally calculated on an annual basis, assuming that the refinery is operating at capacity. The major variable inputs are crude oil, labor, cooling water, electric power, royalties, and catalyst replacement. Assuming that the refinery operates 340 days per year, the refinery will require 10,200,000 barrels of crude oil. If the crude oil to be used sells for $7 per barrel (1973 prices), crude oil costs will be $71,400,000. Using data obtained from other plants, the engineers calculate that this refinery will require a staff of 22 workers. Assuming an average annual wage of $18,000, annual labor costs would be $396,000. Required cooling water and electric power are determined from data on comparable refineries. Multiplying these requirements by the average current costs of the inputs, annual expenditures are obtained. Let us assume that these are, respectively, $16,000 and $140,000. Royalties are paid to patent owners on the basis of the throughput of the refinery. For example, if the royalty rate on the catalytic reformer is 4.5 cents per barrel, the annual royalty is $44,370 ($0.045 \times 2,900 \times 340 = 44,370$). Let us assume that total royalties amount to $66,000 annually. Finally, catalyst replacement is also determined by the amount of crude oil processed. We assume that the annual expenditures for catalyst replacement are $23,000. Combining these, the annual variable costs associated with this refinery are

Crude oil	$71,400,000
Labor	396,000
Cooling water	16,000
Electric power	140,000
Royalties	66,000
Catalyst replacement	23,000
	$72,041,000

*This application is adapted from J. H. Gary and G. E. Handwerk, *Petroleum Refining* (New York: Marcel Dekker, 1975), pp. 214–27.

While an engineering approach to cost estimation is straightforward and useful, we must point out that this approach involves several problems. An obvious difficulty is that the engineering production function may be based on the operation of a pilot plant and the production function may not prove to be valid when the firm expands to a full-scale production facility.

However, we feel that there is an even more serious problem. This problem results from the difference between the engineer's and the economist's view of efficiency. An example should illustrate our concern. Consider a very simple production process: Coal is moved from river barges to the loading hopper for a plant by means of a crane. Suppose that in this process some coal is dropped into the river. It is very likely that the engineer and the economist would differ as to their concept of the efficiency of this process. While the engineer might suggest modifying or replacing the crane to eliminate the "waste," the economist might take a very different view. If the price of coal is low relative to the price of capital, it could be efficient (in the economic sense) to drop coal into the water. The real problem is to determine the optimal amount to drop. The point is that the technologically efficient combination of inputs need not be the economically efficient combination.

Notwithstanding these difficulties, engineering cost functions are widely used. In many instances the manager will obtain estimates of the cost function from the production or engineering division of the firm. And, in these instances, it is very likely that the forthcoming estimates are based on an approach like the one we have described above. (To provide you with a feel for this, in some of our subsequent applications we will use an engineering cost function.)

TECHNICAL PROBLEMS

1. Compare and contrast short-run and long-run cost estimation with respect to:

a. Objectives.

b. Type of data employed.

2. Describe the data problems involved in cost estimation using:

a. Time-series data.

b. Cross-section data.

3. Suppose that an average variable cost function of the form

$$AVC = a + bQ + cQ^2$$

has been estimated. The computer output obtained from this regression is as follows:

a. Determine if the estimated coefficients are as required to yield a U-shaped average variable cost curve.

b. What is the marginal cost function associated with this average variable cost function?

DEPENDENT VARIABLE: AVC		F-RATIO: 214.16
OBSERVATIONS: 30		R-SQUARE: 0.9407
VARIABLE	PARAMETER ESTIMATE	STANDARD ERROR
INTERCEPT	40.0	10.0
Q	−4.0	1.0
Q2	0.2	0.04

c. What is average variable cost at $Q = 10$? What is marginal cost at $Q = 10$?

d. At what output level would average variable cost be at a minimum?

e. What is the minimum average variable cost?

4. Consider the cost function

$$TC = \alpha Q^{\beta} w^{\gamma} r^{\delta}$$

What condition is necessary in order that doubling input prices will double the total cost of producing a given level of output? Explain.

5. Following are the results of an estimation of the cost function

$$(TC/r) = \alpha Q^{\beta} (w/r)^{\gamma}$$

DEPENDENT VAR: LOG(TC/R)		F-RATIO: 265.690
OBSERVATIONS: 35		R-SQUARE: 0.9432
VARIABLE	PARAMETER ESTIMATE	STANDARD ERROR
INTERCEPT	−0.5	0.4
LOGQ	1.6	0.2
LOG(W/R)	0.7	0.3

What do these estimates indicate with respect to economies or diseconomies of scale?

6. Return to our application dealing with an engineering cost function in petroleum refining.

a. Disregarding the output of sulfur, calculate the average variable cost associated with a barrel of finished products.

b. In such an approach, maintenance expense is normally calculated as a percent of total capital cost. Would such a cost be fixed or variable?

c. Note that fuel is not included as a cost of operation. This is because the firm does not purchase any fuel oils; rather, it simply burns some of its own output. Comment on such a practice. How should this be treated in cost estimation?

ANALYTICAL PROBLEMS

1. Suppose that your firm is interested in constructing a new production facility and that you must choose among several alternative plant sizes. What type of cost estimation is required? What type of data are necessary? Explain.

2. Why is a linear specification unacceptable for estimating an average variable cost function?

3. It could be argued that a publicly owned utility (e.g., a water system or a mass transportation system) should operate at that level of output at which average cost is minimized. How would such a firm go about determining this output level? How could regulators check to see if the utility is actually operating at this output level?

4. Suggest a methodology by which an analyst can obtain a measure of the opportunity cost of capital to a firm that owns (rather than leases) its capital stock.

5. We have argued that engineering cost functions may not reflect the economically efficient combinations of inputs. Could this be the case in the instance of the engineering cost function for petroleum refining described in an application? Note that, in this production process, crude oil is completely utilized. Might there exist a circumstance in which it would be economically efficient to ''waste'' crude oil? Suggest the way in which this wastage would most likely occur.

Part 3

Demand

9

Theory of consumer behavior: Individual demand curves

In Chapter 2 we described some of the characteristics of market demand curves. But, in that analysis we did not use the theory of consumer behavior to derive the demand curves or develop their characteristics. Since market demand is directly related to the way consumers are willing and able to act, it is necessary to understand consumer behavior in order to understand the fundamentals of demand. It is useful for managers to be aware of what underlies demand in order to understand, estimate, and forecast the demand for the products they sell. Hence, in this chapter, we will demonstrate how we can derive the demand curve of an individual consumer and examine the determinants of this demand function. Then in Chapter 10 we will aggregate these individual demand curves to obtain a market demand curve.

The basic theory of consumer behavior is really quite simple. As a matter of fact, it follows directly from the constrained optimization we described in Chapter 3. And, it is the mirror image of the firm's constrained cost minimization problem that we described in Chapter 5. (Indeed, as you go through this chapter, you might want to look back at Chapter 5 to see how similar these two problems are.) Very few people have incomes sufficient to purchase as much as they desire of every good or service. Instead, the consumer attempts to attain the most preferred level of consumption—bundle of goods and services—given the constraint of a limited income.

9.1 THE UTILITY FUNCTION

The individual consumer attempts to maximize his or her level of satisfaction—or, as economists call it, *utility*. More precisely, the consumer chooses the goods and services that maximize utility (subject to an income constraint). We define utility as follows:

■ **Definition.** Utility is an individual's perception of his or her own satisfaction from consuming any specific bundle of goods and services.

We can write a consumer's utility function in the form

$$U = f(X_1, X_2, X_3, \ldots, X_n)$$

where X_i is the amount of the i-th good or service to be consumed. If U is some index of utility, the value of this index depends upon the quantities of goods one through n consumed.

As we did in the case of production, we can simplify this n-argument function to a function of only two variables. To this end, let's suppose that the consumer chooses among bundles consisting of only two goods (or services)—X and Y. The utility function can be written as

$$U = f(X,Y),$$

where X and Y are respectively the levels of consumption of the two commodities.

As with all economic models, the theory of consumer behavior employs some simplifying assumptions. These assumptions permit us to go directly to the fundamental determinants of consumer behavior and permit us to abstract away from the less important aspects of the consumer's decision process. Let us briefly describe these assumptions.

Complete information

We assume for now that consumers have complete information pertaining to their consumption decisions. They know the full range of goods and services available and the capacity of each to provide satisfaction (or utility). Further, the price of each good is known exactly, as is each consumer's income during the time period in question.

Admittedly, to assume perfect knowledge is an abstraction from reality. But the assumption of complete information does not distort the relevant aspects of the real world. It allows us to concentrate upon how real consumption choices are made.

Preference ordering

Our second assumption is that consumers are able to rank all conceivable bundles of commodities on the basis of the ability of each bundle to provide satisfaction. When confronted with two or more bundles of goods, consumers can determine their order of preference among them. Let us explain this with an example.

Suppose a consumer is confronted with two bundles consisting of different combinations of two goods. Bundle #1 consists of five candy bars and one soft drink. Bundle #2 consists of three candy bars and three soft drinks. Ranking the two bundles, the person can make one of three possible responses: (1) I prefer bundle #1 to bundle #2. (2) I prefer bundle #2 to bundle #1. (3) I would be equally satisfied with—indifferent between—either.

The same is true when ranking any two bundles of goods and services. The consumer either prefers one bundle to the other or is indifferent between the two. A consumer who is indifferent between two bundles clearly feels that either bundle would yield the same level of utility. A preferred bundle would yield more utility than the other, less-preferred bundle.

■ **Relations.** Consumers have a preference pattern that (1) establishes a rank ordering of all bundles of goods and (2) compares all pairs of bundles, indicating that bundle #1 is preferred to bundle #2, #2 is preferred to #1, or the consumer is indifferent between #1 and #2. In a three-(or more) way comparison, if #1 is preferred (indifferent) to #2, and #2 is preferred (indifferent) to #3, #1 must be preferred (indifferent) to #3. A larger bundle, in the sense of having at least as much of each good and more of another, is always preferred to a smaller one.

9.2 INDIFFERENCE CURVES AND MAPS

A fundamental tool for the analysis of consumer behavior is an indifference curve, defined as follows:

■ **Definition.** An indifference curve is a locus of points—bundles of goods and services—each of which yields an individual the same level of total utility or satisfaction.

For simplicity we continue to assume that the consumer chooses among bundles consisting of only two goods. This assumption enables us to analyze consumer behavior, using two-dimensional graphs.

Figure 9.1 shows a representative indifference curve with the typically assumed slope. The quantity of some good X is plotted along the horizontal axis; the quantity of good Y (possibly some composite of all other goods) is plotted along the vertical axis.

All combinations of goods X and Y along indifference curve I yield the consumer the same level of utility. In other words, the consumer is indifferent among all points such as *A*, with 10 units of X and 50 units of Y; point *B*, with 20X and 35Y; point *C*, with 40*X* and 18*Y*; and so on. At any point on I, it is possible to take away some amount of X and add some amount of Y (though

Figure 9.1
A typical indifference curve

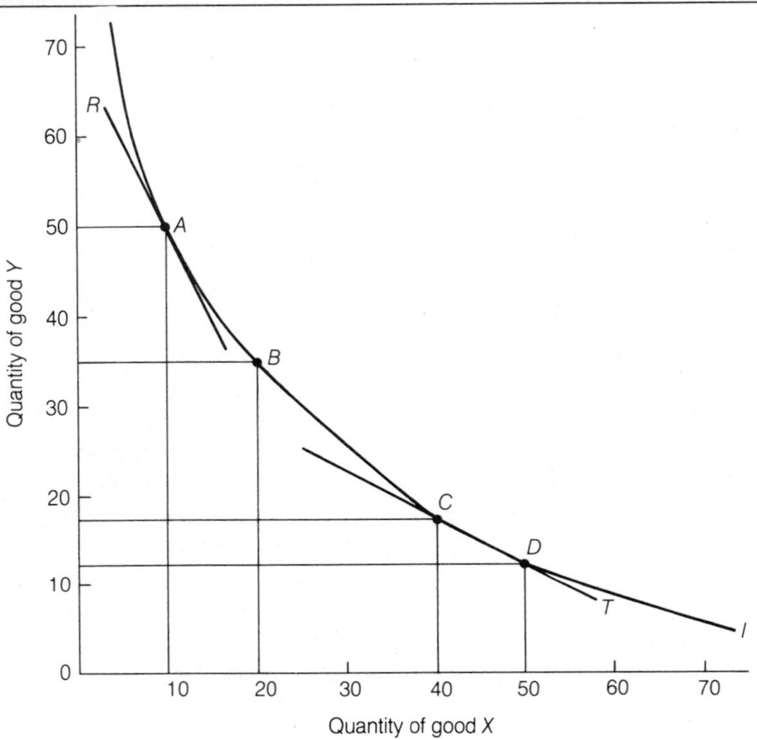

not necessarily the same amount) and leave the consumer with the same level of utility. Conversely, we can add X and take away just enough Y to make the consumer indifferent between the two combinations.

The indifference curve is downward sloping. This reflects the fact that the consumer obtains utility from both goods. Thus, if we add X, we must take away Y in order to keep the same level of utility. If the curve in Figure 9.1 would begin to slope upward at, say, 70 units of X, it would mean that the consumer has so much X that any additional X would reduce utility. In such a case, to keep the consumer at the same level of utility when X is added, more Y would have to be given to compensate for lost utility from having more X. Likewise, if the curve begins to bend backward at, say, 70 units of Y, it would mean that the consumer experiences reduced levels of utility with increases in Y. We might note that unlike the case of isoquants, to which we could assign a specific quantity of output, we generally do not assume that a specific number measuring utility is assigned to an indifference curve.

Indifference curves are convex. This shape requires that as the consumption of X is increased relative to Y, the consumer is willing to accept a smaller reduction in Y for an equal increase in X, in order to stay at the same level of utility. This property is apparent in Figure 9.1. Suppose we begin at point *A* with 10 units of X and 50 units of Y. In order to increase consumption of X by 10 units, to 20, the consumer is willing to reduce consumption of Y by 15 units, to 35. Given indifference curve I, the consumer will be indifferent between the two combinations represented by *A* and *B*. Next begin at *C*, with 40X and 18Y. From this point, to gain an additional 10 units of X (move to point *D*), the consumer is willing to give up only 6 units of Y, much less than the 15 units willingly given up at *A*. The convexity of indifference curves implies diminishing marginal rate of substitution, to which we now turn.

Marginal rate of substitution

An important concept in indifference curve analysis is the marginal rate of substitution, defined as follows:

■ **Definition.** The marginal rate of substitution of X for Y measures the number of units of Y that must be given up per unit of X added so as to maintain a constant level of utility. The marginal rate of substitution is given by the negative of the slope of an indifference curve at a point. It is defined only for movements along a given curve.

Returning to Figure 9.1, we can see that the consumer is indifferent between combinations *A* (10X and 50Y) and *B* (20X and 35Y). Thus the rate at which the consumer is willing to substitute is

$$\frac{\Delta Y}{\Delta X} = \frac{50 - 35}{10 - 20} = -\frac{15}{10} = -1.5$$

The marginal rate of substitution is 1.5, meaning that the consumer is willing to give up 1.5 units of Y for each unit of X added. Since we would find it cumbersome to have the minus sign on the right side of the equation, we define the marginal rate of substitution as

$$MRS = -\frac{\Delta Y}{\Delta X} = 1.5$$

For the movement from *C* to *D* along I, the marginal rate of substitution is

$$MRS = -\frac{\Delta Y}{\Delta X} = -\frac{(18 - 12)}{(40 - 50)} = \frac{6}{10} = .6$$

In this case the consumer is willing to give up only .6 units of Y per additional unit of X added.

Thus we say that the marginal rate of substitution diminishes along an indifference curve. When consumers have a small amount of X relative to Y, they are willing to give up a lot of Y to gain another unit of X. When they have less Y relative to X, they are willing to give up less Y in order to gain another unit of X.

The marginal rate of substitution is, as noted, the negative of the slope of an indifference curve for very small changes in X and Y. For example, the negative of the slope of the tangent *R* at point *A* is the marginal rate of substitution at that point. The same is the case for tangent *T* at point *C*. Looking at these tangents, is easily seen that the slope of the indifference curve, and hence the marginal rate of substitution, declines as X is increased relative to Y.

We can summarize the discussion in the following:

■ **Principles.** Indifference curves are negatively sloped and convex. Therefore, if the consumption of one good is increased, consumption of the other must be reduced to maintain a constant level of utility, and the marginal rate of substitution—the negative of the slope of the indifference curve—diminishes as we move downward along an indifference curve, increasing X relative to Y.

Indifference maps

An indifference map is simply a graph showing a set of two or more indifference curves. Figure 9.2 shows a typical indifference map, made up of four indifference curves, I, II, III, and IV. Any indifference curve lying above and to the right of another represents a higher level of utility. Thus any combination of X and Y on IV is preferred to any combination on III, any

Figure 9.2
An indifference map

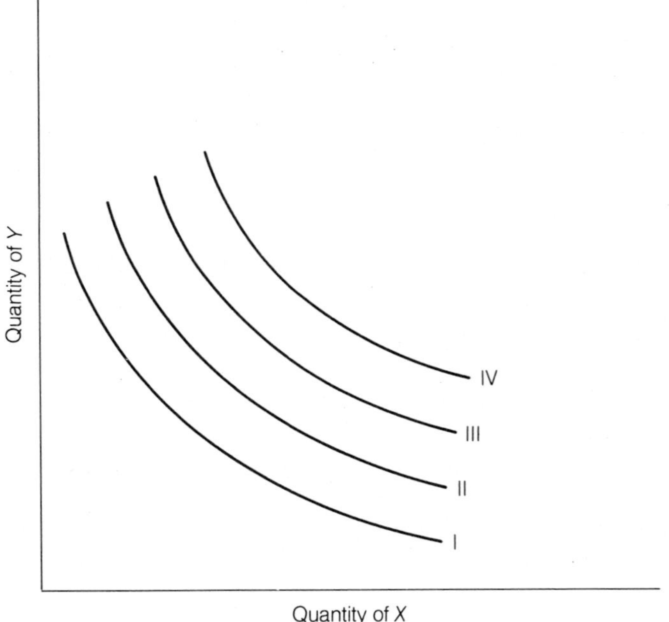

combination on III is preferred to any on II, and so on. All bundles of goods on the same indifference curve are equivalent; all combinations lying on a higher curve are preferred.

The indifference map in Figure 9.2 consists of only four indifference curves. We could have drawn many, many more. In fact, the X-Y space actually contains an infinite number of indifference curves. Each point in the space lies on one indifference curve. Moreover, we can say that each point lies on one and only one indifference curve, since indifference curves—like isoquants—cannot intersect.

We can summarize with the following:

■ **Principles.** An indifference map consists of several indifference curves. The higher (or further to the right) an indifference curve, the greater the level of utility associated with the curve. Combinations of goods on higher indifference curves are preferred to combinations on the lower curves.

Marginal utility approach

The concept of marginal utility can give additional insight into the properties of indifference curves. We define marginal utility as follows:

■ **Definition.** Marginal utility is the addition to total utility that is attributable to the addition of one unit of a good to the current rate of consumption, holding constant the amounts of all other goods consumed.

While many economists object to the concept of marginal utility on the grounds that utility is not measurable, we find it useful to relate marginal utility to the marginal rate of substitution along an indifference curve. Assume for now that utility (U) depends upon the rate of consumption of only two goods, X and Y. The total change in utility resulting from a small change in both X and Y can be represented as[1]

$$\Delta U = [(MU \text{ of } X) \times \Delta X] + [(MU \text{ of } Y) \times \Delta Y]$$

For points on a given indifference curve, all combinations of goods yield the same level of utility; so, ΔU is zero for all changes in X and Y that would keep the consumer on the same indifference curve. From the above equation, if $\Delta U = 0$, it follows that

$$\frac{MU_X}{MU_Y} = -\frac{\Delta Y}{\Delta X}$$

[1]Note that we have violated somewhat one assumption in this analysis. Recall that marginal utility is the increase in utility from a one-unit increase in the rate of consumption in a good, holding the consumption of all other goods constant. In this example, we speak of marginal utility while letting the consumption of both goods change at the same time. However, if the change in each is slight, this presents little or no problem.

where $(-\Delta Y/\Delta X)$ is the negative of the slope of the indifference curve, i.e., the marginal rate of substitution.

9.3 THE CONSUMER'S BUDGET CONSTRAINT

Indifference curves are derived from the preference patterns of consumers. As such, they give us a method of analyzing what consumers are willing to do. But recall from Chapter 2 that demand functions indicate what consumers are both *willing and able* to do. Consumers are constrained in what they are able to do by market-determined prices and their income. We now turn to an analysis of the constraint that consumers face—the determinants of what consumers are able to do.

Budget lines

If consumers had unlimited money incomes there would be no problem of economizing and no jobs for economists. People could buy whatever they want when they want it and would have no problem of choice. But this is not generally the case.

Consumers normally have limited incomes. Thus their problem is to spend this limited income in a way that gives the maximum possible satisfaction. Let's look at this constraint faced by consumers.

We continue to consider only two goods, bought in quantities, X and Y. (We can assume, as before, that there are only two goods in the consumption bundle or that good Y is a composite of all goods other than X.) The consumer has a fixed money income, M, which is the maximum amount that can be spent on the two goods. For simplicity, we assume that the entire income is spent on X and Y.[2] Thus the amount that is spent on X (p_xX) plus the amount that can be spent on Y (p_yY) must equal income (M);

$$M = p_xX + p_yY$$

This equation can be rewritten in the intercept-slope form as,

$$Y = \frac{M}{p_y} - \frac{p_x}{p_y} X$$

Such equations are called budget lines which can be defined as follows:

■ **Definition.** A budget line is the locus of all combinations or bundles of goods that can be purchased if the entire money income is spent.

The first term, M/p_y gives the amount of Y the consumer can buy if no X is purchased. Suppose that income is $1,000 and the price of Y is $5 per unit.

[2]More advanced theories permit consumers to save and borrow between periods. We shall address these more complicated topics below when we analyze the effect of time and the interest rate.

If the consumer spends the entire income on Y, 200 units of Y can be purchased.

The slope of the line ($-p_x/p_y$) indicates the amount of Y that must be given up if one more unit of X is purchased. Suppose the price of Y is \$5, and the price of X is \$10. For every additional unit of X, the consumer must give up \$10 worth of Y, or two units of Y. Thus the rate at which a consumer can trade Y for more X is 10/5, = 2; two units of Y for one of X. If, instead, the price of X is \$2.50, the rate that Y can be traded for X is 2.50/5.00, = 1/2. For every additional unit of X, the consumer must give up 1/2 unit of Y.

A typical budget line is shown in Figure 9.3. The line *BA* shows all combinations of Y and X that can be purchased with the given money income and given prices of the goods. The intercept on the *Y* axis, *B*, is M/p_y; the horizontal intercept, *A*, is M/p_x. The slope of the budget line is $-p_x/p_y$.

Shifting the budget line

If money income (*M*) or the price ratio (p_x/p_y) changes, the budget line changes. Panel A of Figure 9.4 shows the effect of changes in income. Begin with the original budget line *BA*. Next let money income increase, holding the prices of X and Y constant. Since the prices do not change, the slope of the budget line remains the same. But since money income increases, M/p_y, the vertical intercept must increase (shift upward). That is, if the consumer spends the entire income on good Y, more Y can be purchased than before. The result of an increase in income is a parallel shift in the budget line from

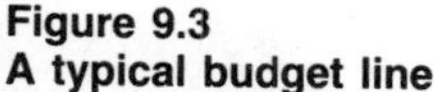
Figure 9.3
A typical budget line

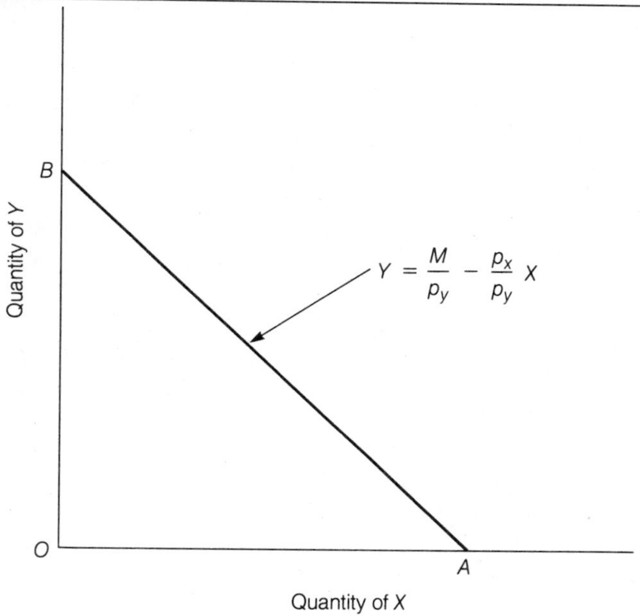

Figure 9.4
Shifting budget lines

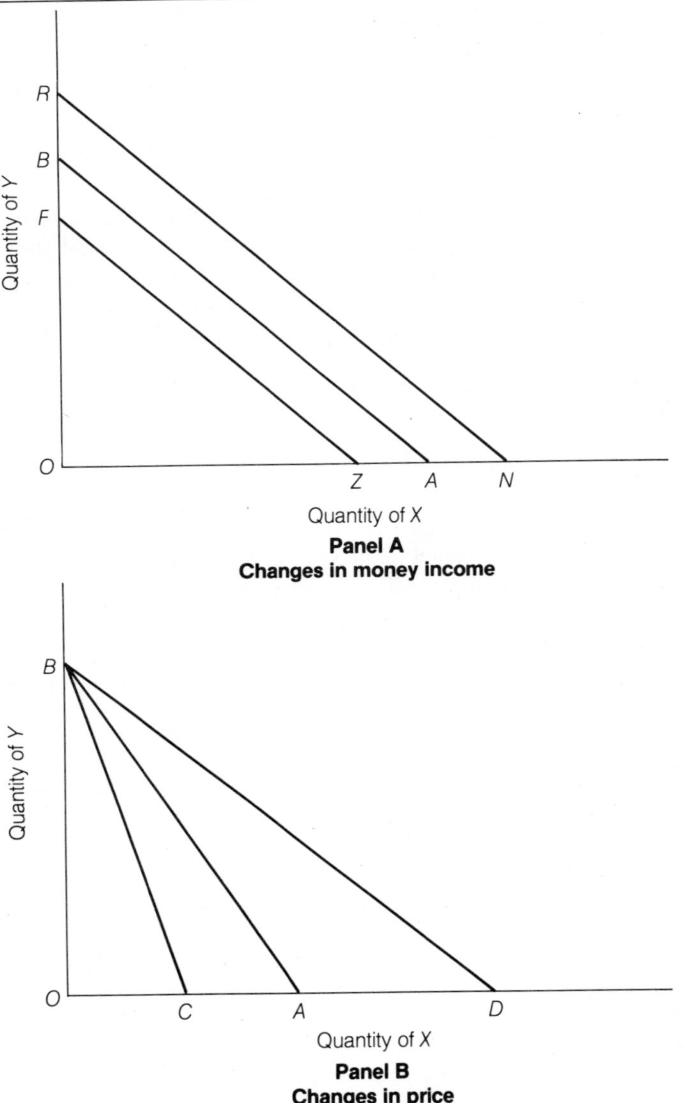

Panel A
Changes in money income

Panel B
Changes in price

BA to *RN*. The increase in income increases the set of combinations of the goods that can be purchased.

Alternatively, begin with budget line *BA* and let money income decline. In this case the set of possible combinations of goods decreases. The vertical intercept decreases, causing a parallel shift in the budget line to *FZ*.

Panel B shows the effect of changes in the price of good X. Begin once more with the budget line *BA*, then let the price of X fall. Since M/p_y does not change, the vertical intercept remains at B. But when p_x declines, the absolute value of the slope, p_x/p_y, must also fall. In this case, the budget line becomes less steep. In Panel B the budget line pivots from BA to BD. In other words, if the price of X falls, more X can be purchased if the entire money income is spent on X. Thus the horizontal intercept increases from A to D.

An increase in the price of good X causes the budget line to pivot backward, from BA to BC. That is, if p_x increases, the absolute value of the slope of the line, p_x/p_y, must increase. The budget line becomes steeper, while the vertical intercept remains constant.

These results can be summarized in the following:

■ **Relations.** An increase (decrease) in money income causes a parallel outward (backward) shift in the budget line. An increase (decrease) in the price of X causes the budget line to pivot backward (outward) around the original vertical intercept.

9.4 UTILITY MAXIMIZATION

We now have the tools to analyze the utility maximization problem. The budget line shows all bundles of commodities that are available to the consumer, given the limited income and market-determined prices. The indifference map shows the preference ordering of all conceivable bundles of goods. The consumer's task is to choose, from all available bundles of goods, the bundle that leads to the highest attainable level of utility.

Maximizing utility subject to a limited money income[3]

The maximization process is shown in Figure 9.5. Indifference curves I–IV represent the indifference map. Budget line BA shows all bundles of X

---

[3]For the mathematically inclined student, the problem can be set forth as a constrained maximization problem. The consumer maximizes the utility function, $U = U(X,Y)$, subject to the income constraint, $M = p_xX + p_yY$. The Lagrangian function to be maximized is

$$L = U(X,Y) + \lambda(M - p_xX - p_yY)$$

Maximization requires that the partial derivatives equal zero:

$$\frac{\partial L}{\partial X} = \frac{\partial U}{\partial X} - \lambda p_x = 0$$

$$\frac{\partial L}{\partial Y} = \frac{\partial U}{\partial Y} - \lambda p_y = 0$$

Combining the two equations

$$\frac{\dfrac{\partial U}{\partial X}}{\dfrac{\partial U}{\partial Y}} = \frac{p_x}{p_y}$$

where $\partial U/\partial X$ and $\partial U/\partial Y$ are the marginal utilities of the two goods, and the ratio is the marginal rate of substitution; p_x/p_y is the absolute value of the slope of the budget line. Thus optimization requires the marginal rate of substitution to equal the price ratio.

and Y available to the consumer. Clearly the highest possible level of satisfaction possible given the consumer's budget is attained at *P* on indifference curve III, where the individual consumes x^* units of X and y^* units of Y. Many bundles of goods, such as combinations on IV, are preferred to the bundle given by *P*, but they are not available because of the consumer's limited money income. All combinations on indifference curves higher than III are unattainable.

Other bundles are attainable but lie on lower indifference curves and are therefore less preferred. Consider the bundle given by point *R*. The consumer could move upward along the budget line, giving up X and adding Y, through combinations such as that at *S*. And the consumer would not stop substituting Y for X until *P* is reached, because such substitution leads to a higher indifference curve.

The consumer would not move beyond *P* to points such as Z, because that would lead to consumption on a lower indifference curve. If the consumer began at combination Z, for example, he or she could substitute X for Y along the budget line and attain higher levels of utility until *P* is reached.

Thus the highest attainable level of utility is reached by consuming the combination at which the marginal rate of substitution (the slope of the indifference curve) equals the price ratio (the slope of the budget line). The mar-

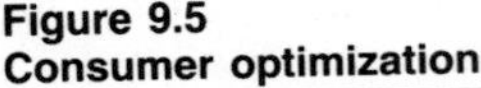
Figure 9.5
Consumer optimization

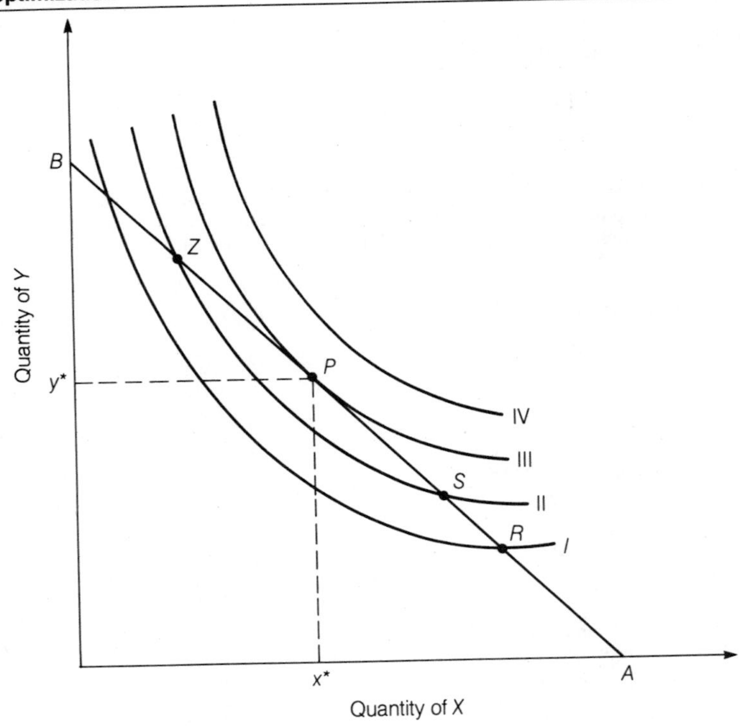

ginal rate of substitution is the rate at which the consumer is *willing* to substitute X for Y. The price ratio is the rate at which the consumer is *able* to substitute X for Y in the market. Thus, equilibrium occurs at the point at which the rate the consumer is willing to substitute equals the rate at which he or she is able to substitute.

To develop the concept further, consider a combination such as *S* in Figure 9.5. At this point, the marginal rate of substitution is less than the price ratio. Suppose at this point $MRS = 2$ and $P_x/P_y = 4$. The consumer is willing to give up one unit of X to get two units of Y. The price ratio allows the consumer to obtain four units of Y for each unit of X given up. Thus the consumer can be made better off by substituting Y for X.

Conversely, suppose the consumer is at a point such as *Z*, where the *MRS* is greater than the price ratio. Suppose at this point the *MRS* is six and the price ratio remains four. The consumer is willing to give up six units of Y to obtain one X. The price ratio allows the consumer to give up only four units of Y to obtain each additional unit of X. Thus the consumer is made better off by substituting X for Y.

We can summarize consumer optimization in the following:

■ **Principle.** The maximization of satisfaction subject to a limited money income occurs at the combination of goods for which the *MRS* of X for Y equals the ratio of the price of X to the price of Y.

Marginal utility interpretation

Recall that the *MRS* can be defined as the ratio of the marginal utilities of the two goods. Therefore, equilibrium occurs when

$$MRS = \frac{MU_X}{MU_Y} = \frac{P_x}{P_y}$$

or

$$\frac{MU_X}{P_x} = \frac{MU_Y}{P_y}$$

This condition means that the marginal utility per dollar spent on good X equals the marginal utility per dollar spent on Y. This principle is certainly plausible. To see this, suppose that the condition did not hold and that

$$\frac{MU_X}{P_x} < \frac{MU_Y}{P_y}$$

The marginal utility per dollar spent on good X is less than the marginal utility per dollar spent on Y. The consumer can take dollars away from X and spend them on Y. As long as the inequality holds, the lost utility from each dollar taken away from X is less than the added utility from each additional dollar spent on Y, and the consumer continues to substitute Y for X. As the consumption of X decreases, we would expect the marginal utility of X to rise.

As Y increases, its marginal utility would decline. The consumer continues substituting until MU_x/p_x equals MU_y/p_y.

Alternatively, if

$$\frac{MU_x}{P_x} > \frac{MU_y}{P_y}$$

the marginal utility per dollar spent on X is greater than the marginal utility per dollar spent on Y. The consumer takes dollars away from Y and buys additional X, continuing to substitute until the equality holds.

■ **Principle.** To obtain maximum satisfaction from a limited money income, a consumer allocates money income so that the marginal utility per dollar spent on each good is the same for all commodities purchased.

APPLICATION

The allocation of retail display space

The preceding concept of consumer equilibrium in conjunction with the concept of the "full price" of a commodity can be used to analyze the way the manager of a retail store should allocate shelf space so as to maximize profit from the limited shelf space available. Suppose a store sells two types of a particular good—a national brand and a generic (store) brand. For example, Kroger food stores sell both Campbell soup and Kroger brand soup (or Tide soap and Kroger soap). In the past, Sears sold both national brand sporting goods and sporting goods carrying their own brand name. Undoubtedly you can think of many other examples. How should the manager of the store display these two types of goods in order to maximize profits?

For generality, let's simply speak of a brand good (B) and a generic good (G) sold by a specific retail store. We would expect that the store is limited by its competitors as to the price it can charge for the brand good B. If Kroger charges too much for Campbell soup and other national brands, it gets a reputation as being a "high-priced store." Shoppers can compare prices of brand goods among stores and, if a store prices its brand name items too high, it will lose practically all its customers. But Kroger can determine the price of Kroger soup. So, the store has flexibility in setting the price of the generic good G (as long as the generic good is priced below the brand good).

How high a price can the retailer charge for the generic good without losing a substantial amount of sales to the brand good? Brand goods generally cost the store more than generic goods and, because of competition, have a lower markup (profit margin). Obviously, the manager wants to obtain as high a markup on G as possible. How does the store induce customers to choose G over B, given that we would expect consumers to prefer the brand good to the generic good, other things being the same?

We know from economic theory that, for any consumer, the equilibrium condition is $MU_G/P_G = MU_B/P_B$; or,

$$\frac{MU_G}{MU_B} = \frac{P_G}{P_B}$$

The retailer has little control over consumers' willingness to substitute (MRS) between G and B. Also, as noted above, the nominal price of B—the price charged at the checkout—is given by competition. But, the retailer does have a choice about the allocation of shelf space. The retailer can raise the "full price" of the brand name good by giving the generic good a more accessible location—possibly by displaying the generic good at eye level and the brand good on one of the bottom shelves. The relative inaccessibility of the brand good increases its full price to consumers by making it relatively more difficult to locate and purchase.

Thus displaying the brand good in a less accessible location in effect raises its price and allows the store to increase the nominal price charged for the generic good. Considering the full prices (price plus transaction cost) the consumer equilibrium is maintained at a higher generic price; and the store increases its profits above those that could be made if the goods were located side by side on the shelf.

If you doubt the analysis, notice the location of brand goods and generic goods when you are shopping. We doubt if you will find many instances where the brand good has a more accessible location than the generic good. There has to be some economic reason for this; and the reason must be to make the full price of the brand good relatively higher so the store can increase the price of the generic good, therefore making more profit.

But you might be thinking, "Hey, wait a minute, I frequently see brand name goods side by side on the shelves with generic goods. Campbell soup is often next to the Kroger soup. How does your theory explain that?"

That's a good question—and there's a good answer. The representatives of the producers of the brand goods also know what's going on; and they don't like it. Poor location lowers the sales of these goods. Campbell soup doesn't sell as well on the bottom shelf as it does when displayed at eye level. So what can the representative of the brand name product do about it?

The answer is obvious. Brand representatives can offer retailers inducements to display the brand goods more prominently. These inducements can and do take the form of discounts on the products. Display Campbell soup at eye level and you get some discount. The discount makes the brand good more profitable. Or the inducement may take the form of pure monetary payments for desirable display space. Again this form of inducement would raise the profit of the retailers.

So, in either case the retailer can increase profit, either by raising the transaction cost of purchasing the lower-profit brand good or by obtaining some form of payment for displaying the brand good more prominently. And the theory of consumer behavior explains the entire process quite well.

9.5 DERIVING DEMAND CURVES

Recall from Chapter 2 that demand was defined as the quantities of a good the consumer is willing and able to purchase at each price, holding other things constant. We have just seen that consumers maximize utility when the rate at which they are willing to substitute one good for another just equals the rate at which they are able to substitute. So it would seem that the two theories are closely related; and they are. The theory of demand can be easily derived from the theory of consumer behavior.

We use Figure 9.6 to see this relation and show how demand curves are derived. We begin with a given money income and prices of good X and good Y. The corresponding budget line is given by budget line 1 in the figure. Let the original price of X be p_1. The consumer maximizes utility where budget line 1 is tangent to indifference curve I, consuming x_1 units of X. Clearly, p_1, x_1 is one point on this consumer's demand for X. This point is illustrated on the price-quantity graph in Figure 9.6.

Now, following our definition of demand, we hold money income and the price of the other good constant, while letting the price of X fall from p_1 to p_2. The new budget line is Budget Line 2. Since money income and the price of Y remain constant, the vertical intercept does not change; but, because the price of X has fallen, the budget line must pivot outward along the X axis. With this new budget line, the consumer now maximizes utility where budget line 2 is tangent to indifference curve II, consuming x_2 units of X. Thus, p_2, x_2 must be another point on the demand schedule.

Next, letting the price of X fall again, this time to p_3, the new budget line is budget line 3. Again the price of Y and money income were held constant. The new equilibrium is on indifference curve III. At the price p_3, the consumer chooses x_3 units of X, another point on this consumer's demand curve.

Thus we have the following demand schedule for good X.

Price	*Quantity demanded*
p_1	x_1
p_2	x_2
p_3	x_3

This schedule is graphed as a demand curve in price-quantity space in the lower part of Figure 9.6. This demand curve is downward sloping. As we let the price of X fall, the quantity of X the consumer is willing and able to purchase increases, following our rule of demand. Furthermore, we followed our definition of demand, holding money income and the price of the other good (goods) constant. Thus we see that an individual's demand for a good is derived from a series of utility-maximizing equilibrium points. We only used three such points, but we could easily have used more in order to obtain more points on the demand curve.

■ **Definition.** The demand curve of an individual for a specific commodity relates utility-maximizing equilibrium quantities purchased to market

Figure 9.6
Deriving a demand curve

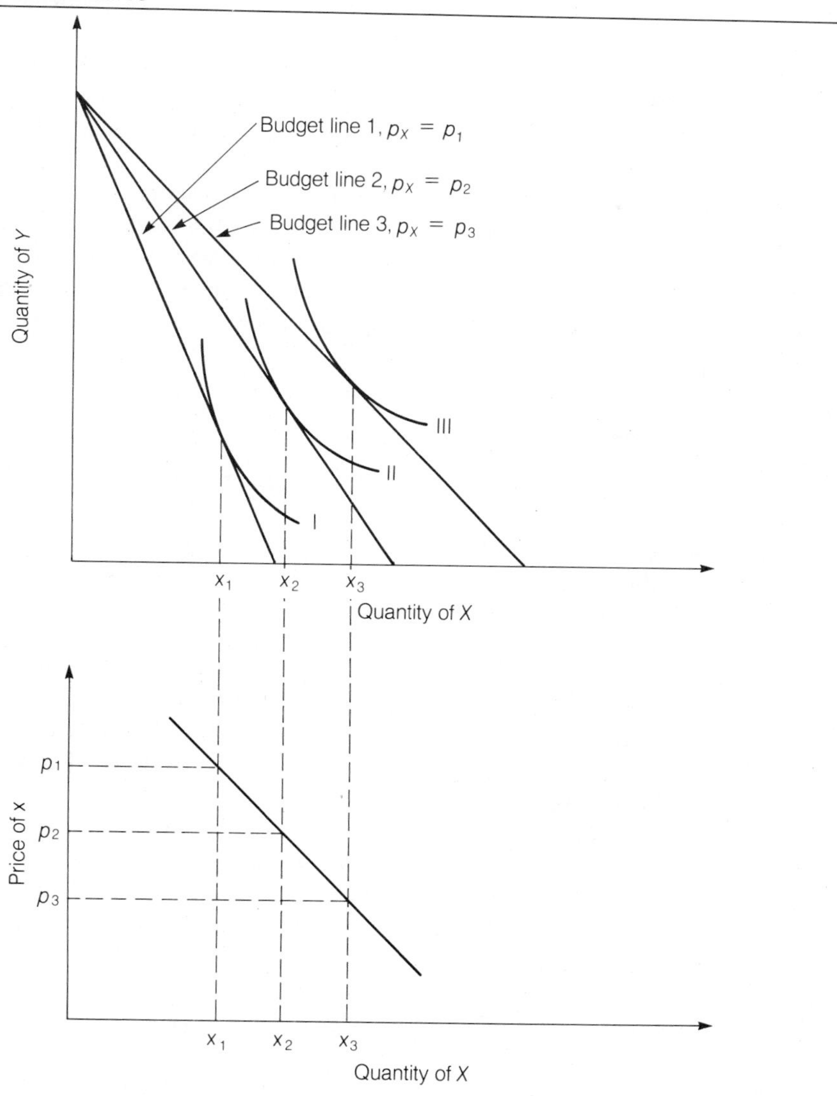

prices, holding constant money income and the prices of all other goods. The slope of the demand curve illustrates the law of demand: quantity demanded varies inversely with price.

9.6 SUBSTITUTION AND INCOME EFFECTS

Recall from Chapter 2, that when the price of a good decreases, consumers tend to substitute that good for other goods, since the good in question has become cheaper relative to other goods. Conversely, when the price of a good rises, it becomes more expensive relative to other goods, and consumers tend to substitute some of the other goods for some of the good with the now higher price. This is called the substitution effect.

But, there is also another effect, called the income effect. If a good becomes cheaper, people who are consuming that good are made better off. Since the price of that good has fallen, people can consume the same amount as before, but, because of the reduced price, they have some income left over, which can be spent on the good with the now lower price and on other goods. The opposite happens when the price of a good increases. The consumers are worse off in the sense that they cannot now afford the bundle they originally chose. They must consume less of the now more expensive good, less of other goods, or less of both. This is called the income effect. Let us analyze each effect in turn.

Substitution effect

We begin our analysis of the substitution effect with a definition:

■ **Definition.** The substitution effect of a change in the price of a good is the change in the consumption of the good that would result if the consumer remains on the same indifference curve.

To develop the substitution effect formally, consider Figure 9.7 in which we consider a reduction in price. Begin with a consumer in equilibrium where the original budget line *AB* is tangent to indifference curve I at point *E*. The consumer chooses x_1 units of good X. Now let the price of X decline so that the budget line pivots outward to *AD*.

The consumer, being better off, can now move to an indifference curve higher than I. But, the substitution effect deals with changes on the same indifference curve; so let's theoretically "take away" just enough of the consumer's income to force the new budget line, *AD*, to become tangent to the original indifference curve I. This is shown as the parallel shift of *AD* to the adjusted budget line *LZ*. It is important to note that the slope of *LZ* reflects the new, lower price of X, but is associated with a lower money income than is the original budget line, *AB*. Since budget line *LZ* is tangent to indifference curve I at point *G*, the consumer now chooses x_2 units of X.

The substitution effect is shown as the distance x_1 to x_2, or the movement along I from *E* to *G*. It is clear that this effect is negative—a decrease in price must result in an increase in consumption of the good when utility is held constant. And this must always be the case, given the shape of our indifference curves. That is, a decrease in price causes the budget line to become less steep; so the budget line, after taking away some income, must be tangent to the original indifference curve at a point with a lower slope (*MRS*) than was the case at the original equilibrium. This can only occur with increased consumption of the good.

Figure 9.7
Substitution effect

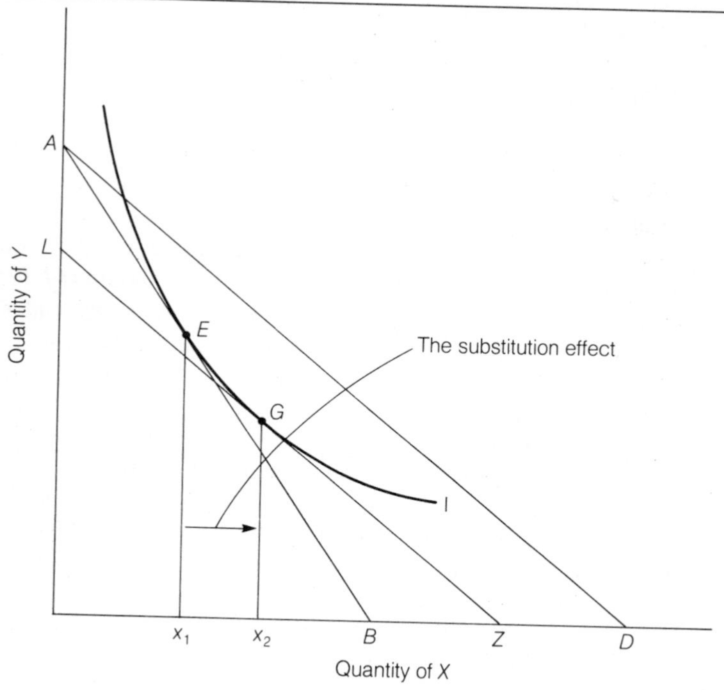

We have established the following principle:

■ **Principle.** The substitution effect is the change in the consumption of a good after a change in its price, when the consumer is forced by a change in money income to consume at some point on the original indifference curve. Considering the substitution effect only, the amount of the good consumed must vary inversely with its price. That is, utility held constant, $\Delta X/\Delta P_x < 0$.

Income effect

We cannot be as certain about the direction of the income effect as was the case for the substitution effect. Before we analyze the income effect, let us define it:

■ **Definition.** The income effect from a price change is the change in the consumption of a good resulting strictly from the change in purchasing power.

When we analyzed the substitution effect we noted that a decrease in the price of a good makes a consumer of that good better off in the sense of being able to purchase the same bundle and have income left over; i.e., the consumer can move to a higher indifference curve. An increase in the price of a good makes a consumer worse off because he or she is unable to purchase the original bundle; i.e., the consumer must move to a lower indifference curve. Since the consumer moves to a higher or lower indifference curve, depending upon the direction of the price change, and the substitution effect takes place along the original indifference curve, the income effect is simply the difference between the total effect of the price change—the movement from one indifference curve to another—and the substitution effect.

We can isolate these effects for a price decrease in Figure 9.8. First consider Panel A. Begin with budget line *AB* and equilibrium at *E* (x_1 units of X) on indifference curve I. Suppose the price of X falls and the budget line pivots to *AC*. The new equilibrium is at point *F* on indifference curve II. The total effect of the price decrease is to increase the consumption of X from x_1 to x_3. As we have already demonstrated, the substitution effect is the movement from x_1 to x_2 (or from *E* to *R*).

Since the total effect is x_1x_3 and the substitution effect is x_1x_2, the remainder of the change—x_2x_3, or the movement from *R* to *F* between indifference curves—must be the income effect. That is, as we return the income that was "taken away" to isolate the substitution effect, the consumer increases the consumption of X from x_2 to x_3.

Note that in Panel A the good is a normal good. Recall from Chapter 2, that consumption of a normal good increases when income increases, prices held constant. This is precisely what we did when we shifted the budget line from *LZ* back to *AC*.

As can be seen from the graph, in the case of a normal good, the income effect reinforces the substitution effect. Thus, for a normal good both effects are negative. When price falls both the substitution effect and the income effect cause the consumer to purchase more of the good. Likewise, when the price of the good rises, both effects will cause the consumer to purchase less of the good.

The situation is different for an inferior good. Recall from Chapter 2 that if a good is inferior, an increase in income, holding prices constant, causes less of the good to be consumed.

The case of an inferior good is illustrated in Panel B of Figure 9.8. Begin, as before, with budget line *AB*. Equilibrium is at *E* on indifference curve I with x_1 being consumed. Let the price of X fall, so that the budget line pivots out to *AC*. The new equilibrium is at *F* on indifference curve II, with x_3 being consumed. The total effect is therefore shown as x_1x_3.

Shifting the new budget line back to *LZ*, we see that the substitution effect is x_1x_2. Note that the substitution effect is greater than the total effect; x_2 is greater than x_3 (or x_1x_2 exceeds x_1x_3). It is apparent that the income effect must have partially offset the substitution effect. Such will always be the case for an inferior good.

To see why this must be so, return the income taken away when isolating

Figure 9.8
The income and substitution effects

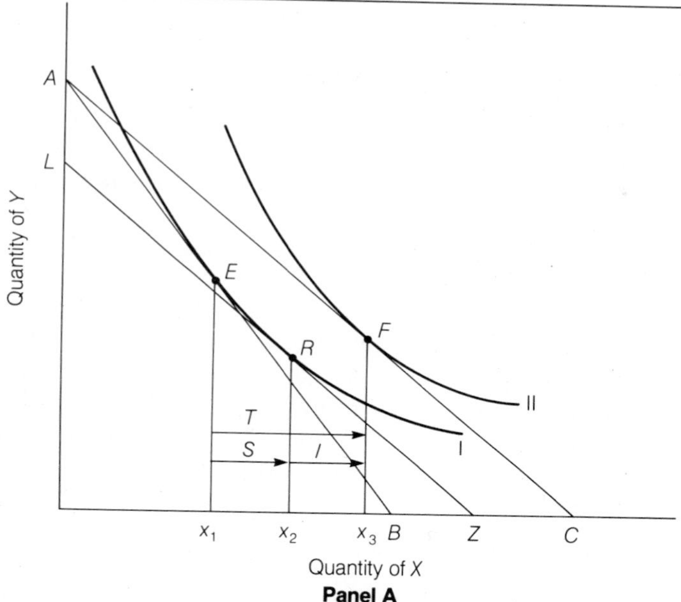

Panel A
Normal good

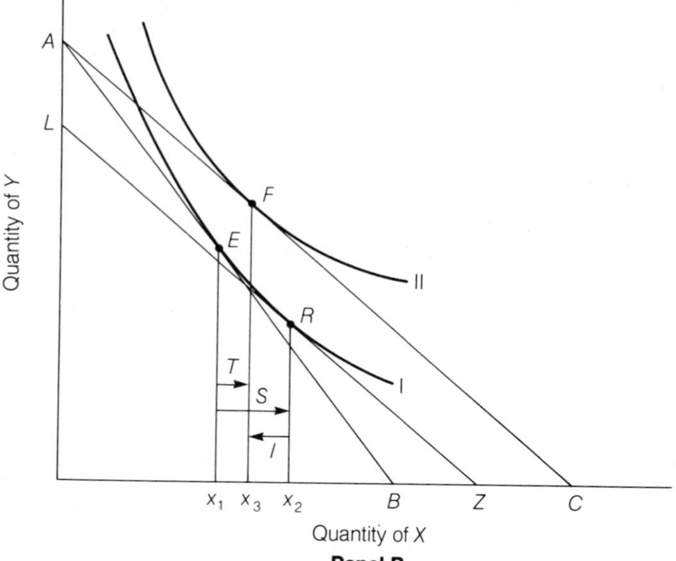

Panel B
Inferior good

the substitution effect. The budget line moves from *LZ* back to *AC*. Since the good is inferior, this increase in income causes less X to be consumed than was the case when the budget line was *LZ*. The income effect is therefore the movement from x_2 back to x_3 (or the movement from *R* to *F* between indifference curves I and II). We can see that in this case the income effect is positive—the decrease in the price of X causes a decrease in the consumption of X (income effect only). As you should be able to demonstrate, if the price of an inferior good rises, the income effect alone leads to an increase in consumption.

Thus we have established the following principle:

■ **Principle.** Considering the substitution effect alone, an increase (decrease) in the price of a good causes less (more) of the good to be demanded. For a normal good, the income effect—from the consumer's being made better or worse off by the price change—adds to or reinforces the substitution effect. The income effect in the case of an inferior good offsets or takes away from the substitution effect.

Why demand slopes downward

In the case of a normal good, it is clear why price and quantity demanded are negatively related. From the substitution effect alone, a decrease in price is accompanied by an increase in quantity demanded. (An increase in price decreases quantity demanded.) For a normal good, the income effect must add to the substitution effect. Since both effects move quantity demanded in the same direction, demand must be negatively sloped.

In the case of an inferior good, the income effect does not move in the same direction, and to some extent offsets the substitution effect. However, looking at Panel B of Figure 9.8 again, we see that the income effect only *partially* offsets the substitution effect, so that quantity demanded still varies inversely with price. And this is the general case: Even if the commodity is inferior, the substitution effect dominates the income effect; so, the demand curve still slopes downward.

It is *theoretically* possible that the income effect for an inferior good could dominate the substitution effect. In this case—the so-called Giffen good—quantity demanded would vary directly with price and the demand curve would be upward sloping. However, in this text, we will ignore Giffen goods. While experimental economists have suggested that a Giffen good may exist for an individual, we have as yet seen no convincing evidence that a Giffen good will exist when a group of consumers is observed in a marketplace.

9.7 ADVERTISING AND INDIFFERENCE CURVES

Advertising is so diverse that it is impossible for us to give you a complete description or classification. Very broadly, we can say that advertising is designed to convey a message about a particular commodity or service; and, of course, these messages are intended to increase the sales of the advertised product. These messages can be divided into two general categories: those intended to convey information about the product and those intended to create an image about the product. (Usually, most ads try to do some of both, but many ads lean more toward one purpose than the other.)

Informative advertising

Purely informative advertising generally conveys pertinent price and quality information. Some examples of this type of advertising are newspaper ads (e.g., food store and drug store ads), catalog ads, and ads in technical publications.

What is the purpose of such advertising? Until now we have assumed in our analyses that consumers have complete information about both product price and the ability of goods to satisfy their wants. But we know that this is not the case in the real world. People do not always have full information about prices or the quality of all products.

We might depict the budget line of a consumer who is only partially informed about the price of a product as in Panel A of Figure 9.9. In that figure we are illustrating the situation confronted by a consumer who is choosing between a particular good, commodity X, and a composite good, i.e., all other goods. This consumer does not know with certainty the price of product X; instead he or she knows that the price of commodity X lies within a certain range. The upper bound of this range would give the budget line *LZ*. This is the budget line if the price of commodity X is the highest that the customer thinks possible. Budget line *LR* is the budget line for the lowest price of X in the potential range. The true budget line would probably lie somewhere in the shaded area between the two.

We have illustrated a similar situation for the indifference curves of a consumer who is only partially informed about the quality of a product in Panel B of Figure 9.9. In this figure, indifference curve I is the indifference curve that would be relevant if the consumer were completely informed about the quality of commodity X. But, with lack of full information, the consumer can't determine exactly where the indifference curve will be located. The perception of this consumer is that the indifference curve could be anywhere between indifference curves I_A and I_B. So, the indifference curve under incomplete information is a band rather than a line.

What would a consumer do when faced with this uncertainty? One possibility is to purchase (or not purchase) under the limited information available. However, as you can tell from Figure 9.9, this could result in a lower level of utility for the consumer than would exist if he or she has complete information. Alternatively, the consumer might elect to search for price and quality information about the product, in order to isolate the true budget line and indifference curve.

Figure 9.9
Budget lines and indifference curves without complete information

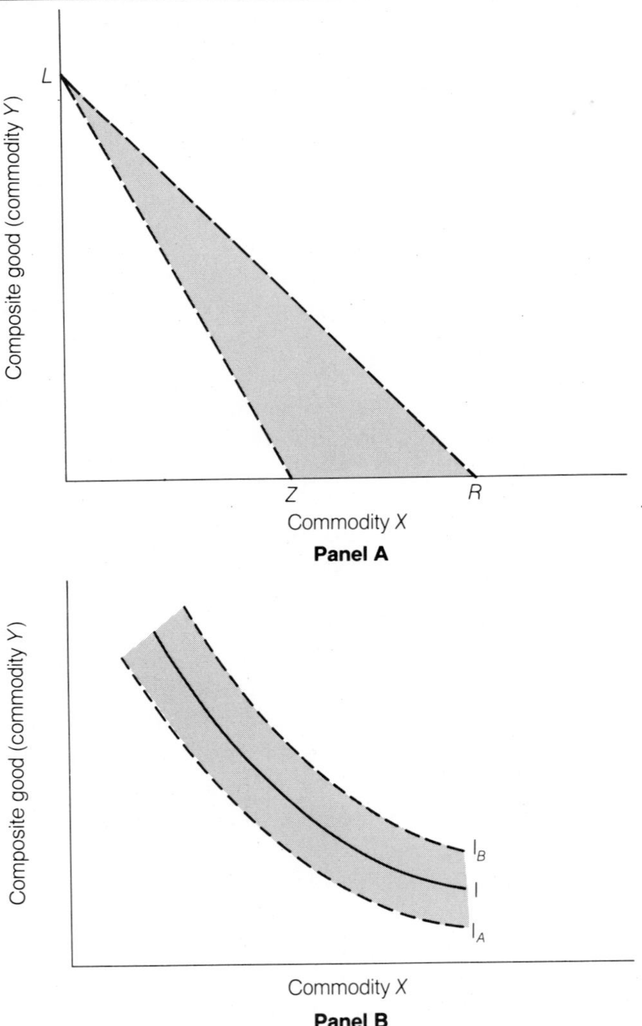

But, if the consumer elects to search for additional information, we have still another economic allocation problem. Gaining additional information about the product takes time, and time is a valuable asset. How much time would a potential consumer spend acquiring information?

The answer to this search decision is found in the general maximization process we described to you in Chapter 3. A consumer should spend time acquiring price and quality information as long as the expected benefit from the additional shopping—searching—time exceeds the expected cost of the time. If the expected cost is greater than the expected gain, the consumer should spend no more time searching.

As an example, suppose someone has decided to buy a particular appliance but is uncertain about the true price of that appliance. Obviously, this consumer wishes to find the lowest available price. The potential consumer has some idea about how much an additional day of price search would be expected to reduce the price that must be paid (e.g., the probability that, by searching another day, he or she could find a lower price). This potential reduction in price is the expected marginal benefit from search. The marginal cost of another unit of search is the value of the person's time. This value is, in general, the wage or salary that could be earned if the person spent his or her time working rather than shopping. This consumer should search an additional day if the expected reduction in price exceeds the opportunity cost of that day spent in shopping. While the expected benefits from additional units of search time for quality information cannot be stated in such a straightforward manner, the principle is identical.

We observe consumers spending a considerable amount of time acquiring information about price and quality. How can the manager of a firm benefit from the fact that acquiring information is costly? If the manager can make it less costly for consumers to acquire information about the firm's product, the manager can increase the probability that the consumer will purchase from the manager's firm rather than continue to search.

This is the reason for pure information advertising. If information about a firm's product is easily available, consumers would be more likely to conserve their valuable search time and purchase the product about which they have information. Thus, the purpose of informative advertising is to lower the search cost of the product, in the expectation that consumers will purchase the advertised product.

To this point, our discussion would imply that informative ads would always contain *both* price and quality information. However, as we are all well aware, a lot of informative ads contain only one type of information. Ads for products with which consumers have a great deal of experience tend to concentrate on price information. An excellent example of this can be found in the newspaper ads run by food and drug stores. Ads for products that are less familiar to the consumer, e.g., personal computers, tend to concentrate on quality information, in an attempt to attract consumers for a "test drive."

Image advertising

While informative and image advertising are frequently combined, image advertising per se is not intended to directly convey information. Image advertising is most often found on television, billboards, and in magazines with a wide and general circulation. Although image advertising presents some information (at the very least telling consumers that a particular product is available), the principal aim of all image advertising is to make consumers associate the advertised image with consumption of the product.

The image is intended to literally become a characteristic of the product.

Marlborough cigarettes use the image of the macho cowboy. Consumers buy this image when they buy the product. Calvin Klein advertises to associate sexiness with their jeans. In its advertising, Cadillac associates its automobiles with successful middle-age men.

In most cases, image advertising is designed to change the consumer's preference patterns, i.e., the consumer's indifference curves. Image advertising is normally designed to make consumers think that other products are not particularly good substitutes for the advertised good. However, some image advertising is designed to increase the amount of expected utility associated with the product. In any case, all image advertising, if successful, will have an effect on consumers' indifference curves. For analytical simplicity, let us decompose the total effect on the indifference map into two effects: (1) the marginal rate of substitution is changed and (2) the indifference map is shifted. Let's analyze each of these effects separately and look at the resulting effect upon the demand for the advertised product.

In Figure 9.10 we have illustrated the desired effect of image advertising on a consumer's marginal rate of substitution. In this figure we consider a commodity, A. Let the solid indifference curve I be the relevant curve if commodity A is not advertised, and let LZ be the consumer's original budget line. Equilibrium is attained at E, with the consumer purchasing A_1 units of commodity A. Next we let the price of commodity A increase relative to the price of the composite commodity.[4] The new budget line, MN, is steeper, because the price ratio, P_A/P_C, has increased. The budget line MN is tangent to indifference curve I at B. The substitution effect is the movement from E to B, and will result in a decrease in the consumption of good A from A_1 to A_2.

The desired effect of image advertising for the commodity is illustrated as the change in the indifference curve from I to the dashed line I$'$. Note that the only thing that has changed is the slope of the indifference curve. With budget line LZ, equilibrium still occurs at E.

With this new indifference curve, let's again let the price of A rise relative to the price of the composite commodity. Since the relative price change is the same as in the preceding case, the slope of the new budget line $M'N'$ is the same as MN. Again isolating the substitution effect, the new budget line $M'N'$ is now tangent to indifference curve I$'$ at C. Now the substitution effect is the movement from E to C along indifference curve I$'$, or the decrease in the consumption of good A from A_1 to A_3. The substitution effect is still negative—an increase in the relative price of A causes a decrease in its consumption—but the decrease in the consumption of commodity A is much less with advertising than was the case without advertising.

The reason for the difference is that image advertising increases the marginal rate of substitution, $\Delta C/\Delta A$. This means that, with advertising, the consumer is willing to give up much less A to obtain an equal amount of the

---

[4]We should note that in this analysis we are considering only the substitution effect from a change in price.

Figure 9.10
Effect of advertising on *MRS*

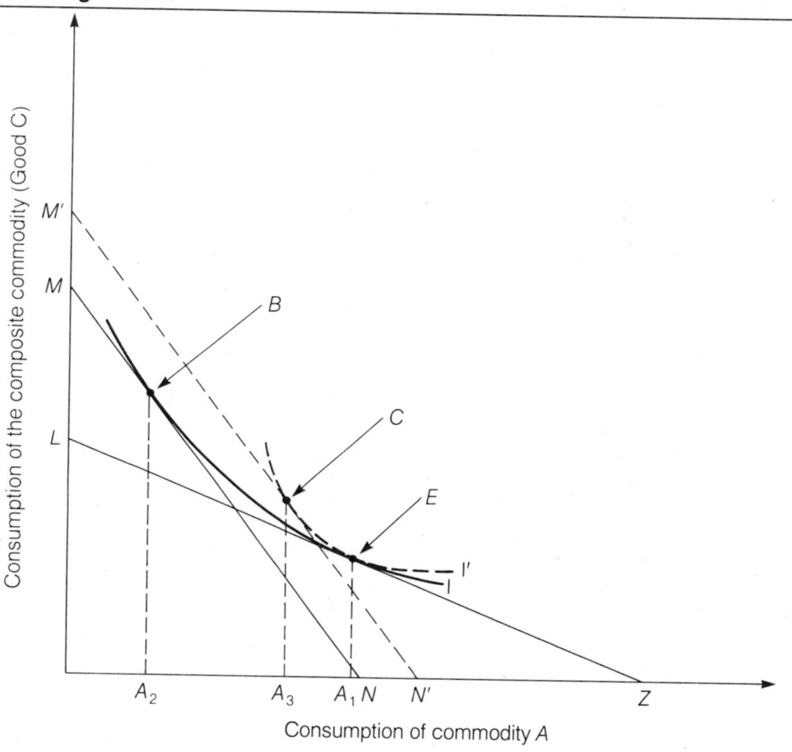

composite good. Thus, if image advertising is successful in increasing the marginal rate of substitution between the advertised product and other products, the firm can increase price with a much lower decrease in sales than would be the case without advertising. Or, the loss in sales would be reduced if the firm's competitors decrease the price of their product.

In other words, image advertising is normally designed to make the demand for the product less elastic. In our analysis, the substitution effect is reduced by image advertising. Looking back at our analysis of an individual's demand curve, we can see that, if the substitution effect is reduced, the demand curve will become less elastic.

So, image advertising can cause the demand for the advertised product to become less elastic by reducing the substitution effect of a price change. But, image advertising can also have another effect on demand. This effect is shown in Figure 9.11. Let's begin with a consumer facing the income constraint given by budget line *LZ*. Again, the solid indifference curves I and II make up a portion of the consumer's original (pre-advertising) indifference map. As we know, the consumer attains utility-maximizing equilibrium at *E* on indifference curve I, consuming A_1 units of good A.

Figure 9.11
Demand increasing advertising

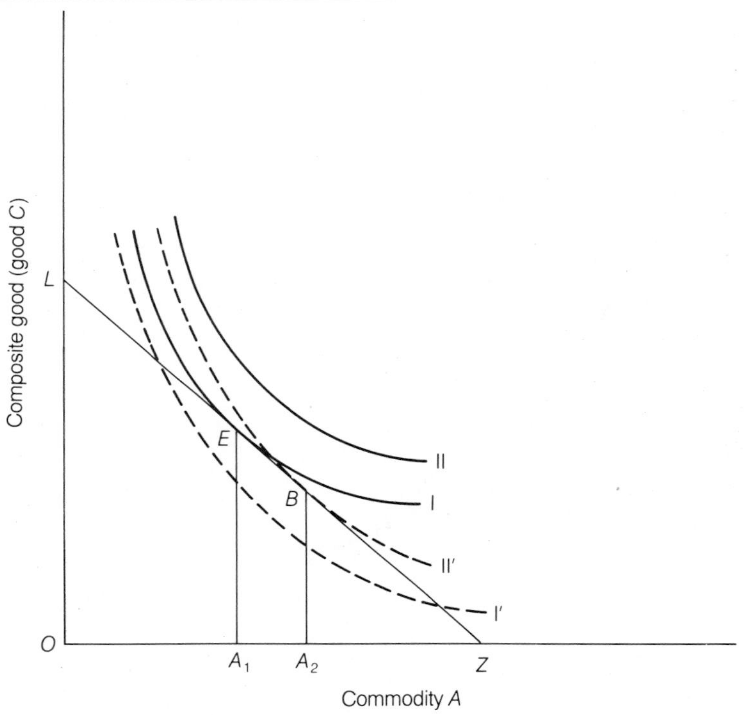

Now suppose that commodity A is advertised and the image advertising is successful in increasing the perceived value of commodity A. In effect, the advertising shifts the indifference map downward. We have illustrated this new indifference map with the dashed indifference curves I′ and II′. Combinations of goods on the new (post-advertising) indifference curve I′ denote the same level of utility as combinations on the original (pre-advertising) indifference curve I. Likewise, combinations on indifference curve II′ give the same utility level as those on indifference curve II. At any given level of consumption of good A, the consumer attains the same level of utility with less of the composite good when A is advertised. Advertising has increased the perceived value of the advertised good, in the sense that the satisfaction is not reduced from having less of good C and the same amount of A. With no change in the budget line, the new equilibrium is reached at B on curve II′, with the consumer purchasing A_2 units of commodity A. The effect of the advertising is to increase the demand for the advertised commodity. The *MRS* still equals the price ratio, but more A and less C are consumed at the new equilibrium.

Thus we see that the effect of image advertising can be decomposed into two effects: The first is to increase the marginal rate of substitution, thereby reducing the substitution effect from a change in relative prices and causing the demand for the product to become less elastic. The second effect is to shift the indifference map downward, which increases the consumer's demand for the advertised product, enabling the firm to sell a greater amount at a given product price.

APPLICATION

Advertising in the home computer market

At the beginning of this section, we noted that it is frequently difficult to distinguish between informative and image advertising. Many advertisements have some of both kinds. But sometimes two types of ad for the same product make the distinction quite well. One sample is found in the advertisements we have seen for home computers.

Many magazines specialize in articles about computers. These periodicals are quite specialized and, therefore, appeal primarily to a particular group of people. The advertising we have seen in these magazines is almost uniformly informative in nature. Firms advertising in these magazines—mail-order firms, retailers, and manufacturers—describe in great detail the specifications of their products. Reading the ads, you can learn almost all you want to know about the size of the memory, number of drives, storage capacity, software availability, display screens, and everything else relevant to the purchase decision.

Furthermore, many of the ads contain very specific price information, going so far as to give prices for various components of the system. In this way the interested reader can compare the different features of the computers and the differences in the relative prices of these features. We have provided a stylized illustration of such an ad in Figure 9.12

Figure 9.12
A stylized computer ad

The Ultimate Computer
ORANGE Model 7S
128K RAM

Fully Compatible With
- **MS-DOS**
- **APPLE**
- **CPM**
- **Radio Shack**

Full System Price of **$1695** Includes

- Orange Model 7S
- Word Processing
- High-Res Monitor
- Spreadsheet
- Two Disk Drives
- Accounting Package

Also Available — **1 Megabyte of RAM!**

Call for other prices and information
(XXX)XXX-XXXX

It is interesting to compare this type of advertising with recent advertising seen on television and in magazines with more general readership. Major computer firms, such as Apple, Commodore, and IBM, have directed their ads toward parents. This advertising presents the *image* that scholastic achievement is tied to early experience with a computer: If parents do not purchase home computers, their children cannot possibly succeed in school. One ad with this kind of message shows a college freshman who has flunked out, apparently because he did not have access to a home computer during high school. Another shows a three-year-old receiving a computer as a birthday present. The message relayed in this ad is that this child will have a distinct advantage over her less-fortunate classmates, or classmates with less-caring parents.

APPLICATION

Advertising cars and cows

Just as it is somewhat difficult to separate informative advertising from image advertising, it is similarly difficult to separate image advertising designed to change the consumer's *MRS* from ads that are intended to increase demand. While most ads attempt to do both, we do see examples of advertising that leans toward one approach or the other.

A major portion of automobile advertising is designed to change the marginal rate of substitution—to make other products less acceptable substitutes for the advertised product. An example is the advertising of Buick automobiles. The advertisements attempt to convince potential purchasers of automobiles that other automobiles are not particularly good substitutes for Buicks. The ads almost seem to take as given that the viewers or readers want to buy a new car. They do not try to convince people that they should purchase a car, but instead imply that, if you are planning to buy, only a Buick will do. Thus the advertising is designed primarily to change the marginal rate of substitution between Buick and other brands.

The ads are designed to create the image of luxury and prestige and associate this with owning a Buick. The views of the automobile show the car as being large on the outside and roomy on the inside (possibly larger and roomier than the car really is). Attractive and obviously successful men and women are shown as Buick owners. The image presented is that successful people buy Buicks. While the price is not given, the ads imply that one can purchase the prestige associated with owning a luxury automobile at a much lower cost by buying a Buick rather than a Cadillac or Lincoln.

The advertising tries to make other luxury cars or smaller more economical cars rather poor substitutes for a Buick at the prevailing set of relative prices.

Thus the image of luxury and success attempts to raise the marginal rate of substitution between Buick and other automobiles. Indeed, the reason we selected Buick as an example rather than another make of automobile is their slogan: "Wouldn't You Really Rather Have a Buick?" This slogan itself demonstrates that the purpose of the ad is to show you how unique—and superior—the Buick is. The ad is meant to convince the customer that there is really no good substitute . . . and wouldn't you really rather have this unique product?

Good examples of demand-increasing advertising (advertising designed to shift consumers' indifference maps) are the ads of producers' trade associations, such as the milk or orange juice producers. Milk producers have followed the post–World War II baby boom generation by pitching their ads to show milk, not just as a drink for children but as a drink for healthy, active—and svelte—adults.

Recent orange juice ads have attempted to portray orange juice as not being "just a breakfast drink." In one ad, school children are shown sitting in class dreaming of the delicious glass of orange juice waiting at lunch. For these children, there is no other lunch drink that is nearly as satisfying, and mothers are reminded that orange juice is more nutritious for their children than any other drink.

In another ad adults are shown ordering and drinking orange juice rather than coffee or soft drinks during the day. All the ads are intended to convey the idea that orange juice should be consumed anytime someone is thirsty, not just at breakfast.

9.8 SUMMARY

The basic principles of consumer behavior and demand have now been developed. The fundamental point of this chapter is that if consumers behave so as to maximize satisfaction from a given money income, quantity demanded will vary inversely with price. Consumers will choose combinations of goods such that the marginal rate of substitution equals the price ratio.

The substitution effect of a price change upon the consumption of that good is always negative; that is, quantity demanded varies inversely with price, holding utility constant and considering the substitution effect only. If the good is normal, the income effect reinforces the substitution effect. If the good is inferior, the income effect to some extent offsets the substitution effect.

TECHNICAL PROBLEMS

1. In the figure below, suppose a consumer has the specified indifference map. The relevant budget line is *LZ*. The price of good Y is $10.

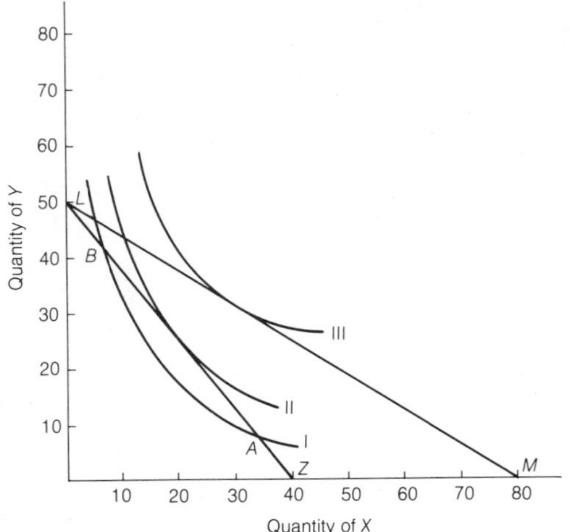

a. What is the consumer's income?
b. What is the price of X?
c. Write the equation for the budget line *LZ*.
d. What combination of X and Y will the consumer choose? Why?
e. What is the marginal rate of substitution at this combination?
f. Explain in terms of the *MRS* why the consumer would not choose combinations designated by A or B.
g. Suppose the budget line pivots to *LM*, money income remaining constant. What combination is now chosen?
h. What is the new *MRS*?

2. The figure below shows indifference maps for two consumers, one in Panel A the other in Panel B. What can you say about the relative preference of the two people for pizzas and hamburgers? Suppose the price of hamburgers falls. If the income effects are the same for each, what can you say about the own-price elasticities of demand for hamburgers for the two consumers? Explain.

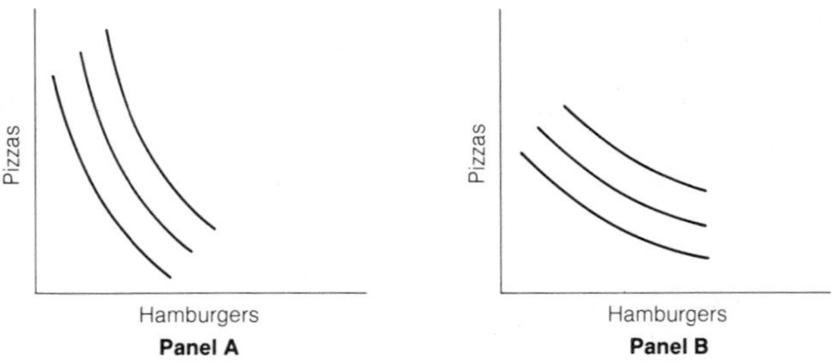

3. If $MU_x/MU_y < P_x/P_y$, the individual would (increase, decrease) the consumption of X relative to Y. Explain your answer.

4. In the figure below, indifference curves I, II, and III make up a portion of an individual's indifference map. The consumer's income is $1,000; the price of Y is $20. Derive three points on the individual's demand curve for good X.

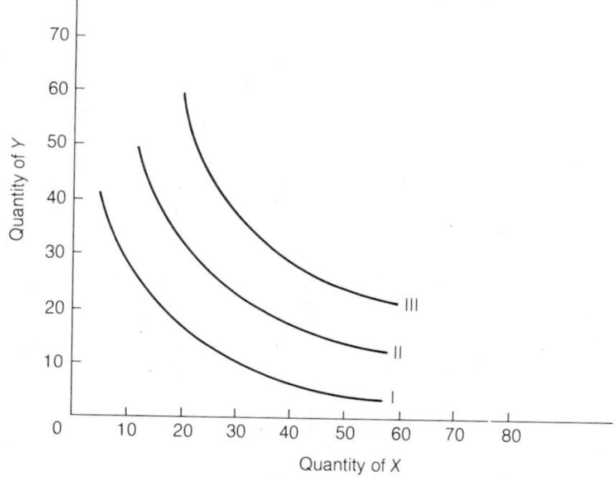

5. A person's marginal rate of substitution between X and Y ($-\Delta X/\Delta Y$) is 4. The price of X is $12 and the price of Y is $3. The consumer is in equilibrium. The price of X rises to $15 and the price of Y rises to $5. Income is varied to restrict the consumer to the original level of utility. Does the person substitute more X for Y, or more Y for X? Explain.

6. The figure below contains a portion of a consumer's indifference map. Income is $600 and the price of Y is $6. The price of X rises from $4 to $10. Derive the total, the substitution, and the income effects on the consumption of good X from the price increase.

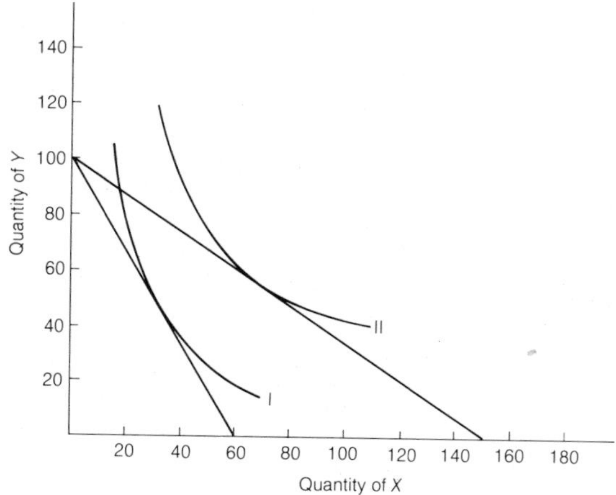

7. What would budget lines look like if consumers received a lower price for a good, the more they purchased during a period? The reduction

varies continuously over the range of quantities of the good. Would the utility-maximizing equilibrium condition be substantially changed from that prevailing under fixed prices?

8. Suppose a consumer spends his or her entire income on some composite commodity (C) and purchases none of good X. What can you say about the marginal utility per dollar spent of the first unit of good X that could be purchased, relative to the marginal utility per dollar of the last unit of C purchased?

ANALYTICAL PROBLEMS

1. Explain what types of effects firms would like their advertising to have upon the indifference curves of purchasers of the products they sell. Why would this be desired by the advertiser?
2. A retailer of video recorders advertises a large price reduction on two of the recorders it sells. How would the retailer allocate display space for the advertised recorders and the merchandise that is not marked down?
3. What methods, other than advertising, can firms use to shift consumers' indifference curves or change the marginal rates of substitution between the product they sell and substitute products?
4. Can you think of hypothetical cases in which someone would not give up a single unit of a good no matter what is offered in exchange? What type of goods would these extreme examples be?
5. Suppose a firm's manager/owner obtains utility from income (profit) and from having the firm be "socially conscious"—possibly making charitable contributions or civic expenditures. Can you set up the problem and derive equilibrium conditions if the manager/owner wishes to obtain a specific level of utility at the lowest possible cost? Do these conditions differ from the utility-maximizing conditions?

10

Market demand and elasticity

For managerial decision making, we are normally more interested in the market demand for a product than in the demand of an individual consumer. Nonetheless, the behavior of individual consumers in the market is the determinant of market demand. Recall that in Chapter 2 we defined market demand as a list of prices and the corresponding quantities consumers are willing and able to purchase at each price in the list, holding constant money income, the prices of other goods, tastes, and expectations. When deriving individual demands in Chapter 9, we pivoted the budget line around the vertical intercept, therefore holding income and the prices of other goods constant. Since the indifference curves remained constant, taste and expectations were unchanged.

Thus the discussion in Chapter 9 meets all of the conditions of market demand. To obtain the market demand function therefore we need only to aggregate the individual demand functions of all potential consumers in the market. In this chapter we will demonstrate this aggregation and analyze some of the more important characteristics of market demand curves.

10.1 AGGREGATING INDIVIDUAL DEMANDS

Suppose there are only three individuals in the market for a particular commodity. The quantities demanded by each consumer at each price in column 1 are shown in columns 2, 3, and 4 of Table 10.1. Column 5 shows the

Table 10.1
Aggregating individual demands

	Quantity demanded			
Price	*Consumer 1*	*Consumer 2*	*Consumer 3*	*Market demand*
$6	3	0	0	3
5	5	1	0	6
4	8	3	1	12
3	10	5	4	19
2	12	7	6	25
1	13	8	8	29

sum of these quantities demanded at each price and is therefore the market demand. Since the demands for each consumer are negatively sloped, market demand is negatively sloped also. Quantity demanded is inversely related to price.

Figure 10.1 shows how a market demand curve can be obtained from individual demand curves. Let D_1D_1' and D_2D_2' be the demand curves for two consumers. As shown in Table 10.1, market demand is simply the sum of the quantities demanded by each consumer. Hence, the market demand curve is the horizontal summation of the individual demand curves. In Figure 10.1,

Figure 10.1
Derivation of market demand

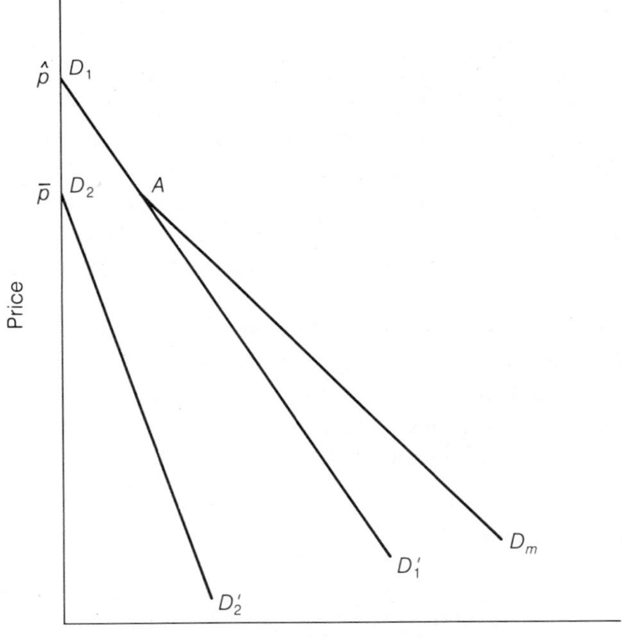

the market demand curve is D_1AD_m. Between the prices $\hat{p}$ and $\overline{p}$, the market demand is the demand of Consumer 1, since Consumer 2 purchases nothing at any price above $\overline{p}$.

10.2 DEMAND ELASTICITY—OWN-PRICE ELASTICITY

We have emphasized that quantity demanded rises when price falls, and vice versa—the law of demand. Those who use economics in decision making are frequently interested how total expenditures on a commodity change when there is a movement along the demand curve. Total expenditures by the consumers (or total revenue, R, to the firm) are simply price times quantity demanded, or

$$R = P \cdot Q$$

Remember that, along a demand curve, P and Q move in opposite directions and, consequently, have offsetting effects on R. For example, an increase in price alone would tend to increase consumer expenditures, whereas the resulting decrease in quantity would tend to decrease expenditures. Thus, the final effect of a price change on total expenditure depends upon which force dominates, the increase in price or the decrease in quantity demanded.

The price effect dominates the quantity effect if the percentage increase in price exceeds the percentage decrease in quantity demanded; in this case, total expenditure rises when price rises. Total expenditure falls, however, if the percentage increase in price is less than the percentage decrease in quantity demanded. Looking at a decrease in the price of the commodity, if the percentage decrease in price exceeds (is less than) the percentage increase in quantity demanded, total expenditure falls (rises). We see, then, that the overall effect of a price change on total expenditures (revenue) depends upon the relative sensitivity of quantity demanded to price along a demand curve. The measure of this relative sensitivity is called the (own-price) elasticity of demand.

This concept is of great interest to both economists and managerial decision makers. Obviously, a manager would like to know the effect of a change in price on sales revenue and what determines such an effect. For some products, a small change in price over a certain range of the demand curve results in a significant change in quantity demanded. In this case, quantity demanded is very responsive to changes in price, and the total revenue collected by a seller falls when price increases. For other products, or perhaps for the same product over a different range of the demand curve, a relatively large change in price leads to a correspondingly smaller change in quantity demanded. That is, quantity demanded is not particularly responsive to price changes.

A graph can help us see how price and quantity interact to determine the effect on total revenue of a movement along the demand curve. In Figure 10.2, suppose a firm sets a price of p_0 and therefore sells quantity x_0. Suppose that the firm then raises price to p_1. As shown in Figure 10.2, the quantity sold falls to x_1. Before the price change, total revenue to the firm or total consumer expenditure was

$$R_0 = p_0x_0$$

In terms of Figure 10.2, total revenue prior to the price change is the area of the rectangle Op_0bx_0. After the price change, total revenue is

$$R_1 = p_1x_1$$

In Figure 10.2 this new total revenue is given by the rectangle Op_1ax_1. The independent effect of the price increase was to increase revenue by an amount shown as rectangle A. However, the consequent reduction in sales reduced total revenue by the amount shown as rectangle B. Total revenue rises if area A is greater than area B; it falls if area A is less than area B; and stays the same if area A equals area B.

Economists have a precise way of classifying demand according to the responsiveness of quantity demanded to a price change and the corresponding effect of changes in price on total revenue. Demand is classified as elastic or inelastic according to its degree of responsiveness. More specifically, demand is said to be *elastic* if total revenue falls with a price increase and rises with a price decrease. It is classified as *inelastic* if total revenue rises with a price increase and falls with a price decrease. Finally if total revenue is unaffected by a price change, demand is said to be *unitary elastic*.

Figure 10.2
Change in revenue from a price increase

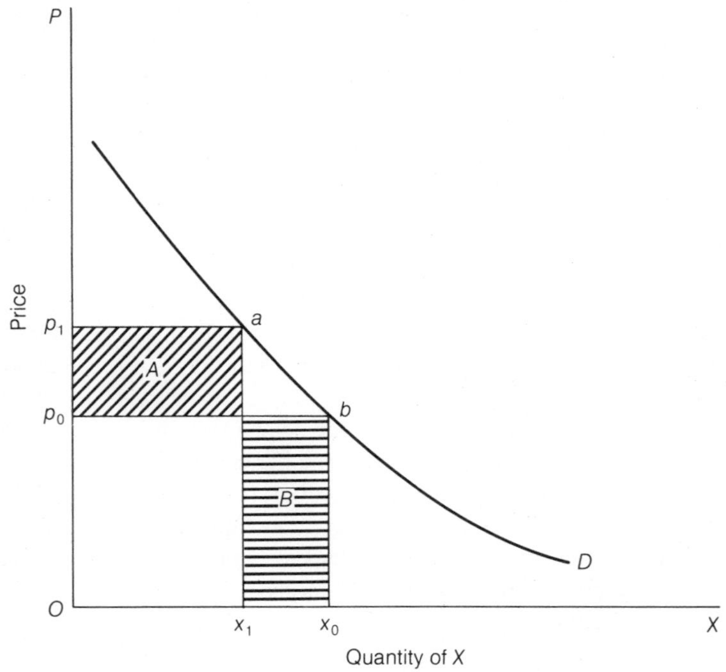

Thus, we can talk about changes in total revenue (or total expenditure) in response to changes in price, using the concepts of demand elasticity or inelasticity. Suppose the price change "outweighs" the quantity change in terms of percent; that is, quantity demanded is not particularly responsive to price. In this case, when price rises and quantity falls, total expenditure increases. Demand is said to be inelastic. If price decreases and quantity demanded increases under the inelastic demand, total expenditure falls. On the other hand, if demand is elastic, the percentage change in quantity demanded exceeds the percentage change in price. In this case, when price rises and quantity falls, total revenue falls because of the greater quantity effect. Clearly, a price decrease leads to an increase in quantity demanded, and, with an elastic demand, total revenue rises.

In summary, we can evaluate the impact of a price change on total revenue (or total expenditure) simply by looking at the relative responsiveness (elasticity) of the demand function. All of the relations we have developed are summarized in Table 10.2. In the table the terms $|\%\Delta P|$ and $|\%\Delta Q|$ are the absolute values of the percentage changes in price and quantity.

Table 10.2
Relations between demand elasticity and total revenue (*TR*)

	Elastic demand $\|\%\Delta Q\| > \|\%\Delta P\|$	*Unitary elasticity* $\|\%\Delta Q\| = \|\%\Delta P\|$	*Inelastic demand* $\|\%\Delta Q\| < \|\%\Delta P\|$
Price rises	*TR* falls	No change in *TR*	*TR* rises
Price falls	*TR* rises	No change in *TR*	*TR* falls

Computation of elasticity

We have thus far talked of elasticity and inelasticity in very general terms. It is useful, at times, to have a specific measure of relative responsiveness rather than merely speaking of demand as being elastic or inelastic. We should emphasize, however, that it is not accurate to say that a given demand curve is elastic or inelastic. In many cases, demand curves have both an inelastic and an elastic range, as well as a point or range of unitary elasticity. Thus, it is more accurate to speak of demand as being elastic or inelastic over a particular range of price and quantity magnitudes. We might wish to determine, over a certain range of prices, which of two demand curves is more elastic. For this we need a measuring device. That device is the coefficient of price elasticity (E):

$$E = -\frac{\text{Percentage change in quantity demanded}}{\text{Percentage change in price}}$$

Since the percentage change in any variable can be expressed as the change in the variable divided by the value of the variable, we can rewrite the coefficient of elasticity as

$$E = -\frac{\Delta Q/Q}{\Delta P/P}$$

or

$$E = -\frac{\Delta Q}{\Delta P} \cdot \frac{P}{Q}$$

Note that since price and quantity vary inversely, a minus sign is used in the calculation of elasticity to make the coefficient positive.

From the formula, we see that the relative responsiveness of quantity demanded to changes in prices (which we summarized in Table 10.2) is reflected precisely in the ratio of the proportional change in quantity demanded to the proportional change in price. That is, if E is less than one, demand is inelastic, since $|\%\Delta Q| < |\%\Delta P|$. Likewise, if E is greater than one, demand is elastic, since $|\%\Delta Q| > |\%\Delta P|$. If E is equal to one, demand has unitary elasticity, since $|\%\Delta Q| = |\%\Delta P|$.

Returning to Figure 10.2 you can see that, for a price increase, if total revenue goes up, demand is inelastic. If total revenue rises, then in Figure 10.2 area $A >$ area B. We can rewrite this inequality as

$$x_1 \cdot (p_1 - p_0) > p_0 \cdot (x_0 - x_1)$$

or, using the Δ sign again, as

$$x_1 \Delta p > p_0 \Delta x$$

Dividing the right side by the left side gives

$$1 > \frac{\Delta x}{\Delta p} \cdot \frac{p_0}{x_1}$$

As you can verify, $(\Delta x/\Delta p) \cdot (p/x)$ is the elasticity coefficient for a price change from p_0 to p_1. This means that

$$E < 1$$

Hence, if total revenue rises when price increases, the measured elasticity of demand must be less than one.

If total revenue goes down when price is increased, we reverse the inequality: area $A < B$. Again rewriting

$$x_1 \Delta p < p_0 \Delta x$$

and, dividing the right side by the left side

$$1 < \frac{\Delta x}{\Delta p} \cdot \frac{p_0}{x_1}$$

Using our definition of the elasticity coefficient,

$$E > 1$$

Table 10.3
Demand and elasticity

Price	*Quantity demanded*	*Total revenue*	*Elasticity*
$1.00	100,000	$100,000	
			ELASTIC
.50	300,000	150,000	
			UNITARY
.25	600,000	150,000	
			INELASTIC
.10	1,000,000	100,000	

So, if total revenue decreases when price increases, the measured elasticity of demand must be greater than one. Using the same type of analysis, it is easy to show that if a price increase has no effect on total revenue (i.e., area A = area B), the measured elasticity of demand must be equal to one.

The process of deriving the coefficient of elasticity between two price-quantity relations involves a simple computation. However there is a problem involved in selecting the proper base. As an example, let us consider the hypothetical demand schedule given in Table 10.3. Suppose price falls from $1 to 50 cents; quantity demanded rises from 100,000 to 300,000 and total expenditure on the commodity rises from $100,000 to $150,000. By the above analysis, we know that demand is elastic over the range of price from $1.00 to 50 cents since total revenue (total expenditures) increases as price decreases.

Let's actually compute the price elasticity for prices between $1.00 and 50 cents. If we consider a price decrease from $1.00 to 50 cents.

$$E = -\frac{\Delta x}{\Delta p} \cdot \frac{p_0}{x_1}$$

$$= -\frac{(100{,}000 - 300{,}000)}{(1.00 - .50)} \cdot \frac{1.00}{300{,}000}$$

$$= 1\frac{1}{3}$$

However, if we consider a price increase from 50 cents to $1.00,

$$E = -\frac{(300{,}000 - 100{,}000)}{(.50 - 1.00)} \cdot \frac{.50}{100{,}000}$$

$$= 2$$

Hence, we get two very different measures for the same region of the demand curve. Which—if either—is correct?

The difficulty lies in the fact that elasticity has been computed over a wide arc of the demand curve but evaluated at a specific point. We can get a much better approximation by using the average values of price and quantity demanded over the arc. That is, for large changes such as this, we should compute elasticity using the "arc formula." Arc elasticity $\bar{E}$ is

$$\bar{E} = -\frac{x_1 - x_0}{(x_1 + x_0)/2} \Big/ \frac{p_1 - p_0}{(p_1 + p_0)/2} = -\frac{x_1 - x_0}{x_1 + x_0} \Big/ \frac{p_1 - p_0}{p_1 + p_0}$$

where subscripts 0 and 1 refer to the initial and the new prices and quantities demanded. Using this formula, we obtain

$$\bar{E} = -\frac{(100{,}000 - 300{,}000)/(100{,}000 + 300{,}000)}{(\$1 - \$0.50)/(\$1 + \$0.50)} = \frac{3}{2}$$

for either a price increase from 50 cents to $1.00 or a price decrease from $1.00 to 50 cents.

■ **Principle.** Demand is said to be elastic, unitary elastic, or inelastic according to the value of E. If $E > 1$, demand is elastic; a given percentage change in price results in a greater percentage change in quantity demanded. Thus, small price changes result in more significant changes in quantity demanded. When $E = 1$, demand has unitary elasticity, meaning that the percentage changes in price and quantity demanded are precisely the same. Finally, if $E < 1$, demand is inelastic. A given percentage change in price results in a smaller percentage change in quantity demanded.

Factors affecting elasticity

To this point in our discussion we have described the importance of price elasticity and have demonstrated a methodology for measuring price elasticity for a specific demand function. We now turn to an examination of the factors that affect the price elasticity of demand. We will indicate those characteristics of a commodity that make it more or less elastic. It follows then that even in the absence of direct estimates of price elasticity, a manager would be able to obtain a subjective measure of the price elasticity of a particular commodity based upon the characteristics of that commodity. As was the case with the determinants of demand, there may well be an infinitely large number of characteristics that affect the price elasticity of demand for a commodity. In this discussion we limit our attention to those factors that appear to be most significant: (1) the number and availability of substitute commodities, (2) the expenditure on the commodity in relation to the consumer's budget, (3) the durability of the product, (4) the number of uses for the commodity, and (5) the length of the time period under consideration.

Of these factors, the number and availability of substitute commodities is the most significant determinant of the price elasticity of demand. The more and better the substitutes for a specific good, the greater its price elasticity will be at a given set of prices. Goods with few and poor substitutes—wheat and salt, for example—will tend to have low price elasticities. Goods with many substitutes—wool, for which cotton and synthetic fibers may be substituted, for instance—will have higher elasticities.

Of course, the definition of a good greatly affects the number of substitutes and thus its elasticity of demand. For example, if all of the gasoline stations in a city raised the price of gasoline by 10 cents per gallon, total sales of gasoline would undoubtedly fall—but probably not by much. If, on the other hand, only the Gulf stations raised the price by 10 cents, the sale of Gulf gasoline would probably fall substantially. There are many good substitutes for Gulf gasoline at the lower price but there are not as many substitutes for gasoline in general. Moreover, if only one service station raised its price, that station's sales would be expected to fall almost to zero in the long run. The availability of so many easily accessible substitutes would encourage most customers to trade elsewhere, since the cost of finding a substitute service station is so small.

The percentage of the consumer's budget that is spent on the commodity is also important in the determination of price elasticity. All other things equal, we would expect the price elasticity to be directly related to the percentage of consumers' budgets spent on the good. For example, we expect that the demand for refrigerators would be more price elastic than the demand for toasters, since the expenditure required to purchase a refrigerator would make up a larger percentage of the budget of a "typical" consumer. Please note in this that we are not saying that price elasticity is determined by the price of the good. Rather, price elasticity is influenced by the relation between total expenditure on the good and the budget of potential consumers of the commodity.

Next, all other things equal, durable goods tend to be more price elastic than nondurable commodities. This relation results simply from the fact that the purchase of a durable good may be postponed. If the price of a durable commodity rises, quantity demanded would be expected to fall by a larger percentage than would be the case for nondurables because potential buyers have the option of "making do" with their existing durables. Returning to an earlier example, this reinforces our assertion that the demand for refrigerators would be more elastic than that for toasters because the refrigerator is more durable. The consumer can make do with the old refrigerator while he or she searches for the lowest price.

The greater the number of uses a commodity has, the greater its price elasticity will be. Thus a commodity such as wool—which can be used in producing clothing, carpeting, upholstery, draperies, tapestries, and so on—will tend to have a higher price elasticity than a commodity with only one or a very few uses—butter, for example.

Finally, the length of the time period under consideration affects the price elasticity of demand. In general, the longer the time period, the more elastic is the demand function. This relation is the result of consumers having more time to adapt to the price change. Excellent examples of the effect of time on demand elasticity are found in the demands for commodities such as gasoline or natural gas. The demand for such commodities is referred to as a "derived demand." That is, consumers do not desire gasoline per se; rather, they desire the services of automobiles or other machines that use gasoline. Hence, for consumers to adjust to changes in the price of gasoline, it is necessary for them to adjust their usage and stock of those machines that use gasoline. In the short run, an increase in the price of gasoline reduces quantity demanded, but this reduction is limited by the fact that the consumers still own their original stock of gasoline-using machinery. The reductions are, therefore, limited to decreased usage. Given a longer period of adjustment, consumers can alter their stock of gasoline-using equipment (for example, by switching to smaller automobiles). The response to the increased price of gasoline would then be more pronounced. Given a still longer period, it is possible that manufacturers will develop machinery that requires less gasoline and the reduction in quantity demanded would become even more significant. The point is that, given a longer time period to adjust, the demand for the commodity exhibits more responsiveness to changes in price—the demand curve is more elastic. Of course, we can treat the effect of time within the framework of the effect of available substitutes on elasticity. The greater the time period available for consumer adjustment, the more substitutes become available and economically feasible. As we stressed above, the more available are substitutes, the more elastic is demand.

APPLICATION

Time and the demand for petroleum

As you are aware, the United States experienced a resource crisis of monumental proportions during the 1970s. The average price of a barrel of oil rose from around \$2 in 1970 to \$35 in 1980. Consequently, the prices of gasoline and heating oil increased dramatically over this decade. After the Arabian oil embargo in 1973–74, most people were predicting disastrous consequences because of the supposed inability, or unwillingness, of consumers to cut back on the amount of oil they were consuming. In other words, the experts thought the demand for gasoline and heating oil was extremely inelastic. As it turned out they were right in the case of the short run, but wrong for the long run. The adaptation to the high energy prices during the 1970s provides an excellent example of the effect of time on the elasticity of demand.

The real price of oil actually fell from 1950 to the early 1970s. It's therefore not surprising that these were the days of the "gas guzzling" automobile. Why would we cut back on gasoline, when it was so cheap? Consumers wanted big cars because gas was cheap. It shouldn't surprise you either that most homes built during this period were not well insulated—they were quite energy inefficient. Insulation cost a lot of money, while heating oil was cheap.

But shortly after 1973, the price of oil tripled. The fact that people did not immediately cut back on consumption led to dismal predictions predicated on an inelastic demand for oil. Experts were saying that Americans were just naturally wasteful. But this prediction turned out to be wrong. Americans did decrease their consumption of oil—substantially. We adapted to the higher prices, but the adaptation took time.

Consider the time that was required to adjust to the higher price of heating oil. When the price went up, people added some insulation to their attics but they did not immediately hire someone to rip out and reinsulate the walls. This costs a considerable amount of money; so, many people simply paid the higher heating bills in order to save the expense of reinsulation. Of course, they did keep their homes a little cooler in winter and a little warmer in the summer, both of which helped conserve some energy. But the new homes that were built were becoming much more energy efficient. And, as people realized that the higher energy prices were going to be around for a long time, many did reinsulate their homes. Likewise, when the price of energy first increased, most people did not immediately replace their home appliances with more energy efficient appliances. But the appliances that were installed in new homes were more energy saving. And when people had to replace their old appliances, the ones they purchased were frequently more energy efficient. This substitution helped decrease the consumption of energy over time.

The same thing was happening in the market for gasoline. Again, when the price of gasoline tripled, people didn't immediately replace their "gas guzzlers" with economy cars. But when it became time to trade, they frequently opted for smaller, more fuel efficient automobiles. The owners of the largest cars generally didn't trade for the smallest compacts. But there was a general movement downward in size. The overall effect was a gradual decrease in automobile size, and a resulting increase in gasoline mileage. From 1973 to 1983 the average fuel efficiency of automobiles increased 18 percent. In addition, driving habits changed. Encouraged in part by lower speed limits and in part by the higher price of gasoline, people began driving more slowly, and consequently decreased their gasoline consumption.

So, the overall result was a decline in the amount of oil consumed. The United States reduced its dependence on imported oil from 50 percent of the total consumed, to 30 percent. And together with the increased production of domestic oil, the decrease in oil consumption significantly reduced the power of the OPEC nations.

The point is, however, that this price-induced decrease in consumption took time. The adaptation did not come overnight. It was practically impossible and certainly not economically feasible to adapt immediately to the change in relative prices. While the demand for energy was relatively inelastic at first, given a sufficient period of time, demand became much more elastic.

10.3 OTHER ELASTICITIES

In addition to own-price elasticity, we should note two other elasticities that are used in economic analysis: income elasticity and cross-price elasticity. Recall that when we derived the demand schedule we held constant the consumers' money income and the prices of other goods. Consequently, these are held constant when deriving market demand curves and evaluating the own-price elasticity of demand. But sometimes economists and business decision makers are interested in the effect of changes in one of these variables on quantity (sales) when the price of the good itself remains constant.

Let's first consider income elasticity, defined as follows:

■ **Definition.** Income elasticity measures the relative responsiveness of quantity purchased when income changes, holding the price of the good and the prices of other goods constant. It is, therefore, the percentage change in quantity purchased in response to a given percentage change in income.

Symbolically, we can express the preceding definition as

$$E_M = \frac{\%\Delta Q}{\%\Delta M} = \frac{\Delta Q/Q}{\Delta M/M} = \frac{\Delta Q}{\Delta M} \cdot \frac{M}{Q}$$

where E_M is income elasticity and M is income. (For market demand, per capita income is normally used.) Note that the sign of E_M depends upon the sign of $\Delta Q/\Delta M$, which may be positive (if the good is normal), negative (if the good is inferior), or zero. Thus, if the good is normal (inferior), the income elasticity is positive (negative).

The cross-price elasticity of a good is defined as follows

■ **Definition.** Cross-price elasticity measures the relative responsiveness of the quantity purchased of some good when the price of some other good changes, holding the price of the good and money income constant. It is, therefore, the percentage change in quantity purchased in response to a given percentage change in the price of another good.

We can express the cross-price elasticity between the good in question, X, and another good, Y, as

$$E_{XY} = \frac{\%\Delta X}{\%\Delta P_Y} = \frac{\Delta X/X}{\Delta P_Y/P_Y} = \frac{\Delta X}{\Delta P_Y} \cdot \frac{P_Y}{X}$$

where X is the amount of commodity X consumed and P_Y is the price of good Y. As was the case for income elasticity, the sign of E_{XY} depends upon the sign of $\Delta X/\Delta P_Y$, which can be positive or negative. Recall from Chapter 2 that if an increase in the price of one good causes the quantity purchased of another good to increase, we say the goods are substitutes (i.e., $\Delta X/\Delta P_Y > 0$). If the rise in the price of one good causes the quantity purchased of another good to fall, the goods are complements (i.e., $\Delta X/\Delta P_Y < 0$). If there is no change in the quantity purchased of the other good, the two goods are independent (i.e.,

$\Delta X/\Delta P_Y = 0$). Thus, E_{XY} is positive (negative) when X and Y are substitutes (complements).[1]

10.4 MARGINAL REVENUE AND ELASTICITY

The concept of marginal revenue will become quite important when we begin to analyze the production and pricing decisions of firms under various market structures in Parts 4 and 5. Let us begin with a definition:

■ **Definition.** Marginal revenue is the addition to total revenue attributable to one additional unit of sales (per period of time),

$$MR = \Delta TR/\Delta Q$$

To show you the relation between marginal revenue and price (i.e., points on the demand curve), let's first use a numerical example. The demand schedule for a product is presented in columns 1 and 2 of Table 10.4. Price times quantity gives the total revenue obtainable from each level of sales, shown in column 3.

Table 10.4
Demand and marginal revenue

(1) Unit sales	(2) Price	(3) Total revenue	(4) Marginal revenue
1	$4.00	$ 4.00	$ 4.00
2	3.50	7.00	3.00
3	3.10	9.30	2.30
4	2.80	11.20	1.90
5	2.40	12.00	.80
6	2.00	12.00	.00
7	1.50	10.50	−1.50

Marginal revenue, shown in column 4, indicates the change in total revenue from an additional unit of sales. Note that marginal revenue equals price only for the first unit sold. At zero sales, total revenue is zero; for the first unit sold total revenue is the demand price for one unit. Thus the change in total revenue is the same as price. However, since price must fall in order to sell additional units, marginal revenue must be less than price at every other level of sales (output).

As shown in column 4, marginal revenue declines for each additional unit sold. Notice that it is positive for each unit 1 through 5. However, marginal revenue is zero for the sixth unit sold, and marginal revenue becomes negative thereafter. That is, the seventh unit sold actually causes total revenue to decline.

---

[1]Note that, because of the possibility of different income effects, the cross-price elasticity of X for Y need not equal the cross-price elasticity of Y for X.

■ **Relation.** Marginal revenue must be less than price for all units sold after the first because price must be lowered in order to sell more units.

Figure 10.3 illustrates the relations between demand, marginal revenue, and total revenue for a linear demand curve. As mentioned above, *MR* is below price at every output level except the first. (Since we have assumed continuous data, the two are equal at an output level that is infinitesimally close to zero.) Also, since demand is negatively sloped, *MR* must also be negatively sloped. Finally, *MR* must at some output equal zero. (In Figure 10.3, *MR* equals zero at output x_0 and price p_0.) At larger levels of output *MR* must be negative.

Figure 10.3
Demand, marginal revenue, and total revenue

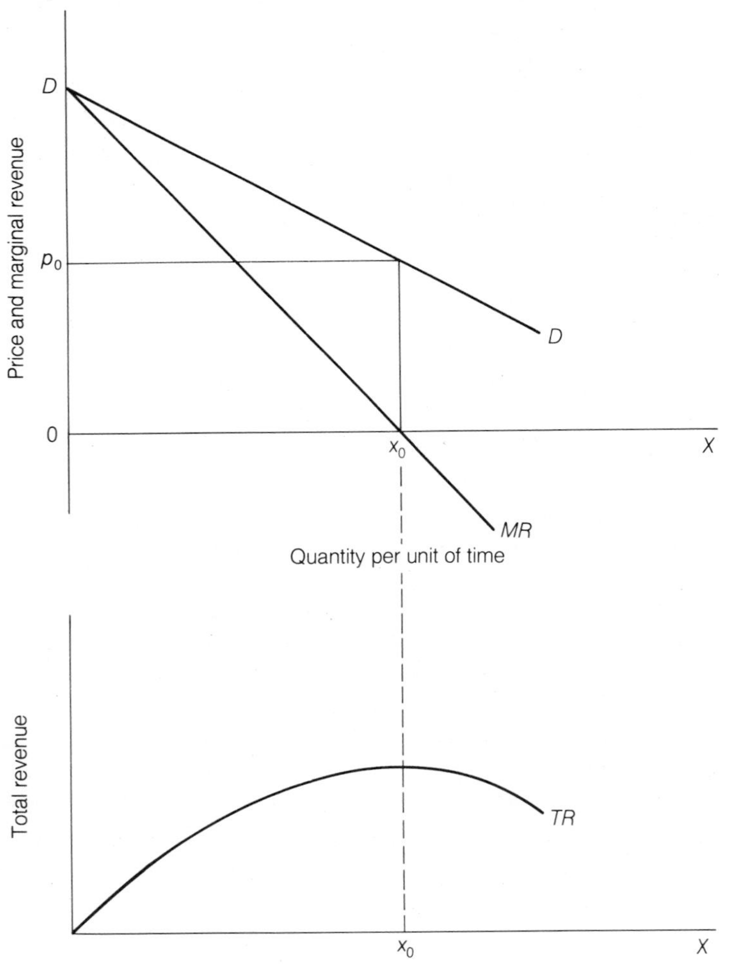

Using the marginal revenue curve, we can obtain information about total revenue and demand elasticity. For example, if marginal revenue is positive, total revenue must increase when price falls and output increases; so, demand must be elastic. Recall that if total revenue rises (falls) when price falls, demand is elastic (inelastic). Conversely, if marginal revenue is negative, total revenue would decline if price was decreased; and demand is therefore inelastic. Finally, if marginal revenue is zero, total revenue does not change when output changes, and the elasticity of demand is unitary. Referring to Figure 10.3 we see that marginal revenue is positive until output x_0 is reached and is negative at greater levels of output. Using the preceding relation, this means that total revenue increases as output increases to x_0 and therefore demand is elastic over the range from zero to x_0. Demand has unitary elasticity at x_0 and is inelastic at outputs larger than x_0, since beyond this point total revenue decreases as output increases.

While demand and marginal revenue are both linear in Figure 10.3, the preceding relations also hold for nonlinear curves. In all cases marginal revenue lies below demand.

The relation between marginal revenue and price at any quantity can be expressed still more precisely. Suppose that at price p_0, quantity demanded is x_0. In order to sell an additional unit, price must fall from p_0 to p_1. That is, as price falls from p_0 to p_1, quantity increases from x_0 to $x_0 + 1$. Since the price has been decreased, the revenue generated by the original level of sales must fall. The decline in total revenue due to the decrease in price is

$$(p_1 - p_0)x_0 = (\Delta p)x_0$$

But this decline is to a greater or lesser extent offset by the revenue generated by the additional unit sold at price p_1. This increase is $p_1 \times 1$, or p_1. Combining the two changes in revenue resulting from the price change, marginal revenue—the change in total revenue—is therefore

$$MR = p_1 + \Delta p \cdot x_0$$

where Δp is negative.

Since $\Delta x = 1$, we can divide Δp by Δx with no change in the value of the expression.

$$MR = p_1 + \frac{\Delta p}{\Delta x} x_0$$

Now, let's factor p_1 out of the right-hand side of this equation

$$MR = p_1\left(1 + \frac{\Delta p}{\Delta x} \cdot \frac{x_0}{p_1}\right)$$

and rewrite this equation as

$$MR = p_1\left[1 - \frac{1}{\left(-\dfrac{\Delta x}{\Delta p} \cdot \dfrac{p_1}{x_0}\right)}\right]$$

At this point you should see what we have been moving toward. The expression

$$-\frac{\Delta x}{\Delta p} \cdot \frac{p_1}{x_0}$$

is a very close approximation to the own-price elasticity of demand. Hence, we can rewrite our equation as

$$MR = p_1\left(1 - \frac{1}{E}\right)$$

or, as long as $p_0 - p_1$ is small,

$$MR = p\left(1 - \frac{1}{E}\right)$$

where E is the own-price elasticity of demand.[2] From this equation it is apparent that when marginal revenue is negative, demand is inelastic ($E < 1$). When marginal revenue is positive, demand is elastic ($E > 1$). Finally, when marginal revenue is zero, demand has unitary elasticity.

APPLICATION

Demand elasticity in the airline industry

Prior to 1979, the airline industry was regulated. The Civil Aeronautics Board (CAB) regulated the prices airlines could charge for tickets, the routes that could be flown, and entry into the industry. In effect, the airlines were protected from price competition. And most experts in the area believed that the regulated prices were above those that would have evolved if an unregulated market had been allowed to function.

This is not to say that the airlines did not compete for passengers. They did. But they didn't compete by changing price. They competed for passengers by increasing the service offered on flights and by increasing the number of flights—lowering the amount of time a passenger had to wait.

After deregulation in 1979, the airlines began to compete for passengers by lowering prices. Frequently, the price reductions took the form of special

---

[2]For the mathematically inclined student, total revenue is simply

$$TR = P \cdot Q$$

so,

$$\frac{dTR}{dQ} = P + \frac{dP}{dQ} \cdot Q$$

$$= P\left(1 + \frac{dP}{dQ} \cdot \frac{Q}{P}\right)$$

Then, using the definition of the own-price elasticity of demand

$$MR = P\left(1 - \frac{1}{E}\right)$$

fares ("super savers") that involved certain restrictions on travel (e.g., certain days of the week, specified flights, and minimum length of stay at the destination). The price reductions were successful for the airlines in the sense that, for a while, airline profits increased. As it turned out, market demand was relatively elastic; so, as fares were reduced, revenues increased for most carriers in the period immediately following deregulation. The fare reductions were aimed primarily at vacation, rather than business, travelers. As we noted, most of the fare reductions were coupled with restrictions on the length of stay and/or advance bookings. Such restrictions would make it less likely for the business traveler to take advantage of the fare reductions. Given this, what can we say about the elasticity of demand for "vacation air travel"?

First, vacation air travel has several good substitutes (alternative modes of transportation), the existence of which would indicate that the demand curve should be elastic. (The time constraint on a business traveler may make alternative modes of transportation less substitutable for airline travel.)

Second, air travel represents a substantial percentage of the typical family's vacation budget. As we have noted, the larger the expenditure on a good or service as a percentage of total budget, the more elastic is the demand for the commodity, if the good is normal.

Finally, vacation travel itself is a "durable" commodity in the sense that it is postponable. Since the consumer can postpone (or forgo) such expenditures, we would expect the demand for vacation airline travel to be more elastic.

But, as time went on, deregulation permitted new entry into the industry. New airlines, in large part regional carriers, began to compete for passengers. These new lines were frequently able to operate at considerably lower cost than the established lines and were therefore able to cut fares on virtually all flights. The major carriers matched these fare reductions, resulting in a series of price wars that proved disastrous to the industry.

Fares dropped sharply from 1981 through the first half of 1983. Over this period the fare decreases were more general than in the period immediately after deregulation. Business travelers were able to fly at the reduced fares; but, for reasons mentioned above, the demand for business travel proved much less elastic than the demand for vacation travel. Thus, total demand was much less elastic—less responsive to these price changes. Since there was very little increase in business travel during this period, revenues for the major carriers fell sharply, as did profits.

And, as we noted, by this time more and more new airlines were competing for the limited number of passengers, cutting further into revenues and profits. The major carriers began to recognize that their price cuts would be followed by other carriers. Consequently, fare reductions did not increase anyone's share of the market. Everyone was worse off if fares were reduced. That is, the demand function facing the *individual* airline was very inelastic.

To get some idea of the effect of the fare wars, note that the average price of airline tickets fell from 13 cents a mile in 1981 to 11 cents a mile by mid-1983. Every one-cent decrease in the average ticket price per mile led to a reduction in yearly revenues for the industry of $2.7 billion. Thus, even very small decreases in ticket prices led to staggering losses for most firms, because each firm faced an inelastic demand curve.*

---

*We will return to this example and discuss what the airlines did about the fare wars in an Application to be presented in Chapter 18.

10.5 SUMMARY

Market demand is simply the aggregation of the demands of individual consumers in the market. Specifically, the market demand function is the horizontal summation of all the individual demand functions. Since the demands of individual consumers are downward sloping, the market demand function must be downward sloping.

Demand elasticity—the own-price elasticity of demand—is the percentage change in quantity demanded in response to a given percentage change in price. Demand elasticity is said to be unitary ($E = 1$), when the two percentage changes are equal. Demand is elastic (inelastic) when the percentage change in quantity demanded is greater (less) than the percentage change in price. If demand is elastic (inelastic) over a range of output, an increase in price and the resulting decrease in quantity demanded cause total revenue (total expenditures on the good by consumers) to fall (rise). A decrease in price causes total revenue to rise (fall) if demand is elastic (inelastic). Several factors affect the own-price elasticity of demand. The most important of these factors is the availability of good substitutes. The better and more numerous are its substitutes, the more elastic is demand.

Two other elasticities are income elasticity, measuring the relative responsiveness of quantity purchased to changes in income, and cross-price elasticity, measuring the relative responsiveness of the quantity purchased of one good to changes in the price of another good. These elasticities can be positive or negative. In the case of income elasticity, the elasticity measure is positive (negative) if the good is normal (inferior). In the case of cross-price elasticity, the elasticity measure is positive (negative) if the two goods are substitutes (complements).

Marginal revenue is the change in total revenue resulting from an additional unit of sales. Marginal revenue declines as output increases and is less than price for every quantity except the first unit, in which case MR equals price. Marginal revenue can be expressed as

$$MR = p\left(1 - \frac{1}{E}\right)$$

where E is the own-price elasticity of demand. Hence, if demand is elastic (inelastic), marginal revenue is positive (negative). If demand is unitary elastic, marginal revenue is equal to zero.

Technical Problems

1. Recall from our definitions that own-price, income, and cross-price elasticities must be calculated holding all other variables constant. Using data from the following table, calculate, were possible, the own-price, income, and cross-price elasticity. Use the averaging method.

Quantity	*Price*	*Price of a related good*	*Per capita income*
10,000	$20	$30	$3,000
12,000	20	30	2,000
12,000	20	40	3,000
10,000	30	40	3,000

Is demand elastic or inelastic? Is the related good a complement or a substitute? Is the good inferior or normal?

2. Use the definition of own-price elasticity to answer the following questions:
   a. You know that the own-price elasticity of demand is 1.5. Price rises by 10 percent. How will quantity demanded change?
   b. Suppose elasticity is still 1.5 but the quantity supplied to the market falls by 10 percent. What will happen to price?
3. The following data table relates the percentage change in the purchase of automobiles to percentage changes in income and the price of automobiles. (The numbers in the body of the table give the percentage change in auto purchases.)

		Percentage change in income				
		−10	−5	0	+5	+10
Percentage change in price	+10	−20	−15	−10	−5	0
	+5	−15	−10	−5	0	+5
	0	−10	−5	0	+5	+10
	−5	−5	0	+5	+10	+15
	−10	0	+5	+10	+15	+20

   a. What is the own-price elasticity of demand for automobiles?
   b. What is the income elasticity of demand for automobiles?
   c. One automaker reduces the price of one of its models from $10,000 to $9,000. Sales of this car increase 10 percent. But at the same time incomes increase by 5 percent. What does this indicate about the own-price elasticity of demand for this particular car?
4. Suppose that government sales of wheat to foreign buyers reduce the amount of wheat available for U.S. consumers.
   a. What will happen to the domestic price of wheat?
   b. What will happen to the amount spent on wheat by U.S. consumers? What additional information must you have?

5. Using the following demand schedule, show the relation between marginal revenue, price, and own-price elasticity.

Price	Quantity demanded
$20	1,000
15	1,400
10	1,800

6. Demand schedules A, B, and C are the aggregate demands for three types of consumers in a market. There are 10 consumers of type A, 5 of type B, and 12 of type C. Derive and graph the market demand for the entire group of consumers.

(A)		(B)		(C)	
Price	Quantity demanded	Price	Quantity demanded	Price	Quantity demanded
$10	2	$10	0	$10	1
8	6	8	4	8	2
6	10	6	8	6	3
4	12	4	10	4	4
2	13	2	12	2	5

7. "I earn $20 a day and spend it all on beer, no matter what the price of beer is." What is this person's elasticity of demand for beer?
8. Seltzer Company sells spring water at a desert oasis; its costs are virtually zero. Seltzer knows that its demand function is $Q = 25 - (3/2)P$. Presently it charges a price of $2. Seltzer wishes to increase its profits. Do you recommend a price change? If so what price would you suggest?

ANALYTICAL PROBLEMS

1. Suppose a quota on imported steel substantially increases the price of steel in the United States. The higher price is expected to last a long time. Discuss the effect of time on the elasticity of demand for steel.
2. Suppose a severe freeze destroys one third of the Florida orange crop, but does not destroy many trees. Discuss the effect of the freeze on the citrus farmers and the effect of time on the elasticity of demand for orange juice.
3. It has often been argued that the demand for agricultural products is (own) price inelastic. Given that farmers want to increase their own incomes, what policies should they try to implement? How could they enforce these policies? What problems might be involved?
4. Consider the demand for automobiles. Would you expect it to be relatively elastic or inelastic? What characteristics of this commodity lead to your assertions?

5. Suppose Saudi Arabia doubles the quantity of oil it puts on the market each year. Describe the adaptive process over time in the United States. Who would benefit and who would lose?
6. You are assistant to the president of a large state university. The university, faced with declining enrollment, is considering a large decrease in tuition. You are asked to forecast the effect. What factors would you have to consider? Explain.

11

Empirical demand functions

We have already talked about the demand function from a theoretical perspective on several occasions: In Chapter 2 we presented a brief overview of demand theory. Chapter 9 demonstrated how an individual consumer's demand function is derived, using the theory of consumer behavior. Then, in Chapter 10, we described the market demand function and the important concept of demand elasticities.

However, we have not yet discussed how demand functions can be estimated or how managers can interpret and use the resulting estimations. From the discussion in the earlier chapters, it should be clear how important knowledge about the demand function is to a manager. In planning and in making policy decisions, managers must have some idea about the characteristics of the demand for their product in order to attain the objectives of the firm or even to enable the firm to survive. In this chapter, we will show you some of the methods used in the estimation and interpretation of demand functions.

We begin with a description of some of the more direct methods of demand estimation—consumer interviews and market studies. We deal rather briefly with these methods, attempting only to point out the strengths and weaknesses in each. The primary topic of the chapter is the use of regression analysis to estimate demand functions. As always, our fundamental concern is with how an analyst can use regression analysis and interpret the results, rather than with the precise statistical concepts underlying the estimation. We will provide some examples to show how actual demand functions have been estimated and interpreted.

11.1 DIRECT METHODS OF DEMAND ESTIMATION

We should note that the following discussion of consumer interviews (surveys) and market studies (or experiments) is meant only to be a brief introduction to these techniques. There are entire courses that deal with these topics. Our purpose here is to provide an overview and mention some of the problems involved rather than to teach you how actually to carry out these direct estimates.

Consumer interviews

It would appear that, since consumers themselves should be most knowledgeable about their individual demand functions for particular commodities, the most straightforward method of demand estimation would be simply to ask potential buyers how much of the commodity they would buy at different prices with alternative values for the determinants of demand (i.e., the price of substitute commodities, the price of complement commodities, and so on). At the simplest level, this might be accomplished by stopping shoppers and asking them how much of the product they would buy at various prices. At a more sophisticated level, this procedure would entail administering detailed questionnaires to a selected sample of the population by professional interviewers. While this procedure appears very simple, there exist several substantial problems. Among these problems are (1) the selection of a representative sample, (2) response bias, and (3) the inability of the respondent to answer accurately. Let us discuss each of these problems briefly.

If the results of a survey accomplished by using a sample of the population are to be reliable, *the sample must be representative* of the total population. More specifically, the sample should be random. In actuality, it is very difficult to obtain a truly random sample. A classic illustration of a bad result from a lack of randomness occurred during the presidential campaign of 1948. A survey was performed that predicted an overwhelming victory for Dewey. In fact Truman won the election. The problem with this survey was that the sample was drawn from the subscription list of a particular magazine. The subscribers were not representative of the entire population of the United States; they were instead a subgroup of the voting population having several important characteristics in common. Thus, the biased sample led to biased results.

A *bias in response* can result simply from the fact that those interviewed are giving hypothetical answers to hypothetical questions. The answers do not necessarily reflect what the individual will do; but, rather, they may reflect intentions or desires. More importantly, however, the responses may be biased by the manner in which the question is asked. In many cases, the questions may be such that the respondents give what they view as a more socially acceptable response rather than reveal their true preferences.

One example of response bias is found in a survey by an automobile manufacturer taken many years ago—during the time of cheap gasoline. The potential consumers were asked if they would be interested in buying small economical cars (i.e., fuel-efficient) which were not flashy, fast, or showy. A large number of people said they would indeed buy such a car. On the basis of this survey, the manufacturer introduced a small, fuel-efficient car—with disastrous results. (Perhaps had the respondents—who indicated that they wanted economy cars—been asked whether their *neighbors* would buy such cars they might have provided more valid responses. It's easier to say that your neighbor wants a flashy car than to admit that you do.) The point is that the wrong question was asked. The way the question was asked induced a response bias. As you might expect, it takes an expert to design a questionnaire that avoids such bias.

Finally, it is quite possible that the respondent is simply *unable to answer accurately the question posed.* Conceptually, the firm performing the survey may want to know about the elasticity of demand for its products. Thus, the firm is interested in the response of consumers to incremental changes. For example, the firm needs to know how the consumers would react to such things as a 1, 2, or 3 percent increase (or decrease) in price or a 5 percent increase (decrease) in advertising expenditures. Obviously, most persons interviewed are not able to answer such questions precisely.

THE WALL STREET JOURNAL

APPLICATION

Problems with consumer interviews

We have mentioned some of the problems that can be encountered in surveys. Let's look at some examples.

As was noted in *The Wall Street Journal,* the food industry has a lot riding on the claims people make about what they eat.* Food companies have, in the past, conducted their market research by asking people what they eat. Based on the results of these surveys, the food manufacturers would develop their new products. But, as the *Journal* noted, there is one big problem: "People don't always tell the truth."

As Harry Balzer (the vice president of a market research firm) put it: "Nobody likes to admit he likes junk food." In this instance, the problem is that there exists a response bias in such surveys. Instead of answering truthfully, the consumer is very likely to give a socially acceptable answer. As Mr. Balzer said, asking a sweet-eater how many Twinkies he eats "is like asking an alcoholic if he drinks much."

A different problem was encountered by Owens-Corning Fiberglass Corporation.† During a home-building convention, the firm commissioned a survey to determine the industry's outlook for 1984. The results were startling: The survey indicated that builders were planning to increase housing starts by an amazing 30 percent!

Owens-Corning convened a news conference to announce their findings; but the star of the news conference turned out to be Michael Sumichrast (chief economist for the National Association of Home Builders). When asked to interpret the bullish forecast he replied that "it shows when you ask stupid questions, you get stupid answers." Mr. Sumichrast's point was that the survey did not use a representative sample. According to the *Journal,* the survey was taken only among the builders who attended the convention and these builders tend to be the larger and more aggressive companies.

*"Study to Detect True Eating Habits Finds Junk-Food Fans in the Health-Food Ranks," by Betsy Morris, *The Wall Street Journal,* February 3, 1984. Reprinted by permission of *The Wall Street Journal*. ©Dow Jones & Company, Inc., 1984. All rights reserved.

†"Stupid Questions," *The Wall Street Journal,* February 7, 1984. Reprinted by permission of *The Wall Street Journal*. ©Dow Jones & Company, Inc., 1984. All rights reserved.

While the survey technique is plagued by these inherent difficulties, we do not wish to imply that it is without merit. Indeed, in many situations, it is extremely useful. A good example of such a situation is when a firm is interested in obtaining information about consumers' views about the commodity in question and related products, as well as their expectations concerning future economic conditions.

Market studies and experiments

An interesting, though somewhat more expensive and difficult, technique for estimating demand and demand elasticity is the controlled market study or experiment. The analyst attempts to hold everything constant during the study except for the price of the good.

Those carrying out these market studies normally display the products in several different stores, generally in areas with differing characteristics, over a period of time. They make certain that there are always sufficient amounts available in every store at each price to satisfy demand. In this way the effect of changes in supply is removed. There is generally no advertising. During the period of the experiment, price is changed in relatively small increments over a range, and sales are recorded at each price. In this way, many of the effects of changes in other things can be removed, and a reasonable approximation of the actual demand curve can be estimated.

THE WALL STREET JOURNAL
APPLICATION

Exhaustive market studies for fast foods

While the results of market studies—e.g., the demand elasticities—are seldom, if ever, publically disclosed, we do see that many firms use this technique. An excellent example is a discussion of market studies in the "fast-food market" that appeared in *The Wall Street Journal*.*

According to this article: "As luring more customers gets more difficult, McDonald's and other fast-food companies are forced to become increasingly sophisticated about how they decide what foods to sell (and what to charge for them). They are adopting the exhaustive market-research techniques more typical of packaged-goods companies and designing elaborate procedures for formulating a product and introducing it into thousands of restaurants."

Before a new product is introduced nationally by one of the fast-food chains, it will have been subjected not only to internal tests in the test kitchens but also to test marketing. By conducting these market studies, the firm can find information regarding the demand for and price elasticity of the new product. Furthermore, a fast-food firm can also use test marketing to evaluate the new product's potential impact on sales of other items (the cross-price elasticity) and on the overall efficiency of the restaurant operation.

The importance McDonald's places on test marketing was indicated by an anecdote. According to the vice president of product development, the late Ray Kroc (founder of McDonald's) insisted on sampling new products: "We always had to include franchises near his home in test markets."

---

*"Fast-Food Firms' New Items Undergo Exhaustive Testing" by John Koten, *The Wall Street Journal,* January 5, 1984. Reprinted by permission of *The Wall Street Journal*.

A relatively new technique for estimating demand is the use of experiments performed in a laboratory or in the field. Such experiments are a compromise between market studies and surveys. In some types of laboratory experiments, volunteers are paid to simulate actual buying conditions without going through real markets. Volunteer "consumers" are given money to go on simulated market trips. The experimenter changes relative prices between trips. After many "shopping trips" by many "consumers" an approximation to demand is obtained. The volunteers have the incentive to act as though they are really shopping, because there is a probability that they may keep their purchases.

Going a step further, some economists have conducted experiments about consumer behavior—with the help of psychologists—in mental institutions and in drug centers, by setting up token economies (which incidentally are supposed to have therapeutic value). Patients receive tokens for jobs performed. They can exchange these tokens for goods and services. The experimenters can change prices and incomes and thus generate demand curves, the properties of which are compared with the theoretical properties of such curves.

In field experiments, the researchers want to be able to change the price of goods and actually observe the behavior of the consumers. To illustrate this type of experiment, let us give you an example.

APPLICATION

The residential demand for electricity*

A question that took on particular importance during the ''energy crisis'' of the 1970s is the own-price elasticity of the demand for energy. While many analysts and researchers used various techniques for examining this issue, some of our colleagues at Texas A & M elected to use an experimental approach.

The researchers selected a random sample of some 100 households in College Station, Texas, and recruited these households to participate in the experiment. The objective of the study was to observe these households' weekly consumption of electric power in June, July, and August—certainly a period in which electricity consumption for cooling in south Texas is substantial. After first establishing the households' baseline levels of usage, the researchers then experimentally changed the price of electric power for part of their sample. They changed the price by paying rebates for reduction in weekly electricity usage.

For example, in one of their subgroups, the researchers paid the household 1.3 cents for every kilowatt hour (kwh) reduction in weekly usage. At the time this study was conducted, the cost of electrical power to the residential consumers was 2.6 cents per kwh. Therefore, for this subgroup, the price of consuming an additional kwh was increased: To consume an additional kwh, the household not only had to *pay* 2.6 cents but also had to *forgo* the rebate of 1.3 cents they could have received had they conserved rather than consumed electricity. Hence, for this subgroup, the price of electricity increased by 50 percent, from 2.6 to 3.9 cents per kwh.

Other subgroups were given other rebate schedules. And one subgroup—the control group—was given no rebate. The researchers could then actually measure the reduction in electricity consumption due to the experimentally-imposed price increase by comparing the change in the consumption of the subgroup receiving the rebate with the change in the consumption of the control group.

The results of this experimental study indicated that the maximum own-price elasticity of the residential demand for electricity was 0.32. That is, the experiment indicated that the residential demand for electricity was very price inelastic. As the researchers indicated, potential users of this estimate should keep in mind that this study measured a very short-run elasticity. (As we noted in Chapter 10, we would expect the price elasticity to increase as the time period for adjustment gets longer.)

*This application is taken from Raymond C. Battalio, John H. Kagel, Robin C. Winkler, and Richard A. Wineh, ''Residential Electricity Demand: An Experimental Study.'' *The Review of Economics and Statistics,* May 1979, pp. 180–89.

11.2 ESTIMATION OF DEMAND USING REGRESSION ANALYSIS

In earlier chapters, we showed how a manager can use the techniques of regression to estimate production and cost functions. We now want to use these techniques to obtain estimates of the market demand function. In the main, this procedure follows the lines of the other estimations we have done. However, there is a special problem that is encountered when we estimate a demand function—the simultaneous equations problem. While the statistics involved in this problem is beyond the level we want to reach in this text, we do want to indicate the nature of the problem and the fact that there are readily available "canned" computer programs that can handle this problem. Again, as we have stressed before, we don't intend to teach you statistics (or econometrics). Instead, we want to give you an idea as to how these techniques can provide the input needed in managerial decision making.

In order to estimate a demand function, it will first be necessary to use a specific functional form. We will consider both linear and nonlinear demand functions. Before proceeding, however, let us simplify the demand function we introduced in Chapter 2 somewhat. We have already noted the difficulties inherent in quantifying taste and price expectations; therefore, let us eliminate those variables for now and rewrite the demand function as

$$Q_{X,t} = f(P_{X,t},\ Y_t,\ P_{R,t})$$

where

$Q_{X,t}$ = quantity purchased of commodity X in period t
$P_{X,t}$ = price of X in period t
Y_t = consumers' income in period t
$P_{R,t}$ = the price of related commodities in period t

A linear demand function

The simplest demand function would be one that specifies a linear relation. That is, using the general demand function above, we could write our empirical demand function as

$$Q_X = a + bP_X + cY + dP_R$$

In this equation, the parameter b measures the change in quantity demanded that would result from a one unit change in the price of X. That is, $b = \Delta Q_X/\Delta P_X$, which is assumed to be negative.[1] Likewise,

---

[1]For the student with a background in mathematics, we should note that b is actually the partial derivative of quantity demanded with respect to price,

$$b = \partial Q_X/\partial P_X$$

$$c = \Delta Q_X/\Delta Y \;\; > 0 \text{ if } X \text{ is a normal good}$$

$$d = \Delta Q_X/\Delta P_R \;\; \substack{> \\ <} \;\; 0 \text{ if commodity } R \text{ is a} \begin{cases} \text{substitute} \\ \text{complement} \end{cases}$$

Using the techniques of regression analysis, this linear demand function could be estimated to provide estimates of the parameters *a, b, c,* and *d*. The *t*-tests would be performed to determine if these parameters are statistically significant.

As we stressed in Chapter 10, the elasticity of demand is a crucial feature. The elasticities of demand—with respect to own price, income, and the prices of related commodities can be calculated from a linear demand function without much difficulty. Consider first the own-price elasticity. In Chapter 10 this was defined as

$$E = -\frac{\Delta Q_X}{\Delta P_X} \cdot \frac{P_X}{Q_X}$$

Incorporating the fact that, in the linear specification, $b = \Delta Q_X/\Delta P_X$, the estimated own-price elasticity is

$$\hat{E} = -\hat{b} \cdot \frac{P_X}{Q_X}$$

The problem is the choice of the price and quantity values to be used. Obviously, this elasticity could be evaluated at any price and output combination. Given the properties of regression analysis, it might be most meaningful to evaluate the elasticity at the mean values for price and output (i.e., at $\bar{P}_X$ and $\bar{Q}_X$). Note that if $\hat{b}$ is statistically significant, the estimated elasticity, $\hat{E}$, will also be statistically significant.

In a similar manner, the income elasticity may be calculated as

$$\hat{E}_Y = \hat{c} \cdot \frac{Y}{Q_X}$$

Likewise, the cross-price elasticity is

$$\hat{E}_{XR} = \hat{d} \cdot \frac{P_R}{Q_X}$$

A nonlinear demand function

The most commonly employed nonlinear demand specification is the log-linear (or constant elasticity) form. Using the general specification above, a log-linear demand function would be written as

$$Q_X = aP_X^bY^cP_R^d$$

The obvious potential advantage of this form is that it would provide a better estimate if the true demand function is indeed nonlinear. Furthermore, as we know from Chapter 4, this specification allows for the direct estimation of the elasticities. Specifically, the absolute value of parameter b measures the own-price elasticity of demand.[2] Likewise, c and d, respectively, measure the income elasticity and cross-price elasticity of demand.

As we know from Chapter 4, in order to obtain estimates from the log-linear demand function, we must convert it to logarithms. Thus, the function to be estimated is

$$\log Q_X = \log a + b \log P_X + c \log Y + d \log P_R$$

The identification problem

To this point we have approached the problem of estimating a demand function as a simple application of regression analysis—i.e., a regression of observed quantity sold on observed price and the other variables. However, a problem arises from the fact that the observed quantities sold and observed prices are not simply points on a specific demand curve but rather represent points of market equilibrium. The observed points are the result of the *simultaneous* interaction of supply and demand.

To illustrate the difficulties that can be encountered, let's consider the following simplified forms of the demand and supply functions

$$\text{Demand: } Q = \alpha + \beta P$$
$$\text{Supply: } Q = a + bP$$

From an empirical standpoint, four situations might exist:

1. Both the demand and supply functions are stable.
2. The supply function is stable; but, the demand function is shifting (due perhaps to changes in income).
3. The demand function is stable; but, the supply function is shifting (due perhaps to changes in the price of inputs).
4. Both the demand and supply functions are shifting.

Let us examine each of these situations in turn to see what happens if we attempt to estimate the demand function simply by regressing observed quantity sold on observed price.

---

[2]As we demonstrated in Chapter 10 own-price elasticity is written as

$$E = -\partial Q_X/\partial P_X \cdot P_X/Q_X$$

with this log-linear specification

$$\partial Q_X/\partial P_X = baP_X^{b-1}Y^cP_R^d = \frac{bQ_X}{P_X}$$

Therefore

$$E = -\frac{bQ_X}{P_X} \cdot \frac{P_X}{Q_X} = -b$$

Figure 11.1
Problems in estimating demand functions

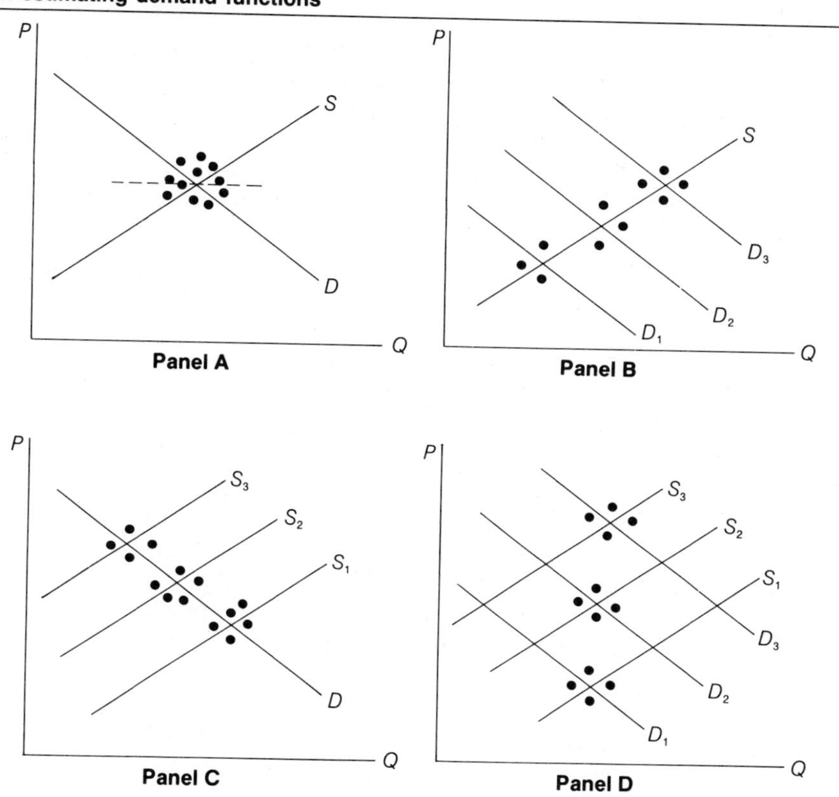

Case 1 is illustrated Panel A of Figure 11.1. If both demand and supply are stable, the equilibrium price and quantity will be subject only to random variation; thus, the observed price and quantity points would be as shown by the scatter of points in this figure. Then, if price were regressed on output, one would obtain simply a horizontal line (as shown as the dashed line in this figure). That is, in this situation, regressing observed output on observed price would result in a conclusion that no relation exists between price and output. Clearly, interpreting this line as a demand function would be a very serious error.

Case 2 is illustrated in Panel B. In this case we have shifted demand from D_1 to D_2 and then to D_3 (as would be the case if the good is normal and income increases). Thus, there are three points of equilibrium. As before, since the actual price-quantity points are subject to random variation about the equilibrium, the observed points would be similar to the scatter presented in this figure. In this instance, attempting to obtain an estimate of the demand function by simply regressing output on price would result in a positive relation between price and output. More specifically, in this case, such a simple estimation would result in an estimate of the supply function rather than the demand function.

In case 3, shown in Panel C of Figure 11.1, supply has shifted from S_1 to S_2 and then to S_3 (as a result, for instance, of increasing input prices), while demand has remained stable. Again, the actual observed price and quantity points are distributed around the equilibrium points. Regressing output on price will indeed result in a good estimation of the demand function. That is, in this case, fitting a regression line through the illustrated scatter of points will provide an estimate of the true demand function, D.

Finally, Panel D illustrates a possible result if both the demand and supply functions are shifting. In this case, we again have three equilibrium points (the intersections of D_1S_1, D_2S_2, D_3S_3) with the observed price-quantity points scattered randomly around these equilibria. It is easily seen that a regression of quantity on price will, in this case, provide an estimate of neither the demand nor the supply function. Such a regression would be analogous simply to connecting the equilibrium points for different demand and supply functions.

From the preceding discussion it would appear that simple regression analysis is useful only in the case in which the demand curve is stable and the supply curve is shifting—a circumstance that is generally not guaranteed. Statistical techniques designed to handle this problem do exist. But, in order to estimate a demand function it must first be *identified*.

To illustrate what we mean by a demand function being identified, look again at Figure 11.1. Only in case 3 (Panel C) would regression analysis provide a meaningful estimate of the true demand function. More specifically, only in case 3 was the demand function identified. Mathematically, this is a case in which the demand curve is stable,

$$D\colon Q = \alpha + \beta P$$

and the supply curve is shifting in response to changes in, say, the price of inputs (P_F),

$$S\colon Q = a + bP + cP_F$$

In this case, since both output, Q, and price, P, are determined in the marketplace, they are both *endogenous* variables. The price of inputs, P_F, is determined outside of this market and is, therefore, *exogenous*. The demand function contains one endogenous variable on the right-hand side; but the supply function contains one exogenous variable not included in the demand function. This set of circumstances causes the demand function to be identified. In more general terms, the necessary conditions for the identification of a demand function can be stated as follows:[3]

[3]In a more general case, if we want to be able to identify one equation in a system of simultaneous equations, the necessary condition for identification is:

> The number of exogenous variables in the system excluded from the equation must be greater than or equal to the number of endogenous variables included on the right-hand side of the equation.

■ **Definition.** The demand function is identified if the supply function contains at least one exogenous variable that is not in the demand function.

Conversely, the supply function will be identified if the demand function contains at least one exogenous variable not in the supply function.

Using this rule, let us return to a more general formulation. In linear form, our demand function is

$$Q_X = a + bP_X + cY + dP_R$$

We could specify a simplified, linear supply function as

$$Q_X = e + fP_X + gT + hP_F$$

where T is the level of technology. Since the output and the price of X are determined within the market, Q_X and P_X are endogenous. The remainder of the variables (Y, P_R, T, P_F) are exogenous because they are determined outside the market. Is the demand function identified? The demand function contains one endogenous variable on the right-hand side, P_X. There exist, however, two exogenous variables in the supply equations that are excluded from the demand equation, T and P_F. Thus, the demand function is identified and can be estimated. (You should be able to see that, in this system of equations, the supply function is also identified.)

If the demand function is log-linear,

$$\log Q_X = \log a + b \log P_X + c \log Y + d \log P_R$$

the same technique applies. We need to specify the supply function; and, for reasons that become more clear in the following discussion, we probably will want to use a log-linear form

$$\log Q_X = \log e + f \log P_X + g \log T + \mathrm{h} \log P_F$$

In this instance, the endogenous variable on the right-hand side of the demand equation is $\log P_X$. Since, however, the supply function contains two exogenous variables ($\log T$ and $\log P_F$) the demand function is again identified.

Estimation of the demand function

Once the demand function has been identified, it can be estimated using any of a number of available techniques. Perhaps the most widely used of these techniques—and the one that is most likely to be preprogrammed into the available regression packages—is two-stage least squares (2SLS).

In the discussion to follow, we will provide only a very brief sketch of the basic technique of 2SLS. Keep in mind what our problem is: Regression techniques normally assume that the right-hand side variables are exogenous. However, in the case of simultaneous equations—like the demand and supply functions considered here—one of the right-hand side variables is endogenous.

Conceptually, what we want to do is to make this endogenous right-hand side variable (in our case, price) behave as if it is exogenous, then use traditional regression techniques to obtain estimates of the parameters. In the example we have been using we have a system of two simultaneous equations:

$$\text{Demand: } Q_X = a + bP_X + cY + dP_R$$
$$\text{Supply: } Q_X = e + fP_X + gT + hP_F$$

In these, P_X is an endogenous variable. To obtain unbiased estimates of *a, b, c,* and *d,* the estimation of the demand function proceeds in two steps or stages.

Stage 1: The endogenous right-hand side variable is regressed on all of the exogenous variables in the system

$$P_X = \alpha + \beta Y + \gamma P_R + \delta T + \theta P_F$$

From this estimation, we obtain estimates of the parameters; i.e., $\hat{\alpha}$, $\hat{\beta}$, $\hat{\gamma}$, $\hat{\delta}$, and $\hat{\theta}$. Using these estimates and the actual value of the exogenous variables, we generate a "new" price series—predicted price—as follows

$$\hat{P}_X = \hat{\alpha} + \hat{\beta} Y + \hat{\gamma} P_R + \hat{\delta} T + \hat{\theta} P_F$$

Note how the predicted price $\hat{P}_X$ is obtained. $\hat{P}_X$ is simply a linear combination of the exogenous variables; so, it follows that $\hat{P}_X$ is also exogenous. However, given the way that we obtained our predicted price series, the values of $\hat{P}_X$ will correspond closely to the original values of P_X. In essence, in this first stage, we have made price behave as if it is exogenous.

Stage 2: We then use the predicted price variable ($\hat{P}_X$) in the demand function we wish to estimate. That is, in the second stage, we estimate the regression equation

$$Q_X = a + b\hat{P}_X + cY + dP_R$$

Note that, in this estimation, we use the exogenous variable we constructed in the first stage. We use predicted price, $\hat{P}_X$, rather than the actual price variable, P_X, in the final regression.

At this point, we probably should remove some of your fears by noting that in the regression programs with which we are familiar, these two stages are done automatically. It is normally necessary for the user only to specify which variables are endogenous and which are exogenous.

Once the estimates for *a, b, c,* and *d* have been obtained from the second stage of the regression, they can be tested for significance (using a *t*-test) in precisely the same manner as for any other regression equation. However, due to the manner in which 2SLS estimates are calculated, the R^2 and *F*-statistics are not meaningful. Indeed, these statistics are usually not even reported in the output of standard regression packages.

APPLICATION

The world demand for copper

In its simplest form, we can define the world demand for copper to be a function of the price of copper, income, and the price of any related commodities. In this example, we will use aluminum as the related commodity because it is the primary substitute for copper in manufacturing. Thus, we can write our demand function as

$$Q_{\text{copper},t} = f(P_{\text{copper},t}, Y_t, P_{\text{aluminum},t})$$

As we have noted, we could specify either a linear or a nonlinear demand function. Let's use a linear form in this application,

$$Q_{\text{copper},t} = a + bP_{\text{copper},t} + cY_t + dP_{\text{aluminum},t}$$

It is tempting simply to regress consumption on the price of copper, income, and the price of aluminum. However, as we have pointed out, such a procedure is normally not appropriate. Instead, it is first necessary to identify the demand function. As we have shown, this requires that we specify the supply function.

In the simplest formulation, the quantity supplied of copper could be specified to be a function of the price of copper, the price of inputs used in extracting copper, and the level of available technology. This can be simplified somewhat by using the real (deflated) price of copper to reflect both the price of copper and the price of inputs. Thus, our supply function would be

$$Q_{\text{copper},t} = g(P_{\text{copper},t}, T_t)$$

However, in this market, inventories are of particular importance. If inventories are rising, we would expect current production to be reduced. Therefore, we will construct an additional variable to reflect inventory changes. We define the ratio of consumption to production in the preceding period (denoted simply as X) to be this variable. As consumption declines relative to production, X will fall, and we would expect a decline in current production. Thus, our supply function becomes

$$Q_{\text{copper},t} = g(P_{\text{copper},t}, T_t, X_t)$$

or, using a linear specification,

$$Q_{\text{copper},t} = e + fP_{\text{copper},t} + gT_t + hX_t$$

We can now turn to the question of whether or not the demand function is identified. Since the supply function includes two exogenous variables that are excluded from the demand equation (T and X), the demand function is identified and may be estimated.

Once we knew that the demand function was identified, we collected the necessary data: (1) The world consumption (sales) of copper in 1,000 metric tons, (2) the price of copper and aluminum in cents per pound, deflated by a price index to obtain the real (i.e., constant dollar) prices, (3) an index of real per capita income, and (4) the world production of copper (in order to calculate our "inventory" variable, X). We used time as our proxy for available technology (i.e., assuming that the level of technology has increased steadily over time). The resulting data set is presented in Table 11.1.[4]

[4]The data in this table are actual values for the period 1951–1975.

Table 11.1
The world copper market (1951–1975)

Year	*(QC)* *World consumption*	*(PC)* *Real price copper*	*(Y)* *Index of real income*	*(PA)* *Real price aluminum*	*X*	*T*
1	3,173.0	26.56	0.70	19.76	0.97679	1
2	3,281.1	27.31	0.71	20.78	1.03937	2
3	3,135.7	32.95	0.72	22.55	1.05153	3
4	3,359.1	33.90	0.70	23.06	0.97312	4
5	3,755.1	42.70	0.74	24.93	1.02349	5
6	3,875.9	46.11	0.74	26.50	1.04135	6
7	3,905.7	31.70	0.74	27.24	0.97686	7
8	3,957.6	27.23	0.72	26.21	0.98069	8
9	4,279.1	32.89	0.75	26.09	1.02888	9
10	4,627.9	33.78	0.77	27.40	1.03392	10
11	4,910.2	31.66	0.76	26.94	0.97922	11
12	4,908.4	32.28	0.79	25.18	0.99679	12
13	5,327.9	32.38	0.83	23.94	0.96630	13
14	5,878.4	33.75	0.85	25.07	1.02915	14
15	6,075.2	36.25	0.89	25.37	1.07950	15
16	6,312.7	36.24	0.93	24.55	1.05073	16
17	6,056.8	38.23	0.95	24.98	1.02788	17
18	6,375.9	40.83	0.99	24.96	1.02799	18
19	6,974.3	44.62	1.00	25.52	0.99151	19
20	7,101.6	52.27	1.00	26.01	1.00191	20
21	7,071.7	45.16	1.02	25.46	0.95644	21
22	7,754.8	42.50	1.07	22.17	0.96947	22
23	8,480.3	43.70	1.12	18.56	0.98220	23
24	8,105.2	47.88	1.10	21.32	1,00793	24
25	7,157.2	36.33	1.07	22.75	0.93810	25

Using these data, we estimated the demand function via 2SLS. In this estimation, the endogenous variable $P_{\text{copper},t}$ is first regressed on all of the exogenous variables, Y_t, $P_{\text{aluminum},t}$, X_t, and T_t. Then, as we described earlier, this estimation is used to generate the predicted value of $P_{\text{copper},t}$. Finally, consumption, $Q_{\text{copper},t}$, is regressed on this predicted price of copper as well as on income and the price of aluminum. The results of these estimations are:

```
SECOND STAGE STATISTICS

DEPENDENT VARIABLE:  QC

OBSERVATIONS:  25

                     PARAMETER          STANDARD
 VARIABLE            ESTIMATE             ERROR

INTERCEPT            -6837.8             1264.5
PC.HAT                 -66.495             31.534
Y                    13997.              1306.3
PA                     107.66              44.510
```

Note that the computer output provides only the results of the second-stage estimation, i.e., estimation of the demand function using $\hat{P}$. Indeed, this printout indicates that a predicted price was used, since it denotes the price of copper as *PC.HAT* rather than *PC*. Note further that, since the R^2 and F values are not meaningful in 2SLS, they are not even reported.

We would predict theoretically that (1) due to a downward-sloping demand curve for copper, $b < 0$; (2) since copper is a normal good, $c > 0$; and (3) since copper and aluminum are substitutes, $d > 0$. Our estimated coefficients conform to this sign pattern:

$$\hat{b} = -66.495 < 0$$
$$\hat{c} = 13997. > 0$$
$$\hat{d} = 107.66 > 0$$

In order to test for the statistical significance of these parameter estimates, we calculated the t-values:

$$t_{\hat{b}} = \frac{-66.495}{31.534} = -2.11$$
$$t_{\hat{c}} = \frac{13997.}{1306.3} = 10.71$$
$$t_{\hat{d}} = \frac{107.66}{44.510} = 2.42$$

We estimated four parameters (a, b, c, and d); so we have $25 - 4$ degrees of freedom and the critical value of t at a 95 percent confidence level is 2.08. Since the absolute values for the calculated values of t for each of the parameter estimates exceed the critical value of t, we know that the estimated parameters are statistically significant.

Now, let's find out about the elasticities of demand. While we know that we can evaluate the elasticity at any point on the demand curve, let's use the sample means. From Table 11.1, the means are

$$\overline{QC} = 5433.63$$
$$\overline{PC} = 37.17$$
$$\overline{Y} = 0.87$$
$$\overline{PA} = 24.29$$

The own-price elasticity of demand evaluated at the sample mean is

$$E = -\hat{b}\frac{\overline{PC}}{\overline{QC}}$$
$$= -(-66.495)\left(\frac{37.17}{5433.63}\right)$$
$$= 0.45$$

Similarly, the income elasticity of demand at the sample mean is

$$E_Y = \hat{c}\left(\frac{\overline{Y}}{\overline{QC}}\right)$$

$$= 13997\left(\frac{0.87}{5433.63}\right)$$

$$= 2.23$$

and the cross-price elasticity of demand at the sample mean is

$$E_{CA} = \hat{d}\left(\frac{\overline{PA}}{\overline{QC}}\right)$$

$$= 107.66\left(\frac{24.29}{5433.63}\right)$$

$$= 0.48$$

In this discussion, we have concentrated our attention on what we think are the two major problems that are encountered in the estimation of a demand function—specification and identification.

As we noted in Chapter 4, specification errors can result from either the selection of variables to be included or the selection of the functional form to be estimated. Obviously, the exclusion of important explanatory variables can lead to unreliability in the estimated coefficients, as can the inclusion of extraneous variables or the selection of incorrect variables. In the case of the selection of the functional form, choosing the incorrect form can reduce the precision of the estimate in the sense that the hypothesized functional form does not "fit" the data. As we noted earlier, this might occur if the analyst uses a linear demand function when the true demand is nonlinear.

In the case of the identification problem, if the analyst fails to recognize that the observed data points are generated by the simultaneous interaction of a demand and supply function, the estimated demand function might well be a supply function or nothing at all. This problem—referred to as simultaneous equations bias—can lead to biased estimates of the parameters of the demand function.

TECHNICAL PROBLEMS

1. Cite the three major problems with consumer interviews or surveys and provide an example of each.
2. Following are four sets of demand and supply functions. For each set, determine if the demand and supply functions are identified and explain why or why not.

a. D: $Q = \alpha + \beta P$
S: $Q = \mathrm{a} + bP$

b. D: $Q = \alpha + \beta P + \gamma Y$
S: $Q = a + bP$

c. D: $Q = \alpha + \beta P$
S: $Q = a + bP + cT$

d. D: $Q = \alpha + \beta P + \gamma Y$
S: $Q = a + bP + cT + dP_F$

3. In our application dealing with the world demand for copper, we estimated the demand elasticities (at the sample means). Using these estimates, evaluate the impact on the world consumption of copper of:

a. The formation of a worldwide cartel in copper that increases the price of copper by 10 percent.

b. The onset of a recession that reduces world income by 5 percent.

c. A technical breakthrough that is expected to reduce the price of copper by 10 percent.

d. A 10 percent reduction in the price of aluminum.

4. A linear demand function of the form

$$Q_X = a + bP_X + cY + dP_R$$

was estimated using 2SLS. (Obviously, this demand function was first identified by specifying the supply function.) The results of this estimation are as follows:

SECOND STAGE STATISTICS

DEPENDENT VARIABLE: QX

OBSERVATIONS: 30

VARIABLE	PARAMETER ESTIMATE	STANDARD ERROR
INTERCEPT	68.38	12.65
PX.HAT	−6.50	3.15
Y	13.926	1.306
PR	−10.77	2.45

The means of the variables are as follows:

$$\overline{Q}_X = 125$$
$$\overline{P}_X = 25$$
$$\overline{Y} = 20$$
$$\overline{P}_R = 25$$

a. Are the signs of $\hat{b}$ and $\hat{c}$ as would be predicted theoretically?
b. What does the sign of $\hat{d}$ imply about the relation between commodity X and the related commodity?
c. Are the parameter estimates $\hat{a}$, $\hat{b}$, $\hat{c}$, and $\hat{d}$ statistically significant?
d. Using the sample means, calculate
1. The own-price elasticity of demand.
2. The income elasticity.
3. The cross-price elasticity.

5. In our examination of the world demand for copper, we used a linear specification. However, we could have estimated a log-linear specification. That is, we could have specified the copper demand function as

$$Q_c = aP_c^b \, Y^c \, P_A^d$$

or

$$\log Q_c = \log a + b \log P_c + c \log Y + d \log P_A$$

The results of such an estimation, using the data in Table 11.1, are as follows:

SECOND STAGE STATISTICS

DEPENDENT VARIABLE: LOGQC

OBSERVATIONS: 25

VARIABLE	PARAMETER ESTIMATE	STANDARD ERROR
INTERCEPT	9.0072	0.97059
LOGPC.HAT	−0.68233	0.30635
LOGY	2.5265	0.28963
LOGPA	0.75246	0.23498

a. Are the parameter estimates consistent with the theoretical predictions made about the signs of *b*, *c*, and *d*?
b. Are the parameter estimates statistically significant?
c. What are the values of the own-price, income, and cross-price elasticities of demand?
d. How do these results compare with these obtained from the linear specification?

ANALYTICAL PROBLEMS

1. Suppose that you want to estimate the demand for automobiles in the United States. Specify a model that you believe might be appropriate.

Check to see if your model is identified. How would the model differ if you wish to estimate the demand for a particular make of automobile?

2. Until the mid-1970s, most estimates of the demand function for automobiles did not include the price of gasoline. Why? Would this exclusion be appropriate today? What kind of an error would this be?
3. In Problem 1, we considered estimation of the demand for automobiles in the United States.
   a. Can you think of some problems—not necessarily statistical problems—involved in estimating the demand for automobiles? What are they?
   b. Is there a problem in defining what is meant by "an automobile" and "the price of an automobile"?
   c. How would you obtain data on the price of automobiles?
4. Suppose that the commodity in Problem 1 is coal rather than automobiles. How would your answers to Problems 1 and 3 differ?
5. In a recent article, a researcher reported that he had found that the demand curve for kerosene sloped upward—as the price of kerosene rose the quantity demanded of kerosene increased. What questions might you have for this researcher?

SUGGESTED ADDITIONAL REFERENCES

Intriligator, Michael D. *Econometric Models, Techniques, and Applications*. Englewood Cliffs, N.J.: Prentice-Hall, 1978.

Kelejian, Harry H., and Wallace E. Oates. *Introduction to Econometrics*. New York: Harper & Row, 1974.

Pindyck, Robert S., and Rubinfeld, Daniel L. *Econometric Models and Economic Forecasts*. New York: McGraw-Hill, 1981.

Rao, Potluri, and Roger LeRoy Miller. *Applied Econometrics*. Belmont, Calif.: Wadsworth, 1971.

Wonnacott, Ronald J., and Thomas H. Wonnacott. *Econometrics*. New York: John Wiley & Sons, 1979.

12

Demand forecasting

In the preceding chapter, we dealt with techniques by which a manager can estimate and analyze the characteristics of demand functions. Information about prevailing demand can help managers decide on the current values for variables such as production scheduling, inventory levels, and advertising. Clearly, knowledge of future demand conditions can also be extremely useful to managers, particularly in making the decision about output and price in future periods and in the firm's investment decisions. In this chapter, we provide some techniques that can be used to forecast future demand conditions.

The range of forecasting techniques is so wide that a complete discussion is quite beyond the scope of this text. Instead, we confine ourselves to a brief description of some of the more widely used techniques. For convenience, we divide forecasting methods into two groups—qualitative models and statistical models. Before proceeding to a discussion of the techniques themselves, it will be useful to provide a general description of these two types of forecasting methods.

Qualitative models are more difficult to describe since there exists no explicit model or method that can serve as a reference point. There is no model that can be used to replicate the initial forecast with a given set of data, and it is this feature, above all others, that distinguishes this approach. It has been said by some that a qualitative model is essentially a "rule-of-thumb" technique. However, you should not infer from this description that qualitative forecasts are naive or unsophisticated. Indeed, it is the very complexity of this method that makes replication so difficult, since such forecasts are typically based on at least some subjective factors. In the final analysis, qualitative forecasts are often based on *expert opinion*. The forecaster will examine the available data, solicit the advice of others, and then sift through this amalgamation of evidence to formulate a forecast. The weights assigned to the disparate bits and pieces of information are subjectively determined and, we might add, separates the neophyte from the expert.

In contrast, a statistical model employs explicit models or methods that can be replicated by another analyst. The results of statistical models can be reproduced by different researchers. An additional advantage of this approach is the existence of reasonably well-defined standards for evaluating such models. The final advantage of statistical models is the ability to use them in simulation models. (Basically, simulation models are models in which the researcher can obtain alternative forecasts for the future values of the endogenous variable, given alternative future trends in the exogenous variables). The statistical models can be further subdivided into two categories—time-series models and econometric models.

This chapter will proceed as follows. First, we will describe briefly some of the data that could be employed in making qualitative forecasts. Next, we consider time-series models. We then introduce econometric models and consider simulation procedures. We close this chapter with a note on some of the more important problems involved in forecasting.

12.1 QUALITATIVE TECHNIQUES

As we noted, qualitative forecasting methods are very difficult to describe in general, due to the subjective elements involved. That is, forecasters combine available data with their knowledge of the firm and industry and, assigning subjective weights to these pieces of evidence, obtain a forecast. While qualitative forecasting may indeed be the best technique, it is difficult, if not impossible, to teach these techniques. In truth, we do not really know how people who do qualitative forecasting well, do it. We can only say that those who are successful know how economics works and know a great deal about their industries.

Skillful forecasters do use data to make these forecasts. While it is impossible to set forth the manner in which their subjective weights are assigned to the data they use, we can, however, describe some of the data that may be observed and used.

Simplifying the qualitative forecasting procedure, it is possible that the analyst has observed through experience (or, perhaps, using regression techniques) that a relation exists between the sales of the firm and the movement in certain aggregate economic variables over time. More specifically, managers know that there are economic variables, changes in which *lead* the changes in the firm's sales. If managers know these variables, they can use these "leading indicators" as a barometer to predict changes in the sales of the firm. The problem then is the isolation of these indicators and the collection of appropriate data.

This problem of data identification and collection has been simplified immensely through the work of the National Bureau of Economic Research and the U.S. Department of Commerce. The U.S. Department of Commerce publishes, monthly, *Business Conditions Digest,* which contains data on a large number of indicators. (More precisely, in 1983, *Business Conditions Digest* contained almost 200 data series that could be used as indicators.) Of these, 12 variables are considered particularly important as leading indicators. These indicators are presented in Table 12.1.

If the forecaster can relate the firm's sales to one or more of the leading indicators, it would then be possible to generate short-term forecasts on the basis of this published data. For example, a firm that manufactures dishwashers would be very interested in the index of new building permits. An increase in building permits precedes housing starts, which precedes the purchase of dishwashers. An experienced forecaster could combine this information with personal knowledge about the firm (e.g., its share of the market) and about the market (e.g., the percentage of new houses that have dishwashers) to provide a forecast of sales for the firm. Again, it is impossible for us to determine the weights that should be assigned to these various pieces of information.

Table 12.1
The 12 leading indicators

1. Average workweek, production workers, manufacturing (hours).
2. Average weekly initial claims, State unemployment insurance—inverted* (thousands).
3. New orders for consumer goods and materials in 1972 dollars (billion dollars).
4. Vendor performance, companies receiving slower deliveries (percent).
5. Net business formation (index: 1967 = 100).
6. Contracts and orders for plant and equipment in 1972 dollars (billion dollars).
7. New building permits, private housing units (index: 1967 = 100).
8. Change in inventories on hand and on order in 1972 dollars, smoothed† (annual rate, billion dollars).
9. Change in sensitive materials prices, smoothed† (percent).
10. Stock prices, 500 common stocks (index: 1941–43 = 10).
11. Money supply (M2) in 1972 dollars (billion dollars).
12. Change in credit—business and consumer borrowing (annual rate, percent).

*This series is inverted, hence a decrease in unemployment claims will lead to an increase in the indicator.

†*Smoothed* means that irregularities in the data have been removed. The purpose in this procedure is to demonstrate the trend in the variable. Many variables exhibit considerable short-term (or seasonal) variation. In order to ascertain the trend in the variable, it is necessary to remove the effects of the short-term variation, that is, smooth the data series.

Source: U.S. Department of Commerce, *Business Conditions Digest.*

Figure 12.1
Composite index of the 12 leading indicators (1965–1983)

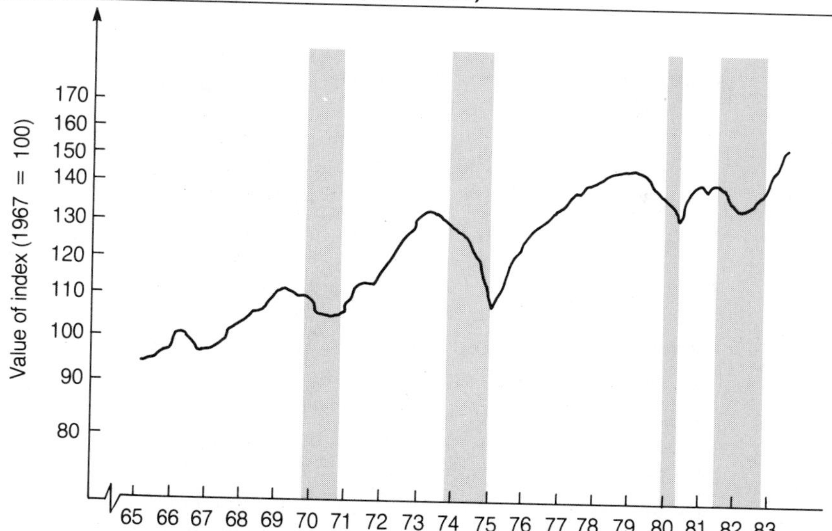

Note: Periods shaded are periods of recession as determined by the National Bureau of Economic Research (e.g., the 1969–70 recession covered the period December 1969 through November 1970).

Source: U.S. Department of Commerce, *Business Conditions Digest.*

There also exist more complex situations in which more than one indicator is used. In some instances, the different indicators could provide conflicting forecasts. To handle this difficulty, two methods are commonly employed. One method is to calculate a composite index. A composite index is simply a weighted average of individual indicators. Indeed, the U.S. Department of Commerce itself publishes several composite indicators, one of which is the weighted average of the 12 leading indicators. In Figure 12.1, we have provided a graph of the behavior of this composite index over the period 1965–83. In this figure, it is easier to see why they are "leading" indicators. Note how the index turned down prior to the recessions of 1969–70, 1973–75, 1980, and 1981–82. Likewise, the upturn in this composite index preceded—led—the upturn in general economic activity.

A second way that multiple indicators are used is to calculate a diffusion index. Using this approach, one would calculate the percentage of the indicators that are rising. For example, if 5 of the 12 leading indicators were rising, the diffusion index would be $5/12$ or 42 percent. Using a diffusion index, one normally defines a critical percentage (usually 50 percent). If the diffusion index is above this critical percentage, one would say that economic activity is rising. Likewise, if the diffusion index is below the critical value, economic activity is said to be declining. In Figure 12.2 we have provided a graph of the diffusion index for the 12 leading indicators for the period 1965–83, and compared it to periods of recession.

Again, let us stress that the procedures outlined above require a great deal

Figure 12.2
Diffusion index for the 12 leading indicators

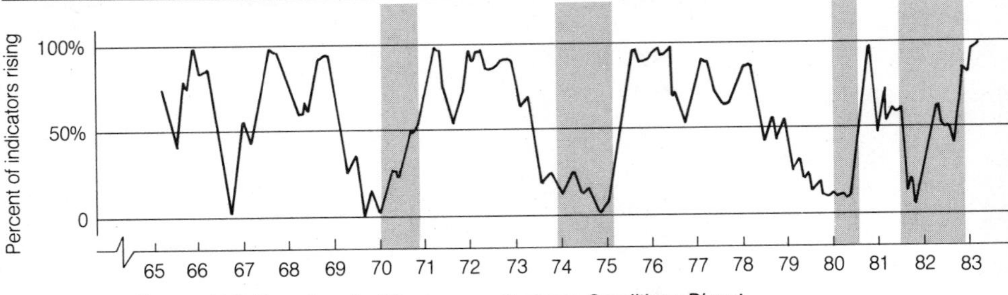

Source: U.S. Department of Commerce, *Business Conditions Digest.*

of subjective input from forecasters. The analyst must determine the appropriate indicators, then interpret them in light of the conditions that will exist in their particular markets and firms. Firstly, these indicators do not always indicate changes in another economic variable (and there also exists some random month-to-month variation in these indicators). Second, the lead times are not necessarily constant. Third, and most important, since these leading indicators predict the *direction rather than the magnitude of changes,* the responsibility for assigning a magnitude rests with the forecaster.

THE WALL STREET JOURNAL

APPLICATION

Qualitative forecasts

Given the subjective nature of qualitative forecasts, we haven't seen instances in which a firm stated that its forecast was based solely on the behavior of the leading indicators. But, we think you might find two stories that appeared on page 2 of *The Wall Street Journal* on February 1, 1984, to be illustrative.

One story announced an increase in the leading indicators:*

> The index of leading economic indicators, the government's main gauge of future economic performance, bounced back in December after dropping slightly in November.
>
> The Commerce Department said the index in December rose 0.6 percent, which is less than the unusually strong average monthly increase of 1.2 percent in 1983, but enough to suggest that the economy will keep growing in the months ahead.
>
> "The 0.6 percent increase is roughly consistent with the kind of slower growth we think the economy will experience in 1984," says Donald Straszheim, chief economist for Wharton Econometrics Forecasting Associates in Philadelphia.

The other story indicated that builders were very optimistic about the coming year:†

> Many builders are bullish about 1984. "The housing market looks good for the next six to nine months," said R. Coleman Whitehead, a Watkinsville, Ga., builder. Builder Wayne Young of Melbourne, Fla., agreed: "The housing market looks brighter than it has in the past few years." And Leon Hickman, an Omaha, Neb., builder, said, "The market is stabilizing and should be good through 1984."
>
> Kevin Villani, chief economist of the Federal Home Loan Mortgage Corp., expects strong sales in the first half, with a slowdown possible in the last half, should interest rates climb then.
>
> The home builders' trade group is revising upward an indicator of housing activity. It expects housing starts this year to rise to about 1.8 million units rather than match last year's 1.7 million, as predicted earlier.

We certainly can not assert that the builders' forecasts were based (solely or otherwise) on the leading indicators. However, it is beyond question that firms do take the behavior of these indicators into account when making forecasts.

---

*"Leading Indicators Rose 0.6 percent in December; New Growth is Seen," by Alan Murray, *The Wall Street Journal,* February 1, 1984.

†"Home Sales Surged 28.5 percent in December from November, Led by Buying in South," by Timothy D. Schellhardt, *The Wall Street Journal,* February 1, 1984. Reprinted by permission of The Wall Street Journal.

12.2 TIME-SERIES MODELS

While we have treated qualitative forecasting rather briefly, we hope we have given some idea of the way such types of forecasts are used and some problems that can arise. We now turn to the second major group of forecasting techniques—statistical forecasting. These methods lend themselves to a more analytical treatment, because the models can be replicated by another researcher. Recall that the statistical methods can be divided into two categories, time-series models and econometric models. We begin with time-series models.

As we noted in Chapter 4, a *time series* is simply a time-ordered sequence of observations on a variable. In general, forecasting via a time-series analysis uses only the time-series history of the variable to be forecasted to develop a model for predicting future values. Time-series analyses involve the description of the process by which these historical data were generated. Thus, to forecast using time series, it is necessary to obtain a mathematical model that represents the generating process.

Several characteristics of time series must be modeled if the resulting forecast is to be reliable. These are illustrated in Figure 12.3, in which the observed variable X is plotted along the vertical axis and time along the horizontal. In Panel A, we show a series that remains at a constant level over time but is subject to random variation from period to period. In Panel B, the series exhibits a time trend in addition to the random variation. Panel C represents a series that is subject to some cyclical variation.

Figure 12.3
Characteristics of time series

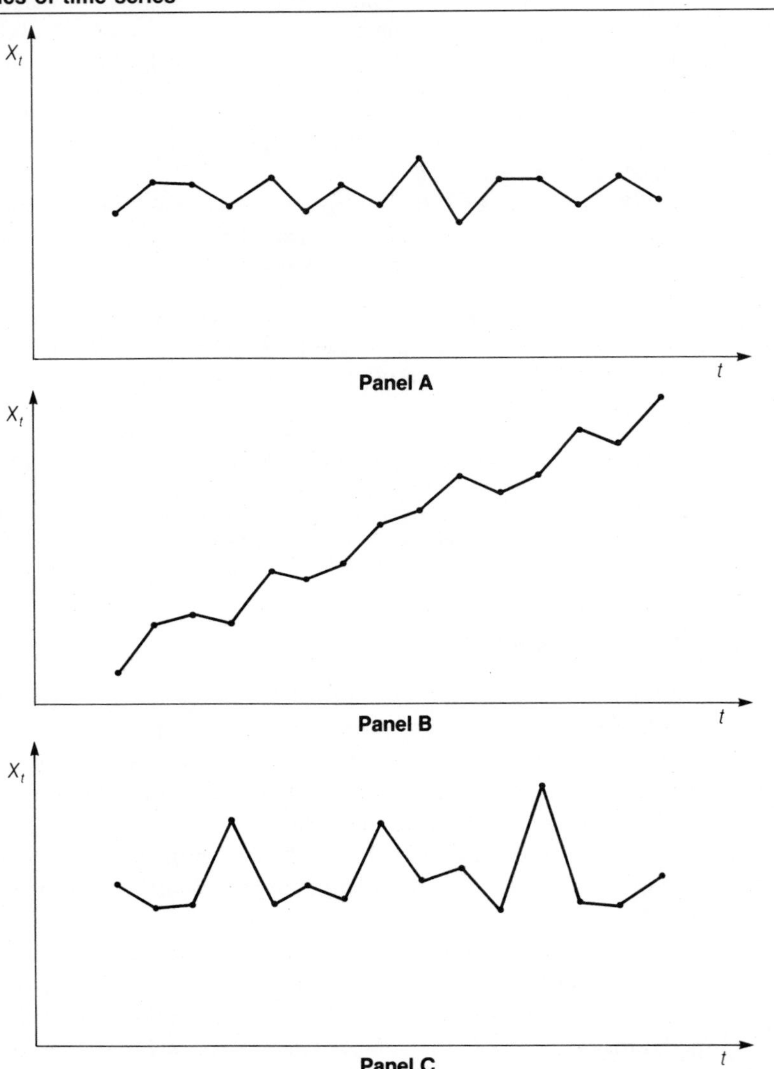

In the following discussion, we will provide a brief overview of some of the more basic techniques used in time-series forecasting to handle trend and cyclical variation. There exist other, more complicated time-series procedures, including the now widely used Box-Jenkins analysis. For those procedures we refer you to the references at the end of this chapter.

Linear trend forecasting

The simplest form of time-series forecasting uses a linear trend. Using this type of forecasting model, we would posit that sales—quantity demanded—

increases (or decreases) linearly over time. To explain this kind of a forecast, let us use a simple example.

Suppose that, for a particular firm, sales for the period 1977–84 were as indicated by the eight data points in Figure 12.4. Using these data points, we could fit a straight line to the data scatter, as is illustrated by the solid line in Figure 12.4. Then, we would forecast sales in the future by extending this trend line and picking the forecast values of sales off this *extrapolated* trend line. We have illustrated sales forecasts for 1985 and 1990 ($\hat{Q}_{1985}$ and $\hat{Q}_{1990}$) in Figure 12.4.

This procedure is, of course, simple to accomplish using regression analysis. We have posited that there is a linear relation between sales and time,

$$Q_t = \alpha + \beta t$$

Using available data, e.g., the eight observations for 1977 through 1984, we can use regression analysis to estimate the values of α and β. That is, we estimate a trend line,

$$\hat{Q}_t = \hat{\alpha} + \hat{\beta} t$$

that best fits the historical data. If $\beta > 0$, sales are increasing over time; and, if $\beta < 0$, sales are decreasing. However, if $\beta = 0$, sales are constant over time. (In this case, the pattern of sales might look like that in Panel A of Figure 12.3). Hence, it is important to determine if there is indeed a *signifi-*

Figure 12.4
A linear trend forecast

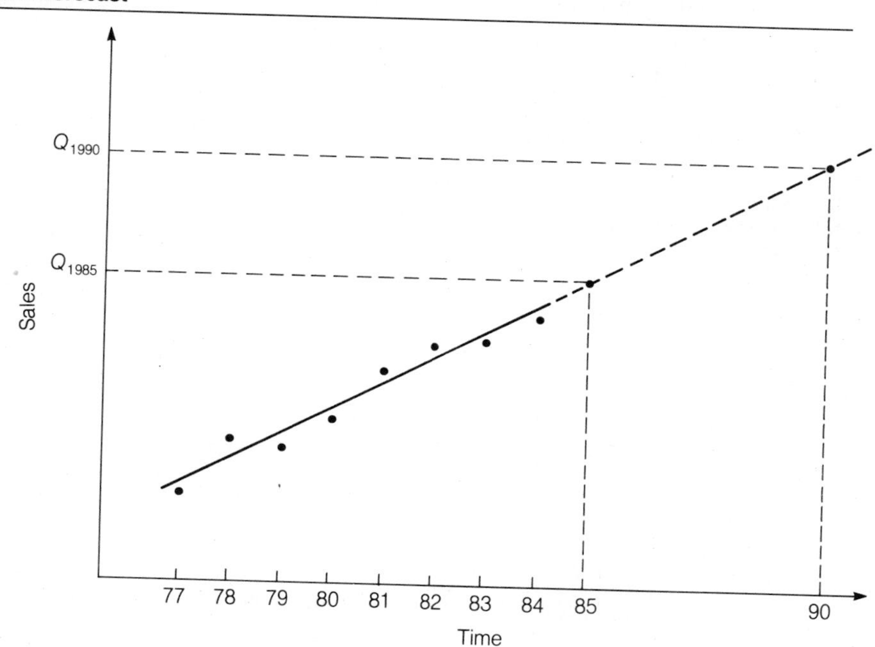

cant trend in sales. From the preceding, this means that we need to determine if $\hat{\beta}$ is significantly different from zero. As always, we would test for significance using a *t*-test.

If the estimation indicates a significant trend, we can use the estimated trend line to obtain forecasts of future sales. For example, if we wanted a forecast for sales in 1985, we simply insert 1985 into our estimated trend line

$$\hat{Q}_{1985} = \hat{\alpha} + \hat{\beta} \times (1985)$$

Likewise, if we wanted a sales forecast for 1990,

$$\hat{Q}_{1990} = \hat{\alpha} + \hat{\beta} \times (1990)$$

Cyclical variation

As we have indicated, time-series data may frequently exhibit regular variation over time, and the failure to take these regular variations into account when estimating a forecasting equation would bias the forecast. Commonly, when using quarterly or monthly sales to forecast sales, seasonal variation may occur—the sales of many products vary systematically by month or by quarter. For example, in the retail clothing business, sales are generally higher around Easter and Christmas. Thus, sales would be higher during the second and fourth quarters of the year. Likewise, the sales of hunting equipment would peak during early fall, the third quarter. In such cases, you would definitely wish to incorporate the systematic variations when estimating the equation and forecasting future sales. We shall describe the technique most commonly employed to handle cyclical variation. The reader interested in additional techniques should look at the references cited at the end of this chapter.

Consider the simplified example of a firm producing and selling a product for which sales are consistently higher in the fourth quarter than in any other quarter. A hypothetical data scatter is presented in Figure 12.5. In each of the

Figure 12.5
Sales with cyclical variation

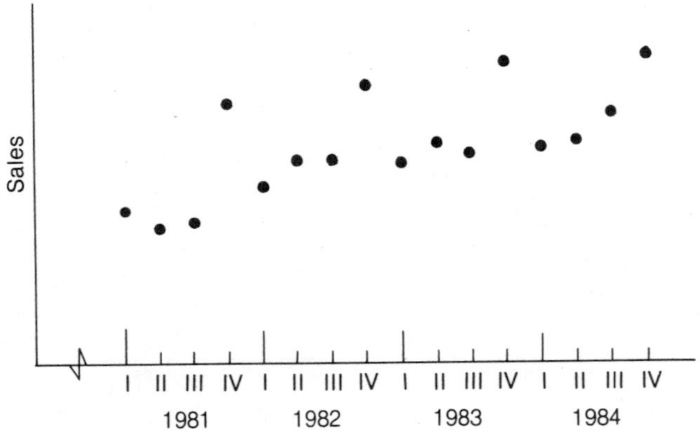

Figure 12.6
Two trend lines

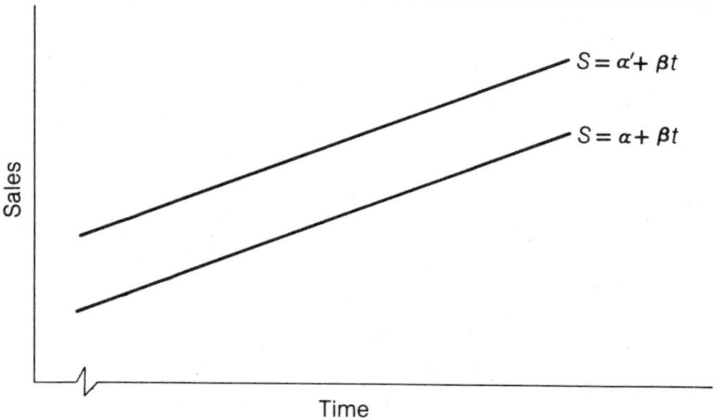

four years, the data point in the fourth quarter is much higher than in the other three. While a time trend clearly exists, if the analyst simply regressed sales against time, without accounting for the higher sales in the fourth quarter, too large a trend would be estimated (i.e., the slope would be too large). In essence, there is an upward shift of the trend line in the fourth quarter. Such a relation is presented in Figure 12.6. That is, in the fourth quarter, the intercept is higher than in the other quarters. In other words, α', the intercept of the trend line for the fourth-quarter data points, exceeds α, the intercept of the trend line for the data points in the other quarters. One way of specifying this relation is to define α' as $\alpha' = \alpha + \delta$, where δ is some positive number. Therefore, the regression line we want to estimate will take the form:

$$Q_t = \alpha + \beta t + \delta$$

where $\delta = 0$ in the first three quarters.

To accomplish the estimation of the preceding equation we use what is commonly referred to as a dummy variable in the estimating equation. A dummy variable is one that can take on only the values *zero* or *one*. In this case, we would assign the dummy variable (D) a value of one if the sales observation is from the fourth quarter and zero in the other three quarters. Our data observations would be as shown in Table 12.2, where S_t represents the sales figure in the tth period. Note that, since we are using quarterly data, we convert time into integers to obtain a continuous time variable. Using these data observations, we would then estimate the equation.

$$Q_t = \alpha + \beta t + \delta D$$

After this equation is estimated, we would have two equations like those shown in Figure 12.6. The slope of the two equations would be the same ($\hat{\beta}$). For quarters I, II, and III, the intercept is $\hat{\alpha}$, while for the fourth quarter, the intercept is $\hat{\alpha} + \hat{\delta}$. This estimation really means that for any future period t_i, the sales forecast would be

$$Q_{t_i} = \hat{\alpha} + \hat{\beta} t_i$$

Table 12.2
Dummy Variable

Q_t	t	D
$S_{1981(I)}$	1	0
$S_{1981(II)}$	2	0
$S_{1981(III)}$	3	0
$S_{1981(IV)}$	4	1
$S_{1982(I)}$	5	0
$S_{1982(II)}$	6	0
$S_{1982(III)}$	7	0
$S_{1982(IV)}$	8	1
$S_{1983(I)}$	9	0
$S_{1983(II)}$	10	0
$S_{1983(III)}$	11	0
$S_{1983(IV)}$	12	1
$S_{1984(I)}$	13	0
$S_{1984(II)}$	14	0
$S_{1984(III)}$	15	0
$S_{1984(IV)}$	16	1

unless period t_i occurs in the fourth quarter, in which the sales forecast would be

$$Q_{t_i} = \hat{\alpha} + \hat{\beta}t_i + \hat{\delta} = (\hat{\alpha} + \hat{\delta}) + \hat{\beta}t_i$$

For example, going back to the data observations in Table 12.2, if we wished to forecast sales in the third quarter of 1985 we would use the equation

$$Q_{1985(\text{III})} = \hat{\alpha} + \hat{\beta}(19)$$

If we wished to forecast sales in the fourth quarter of that year, we would use

$$Q_{1985(\text{IV})} = (\hat{\alpha} + \hat{\delta}) + \hat{\beta}(20)$$

In other words, the mere fact that the forecast is for quarter IV adds the amount δ to the sales that would otherwise be forecast.[1]

Going a step further, it could be the case that there exist quarter-to-quarter differences in sales (i.e., in Figure 12.6, there would be four trend lines). In this case, we would use three dummy variables: D_1 (equal to one in the first quarter and zero otherwise), D_2 (equal to one in the second quarter and zero otherwise), and D_3 (equal to one in the third quarter and zero otherwise).[2] Then, we would estimate the equation

$$Q_t = \alpha + \beta t + \delta_1 D_1 + \delta_2 D_2 + \delta_3 D_3$$

In quarter I the intercept is $\alpha + \delta_1$, in quarter II it is $\alpha + \delta_2$, in quarter III it is $\alpha + \delta_3$, and in quarter IV it is α only.

[1]Throughout this discussion, we have assumed that the trend lines differ only in respect to the intercepts—the slope is the same for all of the trend lines. We should note that dummy variables can also be used to reflect differences in slopes. This procedure is, however, beyond the scope of this text and we refer the interested reader to the references cited at the end of this chapter.

[2]Likewise, if there were month-to-month differences, we would use 11 dummy variables. Note that, in the formulation used here, one would always have one fewer dummy variable than periods considered. For further explanation, see the references at the end of this chapter.

To obtain a forecast for some future quarter, it is necessary to include the coefficient for the dummy variable for that particular quarter. For example, predictions for the third quarter of a particular year would take the form

$$\hat{Q}_t = \hat{\alpha} + \hat{\beta}t + \hat{\delta}_3$$

Perhaps the best way to explain how these dummy variables can be used to account for cyclical variation is to provide an example.

APPLICATION

Use of dummy variables

Consider a firm having sales subject to seasonal variation but having a trend in sales over time. We obtained sales data for 1981–84 by quarter. We wish to predict sales for all four quarters of 1985.

Year	*Quarter*	*Sales ($000)*	t	D_1	D_2	D_3
1981	I	$ 72	1	1	0	0
	II	87	2	0	1	0
	III	87	3	0	0	1
	IV	150	4	0	0	0
1982	I	82	5	1	0	0
	II	98	6	0	1	0
	III	94	7	0	0	1
	IV	162	8	0	0	0
1983	I	97	9	1	0	0
	II	105	10	0	1	0
	III	109	11	0	0	1
	IV	176	12	0	0	0
1984	I	105	13	1	0	0
	II	121	14	0	1	0
	III	119	15	0	0	1
	IV	180	16	0	0	0

From the preceding discussion we know that this desired forecast requires us to estimate an equation containing three dummy variables. One such equation is[3]

[3]This is only one of the specifications that is appropriate. Equally appropriate is

$$\hat{Q}_t = \alpha + \beta t + \delta_2 D_2 + \delta_3 D_3 + \delta_4 D_4$$

or

$$Q_t = \alpha + \beta t + \delta_1 D_1 + \delta_3 D_3 + \delta_4 D_4$$

or

$$Q_t = \alpha + \beta t + \delta_1 D_1 + \delta_2 D_2 + \delta_4 D_4$$

It is necessary only to have *any three* of the quarters represented by dummy variables.

$$Q_t = \alpha + \beta t + \delta_1 D_1 + \delta_2 D_2 + \delta_3 D_3$$

where D_1, D_2, and D_3 are, respectively, dummy variables for quarters I, II, and III.

The data collected are presented on the preceding page. (Note that, since we are using quarterly data, it is necessary to convert time into a continuous variable.) Using these data, the preceding regression equation was estimated. The results of this estimation were as follows:

DEPENDENT VARIABLE: QT		F-RATIO: 794.126
OBSERVATIONS: 16		R-SQUARE: 0.9965
VARIABLE	PARAMETER ESTIMATE	STANDARD ERROR
INTERCEPT	139.63	1.7436
T	2.7375	0.12996
D1	-69.788	1.6895
D2	-58.775	1.6643
D3	-62.013	1.6490

The first thing we might note about these results is that they indicate a positive trend in sales. That is, $\hat{\beta} > 0$. In order to be sure that there is a significant trend, we need to test for the significance of $\hat{\beta}$. The calculated t-value for $\hat{\beta}$ is

$$t_{\hat{\beta}} = \frac{2.7375}{0.12996} = 21.064$$

We have $16 - 5 = 11$ degrees of freedom so, the critical value of t (using a 95 percent confidence level) is 2.201. Since $21.064 > 2.201$, we know that $\hat{\beta}$ is significant; so, we do have evidence of a significant positive trend in sales.

From the preceding discussion of dummy variables we know that the estimated intercept of the trend line is, in the first quarter

$$\hat{\alpha} + \hat{\delta}_1 = 139.63 - 69.788$$
$$= 69.842$$

in the second quarter

$$\hat{\alpha} + \hat{\delta}_2 = 139.63 - 58.775$$
$$= 80.855$$

in the third quarter

$$\hat{\alpha} + \hat{\delta}_3 = 139.63 - 62.013$$
$$= 77.617$$

and, in the fourth quarter

$$\hat{\alpha} = 139.63$$

Therefore, these estimates indicate that the intercepts—and thereby sales—are lower in quarters I, II, and III than in quarter IV. The question that always must be asked is: Are these intercepts *significantly* lower?

To answer this question, let's compare quarters I and IV. In quarter I, the intercept is $\hat{\alpha} + \hat{\delta}_1$; in quarter IV, it is $\hat{\alpha}$. Hence, if $\hat{\alpha} + \hat{\delta}_1$ is significantly lower than $\hat{\alpha}$, it is necessary that $\hat{\delta}_1$ be significantly less than zero. That is, if

$$\hat{\alpha} + \hat{\delta}_1 < \hat{\alpha}$$

it follows that

$$\hat{\delta}_1 < 0$$

we already know that $\hat{\delta}_1$ is negative; to determine if it is significantly negative, we must perform a t-test. The calculated value of t for $\hat{\delta}_1$ is

$$t_{\hat{\delta}_1} = \frac{-69.788}{1.6895} = -41.307$$

Since $|-41.307| = 41.307 > 2.201$, we know that $\hat{\delta}_1$ is significantly less than zero. Therefore, we know that the intercept—and sales—in the first quarter is less than in the fourth. Calculating the t-values for $\hat{\delta}_2$ and $\hat{\delta}_3$,

$$t_{\hat{\delta}_2} = \frac{-58.775}{1.6643} = -35.315$$

$$t_{\hat{\delta}_3} = \frac{-62.013}{1.6490} = -37.606$$

we see that they are both also significantly negative. We know then that the intercepts in the second and third quarters are also significantly less than the intercept for the fourth quarter. Hence, we know that there is a significant increase in sales in the fourth quarter.

We can now proceed to forecasts of sales by quarter in 1985. In the first quarter of 1985, $t = 17$, $D_1 = 1$, $D_2 = 0$, and $D_3 = 0$. Therefore, the forecast for sales in 1985I would be

$$Q = \hat{\alpha} + \hat{\beta} \cdot 17 + \hat{\delta}_1 \cdot 1 + \hat{\delta}_2 \cdot 0 + \hat{\delta}_3 \cdot 0$$
$$= \hat{\alpha} + \hat{\beta} \cdot 17 + \hat{\delta}_1$$
$$= 139.63 + 2.7375 \cdot 17 - 69.788$$
$$= 116.3795$$

Using precisely the same method, the forecasts for sales in the other three quarters of 1985 are as follows:

1985 II:

$$\begin{aligned} Q &= \hat{\alpha} + \hat{\beta} \cdot 18 + \hat{\delta}_2 \\ &= 139.63 + 2.7375 \cdot 18 - 58.775 \\ &= 130.13 \end{aligned}$$

1985 III:

$$\begin{aligned} Q &= \hat{\alpha} + \hat{\beta} \cdot 19 + \hat{\delta}_3 \\ &= 139.63 + 2.7375 \cdot 19 - 62.013 \\ &= 129.6295 \end{aligned}$$

1985 IV:

$$\begin{aligned} Q &= \hat{\alpha} + \hat{\beta} \cdot 20 \\ &= 139.63 + 2.7375 \cdot 20 \\ &= 194.38 \end{aligned}$$

In this discussion, we have confined our attention to quarterly variation. However, exactly the same techniques can be used for any type of cyclical (nonrandom) variation. It should be clear how this technique could be used for monthly data. In addition, this type of technique can be used to account for changes in sales due to forces such as wars and strikes at a competitor's facility.

12.3 ECONOMETRIC MODELS

The other method used in statistical forecasting and decision making is econometric modeling. The primary characteristic of econometric models that differentiates this approach from the preceding approaches is the use of an explicit structural model that attempts to *explain* the underlying economic relations. More specifically, if we wish to employ an econometric model to forecast future sales, it is necessary to develop a model that incorporates those variables that actually determine the level of sales (e.g., income, the price of substitutes, and so on). This approach is in marked contrast to the qualitative approach, in which a loose relation was posited between sales and some leading indicators, and the time-series approach, in which sales are assumed to behave in some regular fashion over time.

The use of econometric models has several advantages. First, econometric models require the analysts to define explicit causal relations. This specification of an explicit model helps rule out problems such as spurious (false) correlation between normally unrelated variables and may help to make the model more logically consistent and reliable.

Second, this approach allows analysts to consider the sensitivity of the variable to be forecasted to changes in the exogenous variables. Using estimated elasticities, forecasters can determine which of the variables are most important in determining changes in the variable to be forecasted. Therefore, the analyst will know to watch the behavior of these variables more closely.

Third, this approach can easily be used in a simulation model. Basically, a simulation procedure is designed to answer "what if" questions. Whereas a single-point forecast uses actual, prevailing data on the values of or trends in the variables, a simulation model allows researchers to consider alternative projections based on hypothetical conditions. Thus, the analyst can get an idea of what could happen if market conditions change. (We will return to a consideration of simulation in the final part of this section.)

Simultaneous equations forecasts

The idea behind simultaneous equations forecasting is really quite simple. We illustrate this methodology, using Figure 12.7. Suppose that, using regression analysis, we have estimated the demand function

$$Q_{X,t} = \hat{a} + \hat{b}P_{X,t} + \hat{c}Y_t + \hat{d}P_{R,t}$$

and the supply function

$$Q_{X,t} = \hat{e} + \hat{f}P_{X,t} + \hat{g}T_t + \hat{h}P_{F,t}$$

Figure 12.7
Simultaneous equations forecasting

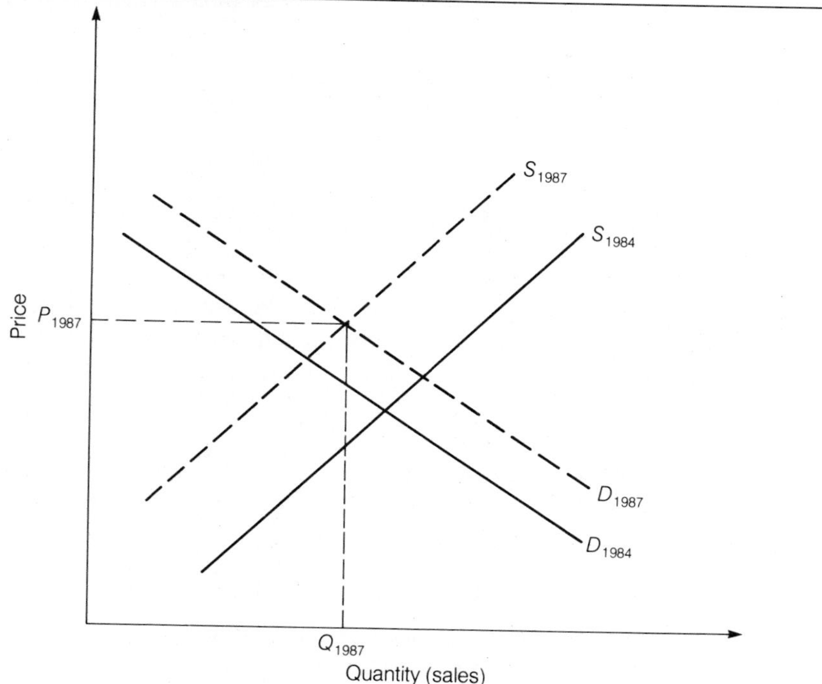

(Note again that the hats on the parameters indicate that they are estimates). Since we know the actual 1984 values for the exogenous variables Y_{1984} and $P_{R,1984}$, we know where the demand function is located in 1984. Likewise, since T_{1984} and $P_{F,1984}$ are also known, we know where the supply function is located in 1984. These demand and supply functions are illustrated in Figure 12.7. Note that their intersection indicates price and sales of X in 1984.

Suppose that in 1984 we want to forecast sales in 1987. As should be clear, in order to obtain this sales forecast, we need to know where the demand and supply functions will be located in 1987. What determines their locations?

From our discussion in Chapter 2 and in the last few chapters, the answer to this question is simple: The values of the exogenous variables determine the location of the demand and supply functions. In the case of our estimated demand function, the values of income and the price of the related good in 1987 will determine the location of the 1987 demand function. For simplicity, let's suppose that, over the period 1984–87, the price of the related good is expected to remain unchanged

$$P_{R,1987} = P_{R,1984}$$

but income is expected to rise

$$Y_{1987} > Y_{1984}$$

As long as X is a normal commodity, this would mean that the 1987 location of the demand curve would be as indicated in Figure 12.7.

In the case of the supply function, its location is determined by the values of T and P_F. Suppose, for purposes of illustration, that comparing 1987 and 1984, we expect

$$T_{1987} = T_{1984}$$

$$P_{F,1987} > P_{F,1984}$$

This set of conditions would yield a 1987 supply function like that illustrated in Figure 12.7.

Once the locations of the 1987 supply and demand functions are determined, the forecast is simple to obtain. We would find the intersection of the two functions and, from that intersection, obtain both forecasted price and forecasted sales in 1987. In Figure 12.7, these are denoted as

$$\hat{P}_{1987} \text{ and } \hat{Q}_{1987}$$

Given this graphical interpretation, let's see how we can actually obtain a forecast, using our estimated demand and supply functions:

$$\text{Demand: } Q_{X,t} = \hat{a} + \hat{b}P_{X,t} + \hat{c}Y_t + \hat{d}P_{R,t}$$
$$\text{Supply: } Q_{X,t} = \hat{e} + \hat{f}P_{X,t} + \hat{g}T_t + \hat{h}P_{F,t}$$

Let's suppose that these functions were estimated for time periods 1,2,...,t and that we want a forecast for period $t + i$.

First, we need to obtain the forecasted values for the *exogenous* variables for period $t + i$. That is, we need to obtain $\hat{Y}_{t+i}$, $\hat{P}_{R,t+i}$, $\hat{T}_{t+i}$, and $\hat{P}_{F,t+i}$. There are several ways in which we might obtain these values. We might simply forecast these values, using the time-series methodology described in Section 12.2. (This approach will be used in the application to follow.)

Alternatively, note that many of these exogenous variables are macroeconomic variables. In the demand function we use income (or per capita income). If we were forecasting the demand for automobiles, we might use the U.S. price of petroleum (or gasoline) as the price of the related good. In our supply function, the price of inputs, P_F, might include things like the wage rate in manufacturing. All of these aggregate (macroeconomic) variables are forecasted by many organizations. In Table 12.3 we have listed some of the more widely known macroeconomic forecasting models. Hence, we might use forecasts from one of these macroeconomic forecasting models as our $t + i$ values of the variables that are exogenous in our model.

Table 12.3
Macroeconomic forecasting models

Public Policy Models
FRB-MIT-Penn Model
Wharton Quarterly Model
St. Louis Federal Reserve Bank Model
Michigan Quarterly Model
Department of Commerce (OBE) Model
Brookings Quarterly Model
Models Supported by Private Firms
Data Resources, Inc.
Chase Econometrics
Wharton Econometrics

Notwithstanding how we obtain the $t + i$ forecasts for Y, P_R, T, and P_F, once we have these values, we can use them to forecast the locations of the demand and supply functions. In the case of the demand function, the values $\hat{Y}_{t+i}$ and $\hat{P}_{R,t+i}$ determine the location of the demand function in time period $t + i$.

$$Q_{X,t+i} = \hat{a} + \hat{b}P_{X,t+i} + \hat{c}\hat{Y}_{t+i} + \hat{d}\hat{P}_{R,t+i}$$

Given that $\hat{Y}_{t+i}$ and $\hat{P}_{R,t+i}$ are now constants, we can simplify this demand function to

$$Q_{X,t+i} = \hat{\theta} + \hat{b}\hat{P}_{X,t+i}$$

where $\hat{\theta} = \hat{a} + \hat{c}\hat{Y}_{t+i} + \hat{d}\hat{P}_{R,t+i}$. Likewise, the supply function in period $t + i$ is

$$Q_{X,t+i} = \hat{e} + \hat{f}P_{X,t+i} + \hat{g}\hat{T}_{t+i} + \hat{h}\hat{P}_{F,t+i}$$

or

$$Q_{X,t+i} = \hat{\phi} + \hat{f}\hat{P}_{X,t+i}$$

where $\hat{\phi} = \hat{e} + \hat{g}\hat{T}_{t+i} + \hat{h}\hat{P}_{F,t+i}$.

Now, since we have determined the locations of the demand and supply functions, we need to find the point at which these functions intersect. As we described in Chapter 2, a market equilibrium exists—demand and supply intersect—when quantity demanded equals quantity supplied. Using the demand and supply functions we have forecast, this condition requires that

$$\hat{\theta} + \hat{b}P_{X,t+i} = \hat{\phi} + \hat{f}P_{X,t+i}$$

Solving this equation for the price of X in period $t + i$,

$$P_{X,t+i} = \frac{\hat{\theta} - \hat{\phi}}{\hat{f} - \hat{b}}$$

This value is our forecasted equilibrium price for period $t + i$. (You may want to look at Figure 12.7 again to verify this.) Let us denote it as $P^*_{X,t+i}$.

Once we have our price forecast, we obtain our sales forecast by simply using this price in either the demand or supply function forecasted for $t + 1$. That is,

$$\hat{\theta} + \hat{b}P^*_{X,t+i} = Q^*_{X,t+i} = \hat{\phi} + \hat{f}P^*_{X,t+i}$$

To help you see how this is accomplished using actual estimations, let us provide an example.

APPLICATION

A forecast for world copper consumption

Returning to the copper data we presented in Chapter 11, let's forecast future copper consumption. To review, we defined the demand function as

$$Q_{\text{copper},t} = a + bP_{\text{copper},t} + cY_t + dP_{\text{aluminum},t}$$

and the supply function as

$$Q_{\text{copper},t} = e + fP_{\text{copper},t} + gT_t + hX_t$$

where time is our proxy for the level of available technology and X is the ratio of consumption to production in the preceding period (to reflect inventory changes). Both of these functions are identified and can be estimated using two-stage least squares.

As you can verify, our estimate for the demand function was

$$Q_{\text{copper},t} = -6837.8 - 66.495\ P_{\text{copper},t} + 13997Y_t + 107.66\ P_{\text{aluminum},t}$$

We also estimated the supply function (via *2SLS*), using the data for $t = 1, 2, \ldots, 25$. The resulting estimated supply function was

$$Q_{\text{copper},t} = 145.623 + 18.154\, P_{\text{copper},t} + 213.88T_t + 1819.8X_t$$

We want to forecast sales in year 26. We will obtain this forecast by proceeding with the steps outlined in our description of simultaneous equations forecasting:

Step 1—Obtain the period 26 values for the exogenous variables. Since time is our proxy for technology, the period 26 value for T is simply

$$\hat{T}_{26} = 26$$

As described in Chapter 11, the value for X in any period is the ratio of consumption to production in the preceding period; and both of these values are known

$$\hat{X}_{26} = \frac{\text{Consumption}_{25}}{\text{Production}_{25}} = \frac{7157.2}{8054.1} = 0.88821$$

However, in the case of Y and P_R, we need forecasted values for year 26. To obtain these, we used the techniques of time-series forecasting and specified a constant growth-rate trend line for each of these variables

$$\log Y_t = \alpha_1 + \beta_1\, t \qquad \log P_{R,t} = \alpha_2 + \beta_2 t$$

Estimating these trend lines for $t = 1, 2, \ldots, 25$, we obtained

$$\log Y_t = -0.4395 + 0.02163t \qquad \log P_{R,t} = 3.2002 - 0.001196t$$

We want to use these estimates to forecast the values for Y and P_R in year 26. Substituting $t = 26$ in the preceding estimated equations, we obtain

$$\log \hat{Y}_{26} = 0.12288 \qquad \log \hat{P}_{R,26} = 3.1691$$

Then, taking the antilogs, we obtain our forecasts

$$\hat{Y}_{26} = 1.13 \qquad \hat{P}_{R,26} = 23.79$$

Step 2—Locate the demand and supply functions for time period 26. Using $\hat{Y}_{26}$ and $P_{R,26}$, the demand function in time period 26 is

$$\begin{aligned} Q_{\text{copper},t} &= -6837.8 - 66.495\, P_{\text{copper},26} + 13997\,(1.13) + 107.66\,(23.79) \\ &= 11540.04 - 66.495\, P_{\text{copper},26} \end{aligned}$$

Likewise, using $\hat{T}_{26}$ and $\hat{X}_{26}$, the supply function in time period 26 is

$$\begin{aligned} Q_{\text{copper},26} &= 145.623 + 18.154\, P_{\text{copper},26} + 213.88\,(26) + 1819.8\,(0.88821) \\ &= 7322.868 + 18.154\, P_{\text{copper},26} \end{aligned}$$

Step 3—Intersect the demand and supply functions. Setting quantity demanded equal to quantity supplied in time period 26.

$$11540.04 - 66.495\, P_{\text{copper},26} = 7322.868 + 18.154\, P_{\text{copper},26}$$

Solving for the forecasted equilibrium price in period 26

$$84.649\, P^*_{\text{copper},26} = 4217.172$$
$$P^*_{\text{copper},26} = 49.82$$

That is, our forecasted equilibrium price for copper is 49.82 cents per pound.

Step 4—Forecast sales in period 26. We can use our equilibrium price in either the demand or supply function to obtain forecasted sales. As a double check, let's use both:[4]

$$\text{Demand: } Q^*_{\text{copper},26} = 11540.04 - 66.495\,(49.82) = 8227.3$$

$$\text{Supply: } Q^*_{\text{copper},26} = 7322.868 + 18.154\,(49.82) = 8227.3$$

A note on simulations

As we noted earlier, the primary objective of a simulation analysis is to answer "what if" questions. This procedure can probably best be explained in the context of the preceding example.

In obtaining our forecasts for the copper market, we assumed that the exogenous variables Y and P_R would continue to follow their historical trends. However, it is quite possible that the exogenous variables will deviate from trend. For example, it may well be the case that real income will grow less rapidly than it has in the past. Thus, we might wish to obtain alternative forecasts under the assumption that the growth rate in income is smaller than that indicated by historical trend.

Adjusting for this type of alternative is precisely what a simulation analysis is designed to do. We would provide alternative forecasts based on alternative projections about the future values of the exogenous variables. In this way, we can examine "what would happen if . . . ." Note that in this way the qualitative and quantitative forecasting techniques are brought together. In a simulation analysis, researchers can impose some subjective evaluations and employ their expertise in the market. For example, in our forecasts of copper consumption, it might be that we think that conditions in the aluminum market are such that price will rise radically. Thus, we could provide an alternate forecast that incorporates this information based on our expertise and knowledge about a particular market.

12.4 SOME FINAL WARNINGS

We have often heard it said in respect to forecasting that "he who lives by the crystal ball ends up eating ground glass." While we do not make nearly so dire a judgment, we do feel that you should be aware of the major limitations

---

[4]As we noted in Chapter 11, the data we have used for our copper market illustration are the actual data for the period 1951–75. Hence, our forecast for year 26 can be interpreted as the forecast for 1976. The actual value for copper consumption in 1976 was 8174.0; so, our forecast error in this application was 0.65 percent—a little more than ½ of 1 percent.

of and problems inherent in forecasting. Basically, our warnings are concerned with three issues—confidence intervals, specification, and change of structure.

To describe the issue of confidence intervals in forecasting, let's look again at the simple linear trend model,

$$Q_t = \alpha + \beta t$$

In order to obtain our prediction model, we must estimate two coefficients, α and β. As you know, we cannot estimate these coefficients with certainty. Indeed, the estimated standard errors reflect the magnitude of uncertainty (i.e., potential error) about the values of the parameters.

In Figure 12.8, we have illustrated a situation in which we have observations on sales for period t_1 through t_n. Due to the manner in which it is calculated, the regression line will go through the mean of the distribution of data points $(\bar{Q}, \bar{t})$. In Panel A, we have illustrated as the shaded area our confidence region if there exist errors only in the estimation of the slope, β. In Panel B, the shaded area represents our confidence region if an error exists only in the estimation of the intercept, α. These two shaded areas are com-

Figure 12.8
Confidence intervals

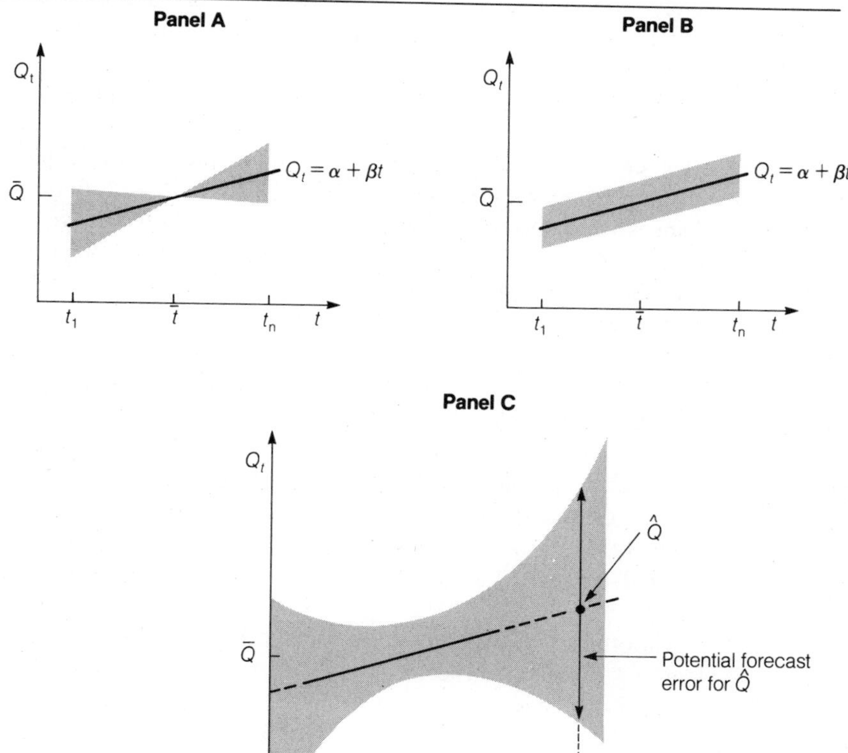

bined in Panel C. As you can see, the further the value of t is from the mean value of t, the wider becomes this zone of uncertainty.

Now consider what happens when we use the estimated regression line to predict future sales. At a future time period, t_{n+k}, our prediction for sales will be a point on the extrapolated regression line (i.e., $\hat{Q}$). However, note what happens to our region of uncertainty about this estimate. The further you forecast into the future, the wider is this region of uncertainty; and this region increases geometrically rather than arithmetically.

This warning applies not just to time-series models. It applies to all statistical techniques. The further the variables used in the forecasts are from the mean values used in the regression, the wider will be the region of uncertainty, and therefore, the less precise will be the forecast. For example, consider our econometric forecasting model for copper. If we attempt to forecast copper sales using a value of per capita income that is much higher than the mean in our data set, the confidence interval for our forecast will be much wider than would be the case if the value of income used in the forecast was close to the mean value in our data set.

We noted the problem of incorrect specification in our discussion of demand estimation; but we feel that it is important enough to deserve another mention here. In order to generate reliable forecasts, the model used must incorporate the appropriate variables. The quality of the forecast can be severely reduced if important explanatory variables are excluded or if an improper functional form is employed (e.g., using a linear form when a nonlinear form is appropriate).

We have saved what we feel to be the most important problem for last. This problem stems from potential changes in structure. Forecasts are widely, and often correctly, criticized for failing to predict "turning points"—sharp changes in the variable under consideration. If it were the case that these changes were only the result of radical changes in the exogenous variables, the simulation approach should be able to handle the problem. However, it is often the case that such changes are the result of changes in the structure of the market itself.

For example, in our consideration of the copper market, there exists the potential for a major change in structure. A major consumer of copper is the telecommunications industry. This industry has been replacing copper transmitting cables with glass fibers. As this change occurs, the demand for copper will be affected significantly. More specifically, any temporal or econometric relation estimated using data before such a change would be incapable of correctly forecasting quantity demanded after the change. In the context of a demand function, the coefficients would be different before and after the change.

Unfortunately, we know of no satisfactory method of handling this problem of "change in structure." Instead, we must simply leave you with the warning that changes in structure are likely. The further you forecast into the future, the more likely is it that you will encounter such a change. To illustrate the warning, let us give you a historical example.

APPLICATION

The dismal science

A classic example of a forecast made invalid by changes in structure is found in the work of Thomas Malthus, an English economist of the late 18th century. According to Malthus, food production was growing at an arithmetic rate while population was expanding geometrically. As is clear in Figure 12.9, such a set of conditions produces a dismal forecast for the future. (Indeed, it was this forecast that led to economics being labeled "the dismal science.") Malthus predicted that population growth would outrun the available food supply, leading to periods of starvation. In the long run, he predicted only a minimum subsistence level of consumption.

Obviously, this dire prediction did not come to pass. Where did Malthus's forecast go wrong? He was unable to foresee changes in structure—particularly in food production. Clearly, technological change in agriculture has increased the rate of growth of food production. The existing trends, which Malthus observed at the time, simply did not hold true in the future.

This example is meant to illustrate a lesson that we feel is extremely important—and one that has not been learned by many people. Compare for a moment Malthus's prediction (which appears ridiculous in retrospect) and the current predictions of doom. Simplifying, the "limits to growth" theories predict that the rate of growth in consumption will outrun the rate of growth in the production of natural resources (particularly energy), leading to a natural resource–based Armageddon for the developed economies—precisely the same sort of argument made by Malthus. This prediction is valid only if there are no changes in structure. However, even the most casual review of history

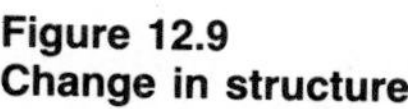

Figure 12.9
Change in structure

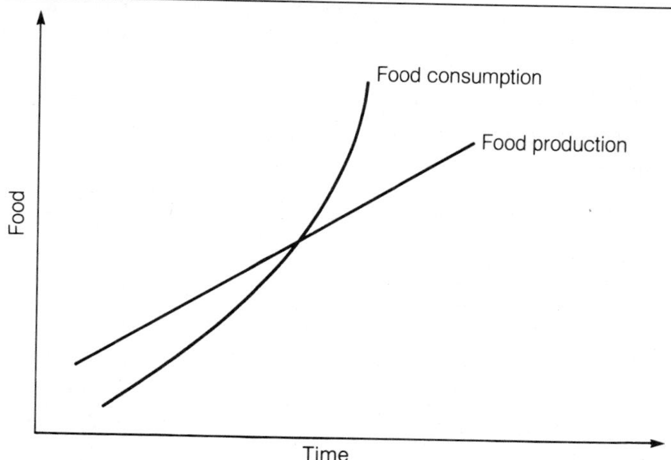

indicates that such circumstances have led to changes in structure in the past. It seems unlikely that none will occur in the future.

TECHNICAL PROBLEMS

1. Contrast and compare qualitative and statistical forecasting methods.
2. A linear trend equation for sales of the form

$$Q_t = \alpha + \beta t$$

was estimated for the period 1970–84 (i.e., $t = 70, 71, \ldots, 84$). The results of the regression are as follows:

DEPENDENT VARIABLE: QT		F-RATIO: 13.1792
OBSERVATIONS: 15		R-SQUARE: 0.8786
VARIABLE	PARAMETER ESTIMATE	STANDARD ERROR
INTERCEPT	73.7146	10.1315
T	3.7621	1.0363

a. Test the estimated coefficients for statistical significance at a 95 percent confidence level. Does this estimation indicate a significant trend?

b. Perform an F-test for significance of the equation at a 95 percent confidence level.

c. Using this equation, forecast sales in 1985 and 1990.

d. Comment on the precision of these two forecasts.

3. Consider a firm subject to quarter-to-quarter variation in its sales. Suppose that the following equation was estimated using quarterly data for the period 1976–84 (the time variable goes from 1 to 36). The variables D_1, D_2, and D_3 are, respectively, dummy variables for the first, second, and third quarters (e.g., D_1 is equal to one in the first quarter and zero otherwise).

$$Q_t = \alpha + \beta t + \delta_1 D_1 + \delta_2 D_2 + \delta_3 D_3$$

The results of the estimation are presented on the following page:

a. Perform t- and F-tests to check for statistical significance of the coefficients and the equation.

b. Calculate the intercept in each of the four quarters. What do these values imply?

c. Use this estimated equation to forecast sales in the four quarters of 1985.

```
DEPENDENT VARIABLE:  QT              F-RATIO:  761.133
OBSERVATIONS:  36                    R-SQUARE:  0.9761

                    PARAMETER            STANDARD
 VARIABLE           ESTIMATE               ERROR

INTERCEPT             51.234               7.163
T                      3.127               0.524
D1                   -11.716               2.717
D2                    -1.424               0.836
D3                   -17.367               2.112
```

4. These supply and demand functions were specified for commodity X:

   Demand: $Q_{X,t} = a + bP_{X,t} + cY_t + dP_{R,t}$
   Supply: $Q_{X,t} = e + fP_{X,t} + gP_{F,t}$

   Using quarterly data for the period 1978I through 1984IV, these functions were estimated (via *2SLS*). The resulting parameter estimates are presented in the following estimated equations.

   Demand: $Q_{X,t} = 50 - 30P_{X,t} + 0.10Y_t - 20P_{R,t}$
   Supply: $Q_{X,t} = -40 + 20P_{X,t} - 10P_{F,t}$

   Predicted values for the exogenous variables (Y, P_R, and P_F) for the first quarter of 1985 were obtained from a macroeconomic forecasting model. These predicted values are:

   Income (Y) = 10,000
   The price of the commodity related in consumption (P_R) = 20
   The price of inputs (P_F) = 6

   a. Are the signs of the estimated coefficients as would be predicted theoretically? Explain.
   b. Predict the price of commodity X in 1985I.
   c. Predict the sales of commodity X in 1985I.

5. Describe the major shortcomings of time-series models.
6. Suppose that you have an estimate of the demand function

$$Q_{X,t} = a + bP_{X,t} + cY_t + dP_{R,t}$$

   Obviously you could use historical trend to forecast the values for *all* of the right-hand side variables and thereby obtain a prediction for sales. What is the major shortcoming in such an approach?

ANALYTICAL PROBLEMS

1. Suppose that your firm produces refrigerators and freezers and you wish to obtain a qualitative forecast of future sales. Consider the 12 leading

indicators published by the U.S. Department of Commerce. Evaluate the effect of changes in these indicators on future sales of your firm. (For example, if the average workweek of production workers in manufacturing increased, what would be the effect on your sales in the future and why?) Which of these indicators would be most important to your firm? Explain.

2. Suppose that a firm's sales are subject to cyclical variation. Describe the effect on estimated trend if the analyst does not account for this variation. Conversely, the analyst might employ a technique such as dummy variables when there exists no cyclical variation. What effect would this have on the estimation?

3. A market in which considerable sales forecasting is done is the automobile market. Clearly, if an automobile firm produces too many units, the costs from holding this inventory are substantial. Alternatively, if too few units are produced, sales are lost and substantial profits are forgone. However, as is evident from the recent experience of U.S. automobile manufacturers, such forecasting is not yet precise.

a. If you were to provide a qualitative forecast, which of the leading indicators would be most relevant? Why? What additional information would you wish to have?

b. Comment on the applicability of time-series forecasting in the automobile market.

c. Let us consider an econometric forecasting model for this market:

(1) Specify the demand and supply functions you think appropriate and explain why they are appropriate.

(2) In our examination of the copper market, we forecasted the values of the exogenous variables, using historical trend. Such an approach might not be advisable in the automobile market—particularly in the case of the complementary good, gasoline. As you may be aware, the real (deflated) price of gasoline fell during most of the 1960s. Only after the mid-70s did it begin its rapid rise. With this circumstance in mind, suggest a methodology for forecasting automobile sales in the future.

4. As you know, the 1930s was the period of the Great Depression (although we fail to see what was so great about it). This period was followed by World War II. Many economists predicted that at the end of the war the U.S. economy would again enter a depression.

These economists could not have been more wrong. The decade of the 1950s was one of the most productive in the history of the United States. (This fact might help to explain the TV series which extolled the 50s as the "happy days.")

Explain why the economists' forecasts went wrong. What factors did they fail to predict correctly and what information did they exclude from their forecasts?

5. Let us consider Coors beer. Until recently, the sale of Coors was rather localized. While the company has expanded its sales into much larger territory, there are still many areas of the nation in which Coors does not distribute. We might note that recently groups such as union members and women's rights activists boycotted Coors beer. Consider the following forecasting problems.
   a. Suppose as is the case, that Coors' management wishes to expand the territory in which it sells and they wish to forecast sales in a particular area in which they presently have no distributorship. How would you set up a forecasting model to predict sales in that area? What variables would you consider important in setting up the model? How important would you expect price to be?
   b. Alternatively, assume that management wishes to find the best area in which to expand out of all the areas not presently served. What kind of a model would you develop in this case? What variables are important?

SUGGESTED ADDITIONAL REFERENCES

Box, G. E. P., and G. M. Jenkins. *Time Series Analysis, Forecasting and Control.* San Francisco: Holden-Day, 1970.

Granger, C. W. J. *Forecasting in Business and Economics.* New York: Academic Press, 1980.

Montgomery, D. C., and L. A. Johnson. *Forecasting and Time Series Analysis.* New York: McGraw-Hill, 1976.

Pindyck, R. C., and D. L. Rubinfeld. *Econometric Models and Economic Forecasts.* New York: McGraw-Hill, 1981.

Part 4

Perfect competition

13

Theory of perfectly competitive firms and industries

Now that we have analyzed both demand and cost, we are prepared to begin our analysis of firms and industries in order to consider the question that is posed by every manager: What can I do to maximize my firm's profits? There are many possible variations of industry structure. On one extreme, an industry could consist of a very large number of firms producing a homogeneous product. On the other extreme, an industry could consist of only one firm. And there are several structures between these two extremes. In this chapter, we consider the first structure, called perfect competition.

We will consider an industry consisting of so many firms that each firm takes the market-determined price as given—no one firm can influence market price. We assume that each firm in the industry attempts to maximize its profit. Certainly managers may have other goals; but, other things equal, managers would prefer more profit to less. In any case, we use the assumption of profit maximization because it works well and because it provides a reasonably good description of the way firms actually behave.

Within this framework of profit maximization under perfect competition, the manager looks at the demand and cost conditions facing the firm in order to answer three fundamental questions: (1) Should I produce or shut down? (2) If I produce, what is the appropriate level of production? (3) What amounts of each input should I use? (Since, as we noted, the perfectly competitive firm must take market price as given, the manager is not faced with the decision concerning what price to charge.)

We should emphasize at the outset that all of the exacting characteristics of perfect competition are generally not met in real-world markets. Although many markets *approach* perfect competition, none that we know of meets *all* of the assumptions. You might therefore ask why such a theory should be considered.

The answer can be given in as much or as little detail as desired. For our purposes, the answer is brief. First, generality can be achieved only by means of abstraction. Hence, no theory can be perfectly descriptive of real-world phenomena. Furthermore, the more accurately a theory describes one specific real-world case, the less accurately it describes all others. Thus, these theories are used in many cases because what is lost in realism is substantially compensated for by the gain in generality.

A second point of great, if somewhat pragmatic, importance is that the conclusions derived from the model of perfect competition (and the theory of pure monopoly to be introduced in Chapter 15) have, by and large, permitted accurate explanation and prediction of real-world phenomena. That is, these models frequently work as theoretical models of economic processes even though they do not accurately describe any specific firm or industry. Thus the fundamentals of the theories are useful not only to theoretical economists but also to managerial decision makers.

To summarize, no market is perfectly competitive; however, the behavior of many markets closely approximates the model. Thus, we can use the model for a first approximation. If necessary, we can revise the predictions of the model to reflect the significant characteristics of the market in question.

13.1 SOME PRINCIPLES

The basic principles of profit maximization are straightforward and follow directly from the discussion of optimization in Chapter 3. The firm will increase any activity so long as the additional revenue from the increase exceeds the additional cost of the increase. The firm will cease to expand the activity if the additional revenue is less than the additional cost.

Suppose that the activity or choice variable is the firm's level of output. As the firm increases its level of output, each additional unit adds to the total revenue of the firm. The change in revenue per unit change in output is, as you will recall, called marginal revenue. As the firm increases its level of output, each unit increase in output increases the firm's total cost. As you will recall from Chapter 7, the added cost per unit increase in output is called marginal cost.

Thus, the firm will choose to expand output so long as the added revenue from the expansion (marginal revenue) is greater than the added cost of the expansion (marginal cost). The firm would choose not to increase output if the marginal cost of the increase is greater than the marginal revenue from the increase. Profit maximization is, therefore, based upon the following principle:

■ **Principle.** Profit is the difference between revenue and cost. If an increase in output adds more to revenue than to cost, the increase in output adds to profit. If the increase in output adds less to revenue than to cost, the increase in output subtracts from profit. The firm, therefore, chooses the level of output at which marginal revenue equals marginal cost. This level maximizes total profit.

In this chapter, we are concerned with the special case in which the price of the produced commodity is given to the firm by the market. In this special case, marginal revenue equals price. For example, if the firm produces plywood, and the market price of plywood is $200 per 1,000 square feet, the marginal revenue from each additional thousand square feet is $200. The owner of the firm would increase plywood production as long as the marginal cost of each additional thousand square feet is less than $200. It would not increase production if each additional thousand square feet costs more than $200 to produce.

Of course, as we mentioned above, we can also analyze profit maximization through the firm's choice of the level of input usage. Again the principle is simple and follows directly from the analysis in Chapter 3. The firm will expand its usage of any input (or factor of production) so long as additional units of the input add more to the firm's revenue than to cost. The firm would not increase the usage of the input if hiring more units increases the firm's cost more than its revenue. From the input side, profit maximization is, therefore, based upon the following principle:

■ **Principle.** If an increase in the usage of an input in the production process adds more to revenue than to cost, the increase in input usage adds to profit. If the increase in usage of the input adds less to revenue than to cost, the increase in usage reduces profit. The firm, therefore, chooses the level of input usage at which the additional revenue per unit change in the input—called marginal revenue product (*MRP*)—equals the additional cost per unit of the input added—called marginal factor cost (*MFC*).

Here, we are interested in the special case in which the price of the input is given to the firm by the market. In this case the input's marginal factor cost is the market-determined price of the input. For example, suppose a manufacturing firm can hire all of the labor it wishes at $10 an hour or $80 a day. The firm would increase labor usage so long as it expects each additional laborer hired to add more than $80 a day to the firm's revenue. It would not increase the number of laborers hired if an additional laborer would add less than $80 a day to revenues. It would follow the same procedure when hiring all other inputs. The marginal revenue product of each must equal its price. In this way profit is maximized.

Let us stress that the term *profit* means return over and above all costs, including implicit costs. Recall from Chapter 7 that implicit costs are included in total cost. Therefore, if the owner manages the firm, the wages that would be paid to an equally qualified manager must be included as a cost of operation. Let us take another example. Suppose the owner has invested his or her own resources in purchasing the capital used in the firm's production process. The return that could be earned from the use of the capital is an opportunity cost and is an implicit cost to the firm.

Economists frequently refer to the opportunity cost of using the owner's capital as a "normal return." Any return over and above the "normal" return is called "pure profit" or "economic profit." To illustrate, suppose the owner has $1 million invested in the firm. Suppose also that the normal return in the economy is 6 percent per year. If the firm earns 10 percent per year, the normal profit, included in cost, is 6 percent; the pure or economic profit is the additional 4 percent return. In this text, when we use the term *profit*, we shall mean pure or economic profit—i.e., profit over and above the normal return on the owner's resources.

13.2 CHARACTERISTICS OF PERFECT COMPETITION

Perfect competition forms the basis of the most important and most widely used model of economic behavior. The essence of perfect competition is that neither buyers nor producers recognize any competitiveness among themselves—i.e., no direct competition among economic agents exists.

Thus, the theoretical concept of competition is diametrically opposed to the generally accepted concept of "competition." One might maintain that the automobile industry or the cigarette industry is quite competitive, since each firm in these industries must consider what its rivals will do before it makes a decision about advertising campaigns, design changes, quality improvements, and so forth. However, that type of market is far removed from the theory of perfect competition, which permits no personal rivalry. (In this, "personal" rivalry is personal in the sense that firms consider the reactions of other firms in determining their own policy.) In perfect competition all relevant economic magnitudes are determined by impersonal market forces.

Several important conditions define perfect competition:[1]

1. The product of each firm in a perfectly competitive market must be identical to the product of every other firm. This condition ensures that buyers are indifferent as to the firm from which they purchase. Product differences, whether real or imaginary, are precluded under perfect competition. Thus, the market is characterized by a homogeneous (or perfectly standardized) commodity.

2. Each firm in the industry must be so small relative to the total market

[1]In addition to the following conditions, perfect competition may also be said to be characterized by perfect knowledge. That is, the consumers and producers have complete knowledge about the product and the market. This assumption is not, however, necessary for our purposes and will not be made.

that it cannot affect market price by changes in output. If all producers act collectively, changes in quantity will definitely affect market price. But, if perfect competition prevails, each producer is so small that individual changes will go unnoticed. In other words, the actions of any individual firm do not affect market supply.

3. There exists free entry and exit of firms into and out of the industry. Hence, there can be no artificial restrictions on entry or exit.

The model can be summarized by the following:

■ **Characteristics.** Perfect competition is an economic model of a market possessing the following characteristics: each economic agent is so small relative to the market that it can exert no perceptible influence on price; the product is homogeneous, and there is free and easy entry and exit of business firms into and out of an industry.

13.3 THE DEMAND CURVE FOR AN INDIVIDUAL FIRM

The marginal revenue of a perfectly competitive firm is the market-determined price of the product it produces and sells. Each firm believes that it can sell all it wishes at the prevailing market price. Thus, the marginal revenue curve is a horizontal line at the market-determined price. This horizontal marginal revenue curve is also the demand facing the firm—demand is said to be perfectly elastic. This condition does not contradict the fact that the demand for the output of the *industry* is negatively sloped. Certainly the law of demand holds in that case.

A perfectly competitive firm faces a horizontal demand because of two of the conditions that must exist in a perfectly competitive market. First, each firm in the industry produces a homogeneous product. Therefore, the product of any firm in the industry is a perfect substitute for the product of every other firm. Second, each firm is small relative to the size of the total market for the product. Thus, no firm acting alone can affect market price and each firm takes the market price, set by total industry supply and demand, as given.

Any firm can sell all it wants at the going market price. For example, if the market price of the product is $10 per unit, the marginal revenue from each additional unit sold is $10. So the marginal revenue curve and hence the demand curve is a horizontal line at $10. Such a curve is shown in Figure 13.1, where marginal revenue equals the price, $10, at any relevant output.

The firm would have no reason to charge any higher or any lower price. Since it can sell all it wants at $10, there would be no reason to lower the price. If the firm raised its price, the availability of perfect substitutes from other firms at $10 means it could sell nothing at the higher price.

Figure 13.2 illustrates the relation between the individual firm's demand and the market-determined price. Panel A shows equilibrium in the market. Supply and demand have the "typically" assumed shapes. Equilibrium price

Figure 13.1
Marginal revenue–demand facing a perfectly competitive firm

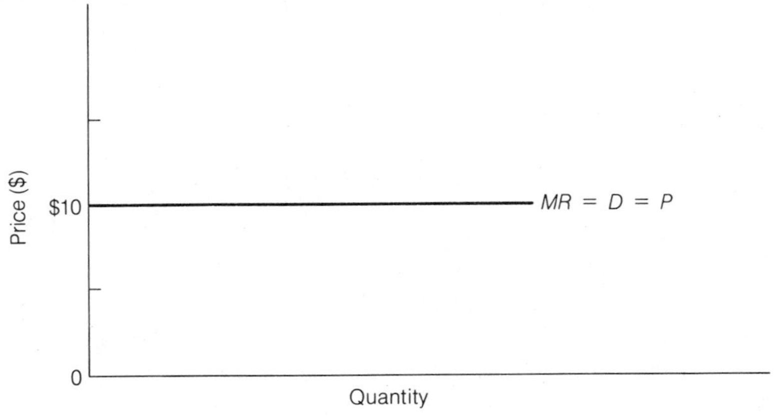

Figure 13.2
Derivation of demand for a perfectly competitive firm

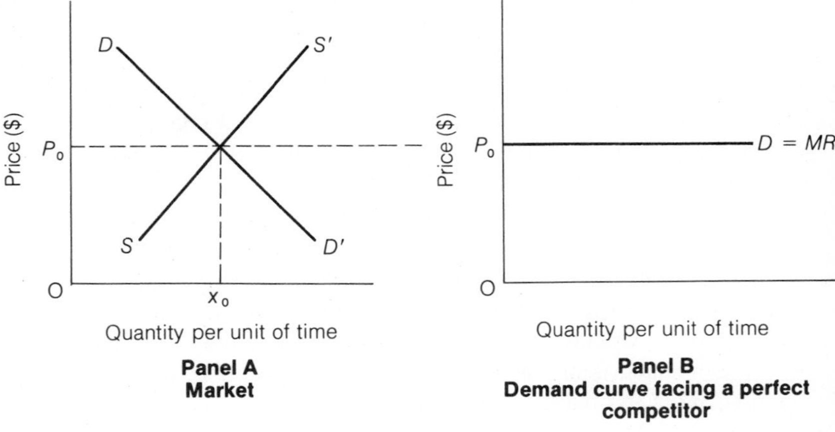

is p_0 and quantity demanded and supplied is x_0. The marginal revenue for any firm in this perfectly competitive industry is shown in Panel B. Each producer knows that changes in the firm's output will have no perceptible effect upon market price. A change in the rate of sales per period of time will change the firm's revenue, but it will not affect market price.

The producer in a perfectly competitive market, therefore, does not have to reduce price in order to expand the rate of sales. Any number of units (per period of time) can be sold at the market equilibrium price.

■ **Relation.** The demand curve facing a producer in a perfectly competitive market is a horizontal line at the level of the market equilibrium price. The output decisions of the individual seller do not affect market price. In this case, the demand and marginal revenue curves are identical (i.e., $D = MR$). Demand is perfectly elastic and the coefficient of price elasticity approaches infinity.

13.4 PROFIT MAXIMIZATION IN THE SHORT RUN

Let us turn now to the output decision of a competitive firm in the short run. Recall from Chapter 7 that, in the short run, the firm has two types of costs—fixed costs, a fixed amount that must be paid regardless of output, and variable costs, which vary with the level of output. In the short run, the firm must make two decisions. The first decision is whether to produce or to shut down, i.e., produce zero output. If the first decision is to produce, the second decision concerns the proper level of output. (As we noted earlier, the firm has no control over price, which is determined in the market; so the individual firm does not have a pricing decision.)

Once the decision to produce is made, the output decision is straightforward. The firm expands output at long as marginal revenue (price) exceeds marginal cost. The firm will maximize profit if it produces that output at which price equals marginal cost.[2]

This situation is illustrated graphically in Figure 13.3. In this figure we have illustrated a typical set of short-run cost curves—marginal cost (*MC*), average total cost (*ATC*), and average variable cost (*AVC*). (Average fixed cost is omitted for convenience and because it is irrelevant for the output decision.) Suppose that the market-determined price, and therefore the marginal revenue, is $10 per unit. Marginal revenue equals marginal cost at point *E*, with 600 units of output being produced and sold.

The firm would not produce less than 600 units. At any lower output, an additional unit sold would add $10 to the firm's revenue; but, since marginal cost is less than $10 for this unit of output, the cost of producing this additional unit is less than the additional revenue. Thus, at any output lower than 600 units, an additional unit of output would increase profit. Likewise, the firm would not produce more than 600 units. Beyond 600 units, any additional unit of production would add more than $10 to cost, because marginal cost is greater than $10. Thus producing any additional unit would decrease profit.

Therefore the firm maximizes profit by producing and selling 600 units of

---

[2]In perfect competition, the firm faces a parametric (fixed) price, $\bar{P}$, and attempts to maximize the profit function

$$\pi = \bar{P} \cdot Q - C(Q)$$

Maximizing this function with respect to output requires

$$\frac{\partial \pi}{\partial Q} = \bar{P} - C'(Q) = 0$$

Thus, profit is maximized at that output at which price (P) is equal to marginal cost [$C'(Q)$].

Figure 13.3
Short-run equilibrium

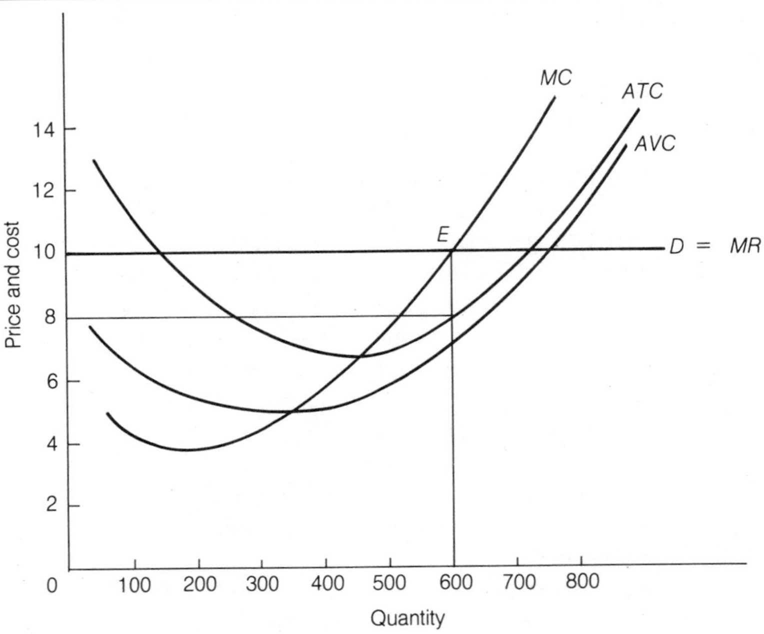

output per period of time. From the figure, we can see that the average total cost of producing 600 units is \$8 per unit. Thus the total cost of production is $\$8 \times 600 = \$4{,}800$. Total revenue is $\$10 \times 600 = \$6{,}000$. The maximum possible profit is therefore $\$6{,}000 - \$4{,}800 = \$1{,}200$.

Looking at Figure 13.3, suppose that the market price was higher than \$10. The demand facing the firm would rise and the profit-maximizing level of output would also rise. If price is higher, the firm will produce a greater output. Conversely, if price is lower, the firm will produce a lower output. It follows then that output varies directly with price.

The equality of price and short-run marginal cost guarantees either that profit is a maximum or that loss is a minimum. Whether a profit is made or a loss incurred can be determined only by comparing price and average total cost at the equilibrium rate of output. If price exceeds unit cost, the firm enjoys a short-run profit. On the other hand, if unit cost exceeds price, a loss is suffered.

Figure 13.4 illustrates four possible short-run situations for the firm. First, if the market-established price is p_1, the demand and marginal revenue facing the firm are D_1 and MR_1. The optimal point for the firm is at point A, where $MC = p_1$, and the firm will produce x_1 units of output. Since ATC is less than price, the firm makes a profit.

Next let the market price fall to p_2. MC now equals price at point B; the

Figure 13.4
Profit, loss, or ceasing production in the short run

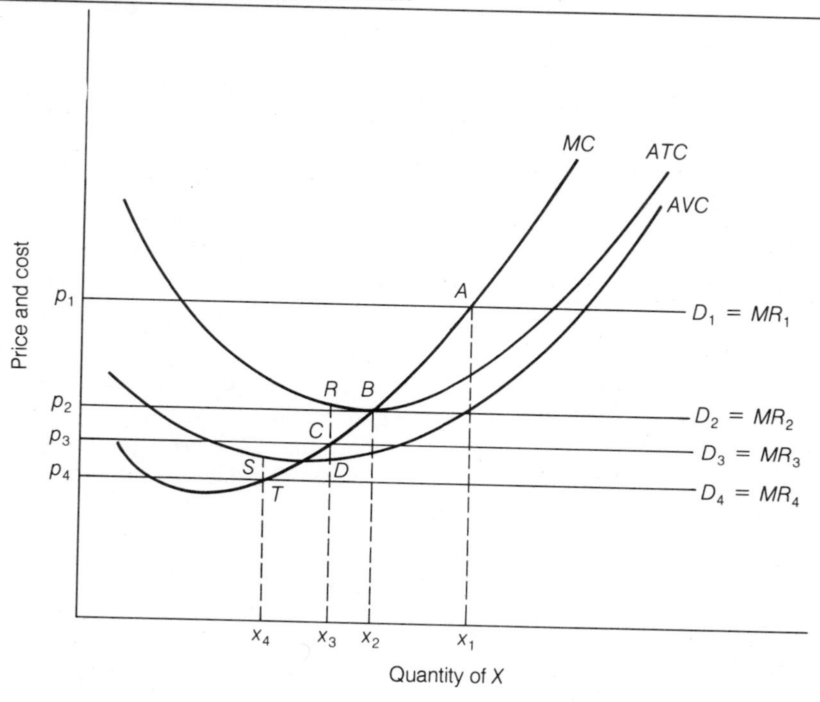

firm produces x_2. Since B is the lowest point on ATC, price just equals average total cost, and the firm makes neither a profit nor a loss. It does cover its opportunity cost, which is included in ATC.

If price falls further to p_3, the firm produces x_3. Price equals MC at point C. Because average total cost is greater than price at this output, total cost is greater than total revenue, and the firm suffers a loss. The amount of loss is the loss per unit (CR) times the number of units produced (x_3).

When price is P_3 and demand is $D_3 = MR_3$ there is simply no way the firm can earn a profit. At every output level, average total cost exceeds price. The firm will continue to produce if, and only if, it loses less by producing than by closing the plant entirely. Recall that there are two types of costs in the short run: fixed costs and variable costs. The fixed costs cannot be changed and are incurred whether the plant is operating or not. Fixed costs are unavoidable in the short run and are the same at zero output as at any other.

If the firm produced zero output, total revenue would also be zero and total cost would be the total fixed cost. The loss would thus be equal to total fixed cost. If the firm can produce where $MC = MR$ and if at this output total revenue is greater than total variable cost, a smaller loss is suffered when production takes place than if the firm were shut down. The firm covers all of its variable cost and some revenue is left over to cover a part of fixed cost. The loss is that part of fixed cost not covered and is clearly less than the entire fixed cost.

Returning to Figure 13.4 you can see more easily why if price is p_3 the firm in the short run would produce at *C* and not shut down. The firm loses *CR* dollars per unit produced. However, not only are all variable costs covered but there is an excess of *CD* dollars per unit sold. The excess of price over average variable cost, *CD*, can be applied to fixed costs. Thus, not all of the fixed costs are lost, as would be the case if production were discontinued. The amount *CD* times x_3 can be applied to fixed costs. Although a loss is sustained, it is smaller than the loss associated with zero output.

To be sure, the firm would not and could not go on for a very long time suffering a loss in each period. In the long run, the firm would leave the industry if it could not cover total costs. However, we shall postpone long-run analysis until we complete our discussion of the short run.

Finally, in Figure 13.4, suppose that the market price is p_4. Demand is given by $D_4 = MR_4$. If the firm were to produce, its equilibrium would be at *T* where $MC = p_4$. Output would be x_4 units per period of time. However, since the average variable cost of production exceeds price, not only would the firm lose all of its fixed costs, it would also lose *ST* dollars per unit on its variable costs as well. The firm could improve its earnings situation by producing nothing and losing only fixed cost. Thus when price is below average variable cost at every level of output, the short-run, loss-minimizing output is zero.

As shown in Chapter 7, average variable cost reaches its minimum at the point at which marginal cost and average variable cost intersect. If price is less than the minimum average variable cost, the loss-minimizing output is zero. For any price equal to or greater than minimum average variable cost, equilibrium output is determined by the intersection of marginal cost and price.

■ **Principles.** (1) Average variable cost tells whether to produce; the firm ceases to produce—shuts down—if price falls below minimum *AVC*. (2) Marginal cost tells how much to produce; if $P >$ minimum *AVC*, the firm produces the output at which $MC = P$. (3) Average total cost tells how much profit or loss is made if the firm decides to produce; profit equals the difference between *P* and *ATC* multiplied by the quantity produced and sold.

From the preceding discussion you probably have seen that the short-run marginal cost curve above the intersection with average variable cost is the firm's short-run supply curve. That is, marginal cost above average variable cost indicates the quantity the firm would be willing and able to supply at each price in a list of prices per period of time, which is the definition of supply. For market prices lower than minimum average variable cost, quantity supplied is zero.

In contrast to market demand curves for commodities, which we described in Chapter 10, the industry supply curve cannot always be obtained by simply summing (horizontally) the marginal cost curves of each producer. The reason is that the short-run supply curve for each firm is derived assuming that the prices of variable inputs are given. No change in input usage by an individual firm acting alone can change an input's unit cost to the firm, because a single competitive firm is so small, relative to all users of the resource. But if all producers in an industry were to simultaneously expand output and thereby their usage of inputs, there may be marked effects in resource markets. When all firms attempt to increase output, the prices of some variable inputs may be bid up and the increase in these input prices causes an increase in all firms' cost curves, including marginal cost. As a consequence, the industry's short-run supply curve usually is somewhat more steeply sloped and somewhat less elastic when input prices increase in response to an increase in industry output than when input prices remain constant (as would be the presumption if we simply summed the marginal cost curves). In any case, in the short run quantity supplied by the industry does vary directly with price.

We can summarize the theory of the competitive firm in the short run as follows: In the short run, some costs are fixed regardless of the level of production. The firm will produce some positive output in the short run so long as the price is high enough that it can cover all of average variable cost and at least some portion of average fixed cost. For the individual firm, market price is equal to marginal revenue because each unit sold adds an amount equal to the market price to the firm's revenue. Equilibrium output is that at which marginal revenue equals marginal cost. The firm's short-run supply curve is its marginal cost above average variable cost.

If price equals marginal cost above average total cost, a pure economic profit is earned. Profit is price minus *ATC* times output. If price equals marginal cost between *ATC* and *AVC*, the loss to the firm is *ATC* minus price times output. If price falls below minimum *AVC*, the firm produces nothing and loses all of its fixed cost.

13.5 PROFIT MAXIMIZATION IN THE LONG RUN

In the short run the firm is limited by past decisions, i.e., its fixed costs. In the long run all inputs are variable; the firm is not bound by the past. The long run may be viewed as the planning stage, prior to the firm's entry into the industry. In this stage the firm is trying to decide how large a production facility to construct, i.e., the optimal amount of fixed cost. Or, if a firm is operating in the short run at a scale such that it is not obtaining maximum possible profits, the long run is the period of time necessary for the firm to readjust its scale. Once the plans have congealed, the firm operates in a short-run situation again. It operates in the short run until it makes another long-run change in the scale of operation.

In the long run, just as in the short run, the firm attempts to maximize profits. We use exactly the same approach, except in this case there are no fixed costs; all costs are variable. As before, the firm takes a market-determined price as given. This market price is again the firm's marginal revenue. As in the preceding section, the firm would increase output as long as the marginal revenue from each additional unit is greater than the marginal cost of that unit. It would contract output when marginal cost exceeds marginal revenue. The firm will maximize profit by equating cost and marginal revenue.

Profit maximizing equilibrium

Let us examine the long-run relations graphically. In Figure 13.5, *LAC* and *LMC* are the long-run average and marginal cost curves. The demand curve (*D*) indicates the equilibrium market price (p_0) and is equal to marginal revenue. As long as price is greater than long-run average cost the firm can make a profit. Thus any output between x_0 and x_1 yields some profits. These levels of output are sometimes called break-even points.

Maximum profit occurs at point *S* where marginal revenue equals long-run marginal cost. The firm would want to select that plant size that would produce x_m units of output. Note that the firm would not under these circumstances try to produce at point *M*, the minimum point of long-run average cost. At *M*, marginal revenue exceeds marginal cost; so, the firm can gain by producing more output. In Figure 13.5 total revenue (price times quantity) is

Figure 13.5
Profit maximization in the long run

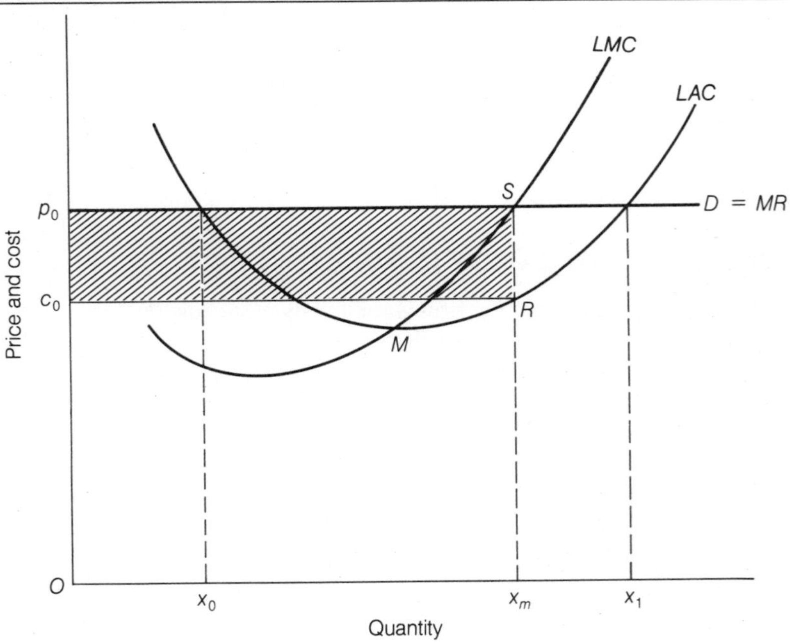

given by the area of the rectangle Op_0Sx_m. Total cost (average cost times quantity) is the area Oc_0Rx_m. Total profit ($TR - TC$) is the shaded area c_0p_0SR.

To summarize, the firm will plan to operate at a scale (or plant size) such that long-run marginal cost equals price. This is the most profitable situation with the given market price. Of course, if market price changes, the point of long-run profit maximization will change also. Thus it follows that the firm's long-run supply is its long-run marginal cost curve.

THE WALL STREET JOURNAL

APPLICATION

How long can a firm suffer losses?

In our discussion of the short-run decisions of competitive firms, we emphasized that firms should continue producing, even though they are making losses, so long as revenue exceeds variable cost. We also noted that such situations in which the firm makes losses cannot continue forever. The firm must either go out of business or find some way to eliminate the losses. But, for many firms, this period of making negative profits can be rather long.

A good example of such a situation was provided in *The Wall Street Journal*.* According to the *Journal*, Massey-Ferguson Ltd., a Canadian farm equipment firm, reported losses every year from 1978 through 1983 (when it lost more than $41 million). A spokesman for the company was somewhat optimistic about 1984, partly because of the forecasted improvement in the farm-equipment market. However, even he was not looking for a major resurgence.

The primary reason for the company's guarded optimism was the effort being made to improve Massey-Ferguson's productivity. In 1984, Massey-Ferguson's management was beginning to think of the firm more as a *marketer* of farm machinery than as a *manufacturer*. Although the company was still making large numbers of tractors and harvesters, its implements were increasingly being manufactured by other firms. It had cut its own work force from 58,000 in 1978 to 25,000 in 1983, and its capital assets had declined from $2.57 billion to $1.64 billion over the same period.

Massey-Ferguson began purchasing many of its component parts overseas, since it could buy them more cheaply than it could make them. And they had entered into joint manufacturing ventures with other Canadian firms. All of the adjustments were designed to reduce costs—a move to a more efficient scale of operation, in the long run.

This adjustment process illustrates two points we have made in this chapter. First, Massey-Ferguson continued to operate for a long time—five years—while making substantial losses. Thus, it must have been at least covering its variable costs during this period. In this case the short run lasted for a considerable period of time.

Second, Massey-Ferguson adjusted its scale in the long run in order to attain a more optimal (and they hoped a profitable) size. In this case, it is clear that the company management felt that its former scale of operation was much too large for efficient operation.

*"Massey-Ferguson 'Hopes' for Return to Profitability in '84," *The Wall Street Journal*, January, 1984. Reprinted by permission of The Wall Street Journal.

Long-run competitive equilibrium

If firms in a competitive industry are making above-normal returns (i.e., pure profit), there is strong reason to believe that the market price will fall. Profits attract new firms into the industry and the new firms will increase industry supply. This increased supply drives down price. In fact, price may even be driven below long-run average cost and cause temporary losses. But if losses occur, some firms would leave the industry, thereby reducing supply and driving up price. As we shall show, free entry and exit will result in a long-run equilibrium at which each firm produces at the minimum point on its long-run average cost curve. All pure profits are eliminated.

The adjustment process is shown in Figure 13.6. In Panel A, DD' is the market demand for the product and S_1S_1' is the original long-run market supply with a given number of firms in the industry.[3] Suppose that all firms are

Figure 13.6
Long-run equilibrium adjustment in a perfectly competitive industry

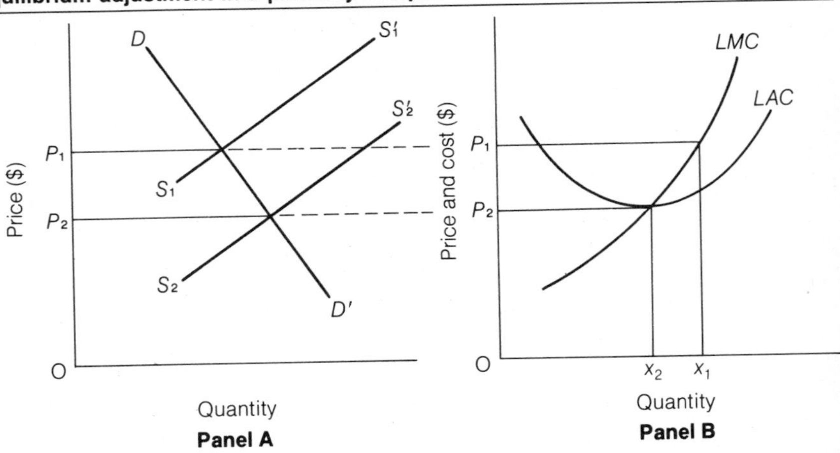

[3]We ignore for now the problem that firms would exit if price falls below minimum average cost, and assume the firm's supply curve is its marginal cost. We could simply let this supply be marginal cost above average cost. We will assume for now that the industry's usage of any input does not affect the price of that input. S_1S_1' is therefore the horizontal summation of the long-run marginal cost curves of all firms in the industry at the time.

[4]Some people may object to the concept of long-run equilibrium because it is apparently

alike and have identical cost curves as illustrated by those shown in Panel B. Demand and supply in the market result in a market price of p_1. Taking this price as given, each firm produces x_1 and obviously makes a pure profit.

This profit induces entry, which causes supply to increase as more firms enter the industry, thereby driving down price in the market. Entry will continue as long as firms are earning economic profit, and price will continue to decline. In other words, entry will continue until supply increases to S_2S_2' and price falls to p_2. At this price each firm will produce x_2. Price will equal long-run average cost at its minimum point (where $LAC = LMC$). Each firm covers all of its costs, but no firm makes an economic profit. All profits are competed away. This situation is called long-run competitive equilibrium.

■ **Definition.** In long-run competitive equilibrium, price equals long-run marginal cost, which equals long-run average cost at the minimum point on the latter. No firm makes an economic profit.

If too many firms enter and price falls below each firm's long-run average cost, the opposite situation occurs. All firms make losses and exit occurs. As firms exit, supply decreases and price increases. Exit would continue until supply rises to S_2S_2' and price to p_2. The same equilibrium results and all losses are competed away. Each firm is in long-run competitive equilibrium.

The long-run equilibrium is summarized in Figure 13.7. The point of long-run equilibrium occurs at point E in this figure. Each firm in the industry makes neither economic profit nor loss. Each firm is earning a normal profit. There is no incentive for further entry because the rate of return in this industry is the same as in the best alternative. For the same reason, there is no

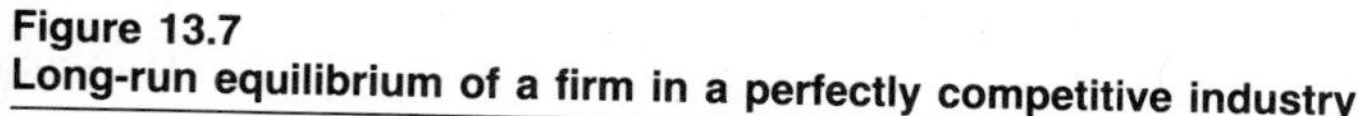

Figure 13.7
Long-run equilibrium of a firm in a perfectly competitive industry

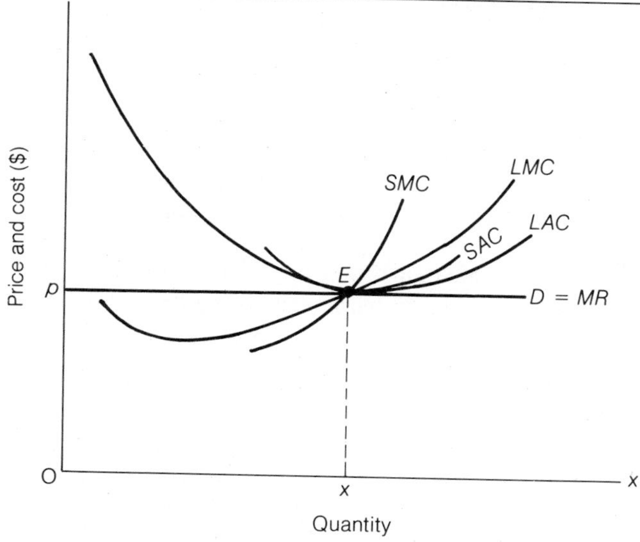

incentive for a firm to leave the industry. The number of firms stabilizes, each firm operating with a plant size represented by *SAC* and *SMC*.[4]

Firms will enter or leave the industry if there is either pure profit or pure loss. Therefore, since the position of long-run equilibrium must be consistent with zero economic profit (and zero loss), it is necessary that price equal average cost. For a firm to attain its individual equilibrium, price must be equal to marginal cost. Therefore, price must equal both marginal and average cost. This can occur only at the point where average and marginal cost are equal—the point of minimum long-run average cost.

13.6 PROFIT-MAXIMIZING INPUT USAGE

Thus far, we have analyzed the firm's profit maximizing decision in terms of the output decision. But, as noted in the introduction, we can also consider profit maximization from the input side. Of course, when we develop profit maximization from the output decision, we implicitly have determined the input usage of the firm. Recall from Chapter 7 that from cost minimization the cost function is directly related to the production function. Thus, when we determine a unique profit-maximizing level of output, we also determine the quantity of each input that is used in the production process.

But, it is possible to determine a profit-maximizing equilibrium directly from the input decision. In this way, we are able to develop the firm's demand for factors of production.

Value of marginal product

Recall that in the introduction to this chapter we argued that the firm would increase its usage of an input so long as the addition to total revenue per unit of the input, which we called marginal revenue product, exceeds the price of the input. The firm would not expand input usage if its price is greater than its marginal revenue product.

For a perfectly competitive firm the marginal revenue product of an input is called the value of marginal product, defined as follows:

■ **Definition.** The value of marginal product (*VMP*) of a factor of production is the additional revenue that one additional unit of the input contributes to the firm. For a competitive firm, *VMP* is therefore the price of the output produced times the marginal product of the input.

For example, if one additional unit of an input, say labor, has a marginal product of 10 and the price of the product being produced is \$5, the value of the marginal product is \$50.

As we showed in Chapter 5, the "typical" marginal product curve first increases, reaches a maximum, then declines thereafter. Therefore, the *VMP*

[4]Some people may object to the concept of long-run equilibrium because it is apparently based upon the "unrealistic" assumption that all firms have identical cost curves. We have made that assumption simply to make the graphs more simple. This assumption is not necessary to obtain long-run equilibrium, in which no firm is making economic profit.

curve, which is simply price times marginal product, also rises then declines. At the level of input usage at which marginal product becomes negative, the value of marginal product becomes negative also. Since an input's marginal product depends upon the usage of the other inputs, the value of marginal product also changes when the quantities of other inputs change.

A "typical" *VMP* schedule for a single variable input is given in Table 13.1, assuming that the price of the product is \$10. This schedule shows the value of marginal product first rising, reaching a maximum, then declining and becoming negative at 10 units of the input. If the price of the product increases, *VMP* will increase for each level of input usage. If the price of the product falls, *VMP* falls also.

Table 13.1
VMP schedule

Units of variable Input	*Output*	*Marginal product*	*Value of marginal product*
1	20	20	\$200
2	50	30	300
3	90	40	400
4	120	30	300
5	138	18	180
6	150	12	120
8	155	5	50
9	158	3	30
10	154	−4	−40

VMP and the hiring decision

As you would expect from our previous discussion, the quantity of an input the firm will hire depends on the marginal benefit and the marginal cost of the input. The marginal benefit is the value of marginal product—the addition to total revenue. The marginal cost is the amount that must be paid to hire another unit of the input—the addition to total cost. If the *VMP* of an additional unit of the input is \$50, the firm would hire another unit as long as the wage rate is less than \$50. In this instance, the additional unit would add more to revenue than to costs. If the wage rate is more than \$50, the additional cost is greater than the additional revenue and no more of the input would be hired.

This employment decision is illustrated graphically in Figure 13.8. In this example, labor is the only variable input. If the wage rate is w_1, the firm would wish to hire L_1 units of labor. The firm would not stop short of L_1, because up to employment level L_1 an additional unit of labor would add more to revenue than to cost. It would not hire more than L_1, because beyond L_1 the added cost would exceed the added revenue. If the wage rate falls to w_2, the firm would increase its labor usage to L_2 units.[5]

[5]Note that we did not include the upward-sloping portion of the *VMP* curve, because this segment is not relevant to the hiring decision. If the wage equals *VMP* and *VMP* is increasing, the firm could hire additional units, and the value of the marginal product of these added inputs would be greater than the wage. Thus this would not be a profit-maximizing situation.

Hence, if labor is the firm's only variable input, the firm will maximize profit or minimize loss by employing that amount of labor for which the value of the marginal product of labor is equal to the wage rate,

$$VMP_L = w$$

More generally, if the firm has a single variable input—let's denote it as I—the firm will maximize profit or minimize loss by using the amount of the input at which the value of its marginal product is equal to the input's price,

$$VMP_I = P_I$$

This condition is directly comparable to the $P = MR = MC$ condition for the optimal output level.[6]

Clearly the firm would never hire labor beyond the point at which *VMP* is zero. Furthermore, the firm would hire no labor if, at the point where the wage rate equals *VMP*, average product is less than marginal product. If $AP < MP$, the value of the average product would be less than the wage rate. Therefore, the total cost of labor would be greater than total revenue. In terms of our previous analysis, price would be less than average variable cost and the firm would shut down.[7]

Thus the demand for a single variable input by a competitive firm is the positive portion of the value of marginal product curve below the point at which the marginal product and the average product curves are equal. *VMP*

---

[6]To see this, suppose labor is the only variable input. From Chapter 7, we know that, in this case,

$$MC = \frac{w}{MP_L}$$

Therefore, the optimizing condition for output becomes

$$P = MC = \frac{w}{MP_L}$$

or

$$P \cdot MP_L = w$$

[7]The total variable cost of hiring L units of labor is

$$TVC = w \times L$$

The total revenue generated by employing L units of labor is

$$\begin{aligned} \text{TR} &= P \times Q \\ &= P \times (AP_L) \times L \end{aligned}$$

If, at the point at which $P \times MP_L = w$, $AP_L < MP_L$, it follows that

$$P \times AP_L < P \times MP_L = w$$

and

$$TR < TVC$$

Thus, since *TR* is less than *TVC* at this level of output, price must be less than *AVC* and the firm would shut down in the short run.

Figure 13.8
A competitive firm's demand for labor

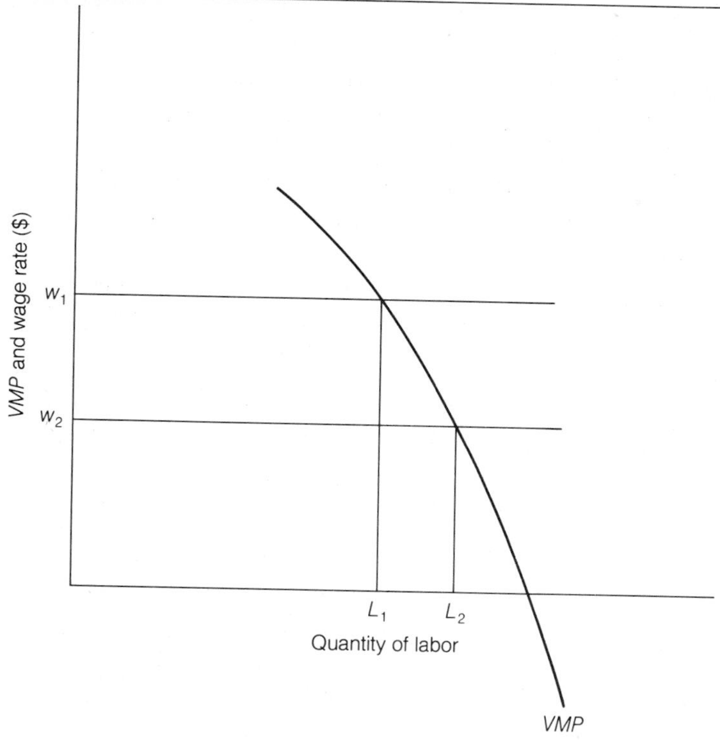

gives the quantity of the variable input that will be hired at each price of the input.

When there is more than one variable input, the firm's demand function for a particular input is slightly different. For example, if the quantities of other inputs are also variable, when wages fall from w_1 to w_2 in Figure 13.8, the firm will use more labor but it may use more or less of the other variable inputs. For this reason, the *VMP* curve of labor may shift—either outward or inward. Thus, the firm may use more than or less than L_2 units of labor at wage w_2.

Notwithstanding this, two things are certain: (1) the firm will hire more labor when the wage falls and (2) it will hire labor up to quantity at which the wage equals the value of marginal product, even though *VMP* may shift. Thus, for every variable input, the firm will hire the quantity of the input at which its *VMP* equals its price. If, for example, the firm has two variable inputs, denoted *I* and *J*, the firm will maximize profits by using both inputs at such levels that

$$VMP_I = P_I$$
$$VMP_J = P_J$$

Since the marginal products of either input shift according to the level of usage of the other, these conditions must hold *simultaneously*.

Input demand by a competitive industry

Any one competitive firm can vary its level of use of an input in response to a change in the input price and can therefore vary output without affecting the price of the commodity produced. However when all firms respond to a change in the price of an input by changing the level of usage of the input, commodity price (i.e., the price of their output) does change. Since each firm's demand for the input is derived holding commodity price constant, all firms' input demands shift when all firms change simultaneously.

To illustrate the process, we use labor as the variable input (although all of the following holds for any input). Let's suppose that a typical firm having only labor as a variable input is depicted in Figure 13.9, Panel A. At the existing market price of the commodity produced, d_1d_1' is the firm's demand curve for labor. If the market wage rate is w_1, the firm uses l_1 units of labor. Aggregating over all the firms in the industry, L_1 units of labor are employed. Thus, point *A* in Panel B is one point on the industry demand curve for labor.

Next, suppose the price of labor declines to w_2. Other things equal, the individual firm would move along d_1d_1' to point b' and would employ l_2' units of labor. But, other things are *not* equal. When all firms expand their use of the input, total output expands. Stated differently, the market supply curve for the commodity shifts to the right because of the decline in the input's price. For a given commodity demand, commodity price must fall; and when it

Figure 13.9
Derivation of the industry demand for a variable input

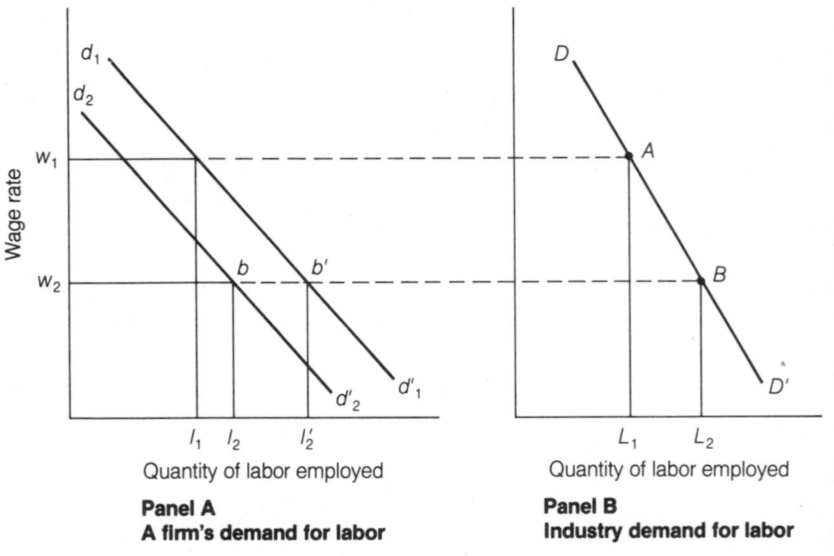

Panel A
A firm's demand for labor

Panel B
Industry demand for labor

does, the individual demand curve for labor—the *VMP* curve—also falls.

In Panel A, the decline in individual input demand attributable to the decline in commodity price is represented by the shift leftward from d_1d_1' to d_2d_2'. At wage rate w_2, b is now the equilibrium point, with l_2 units employed. Aggregating for all employers, L_2 units of labor are used (Point B is obtained in Panel B.) Any number of points such as A and B can be generated by varying the market price of the input. Connecting these points, you can obtain DD', the industry demand for the input, which must be negatively sloped.

Thus the wage rate that firms in the industry must pay for any type of input is determined by supply and demand in the market for that input. The demand for the input is the industry's demand plus the demand or demands of all other industries using that input. Since each industry's demand is negatively sloped, the total demand for the input must be negatively sloped also.

The supply of the input in the market would be positively sloped. Since additional units of the input—say, some type of labor—must be bid away from other occupations, presumably a higher price must be paid to obtain additional units of the input in the market. For example, if the construction industry in a particular area wants to hire more electricians, the added electricians must be bid away from other areas—at a higher wage.

Supply and demand in the market, therefore, determine the wage rate that firms in the industry must pay. Anything that increases (decreases) the demand for the input must increase (decrease) the price that firms must pay for the input. To see this effect, let's look at the following application.

THE WALL STREET JOURNAL

APPLICATION

Supply and demand in high-wage labor markets

In our theoretical discussion of wage determination we used the example of labor markets. We do not want to give the impression that the theory applies solely to low-wage, relatively unskilled labor. The same type of analysis applies equally well to occupations paying extremely high salaries.

To see this, let us consider what was happening to brokerage firms during 1983 and early 1984. According to an article in *The Wall Street Journal*,* by early 1984 experts were warning that the operating costs of brokerage firms had risen out of control. Major firms such as Merrill Lynch, Paine Webber, and E. F. Hutton reported sharply reduced operating profits during the last quarter of 1983 due to rising costs. Several companies instituted hiring freezes.

The cost spiral began early in 1983, during the tremendous rally in the stock market. In general, brokers expand rapidly during stock market rallies. Costs tend to rise less rapidly than revenues until the rally begins to slow down. The effect was extreme in early 1984 because the market boom was particularly strong in 1983, then ended rather abruptly. It was estimated that revenues were $28 billion in 1983, compared with the previous high of $23.2 billion in 1982. But, over the same period, costs rose 31 percent, despite the sharp reduction in inflation.

The *Journal* pointed out that "Hiring binges and wild competition for talent account for much of the soaring costs." One analyst estimated that as much as three fourths of the 1983 increase in costs was due to bigger payrolls. During a 12-month period, Merrill Lynch added 6,000 employees to bring its staff up to 44,000. E. F. Hutton added 2,400 for a total staff of almost 16,000. Prudential Bache hired 800 brokers from competing firms to bring its sales staff to 4,700.

To hire these additional brokers, the companies had to pay huge increases in salary. Prudential Bache was reported to have offered tens of thousands of dollars—as much as 30 percent to 50 percent of a broker's annual commissions—to persuade brokers to switch firms. Bonuses of $50,000 just "to get a broker to walk through the door" were being paid. Obviously other firms were forced to make counter bids to keep or hire talented salespeople.

Top security analysts were enjoying the same type of market and even higher salaries. Some analysts were switching companies for double their salary—$500,000 or more in some cases. To give you some idea of the extent of the increase, a senior brokerage executive said that, "Three or four years ago, we paid $100,000 to $150,000 for top-flight analysts, and that seemed like a lot." Compare that with $500,000 or more.

Many of the larger firms, worried about the huge increases in costs, began trying to hold down hiring and to put a lid on the number of new employees. This was easier to carry out because of the concurrent slump in the stock market. If the market had continued to surge, it would have been much more difficult to resist the urge to increase staffs, and salaries would have continued to rise.

But our point is that the market for high-wage employees behaves just like the market for ordinary labor. An increase in demand for the product—the rapid rise in the stock market—substantially increased the demand for workers—brokers and analysts. This increase in the demand for workers increased salaries, as firms bid among themselves for available employees. As the boom in sales leveled off, the demand for workers leveled off also, which in turn stopped the rapid rise in salaries.

---

*Scott McMurrary, "Brokerage Firm's Spiraling Costs Are Blamed for Decline in Earnings," *The Wall Street Journal*, February 3, 1984. Reprinted by permission of *The Wall Street Journal*.

13.7 SUMMARY

Perfectly competitive markets exist when there are a large number of buyers and sellers, identical products, easy entry and exit by producers, and prices freely determined by the interaction of supply and demand. In the short run, the firm produces the quantity at which short-run marginal cost equals price, so long as price exceeds average variable cost. Therefore, marginal cost above average variable cost is the firm's short-run supply curve. If all input prices are given to the industry, industry short-run supply is the horizontal summation of all marginal cost curves. If the industry's (although not the individual firm's) use of the inputs affects the prices of some inputs, industry supply is less elastic than this horizontal summation.

In the long run, the entry and exit of firms force each firm to produce at minimum *LAC*. That is, the firm will produce where $LAC = LMC = SAC = SMC$. Economic or pure profit is zero at this output. (Although each firm earns a normal profit.)

The salient feature of perfect competition is that, in long-run market equilibrium, market price equals minimum average cost. This means that each unit of output is produced at the lowest possible cost, either from the standpoint of money cost or of resource use. The product sells for its average (long-run) cost of production; each firm, accordingly, earns the going rate of return in competitive industries, nothing more or less.

It should be emphasized that firms do not choose to produce the quantity with the lowest possible long-run average cost simply because they believe this level of production is optimal for society and they wish to benefit society. The firms are merely trying to maximize their profits. Given that motivation, the market forces firms to produce at that point. If society benefits, it is not through any benevolence of firms but through the functioning of the market.

Finally, no matter how many factors of production are variable, the firm hires each variable input so that the value of the marginal product of the input equals its price. If only one input is variable, the firm's demand for that input is its *VMP* curve.

It should be emphasized that the theory of perfect competition is not designed to describe specific real-world firms. It is a theoretical model that is frequently useful in explaining real-world behavior and in predicting the economic consequences of changes in the different variables contained in the model. The conclusions of the theory, not the assumptions, are the crucial points when analyzing economic problems.

TECHNICAL PROBLEMS

1. Consider the following cost curves for a perfectly competitive firm:

a. If price is \$9 per unit of output, the firm should produce ________ units.

b. Since average total cost is \$________ for this output, total cost is \$________.

c. The firm makes a profit of \$________.

d. Price falls to \$5. The firm now produces ________ units.

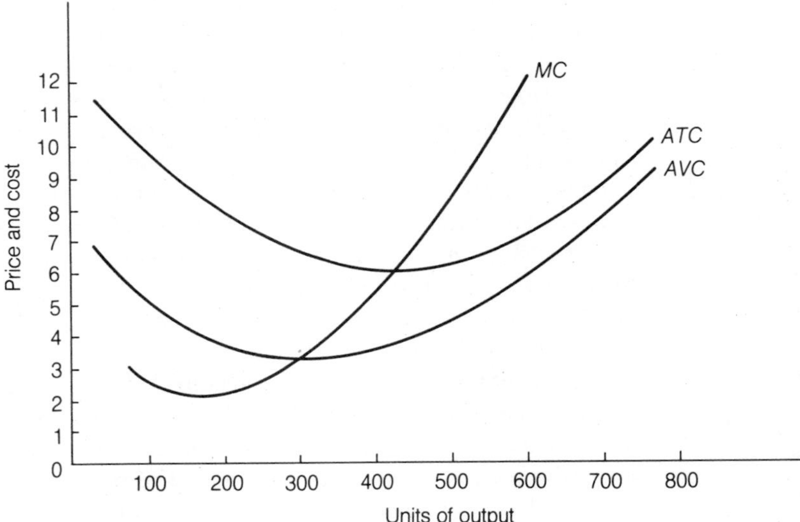

e. Total revenue is now $________ and total cost is $________. The firm makes a loss of $________.

f. Total variable cost is $________, leaving $________ to apply to fixed cost.

g. If price falls below $________ the firm will produce zero output. Explain why.

2. If, in the above problem, price remains at $5, the firm in the long run will do one of two things. What are these and under what circumstances will each be done?

3. Describe a position of long-run competitive equilibrium for a perfectly competitive firm and industry. How and why does such an equilibrium come about.

4. The figure to follow shows a perfectly competitive firm's short-run cost structure.

a. Label the three curves.

b. Show a price at which the firm would make a pure profit. Show the quantity it would produce and the amount of pure profit that would be earned.

c. Show a price at which the firm would continue to produce in the short run but would suffer losses. Show the output and losses at this price.

d. Show the price below which the firm would not produce in the short run.

5. Explain why the short-run supply curve of a perfectly competitive in-

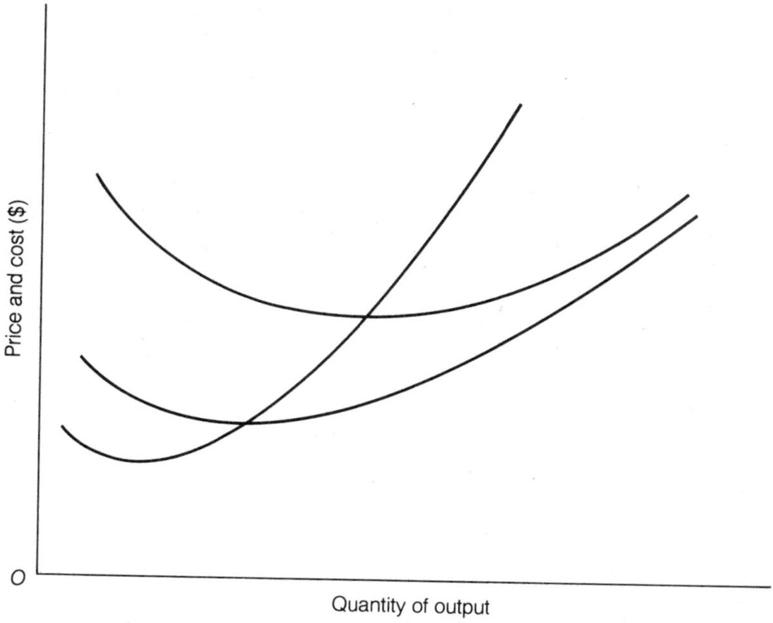

dustry could be less elastic than the horizontal summation of the supply curves of all the firms in the industry.

6. Draw and label the following curves: long-run average cost, and long-run marginal cost; short-run average cost, and short-run marginal cost.

   Let the short-run profit-maximizing output be greater than minimum long-run average cost. The firm is a perfect competitor making short-run profits. It could, however, increase profits (maximize profits) by decreasing plant size.

   a. Show the current output, price, and profit.

   b. Show the profit that could have been earned and the optimal output, if at the same price, the firm was maximizing long-run profit.

   c. Show price and output of this firm after the industry attains its long-run equilibrium.

   d. Explain how this long-run competitive equilibrium situation is attained.

7. The supply of labor to all firms in a perfectly competitive industry is reduced. Explain the effects on the wage rate, the quantity of labor employed, total industry supply of the commodity produced, and the price of the output.

8. The following figure shows the relevant portion of the marginal product curve for labor (the only variable input) of a perfectly competitive firm.

   a. In a separate graph draw the associated marginal revenue product

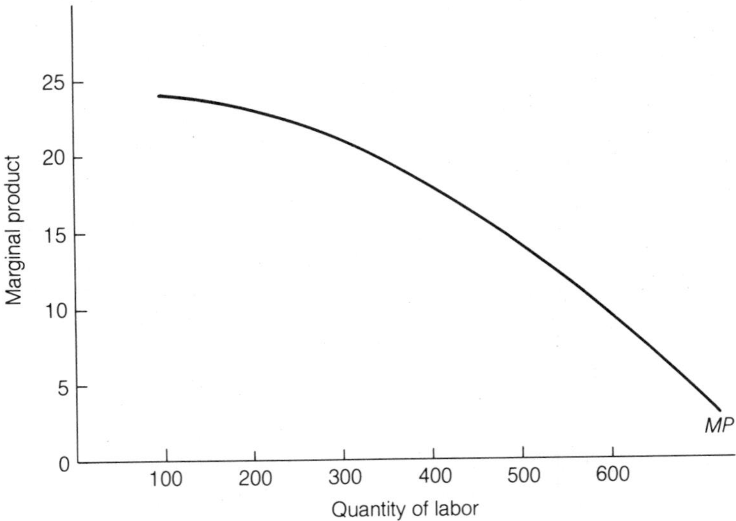

curve (value of marginal product) over the relevant range of labor usage. The price of the product produced is $2 per unit.

b. At a wage rate of $30 how much labor will the firm hire? What if the wage rate falls to $25?

c. Suppose the price of the product falls to $1. Draw the new *VMP* curve.

d. How much labor is hired now at each of the two wage rates?

9. Explain why the industry's demand for an input is less elastic than the horizontal sum of all firms' demands for the input.

10. Explain why, when there is more than one variable input, the firm's demand for one of the inputs is not the *VMP* curve, but every input is hired so that its *VMP* equals its price.

11. Suppose a perfectly competitive firm has a total revenue during a particular year of $4 million. Its total payments to factors of production are $3 million. The firm's owner also owns $4 million dollars worth of capital used by the firm. The going rate of return on capital is 10 percent. What is the firm's economic profit? The owner does not manage the firm. What is the owner's rate of return on the capital?

ANALYTICAL PROBLEMS

1. We have said that the exacting characteristics of perfect competition are not met in real-world markets. Can you think of any real-world industries that closely approximate the model? What characteristic(s) do you think would most likely not be met?

2. Grocery stores and gasoline stations in a large city would appear to be an example of perfectly competitive markets—there are numerous sellers, each seller is relatively small, and the products sold are quite similar. How would we argue that these markets are not perfectly competitive (leaving out the assumption of perfect knowledge)? Could each firm have some monopoly power? How do you think the theory of perfect competition would permit us to make predictions about the behavior of such firms.
3. Insurance agents receive a commission on the policies they sell. Many states regulate the rates that can be charged for insurance. Would higher or lower rates increase the incomes of agents? Explain, distinguishing between the short run and long run.
4. Suppose an excise tax is placed on the products sold in a perfectly competitive market. That is, for every unit sold, each firm must pay the state \$$k$ per unit. What would be the effect on each firm's marginal cost? Output? Industry supply? The price of the product?
5. The beef market is competitive. During periods of rising prices, ranchers keep more heifers from market to breed them and expand their herds rather than fattening them to slaughter. It, of course, takes time for heifers to produce calves. Because of this, would you expect beef prices to fluctuate greatly or remain relatively stable? Explain.
6. If all of the assumptions of perfect competition hold, why would firms in such an industry have little incentive to carry out technological change or much research and development? What conditions would encourage research and development in competitive industries?
7. Suppose you manage a small manufacturing firm that has been making short-run losses for almost two years. The board of directors directs you to remedy the situation. What steps would you try to take? What information would you want to get?
8. Would your answer to problem 7 differ if the firm in question was a small-to-medium-sized stock brokerage firm? If so, in what way?
9. At the present time the oil business is somewhat depressed. Suppose that oil prices increase rather rapidly over the next few years. What will happen to the salaries of petroleum engineers and oil geologists? Distinguish between the short run and long run.

14

Implementation of the competitive profit-making decisions

In the preceding chapter, we described the theoretical relations that must exist when a firm in a perfectly competitive market maximizes its profit in the short run. As we demonstrated, the firm can attain maximum profits through the selection of either the optimal level of output or the optimal level of usage of its inputs.

In this chapter, we will show you the basics of the way in which the manager of a firm can actually implement these theoretical relations. Using what we have already described about the estimation and forecasting of production, cost, and demand functions, we can estimate (forecast) the levels of output or input usage that will maximize the firm's profit in the short run. In essence, this chapter is the first "payoff" from all the discussions we have presented in preceding chapters: We have spent a lot of time describing the estimation of the various functions; now we can put these techniques to use to answer the primary question in the mind of the manager: What can I do to maximize profit?

Following the outline we set forth in Chapter 13, we will first describe the profit-maximizing output decision. Then, we will turn to a brief description of the profit-maximizing input decision.

14.1 PROFIT-MAXIMIZING OUTPUT

As we described in Chapter 13, the manager of a firm must answer two questions. Let's begin by restating these questions and the answers we found in our theoretical discussion:

1. Do I produce or shut down? *The firm should produce as long as the market price exceeds the minimum of average variable cost—$P > AVC$.*
2. If I produce, how much should I produce? *The output that will maximize profit or minimize loss is that at which market price is equal to marginal cost—$P = MC$.*

It follows that in order to be able to determine or forecast the profit-maximizing level of output for the firm, we need estimates of or forecasts for the market price of the commodity being produced by the firm, the firm's average cost function, and the firm's marginal cost function. Let's first review how we are able to obtain these components before showing you how we can obtain actual answers to the questions facing the manager.

Price forecasts

As we described in Chapter 12, there exist several methods by which we could forecast the market price that will exist in the next (or some future) period. We could use some kind of a qualitative forecast. Or, we might use a time-series forecast in which price follows a trend or a trend with cyclical (e.g., quarterly) variations.

However, our experiences have been such that we normally use an econometric model to obtain market price forecasts. As we described in Chapter 12, this requires that we specify and estimate both the market demand and market supply functions.

Once we have these functions estimated, we must obtain the forecasted values for the exogenous variables (e.g., income and the prices of inputs). Inserting these forecasts into our estimated demand and supply functions, we can solve the equations simultaneously to obtain the price forecast. To illustrate this technique again, let's use an example.

APPLICATION

An econometric price forecast

The manager of Beau Apparel, Inc.—a manufacturer of men's clothing—was preparing the firm's production plan for the first quarter of 1985. One of the firm's divisions produces moderately priced men's shirts and the manager wanted to obtain a price forecast for this product for 1985I that would subsequently be used in making the production decision for this division.

The manager realized that, in this particular segment of the shirt market, Beau Apparel was only one of many firms that produced a fairly homogeneous product and that none of the firms in this "moderate price shirt market" engaged in any significant advertising. Hence, this market approximated the conditions of a perfectly competitive market. Therefore, the manager specified a simplified demand-supply system for the market.

$$\text{Demand: } Q_t = a + bP_t + cY_t$$
$$\text{Supply: } Q_t = e + fP_t + gP_{F,t}$$

Using quarterly data for the period 1981I–1984IV, these equations were estimated. The estimated demand and supply functions were as follows:

$$\text{Demand: } Q_t = 125 - 2P_t + 12.5Y_t$$
$$\text{Supply: } Q_t = 250 + 8P_t - 5P_{F,t}$$

In this estimation, sales (Q) were expressed in thousand units, the price of the product (P) in dollars per unit and income (Y) and the price of factors (P_F) in \$1,000.

To obtain 1985I forecasts for the exogenous variables, the manager purchased forecasts of income and input prices from a large econometric forecasting firm. The 1985I forecast for the price of inputs was \$10,000. So, in the model, the forecasted 1985I value for P_F was 10.

However, in the case of an income forecast for 1985I, the forecasting firm was less sure. Indeed, the firm provided three different forecasts, each predicated on different assumptions about legislation pending in Congress. These income forecasts were as follows:

High = \$22,000
Best = \$18,000
Low = \$14,000

In forecasting the price of shirts in the first quarter of 1985, the manager of Beau Apparel would then have three alterantive values of $\hat{Y}_{1985\text{I}}$: 22, 18, and 14.

To obtain price forecasts for shirts, it was then necessary for the manager to insert the forecasted values for the exogenous variables into the estimated demand and supply functions. Using the high forecast for income.

$$\begin{aligned}\text{Demand:}\quad Q_{1985\text{I}} &= 125 - 2P_{1985\text{I}} + 12.5(22)\\ &= 400 - 2P_{1985\text{I}}\\ \text{Supply:}\quad Q_{1985\text{I}} &= 250 + 8P_{1985\text{I}} - 5(10)\\ &= 200 + 8P_{1985\text{I}}\end{aligned}$$

Establishing an equilibrium, i.e., setting quantity demanded equal to quantity supplied,

$$400 - 2\hat{P}_{1985\text{I}} = 200 + 8\hat{P}_{1985\text{I}}$$

Solving this equation for price,

$$\hat{P}_{1985\text{I}} = 20$$

Hence, the manager of Beau Apparel found that the 1985I forecast for the price of shirts, assuming the high-income forecast, is \$20 per unit.

In precisely the same way, using the ''best'' forecast for income in 1985I, the forecasted price of shirts in the first quarter of 1985 would be \$15 per unit.

And, using the low-income forecast, the 1985I price forecast would be \$10 per unit. So, the manager of Beau Apparel has three price forecasts for shirts for the first quarter of 1985:

High = \$20
Best = \$15
Low = \$10

Estimation of average variable cost

To obtain an estimate of the firm's average variable cost curve, several methods can be used. However, let us continue to consider regression analysis and employ the technique we described in Chapter 8. Using time-series data for a period short enough that the firm's fixed costs (e.g., the firm's capital stock) have not changed, we can estimate the function

$$AVC = a + bQ + cQ^2$$

To remind you of the way this function is used, let's return to our application dealing with a competitive firm.

APPLICATION

An average variable cost function

The manager of Beau Apparel also wanted to obtain an estimate of the shirt division's average variable cost function. The manager knew that the last major change in the division's capital stock had occurred in the second quarter of 1982; so, using quarterly data for the division for 1982III through 1984IV, the function

$$AVC = a + bQ + cQ^2$$

was estimated. Again output was expressed in thousand units and average variable cost was expressed in dollars per unit. The estimated AVC function obtained from the computer printout was

$$AVC = 20 - 3Q + 0.25Q^2$$

The value for R^2 was 0.8952 and the F value was 29.897. All of the estimated coefficients ($\hat{a}$, $\hat{b}$, and $\hat{c}$) were of the required sign and were statistically significant.

Derivation of the marginal cost function

As we demonstrated in Chapter 8, if the average variable cost function is

$$AVC = a + bQ + cQ^2$$

the marginal cost function is simply

$$MC = a + 2bQ + 3cQ^2$$

Hence, once the analyst has estimated the average variable cost function, it is a trivial matter to obtain the corresponding marginal cost function. Let's see how our shirt manufacturer did this.

APPLICATION

A marginal cost function

In the preceding application, the manager of Beau Apparel had estimated an average variable cost function for the shirt division as

$$AVC = 20 - 3Q + 0.25Q^2$$

Therefore, the marginal cost function for shirts is

$$\begin{aligned} MC &= 20 + 2(-3)Q + 3(0.25)Q^2 \\ &= 20 - 6Q + 0.75Q^2 \end{aligned}$$

The shutdown decision

We are now in a position to answer the manager's first question: Do I produce or should I shut down? As we know from Chapter 13, the firm should produce as long as price exceeds minimum average variable cost.

From the preceding discussion, we already know how to obtain a forecast for price. Hence, to consider the shutdown decision, we need only find the minimum average variable cost. As we demonstrated in Chapter 8, the average variable cost curve will be at its minimum when $AVC = MC$; so, the output at which AVC is a minimum is

$$\tilde{Q} = -b/2c$$

Then, to find minimum average variable cost, we simply substitute this output level into the estimated average variable cost function:

$$AVC_{MIN} = a + b\tilde{Q} + c(\tilde{Q})^2$$

The firm should produce as long as $P \geqq AVC_{MIN}$. If $P < AVC_{MIN}$, the firm should shut down—produce zero output. To see how this decision is implemented, let's return to our application.

APPLICATION

Should I produce?

As we noted earlier, the manager of Beau Apparel estimated the average variable cost function for shirts to be

$$AVC = 20 - 3Q + 0.25Q^2$$

Therefore, the manager knows that this average variable cost curve is at its minimum when output is

$$Q = -(-3)/2(.25) = (3)/(0.5) = 6$$

(i.e., an output of 6,000 units). Substituting this output level into the estimated average variable cost function, the minimum average variable cost is

$$AVC_{MIN} = 20 - 3(6) + 0.25(6)^2 = 11$$

That is, minimum average variable cost is $11 per unit.

The manager of Beau Apparel then compares this minimum average variable cost with the three price forecasts described in an earlier application. With the high forecast,

$$\hat{P} = \$20 > \$11 = AVC_{MIN}$$

so the firm should produce. Likewise, with the "best" forecast

$$\hat{P} = \$15 > \$11 = AVC_{MIN}$$

and the firm should again produce. However, if it turns out that the low forecast is correct, the firm should shut down—produce zero output—since

$$\hat{P} = \$10 < \$11 = AVC_{MIN}$$

The output decision

If price exceeds minimum average variable cost, we know that the firm will produce; but, the question is: how much? We can answer this question easily, since we know that the firm will maximize its profit or minimize its loss if it produces that output at which $P = MC$.

In the context of the average variable cost function we have been using (i.e., $AVC = a + bQ + cQ^2$), the profit-maximizing (or loss-minimizing) output is determined by setting forecasted price equal to estimated marginal cost:

$$\hat{P} = \hat{a} + 2\hat{b}Q + 3\hat{c}Q^2$$

Solving this equation for Q gives us the optimal output for the firm. To see how this would work in the context of actual estimates, we return to our shirt manufacturer.

APPLICATION

How much should I produce?

The manager of Beau Apparel found that the firm's shirt division should produce if the market price is $20 (the high forecast) or $15 (the "best" forecast). The next question is, of course: How much should I produce at either of these two prices?

Looking first at the high forecast, optimal output is that at which the price forecast is equal to marginal cost. That is

$$20 = 20 - 6Q + 0.75Q^2$$

Solving this equation for Q (by factoring), the optimal—profit-maximizing or loss-minimizing—output is $Q = 8$. Since output was expressed in thousand units, this gives an output of 8,000 units. That is, if the price is expected to be \$20 per unit, the optimal level of output is 8,000 units.

With the "best" forecast, the optimal output is again determined by equating the price forecast with the estimated marginal cost function:

$$15 = 20 - 6Q + 0.75Q^2$$

or

$$0.75Q^2 - 6Q + 5 = 0$$

As luck would have it, the solution to this equation is not as simple as was the preceding case. To solve this equation, we must resort to the quadratic formula:*

$$Q = \frac{-(-6) \pm \sqrt{(-6)^2 - 4(0.75)(5)}}{2(0.75)} = \frac{6 \pm 4.6}{1.5}$$

Using the quadratic formula, the equation has two solutions—$Q = 0.93$ and $Q = 7.1$. Which is correct? That is, which one of these is the optimal output for a price of \$15 per unit? If you look again at Figure 13.3, you should be able to see that the correct output is the higher output, 7.1. However, an alternate way of checking is to look at the average variable costs for the two outputs:

$$AVC_{Q=0.93} = 20 - 3(0.93) + 0.25(0.93)^2 = \$17.43$$
$$AVC_{Q=7.1} = 20 - 3(7.1) + 0.25(7.1)^2 = \$11.30$$

Since \$17.43 exceeds the price of \$15 per unit, the output level of $Q = 0.93$ cannot be optimal; so, the optimal level of output for a price of \$15 is 7.1. That is, if the price is expected to be \$15 per unit, the firm would produce 7,100 units.

---

*For an equation of the form

$$aY^2 + bY + c = 0$$

the solutions for Y are found as

$$Y = \frac{-b \pm \sqrt{b^2 - 4ac}}{2a}$$

Total profit or loss

Once the firm's output decision is made, the calculation of total profit or loss is very simple. Total profit (loss) is simply total revenue minus total cost.

Total revenue for a competitive firm is price times quantity sold. Total cost is the sum of total variable cost and total fixed cost, where total variable cost is average variable cost times the number of units sold. Hence, total profit (loss) is

$$\begin{aligned}\text{Profit} &= TR - TC \\ &= (P \times Q) - [(AVC \times Q) + TFC]\end{aligned}$$

APPLICATION

What's the bottom line?

In the applications in this section, the manager of Beau Apparel has been attempting to determine the optimal production level for the firm's shirt division for 1985I. So far, this manager has looked at the shutdown and production questions. As you might expect, the final question this manager has is: What is the profit or loss associated with each of the alternative price forecasts?

As we have shown, total profit or loss is

$$\text{Profit} = (P \times Q) - [(AVC \times Q) + TFC]$$

Based on actual costs in the fourth quarter of 1984, the manager expects total fixed costs for the shirt division for 1985I to be $30,000. The values for total revenue and total variable cost depend on the price forecast and corresponding optimal output. Let's look at each of the three price forecasts in turn:

High forecast—$\hat{P}$ = $20: In this case, the manager has determined the optimal level of production to be $Q = 8$, i.e., 8,000 units. The average variable cost associated with the production of 8,000 units is

$$AVC_{Q=8} = 20 - 3(8) + 0.25(8)^2 = \$12$$

Therefore, profit will be

$$\text{Profit} = (\$20)(8{,}000) - [(\$12)(8{,}000) + \$30{,}000] = +\$34{,}000$$

That is, if price is $20 per unit, the shirt division would be expected to earn a profit of $34,000 in the first quarter of 1985.

Best forecast—$\hat{P}$ = $15: We have seen that, with a price of $15 per unit, the optimal output is $Q = 7.1$, i.e., 7,100 units. The average variable cost for this output level is

$$AVC_{Q=7.1} = 20 - 3(7.1) + 0.25(7.1)^2 = \$11.30$$

and total profit is

$$\text{Profit} = (\$15)(7{,}100) - [(\$11.30)(7{,}100) + \$30{,}000] = -\$3{,}730$$

That is, if price is $15 per unit, the shirt division of Beau Apparel will be expected to suffer a *loss* of $3,730 in the first quarter of 1985. However, the firm will continue to produce since, as should become more clear in the next case, this is the minimum loss that would be possible in the short run.

Low forecast—$\hat{P}$ = $10: In an earlier application, we showed that with this price, the division should shut down—produce zero output. Hence,

$$\text{Profit} = 0 - [0 + \$30{,}000] = -\$30{,}000$$

In this case, the division would be expected to suffer a loss equal to its fixed costs ($30,000) in the first quarter of 1985.

In the applications presented in this section we have looked at the way the manager of a competitive firm would make decisions when faced with three alternative price forecasts. Our purpose in using the three price forecasts was to reinforce the material presented in Chapter 13. As we showed there, in the short run, a firm would make one of the choices below.

1. Produce a positive level of output and earn an economic profit (if $P < ATC$).
2. Produce a positive level of output and suffer an economic loss less than the amount of total fixed cost (if $AVC < P < ATC$).
3. Produce zero output and suffer an economic loss equal to total fixed cost (if $P < AVC$).

Thus, the applications presented here have mirrored the discussion and graphical exposition of Chapter 13.

A note on decision making under uncertainty

By introducing the three alternative price forecasts we have also implicitly introduced another topic—decision making under uncertainty. Faced with these three different price forecasts and the correspondingly very different conclusions as to the optimal level of production and the resultant profits, what should the manager do? Put another way, which of the three price forecasts should the manager act on?

The type of uncertainty we have introduced is one that is continually faced by decision makers. Managers do not know with certainty what the future will hold, e.g., precisely where the demand function will be located in some future period. Obviously the manager could try to collect information in order to reduce this uncertainty. But, since collecting information is costly, we would never expect the manager to eliminate all uncertainty. Indeed, as we know from the optimization rules in Chapter 3, the manager will collect additional information only so long as the marginal benefit from the information (the gain in profit to the firm from reduced uncertainty) exceeds the marginal cost of collecting additional information.

APPLICATION

Acquiring information to reduce uncertainty

In the applications so far, the manager of Beau Apparel has been faced with three forecast prices for shirts. Suppose that the manager has no information about the true probabilities that any one of the prices will occur and has therefore presumed that all three are equally likely. That is, the manager presumed that the probability of any of these prices occurring is 1/3. Hence, in a very simplistic manner, the *expected* profit for the shirt division of Beau Apparel was

$$\text{Expected profit} = 1/3(-30{,}000) + 1/3(-3730) + 1/3(34{,}000) = \$90$$

By acquiring information, the probabilities of the different prices can be estimated more precisely. And, as more information is acquired, the estimates get closer to the true probabilities. Suppose that Beau Apparel spent $3,000 collecting information and in the process found that better estimates of the probabilities were 1/8 for $10, 5/8 for $15, and 2/8 for $20. Was this a potentially profitable expenditure?

As it turns out, it was not. With the new probabilities, expected profit for the shirt division was

$$\text{Expected profit} = 1/8(-30{,}000) + 5/8(-3730) + 2/8(34{,}000) = \$2{,}419$$

The marginal benefit of the information was the increase in expected profit, $\$2{,}419 - 90 = \$2{,}329$. And, since the marginal benefit was less than the marginal cost of acquiring the information ($\$2{,}329 < \$3{,}000$), too much information had been acquired. The firm would have been better off with more uncertainty.

Since the elimination of uncertainty is not an optimal (or even feasible) choice for the firm, the manager is forced to make decisions facing uncertainty. How the decision is made depends on a number of factors, including the manner in which the manager is compensated. (For example, you might think about the way the manager would approach the decision if the manager was paid a given salary with a bonus based on profits and then compare this with the case in which the manager is notified that he or she will be fired if the firm suffers a loss.)

Nonetheless, a strategy for decision making under uncertainty that has received a great deal of attention is one referred to as "MiniMax." In essence, this strategy might be characterized as "making the best out of the worst possible outcome." To show you how a manager might apply this strategy, let's look again at Beau Apparel.

APPLICATION

A minimax decision

By collecting some additional information on the legislation pending in Congress, the manager of Beau Apparel eliminated the econometric forecasting firm's low-income forecast as a possibility. Hence, the price forecast of \$10 was ignored.

The manager then had two options remaining: Option 1—Use the price forecast of \$15 and produce 7,100 units. Option 2—Use the \$20 price forecast and produce 8,000 units. If the manager selects option 1 and it turns out that \$15 is, in fact, the true price, we know that the firm will lose \$3,730. However, if the manager selects option 1 and the true price turns out to be \$20, the firm will earn a profit of \$31,770. That is,

$$(\$20) \times (7{,}100) - [(\$11.30) \times (7{,}100) + \$30{,}000] = \$31{,}770.$$

Likewise, if the firm selects option 2, the firm will earn a profit of \$34,000 if \$20 is the true price or suffer a loss of \$6,000 if \$15 is the true price. Thus there are four possible outcomes, which are summarized in the following table.

Manager's strategy	Actual price in 1985l		Worst possible outcome
	\$15	*\$20*	
Option 1	−3,730	+31,770	−3,730
Option 2	−6,000	+34,000	−6,000

With option 1, the worst the firm could do is to lose \$3,730. With option 2, the worst the firm could do is to lose \$6,000. If the manager of Beau Apparel followed the MiniMax strategy, the option selected would be that which provides the minimum of the worst possible outcomes—option 1 would be selected.

As indicated in the preceding example, using the MiniMax strategy, the manager selects the option that maximizes the minimum profits (or minimizes the maximum loss). Because of this characteristic, this view of the way decision makers behave when faced with uncertainty has been criticized as being overly conservative. Nonetheless, this strategy does provide some insight into the problems involved when uncertainty exists.

14.2 PROFIT-MAXIMIZING LEVELS OF INPUT USAGE

A firm can also attain profit-maximization through selection of the optimal level of employment of its inputs. That is, a firm can maximize profits by selecting the optimal value for *either* output *or* input usage.

To show how profit-maximization can be attained by selection of the optimal level of input usage, we will begin by looking at the case of a single variable input. Once we complete this, we will look at the more complex situation in which a firm has several inputs that are variable.

One variable input

To be consistent with our discussion in Chapter 13, let the variable input be labor, although the techniques shown can be used for any input. We know that the firm will maximize profit if it employs labor at the level at which the value of the marginal product of labor equals the wage rate,

$$VMP_L = w$$

As was described in Chapter 13, for a firm in a competitive market, VMP_L is equal to the price of the firm's output times the marginal product of labor. The wage rate is determined in the aggregate labor market; so, an individual firm treats the wage rate as given (parametric).

Therefore, to implement this decision, the firm needs three pieces of information: (1) the market wage rate, (2) the price of its output, and (3) the marginal product function for labor. The market wage rate can be determined directly by the firm or forecasted using the techniques we described in Chapter 12. The price of the firm's output can be determined or forecasted by the firm in precisely the manner we described in section 14.1. Hence, the only potential difficulty is in finding the marginal product function for labor.

Essentially, as we described in Chapter 5, we have a production function with a single variable input, $Q = f(L)$. For the reasons described in Chapter 6, an appropriate empirical production function would be a log-linear function,

$$Q = AL^{\beta}$$

where $0 < \beta < 1$. With this short-run production function, the marginal product function for labor is[1]

$$MP_L = \beta AL^{\beta-1}$$

Once we have obtained the price forecast for the firm's output ($\hat{P}$), the forecasted wage rate ($\hat{w}$), and estimates of the parameters of the production function ($\hat{\beta}$ and $\hat{A}$), we can express the profit-maximizing condition as

$$(\hat{P}) \times (\hat{\beta}\hat{A}L^{\hat{\beta}-1}) = \hat{w}$$

To obtain the profit-maximizing employment level for labor, the analyst then needs to solve this equation for L. To show you how this is done using estimates and forecasts, let's turn to an example.

---

[1]More precisely,

$$MP_L = \frac{\partial Q}{\partial L} = \beta AL^{\beta-1}$$

APPLICATION

How many workers should I hire?

We have already seen how the manager of Beau Apparel selected the optimal output level for the firm's shirt division. Now let's see how the manager selected the optimal level of use of the variable factor of production—labor.

In order to determine the profit-maximizing (or loss-minimizing) level of usage of labor in 1985I, the manager needs to know three things:

1. *Forecasted price for the firm's output—the market price of output—in 1985I.* In an earlier application, we saw how such a forecast was obtained. For this application, let's use only the high forecast; so, $\hat{P}_{1985\text{I}} =$ \$20.
2. *Forecasted wage rate in 1985I.* As with price, various forecasting techniques could be used to obtain a forecast for the wage rate. In this case, the manager of Beau Apparel purchased a wage forecast for the geographic region in which its plant is located from an economic forecasting firm. The forecast provided by the consulting firm was \$16 per hour; so, $\hat{w}_{1985\text{I}} = 16$.
3. *The firm's short-run production function.* Using the available quarterly data for the division for the period 1982II–84IV, the manager estimated a production function of the form

$$Q = AL^{\beta}$$

More specifically, the manager used the 10 quarterly observations to estimate

$$\log Q = \log A + \beta \log L$$

where output (Q) was expressed in thousand units and labor usage (L) was in thousand hours. Using the estimated coefficients from the computer printout, the estimated production function was

$$\log Q = 1.004 + 0.6 \log L$$

This equation had an R^2 of 0.9210 and an F value of 93.266. The appropriate t-tests were performed to determine that the estimate of β was significantly greater than zero and less than one.

Rewriting the estimated production function in its exponential form, the empirical production function was

$$Q = (2.73)L^{0.6}$$

From this estimated production function, the marginal product function for labor was

$$MP_L = (0.6)(2.73)L^{0.6-1.0} = (1.638)L^{-0.4}$$

Using the price and wage forecasts and the estimated marginal product function, the profit-maximization condition ($P \times MP_L = w$) can be expressed as

$$(20) \times (1.638L^{-0.4}) = 16$$

or

$$L^{-0.4} = 0.4884$$

Taking logarithms of both sides of the preceding equation,

$$-0.4 \log L = -0.717$$

so $\log L = 1.792$ and it follows that (using natural logs) $L = 6.0$.[2] That is, the profit-maximizing level of labor usage in the first quarter of 1985 is 6,000 hours. (This is the equivalent of 12 full-time employees.)

As we noted in Chapter 13, the firm would actually hire this amount of labor—6,000 hours—only if the average product of labor exceeds the marginal product. If $AP_L < MP_L$, the firm would shut down. Hence, in order to make sure that $L = 6.0$ is indeed optimal, we must be sure that $AP_L \geq MP_L$. Using $L = 6.0$ in the estimated marginal product function, $MP_L = 0.8$. The average product of labor is

$$AP_L = Q/L = [(2.73)L^{0.6}]/L = (2.73)L^{-0.4}$$

Using $L = 6.0$ in this average product function, $AP_L = 1.33$. Hence, at $L = 6.0$, $AP_L > MP_L$ and 6,000 hours of labor usage is indeed optimal.

Using this optimal employment level in the estimated production function, the profit-maximizing output level is

$$Q = (2.73)6^{0.6} = 8$$

That is, the profit-maximizing output level is 8,000 units.

Further, since the level of labor usage and the wage rate are both known, the manager can calculate total variable cost:

$$TVC = w \times L = \$16 \times 6{,}000 = \$96{,}000$$

And, since total fixed cost in 1985I is $30,000, the manager expected profit for the shirt division of Beau Apparel is:

$$\text{Profit} = (\$20 \times 8{,}000) - [\$96{,}000 + \$30{,}000] = \$34{,}000$$

This is precisely the same result that was obtained via the optimal output determination.[3]

---

[2]In this application, natural logarithms were used. Therefore, if $\log L = 1.792$,

$$L = e^{\log L} = e^{1.792} = 6.001$$

[3]The results in this application correspond precisely to those obtained by equating $P = \$20$ to marginal cost in an earlier application. This correspondence was accomplished via a "judicious" selection of the parameters of the short-run production function, i.e., A and β. However, since the production function exhibits only diminishing returns to the variable factor, it would not generate a U-shaped average variable cost curve and this correspondence is not guaranteed for other prices.

Several variable inputs[4]

If the firm hires several variable inputs, the profit-maximization condition remains unchanged. However, the profit-maximization conditions for the inputs must be solved simultaneously, so the computation is somewhat more complex.

Let's look at a case in which the firm has two variable inputs—capital and labor. The profit-maximization conditions require that the value of the marginal products for the inputs be equal to the respective input prices. That is,

$$P \times MP_L = w \quad \text{and} \quad P \times MP_K = r$$

where r is the user cost of capital, i.e., the cost to the firm of using a unit of capital.

We have already talked about the way in which the firm can obtain its price forecast ($\hat{P}$). And, the firm can obtain forecasts of the price of capital ($\hat{r}$) in much the same way it obtains forecasts for the wage rate ($\hat{w}$). Hence, the remaining question is the determination of the marginal product functions for labor and capital.

In this case, we have a two-input production function, $Q = f(K,L)$. As we described in Chapter 6, we can use a Cobb-Douglas production function; so, we can write our empirical production function as

$$Q = AK^{\alpha}L^{\beta}$$

where $0 < \alpha,\ \beta < 1$. As we noted in Chapter 6, with this production function, the marginal product functions are

$$MP_K = \alpha\frac{Q}{K} = \alpha AK^{\alpha-1}L^{\beta}$$

$$MP_L = \beta\frac{Q}{L} = \beta AK^{\alpha}L^{\beta-1}$$

Once the production function has been estimated (i.e., we have the estimates $\hat{A}$, $\hat{\alpha}$, and $\hat{\beta}$) it can be used in conjunction with the forecasts of the output price and the prices of inputs to express the two profit-maximizing conditions as

$$(\hat{P}) \times (\hat{\beta}AK^{\hat{\alpha}}L^{\hat{\beta}-1}) = \hat{w}$$

and

$$(\hat{P}) \times (\hat{\alpha}AK^{\hat{\alpha}-1}L^{\hat{\beta}}) = \hat{r}$$

To determine the profit-maximizing levels of wage of labor and capital, we need to solve these two equations simultaneously for L and K. To show you how this is done, let's go to an example.

---

[4]This discussion and the application to follow are more computationally complex than most of the material presented in this text. This subsection can be skipped with no loss in continuity.

APPLICATION

A more complicated employment decision

Phoenix Manufacturing produces a small machine part that is sold in a market that approximates perfect competition. In its short-run production process, Phoenix is able to vary not only its usage of labor but also the usage of a portion of its capital, since it leases some of its machinery on a short-term basis. The firm does, however, have some inputs, e.g., its building, that are not variable in the short run.

The manager of Phoenix Mfg. wanted to determine the profit-maximizing (or loss-minimizing) levels of usage of the two variable inputs in 1985. From an econometric forecasting firm, the manager obtained a forecast for the market price of the firm's output in 1985 of $18 per unit.

From the same consulting firm, the manager obtained forecasts for the wage rate in the region in which the plant is located and the rental price of capital in 1985. The wage rate was forecasted to be $16 per hour. The forecast for the 1985 rental price (user price) of capital was 12 percent, i.e., the annual cost of using $1 worth of capital for one year is 12 cents; so $\hat{r} = 0.12$.

The manager collected historical data for Phoenix Mfg. on the firm's levels of usage of labor and the variable capital input and the resulting output. Using these data, a production function of the form

$$Q = AK^{\alpha}L^{\beta}$$

was estimated in which Q was expressed in thousand units, K in thousand dollars, and L in thousand hours of labor usage. The resulting estimate was

$$\log Q = -1.6 + 0.5 \log K + 0.4 \log L$$

or

$$Q = (0.2)K^{0.5}L^{0.4}$$

From this production function, the marginal product functions for labor and capital were

$$MP_L = (0.4)(0.2)K^{0.5}L^{(0.4-1.0)} = (0.08)K^{0.5}L^{-0.6}$$

and

$$MP_K = (0.5)(0.2)K^{(0.5-1.0)}L^{0.4} = (0.1)K^{-0.5}L^{0.4}$$

Since the manager knew that profit maximization occurs when the levels of usage of the inputs are such that the values, marginal products are equal to the input prices, the profit-maximizing conditions for Phoenix Mfg. in 1985 are

$$(18) \times [(0.08)K^{0.5}L^{-0.6}] = 16$$

$$(18) \times [(0.1)K^{-0.5}L^{0.4}] = 0.12$$

After performing some arithmetic and taking logarithms, these equations can be written as

$$0.5 \log K - 0.6 \log L = 2.41$$
$$-0.5 \log K + 0.4 \log L = -2.71$$

Solving these equations for log K and log L,

$$\log K = 6.62$$
$$\log L = 1.5$$

it follows then that $K = 750$ and $L = 4.5$. That is, the profit-maximizing levels of use of the two inputs are 4,500 hours of labor and $750,000 of capital.

In the preceding discussion and application we have confined ourselves to two inputs. However, this technique can be expanded to any number of variable inputs. The methodology will not change. The only thing that happens when you add more inputs is that the computation of the solution becomes more complex.

TECHNICAL PROBLEMS

1. In a perfectly competitive market, under what condition will a firm produce rather than shut down in the short run? If the decision is to produce, how is the optimal level of production determined?

2. Suppose that the manager of a firm operating in a perfectly competitive market has estimated the firm's average variable cost function to be

$$AVC = 10.0 - 3.0Q + 0.5Q^2$$

where AVC was expressed in dollars per unit and Q was measured in 100 units. Suppose that total fixed cost is $600.

a. What is the corresponding marginal cost function?
b. At what output is AVC a minimum?
c. What is the minimum value for AVC?

If the forecasted market price of the firm's output is $10 per unit,

d. How much output will this firm produce in the short run?
e. How much profit (loss) is this firm expected to earn?

If the forecasted market price of the firm's output is $5 per unit,

f. How much output will this firm produce in the short run?
g. How much profit (loss) is this firm expected to earn?

3. To find the optimizing level of usage of a single variable input, what condition must be satisfied for a firm in a perfectly competitive market? In order that the level of usage indicated by the preceding condition actually be optimal, what must be the relation between the average and the marginal products?

4. Suppose a firm operating in a perfectly competitive market has only one variable input—labor. The manager of the firm estimated a short-run production function for the firm of the form

$$Q = AL^{\beta}$$

The resulting estimated function was

$$\log Q = 1.176 + 0.7 \log L$$

where Q was measured in 1,000 units and L was measured in 1,000 hours of labor input.

a. Using the estimates obtained, rewrite the production function in the form $Q = AL^{\beta}$.

b. What is the marginal product of labor function?

The manager has forecasted the price of the firm's output to be $10 per unit and the price of labor (the wage rate) to be $14 per hour.

c. What is the firm's value of the marginal product function?

d. What is the indicated optimal level of usage of labor?

e. Ensure that this level of usage is indeed optimal (i.e., compare AP_L and MP_L at this level of usage of labor).

5. Using your results in Problem 4,

a. How much output will this firm produce?

b. What is the firm's total revenue?

c. What is the firm's total variable cost?

If total fixed cost for the firm is $50,000,

d. How much profit (loss) will the firm earn?

e. If the firm had elected to shut down, how much profit (loss) would it have earned?

ANALYTICAL PROBLEMS

1. Suppose you are the manager of a firm. If you wanted to determine the profit-maximizing level of output or input usage for your firm, how might you decide whether or not the competitive model is appropriate?
2. As in the applications in this chapter, many times the manager does not have a single forecast for future price. Instead, he or she will be faced with a range of price forecasts, e.g., high, best, low. How might the manager go about deciding which of these forecasts to base the production decision on?
3. In this chapter, we used estimates of the cost function obtained from regression analysis. Could the manager use estimates obtained using the engineering cost function approach? Discuss your answer, i.e., explain how or why not.
4. If a firm is suffering losses (or is shut down) in the short run, what decisions must it make for the long run? What are the firm's alternatives?

What kind of data would the manager need to look at to make the necessary decision?

5. "The most a firm could ever lose is the amount it has invested (its fixed cost)." Is this true or false? Explain.
6. Given the kind of production functions we used in this chapter,

$$Q = AL^{\beta},\ 0 < \beta < 1$$

and

$$Q = AK^{\alpha}L^{\beta},\ 0 < \alpha,\ \beta < 1$$

the average product of the input is guaranteed to exceed the marginal product. Why?

7. In our application titled "How Many Workers Should I Hire?" we obtained precisely the same results for a forecasted price of \$20 that we obtained earlier by equating price to marginal cost. As you might wish to verify, this correspondence does not hold for other prices, e.g., \$15 per unit. The reason for this is that the form of the average variable cost function we estimated,

$$AVC = a + bQ + cQ^2$$

does not "match" the form of the production function we estimated,

$$Q = AL^{\beta}$$

In what sense do these two functions not "match"?

Part 5

Firms with market power

15

Monopoly and monopolistic competition

Just as perfect competition lies at one extreme of the spectrum of market structures, pure monopoly lies at the other. A pure monopoly exists if and only if a single firm produces and sells a particular, well-defined commodity or service. Since the monopoly is the only seller in the market, it has neither rivals nor direct competitors. Furthermore, no new sellers can enter the market. Therefore, the demand function facing a monopolist is the market demand for the product.

An intermediate market structure that combines characteristics of both the perfectly competitive and monopoly structures is monopolistic competition. As is the case for perfect competition, under monopolistic competition the market consists of a large number of firms. But, unlike perfect competition, the products produced under monopolistic competition are differentiated rather than homogeneous. Each firm in the market produces a product that is distinguishable in one way or another from the products sold by the other firms in the market. But, these products, while different, are quite closely related. There is no good substitute for the product sold by a pure monopolist; but the products of the other firms in the market are good (but not perfect) substitutes for the product sold by a monopolistically competitive firm. Monopolistic competition is monopolistic in the sense that each firm has some monopoly—market—power. No other firm produces exactly the same product as that produced by a particular firm. But it is competitive because other firms produce close substitutes. Like perfect competition but unlike monopoly, under monopolistic competition there is free entry into and exit from the market. If profits are being made, firms can freely enter, selling a similar, though somewhat differentiated product. Likewise, if losses occur, firms can freely leave the market.

In this chapter we will analyze decision making under both of these market structures. We first discuss profit maximization by a pure monopolist in terms of the output and price decision and the input decision. We then turn to profit maximization under monopolistic competition and compare the results with those obtained under monopoly and perfect competition.

15.1 PROFIT MAXIMIZATION UNDER MONOPOLY— THE OUTPUT AND PRICE DECISIONS

As was the case for the perfectly competitive firm, we assume that the monopolist wishes to maximize profit, given prevailing cost and demand conditions. As you know, *any* firm can increase profit by expanding output so long as the marginal revenue from the expansion exceeds the marginal cost of expanding output. The firm would not expand if marginal revenue is less than marginal cost. The basic principle of profit maximization—profit is maximized by producing and selling the output at which marginal cost equals marginal revenue—is the same for the monopoly as for the perfectly competitive firm.

The fundamental difference is that, for the monopolist, marginal revenue is not equal to price. Instead, the marginal revenue for additional units sold is less than the price at which these units sell. Unlike the firm in a perfectly competitive market, the monopoly firm cannot sell all it desires to sell at the prevailing market price. Since a monopolist is the only firm selling in the market, the demand curve facing the monopolist is the market demand curve. Additional sales by a competitive firm do not lower the market price; but a monopoly firm can sell more only by lowering the price charged. Therefore, the marginal revenue from additional units sold is the price of those units *less* the reduction in the price of those units that could have been sold at the higher price. We will say more about the relation between price and marginal revenue for a monopolist, but first let us reemphasize that the basic principle of profit maximization is the same for the monopoly as for the perfectly competitive firm: profit is maximized at the output at which marginal revenue equals marginal cost.

Demand and marginal revenue under monopoly

As we showed in Chapter 10, if the demand curve is downward sloping, the marginal revenue from each additional unit sold is less than price (beyond the first unit). Thus the marginal revenue curve lies below the demand curve.

Figure 15.1
Demand and marginal revenue facing a monopolist

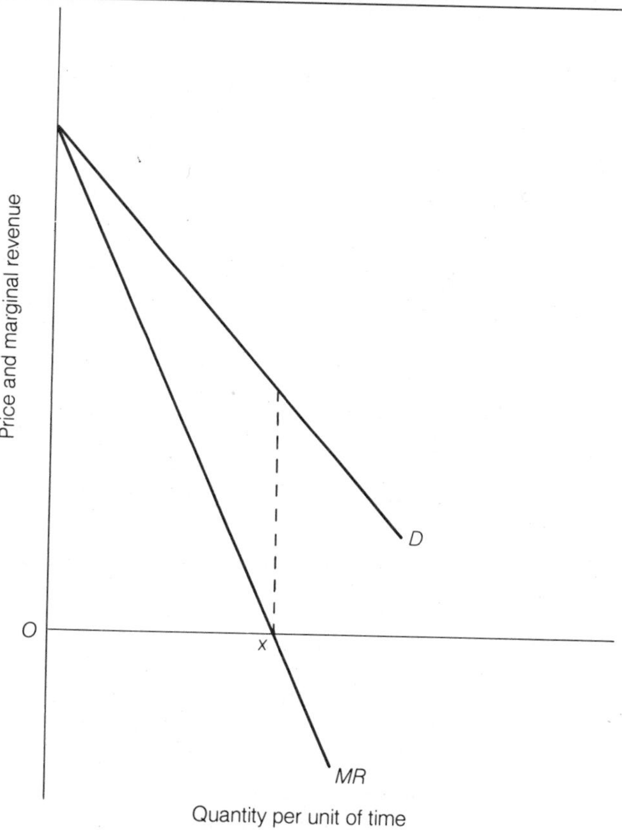

As we noted above, the demand function facing a monopolist is the market demand for the product. The market marginal revenue curve is, therefore, the marginal revenue curve of the monopolist.

A typical demand curve and marginal revenue curve are shown in Figure 15.1. As we showed in Chapter 10, when marginal revenue is positive, demand is elastic (at outputs between zero and x). When marginal revenue is negative, demand is inelastic (at outputs greater than x). We might note that in the case of a straight-line demand curve (as in Figure 15.1) the marginal revenue curve lies halfway between the vertical axis and the demand curve.

We can identify a monopoly firm or ascertain the amount of market power possessed by a firm by looking at the effect of changes in the prices of other products upon the firm's demand function. All firms, except for perfect competitors, possess some monopoly power. That is, they do not face horizontal demand curves. But the point at which a firm with monopoly power is called a monopolist is somewhat arbitrary.

A helpful measure of monopoly power is the cross elasticity of demand. This measure tells us directly which products are in the same market, and, therefore, whether a firm's product has good substitutes.

You will recall from Chapter 10 that the cross elasticity of demand measures the sensitivity of the quantity purchased of one good to a price change in another good. It is defined as

$$E_{XY} = \frac{\%\Delta X}{\%\Delta P_y} = \frac{\Delta X}{\Delta P_y} \cdot \frac{P_y}{X}$$

Where X is the quantity purchased of the good under consideration and P_y is the price of the other good. This term is positive, negative, or zero, as the goods are substitutes, complements, or independent. The cross elasticity of demand helps us determine whether two products are in the same market. A large positive cross elasticity means the goods are easily substitutable. Monopoly power is therefore likely to be weak. However, if a firm produces a product for which we cannot find other products with a high cross elasticity, we can be reasonably sure that the firm is alone in its market—there are no good substitutes available. This firm would, therefore, have considerable market power and could be classified as a monopolist.

Short-run equilibrium

The short-run cost curves confronting a monopolist are derived in exactly the same fashion as those faced by a perfectly competitive firm. From the theory of cost developed in Chapter 7, we know that cost depends upon the production function and input prices. The chief difference between a monopolist's cost curves and those for a perfect competitor is found in the potential impact of output changes on factor prices.

In the theory of perfect competition we assumed that each firm is very small relative to the total factor market and can, therefore, change its own rate of output without affecting factor prices, just as any one consumer can change the amount of a good purchased without affecting its price. But recall that, if all firms in the industry change output and, therefore, the use of all inputs, the prices of some of those inputs may change. The output of the monopolist, the sole firm in the industry, is accordingly the output of the industry. Certainly a monopolist, just as a competitive industry, may be so small relative to the demand for all inputs that its input use will have no effect on the price of any input. To be sure, even a very large monopolist will purchase some inputs (such as unskilled labor) the prices of which are not affected by the monopolist's rate of use. On the other hand, there is a possibility that a monopoly firm will purchase certain inputs for which the firm's rate of purchase will have a definite effect on the prices of these factors of production.

Notwithstanding the monopolist's possible effect upon factor prices, the cost curves for a monopoly firm are assumed to have the general shapes

Figure 15.2
Short-run equilibrium under monopoly

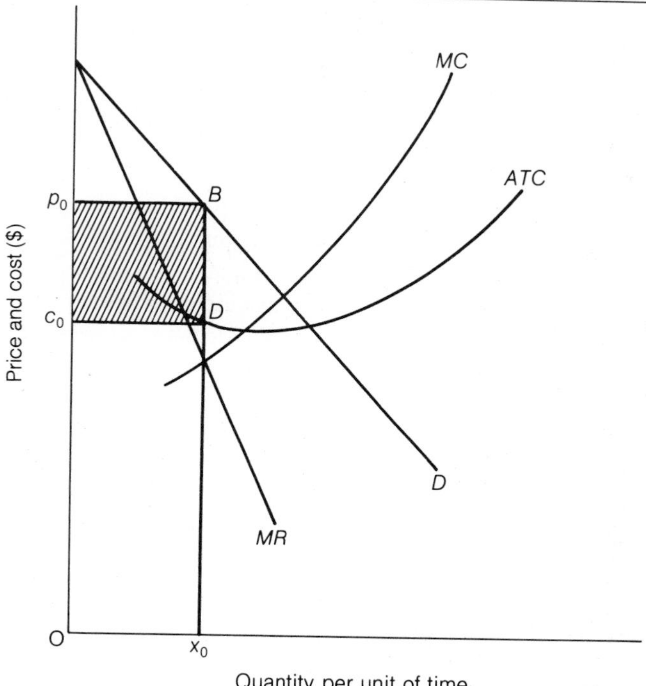

described in Chapter 7. The primary implication of rising supply prices of variable inputs is that the average and marginal cost curves rise more rapidly or fall less rapidly than if input prices were constant. Thus, for example, marginal cost may rise not only because of diminishing marginal productivity, but also because input prices rise with increased use.

A monopolist, just as a perfect competitor, attains maximum profit (or minimum loss) by producing and selling at that rate of output for which the positive (negative) difference between total revenue and total cost is greatest (least). This condition occurs when marginal revenue equals marginal cost.[1]

Using this proposition, the position of short-run equilibrium is easily described. Figure 15.2 shows the relevant cost and revenue curves for a monop-

---

[1]This can easily be shown mathematically. Since revenue and cost are both functions of output, we can write the monopolist's profit function as

$$\pi = R(x) - C(x) - F$$

where F denotes fixed cost and x is units of output. Profit maximization requires

$$\frac{d\pi}{dx} = \frac{dR}{dx} - \frac{dC}{dx} = 0$$

or $MR = MC$, since $\frac{dR}{dx}$ is marginal revenue and $\frac{dC}{dx}$ is marginal cost.

olist. (Since *AVC* and *AFC* are not necessary for exposition, they are omitted.) The profit-maximizing monopolist produces x_0 units of output, since at this level of production $MC = MR$. From the demand curve we see that price must be p_0 in order to ration the x_0 units among those who wish to buy the commodity. Total revenue is p_0 times x_0, or the area of the rectangle Op_0Bx_0. The unit cost of producing this amount of output is c_0. Total cost is then c_0 times x_0, or the area Oc_0Dx_0. Profit is $TR - TC$, or the shaded area c_0p_0BD.

In the example of Figure 15.2, the monopolist earns a pure profit in the short run. This need not be the case. A monopolistic position does not assure profit. If demand is sufficiently low, a monopolist may incur a loss in the short run, just as a pure competitor may. Figure 15.3 shows a loss situation. Marginal cost equals marginal revenue at output x_1, which can be sold at a price p_1. Average cost is c_1. Total cost, Oc_1Dx_1, exceeds total revenue, Op_1Bx_1; hence the firm suffers a loss shown as the shaded area p_1c_1DB.

Note that in Figure 15.3 the monopolist would produce rather than shut down in the short run, since total revenue (Op_1Bx_1) exceeds total variable cost ($OvNx_1$). After all variable costs have been covered, there is still some revenue (vp_1BN) left to apply to fixed cost. However, if demand decreases so that the monopolist cannot cover all of variable cost at any price, the firm would shut down and lose only fixed cost. This situation is analogous to that of the perfect competitor.

In the short run, the primary difference between a monopoly and a perfect competitor lies in the slope of the demand curve. Either may earn a pure profit; either may incur a loss.

Figure 15.3
Short-run losses under monopoly

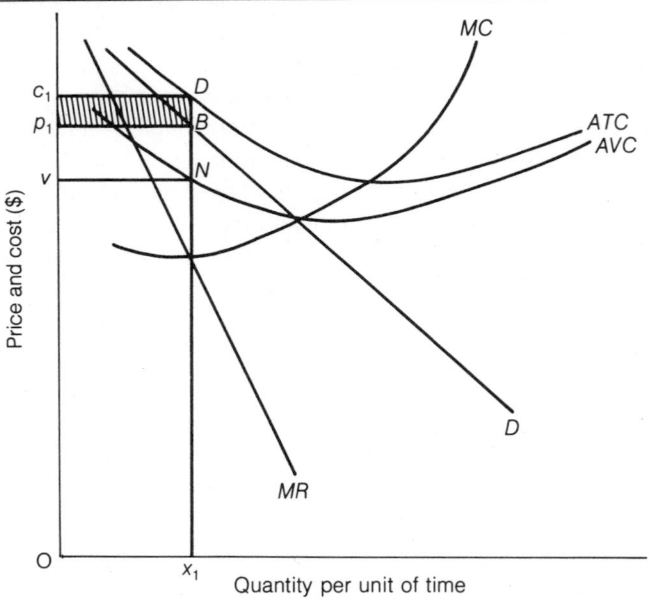

Table 15.1
Marginal revenue–marginal cost approach to profit maximization

(1) Output and sales	(2) Price	(3) Total revenue	(4) Total cost	(5) Marginal revenue	(6) Marginal cost	(7) Profit
5	$2.00	$10.00	$12.25	—	$0.45	$− 2.25
13	1.10	14.30	15.00	$0.54	0.34	− 0.70
23	0.85	19.55	18.25	0.52	0.33	+ 1.30
38	0.69	25.92	22.00	0.42	0.25	+ 3.92
50	0.615	30.75	26.25	0.35	0.35	+ 4.50
60	0.55	33.00	31.00	0.23	0.48	+ 2.00
68	0.50	34.00	36.25	0.13	0.66	− 2.25
75	0.45	33.75	42.00	−0.03	0.82	− 8.25
81	0.40	32.40	48.25	−0.23	1.04	−15.85
86	0.35	30.10	55.00	−0.46	1.35	−25.10

■ **Principle.** A monopoly will produce a positive output as long as some price on the demand curve exceeds average variable cost. It maximizes profit or minimizes losses by producing the quantity for which $MC = MR$. Since the monopolist's demand curve is above its marginal revenue curve at every positive output, equilibrium price exceeds MC.[2]

A numerical example can help to illustrate the principal points of this discussion. In Table 15.1 the demand schedule in columns 1 and 2 yields the total revenue schedule in column 3. We can simply subtract the total cost of producing each relevant level of sales from total revenue to obtain the profit from that output (column 7). Examination of the profit column shows that maximum profit ($4.50) occurs at 50 units of output. Marginal revenue and marginal cost, given in columns 5 and 6, give the same result. The monopolist can increase profit by increasing sales so long as marginal revenue exceeds marginal cost. If, on the other hand, marginal cost exceeds marginal revenue, profit falls with increased sales. Hence, the monopolist produces and sells 50 units, the level at which marginal cost and marginal revenue are equal.

Long-run equilibrium

We have said that a monopoly exists if there is only one firm in the market. Among other things, this statement implies that entrance into the market is closed. Thus, if a monopolist earns a pure profit in the short run, no new producer can enter the market in the hope of sharing whatever pure profit potential exists. Therefore, economic profit is not eliminated in the long run, as was the case under perfect competition. The monopolist will, however,

[2]We should note that a monopolist would never choose a situation in which it was producing and selling an output on the inelastic portion of its demand. When demand is inelastic marginal revenue is negative. Since marginal cost is always positive, it must equal marginal revenue when the latter is also positive. Thus the monopolist will always be on the elastic portion of demand.

make adjustments in plant size as demand conditions warrant them, even though entry is prohibited.

Clearly, in the long run, a monopolist would use the plant size designed to produce the quantity at which long-run marginal cost equals marginal revenue. Profit would be equal to the product of output times the difference between price and long-run average cost. New entrants cannot come into the industry and compete away profits—entry will not shift the demand curve facing the monopolist.

But demand conditions can change for reasons other than the entry of new firms; and such changes cause the monopolist to make adjustments. Suppose that demand for the product changes, due perhaps to a change in consumers' incomes. At first the firm will adjust without changing plant size. It will produce the quantity at which the new marginal revenue curve equals short-run marginal cost, or it will shut down in the short run if it cannot cover variable costs. In the long run, however the monopolist can adjust to the change in demand by changing plant size.

Long-run equilibrium adjustment for a monopoly firm must take one of two possible courses: (1) If the monopolist incurs a short-run loss and if there is no plant size that will result in pure profit (or, at least, no loss), the monopoly will go out of business; or (2) If it suffers a short-run loss or earns a short-run profit with the original plant, the manager must determine whether a plant of different size (and thus a different price and output) will lead to a larger profit. If the latter course of action is followed, the firm will select the plant size designed to produce the output at which the new marginal revenue equals long-run marginal cost.

Figure 15.4
Long-run equilibrium under monopoly

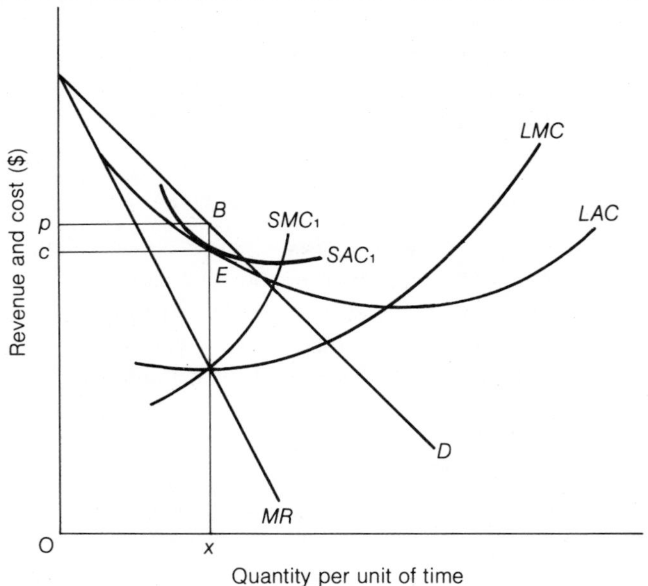

Generalizing, we have the following:

■ **Principle.** A monopolist maximizes profit in the long run by producing and marketing that rate of output for which long-run marginal cost equals marginal revenue. The optimal plant is the one whose short-run average cost curve is tangent to the long-run average cost curve at the point corresponding to long-run equilibrium output. At this point, short-run marginal cost equals marginal revenue.

This proposition is illustrated in Figure 15.4. The monopolist would build a plant to produce the quantity at which long-run marginal cost equals marginal revenue. In each period, x units are produced, costing c per unit and selling at a price of p per unit. Long-run profit is $cpBE$. By the now familiar argument, this is the maximum profit possible under the given revenue and cost conditions. The monopoly operates in the short run with the plant size indicated by SAC_1 and SMC_1. This is the best the monopolist can attain; and it can be attained because in the long run plant size is variable and the market is effectively closed to entry.

THE WALL STREET JOURNAL
APPLICATION

The decline of a monopoly

In 1983 the U.S. government in essence broke up the American Telephone and Telegraph Company (AT&T). To briefly summarize an extremely complex ruling, AT&T was permitted to continue providing long-distance service but was required to divest itself of its local service. Because of the sheer size of the company, this divestiture caused extensive turmoil in the industry and in the financial community, as you would expect.

There was no question that for most of its history AT&T was a classic monopoly. And it was generally the example of monopoly cited in textbooks. Neither is there any question that it was the most efficient large telephone company in the world. In fact, given its service record, many people wondered why AT&T was broken up.

A question that has been asked is whether the breakup was a result of government policy or whether the government action merely represented a "public notice" that Bell Telephone's monopoly position no longer existed. To look at this question, let's first examine the growth of Bell, then point out two recent events that may have brought about a deterioration of Bell's monopoly position.

In an article in *The Wall Street Journal,* Lindley H. Clark, Jr., noted that, from its beginning, good service was a calculated AT&T tactic.* This tactic was devised and implemented by Theodore Vail, who became Bell's general manager in 1878. The policy was to put telephones in American homes and make sure they worked. Good service would discourage competition.

Mr. Clark also noted that, around the turn of the century—during the "trust busting" era—Mr. Vail devised a survival formula for AT&T. He believed that AT&T *had to have* a monopoly position, or something close to it. And, to maintain the monopoly position, it had to provide good service at low rates. This became company policy.

Rather than resisting it, he actually encouraged governmental regulation. This helped entrench Bell's reputation as a public service company. Nonetheless, competitors were beginning to enter the business. Mr. Vail's policy was to cooperate with the new entrants, but charge a fee for connecting with AT&T's lines. The strategy was that Bell would provide such good service at such low rates that customers "would drift away from the competitors and back into the arms of Ma Bell."

Stockholders were also kept happy—with good dividends—and the company continued to try to get as many stockholders as possible. As Clark pointed out, "If you want to make a monopoly palatable to the public, the best way to do it is to have millions of contented customers and stockholders. To do that you have to run a good company."

After suffering through the depression of the 1930s, Bell's growth after World War II, both in revenues and productivity, was phenomenal. But the growth may have been a little too fast. In some areas, the increase in the number of phones resulted in some deterioration in service. Many of the customers had been somewhat less than contented.

Naturally, competitors began to enter, and Bell didn't react in the old way—cooperate with them but always try to out-compete them. Bell began to look more like a monopoly. As Lindley Clark noted, "Bell was vulnerable, and when big businesses are vulnerable there is always someone in Washington who is sure that it is time for government to do something."

At the time of the divestiture Ma Bell was not as secure as she once had been. Let's examine two types of competition Bell was faced with at the time. This competition suggests that Bell's monopoly position was in some danger even in the absence of the government's actions.

By 1983 the competition for long-distance customers had become quite intense. According to an article in *The Wall Street Journal*,† AT&T was losing customers to discount carriers such as MCI Communications Corporation and GTE Corporation's Sprint service. Given the revenues generated by long-distance calls—$40 billion in 1982—the small (5 percent) market share captured by Bell's competitors represented a substantial reduction in Bell's profits.

The smaller firms not only were under-pricing Bell on long-distance calls but also were mounting aggressive advertising and marketing campaigns. For example, in addition to making telephone solicitations for additional customers, MCI was planning a door-to-door sales campaign. (It's interesting to note that MCI's vice president for marketing had spent 13 years as an executive at Avon.) In addition to all of this, MCI and the other competitors were improving their service dramatically and making it easier for callers to use their service.

Obviously, all of this aggressive competition forced AT&T to begin competing for customers in order to keep the shares of the smaller firms from increasing even further. Bell started extensive advertising campaigns and telephone solicitations itself. All of this marketing was very expensive, consequently cutting into profits.

Certainly AT&T was still quite profitable during divestiture. Nonetheless the additional competition was beginning to cut into Bell's sheltered monopoly position.

Moreover, in the early 1980s, a new and potentially far more dangerous competition had emerged. This new competition was not from smaller companies, but from a giant, quite able to match Ma Bell in strength. The competitor was IBM. As *The Wall Street Journal* stated in 1981, the world's biggest phone company and the world's biggest computer maker seemed to be treading on each other's toes.‡

By 1981, IBM was selling a telephone system that had capabilities not available on AT&T telephones. According to the *Journal,* "Telephones and computers have grown all but inseparable, with most businesses now requiring advanced communications systems marrying both technologies." It was so difficult to separate the two systems that in 1980 the Federal Communications Commission formally gave up trying to draw a fine line between data processing and message carrying. AT&T was now free to compete in the data processing industry. But IBM also benefitted from the ruling: it now could enter the communications business, because all services that combined data processing and data transmission were deregulated.

The *Journal* predicted open competition between AT&T and IBM. An expert in the area forecast big benefits for consumers as the two giants began competing for the rapidly expanding business-communications market.

And the potential for computers as a communications tool had only begun to be tapped. The market was expected to expand to $59 billion by 1985. Although it is unlikely that AT&T would sell large computers or that IBM would sell traditional telephones, The *Journal* expected the future growth of each company would lie on the other's "traditional turf" and stressed the overlap: AT&T's telecommunications system was nothing more than a computer network and IBM was operating a sophisticated telephone network that transmits information by satellite throughout the country. Both companies saw, as a primary goal, enabling computers to be used by those with little or no training in their operation and to one day make data transmission as simple and accessible as voice transmission by telephone.

So, while the consent decree breaking up Ma Bell is very important, the government action was not the only factor in the decline of AT&T's monopoly position. Bell's monopoly position had been and was continuing to be eroded by the entry of new communications—not necessarily telephone—firms.

---

*"Where Was Theodore Vail When We (and AT&T) Needed Him?" by Lindley H. Clark, Jr., (Speaking of Business), *The Wall Street Journal,* January 31, 1984. Reprinted by permission of *The Wall Street Journal.*

†Virginia Inman, "AT&T Tells Everyone Its Long-Distance Calls Are Better than MCI's," *The Wall Street Journal,* October 27, 1983. Reprinted by permission of *The Wall Street Journal.*

‡Susan Chance, "AT&T and IBM Tread on Each Other's Toes as Courses Converge," *The Wall Street Journal,* September 4, 1981. Reprinted by permission of *The Wall Street Journal.*

15.2 INPUT DEMAND FOR A MONOPOLIST

Thus far we have analyzed profit maximization for a monopoly firm in terms of the output decision. As was the case for perfectly competitive firms, we can also analyze profit maximization in terms of input usage. We will first look at the monopoly firm's input decision assuming that it faces given (constant) prices for the inputs it purchases. Then, given our earlier discussion of the possibility that the monopoly firm's employment decision may affect the prices of the inputs, we will look at input decisions with an upward-sloping supply function for the input.

Input prices given

The analytical principles underlying the demand for a single variable input for a monopolist are the same as those for perfectly competitive firms. But, since price does not equal marginal revenue for a monopoly, there is one methodological difference.

To illustrate this difference, let's assume a monopoly hires a single variable input and faces a market-determined price for that input. As in the case of competition, when a monopoly employs an additional unit of the input, output increases by an amount equal to the marginal product of the input. However, to sell the larger output, commodity price must be reduced. Hence, total revenue is not augmented by price times the marginal product of the input. Instead, total revenue changes by marginal revenue times marginal product. We call this the *marginal revenue product* of the input.

■ **Definition.** Marginal revenue product for a monopolist is the additional revenue attributable to the addition of one unit of the variable input (V). It is equal to per-unit marginal revenue times marginal product.

$$MRP_v = \Delta TR/\Delta V = MR \times MP_v$$

Since price is greater than marginal revenue, marginal revenue product is less than the value of the marginal product (price times marginal product).

In the case of a competitive firm, *VMP* declines because marginal product declines. For a monopolist, marginal revenue product declines with increases in the usage of the input not only because marginal product declines but also because marginal revenue declines as output is increased.

For example, assume that increasing the usage of the variable input by one unit increases output from 30 to 38 units; thus $MP = 8$. Suppose that the firm could sell 30 units at a price of \$25 each; but, to sell 38 units, price must fall to \$22.

Thus the *gross* addition to total revenue from hiring the additional unit of the input is 8 (the added production) times \$22 (the new selling price) or \$8 × \$22 = \$176. But to sell the additional 8 units, the price of the 30 units that could have been sold at \$25, must fall by \$3. Thus the lost revenue from the price reduction is \$3 × 30 = \$90. This loss must be subtracted from the gross gain to give a *net* gain of \$176 − \$90 = \$86. This net gain—\$86—is the marginal revenue product of the input.

A monopolist's demand for a single variable input is the positive portion of the *MRP* curve.[3] Since both *MP* and *MR* decline, the input demand function must also decline.

In Figure 15.5, the relevant portion of *MRP* is shown. Begin with the price of the input at w_0. The firm will hire v_0 units of the input at this price. It would not hire fewer than v_0, because an additional unit of input would add more to the firm's revenue (*MRP*) than it costs (w_0). Clearly it would not hire more than v_0, because an additional unit of the input would add less than it costs the firm to hire that unit.

If the price of the input rises to w_1, the firm decreases its usage of the input to v_1 units, the amount at which *MRP* equals w_1. Thus we see that within the relevant range the *MRP* curve is the monopolist's demand curve for a single factor of production.

■ **Principle.** A monopolist who purchases a variable productive resource or input in a perfectly competitive input market (the price of the input is given to the firm) will employ that amount of the input for which marginal revenue

---

[3]For the same reasons as those discussed in the case of a perfect competitor, a monopolist would not use an amount of a variable at which the average revenue product is less than marginal revenue product. Since

$$ARP = \frac{Q}{V} \cdot P$$

and

$$MRP = w$$

in equilibrium, where w is the price of the variable input, V, and P is the price of the product. If

$$ARP = \frac{Q \cdot P}{V} < MRP = w$$

$$P \times Q < wV$$

so total revenue is less than total variable cost.

Figure 15.5
Marginal revenue product and input demand

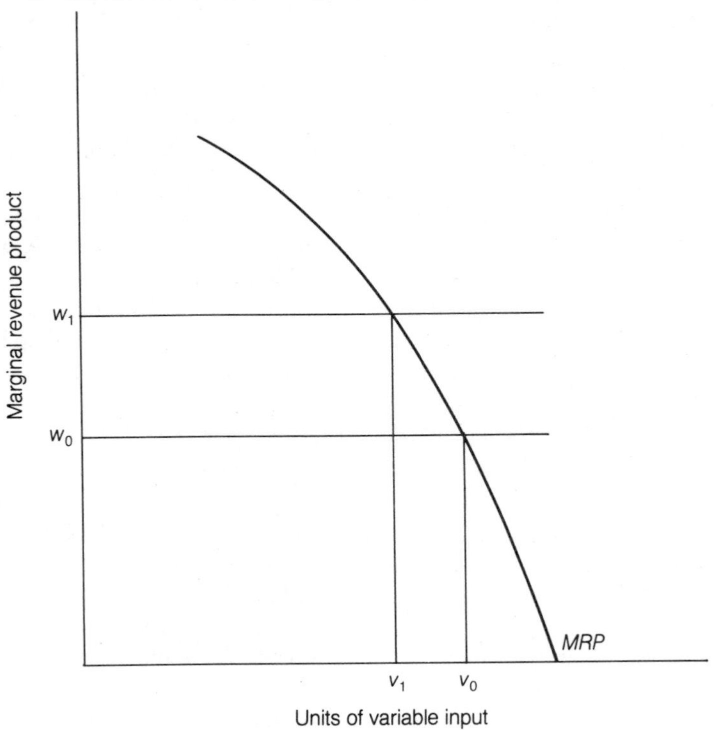

product equals the price of the input. Consequently, the marginal revenue product curve, within the relevant range, is the monopolist's demand curve for the variable input when only one variable input is employed. Marginal revenue product declines for two reasons: (1) the marginal product of the input declines as more units of the variable input are added and (2) to sell the additional output, the monopoly must lower the price of its output.

As was the case for perfect competition, the derivation of input demand curves is more complicated when production involves more than one variable input. The *MRP* curve is no longer the demand for the productive service, because the inputs are interdependent in the productive process. A change in the price of any one input leads to a change not only in the usage of that input but also in the use of other inputs as well. Recall that the marginal product curve for an input is derived assuming the usage of all other inputs is held constant. Thus changes in the rates of usage of other inputs shift the *MRP* curve.

Nonetheless, the monopolist's demand for an input is still downward sloping. And, most important, the monopolist still uses the amount of each variable input at which its marginal revenue product equals its price.[4] For instance, if the monopoly firm uses three variable inputs—v_1, v_2, and v_3—all of which have given, market-determined prices—w_1, w_2, and w_3—the firm will maximize profit (or minimize loss) by employing each input so that

$$MRP_{v_1} = w_1$$
$$MRP_{v_2} = w_2$$
$$MRP_{v_3} = w_3$$

Since the inputs are interdependent in the production process, these conditions must hold simultaneously; so this means that the optimal levels of usage of the inputs must be determined simultaneously.

Thus, if an input's price is given to the monopoly we have the following:

■ **Principle.** A monopolist's demand for a variable productive resource must be negatively sloped. Even though input demand, when more than one input is variable, is not the *MRP* curve, it should be stressed that at every point on the demand curve the price of the input equals its marginal revenue product.

Upward-sloping input supply

Thus far we have assumed that the price of an input is determined by supply and demand in the resource market and is independent of the level of

---

[4]These results can be easily shown mathematically. Let the production function be

$$q = f(V_1, V_2, \cdots, V_m)$$

where q is output and the V_i are the quantities of the variable inputs used.

Since the firm is a monopolist we can write the demand function as,

$$p = h[q] = h[f(V_1, V_2, \cdots, V_m)]$$

where $h' < 0$. Let w_i be the price of input V_i. Profit is therefore,

$$\pi = h[f(V_1, V_2, \cdots, V_m)]f(V_1, V_2, \cdots, V_m) - \sum_{i=1}^{m} w_i V_i$$

Profit maximization requires

$$\left(\frac{dP}{dq}q + p\right)f_1 = w_1$$
$$\vdots \qquad \vdots \qquad \vdots$$
$$\left(\frac{dP}{dq}q + p\right)f_m = w_m$$

Since total revenue is $h(q) \times q$, marginal revenue is $\frac{dP}{dq}q + p$. Therefore, profit maximization requires that for each input, V_i, $\left(\frac{dP}{dq}q + p\right)f_i = w_i$. Since f_i is the marginal product of the i-th input, $MR \times MP_i = MRP_i = w_i =$ input price.

usage of the input by an individual firm. But, as we noted earlier in this chapter, a monopoly firm may well be large enough to have an effect upon the prices of some of the inputs it uses.

In such instances, the firm must pay a higher price if it wishes to hire more units of the input. And, it not only has to pay more to the additional units of the resource hired but also must pay the higher price for those units that it could have hired (or was hiring) at the lower price. Thus the addition to cost is the cost of the added units hired plus the cost of paying more to the other units already being used. This added cost is called the *marginal factor cost* of an input. Marginal factor cost is greater than the price of the input. Therefore, if the monopoly firm faces an upward-sloping input supply function, it will make its employment decision by equating the marginal revenue product of the input with the marginal factor cost of the input (rather than the input price):

$$MRP = MFC$$

In this case, the input price will be less than MFC.

APPLICATION

A monopoly of another sort

When most people think of monopolies, the first examples that come to mind are corporate giants like AT&T. While you may not become the CEO of such a company—at least not for a few years—you are quite likely to deal with another type of monopoly, one which is pervasive in the American economy but not generally recognized as a monopoly. These monopolies are labor unions.

Established labor unions can be thought of as the single seller of particular types of labor service to a firm. Once a labor contract is put into effect, the firm can hire only union labor under the conditions specified by the labor contract.

In essence, unions can use their monopoly power to do one of two things: (1) they can set a wage rate (or a package of wage rates), then let the firm or industry determine the amount of labor hired; or (2) they can set the number of workers available to the firm or industry, and then let market forces determine the wage rate (or rates). These actions are illustrated in Figure 15.6. The firm's (or industry's) demand for labor is DD'. If the pre-union wage rate is w_0, L_0 units of labor are hired.

Suppose a labor union is organized and it sets a higher wage rate of w_1. At this wage, L_1 units of labor are hired. Obviously, given the downward-sloping demand for labor, fewer workers will be hired at the higher wage.

Alternatively, if the union wants to establish a wage of w_1, it could make available only L_1 units of labor. No more workers are permitted to join the union, and under the contract only union labor can be employed. The reduction in the amount of available labor drives the wage up to w_1.

Figure 15.6
The effect of unions

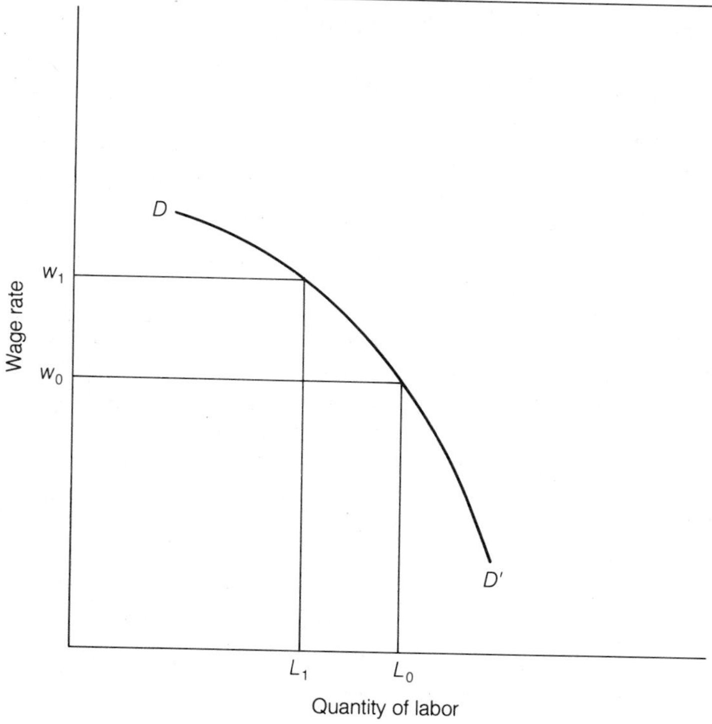

In this simplified analysis, if the union wishes to obtain increased wages, it can do so only with a reduction in the number of workers hired. Increased wages would be obtained only by reducing employment.

This is not to say that workers cannot be made better off by the formation of a union and the increase in wages. If the demand for labor is inelastic over the range L_0 to L_1, the increase in the wage rate from w_0 to w_1 would increase the total amount of wage income received by labor. The union could decrease the number of hours worked by each union member and keep all L_0 workers employed. (Of course, if demand is elastic, the wage bill would decrease. Those workers who keep their jobs would be better off, but some workers would have to find employment elsewhere.)

While the union possesses monopoly power, it might not be able to obtain as high a wage as desired. The union can always use the threat of a strike if the firm's management does not accept the wage asked for. But, although a strike generally causes the firm to suffer losses, workers also suffer reduced incomes during a strike. These reduced incomes may well offset any wage increases.

In addition, the union must also consider the reduction in employment associated with a higher wage. If too many workers are forced into unemployment, there is the possibility that this unemployed labor could cause the union to break up.

The effect on wages alone is not the entire story of the effect of labor unions. In fact, there is considerable controversy among economists about the overall impact of unions on productivity and costs.

No one denies that when unions obtain wage increases above the level that would otherwise exist, firms substitute other resources—most notably capital—for labor, and employment declines. But one group of economists argues that unions increase labor productivity through decreased turnover and the establishment of grievance procedures, seniority systems, work rules, and so on. They also argue that unions somehow shock management into becoming more efficient.

Opponents of this view argue that unions lead to an inefficient input mix, reduce management flexibility, bring about inefficient work rules, and limit competition based upon individual productivity. Thus far the evidence is somewhat inconclusive.*

One prominent labor economist, Morgan Reynolds, stressed the direct restrictions imposed by unions.† He pointed out several examples: Electrical unions refused to install switchboards unless factory wiring was torn out and rewired by union members. A typographical union required resetting existing plates of newspaper advertising. An operating engineer's union required one of its members to operate each machine or engine on a construction site, even if only one switch needed to be turned on for the entire day's work. Reynolds also pointed out that unions have consistently resisted labor-saving technological change.

As an example of the effect of union work rules on productivity, Reynolds cited a study of the effect of a 1960 agreement with the West Coast longshoremen's union that eliminated work rules requiring multiple handling of goods and redundant crews. Following unionization in the 1930s, productivity had dropped and remained relatively constant at this lower level until 1960 when the work rules were eliminated. Productivity increased 40 percent over the five years following the elimination of the work rules. Workers earned higher pay, no fewer longshoremen were employed, and industry volume increased.

But the jury is still out on the effects of unionization on productivity. Much more empirical evidence will be presented on both sides of the question.

*A summary of the evidence may be found in Barry T. Hirsch and Albert N. Link, "Unions, Productivity, and Productivity Growth," *Journal of Labor Research,* Winter, 1984, pp. 29–37.

†Morgan O. Reynolds, *Power and Privilege* (New York: Universe Books, 1984), pp. 83–88.

15.3 MONOPOLISTIC COMPETITION

Between the extremes of perfect competition and monopoly come a large number of theoretical market structures. For convenience, economists normally classify all of these "intermediate" market structures into two categories: monopolistic competition and oligopoly. Given its similarities to monopoly, we will consider monopolistic competition in this chapter. We will defer our discussion of oligopoly to Chapter 18.

The theory of monopolistic competition was developed to analyze cases in which a large number of firms produce and sell commodities that are similar, but not identical. The various commodities have some distinguishing characteristics. Competition exists in the sense that the firms compete with one another to sell closely related products. Monopoly power is present because each firm produces a product that is distinguishable from the product of every other firm. Each firm's product is a close but not perfect substitute for the products of the other firms. Even though there are many firms in the market, product differentiation prevents the individual firm's demand curve from being horizontal (perfectly elastic). Each seller possesses some market power.

Short-run equilibrium

The theory of monopolistic competition is essentially a long-run theory. In the short run, there is virtually no difference between the analysis of monopoly and of monopolistic competition. Each firm attempts to maximize profit. With a given, down-sloping demand curve, the firm maximizes profit or minimizes loss by equating marginal cost with marginal revenue.

In Figure 15.7, we have illustrated a short-run equilibrium for a firm in a monopolistically competitive market. Since the firm produces and sells a

Figure 15.7
Short-run equilibrium under monopolistic competition

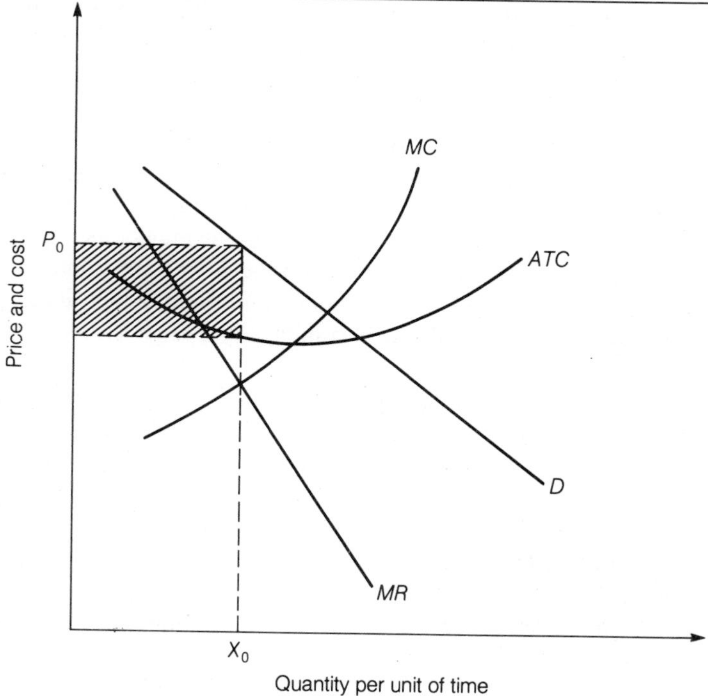

differentiated product, the demand curve facing the firm is downward sloping. So, the firm will select its optimal level of production and sales by equating the marginal revenue curve corresponding to this demand function with its marginal cost function. In Figure 15.7, the optimal output is X_0 and the corresponding price is P_0.

In the situation illustrated, the firm will earn an economic profit (shown as the shaded area). However, as was the case for perfect competition and for monopoly, in the short run the firm could operate with a loss, if the demand curve was below *ATC* but above *AVC;* or, if the demand curve was below *AVC,* the firm would shut down.

So far as the short run is concerned, there appears to be very little competition in monopolistic competition. Indeed, Figure 15.7 is virtually identical to the figure illustrating short-run equilibrium under monopoly (Figure 15.2). But when a longer view is taken, one essential element of monopoly is missing. In particular, a monopoly cannot be maintained if there is free entry. If pure profit is present in the short run, other firms will enter and produce the product, and they will continue to enter until all pure profits are eliminated. This feature leads us to a discussion of the long-run equilibrium for a monopolistically competitive firm.

Long-run equilibrium

While the short-run equilibrium for a firm under monopolistic competition is the same as that under monopoly, the long-run equilibrium is more closely related to the equilibrium position under perfect competition. Because of free and easy entry, all economic profit must be eliminated in the long run. Such a zero-profit equilibrium can only occur at an output at which price equals long-run average cost. This occurs when the firm's demand is tangent to long-run average cost. The only difference between this equilibrium and that for perfect competition is that, for a firm in a monopolistically competitive market, the tangency cannot occur at minimum average cost. Since the demand curve facing the firm is downward sloping under monopolistic competition, the point of tangency must be on the downward-sloping range of long-run average cost. Thus, the long-run equilibrium output under monopolistic competition is less than that forthcoming under perfect competition in the long run.

This result is shown in Figure 15.8. *LAC* and *LMC* are the long-run average and marginal cost cures for a typical monopolistically competitive firm. Suppose that the short-run demand curve is given by D_m. In this case the firm would be making substantial economic profits; and if this firm is making profits, we would expect that other firms in the market are also earning economic profits. Thus we would expect these profits to attract new firms into the market. While the new firms would not be selling exactly the same products as existing firms, their products would be very similar. So as new firms enter, the number of substitutes would increase and the demand facing the typical

Figure 15.8
Long-run competitive equilibrium under monopolistic competition

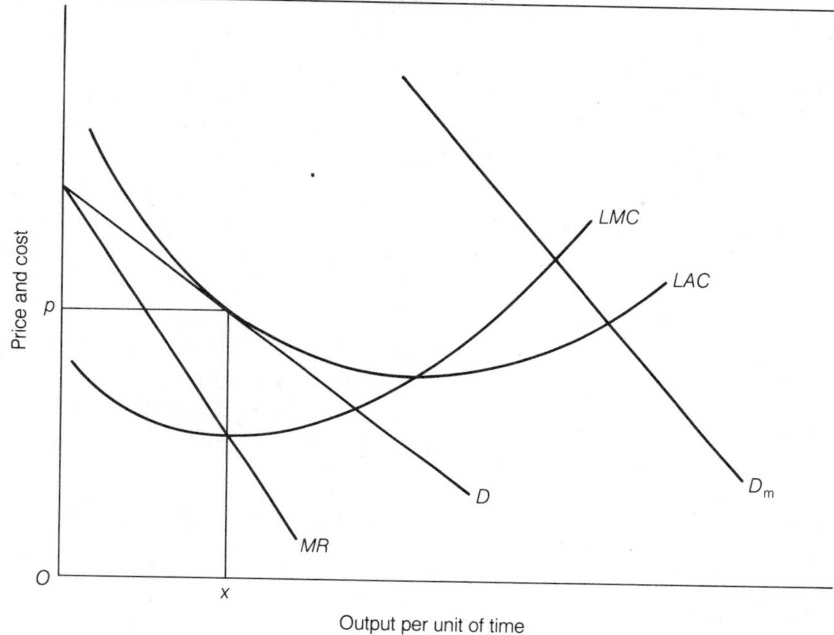

firm will shift backward and probably become more elastic (though not perfectly elastic). Entry will continue as long as there is some economic profit being earned. Thus entry causes each firm's demand curve to shift backward until a demand curve such as D in 15.8 is reached. This long-run demand curve, D, is tangent to LAC at a price of p and output of x.

In such an equilibrium either an increase or a decrease in price by the firm would lead to losses. No more entry would occur since there are no pure profits to be earned in this market.

If "too many" firms enter the market, each firm's demand curve would be pushed so far back that demand falls below LAC. Firms would be suffering losses and exit would take place. As this happened, the demand curve would be pushed back up to tangency with LAC. Free entry and exit under monopolistic competition must lead to a situation where demand is tangent to LAC—where price equals average cost—and no economic profit is earned.

The equilibrium in Figure 15.8 must also be characterized by the intersection of LMC and MR. Only at output x can the firm avoid a loss; so, this output must be optimal. But we also know that the optimal output requires marginal cost to equal marginal revenue. Thus, at x, it must be the case that $MR = LMC$.

■ **Principle.** Long-run equilibrium in a monopolistically competitive market is attained when the demand curve for each producer is tangent to the long-run average cost curve. Free entry and exit force this equilibrium. At the equilibrium output, price equals long-run average cost and marginal revenue equals long-run marginal cost.

We might note that short of getting the government to prevent entry, there is nothing the firms in a monopolistically competitive market can do about having their profits competed away. Even if the firms were to conspire to fix a price, new firms would enter. Each firm would find its sales reduced until price equaled average cost and zero economic profits would result, although possibly at a higher price than would occur in the absence of the price-fixing agreement.

We have emphasized that, under monopolistic competition, profits are competed away in the long run. While this is certainly correct in general, we do not mean to imply that there is no opportunity for astute managers to postpone this situation far into the future by innovative decision making. As an example, let us examine the experience of a trucking firm.

THE WALL STREET JOURNAL

APPLICATION

"Iowa Trucker Prospers after Deregulation"*

The trucking industry fits rather well into the structure of monopolistic competition. There are a very large number of firms and each firm is small relative to the total market. But the services of the different firms are distinguishable, i.e., the products (services) are not homogenous.

Prior to the Motor Carrier Act of 1980, the Interstate Commerce Commission (ICC) rigidly regulated who could carry what freight to what places at what rates. Entry was also regulated. And, as you would expect, the established trucking companies prospered under these regulations.

During the three years after deregulation, 9,000 new carriers entered the industry. Moreover, the 1982 recession substantially reduced the amount of freight being shipped. Firms began discounting and cutting rates—a tactic previously not permitted under regulation. More than 100,000 drivers lost their jobs and most companies lost money. Even during the recovery of 1983, the American Trucking Association estimated that 25 percent of all firms operated in the red. With the larger number of firms, there just wasn't enough business to go around.

But, according to the *Journal,* a few companies were expanding their volume, despite excess capacity in the industry. And, despite the reduced freight rates, a few companies continued to earn economic profits. One of these profitable companies was CRST (formerly Cedar Rapids Steel Transportation). This was remarkable because CRST was not one of the largest companies and it was a full-load carrier, a field in which competition was the most fierce. The *Journal* noted that CRST moved from 134th in revenues in 1979 to 65th in 1982, and predicted an even higher position after the figures for 1983 came in. Even in 1982, when hundreds of trucking companies suffered losses or went bankrupt, CRST made a profit. In 1983 its profits rose 35 percent, and its president predicted another 30 to 35 percent increase in 1984.

CRST must have been doing something right. *The Wall Street Journal* pointed out that one tactic employed by CRST and the few other successful firms was offering shippers special packages and rates that benefitted both the trucker and the shipper. As a result, many giant shippers (e.g., Sears, DuPont, General Mills, and General Electric) increasingly began using many of these efficient truckers.

As an example of innovative scheduling, the *Journal* noted that General Mills was paying 40 to 50 percent below the usual single-haul rates by giving CRST "connected hauls"—hauls that eliminated empty, unpaid deadheading after products were delivered. The CRST sales plan revolved around keeping empty trips to a minimum. This was the key to profitable trucking, according to the firm's marketing director. He noted that many trucking companies hadn't known how much deadheading they had—much less how to control it—under ICC regulation.

DuPont, another corporate giant, began using relatively small but efficient carriers like CRST. By 1984 they were using only 40 carriers—down from hundreds a few years before. DuPont's logistics director was quoted as saying that CRST's cost effectiveness was the reason the firm was a winner.

The *Journal* pointed out that such marketing emphasis was a new idea for most truckers. Shielded by ICC regulation and not needing to compete, truckers' marketing efforts were described in one 1981 survey of shippers as "horrible," "subpar," and "dismal." As late as 1984, one industry executive stated that only about 15 percent of all firms were "selling their services with vigor." But at the time, industry analysts were predicting that "The trucker who doesn't make a special effort to present a freight program specially designed for his customers will be frozen out."

To summarize, CRST and a few other profitable carriers took advantage of deregulation by selling shippers freight packages that offered them savings, in return for reduced or paid-for deadhead mileage for the trucker. According to the *Journal,* "Discounting without serious profit damage was possible only because of CRST's close control of truck operations. The aim: Load the truck, deliver it in a set time based on mileage, unload—the same day if possible—and reload quickly." Such efforts paid off, even when many other trucking firms were losing money.

---

*Albert R. Karr, "Iowa Trucker Prospers after Deregulation Eases Rules on Routes," *The Wall Street Journal,* February 13, 1984. Reprinted by permission of *The Wall Street Journal.*

15.4 SUMMARY

A monopoly is a firm that is the sole seller of a well-defined product. The demand curve facing the monopolist is the market demand curve for the product. The monopolist faces no direct competition but does have indirect competition. The degree of monopoly power is measured by the cross elasticity of demand for the product.

The monopoly maximizes profit by equating marginal revenue with marginal cost. Since the demand is downward sloping, the price charged is greater than the marginal cost in equilibrium. In its hiring decision a monopoly purchases every input so that the marginal revenue product for each input equals its price or marginal factor cost.

Monopolistic competition is a market structure consisting of many firms that are selling similar but differentiated products. Thus each firm faces a great deal of direct competition. Nonetheless, because of product differentiation, each firm faces a downward sloping demand.

In the short run, monopolistic competition is identical to monopoly; each firm equates marginal revenue with marginal cost. In the long run, all pure profit is competed away. Each firm produces the quantity at which its demand is tangent to its long-run average cost. Since price equals average cost, this gives a zero-profit equilibrium; but because demand is downward sloping, the firm does not produce at minimum long-run average cost, as is the case under perfect competition. In this long-run equilibrium, marginal revenue equals long-run marginal cost.

TECHNICAL PROBLEMS

1. Consider a monopoly firm with the demand and cost curves shown in the following figure. Assume that the firm is operating in the short run with the plant designed to produce 400 units of output optimally.

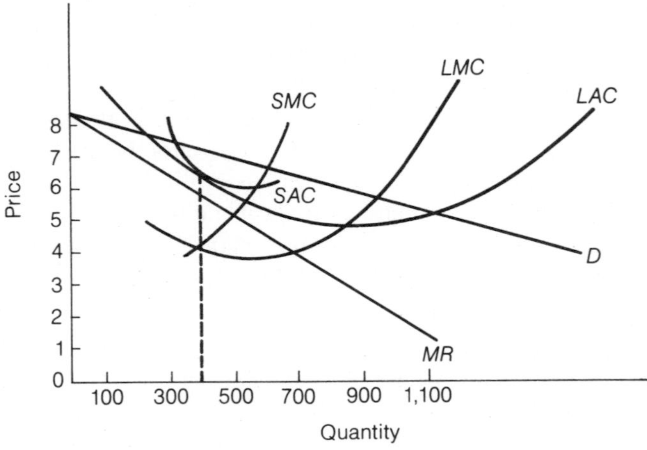

a. What output should be produced?
b. What will be the price?
c. How much profit is made?
d. If the firm can change plant size and move into the long run, what will be output and price?
e. Will profit increase? How do you know?
f. Draw in the new short-run average and marginal cost curves associated with the new plant size.

2. Explain why a profit maximizing monopolist always (in theory) produces and sells on the elastic portion of the demand curve. If costs are zero what output will the monopolist produce?

3. A monopolist has the short-run cost configuration shown below. The firm is making losses but continues to produce in the short run.

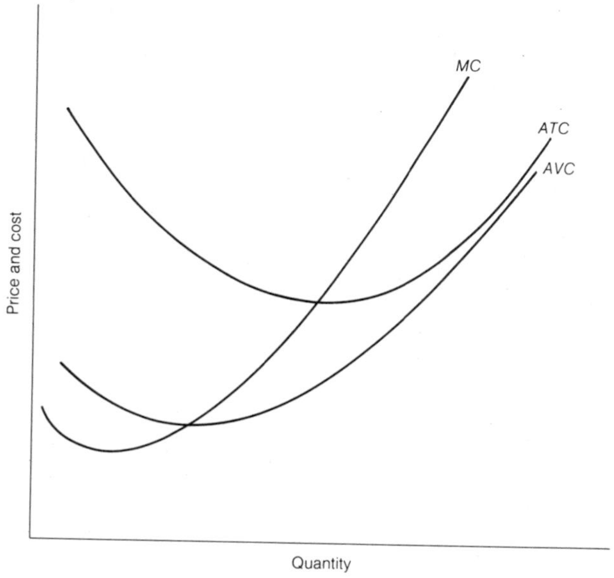

a. Draw in accurately the appropriate demand and marginal revenue curves for this situation.
b. Show and label price and quantity.
c. Show and label the loss being made.
d. If this demand situation persists, what two things can the firm do in the long run?

4. Compare the perfectly competitive firm and the monopolist as to how each makes the following decisions:
a. How much to produce.
b. What to charge.
c. Whether or not to shut down in the short run.

5. If a monopolist is not making enough profit it can simply raise price until it does. Comment critically.
6. Suppose there is a natural monopoly; that is, economies of scale are experienced over the entire range of output. Show long-run average and marginal costs in a graph. Now add demand and marginal revenue curves. Show the output and price that maximize profits. If the monopolist is forced to produce where demand equals long-run marginal cost, would it continue to operate? Why or why not? Analyze the situation if it is forced to operate where demand equals average cost.
7. Describe the features of monopolistic competition:
    a. How is it similar to monopoly?
    b. How is it similar to competition?
    c. What are the characteristics of short-run equilibrium?
    d. What are the characteristics of long-run equilibrium?
    e. How is long-run equilibrium attained?
8. The figure below shows the long-run average and marginal cost curves for a monopolistically competitive firm.

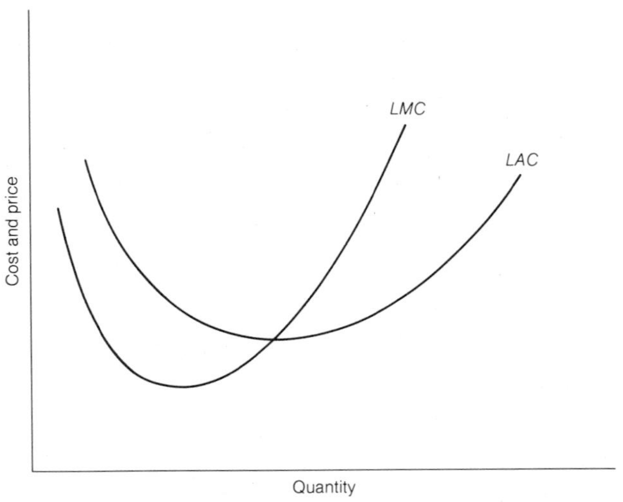

    a. Assume the firm is in the short run and making profits. Draw in the demand and marginal revenue curves. Show output and price.
    b. Now let the firm reach long-run equilibrium. Draw in the new demand and marginal revenue curves. Show output and price.
9. How might advertising to make the demand curve less elastic be useful to a firm that desires to raise the price of the product it sells without encouraging entry?
10. Discuss the difference between a monopolist's demand for an input and the input demand for a perfectly competitive firm. Contrast this with input demand for a perfectly competitive industry.

11. How can we say that when more than one input is variable, the monopolist's demand for an input is not its marginal revenue product curve, yet in equilibrium the monopolist hires each input so that its *MRP* equals its price?
12. The demand for a factor of production depends to a certain extent on the demand for the product produced by the input. Explain the connection.

ANALYTICAL PROBLEMS

1. One sure test that an industry is competitive is the absence of any economic profit. Comment critically.
2. An industry said to be characterized by monopolistic competition is the apparel industry. Suppose you are hired as a consultant by a firm in this industry. How would you advise the firm as to the levels of output, price, input usage, and levels of advertising? What problems might you encounter?
3. In the Application concerning AT&T, how can AT&T and IBM be so competitive when AT&T produces no pure computers and IBM sells no pure telephones?
4. Why would labor unions seek restrictive work rules, such as those described in the union Application? Given your answer, can you think of any other type of work rules a union might desire? Why would management agree to such rules?
5. Discuss the argument that unionization somehow "shocks" management into becoming more efficient. Some evidence is that after unionization, firms frequently purchase more capital to use with labor. Comment.
6. You are attempting to unionize the workers in a particular plant. What economic conditions would make your job easier? What would make your job harder? Analyze the case of an entire industry; an entire trade or profession; a government employees union.
7. The patent system conveys monopoly rights to some good or process. It is often claimed to be beneficial to economic growth because it encourages research. But, in general, it is asserted that monopolies result in inefficient resource allocation. Discuss.
8. Neighborhood grocery stores in a large city would appear to be an example of a perfectly competitive market—there are numerous sellers, each seller is small, and each store carries generally the same products (i.e., homogeneous outputs). However, it can be argued that these are monopolies. Comment on this issue.
9. In monopolistic competition, the entry of new firms eliminates economic profit. Obviously, the firms in such a market would desire to maintain these above-normal profits. What policies might be suggested to keep profits from being eliminated? Why is it impossible to implement such policies in a perfectly competitive market?

10. In what sense is the only bank in a small town a monopoly? In what sense is it not? In what sense is GM or Exxon a monopoly? In what sense is it not? How about the U.S. Postal Service or your local electric company? If you were an adviser to a Supreme Court justice, how would you decide what does or does not constitute a monopoly? How could cross elasticity of demand help you decide?
11. In 1945, ALCOA was found guilty of attempting to monopolize the aluminum market. Up to that time, the company maintained low markups and had a modest profit rate. Ironically, if ALCOA had set high markups and realized a high profit rate before World War II, it probably would not have been found guilty. Can you explain why?
12. Can a firm have any control over the cross elasticity of demand of its output with other products? To put the question another way, can a seller lower a high positive cross elasticity of demand? Discuss.
13. Oil companies advertise that they are very pollution conscious. Why do they do so? Why don't individual farmers advertise that they use pollution-free insecticide?
14. Firms and their unions frequently agree on policy. Why would the big-three auto manufacturers and the United Automobile Workers both lobby for tariffs and quotas on foreign cars?

16

Implementation of the profit-maximizing decisions for firms with market power

Now that we have described the theoretical relations by which firms with market power can maximize profit (or minimize loss), we are in a position to show how these relations can actually be implemented. In this chapter, we will describe how the manager of the firm can use estimates of the firm's production function, cost function, and demand function to determine the firm's optimal levels of output, price, and input usage.

As was the case in Chapter 14, the objective of this chapter is to show how a manager can combine the principles of microeconomic theory and some relatively simple empirical estimates to obtain forecasts or estimates that will aid in maximizing the firm's profits. While this discussion will get a little technical, our objective is *not* to turn you into a ''technocrat''; rather, we want you simply to understand how the theoretical principles of profit maximization can be and are implemented.

We will begin by first looking at the output and price decisions for a monopoly firm. Following this, we look at the modifications/complications that are involved in the same decision for a firm in a monopolistically competitive market. Then we will turn to the alternative manner in which the firm can attain profit-maximization—the selection of the optimal levels of usage of its inputs.

16.1 MONOPOLY OUTPUT AND PRICE

From the discussion in Chapter 15, we know that the profit-maximizing or loss-minimizing output for a monopoly firm is that at which marginal revenue is equal to marginal cost. Once this output level is determined, we know that the unit price of the output is taken directly from the demand curve. And, we know that the monopoly firm will *actually* produce in the short-run—rather than shut down—as long as this price exceeds average variable cost at the output level selected. Let's see how a monopoly firm might actually go about implementing these decisions.

In order to determine the optimal output for the firm, the manager must employ the condition $MR = MC$. We have already had a great deal to say about the estimation of a firm's marginal cost function and there is nothing unusual about the marginal cost function for a monopoly firm. However, obtaining an estimate of the marginal revenue function for a monopoly differs from the case of perfect competition we described in Chapter 14. As we stressed in Chapter 15, the monopoly firm does not face a horizontal demand curve but instead faces a down-sloping market demand function.

Let's write the estimated demand function facing the monopoly firm as a linear function

$$Q = a + bP + cY + dP_R$$

As before, in order to isolate the demand curve that is relevant for the period in question, we must have forecasts for (or estimates of) the values of the exogenous variables, Y and P_R, in that period. If we denote these forecasts as $\hat{Y}$ and $\hat{P}_R$, we can rewrite the demand function for the specific period in question as

$$Q = a' + bP$$

where $a' = a + c\hat{Y} + d\hat{P}_R$.

If we solve this demand function for P, we obtain what is referred to as the *inverse demand function:*

$$P = \frac{-a'}{b} + \frac{1}{b}Q$$

Total revenue for the firm is simply price times quantity sold; so, in terms of our estimated demand function,

$$TR = \frac{-a'}{b}Q + \frac{1}{b}Q^2$$

Finally, since $MR = \Delta TR/\Delta Q$, it follows that[1]

---

[1]More precisely, $MR = \partial TR/\partial Q$; so, if the inverse demand function is

$$P = \alpha + \beta Q$$

total revenue is

$$TR = \alpha Q + \beta Q^2$$

and marginal revenue is

$$MR = \alpha + 2\beta Q$$

$$MR = \left(\frac{-a'}{b}\right) + 2\left(\frac{1}{b}\right)Q$$

To make this procedure somewhat more clear, let's look at a stylized example.

APPLICATION

Estimation of a marginal revenue function

By virtue of patents it owns, Aztec Electronics possesses substantial monopoly power in the product it manufactures. The manager of Aztec wished to determine the optimal values for output and price for 1985.

The demand for the firm's product was specified as a function of the price of the product, income of the customers, and the price of a complementary good,

$$Q = f(P,Y,P_R)$$

Using data available for the period 1975–84, a linear form of this function was estimated. The resulting estimated demand function was

$$Q = 41 - 0.5P + 1.5Y - 0.4P_R$$

where output (Q) was measured in 100,000 units, average annual family income (Y) in thousand dollars, and the two prices (P and P_R) in dollars per unit.

From an economic consulting firm, the manager obtained 1985 forecasts for income and the price of the complementary good as, respectively, \$18,000 and \$45. Using these values—$\hat{Y} = 18$ and $\hat{P}_R = 45$—the estimated (forecasted) demand function in 1985 was

$$Q = 50 - 0.5P$$

The inverse demand function corresponding to this demand function was obtained by solving for P,

$$P = 100 - 2Q$$

And, from this inverse demand function, the manager knew that the marginal revenue function was

$$MR = 100 - 4Q$$

Once you have obtained the marginal revenue function, the determination of the optimal level of output is made by equating marginal revenue and marginal cost, then solving for Q. It's been our experience that it is much easier to see this with an example; so let's go to one now.

APPLICATION

How much do I produce?

The manager of Aztec Electronics also obtained an estimate of the firm's average variable cost function:

$$AVC = 28 - 5Q + 1Q^2$$

In this estimation, AVC was measured in dollars per unit and Q was again measured in 100,000 units. Given this average variable cost function, the marginal cost function is

$$MC = 28 - 10Q + 3Q^2$$

In order to determine the optimal level of production, the manager equated the 1985 marginal revenue function with the firm's marginal cost function

$$100 - 4Q = 28 - 10Q + 3Q^2$$

Solving this equation for Q, two solutions were obtained—$Q = 6$ and $Q = -4$. Since $Q = -4$ is an irrelevant solution (we can not have negative outputs), the optimal level of production is $Q = 6$. That is, the profit-maximizing (or loss-minimizing) output level for 1985 is 600,000 units.

Given that you know the optimal level of production, determination of the optimal price is really nothing more than finding the price on the demand curve that corresponds to the optimal output level. In terms of the functions we have been working with, this means that the optimal output—let's call it Q^*—is plugged into the inverse demand function to give the optimal price, P^*

$$P^* = \left(\frac{-a'}{b}\right) + \frac{1}{b}Q^*$$

To see how this works, let's continue with our example.

APPLICATION

What price do I charge?

In the preceding Application, we saw that the manager of Aztec Electronics had determined the optimal output in 1985 to be 600,000 units (i.e., $Q^* = 6$). Inserting this value into the inverse demand function,

$$P^* = 100 - 2(6) = 88$$

Hence, the optimal price for 1985 was found to be \$88 per unit.

Remember that there is nothing that *guarantees* that a monopoly firm will make a profit in the short run. It is possible, as we showed in Chapter 15, for a monopoly firm to suffer a loss in the short run if the optimal price is below average total cost. However, if the optimal price is above average variable cost, it is still in the best interest of the firm to continue producing, since the loss will be smaller than the loss would be if the firm simply shut down—produced zero output. Only if the optimal price is below average variable cost at that output level should the firm shut down.

APPLICATION

The shutdown decision

In the preceding applications, we have seen that the manager of Aztec Electronics found the optimal 1985 output to be 600,000 units, which would be priced at \$88 per unit. But, isn't it possible that this price would yield a total revenue that is less than variable cost and that the best policy is to shut down? To consider this, the manager compared the optimal price with the average variable cost of producing the 600,000 units.

Using the estimated average variable cost function, *AVC* per unit for 600,000 units was calculated as

$$AVC = 28 - 5(6) + 1(6^2) = \$34$$

Since \$88 > \$34, the manager knows that all of the variable costs will be covered and the best policy is to produce.

Put another way, the firm's expected total revenue in 1985 was \$52.8 million (i.e., \$88 × 600,000) and total variable cost was forecasted to be \$20.4 million (i.e., \$34 × 600,000). Since total revenue exceeds total variable cost, the firm should continue to produce.

On the basis of actual 1984 data, the manager of Aztec Electronics would have had a very good estimate of the firm's fixed costs in 1985. Suppose that projected 1985 fixed costs were \$27 million. In this case, with an output of 600,000 units priced at \$88 per unit, the expected profit is \$5.4 million. Clearly, the firm should continue to produce since it can earn an economic profit.

If, on the other hand, projected fixed costs for 1985 were \$35 million, the firm would be expected to suffer a loss of \$2.6 million. Should the firm continue to produce? Yes. If it produces the 600,000 units, its loss would be \$2.6 million. But, if it shuts down, the loss in 1985 would be \$35 million. (If it shuts down, Aztec would have a loss equal to its fixed costs.)

In the preceding, we have considered only a linear demand function. Given the form of the marginal cost function, a linear demand function is somewhat easier to use in determining the optimal level of production. However, we could use a log-linear demand function. Let's look briefly at how we would obtain the marginal revenue function.

We begin by estimating a log-linear demand function

$$Q = aP^bY^cP_R^d$$

Once we have estimates of a, b, c, and d, we can obtain forecasts for the exogenous variables—$\hat{Y}$ and $\hat{P}_R$—to give us a forecasted demand function for some future period, e.g., the demand function for 1985III. We can write this forecasted demand function as

$$Q = BP^b$$

where $B = a\hat{Y}^c\hat{P}_R^d$

Solving for the price of the commodity (P), the inverse demand function is

$$P = B^{-1/b}Q^{1/b}$$

Then, total revenue ($P \times Q$) is

$$TR = B^{-1/b}Q^{(1/b)+1}$$

From this total revenue function, the marginal revenue function is

$$MR = \left(\frac{b+1}{b}\right) B^{-1/b}Q^{1/b}$$

Let's look at an example using this log-linear form of the demand function.

APPLICATION

Marginal revenue for a log-linear demand function

In preparation for forecasting the optimal level of service and the optimal monthly service fee for 1985 (a question we will return to in a subsequent application), the manager of Allied Cable TV, Inc., elected to estimate a demand function of the form

$$Q = aP^bY^c$$

The manager was able to obtain a cross-section data set in which Q was measured as the number of households served (in thousands), P as the (monthly) service fee, and Y as the average annual family income of households in the service area (in thousand dollars). Using these data, the estimated demand function was

$$\log Q = 2.785 - 2.0 \log P + 3.0 \log Y$$

or

$$Q = 16.2P^{-2}Y^3$$

From an economic consulting firm, the manager obtained an estimate of average annual family income for Allied's service area in 1985 of $20,000, i.e., $\hat{Y} = 20$. Using this forecast in the estimated demand function, the forecasted demand function for Allied Cable TV in 1985 was

$$Q = 16.2P^{-2}(20)^3 = 129{,}600P^{-2}$$

Solving this equation for P, the inverse demand function for 1985 was

$$P = 360Q^{-1/2}$$

Forecasted total revenue was $P \times Q = 360Q^{1/2}$; so, the forecasted marginal revenue function was

$$MR = 180Q^{-1/2}$$

16.2 OUTPUT AND PRICE FOR MONOPOLISTICALLY COMPETITIVE FIRMS

In Chapter 15 we noted that there is essentially no difference in the short-run analysis of monopoly and monopolistic competition: A firm in a monopolistically competitive market faces a downward-sloping demand curve. So, the firm maximizes profit or minimizes losses by producing the output at which marginal revenue equals marginal cost. Once this output is selected, the price to be charged is taken directly from the firm's demand curve.

Therefore a monopolistically competitive firm will follow the steps we outlined in the preceding section to determine its optimal output level and price:

1. Given an estimate of the demand function facing the firm, obtain the inverse demand function and the marginal revenue function.
2. From the estimated average variable cost function, obtain the marginal cost function.
3. Determine the optimal output level by equating the marginal revenue and marginal cost functions.
4. Use the optimal output level in the inverse demand function to obtain the optimal price.
5. To make sure that the firm should actually produce, compare the optimal price and average variable cost at the optimal output level. The firm should continue to produce as long as the optimal price is greater than average variable cost and would shut down only if average variable cost exceeds price.

Complications

In general, the implementation of the output and pricing decision is the same for a monopolistically competitive firm as for a monopoly firm. However, a complication arises in the estimation of the demand function facing the individual firm. For any one firm, demand is determined not only by the firm's own price, the income of the consumers, the price of related goods, and the firm's level of advertising, but also by the prices charged by its competitors and their advertising. That is, the demand function facing firm i may be written as

$$Q_i = f(P_i, Y, P_R, A_i, P_j, A_j, P_k, A_k, \ldots)$$

where

$$\begin{aligned}
Q_i &= \text{the sales of firm } i \\
P_i &= \text{the price charged by firm } i \\
Y &= \text{income of the consumers} \\
P_R &= \text{the price of related goods} \\
A_i &= \text{advertising by firm } i \\
P_j,\ P_k, \ldots &= \text{the prices charged by competitors} \\
A_j,\ A_k, \ldots &= \text{advertising by competitors}
\end{aligned}$$

Thus, to obtain estimates of the individual firm's demand function, a very substantial amount of data is required.

And, in order for this technique to be useful, we need to forecast demand in the future. As you are aware, in order to do this, we need the future values for the competitors' prices and advertising. A precise prediction is simply impossible. These values are not constant, nor do they follow some trend. Hence, in order to obtain an accurate forecast of future demand, the manager must be able to predict the pricing and advertising policies of its competitors.

The upshot of all this is simply that it is much more difficult to obtain an accurate estimate of and forecast for an individual firm's demand function in a monopolistically competitive market. On a practical basis, this would suggest that the firm might consider doing simulation analyses like those outlined in Chapter 12. That is, given its best estimate of its demand function from historical data, the firm might consider several alternative demand forecasts based on alternative assumptions about the policies of the other firms in the market.

Cost-plus pricing

It should be clear to you that the short-run pricing decision based on the equality of marginal revenue and marginal cost is the one that will give maximum profit (or minimum loss). However, there is considerable evidence to suggest that many firms—particularly those in monopolistically competitive markets—use a pricing technique based on average rather than marginal cost. This technique is called cost-plus pricing.

The basic concept is deceptively simple. In cost-plus pricing, the firm determines its average total cost then adds a percentage markup (or margin) for profits. Thus, price would be

$$P = ATC + (m \cdot ATC)$$
$$= (1 + m) \cdot ATC$$

where m is the markup on cost. For example, if the markup is 20 percent, price would be (1.2) ATC.

This very basic description of cost-plus pricing glosses over two major difficulties. First, how does the firm determine average total cost? Second, how does the firm select the "appropriate" markup (or margin)?

Given that costs vary with the level of output produced, determination of average cost requires that the firm first specify the level of output that will be produced. Obviously, a precise determination of this output would require consideration of the prevailing demand conditions—a feature not incorporated in cost-plus pricing. Instead, firms typically specify a "standard" volume of production, based on some assumption about the percentage of the firm's capacity that will be utilized. Furthermore, the costs used are derived from accounting data. As we have noted in earlier chapters, the use of accounting data may not be valid, since accounting costs do not always reflect opportunity costs. Also, such historical data would not reflect recent or potential changes in input prices.

Notwithstanding the difficulties involved in determining average cost, a potentially more troublesome problem is the selection of the markup percentage. While the firm might arbitrarily select some target rate of return on invested capital, recent empirical evidence suggests that the firms use a more subjective approach. It appears that the markups for different products differ according to such factors as the degree of competitiveness in the market and the price elasticity of demand. Apparently, the manager employs knowledge about the market to determine the markup that maximizes profits.

Cost-plus pricing has been criticized on two grounds. First, it employs average rather than marginal cost. As we know from Chapter 3, marginal (or incremental) cost rather than total cost should be used in making any optimizing decision. Second, cost-plus pricing does not incorporate a consideration of prevailing demand conditions. Using the $MR = MC$ pricing rule, demand conditions enter explicitly through the marginal revenue function; but cost-plus pricing does not embody this information.

These criticisms are valid. However, it should be noted that, *under certain circumstances,* cost-plus pricing may approximate $MR = MC$ pricing. Let us show you how this can occur. As we have shown in an earlier chapter, marginal revenue may be written as

$$MR = P\left(1 - \frac{1}{E}\right)$$

where E is the own-price elasticity of demand. Setting marginal revenue equal to marginal cost, our optimization condition may be written as

$$P = \left(\frac{E}{E - 1}\right) MC$$

If the firm has a flat average cost curve (e.g., if the firm's long-run cost relation is characterized by constant returns to scale) average cost is constant and is equal to marginal cost. In this case, we could write the preceding condition as

$$P = \left(\frac{E}{E - 1}\right) AC$$

Note the similarity between this equation and the equation for cost-plus pricing, $P = (1 + m)AC$. Setting these equations equal (i.e., assuming that cost-plus pricing is equivalent to $MR = MC$ pricing), the markup would be

$$m = \frac{1}{E - 1}$$

That is, if firms are using cost-plus pricing as an approximation to pricing based on profit maximization, the markup would be determined by the price elasticity of demand—precisely the relation indicated in the empirical investigations mentioned earlier. While we are limited to the elastic portion of the demand function (i.e., where $E > 1$), this formulation indicates that, as the demand curve is more elastic (i.e., as E increases), the profit-maximizing markup decreases. For example, if $E = 2$, the profit-maximizing markup would be 100 percent. However, if the demand curve were more elastic, say, $E = 5$, the profit-maximizing markup would fall to 25 percent. The point is that if the firm's average cost is constant, cost-plus pricing *could* be equivalent to pricing based on profit maximization. Moreover, the size of the markup would depend on the own-price elasticity of demand, which of course depends upon the availability of good substitutes for the product. The better the substitute, the lower the markup.

16.3 PROFIT-MAXIMIZING INPUT USAGE

Firms with market power can also attain their profit-maximizing (or loss-minimizing) position via the selection of the optimal levels of usage of their inputs. To see how this can be done—and to demonstrate that this situation is very similar to the situation we described for a perfectly competitive firm—let's begin by looking at the case where the firm employs a single variable input and pays a fixed (constant) price for that input. After looking at this case, we can briefly describe the implementation of the more complicated cases—multiple variable inputs and an upward-sloping supply function for inputs.

One variable input with a fixed input price

In this case we consider a firm that has market power in its output market—it faces a downward-sloping demand function for its output. However, the firm is one of many purchasers of the input; so, its employment decision will have no effect on the input price. As an example, you might think of the single electric utility firm or cable TV firm in your city. This kind of a firm has substantial market power (albeit in its own small market) so it faces a downward-sloping demand curve. The firm uses a variable input—labor—in conjunction with its fixed capital stock to produce its output. But, since it is only one of many firms hiring labor in the city, its employment decision—how much labor it hires—would not be expected to change the city-wide wage rate.

As we know from Chapter 15, in this case, the optimum level of employment for the firm is that at which the marginal revenue product of the input is equal to the price of the input. Since we are using labor as an example, we can express this condition as

$$MRP_L = w$$

where MRP_L is the marginal revenue product of labor and w is the market-determined wage rate. From Chapter 15 we know that, for a firm with market power, MRP is equal to the product of the firm's marginal revenue function and the marginal product function for the input,

$$MRP_L = MR \times MP_L$$

As in Chapter 14, let's use a one-input (short-run) production function of the form

$$Q = AL^{\beta}$$

where $0 < \beta < 1$. As we know, the marginal product function for labor is

$$MP_L = \beta AL^{\beta-1}$$

To "match" this log-linear production function, let's also use a log-linear demand function

$$Q = P^b Y^c P_R^d$$

As we demonstrated earlier in this chapter, after we have estimated this demand function and obtained forecasts for the exogenous variables—$\hat{Y}$ and $\hat{P}_R$—the forecasted demand function may be written as

$$Q = BP^b$$

and the marginal revenue function as

$$MR = \left(\frac{b+1}{b}\right) B^{-1/b} Q^{1/b}$$

If, however, we want to solve for the optimal level of usage of labor, the marginal revenue function must be expressed in terms of L rather than Q. To accomplish this, let's substitute the production function ($Q = AL^{\beta}$) into our MR function. Via this substitution, the marginal revenue function becomes

$$MR = \left(\frac{b+1}{b}\right) B^{-1/b}(AL^{\beta})^{1/b}$$

$$= \left(\frac{b+1}{b}\right) B^{-1/b}A^{1/b}L^{\beta/b}$$

We can obtain the marginal revenue product function as

$$MRP_L = MR \times MP_L$$

where the MR and MP_L functions are those derived above. Then, to determine the optimal level of usage of labor, we equate this marginal revenue product function to the price of labor, w, and solve for L. To make this somewhat complicated procedure more understandable, let's look at an example.

APPLICATION

The employment decision

Allied Cable TV, Inc., is a firm that (1) has substantial monopoly power in its local market, (2) uses a single variable input—labor, and (3) faces a fixed, market-determined price for labor. The manager of Allied wants to determine the optimal level of labor usage for 1985. As we know, in order to make this determination, the manager must have estimates/forecasts of the marginal product function for labor, the firm's marginal revenue function, the marginal revenue product function for labor, and the wage rate. Let's take these in order.

Marginal product

The manager used available historical data to estimate a short-run production function of the form

$$Q = AL^{\beta}$$

Measuring output in thousand households served and labor usage in thousand hours per month, the estimated function was

$$\log Q = 3.892 + 0.4 \log L$$

Rewriting this function in its exponential form, the short-run production function was

$$Q = 49L^{0.4}$$

and the corresponding marginal product function was

$$MP_L = (0.4)(49)L^{0.4-1} = 19.6L^{-0.6}$$

Marginal revenue

We introduced the forecasted 1985 marginal revenue function for Allied Cable TV in an earlier application. As we saw, the forecasted inverse demand function in 1985 was

$$P = 360Q^{-1/2}$$

(where price was expressed in dollars per household per month and output was expressed in thousand households serviced per month) and the marginal revenue function was

$$MR = 180Q^{-1/2}$$

Substituting the estimated production function into this marginal revenue function,

$$\begin{aligned} MR &= 180(49L^{0.4})^{-1/2} \\ &= 25.714L^{-0.2} \end{aligned}$$

Marginal revenue product

Using the preceding estimates/forecasts of MP_L and MR, the manager of Allied Cable TV calculated the marginal revenue product of labor as

$$MRP_L = (25.714L^{-0.2}) \times (19.6L^{-0.6}) = 504L^{-0.8}$$

Wage rate

From a econometric forecasting firm, the manager obtained a forecast for the 1985 wage rate of $18 per hour.

Optimization

To determine the optimal monthly employment level for Allied Cable TV in 1985, the manager equated the forecasts for MRP_L and w:

$$504L^{-0.8} = 18$$

Solving this equation for L,

$$L^{-0.8} = 0.0357$$

or, taking logarithms,

$$-0.8 \log L = -3.332$$

Therefore, $\log L = 4.165$; so, $L = 64.4$. That is, the optimal monthly level of labor usage in 1985 is forecasted to be 64,400 hours; or, an annual level of usage of 772,800 hours. (This is approximately 386.4 full-time employees.)

Given $L = 64.4$, the output of the firm in 1985 would be obtained from the production function as

$$Q = 49(64.4)^{0.4} = 259.3$$

Then, the price of the output is, from the inverse demand function,

$$P = 360(259.3)^{-1/2} = 22.36$$

That is, these estimates indicate that Allied should serve 259,300 households and charge a monthly fee of $22.36.

Several variable inputs with fixed input prices

As we saw in the case of the input decision for a perfectly competitive firm, if the firm has several variable inputs, the optimizing condition for each input remains unchanged. However, there is an additional complication: the optimizing conditions must be solved simultaneously. Precisely the same thing happens for the input decision for firms with market power.

Without going into a great deal of detail, let's look at how the firm might approach the input decision if it employs two variable inputs—capital and labor. From our discussion thus far we hope that you can see that, if the production function is of the Cobb-Douglas form,

$$Q = AK^{\alpha}L^{\beta}$$

and the forecasted demand function is log-linear,

$$Q = BP^{b}$$

the marginal revenue product of labor will take the form

$$MRP_L = ZK^{\theta}L^{\phi}$$

where Z, θ, and ϕ are known parameters. Likewise, the marginal revenue product of capital will take the form

$$MRP_K = WK^{\delta}L^{\eta}$$

where W, δ, and η are also known parameters.[2]

Then, the optimizing conditions for the two inputs are

$$ZK^{\theta}L^{\phi} = w$$
$$WK^{\delta}L^{\eta} = r$$

To obtain the optimal levels of usage of the input, these conditions must be solved simultaneously for K and L. As you remember from our discussion in Chapter 14, such a solution involves substantial mathematical manipulation. But, the primary point we want you to keep in mind is that, given estimates of the production function and the demand function, a determination of the optimal values can be obtained. And, this same technique could be extended to consider three or more variable inputs.

Upward-sloping input supply

Thus far, we have presumed that the individual firm's employment decision will have no effect on the price it will have to pay for the inputs it

[2]Specifically, the marginal revenue products of the inputs are

$$MRP_L = \left(\frac{b+1}{b}\right)\beta B^{-1/b}A^{1+1/b}K^{\alpha/b+\alpha}L^{\beta/b+\beta-1}$$

$$MRP_K = \left(\frac{b+1}{b}\right)\alpha B^{-1/b}A^{1+1/b}K^{\alpha/b+\alpha-1}L^{\beta/b+\beta}$$

employs. We have been considering a labor market sufficiently large that the individual firm can hire as much or as little of the input as it desires at a constant input price. However, as we noted in Chapter 15, it is possible that a firm with market power may be large enough that its employment decision will affect the market price of the input. In this case, if the firm wishes to employ more of the input, it will be required to pay more for the input—the price of the input will rise.

To see how this complication influences the employment decision, let's look at a firm that employs only a single variable input, labor. In this case, the price of the input (the wage rate) is not constant. Instead, the wage rate depends on the amount of labor the firm hires,

$$w = f(L)$$

As the firm hires more labor, the wage rate rises; so we would want our function—the labor supply function—to reflect this positive relation. The simplest such function is a linear function, $w = m + nL$, where m and n are both positive. With this function, total factor (labor) cost is $w \times L = mL + nL^2$ and the marginal factor cost function is $MFC = m + 2nL$.

The linear specification is completely acceptable. But, given the way in which we have calculated our marginal revenue product function, a more useful specification of the firm's labor supply function is a log-linear form,

$$w = mL^n$$

With this form, the total factor cost function ($w \times L$) is

$$TFC = mL^{n+1}$$

and the marginal factor cost function is

$$MFC = (n + 1)mL^n$$

Equating this marginal factor cost function with the firm's marginal revenue product function for labor, the manager can determine the firm's optimal level of usage of labor. To show you how this can be done, let's look at an example.

APPLICATION

The employment decision with an upward-sloping labor supply

In an earlier Application we looked at Allied Cable TV's employment decision presuming that the firm faced a constant wage rate for labor. Alternatively, suppose that the manager had discovered that the labor required by Allied was specialized and in limited supply in the city. Therefore, if Allied were to increase its employment, it would have to raise the wage rate it paid.

To reevaluate the employment decision under this altered situation, the manager obtained an estimate of the labor supply function facing Allied. The estimated labor supply function was

$$w = 8.55L^{0.17}$$

where the wage rate was measured in dollars per hour and labor usage was measured in thousand hours per month. From this estimated labor supply function, the marginal factor cost function for Allied is

$$MFC = 10L^{0.17}$$

Equating this marginal factor cost function with the firm's marginal revenue product function for labor (as obtained in the preceding Application), the profit-maximization condition is obtained:

$$504L^{-0.8} = 10L^{0.17}$$

Then, the manager was able to solve this equation to determine the optimal level of usage of labor. That is,

$$L^{0.97} = 50.4$$

or, converting to logarithms,

$$0.97 \log L = 3.92$$

Therefore, $\log L = 4.04$ and it follows that $L = 56.9$. That is, with this upward-sloping supply curve for labor, the optimal monthly labor usage for Allied in 1985 was forecasted to be 56,900 hours (on an annual basis, 341.4 full-time employees).

TECHNICAL PROBLEMS

1. The manager of a monopoly firm obtained the following estimate of the market demand function for its output:

$$Q = 26 - 1P + 2Y - 5P_R$$

where Q was measured in 100 units, prices in dollars per unit, and income (Y) in thousand dollars. From an econometric forecasting firm, the manager obtained forecasts for the 1985 values of Y and P_R as, respectively, \$20,000 and \$2. For 1985, what is

a. The forecasted demand function?
b. The inverse demand function?
c. The marginal revenue function?

2. For the firm in Problem 1, the manager estimated the average variable cost function as

$$AVC = 20 - 7Q + 1Q^2$$

where AVC was measured in dollars per unit and Q was measured in 100 units.

a. What is the estimated marginal cost function?
b. What is the optimal level of production in 1985?
c. What is the optimal price in 1985?
d. Check to make sure that the firm should actually produce in the short run rather than shut down.

In addition, the manager expects fixed costs in 1985 to be $22,500.

e. What is the firm's expected profit or loss in 1985?

3. The manager of a monopoly firm estimated a demand function of the form

$$Q = aP^bY^cP_R^d$$

The estimated function was

$$\log Q = 2.303 - 2.0 \log P + 2.0 \log Y - 0.5 \log P_R$$

The manager obtained forecasts for the 1985 values of the exogenous variables as $\hat{Y}_{1985} = 20$ and $\hat{P}_{R,1985} = 100$.

a. What is the forecasted demand function for 1985?
b. What is the inverse demand function?
c. What is the marginal revenue function?

4. Under what condition(s) would cost-plus pricing be equivalent to profit-maximization, i.e., $MR = MC$ pricing?

5. If the condition(s) in Problem 4 are satisfied and if the own-price elasticity of the demand function facing the firm is equal to 1.5, what is the profit-maximizing markup? What is the profit-maximizing markup if the own-price elasticity is equal to 3?

6. Return to the firm introduced in Problem 3. The manager of the firm estimated the short-run production function as

$$\log Q = 4.605 + 0.6 \log L$$

Using these results with the marginal revenue function obtained in Problem 3, obtain the firm's marginal revenue product function for labor.

7. Using your results from Problem 6, if the expected wage rate for 1985 is $20,

a. What is the optimal level of usage of labor?
b. What are the values of output and price that correspond to that level of usage of labor?

8. Suppose that the firm introduced in Problem 3 faces an upward-sloping labor supply function that has been estimated as

$$w = 11.54L^{0.3}$$

a. What is the marginal factor cost function facing the firm?
b. Using the marginal revenue product function obtained in Problem 6, what would be the optimal level of usage of labor?

ANALYTICAL PROBLEMS

1. In this chapter, we used both linear and log-linear demand function estimates in our applications. On a practical basis, how would the analyst choose between these specifications? (In what situation would one or the other be easier to work with?)
2. In our discussion of monopolistic competition, we noted that a monopolistically competitive firm is faced with much more uncertainty. What kind of uncertainty might a monopolistically competitive firm face?
3. Suppose a manager wanted to use cost-plus pricing. How might he or she determine if the characteristics of the firm are such that cost-plus pricing can approximate profit-maximization? How might the manager obtain the estimate of own-price elasticity necessary to determine the optimal markup?
4. In our discussion of the employment decision with an upward-sloping input supply function, we said that the log-linear form, e.g.,

$$w = mL^n$$

is more "useful." We might have said "easier to use." Why?
5. In our discussion of the employment decision, we used estimates of the production relation obtained from regression analysis. Could the manager use some other method of estimating the production relation, e.g., linear programming? Explain your answer.

17

Multiple plants, markets, and products

Until now we have only considered—at least implicitly—a very simple firm. We have been looking at a firm that has a single plant in which it produces a single product that is sold in a single market. Clearly, this is frequently not the situation actually faced by real-world firms or corporations.

Therefore, in this chapter, we want to show how these complications—multiple plants, multiple markets, and multiple products—affect the profit maximization principles we have described. The discussion of each of these topics will of necessity be brief. It is not our intention to provide an exhaustive discussion of these complications; such a discussion could and does form the basis for entire courses. Rather, it is our intention to show that these complications do not alter the principles of profit maximization we have set forth: The firm continues to produce that output at which marginal revenue equals marginal cost (or marginal revenue product is equal to marginal factor cost). The effect of these complications does, however, make the implementation of these principles more computationally complex: "The rule's the same but the arithmetic is a little harder."

In this discussion, we limit our attention to firms with market power; so, we will be looking at monopoly and monopolistically competitive firms. Since we will be concerned with the firm's output and pricing decision—the firm's short-run decisions—we know that those two market structures are analytically the same. Hence, in our discussion, we will normally consider a monopoly firm; but, the conclusions also apply to monopolistic competition (and to some extent to the oligopoly markets we will describe in Chapter 18).

We begin with a discussion of multiplant firms. This will be followed by a discussion of firms with multiple markets and then a discussion of firms that produce multiple products.

17.1 MULTIPLANT FIRMS

A situation likely in the case of a monopoly is that the firm produces output in more than one plant. In this situation, it is likely also that the various plants will have different cost conditions. The problem facing the firm is, therefore, how to allocate the firm's desired level of production among these plants.

For simplicity, let's assume there are only two plants, A and B. Suppose at the desired level of output, the following situation holds

$$MC_A < MC_B$$

Clearly the firm should transfer output from the higher cost Plant B to the lower cost Plant A. If the last unit produced in Plant B costs \$10, but one more unit produced in Plant A adds only \$7 to A's cost, that unit should be transferred from B to A. The transfer results in a cost reduction of \$3. In fact, output should be transferred from B to A until

$$MC_A = MC_B$$

Eventual equalization occurs because of increasing marginal cost. As output is transferred out of B into A, the marginal cost in A rises, and the marginal cost in B falls. It is simple to see that exactly the opposite occurs in the case of

$$MC_A > MC_B$$

Output is taken out of A and produced in B until

$$MC_A = MC_B$$

The total output decision is easily determined. The horizontal summation of all plants' marginal cost curves is the firm's total marginal cost curve. This total marginal cost curve is equated to marginal revenue in order to determine the profit-maximizing output and price. This output is divided among the plants so that the marginal cost is equal for all plants.[1]

---

[1]In this case, the firm's profit function is

$$\pi = R(Q) - C_A(Q_A) - C_B(Q_B)$$

where $Q = Q_A + Q_B$. Maximizing this function with respect to the outputs of the two plants requires

$$\frac{\partial \pi}{\partial Q_A} = \frac{\partial R}{\partial Q} - \frac{\partial C_A}{\partial Q_A} = 0$$

$$\frac{\partial \pi}{\partial Q_B} = \frac{\partial R}{\partial Q} - \frac{\partial C_B}{\partial Q_B} = 0$$

Combining these conditions, profit is maximized when

$$MR = MC_A = MC_B$$

Figure 17.1
Multiplant monopoly

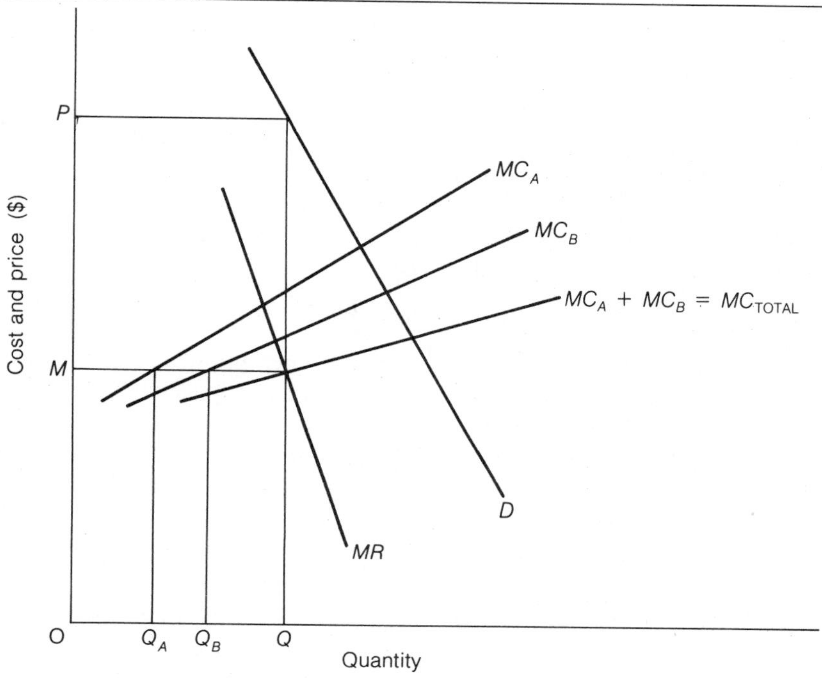

The two-plant case is illustrated in Figure 17.1. Demand for the product is D, and marginal revenue for the firm is MR. The marginal cost curves for plants A and B are respectively MC_A and MC_B. The total marginal cost curve for the firm is the horizontal summation of MC_A and MC_B, labeled MC_{Total}. Profit is maximized when this curve equals marginal revenue, giving an output of Q and a price of P. Marginal cost at this output is M. Equalization of marginal costs requires Plant A to produce Q_A and Plant B to produce Q_B. This allocation equalizes marginal costs and is consequently the least-cost method of production for the desired level of output.

Hence, in this case, the principle of profit-maximization has been expanded to include the allocation decision: The firm with plants A and B will maximize profits if it produces the level of output and allocates production between the plants so that

$$MR = MC_{\text{TOTAL}} = MC_A = MC_B$$

This principle can certainly be expanded to consider production in three or more plants. But, in order to see how this principle could be implemented by a firm, let's look at a simplified, two-plant example.

APPLICATION

Allocation of production between two plants

Mercantile Enterprises—a firm with some degree of market power—produces its product in two plants. Hence, when making production decisions, the manager of Mercantile must decide not only how much to produce but also how to allocate the desired production between the two plants.

The production engineering department of Mercantile was able to provide the manager with simple, linear estimates of the incremental (marginal) cost functions for the two plants:

$$MC_A = 28 + 4Q \qquad MC_B = 16 + 2Q$$

where the marginal costs were measured in dollars per unit and output was measured in thousand units. Note that the estimated marginal cost function for Plant A (a plant built in 1948) is higher for every output than that for Plant B (a plant built in 1967); so, Plant B is more efficient. Summing horizontally (and, after some algebraic manipulation), the total marginal cost function is

$$MC_{\text{TOTAL}} = 20 + \frac{4}{3}Q$$

for outputs in excess of 6,000 units. (We will discuss the total marginal cost function for outputs less than 6,000 units below.)

Suppose that the estimated demand curve for Mercantile's output is

$$Q = 114 - 3P$$

where output was measured in thousand units and price was measured in dollars per unit. Using techniques described earlier in this text, the corresponding marginal revenue function is

$$MR = 38 - \frac{2}{3}Q$$

Equating marginal revenue and total marginal cost,

$$38 - \frac{2}{3}Q = 20 + \frac{4}{3}Q$$

the profit-maximizing output for the firm is $Q = 9$ (i.e., 9,000 units). At this level of output, marginal revenue and total marginal cost are both \$32. In order to maximize profit, the production of the 9,000 units should be allocated between Plants A and B so that the marginal cost of the last unit produced in either plant is \$32:

$$MC_A = 28 + 4Q = 32 \qquad MC_B = 16 + 2Q = 32$$

Hence, for Plant A, $Q = 1$. This is, 1,000 units will be produced in Plant A. Likewise, for Plant B, $Q = 8$; so, 8,000 units will be produced in Plant B.

Now, suppose that forecasted demand decreases. Let's suppose that a new forecast of the demand for Mercantile's output is

$$Q = 96 - 3P$$

Given that the corresponding marginal revenue function is

$$MR = 32 - \frac{2}{3}Q$$

the firm's profit-maximizing output declines to 6,000 units. At this output, marginal revenue and marginal cost are both \$28. Equating MC_A and MC_B to 28, the manager found that for Plant A, $Q = 0$ and for Plant B, $Q = 6$. That is, Plant A will be shut down and all of the output will be produced in Plant B.

As you can verify, were demand to decline any further, Mercantile would produce using only Plant B. So, for output levels less than 6,000 units, the total marginal cost function is MC_B. That is, for outputs less than 6,000 units, Mercantile becomes a single-plant firm.

From the preceding discussion and application, you should be able to see how a firm decides to allocate production among multiple plants. As we have seen, the allocation is determined both by the marginal cost functions of the various plants and the demand function facing the firm. It may be the case that a firm will use several plants to produce its output. But, it can also be the case that if demand declines, the firm may shut down one or more of its plants.

THE WALL STREET JOURNAL

APPLICATION

U.S. Steel closes 23 mills

So far we have seen that a multiplant firm will produce a larger percentage of its output in those plants that are more efficient, i.e., have lower marginal costs. We have also seen that if demand declines sufficiently, the firm will be induced to shut down its less efficient plants. This is apparently what happened to U.S. Steel Corporation.

In December of 1983, *The Wall Street Journal* reported that U.S. Steel had undertaken still another retrenchment of its steel operations.* The firm had announced the closing of nearly one fifth of its steel-making capacity and 23 finishing and fabricating mills. The closings were expected to affect a total of more than 15,000 employees.

This behavior is entirely predictable given the preceding discussion of profit-maximization in a multiplant firm. The demand facing U.S. Steel had declined, due in part to the lower price charged for imported steel. This decline in demand led to a decline in output, and the facilities that bore the brunt of the cuts were the least efficient plants. Indeed, that is what the *WSJ* article concluded: The plants closed were those that had higher (marginal) costs.

---

*"U.S. Steel to Trim Output Capacity by Almost 20 Percent," by Thomas F. O'Boyle and J. Ernest Beazley, *The Wall Street Journal*, December 28, 1983. Reprinted by permission of *The Wall Street Journal*.

17.2 FIRMS WITH MULTIPLE MARKETS—PRICE DISCRIMINATION

Thus far our analysis has been under the assumption that market demand is simply the horizontal summation of the demands of all consumers and every consumer is charged the same price for the product. But, since consumers are different, we would expect their demands to differ. At times, firms can take advantage of these differences in demand in order to increase their profit. Price discrimination—pricing in multiple markets—is the method through which this is accomplished. Basically, price discrimination means that the firm charges different consumers different prices (with no corresponding differences in costs). For example, price discrimination can occur when a firm charges different prices in its domestic and foreign markets or perhaps when a doctor charges one fee for an operation to low-income patients and another fee for the same operation to high-income patients.

Certain conditions are necessary for the firm to be *able* to price discriminate. First, the firm must possess some market power. We normally think of price discrimination in the context of a monopoly firm; but, since they have market power, monopolistic competitors (and oligopolists) may also be able to price discriminate. Second, the demand functions for the individual consumers or groups of consumers must differ. (As we will demonstrate later, this statement can be made more specific to require that the own-price elasticities must be different.) Third, the different markets must be separable. The firm must be able to identify the individuals or groups of individuals and separate them into submarkets. This leads to the final requirement. Purchasers of the product must not be able to resell it to other customers. If consumers could buy and sell the product among themselves, there is no way that the firm can keep the submarkets separated. (You don't want the low-price buyers to sell your product to the high-price buyers.)

Normally, economists speak of three degrees of price discrimination. However, because we only want to provide a brief overview of this topic, we will limit our discussion to what is referred to as "third-degree" price discrimination. This is the form most commonly employed and is the form that best illustrates our primary concern in this section: profit-maximization with multiple markets.

The analysis is a straightforward application of the $MR = MC$ rule. As a first step in that analysis, let us assume that a firm has two separate markets

Table 17.1
Allocation of sales between two markets

Quantity	Marginal revenue, Market I	Order of Sales	Marginal revenue, Market II	Order of Sales
1	$45	(1)	$34	(3)
2	36	(2)	28	(5)
3	30	(4)	22	(7)
4	22	(6)	13	(10)
5	17	(8)	10	(12)
6	15	(9)	6	
7	10	(11)	7	
8	7		4	
9	4		2	
10	0		1	

for its product. Demand conditions in each market are such that the marginal revenues from selling specified quantities are as given in Table 17.1. Assume also that for some reason the firm decides to produce 12 units. How should it allocate sales between the two markets?

Consider the first unit; the firm can increase revenue by $45 by selling it in Market I or by $34 by selling in Market II. Obviously, the firm will sell the first unit in Market I. So, the first unit (1) is sold in Market I. The second unit is also sold in Market I since its sale there increases revenue by $36, whereas it would only increase revenue by $34 in Market II. Since $34 can be gained in II but only $30 in I, unit three is sold in Market II. Similar analysis shows that the fourth unit goes to I and the fifth to II. Since unit six adds $22 to revenue in either market, it makes no difference where it is sold; six and seven go one to each market. Eight and nine are sold in I because they yield higher marginal revenue there; ten goes to II for the same reason. Unit 11 can go to either market, since the additional revenues are the same, and unit 12 goes to the other. Thus we see that the 12 units will be divided so that the marginal revenue is the same for the last unit sold in each market; the firm sells seven units in Market I and five in Market II. Thus, the discriminating firm allocates a given output in such a way that the marginal revenues in each market are equal.

The results from Table 17.1 indicate that the firm will maximize profit if it allocates its output such that

$$MR_{\mathrm{I}} = MR_{\mathrm{II}}$$

This condition should not be surprising since it is nothing more than another application of the principle of constrained optimization that we presented in Chapter 3: If the firm wants to maximize profit subject to the constraint that there is only a limited number of units to sell, the firm will allocate sales so that the marginal revenues (marginal benefit) per unit are equal in the two markets. (The marginal cost of selling one unit in Market I is the unit not available for sale in Market II.)

Although the marginal revenues in the two markets are equal, the prices charged are not. The higher price will be charged in the market with the more inelastic demand; the lower price would be charged in the market having the more elastic demand. In the more elastic market, price could be raised only at the expense of a large decrease in sales. In the inelastic market higher prices bring less reduction in sales.

This assertion can be demonstrated as follows. Let the prices in the two markets be P_{I} and P_{II}. Likewise, let E_{I} and E_{II} denote the own-price elasticities. As we know, we can express marginal revenue as

$$MR = P\left(1 - \frac{1}{E}\right)$$

We noted above that the firm will maximize profit if it allocates output so that $MR_{\mathrm{I}} = MR_{\mathrm{II}}$. That is,

$$P_{\mathrm{I}}\left(1 - \frac{1}{E_{\mathrm{I}}}\right) = P_{\mathrm{II}}\left(1 - \frac{1}{E_{\mathrm{II}}}\right)$$

Now, suppose Market I has the more elastic demand,

$$E_{\mathrm{I}} > E_{\mathrm{II}}$$

It follows that

$$\left(1 - \frac{1}{E_{\mathrm{I}}}\right) > \left(1 - \frac{1}{E_{\mathrm{II}}}\right)$$

So,

$$\frac{P_{\mathrm{I}}}{P_{\mathrm{II}}} = \frac{\left(1 - \frac{1}{E_{\mathrm{II}}}\right)}{\left(1 - \frac{1}{E_{\mathrm{I}}}\right)} < 1$$

That is,

$$P_{\mathrm{I}} < P_{\mathrm{II}}$$

Therefore, if a firm price discriminates, it will always charge the lower price in the market having the more elastic demand curve.

The demand and marginal revenue curves for two markets are shown in Panel A, Figure 17.2. D_1D_1' and MR_1 are demand and marginal revenue in Market I; D_2D_2' and MR_2 are demand and marginal revenue in Market II. Panel B shows the horizontal summation of the two demand curves. For example, at a price of $\overline{p}$, consumers in Market I would purchase x_1 and consumers in Market II would buy x_2. The total quantity demanded at $\overline{p}$ is accordingly $x_1 + x_2 = x_T$, shown in Panel B. All other points on D_mD_m' are derived similarly.

Figure 17.2
Submarket and total market demand

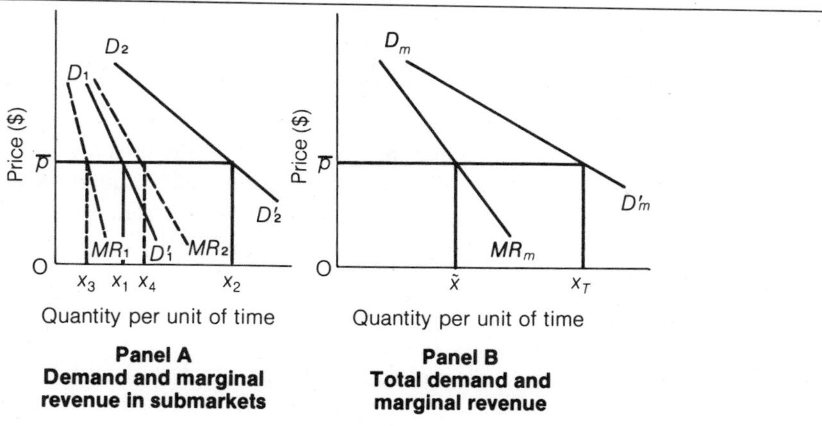

Panel A
Demand and marginal revenue in submarkets

Panel B
Total demand and marginal revenue

Panel B of Figure 17.2 also shows the horizontal summation of the marginal revenue curves in the two markets. Again looking at $\bar{p}$, $MR_1 = \bar{p}$ at output x_3; $MR_2 = \bar{p}$ at x_4. Therefore, in Panel B, $MR_m = \bar{p}$ at a quantity of $x_3 + x_4 = \tilde{x}$. Other points on MR_m (the total market MR curve) are derived similarly.

These demand and marginal revenue relations are reproduced in Figure 17.3 along with the average and marginal costs of production. The profit-maximizing output is $\bar{x}$, the quantity at which the total market marginal reve-

Figure 17.3
Profit maximization with two markets

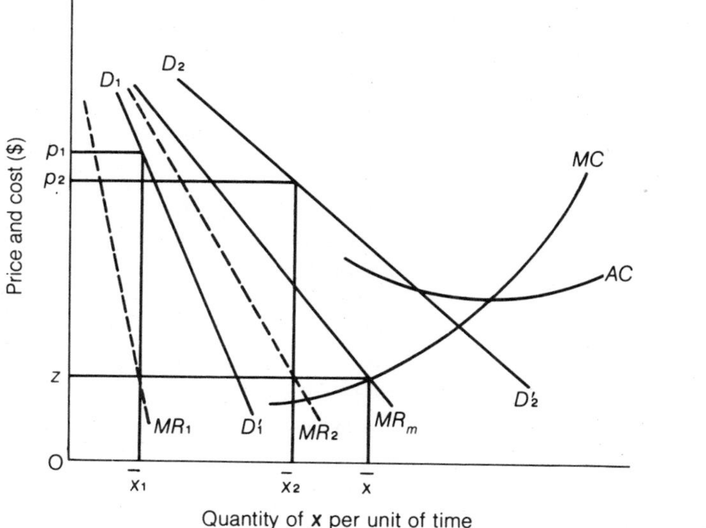

nue, MR_m, equals marginal cost. Note that, at output level $\bar{x}$, total market marginal revenue and marginal cost are both equal to the dollar amount denoted as Z in Figure 17.3.

The market allocation rule, previously determined, requires that marginal revenue be the same in each submarket. Since the total market marginal revenue is the added revenue from selling the last unit in either submarket, $MR_1 = MR_2 = Z$. At a marginal revenue of Z, the quantity sold in Market I is $\bar{x}_1$; in Market II, $\bar{x}_2$. Since MR_m is the horizontal summation of MR_1 and MR_2, $\bar{x}_1 + \bar{x}_2 = \bar{x}$, the total output. Furthermore, from the relevant demand curves, the price associated with output $\bar{x}_1$ in Market I is p_1, the price associated with $\bar{x}_2$ in Market II is p_2.

Summarizing these results, if the aggregate market for a firm's product can be divided into submarkets with different price elasticities, the firm can profitably practice price discrimination. Total output is determined by equating marginal cost with aggregate marginal revenue. The output is allocated among the submarkets so as to equate marginal revenue in each submarket with aggregate marginal revenue at the profit-maximizing level of output. That is, with two markets, the profit-maximization criterion for the firm is expanded to become

$$MR_{\text{TOTAL}} = MC = MR_{\text{I}} = MR_{\text{II}}$$

Finally, price in each submarket is determined from the submarket demand curve.[2]

---

[2]Using mathematics, we can summarize the conclusions of this section. Revenues in each of the submarkets are functions of the quantities sold in those submarkets,

$$R_1 = R_1(Q_1)$$
$$R_2 = R_2(Q_2)$$

Cost, however, is a function of total output, that is,

$$C = C(Q)$$

where

$$Q = Q_1 + Q_2$$

Thus, the firm maximizes profit,

$$\pi = R_1(Q_1) + R_2(Q_2) - C(Q)$$

with respect to the levels of output sold in the two markets. In order to maximize profit, the derivatives of the profit function with respect to these outputs must be equal to zero,

$$\frac{\partial \pi}{\partial Q_1} = \frac{\partial R_1}{\partial Q_1} - \frac{\partial C}{\partial Q_1} = MR_1 - MC = 0$$
$$\frac{\partial \pi}{\partial Q_2} = \frac{\partial R_2}{\partial Q_2} - \frac{\partial C}{\partial Q_2} = MR_2 - MC = 0$$

Thus, profit maximization requires that the marginal revenues in the submarkets be equal, and equal to total marginal cost,

$$MR_1 = MR_2 = MC$$

APPLICATION

Examples of price discrimination

Many drugstores offer discounts on drugs to persons 65 and over. Thus, the drugstores price discriminate. Retired persons probably have a more elastic demand for drugs, because the market value of their time is lower. Retired persons would tend to shop around more for lower prices, and differences in price among different age groups can be explained by different price elasticities, resulting from different evaluations of time.

Movies, plays, concerts, and similar forms of entertainment practice price discrimination according to age. Generally, younger people pay lower prices. Supposedly, in this case, younger people have more elastic demands for such tickets, possibly because of the availability of more substitute forms of entertainment. (It is not correct to say that different ticket prices for afternoon and evening performances are evidence of price discrimination. These are different products in the eye of the consumer.)

Airlines frequently discriminate between vacation and business travel. Vacation travelers would have a more elastic demand than business travelers, probably because the value of time in business travel is greater. Other examples of price discrimination are electric companies that charge lower rates to industrial users than to households (although this may be, in part, due to differences in costs), and university bookstores that charge lower prices to faculty than to students.

In order to implement profit maximization with multiple markets, it would be necessary for the manager to estimate demand functions for each of the markets. After summing to obtain a total demand function, total output would be that at which total marginal revenue is equal to total marginal cost. Then, this output would be allocated to the various markets so that the marginal revenues are all equal to total marginal revenue at the profit-maximizing output. Let's illustrate this procedure with a simplified example.

APPLICATION

Profit maximization with multiple markets

The manager of Galactic Manufacturing—a firm with substantial monopoly power—knows that the firm faces two distinct markets. Using the techniques described earlier in this text, the demand curves for these two markets were forecasted to be

$$\text{Mkt I: } Q = 100 - 2P \qquad \text{Mkt II: } Q = 50 - 0.5P$$

where output was measured in thousand units and price in dollars per unit. Summing these, the firm's total demand was forecasted to be

$$Q = 150 - 2.5P$$

The manager solved these for the inverse demand functions, then obtained the corresponding marginal revenue functions:

$$\text{Mkt I: } MR = 50 - 1Q \qquad \text{Mkt II: } MR = 100 - 4Q$$
$$\text{Total: } MR = 60 - 0.8Q$$

From the engineering department, the manager obtained a linear estimate of the firm's incremental (marginal) cost of production per thousand units,

$$MC = 10 + 0.2Q$$

Equating total marginal revenue and this estimate of marginal cost,

$$60 - 0.8Q = 10 + 0.2Q$$

the profit maximizing level of production is $Q^* = 50$ (i.e., 50,000 units.) At this output level, total marginal revenue and marginal cost are both equal to \$20.

To allocate the output between the two markets, the marginal revenues in both markets must be equal to total marginal revenue, i.e., \$20. The manager must, therefore, solve two equations:

$$\text{Mkt I: } 50 - 1Q = 20 \qquad \text{Mkt II: } 100 - 4Q = 20$$

Hence, for Market I, $Q = 30$ (i.e., 30,000 units) and for Market II, $Q = 20$ (i.e., 20,000 units). Finally, substituting these quantities into the respective demand functions, the profit-maximizing prices will be \$35 in Market I and \$60 in Market II.

17.3 FIRMS WITH MULTIPLE PRODUCTS

To this point, we have assumed that the firm produces a single product. However, even a very cursory survey of the existing firms in the United States would show that many produce and sell several different products or at least several different models. While it is possible that the firm's products could be unrelated, it is more likely that the products produced are related either in consumption or production. When the products are related, the firm's output and pricing decision must incorporate the interrelations.

In this section we provide a brief overview of profit-maximization in a multiple-product firm. We consider three possibilities: First, we examine the case of products that are related in consumption. We then turn to a consideration of products that are complements in production. We conclude this section with a discussion of products that are substitutes in production.

Multiple products related in consumption

Recall that the demand for a particular commodity depends not only on the price of the product itself but also on the price of any related commodities, income, taste, and so on. For simplicity, let us ignore the other factors and write our demand function as

$$Q_x = f(P_X,P_Y)$$

where Q_X is the quantity demanded of commodity X, P_X is the price of X, and P_Y is the price of the related commodity Y—either a substitute or complement.

In our discussion so far, we have treated P_Y as if it were given to the firm. That is, we assumed P_Y to be a parameter (i.e., a constant) determined outside of the firm. Thus, the firm would maximize its profits by selecting the appropriate level of production and price for X. If, however, the firm in question produces *both* commodities X and Y, the price of the related commodity Y is no longer parametric—exogenous—but is controlled by the firm. The profitability of X would then depend on the price of Y and vice versa.

An example might help to clarify this issue. Consider a firm such as Coleman, which produces several commodities that are complementary—tents, lanterns, stoves, iceboxes, and so forth. Consumers in this market for outdoor recreation equipment frequently wish to purchase the ''bundle'' of commodities. Therefore, we would expect the sales of, say, lanterns to depend to some extent on the price charged for a good that is used in conjunction, perhaps tents. It follows then that the price charged for tents would affect the profits of the division producing lanterns, and the firm as a whole.

The point is, in order to maximize the profit of the firm, the levels of output and prices for the related commodities must be determined *jointly*. Hence, for a two-product firm, the profit-maximization conditions remain the same,

$$MR_X = MC_X \text{ and } MR_Y = MC_Y$$

However, the marginal revenue of X will be a function of both the prices of X and Y, as will the marginal revenue of Y. Hence, these marginal conditions must be satisfied *simultaneously*. To see how this could be accomplished, let's look at another stylized example. (In this example we will look at a firm that produces products that are substitutes in consumption; but the same technique would apply for products that are complements in consumption.)

APPLICATION

Profit maximization with substitutes in consumption

Zicon Manufacturing produces two types of automobile vacuum cleaners. One, which we denote as product X, plugs into the cigarette lighter receptacle; the other—product Y—has rechargeable batteries. Assuming that there is no other relation between the two products other than the apparent substitutability in consumption, the manager of Zicon wanted to determine the profit-maximizing levels of production and price for the two products.

Using the techniques described in this text, the demand functions for the two products were forecasted to be

$$Q_X = 80 - 8P_X + 6P_Y \qquad Q_Y = 40 - 4P_Y + 4P_X$$

where the outputs were measured in thousand units and the prices in dollars per unit. Solving these two forecasted demand functions simultaneously, the manager obtained the corresponding inverse demand functions,

$$P_X = 70 - \frac{1}{2}Q_X - \frac{3}{4}Q_Y \qquad P_Y = 80 - 1Q_Y - \frac{1}{2}Q_X$$

so, the marginal revenue functions were

$$MR_X = 70 - 1Q_X - \frac{3}{4}Q_Y \qquad MR_Y = 80 - 2Q_Y - \frac{1}{2}Q_X$$

From the production manager, estimates of the incremental cost (marginal cost) functions were obtained;

$$MC_X = 10 + \frac{1}{2}Q_X \qquad MC_Y = 20 + \frac{1}{4}Q_Y$$

where output was again measured in thousand units.

To determine the outputs that will be expected to maximize profit, the manager of Zicon equated *MR* and *MC* for the two products,

$$70 - 1\,Q_X - \frac{3}{4}Q_Y = 10 + \frac{1}{2}Q_X$$

$$80 - 2\,Q_Y - \frac{1}{2}Q_X = 20 + \frac{1}{4}Q_Y$$

Solving these equations simultaneously, the profit-maximizing outputs were found to be $Q_X = 30$ (i.e., 30,000 units) and $Q_Y = 20$ (i.e., 20,000 units.) Finally, using these outputs in the inverse demand functions, the manager of Zicon found that the profit-maximizing price for X was $40 and for Y was $45.

From the preceding discussion and illustration, the point we wish to stress is that if a firm produces products that are related in consumption, profit maximization requires that output levels and prices be determined jointly. Specifically, in such a firm, the profit-maximizing price for a particular commodity will be determined not only by its own demand and cost conditions but also by those of the related commodities.

Multiple products that are complements in production

In the preceding, we considered products that are related in consumption. We now turn to products that are related in production. We begin by considering a firm that produces products that are complements in production.

For simplicity, we limit ourselves to the case of products that are produced in fixed proportions. The classic illustration is that of beef carcasses and hides. Clearly, these products are complements in production. Furthermore, this joint production of the two products is characterized by fixed proportions—for each additional beef carcass produced, one additional hide will be produced. Note, however, that there exist other instances of joint production characterized by fixed proportion. Indeed, petroleum refining has such characteristics. With an existing refinery and the prevailing mix of input crude oils, production of an additional barrel of one of the lighter distillates, such as gasoline, would require that the refinery produce some additional amount of the heavier distillates, like fuel oil.

We again assume that the firm produces only two products, X and Y. Our problem is to determine the level of production and the price for each of these complementary products.

In Figure 17.4, we have provided a graphical analysis of this problem. In this figure, the demand curves for the two products are denoted as D_X and D_Y and the corresponding marginal revenue curves are shown as the dashed lines MR_X and MR_Y. The marginal cost curve shown is the marginal cost of producing the joint product.

In order to determine how much of the joint product to produce, we need to obtain the demand curve and the marginal revenue curve for the joint product. To obtain the joint product demand curve, we sum the individual demand curves *vertically*: For example, given some level of production of beef carcasses and hides, the total price received is equal to the sum of the prices received for the carcasses and hides.

The marginal revenue curve for the joint product is also obtained via the *vertical* summation of MR_X and MR_Y; but, there is one major difference. In Figure 17.4, note that MR_Y becomes zero at an output we have denoted as Q_Y. For sales of commodity Y in excess of Q_Y, the marginal revenue for Y would be negative. Clearly, no firm would wish to sell a unit of a product for which the marginal revenue is negative; so, the maximum amount of Y the firm will *sell* is Q_Y. Therefore, the marginal revenue curve for the joint product is the vertical sum of MR_X and MR_Y until MR_Y equals zero. For outputs in excess of Q_Y, only commodity X would be sold, so the joint marginal revenue curve corresponds to MR_X. The result is the "kinked" joint product marginal revenue curve shown in Figure 17.4

The profit-maximizing level of production for the firm is determined at that level of output at which the joint marginal revenue is equal to the joint marginal cost. In Figure 17.4, this means that the firm will produce Q units of the joint product. The firm will then sell Q units of product X at a price of P_X and Q units of product Y at a price of P_Y.

Figure 17.4
Profit maximization with joint products

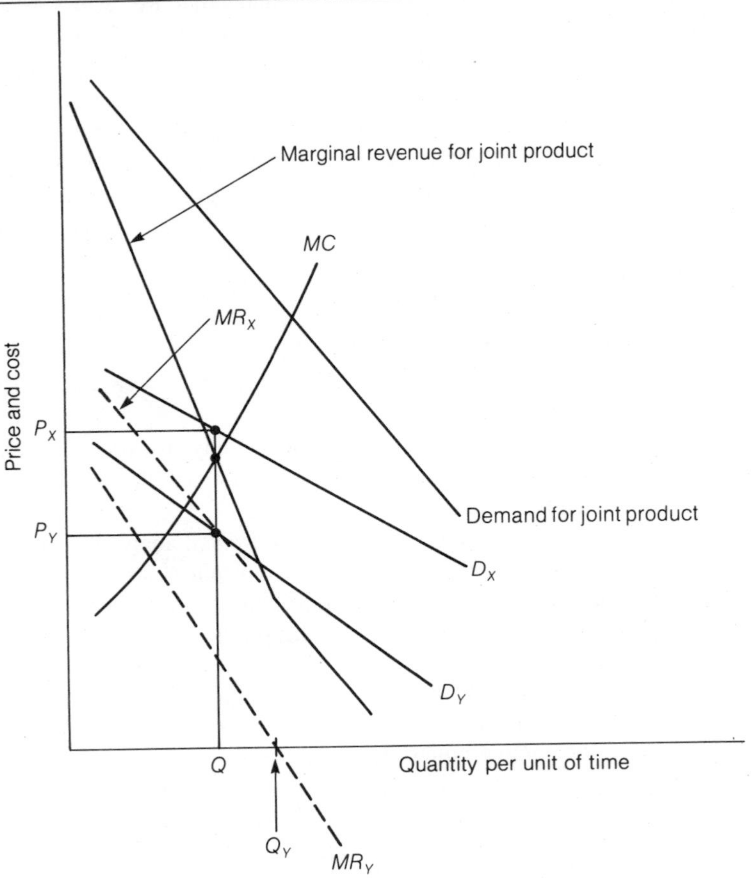

To see how the firm can implement profit-maximization with joint products, as illustrated in Figure 17.4, let's turn to still another stylized example.

APPLICATION

Profit maximization with joint products

The Horizon Corporation produces refined chemicals. In one of its divisions a joint product is produced. That is, as it refines the raw chemical input, the processes will yield equal amounts of two products which we will denote simply as products X and Y. The question facing the manager is, of course, how much of products X and Y the firm should sell and at what prices?

The demand functions for the two products had been forecasted as

$$Q_X = 285 - P_X \qquad Q_Y = 150 - 2P_Y$$

where the outputs were measured in thousand pounds and the prices in cents per pound. The marginal revenue curves associated with these demand functions are

$$MR_X = 285 - 2Q_X \qquad MR_Y = 75 - Q_Y$$

Note that the marginal revenue function for Y is equal to zero at an output of 75 (i.e., 75,000 pounds.) So, for output levels of the joint product less than or equal to 75, the marginal revenue function for the joint product is the vertical summation of the two marginal revenues,

$$MR = 360 - 3Q$$

For output levels in excess of $Q = 75$, the joint product marginal revenue function would coincide with MR_X.

Given the existing capital stock, the firm's engineers have estimated the incremental (marginal) cost function for refining the raw chemical input to be

$$MC = 10 + 2Q$$

where marginal cost is measured in cents per pound and output (Q) is in thousand pounds.

Equating marginal revenue and marginal cost for the joint product,

$$360 - 3Q = 10 + 2Q$$

the profit-maximizing level of production of the joint product is $Q = 70$ (i.e., 70,000 pounds.) Using $Q = 70$ in the two demand curves, the manager of Horizon found that the firm should sell 70,000 pounds of X at \$2.15 per pound and 70,000 pounds of Y at \$0.40 per pound.

So far, our results have indicated that the firm will produce *and sell* equal amounts of the two products. This need not always be the case. The joint product nature of the production relation we have been considering does require that the firm will always *produce* equal amounts of the two products. (You can't produce an additional beef carcass without producing an additional hide.) But, there is nothing that requires the firm to *sell* equal amounts of the two products.

We have illustrated this situation in Figure 17.5. The only difference between this figure and Figure 17.4 is the location of the marginal cost curve for the joint product. In this case, the firm will *produce* Q' units of the joint product. And, since MR_X is positive at Q', the firm will *sell* Q' units of X at the price P'_X. However, at Q', MR_Y is negative. Clearly the firm will not sell Q' units of Y. Instead, the firm will *sell* only Q_Y units of commodity *Y* at the price of P'_Y. Since it has produced Q' units of Y but only sells Q_Y units, what will the firm do with the remainder (i.e., $Q' - Q_Y$ units of Y)? The answer is simple but somewhat surprising: The firm will destroy the remainder, since marketing these units would reduce the firm's revenues.

Figure 17.5
Profit maximization with joint products—destruction of one product

APPLICATION

Profit maximization with joint products—continued

Look again at the decision faced by the manager of Horizon Corporation. Suppose that the engineers had instead estimated the incremental (marginal) cost of refining the joint product to be

$$MC = 80 + \frac{1}{2}Q$$

How would this alternative marginal cost function affect the firm's decisions?

Setting this marginal cost function equal to the joint product marginal revenue function used before,

$$360 - 3Q = 80 + \frac{1}{2}Q$$

the *implied* optimal output would be Q = 80. However, as the manager is aware, at this production level, the marginal revenue for product Y would be negative. Hence, in this range of production, the joint product marginal revenue function coincides with MR_X; so, to determine optimal production, the manager must equate marginal cost to the marginal revenue for product X,

$$285 - 2Q = 80 + \frac{1}{2}Q$$

Hence, in this situation, the optimal level of production of the joint product is $Q = 82$. That is, the firm will produce 82,000 pounds of chemicals X and Y.

Since MR_X is positive at $Q = 82$, the firm will sell the 82,000 pounds of X. From the demand function for X, the price charged will be $2.03 per pound.

However, Horizon will sell chemical Y only to that point at which its marginal revenue is zero. That is, since $MR_Y = 0$ when $Q = 75$, the firm will sell only 75,000 pounds of chemical Y and will destroy the remaining 7,000 pounds. From the demand function for Y, the price that will be charged for the 75,000 pounds of Y that is sold is 37.5 cents per pound.

Summarizing, if a firm produces products that are complements in production and are characterized by fixed proportions production, the profit-maximizing firm will select the level of output of the joint product at which total marginal revenue equals total marginal cost. Given this level of production, the prices for the individual products would be taken from the individual demand curves. However, it is possible that, at the profit-maximizing level of output for the joint product, the marginal revenue for one or more of the individual products is negative. In such an instance, the firm would sell that product only to the point at which marginal revenue becomes zero and destroy the excess.

The theoretical principles and implementation techniques we have presented here can be expanded to consider products that are complements but not in the fixed (one-to-one) proportions we have used in this analysis. The principles remain the same but the solution becomes more complex.

Multiple products that are substitutes in production

While the case of products that are complementary in production is clearly possible, a potentially more common situation is the multiproduct firm that produces products that are substitutes in production. This situation is most easily seen in the case of a firm that produces several models of the same basic product. These different models compete for the limited production facilities of the firm and are therefore substitutes in the firm's production process. In the long run, the firm can adjust its production facility in order to produce the profit-maximizing level of each product. However, in the short run, the firm must determine how to allocate its limited production capacity among the competing products in order to maximize profit.

As you should recognize, the short-run case is still another example of constrained optimization. The firm must maximize profit subject to the constraint imposed by the limited production facility. For simplicity, let us consider a firm that produces only two products, which we will denote as X and Y. Further, we assume that the two products are produced using the same production facility and that the cost of operating this facility is invariant to the product produced. The marginal benefit accrued from producing an additional unit of either product is the marginal revenue that would be generated. In the case of product X, this is MR_X. The marginal cost of producing an additional unit of one product is the reduction in output of the competing product. For product X, the marginal cost is the corresponding reduction in the production of Y, ΔY. Conversely, the marginal cost of producing an additional unit of Y is ΔX. As we demonstrated in Chapter 3, a firm will maximize its objective function subject to a constraint when the ratios of marginal benefit to marginal cost are equal for all decision variables. In the case in question, this means that profit will be maximized when the levels of production of the two products are such that

$$\frac{MR_X}{\Delta Y} = \frac{MR_Y}{\Delta X}$$

To see how this condition can be utilized, let's look at a very simplified example

APPLICATION

The allocation of assembly line time

A division of Surefire Products, Inc., manufactures two products, X and Y, that are unrelated in consumption but are substitutes in production. More specifically, these two products are produced on the same assembly line; so, they compete for the limited time available. The question facing the manager of the parent company—Surefire Products—is: How should an eight-hour production day be allocated between the production of X and the production of Y?

The demand functions for the two products were forecasted to be

$$Q_X = 60 - \frac{1}{2} P_X \qquad Q_Y = 40 - \frac{2}{3} P_Y$$

where the quantities were the number of units demanded per day and the prices were expressed in dollars per unit. From these forecasted demand functions, the marginal revenue functions were

$$MR_X = 120 - 4Q_X \qquad MR_Y = 60 - 3Q_Y$$

Discussions with the plant supervisor indicated that, in one hour of production time, either two units of X or four units of Y could be produced. In a sense, the "production functions" for the two products are

$$Q_X = 2H_X \qquad Q_Y = 4H_Y$$

where H_X and H_Y denote, respectively, one hour of assembly line time in the production of X and Y. From this, the marginal cost of using an additional hour in the production of X is $\Delta Y = 4$. That is, if this plant devotes an additional hour to the production of X, it must forgo the production of four units of Y. Likewise, the marginal cost of an additional hour in the production of Y is $\Delta X = 2$.

Hence, the firm will maximize profit subject to the limitation of the eight-hour production day if it produces amounts of X and Y such that the condition

$$\frac{120 - 4Q_X}{4} = \frac{60 - 3Q_Y}{2}$$

is satisfied. This condition requires that $Q_X = \frac{3}{2} Q_Y$. Using the "production functions" above, this profit-maximization condition can be rewritten in terms of the hours devoted to the production of the two products, i.e., $Q_X = \frac{3}{2} Q_Y$ may be rewritten as

$$H_X = 3H_Y$$

For profit maximization, the firm should devote assembly line time to X and Y in the ratio 3:1.

Using this optimality condition with the time constraint (i.e., $H_X + H_Y = 8$), it follows that to maximize profits, six hours will be devoted to product X and two hours to product Y. That means that Surefire Products will produce 12 units of X per day and 8 units of Y; so, the optimal prices are \$96 per unit for X and \$48 per unit for Y.

As you may have guessed from the preceding Application, there is another way of expressing the optimization condition for the allocation of the production facility between the production of X and Y. Let's define F as the level of usage of the production facility. Then $\Delta X/\Delta F$ is the marginal product of the production facility in the production of X. Likewise, $\Delta Y/\Delta F$ is the marginal product of the production facility in the production of Y. Then, dividing both sides of the previous condition by ΔF, the optimization condition can be written as

$$(MR_X) \times (MP_{F,X}) = (MR_Y) \times (MP_{F,Y})$$

or

$$MRP_X = MRP_Y$$

Figure 17.6
Profit-maximizing allocation of production facilities

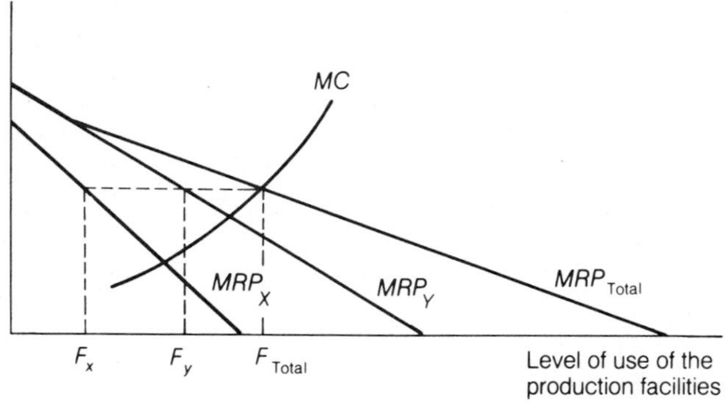

If, in the longer run, the firm has some ability to vary its usage of its production facilities, we can generalize this condition. In Figure 17.6 the horizontal axis measures the level of usage of the limited production facilities. We have illustrated the marginal revenue product curves for the production facility in the production of the two products and, summing horizontally, the total marginal revenue product curve. In this situation, we continue to consider a single marginal cost curve—that is, we assume that costs depend only on the level of usage of the production facility and are not affected by the type of product produced. We know that profit will be maximized at the point at which marginal cost is equal to total marginal revenue product. Thus, the usage level of the production facility will be F_{TOTAL}. The question then becomes how this level of usage (e.g., machine hours) is to be divided between the two products.

From our discussion to this point, the answer is probably obvious. If the allocation were such that $MRP_X > MRP_Y$, profit could be increased by reallocating from the production of Y to the production of X. This would reduce MRP_X and increase MRP_Y. Such a reallocation would continue until the marginal revenue products are equal, $MRP_X = MRP_Y$. Further, since the total marginal revenue product is simply the sum of the two individual curves, the profit-maximizing condition is

$$MRP_{\text{TOTAL}} = MC = MRP_X = MRP_Y$$

Thus, profits will be maximized when production is allocated such that the marginal additions to revenue are the same for the two products. To show you how this decision rule could be implemented, let's return to our simplified example.

APPLICATION

Optimal usage of a production facility

The manager of Surefire Products, Inc., also wanted to consider changing the daily production schedule for the plant producing X and Y from a strict eight-hour-per-day schedule. That is, the manager wanted to know the answers to two questions: (1) What is the optimal level of usage (hours of operation) of the plant? (2) How should this level of usage be allocated between the production of the two products?

Using the demand forecasts and the estimates of the "production functions" provided by the plant supervisor, estimates/forecasts of the marginal revenue product of the production facility in the production of X and Y were

$$MRP_X = [120 - 4\ (2H_X)] \times (2) \qquad MRP_Y = [60 - 3\ (4H_X)] \times (4)$$
$$= 240 - 16H_X \qquad = 240 - 48H_Y$$

To obtain the total marginal revenue production function, these two curves were summed horizontally, i.e., these functions were inverted to find H_X and H_Y; then the hours were summed ($H_{\text{Total}} = H_X + H_Y$). The resulting total MRP was

$$MRP_{\text{Total}} = 240 - 12H_{\text{Total}}$$

Working with the engineers for Surefire, the plant supervisor was able to come up with an estimate of the additional cost of operating the plant an additional hour—an incremental (marginal) cost for usage of the plant. This estimate was

$$MC = 72 + 2H$$

Equating the total marginal revenue product of an hour's usage of the plant with the marginal cost of an additional hour's usage,

$$240 - 12H = 72 + 2H$$

the manager of Surefire Products found that the optimal level of usage of the plant was 12 hours per day. At this level of usage, $MRP_{\text{Total}} = MC = \$96$. To allocate these hours between the production of X and Y, the marginal revenue products for the production facility in the production of X and Y must both be equal to 96:

$$240 - 16H_X = 96 \qquad 240 - 48H_Y = 96$$

So, the optimal allocation would be nine hours in the production of X and three hours in the production of Y.

17.4 SUMMARY

In this chapter, we have looked at a lot of "special cases." While it might seem that we have introduced a lot of new conditions, we really haven't. Essentially, all we have done is apply the basic principles of profit maximization to instances in which the firm has more than one plant or market or product. To see that the resulting rules for profit maximization have much in common, let's review them briefly:

1. *Multiple plants*—If a firm produces in two plants, A and B, it should allocate production between the two plants so that $MC_A = MC_B$. The optimal

total output for the firm is that at which $MR = MC_{\text{TOTAL}}$. Hence, for profit-maximization, the firm should produce that level of output and allocate the production of that output between the two plants so that

$$MR = MC_{\text{TOTAL}} = MC_A = MC_B$$

2. *Multiple markets*—If a firm sells in two distinct markets, I and II, it should allocate output (sales) between the two markets such that $MR_{\text{I}} = MR_{\text{II}}$. The optimal level of total output for the firm is that at which $MR_{\text{TOTAL}} = MC$. Hence, for profit-maximization, the firm should produce that level of output and allocate the sales of this output between the two markets so that

$$MR_{\text{TOTAL}} = MC = MR_{\text{I}} = MR_{\text{II}}$$

3. *Multiple products/related in consumption*—Defining the two products to be X and Y, the firm will produce and sell those levels of output for which

$$MR_X = MC_X \text{ and } MR_Y = MC_Y$$

Since the products are related in consumption MR_X is a function not only of Q_X but also of Q_Y and vice versa. Therefore, the marginal conditions for the two products must be satisfied simultaneously.

4. *Multiple products/complements in production*—If the firm produces two products, X and Y, that are joint products, the optimum level of production is that at which

$$MR_{\text{TOTAL}} = MC$$

where MR_{TOTAL} is the *vertical* summation of MR_X and MR_Y. The only complication introduced is that at this optimum level of production if the MR for either of the two products is negative, the firm will sell only the amount of that product for which $MR = 0$ and will destroy the remainder.

5. *Multiple products/substitutes in production*—If a firm produces two products, X and Y, that compete for the firm's limited production facilities, the firm should allocate the production facility so that the marginal revenue product of the production facility is equal for the two products, $MRP_X = MRP_Y$. If in the longer run the firm can vary its usage of or size of the production facility, the optimal level of usage of the facility is that at which $MRP_{\text{TOTAL}} = MC$. Hence, for profit maximization the firm should select that level of usage of its production facility and allocate that level of usage between the production of the two products so that

$$MRP_{\text{TOTAL}} = MC = MRP_X = MRP_Y$$

Note, in particular, the similarities between cases 1, 2, and 5. All of these are allocation problems; so they share a common solution. Case 3 requires only that the basic profit-maximization conditions for the related products be solved simultaneously. Case 4 is unique only in that it requires a vertical (rather than horizontal) summation and does permit a firm to destroy some of its own output.

So, the view we want to leave you with is that the complications introduced in this chapter do not change the basic rules of profit maximization. As we noted at the outset, the only thing these real-world complications do is to make profit maximization a little more computationally complex.

TECHNICAL PROBLEMS

1. Look again at Mercantile Enterprises—our example of a multiplant firm.

a. Suppose the forecasted demand function is

$$Q = 78 - 1.2P$$

How many units will be produced? How will these units be allocated between Plants A and B?

b. Suppose the forecasted demand function is

$$Q = 88 - 3P$$

How many units will be produced? How will these units be allocated between Plants A and B?

2. What conditions are necessary for a firm to be able to price discriminate?

3. Using our Application dealing with profit maximization in multiple markets (Galactic Manufacturing), what price would be charged if the firm does not price discriminate? Demonstrate that the firm will have a higher profit if it price discriminates than if it charges the same price in both markets.

4. Suppose a firm serves two distinct markets. The forecasted demand functions in the two markets are

$$\text{Mkt I: } Q = 50 - 0.25P \qquad \text{Mkt II: } Q = 100 - 1.0P$$

and the firm's incremental (marginal) cost function has been estimated to be

$$MC = 20 + 0.4Q$$

a. What is the profit-maximizing total level of output?
b. How should this output be allocated between the two markets?
c. What are the profit-maximizing prices in the two markets?
d. Which market has the more elastic demand?

5. How would the profit-maximization decision for a firm that produces two products that are related in consumption differ from that for a firm whose two products are unrelated?

6. Look again at Zicon Manufacturing—a firm that produces products that are substitutes in consumption. Suppose that the production manager changed the estimates of the incremental (marginal) cost functions to

$$MC_X = 20 + \frac{1}{4} Q_X \qquad MC_Y = 16 + \frac{1}{2} Q_Y$$

Calculate the new profit-maximizing levels of output and price for the two products.

7. Describe the circumstances under which a firm might produce a product and then destroy it.

8. Suppose that a firm produces two joint products in fixed, one-to-one proportions. The demand functions for the two products have been estimated as

$$Q_X = 110 - P_X$$

$$Q_Y = 10 - \frac{1}{4} P_Y$$

and the incremental (marginal) cost function for the joint product has been estimated to be

$$MC = 30 + 2Q$$

a. What is the profit-maximizing level of production for the joint product?
b. How much of each product will be sold?
c. What are the profit-maximizing prices for the two products?

9. Look again at the division of Surefire Products, Inc., that produces two products that are substitutes in production. Suppose that the forecasted demand function was changed to

$$Q_X = 76 - \frac{1}{2} P_X$$

a. How will an eight-hour production day be allocated between the production of the two products?
b. What will be the daily outputs?
c. What prices will be charged?

10. In our Application dealing with the optimal usage of a production facility (Surefire Products, Inc.) suppose that the plant supervisor changes the estimate of the incremental (marginal) cost for usage of the plant to

$$MC = 150 + 3H$$

a. What is the optimal level of usage for the plant (hours per day)?
b. How will this level of usage be allocated between the production of the two products?
c. What will be the daily outputs?
d. What prices will be charged?

ANALYTICAL PROBLEMS

1. Consider a monopoly firm with two plants. One of the plants has a distinct cost advantage in the sense that, at every output, average cost per unit is lower. Why would the firm elect to produce any output from the plant with the higher average costs?
2. Do price differences always indicate price discrimination? Put another way, could there exist a situation in which two groups of consumers were being charged different prices yet the firm was not price discriminating?
3. Although there exists relatively little difference in the cost of producing hardcover and paperback books, they sell for very different prices. Explain this pricing behavior.
4. In 1980, *The Wall Street Journal* reported on dating services, noting that the fees were $300 for men and $250 for women. The owner of the service said that the differences in fees was to compensate for inequalities in pay scales for men and women. Can you suggest any alternative reasons for this difference?
5. Currently, many firms are expanding into product lines that are related to their primary product. Consider, for example, the AMF sporting goods group. Why would you expect this type of behavior?
6. Provide some examples of products that are complements in production. Can you provide any examples of products that have been produced and destroyed in a joint production process?
7. Not too long ago the evening news showed us pictures of dairy farmers dumping milk on the ground. Is this a result of some joint product profit maximization? If so, explain why this is happening. If not, provide a rationale for such behavior.
8. In the case of substitutes in production, we assumed that production costs, e.g., cost of running the assembly line, were invariant to the product produced. How would the problem and the optimization condition change if production costs were different for the different products?
9. Can you think of examples of firms that produce products that are both related in consumption and substitutes in production? In general, how would this additional complication affect the optimization condition?

SELECTED ADDITIONAL REFERENCES

Koch, J. V. *Industrial Organization and Prices*. Englewood Cliffs, N.J.: Prentice-Hall, 1980.

Mahanty, A. K. *Intermediate Microeconomics with Applications*. New York: Academic Press, 1980.

Scherer, F. M. *Industrial Market Structure and Economic Performance*. Chicago: Rand McNally, 1980.

Stigler, G. J. *The Theory of Price*. London: Macmillan, 1966.

18

Oligopoly

Oligopoly is the name given to another market structure between the extremes of perfect competition and monopoly. It differs from monopolistic competition in that the number of firms is not so large as to render negligible the contribution of each firm. Recall that under monopolistic competition the number of firms is large enough that no firm has significant market power. Each firm acts as though its activities have no effect upon the actions taken by other firms. An oligopolist has more market power than monopolistic competitors.

How small must the number of firms be to make a market oligopolistic? The answer is that a market has few enough sellers to be considered oligopolistic if the firms recognize their *mutual interdependence*. In all of the other market structures, firms make decisions and take action without considering how these actions will affect other firms and how, in turn, other firms' reactions will affect them. Oligopolists must take these reactions into account in their decision-making process.

For example, when contemplating a price change, a design innovation, or a new advertising campaign, Ford Motor Company must anticipate how General Motors and the Chrysler Corporation will react, because, without doubt, Ford's actions will affect the demand for Chevrolets and Chryslers. Likewise, Dow Chemical must consider how DuPont will react when making price, output, and research decisions.

This, in short, is the central problem in oligopoly analysis. The oligopolistic firm is large enough to recognize (*a*) the mutual interdependence of the firms in the oligopoly market and (*b*) that its decisions will affect the other firms, which in turn will react in a way that affects the initial firm. The great uncertainty is how one's competitors will react.

Many real-world industries satisfy the general description of oligopoly. However, there as yet exists no *general* theory of oligopoly behavior. The problem in developing oligopoly theory is the oligopoly problem itself. Mutual interdependence and the resulting uncertainty about reaction patterns of rivals make it necessary for economists to make specific assumptions about behavioral patterns—how oligopolists believe their competitors will react and how their competitors actually react.

Therefore, as we shall see, the decisions made in the oligopoly model (e.g., price and output) depend critically upon the assumptions made about the behavioral reactions of rival managers. Since many different assumptions can and have been made, many different solutions can and have been reached. Thus, there is no single "theory of oligopoly."

We can classify oligopoly markets by whether or not the firms "cooperate." A noncooperative oligopoly market simply means that each firm considers the possible reactions of its rivals when making decisions, but each firm acts independently. Cooperation can take many forms, from overt collusion (e.g., price fixing), to implicit collusion and price leadership. We will analyze the different forms of collusion in more detail in a later section.

18.1 BARRIERS TO ENTRY

Before analysing oligopoly behavior, let us first examine briefly why some industries are oligopolistic (or approach a monopoly structure) while others are much closer to perfect or monopolistic competition. The question that must be addressed is: Why in some industries do the few largest firms produce a large percentage of total output while in other industries no firm has a substantial share of the total market?

One of the more important barriers to entry is the control of raw material supplies. If one firm (or perhaps a few firms) controls all of the known supply of a necessary ingredient of a particular product, the firm or firms can refuse to sell that ingredient to other firms at a price low enough for them to compete. Since no others can produce the product, a monopoly or oligopoly results. For example, for many years the Aluminum Company of America (Alcoa) owned almost every source of bauxite, a necessary ingredient in the production of aluminum. The control of resource supply, coupled with certain patent rights, provided Alcoa with an absolute monopoly in aluminum production.

Another source of monopoly (oligopoly) power—barrier to entry—lies in the patent laws of the United States. These laws make it possible for a person to apply for and obtain the exclusive right to produce a certain commodity or to produce a commodity by means of a specified process. Obviously, such exclusive rights can easily lead to monopoly or, if a few firms hold the patents, to oligopoly. As noted, Alcoa was an example of a monopoly based upon both resource control and patent rights. E. I. DuPont de Nemours & Co. enjoyed patent monopolies over many commodities, cellophane being perhaps the most notable. And, at one time the Eastman Kodak Company enjoyed a similar position.

A third source of an oligopoly or monopoly position, clearly related to the two sources just discussed, lies in the cost of establishing an efficient production plant. A "natural" monopoly or "natural" oligopoly is said to exist when the minimum average cost of production occurs at a rate of output so large that one or a few firms can supply the entire market at a price covering full cost. To illustrate this situation, suppose there exists a market in which a few firms supply the entire market, and each enjoys a pure profit. Because of the existence of substantial economies of scale, the average cost at smaller rates of output is so high that entry is not profitable for small-scale firms. On the other hand, the entry of another large-scale producer is also discouraged because the added production of this firm would increase the quantity supplied and drive price below the pure-profit level for all firms. Therefore, entry is discouraged and a "natural" oligopoly market exists.

Another basis for oligopoly position (barrier to entry) is the advantage that established firms sometimes have over new firms. On the cost side, the established firms may be able to secure financing at a more favorable rate than new firms (perhaps because of a history of good earnings). On the demand side, older firms may have built up the allegiance of a group of buyers. Buyer allegiance for durable goods can be built by establishing a reputation for service. No one knows what the service or repair policy of a new firm may be. Or, the allegiance of buyers can be built by a long, successful advertising campaign. (This type of allegiance is also probably more prevalent for durable goods.) New firms might have considerable difficulties establishing a market organization and overcoming buyer preference for the established firms.

The role of advertising in fostering oligopoly has, however, been a source of controversy. Some argue that advertising acts as a barrier to entry by strengthening buyer preferences for the products of established firms. On the other hand, consider the great difficulty of entering an established industry without access to advertising. A good way for entrenched oligopolists to discourage entry would be, in fact, to get the government to prohibit advertising. The reputation of the old firms would enable them to continue their dominance. A new firm would have difficulty informing the public about the availability of a new product unless it was able to advertise. Thus advertising may be a way for a new firm to overcome the advantages of established firms. The effect of advertising on oligopoly remains a point of disagreement among economists.

A final source of an oligopoly (or monopoly) position is government. Although the United States does enforce antitrust laws with varying degrees of severity, government (at all levels) frequently acts so as to erect barriers to entry. One method is the granting of a market franchise. Use of a market franchise is frequently associated with natural monopolies, but it need not be. A market franchise is actually a contract entered into by some governmental body (for instance, a city government) and a business concern. The governmental unit gives a business firm the exclusive right to market a good or service within its jurisdiction. The business firm, in turn, agrees to permit the governmental unit to control certain aspects of its market conduct.

18.2 PRICE AND OUTPUT UNDER NONCOOPERATING OLIGOPOLY

Again, the distinguishing characteristic of oligopoly is the recognition by each firm that its actions will have a perceptible effect upon other firms and that these rivals will react accordingly. Thus, the potential reactions of other firms must be taken into account when an individual firm makes decisions, especially decisions about price and output.

The managers of oligopolies do use the marginal benefit–marginal cost rule when making decisions, even given the uncertainty that exists about the reactions of rivals. A firm would reduce price and increase output as long as expected marginal revenue exceeds expected marginal cost. It would not continue to reduce price and increase output if expected marginal revenue is less than expected marginal cost.

The problem is, of course, accurately forecasting marginal revenue and marginal cost, i.e., how to form accurate expectations. Any change in price and output by one firm will have a noticeable effect upon the sales of other firms. These rival firms may react by changing *their* prices and levels of output. Or, it is possible they may not react at all. In any case, the firm making the price and output decision must take into consideration these potential changes by rivals, because any price changes by rival firms would be expected to shift the firm's original demand curve and therefore its marginal revenue curve.

This differs from the cases of monopoly and monopolistic competition. Firms in those two types of markets can change price and output under the assumption that their demand and marginal revenue functions will remain constant. Oligopolists cannot make changes under the same assumption. There is a good chance that these curves will not stay put for very long.

So there is the problem. The oligopolist equates marginal revenue to marginal cost, but must consider what will happen to demand when rivals react to the change. In making price and output decisions, the oligopolist's expectations about the reaction of other firms generally depend upon several factors. The more important of these are the nature of the industry, the way rivals have reacted to past changes, the market share of the firm, and the type of product sold. Thus we have no general theory of oligopoly. Instead we have a large number of *ad hoc* analyses of specific industries and their pricing policies—which make up the subject matter of one or more entire courses in economics.

Price rigidity under oligopoly

Some economists have argued that the very nature of the oligopoly problem—the expected reaction of rivals—causes oligopoly markets to be characterized by a great deal of price rigidity. That is, prices under oligopoly would not be very responsive to changes in demand or cost conditions.

Many theories have been set forth to explain why prices are supposedly inflexible in an oligopoly market structure. The most frequently cited hypothesis took the following form: If one oligopolist increases its price, competing oligopolists will hold their prices constant; so, the oligopolistic firm that raises its prices will lose considerable sales to rivals. On the other hand, if one oligopolist lowers its price, the rival firms, fearing substantial losses in sales, will also lower their prices. Thus, the oligopolist that lowers the price will experience only an insignificant increase in sales, because of the price competition.

If the preceding hypothesis is true, oligopolists would have little motivation to change prices. Thus oligopoly is supposedly not as adaptable as other market structures, since prices are rigid. This theory is supposed to explain why oligopoly markets are characterized by ''sticky'' prices, but of course it cannot explain why price is where it is in the first place. It must, therefore, be regarded as an (ex post) rationalization of market behavior rather than an (ex ante) explanation of market behavior.

Nonprice competition in oligopoly markets

Although the preceding discussion indicates that there is a certain amount of debate among economists as to the amount of price competition in industries characterized by oligopoly, most would agree that oligopoly is characterized by considerable nonprice competition, particularly when the product is differentiated. The alternative forms of nonprice competition are as diverse as the minds of inventive managers can make them. Yet there is one central feature: an oligopoly attempts to attract customers to its own product (and, therefore, away from that of rivals) by some means other than a price differential.

Nonprice competition accordingly involves the differentiation of a product, even when the product is fundamentally homogeneous. The ways of differentiating are diverse, but the two principal methods of nonprice competition are advertising and product quality.

Using advertising and product quality, the firm wishes to increase the demand for its product and make it less elastic. As we know, the firm chooses the amount of advertising and product quality at which the marginal cost of advertising (quality) equals the marginal revenue from increased advertising (quality). The oligopolist then allocates its advertising budget so that the marginal revenue per dollar spent is the same for all media.

These choices, however, are not as simple for oligopolists as for firms in a monopolistically competitive market. The problem is the same as we have for price and quantity choices: Any one firm's change in its advertising or quality will have a noticeable effect on the sales of other firms, and these rivals would be expected to react by changing their own advertising or quality. Thus each firm has to take into account the reaction of other firms when making its decisions. As was the case for price, this interdependence complicates the decision considerably.

In the case of advertising, oligopolistic interdependence has an additional complicating effect. It can lead to excessive—greater than the optimal—amounts of advertising. In such cases, it would be possible that sellers in an oligopolistic market could increase their profits if they could cooperate and reduce the amount of advertising done by each. Advertising is, in certain cases, excessive (to advertisers) because it is frequently a defensive measure taken to counteract the advertising of rival firms.

How rivalry leads to unprofitable amounts of advertising can be illustrated by a model known as "the prisoner's dilemma." The model is best described by the story for which it is named. Suppose a crime is committed and two suspects are apprehended and questioned by the police. Unknown to the suspects, the police do not have enough evidence to convict the suspects without at least one of them confessing. So the police separate them and make each one an offer known to the other. The offer is, if one suspect confesses to the crime and turns state's evidence, the one who confesses receives only a 2-year sentence, while the other (who does not confess) gets 10 years. If both prisoners confess, each receives a 2-year sentence. If neither confesses, the probability is very high both will go free. Thus, each prisoner could receive 2 years, 10 years, or go free, depending upon what the other does.

Figure 18.1 shows the four possibilities. The upper-left and lower-right cells show the results if both, respectively, do not confess or confess. The upper-right and lower-left cells show the consequences if one confesses and the other does not.

The problem is that the suspects cannot collude. If they could, it is clear that neither would confess. However, they must make their decisions independently. If either suspect pleads innocent, he stands a chance of 10 years in

Figure 18.1
The prisoner's dilemma

		Suspect 1	
		Does not confess	*Confesses*
Suspect 2	*Does not confess*	A 1: 0 years 2: 0 years	B 1: 2 years 2: 10 years
	Confesses	C 1: 10 years 2: 2 years	D 1: 2 years 2: 2 years

prison if the other confesses. However, the worst that could happen if a suspect confesses to the crime is two years imprisonment regardless of what the other does.

Whether or not the crime was committed by these suspects, the less each knows about the other, the more likely he or she will confess to the crime. In other words, the less information these accused felons possess about each other, the less certainty they have about going free—settling in cell A. Each wants to avoid cells B and C. Each can get two years in prison with certainty by confessing. Thus, the safest tactic is for both to confess, and they end up in cell D.

Oligopolists are often caught in a similar dilemma in the case of nonprice competition—particularly with advertising. Suppose there are only two choices: spend a small amount of money on advertising or spend a lot. If all firms are spending a small amount on advertising, a single firm could increase its profits at the expense of the other firms if it increased its advertising while the others do not. Conversely, if any firm does little or no advertising while the other firms advertise heavily, that firm loses a substantial share of the market. However, as in many imperfectly competitive markets, the total amount of advertising by all firms has little effect on total sales in the market. That is, market demand is relatively inelastic with respect to advertising.

To illustrate this situation, let's assume that there are only two rival firms. As with the prisoner's dilemma, each firm has two choices; so, there are four possible outcomes for the rival firms. We have provided a hypothetical example in Figure 18.2. In cells A through D of Figure 18.2, the profitability (π) of each outcome is shown for the firms. If both firms have low advertising budgets, profits are \$100 for each firm. But you can see that there is a big temptation for one firm to increase its advertising relative to that of the rival. If only one firm switches to high advertising expenditures, its profits jump to \$150, largely because it attracts business away from the firm with a low advertising budget—whose profits fall to \$60. (Note that, to a small extent, total market profits also rise because the total market expands as a result of more total advertising.) However, neither outcome B nor C is equilibrium.

Figure 18.2
The advertiser's dilemma

		Firm 1	
		Low expenditures	*High expenditures*
Firm 2	*Low expenditures*	A π_1: 100 π_2: 100	B π_1: 150 π_2: 60
	High expenditures	C π_1: 60 π_2: 150	D π_1: 80 π_2: 80

The low advertiser can at least raise profits to $80 by matching its rival's high advertising budget. In the long run, both firms end up with high advertising expenditures—and lower profits. From each seller's perspective, there is too much advertising.

Once a firm decides to increase advertising, it is very difficult to avoid cell D in Figure 18.2. And it is quite unlikely that, without an explicit agreement, firms will return to cell A. The uncertainty inherent in an oligopoly market will result in lower profits than might otherwise be earned.

APPLICATION

The ban on broadcast advertising of cigarettes

Oligopoly interdependence was clearly demonstrated by James L. Hamilton when he examined the degree to which cigarette smoking in the United States was affected by the Congressional ban on TV and radio advertising of cigarettes.* In order to examine statistically the demand for cigarettes, he estimated the effect on cigarette consumption of (1) per capita income, (2) a cigarette price index, (3) advertising expenditures, and (4) several variables representing the cigarette health scare. It was shown that cigarette advertising expenditures—both per capita and aggregate—had very little, if any, effect on total cigarette consumption.

Why would cigarette manufacturers advertise at all if advertising does not affect sales significantly? This is a case of the prisoner's dilemma—or advertiser's dilemma—that we noted. Any one firm that stopped advertising would experience a substantial loss in sales to the other firms. On the other hand, all firms together could increase or decrease total advertising without much change in total sales. While total cigarette consumption may not be significantly affected by advertising, the sales of any one manufacturer are strongly related to its own advertising.

Quite possibly the ban on TV and radio cigarette advertising increased profits for most of the established firms. The firms' expenses fell while total sales dropped very little—total cost declined substantially but total revenue was almost unchanged.

Indeed, Hamilton pointed out that cigarette advertising fell 20 to 30 percent in 1971 while per capita consumption increased noticeably after being sluggish for several years. The statistics seem to suggest that the ban increased consumption above the level that would have existed with both broadcast cigarette advertising and subsidized health scare advertising. Furthermore, the ban seemed to strengthen the existing manufacturers, since the easiest way for a new company to enter the market had been through large-scale broadcast advertising.

---

*James L. Hamilton, "The Demand for Cigarettes: Advertising, the Health Scare, and the Cigarette Advertising Ban," *The Review of Economics and Statistics,* November 1972, pp. 401–11.

As we noted, oligopolists also can use changes in product quality as a means of nonprice competition—i.e., to differentiate their product from those of rival firms. The product quality change may be real or perceived. In either case, such decisions are made employing the same process as that used in the case of advertising—evaluating marginal revenue and marginal cost.

As was true for advertising, the firm must take into consideration the reaction of its rivals to any quality changes. Thus, quality changes that will be noticed by consumers but cannot be quickly copied by rivals are frequently attempted. A wine that is aged longer to give it a better taste, a few added inches between seats on an airplane, or fewer defective parts in a large shipment of equipment are quality changes not easily copied by rivals.

Product-quality competition is particularly intense in service oligopolies, where product quality is difficult to judge. Doctors and dentists, for instance, do not usually compete via the prices they charge patients, but the quality of their services and the waiting time in their offices vary a great deal.

The annual style change made by manufacturers of consumer durables is another method of product quality competition. We see such changes in automobiles, household appliances, TVs, stereos, and sporting goods. Until the new models are put on the market, these style changes are closely guarded secrets. If other firms do not know what the new model is going to look like, it may take a year or more for the rivals to copy. (If, in fact, the style change is successful.)

We could go on with many other examples, but we are sure you have seen our point. The types of quality competition are practically as numerous as the oligopolistic industries themselves.

18.3 PRICE AND OUTPUT UNDER COOPERATING OLIGOPOLY

Thus far, we have discussed oligopoly behavior under the assumption that rival firms do not cooperate or collude. But we know that firms can and do reach agreements—cooperate—to raise prices. And, in such cases, the effect is to increase all firms' profits whereas any one firm, acting alone, would lose a considerable amount of its sales if it raised price when its rivals kept their prices low. Such a situation is shown in Figure 18.3.

In this figure an oligopolist is charging a price p_0 and selling x_0. DD is the firm's demand when all rivals hold their prices constant. Let the oligopolist increase its price to p_1, while all other firms hold their prices constant. The firm's sales fall to x_2. The firm loses a great part of its sales to rivals.

But, let all the rivals increase their prices by the same amount. With the price of all rival firms higher, we would expect the demand of this firm to be much less elastic—other products are not as good substitutes at the higher prices. The relevant demand segment under this assumption is dA. Now when the firm increases its price to p_1, sales fall only to x_1.

Figure 18.3
Quantity responses from a price increase

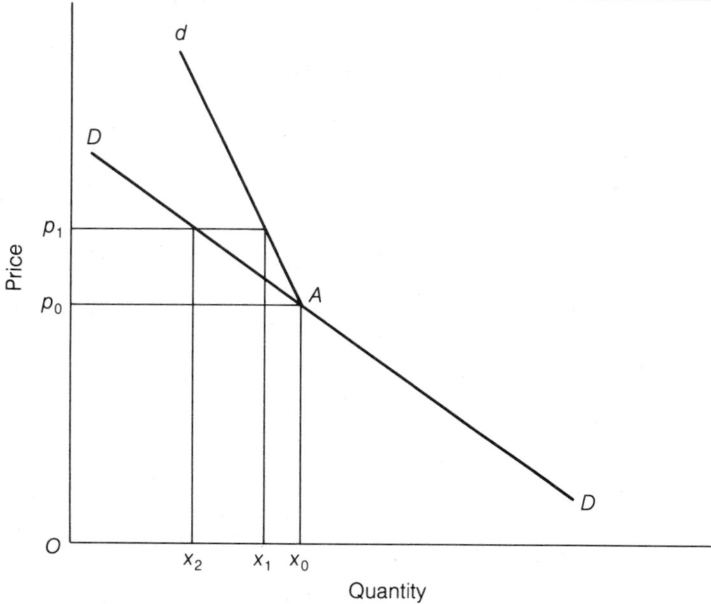

Thus it is possible for all firms to make themselves better off by cooperative agreements. Such agreements are called collusive agreements. The most extreme form of collusion is called a *cartel.*

Cartel profit maximization

A cartel is a combination of firms whose objective is to limit the competitive forces within a market. It may take the form of open collusion, with the member firms entering into contracts about price and other market variables. Or, the cartel may involve secret collusion among members with no explicit contract. Or it can operate like a trade association or a professional organization. At this time, the most famous cartel is OPEC (The Organization of Petroleum Exporting Countries), an "association" of the major oil-producing nations.

Let's consider an *ideal* cartel. Suppose a group of firms producing a homogeneous commodity forms a cartel. A central management body is appointed, its function being to determine the uniform cartel price. The task, in theory, is relatively simple, as illustrated in Figure 18.4. Market demand for the homogeneous commodity is given by DD', so marginal revenue is given by the dashed line MR. The marginal cost curve for the cartel must be determined by the management body. If all firms in the cartel purchase their inputs in per-

Figure 18.4
Cartel profit maximization

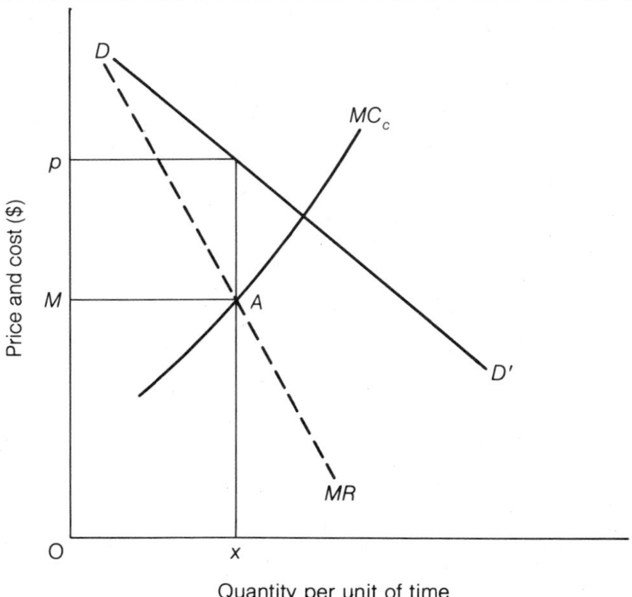

fectly competitive markets, the cartel marginal cost curve (MC_c) is simply the horizontal sum of the marginal cost curves of the member firms. Otherwise, allowance must be made for the increase in input price accompanying an increase in input usage; MC_c will be more inelastic than would be the case if all input markets were perfectly competitive. (Recall the discussion of short-run supply in Chapter 13.)

In either case, once the management group determines the cartel marginal cost curve (MC_c), the problem is the simple one of determining the price that maximizes cartel profit—the monopoly price. In Figure 18.4 marginal cost and marginal revenue intersect at A. This gives the level of output, x, and the price, p, that maximize total profit for the cartel.

Once the profit-maximizing price and total sales are determined, the problem confronting cartel management is how to allocate the total sales among the member firms. Two fundamental methods of allocation are possible: market sharing (or quotas) and nonprice competition.

There are several possible variants of market sharing or quotas. Indeed there is no uniform principle by which quotas can be determined. In practice, the bargaining ability of a firm and the importance of the firm to the cartel are likely to be extremely important elements in determining a quota. However, one method of allocating the market is to use either the relative sales of each firm in some pre-cartel period or the "productive capacity" of the firm as a basis for allocating shares of the cartel sales. As a practical matter, the choice of which pre-cartel period or what measure of capacity to use is a matter of bargaining among the members. The most skillful bargainer is likely to come out best.

Another method of market sharing is geographical division of the market. Some of the more dramatic illustrations involve international markets. For example, an agreement between DuPont and Imperial Chemicals divided the market for certain products so that DuPont had exclusive sales rights in North and Central America (except for British possessions) and Imperial had exclusive rights in the British Empire and Egypt. Another example is an agreement between the American company Rohm and Haas and its German counterpart Roehm und Haas. The former was given exclusive rights in the Americas, Australia, New Zealand, and Japan; the latter was given Europe and Asia (except for Japan).

APPLICATION

A case of market sharing*

The market for steam turbine generators in the United States is extremely concentrated, composed primarily of two producers—General Electric and Westinghouse. From 1951 to 1959, this industry was characterized by a cartel. This cartel was eliminated in 1959. However, there exists evidence of tacit collusion, at least in the period 1963–72.

Let's first look at prices over this period. In Table 18.1 the quoted prices of comparable generators are presented. There is, to say the least, a remarkable degree of consistency. It would appear, at the very least, that the firms were following some common course of conduct.

Table 18.1
Prices of comparable generators, 1963–1971

	Quoted price ($000)	
Date	*General Electric*	*Westinghouse*
May 1963	$10,722	$10,722
January 1964	11,286	11,286
June 1964	11,004	11,851
November 1964	11,817	11,817
July 1966	12,566	12,566
October 1966	13,306	13,306
May 1967	14,245	14,245
August 1968	14,858	14,858
June 1969	15,733	15,733
February 1970	16,659	16,659
December 1970	17,584	17,584
August 1971	18,201	18,201

Table 18.2
Relative shares, 1963–1972

	General Electric	*Westinghouse*
1963–64	55%	45%
1964–65	67	33
1965–66	56	44
1966–67	56	44
1967–68	61	39
1968–69	55	45
1969–70	59	41
1970–71	64	36
1971–72	60	40

Given this agreement on price, it would then be necessary for the firms to agree on the manner in which output will be allocated. As we have described, allocation of a market could be accomplished through either nonprice competition or some form of market sharing. In the instance of steam turbine generators, the firms apparently resorted to some sort of market sharing. The relative shares of the two firms (eliminating all others) are presented in Table 18.2. While the shares are not constant, there does not appear to be any evidence of a significant shift in favor of one or the other. Thus, it would appear that these firms applied a policy of sharing the market rather than competing on some nonprice basis.

*This application is taken from Bruce T. Allen, "Tacit Collusion and Market Sharing: The Case of Steam Turbine Generators," *Industrial Organization Review,* vol. 4 (1976).

While market sharing or quota agreements may be difficult in practice, some guidelines can be set forth. If the cartel produces a homogeneous product, a reasonable objective for the cartel is to produce the optimal output at the minimum total cost. In this way, total cartel profit is maximized.

Minimum cartel cost is achieved when each firm produces that output for which its marginal cost equals the common cartel marginal cost and marginal revenue. Returning to Figure 18.4, we see that each firm would produce the amount at which its marginal cost is equal to M. Summing to obtain MC_c, total cartel output will be x and total profit is maximized.

To reinforce this conclusion, suppose that two firms in the cartel are producing at different marginal costs; that is, assume

$$MC_1 > MC_2$$

for Firms 1 and 2. In this case the cartel manager could transfer sales from the higher cost Firm 1 to the lower cost Firm 2. So long as the marginal cost of producing in Firm 2 is lower, total cartel cost can be lowered by transferring production. Thus in equilibrium the marginal costs will be equal for all firms.[1] (Not surprisingly, this is precisely the same solution we obtained for the multiplant monopolist in Chapter 17. In this case, the cartel management is acting as the monopoly and is allocating production to the various member firms.)

The difficulty involved with this method of allocation is that, if firms differ in their cost structures, the lower-cost firms obtain the bulk of the market and therefore the bulk of the profits. To make this method of allocation acceptable to all members, a profit sharing system, more or less independent of sales quota, must be devised.

In some cases the member firms will be able to agree upon the share of the market each is to have. This is illustrated in Figure 18.5 for an "ideal" situation. Suppose only two firms are in the market and they decide to divide the market evenly. The market demand curve is DD', so the half-share curve for each firm is Dd. The curve marginal to Dd is the dashed line MR, the half-share marginal revenue for each firm. Suppose each firm has identical costs, represented by SAC and SMC.

With these individual marginal revenue, marginal cost, and demand curves, each firm will decide to produce x units of output, where MR and SMC intersect. A uniform price of p is established on each firm's demand. At p a total output of x_c is supplied (x_c is twice x). This is a tenable solution because the market demand is consistent with the sale of x_c units at a price of p.

To see this, let's go the other way around. Suppose a cartel management group is formed and given the task of maximizing cartel profit. With the demand curve DD', the cartel management views Dd as the marginal revenue curve; i.e., Dd lies halfway between market demand, DD', and the vertical axis. Next, summing the identical marginal cost curves, it obtains cartel marginal cost MC_c. The intersection of cartel marginal cost and cartel marginal revenue occurs at the level F, corresponding to output x_c and price p. Since, this is the same solution arrived at by the identical firms, the firms' decision to share the market equally is consistent with the objective of the cartel.

In this example we have assumed firms with identical cost functions. The solution is more complex when cost conditions differ, as we noted above.

---

[1]Mathematically, we can describe this condition as follows. The cartel attempts to maximize total industry profit

$$\pi_T = P \cdot (Q_1 + Q_2) - C_1(Q_1) - C_2(Q_2)$$

Maximizing with respect to the outputs of the two firms, the first order conditions are

$$\frac{\partial \pi_T}{\partial Q_1} = \frac{\partial P}{\partial Q}(Q_1 + Q_2) + P - \frac{\partial C_1}{\partial Q_1} = MR_T - MC_1 = 0$$

$$\frac{\partial \pi_T}{\partial Q_2} = \frac{\partial P}{\partial Q}(Q_1 + Q_2) + P - \frac{\partial C_2}{\partial Q_2} = MR_T - MC_2 = 0$$

Combining these conditions, it follows that, for maximization of total industry profits,

$$MR_T = MC_1 = MC_2.$$

Figure 18.5
Ideal market sharing

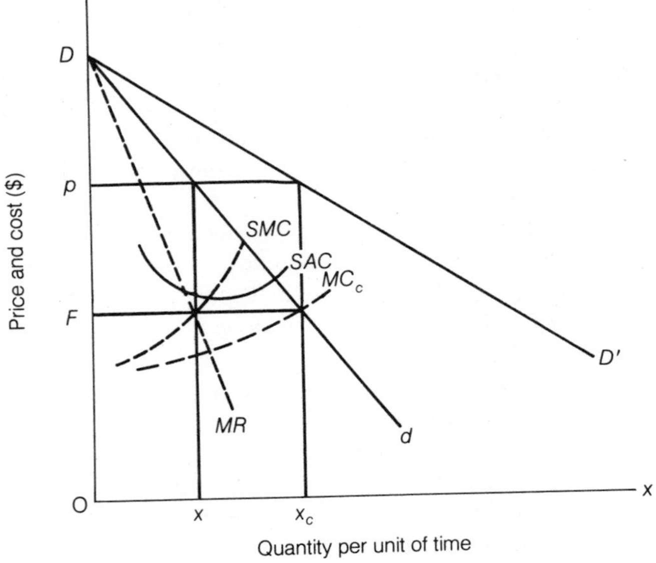

Nonetheless, cartel profit is maximized when total cartel output is chosen so that market marginal revenue equals the horizontal sum of all firms' marginal costs—the cartel's marginal cost curve. Price is determined from the market demand curve at the chosen output. Output is allocated to the firms so that each firm's marginal cost equals market marginal revenue (which is also equal to the cartel's marginal cost) at the chosen level of output.

Ideal situations like the one described above are rare. More likely, cost conditions will differ among firms. Yet another problem arises when firms produce a differentiated product. In such cases a cartel frequently allocates sales through nonprice competition. This type of allocation is frequently associated with "loose" cartels.

In such cases, a uniform price is fixed and each firm is allowed to sell all it can at that price. The only requirement is that firms do not reduce price below the cartel price. There are many examples of this type of cartel organization in the United States today. For instance, in most localities both medical doctors and lawyers have associations whose code of ethics is frequently the basis of price agreement. The patient market, for example, is divided among the various doctors on the basis of nonprice competition: each patient selects the doctor of his or her choice. Similarly, the generally uniform prices of haircuts, major brands of gasoline, and movie tickets do not result from perfect competition within the market. Rather, they result from tacit, and sometimes open, agreement upon a price. The sellers compete with one another in various ways; but not by price variations. This type of cartel arrangement is rather common in the sale of services.

Tacit collusion

A less extreme form of cooperation among oligopoly firms is tacit collusion—agreement without communication. For instance, the producers in a market may restrict their sales to specific geographical regions without meeting and explicitly designating marketing areas on a map. One firm's market area is understood from the ongoing relations it has had with its rivals. As opposed to the formation of a cartel in an attempt to monopolize a market, tacit collusion is not per se (categorically) illegal. However, evidence of agreement would quickly tip the legal balance against accused participants.

Examples consistent with tacit collusion are evident among manufacturers of consumer durables. For instance, oligopolists will often act together (cooperatively) by changing their models annually at the same time. Washing machines, refrigerators, cooking ranges, and lawn mowers have annual model changes that are announced by manufacturers at nearly the same time. Without any known agreement, there is a surprising amount of uniformity in such behavior. The same holds true for fashions, i.e., when spring and fall designs are announced. Why do makers of soft drinks and beer all use the same size cans and bottles (or makers of breakfast cereal package their product in the same size boxes)? Certainly, all consumers do not have a preference for the 12-ounce size. But, as far as anyone knows, cereal makers and bottlers have no explicit agreement that only certain container sizes are allowable.

Probably the strongest evidence consistent with tacit collusion is found in the prices oligopolists charge. Particularly in the service sector of our economy, there is surprising price uniformity, even though there is a wide variance in the quality of services. For instance, lawyers and real estate agents by and large charge the same prices for their services even though the quality of services varies from lawyer to lawyer and broker to broker. Explicit collusion is illegal in these industries and presumably does not take place, but a substantial amount of price uniformity exists.

How does tacit collusion arise? What makes oligopolists cooperate without an explicit arrangement? The answer lies in the consequences of noncooperation. As we know, each oligopolist realizes that what it does will cause its rivals to react. The expected reaction is likely to leave sellers no better off than they were before the move. Oligopolists know that they are related to rivals in what we referred to earlier as the prisoner's dilemma. A new style or a lower price may increase profits in the short run, but may reduce profits in the long run.

Thus, whether or not an oligopolist makes a change depends upon the relative expected costs and benefits of making the change. Profits may increase substantially at first as a result of a change, but decrease after rivals react. How quickly rivals react in large measure determines how profitable a change will be. Moreover, since each oligopolist knows that its rivals may have the same motivation to make a change, there is the temptation to move first.

In many cases ''patterns of behavior'' are established among rivals. Oligopolists cooperate because, given the expected reaction of rivals to one firm's attempt to raise profits, long-run profits are more likely maximized by stable behavior. This is particularly true because other behavior in the long run will raise the costs to producers, and revenues are not likely to go up after rivals have adjusted.

THE WALL STREET JOURNAL

APPLICATION

Tacit collusion in the airline industry

In an application in Chapter 10 we described the reaction of the airlines to the deregulation that took place in 1979. Recall that after deregulation the airlines first introduced fare reductions aimed primarily at vacation travelers. Because the demand for vacation travel was relatively elastic, revenues increased for a short time. But, because of the pressure from new lines, the major carriers began to cut ticket prices in general. Most of the previous restrictions were removed. But this time the demand for air travel as a whole proved to be rather inelastic. Revenues decreased sharply. Because of the reduced revenues and increased competition from new carriers, many airlines began making staggering losses in 1982 and the first half of 1983.

The airline executives recognized the problem and began raising fares and eliminating special fares like Super Savers. By October 1983, fares had risen to their highest level in two and a half years. Profits therefore improved for most airlines.

Nonetheless, by December 1983, there was growing pressure in the industry for another fare war. This time, however, the airlines seemed to have learned their lesson.

William M. Carley discussed the situation facing the airlines in *The Wall Street Journal*.* Carley pointed out that while other airlines were increasing their ticket prices, Continental Airlines was reducing their fares substantially. After filing bankruptcy proceedings in September 1983, Continental had been able to cut salaries by 50 percent. And, even in the face of a strike by pilots and machinists, Continental was able to keep 54 of its 106 jets flying. Thus Continental Airlines was in a good position to cut fares. Continental and many of the new, smaller lines had much lower costs than the major carriers.

According to Carley, many airline executives were arguing for matching fares. In fact, a few major carriers—Pan American, Eastern, and Delta—did drop their ticket prices on a few routes. But, the reductions were temporary and only for very limited flights. In general, most of the major airlines were resisting fare reductions and, in some cases, actually increased fares slightly. They recognized that their individual demand curves were not very elastic.

They realized that their price cuts would be matched by other carriers. Consequently a fare reduction would not increase anyone's share of the market. Everyone would be worse off.

To see the situation look at Figure 18.6. Suppose that one firm is selling x_0 units at a price of p_0. Now let the firm drop its price to p_1. If DD' is the demand curve when everything remains the same—that is, if rival firms do not match the price reduction—this firm's sales increase to x_2, a substantial expansion. But competitors would not be expected to hold their prices constant in the face of such a loss in their sales. After all, the huge increase in the sales of the firm that first lowered its price must have, in large part, come at the expense of the rivals. Thus the rival firms would have every incentive to lower their prices also and "everything else" does not remain constant for the firm that originally lowered its price.

In this case, DD' cannot be the firm's demand. When one firm lowers its price other firms will follow the price decrease. In Figure 18.6 the firm's rivals match its price cuts. In this case the firm's demand is the much steeper curve, Dd. With demand curve Dd, when the firm decreases price from p_0 to p_1 its sales increase only from x_0 to x_1, a significantly smaller expansion.

The airlines realized that they were in a prisoner's dilemma. All of the major airline executives quoted by Mr. Carley recognized that if a few of the major carriers matched Continental's fares on a large-scale basis, a severe price war would result and all would make losses. In effect, they realized that the demand for flights on each of their lines would be affected by changes in

Figure 18.6
Two demand curves

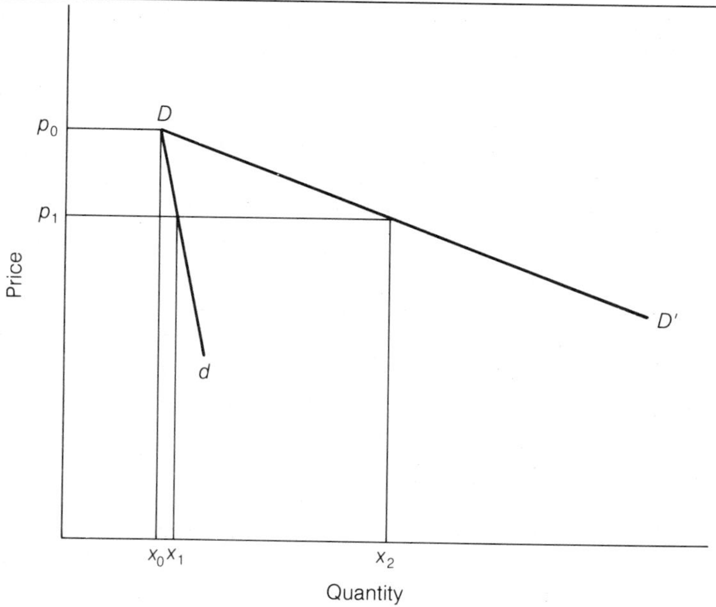

the prices charged by other carriers. At the time the article was written, the major airlines had resisted the temptation to cut fares in order to regain the revenues lost to Continental and the regional carriers.

But the article concluded by noting that the planned increase in capacity by United and American could well trigger a price cut if those airlines found themselves with excess capacity. As Carley stated, ''With all that added capacity, the temptation to cut fares will be strong. And fare cuts, says an industry executive, are like measles: They spread rapidly.''

So it appears that after the disastrous fare wars of 1982 through mid-1983 the airlines entered a period of tacit collusion, even though Continental and a few of the smaller carriers did cut ticket prices substantially. But, the major carriers were able to resist the temptation to slash prices in response, because the fare cutters were not large enough to have a significant impact upon their business. At the time, however, it remained to be seen whether the major carriers, faced with the excess capacity caused by the expansion of American and United, would be caught once again in the prisoner's dilemma and begin reducing fares, to the detriment of all (that is, all except the passengers who would enjoy the reduced fares).

---

*''Airlines Resist Mounting Pressure to Resume Disastrous Fare Wars,'' December 23, 1982. Reprinted by permission of *The Wall Street Journal*.

Price leadership

Another cooperative solution to the oligopoly problem is price leadership. This solution does not require open collusion, but the firms in the market must tacitly agree to the solution. Price leadership has been quite common in certain industries. It was characteristic of the steel industry some time ago. At times it has characterized the tire, oil, and cigarette industries.

Any firm in an oligopoly market can be the price leader. While it is frequently the dominant firm in the market, it may be simply the firm with a reputation for good judgment. There could exist a situation in which the most efficient—the least cost—firm is the price leader, even though this firm is not the largest. In any case, the price leader sets a price that will maximize industry profits; and all firms in the industry compete for sales through advertising and other types of marketing. The price remains constant until the price leader changes the price, or one or more other firms break away.

Possibly the simplest form of price leadership is ''barometric'' price leadership. In this case the price leader is a firm with a reputation for good decision making. (In reality, most price leaders have been one of the larger firms.) The price leader acts as a barometer for prevailing market conditions and sets the price so as to maximize profits under these conditions. For example, if consumers' incomes increase (and the commodity in question is normal), the price leader would note an increase in demand and would respond by raising price. If all of the other firms in the industry follow with price increases, the result will be that the industry moves to a new position of equilibrium with a minimum of interfirm competition. It is important to note that, in this case, the price leader has no power to coerce the other firms into following its lead. Instead, the rival firms will follow this lead only so long as they believe that the price leader's behavior accurately and promptly reflects changes in market conditions.

A much more structured form of price leadership is *dominant firm* price leadership. In this case, there is one firm in the oligopoly market that has the capability of becoming a monopoly. Hence the market is composed of one dominant firm and numerous small ones.

The dominant firm could possibly eliminate all its rivals by a price war. But in addition to being costly, this would establish the firm as a monopoly, with its attendant legal problems. Possibly a more desirable course of action for the dominant firm is to become the price leader and set the market price so as to maximize its own profit, at the same time letting the small firms sell all they wish at that price. Note that, given the size of the dominant firm, in this type of price leadership the price leader—the dominant firm—does have the ability to enforce the price it sets. It does not have to rely on its reputation or the trust of the smaller firms. The small firms, recognizing their position, will behave as do perfectly competitive firms. That is, they will regard their demand curve as a horizontal line at the price set by the dominant firm and sell that amount for which marginal cost equals price. Notice, however, that this does not necessarily entail the long-run, zero-profit solution for the smaller firms, because the dominant firm may set price above (minimum) average cost.

There are many variations of dominant firm price leadership. One may allow for the existence of two or more dominant firms, for product differentiation, for geographically separated sellers, for transportation costs, and so on. In all cases, however, the dominant firm is allowed to set price, since it controls such a large share of the market.

18.4 CONCLUDING REMARKS

As we have tried to demonstrate, while the oligopoly market structure is perhaps more "realistic" than perfect competition or monopoly (or monopolistic competition), this increase in realism cannot be gained without a cost. The increased complexity of the firm's decisions in an oligopoly market effectively precludes straightforward solutions.

We have emphasized that the primary feature differentiating oligopoly from the other market structures is that the *firms recognize their mutual interdependence*. In contrast to the other market structures, it is not sufficient for a firm in an oligopoly market to make its output and pricing decisions on the basis of its own demand and cost conditions. In addition, an oligopolist must consider the potential reactions of its rivals. In this chapter we discussed some possible ways in which the oligopoly firms could resolve this difficulty. However, as you have seen, the determination of the profit-maximizing levels of output and/or price for a specific firm becomes extremely difficult. (Furthermore, as we have shown, oligopolistic firms would be expected to compete frequently with one another on a nonprice basis.)

The important point then is that, for the oligopoly market structure, we are unable to provide a simple profit-maximization rule of the type presented in Chapters 13 and 15. In the oligopoly market, the answer to the question of the profit-maximizing levels of output and price is: "It depends." In the cases of perfect competition and monopoly we could show you the forest. In our discussion of the oligopoly market, the best we have been able to do is to bump into several of the trees.

TECHNICAL PROBLEMS

1. Compare and contrast oligopoly with perfect competition, pure monopoly, and monopolistic competition. What is the principal distinguishing characteristic of oligopolies?

2. What types of barriers to entry might permit a profitable oligopoly to last a long time?

3. What forms of nonprice competition might exist in an oligopoly market?

4. At one time, the Federal Trade Commission was being urged to eliminate ads directed toward children. Of particular concern to the proponents of this proposal were the TV ads for breakfast cereals. While there are obviously many brands of breakfast cereals, there are relatively few firms in this market.

a. How responsive would you expect *total* consumption of breakfast cereal to be to changes in *total* advertising by the industry?

b. How responsive would consumption of an *individual* brand of cereal be to changes in the level of advertising *for that brand?*

c. Given your answers to *a* and *b* above, would you expect advertising in this market to be at its optimal level? Why?

d. What would you expect would be the effect on the industry of a total ban on the advertising of breakfast cereals on TV?

5. Consider the bituminous coal industry to be a competitive industry in long-run equilibrium. Suppose that the firms in the industry were able to form a cartel.

a. What will happen to the equilibrium output and price of coal? Why?

b. How might the output be allocated among the individual firms?

c. After the cartel is operating, are there incentives for the individual firms to cheat? Why (or why not)?

6. What is "tacit collusion"? How would the behavior of the firms differ from that of members of a cartel? Why would tacit collusion exist?

7. Contrast barometric price leadership and dominant firm price leadership.
8. What is the basic difference between noncooperating and cooperating oligopoly?
9. Would you expect the competitive strategies of oligopolists who produce a homogeneous product to differ from the strategies of oligopolists producing a differentiated product? Explain.
10. Why would you expect prices might be more rigid (exhibit less fluctuation) in an oligopoly market than in a monopoly or competitive market?

ANALYTICAL PROBLEMS

1. Suppose you were attempting to establish a price-fixing cartel in an industry.
   a. Would you prefer many or few firms? Why?
   b. How could you prevent cheating (price cutting) by cartel members? Why would members have an incentive to cheat?
   c. Would you keep substantial or very few records? What are the advantages and disadvantages of each?
   d. How could you prevent entry into the industry?
   e. How could government help you prevent entry and even cheating?
   f. How would you try to talk government into helping? Under what conditions might this work?
2. In an Application, we cited the behavior of General Electric and Westinghouse as a possible case of collusive market sharing. Could this behavior be instead a case of price leadership? Explain.
3. During the "energy crisis" of the 1970s, many people accused the "big three" automobile manufacturers of deliberately withholding small, fuel-efficient automobiles and forcing large "gas guzzlers" on the consumers, when there was in fact a demand for fuel-efficient cars. Suppose that there was some demand for these small cars, and suppose also (as was probably the case) that the large manufacturers did have plans to make these cars and could have manufactured them. Use your knowledge of oligopolistic interdependence to explain why it took a relatively long time for the big three to introduce the fuel-efficient cars. What would Ford and Chrysler have had to do if GM introduced these automobiles? How would each firm's determination of the size of the market for such cars affect the decision?
4. Many economists argue that more research, development, and innovation occurs in the oligopolistic market structure than in any other. Why might this conclusion be true?
5. In the application concerning tacit collusion in the airline industry, we noted that many observers expected the greatly expanded capacity of

American and United to bring about another price war. Why would they expect this to occur?

6. In the absence of long-run economies of scale, what conditions would cause an oligopoly structure to evolve and be maintained over a long period of time?

SELECTED ADDITIONAL REFERENCES

Greer, D. F. *Industrial Organization and Public Policy*. New York: Macmillan, 1980.

Koch, J. V. *Industrial Organization and Prices*. Englewood Cliffs, N.J.: Prentice-Hall, 1980.

Scherer, F. M. *Industrial Market Structure and Economic Performance*. Chicago: Rand McNally, 1980.

Stigler, G. J. *The Organization of Industry*. Homewood, Ill.: Richard D. Irwin, 1968.

Part 6

The firm over time

19

Decision making over time

Until now we have set forth economic theories and analyzed managerial decision making within the context of single-period models. Certainly this type of analysis is of great importance, but we know that many decisions involve longer periods of time. Thus we need additional tools to analyze decision making when more than one period is involved. In this chapter we will add a time dimension.

Decisions made now can have an effect in the future. Such decisions often involve investments or purchases that yield a stream of future income (or require a stream of future payments). When considering an investment, a firm must evaluate the stream of future returns from the investment and compare it to the current dollar price of the investment. A consumer makes the same type of decision when considering the purchase of a durable good—for example, an automobile or appliance. The consumer compares the price of the good with the value of the future stream of services.

As we shall show, the rate of interest is a crucial element in decisions that involve a time dimension. This dependence is easy to understand when we note that the opportunity cost of spending now is the interest that could have been earned had the money not been spent now but invested at the prevailing interest rate. Interest is forgone when income is spent rather than saved. Thus higher interest rates raise the opportunity cost of purchasing something now.

This chapter sets forth the simple but powerful theory necessary to analyze multiperiod decision making. We first discuss the role of interest rates by introducing the concepts of future and present value. We then use these concepts to examine some examples of multiperiod decision making. The tools of this chapter are essential to an understanding of the theory of investment, the topic of the next chapter.

19.1 FUTURE VALUE AND PRESENT VALUE

To introduce the role played by interest rates in making multiperiod decisions, we begin by considering the rate at which a monetary asset appreciates in value over time. This appreciation determines the future value of an asset.

Future value

Suppose you have \$100 today and the interest rate is 12 percent. If you invest the \$100 at 12 percent interest, you would have in one year

$$\$100 + .12(\$100) = \$100(1.12) = \$112$$

Thus the future value of \$100 in one year is \$112. Obviously if the interest rate is higher than 12 percent the future value is higher. If you kept the investment for two years, the future value would be

$$\$112 + .12(112) = \$112(1.12) = \$125.44$$

since you had \$112 at the end of one year and invested this amount at 12 percent. We can rewrite this expression for future value as

$$(1 + .12)\$112 = (1 + .12)(1 + .12)\$100 = (1 + .12)^2\$100 = \$125.44$$

Similarly, the future value of the investment in three years is

$$(1 + .12)[(1 + .12)^2\$100] = (1 + .12)^3\$100$$

More generally, in n years the value of the investment would be

$$(1 + .12)^n\$100$$

Generalizing further, the future value of investing \$$A$ at an interest rate r for n years is

$$FV = A(1 + r)^n$$

Figure 19.1 shows a comparison of future values over a 25-year-period for four different rates of interest. It is easily seen that the future values increasingly diverge for higher interest rates as the time period becomes longer.

We can use the concept of future value to analyze again the cost of holding an asset, a point we first discussed in Chapter 3. For simplicity, assume that someone owns a sterile asset (i.e., ownership yields absolutely no utility to the owner). But the asset is expected to appreciate in value. Examples might be a bar of gold, a ton of coal, or a case of fine wine.[1]

[1]Examples of nonsterile assets, assets that give utility to the owner while appreciating in value, might be paintings or antique furniture.

Figure 19.1
Future values at different rates of interest

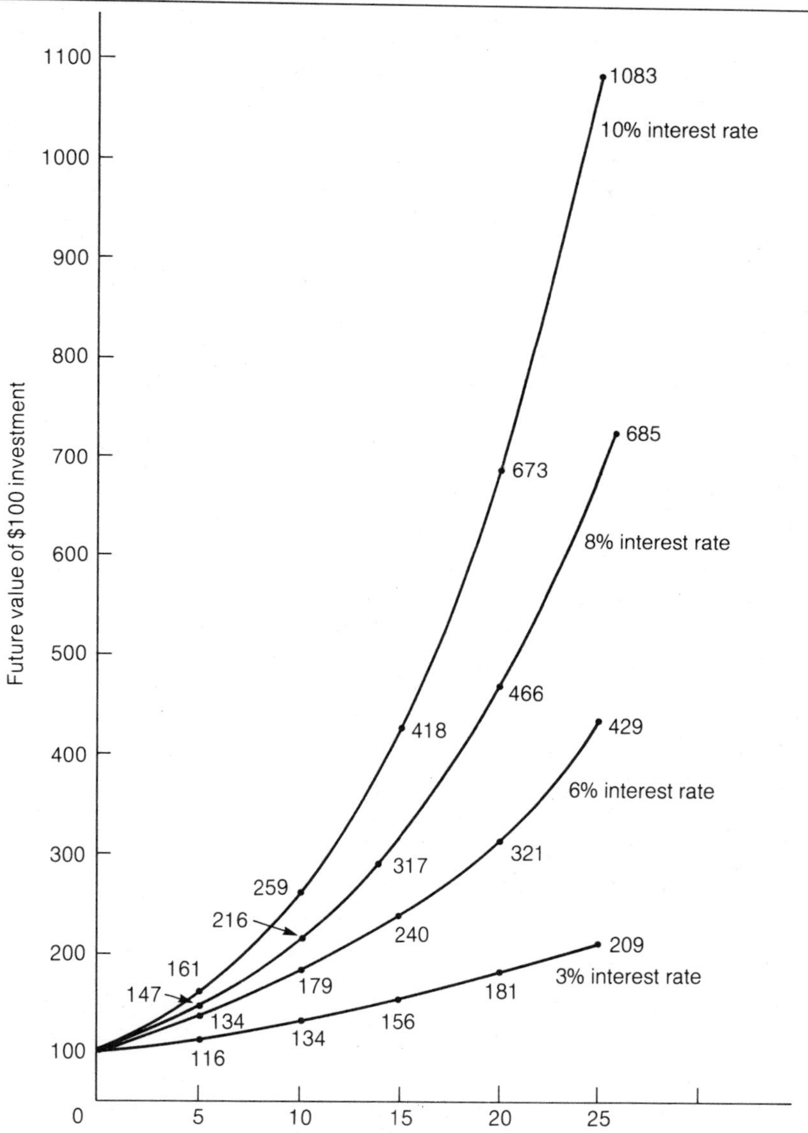

The question is: Should the owner keep the asset and sell it later or sell it now? The answer depends upon the future value of the asset. (For simplicity we assume that the asset costs nothing to store.)

Suppose the asset could be sold now for $10,000 or could be held for one year and sold for $11,000, an appreciation rate of 10 percent. As we know from Chapter 3, if the interest rate is above 10 percent, the asset should be sold. For example, if the interest rate is 12 percent, the owner could sell the asset now, invest the $10,000 at 12 percent, and have $11,200 at the end of the year. The owner would be $200 better off than if he or she had held the asset. The opportunity cost of holding the asset is the potential $1200 that could be earned as interest.

On the other hand, if the interest rate is below 10 percent, the asset should be held. If, for example, the interest rate is 8 percent, the $10,000 would bring only ($10,000)(1.08) = $10,800, which is $200 less than the potential gain from keeping the asset.

Hence, for sterile assets, the rule is: Hold the asset if it is expected to appreciate at a rate greater than the relevant rate of interest. Sell the asset if it is expected to appreciate at a rate less than the rate of interest.

Present value

Now that we have the concept of future value, we can translate future values to present values. To get at the concept of present value, consider how much you would be willing to pay for the right to receive $1,000 one year from now. Clearly, $1,000 one year in the future is worth less to you than $1,000 today. If you had $1,000 now, you could invest it at some rate of interest and have more than $1,000 in one year.

So how much less than $1,000 would you be willing to pay? At a 12 percent rate of interest, if you invest $892.86 now you would receive $1,000 in one year,

$$(1 + .12)\$892.86 = \$1{,}000$$

Thus, you would be willing to pay no more than $892.86 for the right to receive $1,000 one year in the future.

At the same rate of interest—12 percent you would be willing to pay no more than $797.19, for $1,000 that would be received in two years. That is because

$$(1 + .12)^2\$797.19 = \$1{,}000$$

These amounts, $892.86 and $797.19, are the present values of $1,000 in one and two years, respectively. Generalizing, for the right to receive $1,000 n years in the future with an interest rate of 12 percent, a person would be willing to pay no more than the present value (PV), where

$$(1 + .12)^n PV = \$1{,}000$$

or

$$PV = \frac{\$1000}{(1 + .12)^n}$$

Generalizing further, the present value of a return (R) in n years with an interest rate of r is given by

$$PV = \frac{R}{(1 + r)^n}$$

We say that present value is the "discounted value" of a future income payment. As you can see, discounting means dividing the return by $(1 + r)^n$. Thus the concepts of present and future values are linked by the rate of interest.

Let's expand our analysis to consider the present value of a *stream* of future income payments. How much would someone pay for the following stream of income payments (each payment payable at year end)?

Year	*Income*
1	$1500
2	2000
3	2200
4	3000
5	3400

Clearly, no one would pay $12,100, the sum of the yearly incomes. The amount someone will be willing to pay depends on the present value of the income stream. Suppose the relevant rate of interest is 10 percent. Then the present value of this income stream is

$$\begin{aligned} PV &= \frac{\$1{,}500}{(1 + .10)} + \frac{\$2{,}000}{(1 + .10)^2} + \frac{\$2{,}200}{(1 + .10)^3} + \frac{\$3{,}000}{(1 + .10)^4} + \frac{\$3{,}400}{(1 + .10)^5} \\ &= \$1{,}363.64 + \$1{,}652.89 + \$1{,}652.89 + \$2{,}049.18 + \$2{,}111.13 \\ &= \$8{,}829.83 \end{aligned}$$

Generalizing, let R_t be the income in the t-th year and r be the rate of interest. The present value of the stream of income is

$$PV = \frac{R_1}{(1 + r)} + \frac{R_2}{(1 + r)^2} + \frac{R_3}{(1 + r)^3} + \cdots + \frac{R_n}{(1 + r)^n} = \sum_{t=1}^{n} \left(\frac{1}{1 + r}\right)^t R_t$$

■ **Principle.** The future value of investing $A for n years with an interest rate of r is

$$FV = A(1 + r)^n$$

■ **Principle.** The present value of (the maximum amount that would be paid for) a future payment of R in n years is

$$PV = \frac{R}{(1 + r)^n}$$

■ **Principle.** The present value of an income stream is

$$PV = \sum_{t=1}^{n} \frac{R_t}{(1 + r)^t}$$

where R_t is the income to be received in year t.

Note that the more heavily weighted toward the future are the income payments, the lower is the present value of a stream of income. To see this, consider the following two streams of income, both of which sum to $10,000.

Year	*Stream 1*	*Stream 2*
1	$1,000	$4,000
2	2,000	3,000
3	3,000	2,000
4	4,000	1,000

At a 10 percent rate of interest the present value of stream 1 is

$$PV = \frac{\$1{,}000}{(1 + .10)} + \frac{\$2{,}000}{(1 + .10)^2} + \frac{\$3{,}000}{(1 + .10)^3} + \frac{\$4{,}000}{(1 + .10)^4} = \$7{,}547.97$$

The present value of stream 2 with the same rate of interest is

$$PV = \frac{\$4{,}000}{(1 + .10)} + \frac{\$3{,}000}{(1 + .10)^2} + \frac{\$2{,}000}{(1 + .10)^3} + \frac{\$1{,}000}{(1 + .10)^4} = \$8{,}301.34$$

The present value of income stream 2 is almost $1,000 more than that for stream 1, even though the sums of the incomes are equal. The high incomes are closer to the present in stream 2. This means that they are discounted by a lower number than the high incomes in stream 1. For example, in stream 1, the $4,000 income is divided by $(1.1)^4 = 1.464$ while the $4,000 in stream 2 is divided by 1.1. Thus income closer to the present is worth more now than the same income further in the future. Figure 19.2 shows the present value of $100 in years from the present to 25 years at four selected interest rates.

When we speak of "the value of an asset" we generally mean the price that the asset will sell for in the market. In the case of an income-yielding asset, this value is determined by the present value of the stream of income the asset will yield over the relevant time horizon. Unless the asset is expected to yield utility to its owner in addition to the expected income, no one would pay more than its present value for the asset. If the price of the asset is greater than its present value, a prospective purchaser could simply invest the money at the relevant interest rate and derive a net return greater than that which would be expected from purchasing the asset. On the other hand, if the price is lower than the present value, the asset would be expected to yield a net return

Figure 19.2
Present value over time

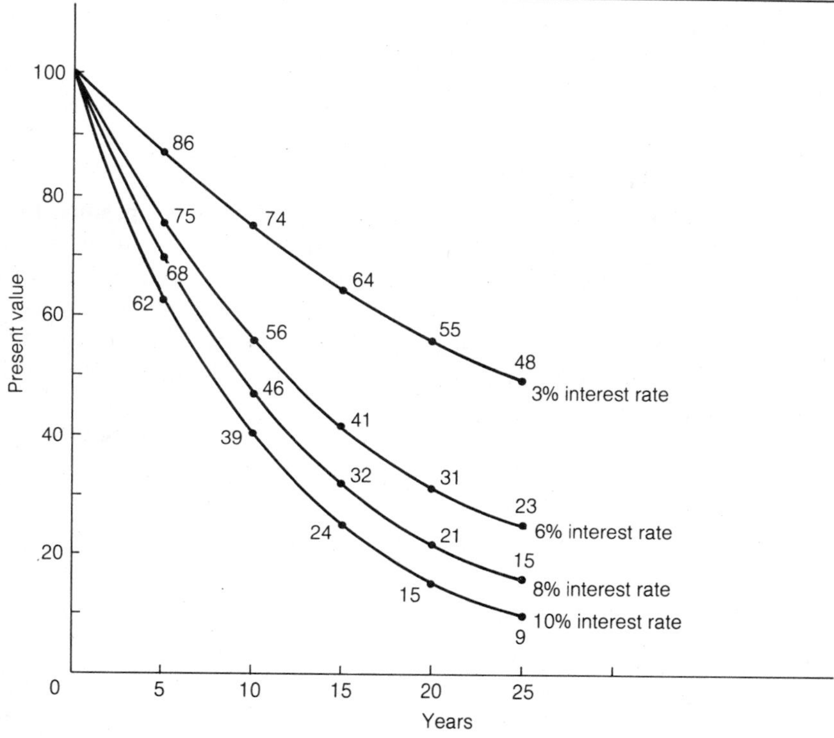

greater than could be acquired from investing the money at market rate of interest. Hence, the market price of the asset will be bid up or down until it is equal to the present value of the asset.

APPLICATION

The value of an asset

Metroplex Properties can buy a building for $1 million and can lease office space in the building to generate a net income of $50,000 a year for five years. (For analytical simplicity, assume that the rent is paid at the end of each year.) It is estimated that the wear and tear from lessees' using the building (depreciation) will exactly offset appreciation in value due to inflation and that the building will sell for $1 million at the end of five years.

If the market rate of interest is 10 percent, the present value of the building is

$$PV = \sum_{t=1}^{5} \left(\frac{1}{1.1}\right)^t 50{,}000 + \frac{1{,}000{,}000}{(1.1)^5} = \$810{,}461$$

Hence, the asking price of this asset exceeds the value of the asset—the present value of the income stream. At a 10 percent interest rate, Metroplex would pay no more than $810,461 for the office building. Unless, the present owner is willing to lower the price of the building, Metroplex would be better off investing in bonds.

19.2 MAXIMIZING THE VALUE OF A FIRM

Using the preceding discussion, we are now in a position to examine a firm's decision process when it takes time into consideration. When time is a factor, we can define the objective of the firm as the maximization of the present value of the firm over the relevant time horizon. What would this objective imply about the previously derived (single-period) profit maximizing conditions? To answer this question, let's look at the way a firm would behave over time.

Consider a firm with a time horizon of H years. If the prevailing interest rate is r, the present value of the firm is

$$PV = \sum_{t=1}^{H} \left(\frac{1}{1 + r}\right)^t (R_t - C_t)$$

where R_t and C_t are, respectively, revenue and cost in period t. Note that $R_t - C_t$ is the firm's profit in the t-th period, and the maximum possible profit in year t (or any other year) would be achieved by producing the output at which marginal revenue equals marginal cost. If in any one period, the firm chooses some other level of output, profit in that period would not be maximized; so, the present value of the stream of profits would be less than the maximum. Thus, the firm could maximize its present value by producing in each year (period) that output for which MR equals MC. In this instance, the single-period, profit-maximizing rules are not changed when the time dimension is added.

In the preceding case, note that the firm's output decision in one period did not affect revenue or cost in any other period. But, in certain cases, output in one period may affect revenue or cost in future periods. The extraction of a natural resource is an example of this situation—if more of the resource is extracted in period t, the cost of extracting in period $t + 1$ is increased. In these cases, when decisions in one period affect future revenues and/or costs, maximizing profit in each period may not result in maximizing the present value. But in the more typical case, maximization of present value implies maximization of profit in each period.

The concept of present value allows us to address the question of profitability of a monopolist or an oligopolist. Recall that for perfect and monopolistic competition, each firm's above-normal profit (profit above opportunity cost) would be competed away in the long run. In a sense this is also the case for monopoly and oligopoly.

Consider a monopoly that is expected to yield above-normal profits over its time horizon. As we have seen, the value of this monopoly—the price a potential purchaser would be willing to pay to acquire this firm—would be the present value of the stream of profits. Anyone who purchased the monopoly by paying the present value would only make normal profits on the investment. The original owner captures all of the above-normal returns when the firm is sold.

And, even if the owner elects not to sell the firm, this above-normal return is embedded in the owner's opportunity cost, because there is always the opportunity of selling the firm. In this sense, the owner of the monopoly firm makes only normal profits, when the opportunity cost of the sale is capitalized into the cost of the firm.

The same thing holds when the owner of a firm possesses a government license, subsidy, or other type of benefit. In many instances, the owner of a firm must possess a license to do business. The necessity of having a license limits entry into the market. But the value of the license is captured in the present value of the firm. The owner of the firm would sell the firm for its present value, including the value of the license, and the new owner would make only normal profits. Thus the value of license, like the value of a monopoly position, is capitalized into the value of firm. The same thing is true in the cases of farms that receive a subsidy or acreage allocations from the government. The benefits from these valuable assets are capitalized into the worth of the farm.

You might ask why would one firm purchase or merge with another firm, if it must pay the present value of the firm? It must be the case that the acquiring firm believes that, under new management, the present value of the acquired firm will be higher. This might be the case when the purchased firm is poorly managed or when the purchasing firm thinks that joint ownership could lead to economies of scale and lower costs.

19.3 LIMIT PRICING

One strategy that firms with market power can use to increase their profits over time is called limit pricing—pricing to deter or limit entry. Under such a strategy a firm would set its price so as to prevent, discourage, or delay the entry of rival firms into its market. Such a price would be below the price that maximizes the firm's single-period profit.

The basic philosophy behind limit pricing is simple. The firm could use the $MR = MC$ rule to determine the price that will maximize profit in the current period. However, if this price is high enough to encourage the entry of new firms, profits will decline over time as these additional competitors enter the market. Thus, the existing firms may be willing to forgo some profit in the current period in favor of maintaining their market power and having a larger stream of profits in the future. Consequently, these firms may be willing to set a price below the short-run profit-maximizing level in order to discourage new entrants, thereby maximizing long-run profit. To illustrate our assertion that pricing below the short-run profit-maximizing level can, with the threat of potential competition, increase a firm's profits over time, consider the following example.

APPLICATION

A long-run pricing decision

Zephyr Products—a firm providing industrial services—was the first firm to enter a new market and therefore enjoys the position of being the "established firm". On the basis of prevailing demand and cost conditions, the manager of Zephyr has determined the single-period profit-maximizing price to be \$2,000. With this price, forecasted annual profit is \$80,000.

However, the manager of Zephyr knows that, if price is set at \$2,000, additional firms will enter the market. It is expected that entry would eventually drive price to \$1,200 and Zephyr's annual profit to \$30,000. Using experience in other markets, Zephyr's manager expects Zephyr's profits over its five-year planning horizon in this case to be

Year:	1	2	3	4	5
Profit:	\$80,000	\$50,000	\$40,000	\$30,000	\$30,000

Alternatively, Zephyr can limit price. The manager of Zephyr Products believes that if price were set at \$1,400, no firms would enter the market. With this price, Zephyr's annual profit would be \$50,000; and this level of profit could be maintained over the five-year planning horizon.

Hence, the manager of Zephyr is faced with a choice of two strategies—two income streams. Which would be chosen? The manager will select that stream of income that has the higher present value. If the prevailing rate of interest is 12 percent, the present values are as follows:

Limit Price:

$$PV = \sum_{t=1}^{5} \frac{50,000}{(1.12)^t} = \$180,239$$

Permit Entry:

$$PV = \frac{80,000}{(1.12)} + \frac{50,000}{(1.12)^2} + \frac{40,000}{(1.12)^3} + \frac{30,000}{(1.12)^4} + \frac{30,000}{(1.12)^5}$$
$$= \$175,848$$

In this case, the present value of the firm's profit stream is maximized by limit pricing; so, the manager would elect to set a price below its single-period profit-maximizing price, in order to maximize long-run profit.

As the preceding application illustrates, limit pricing involves multiperiod profit maximization; so, the manager must use present value—discounting a profit stream over time. Clearly, to determine if limit pricing is *desirable,* the manager must compare the present value of the firm's profit streams under limit and nonlimit pricing. However, we should also consider the conditions necessary for the firm to be *able* to limit price.[2]

Conditions necessary for limit pricing

Conceptually, the problem is simple. In order for the firm to maintain a stream of profit in the future, the price set must exceed its own average cost. On the other hand, if entry is to be discouraged, the price must be less than the average cost of potential entrants. Therefore, in order to be able to limit price, the firm's own average cost must be less than that of potential entrants. We illustrate this situation in Figure 19.3. Let us for simplicity consider a monopoly firm. Short-run profit would be maximized at a price of p_0. The question is then whether entry is profitable at this price. Specifically, a new firm would be expected to enter if p_0 exceeds the minimum point on the potential entrant's average total cost curve. Suppose, for example, that the minimum of the potential entrant's average total cost curve occurs at p_1. The existing firm could deter entry by setting a price slightly below p_1 and producing an output slightly larger than Q_1. As you can easily verify, this strategy would result in reduced *current* profits. The decision whether or not to use this limit price would again be determined on the basis of the present value of future income streams. Alternatively, suppose that the minimum point on the potential entrant's average total cost curve occurs at p_2. In this case, it is not possible for the existing firm to limit price. In order to discourage entry, price would have to be set below its own average total cost curve. Thus, the existing firm would be suffering a loss—a situation that is clearly not in its own best interests. Finally, suppose that the minimum point on the potential entrant's average total cost curve occurs at p_3. In this situation, the short-run profit-maximizing price, p_0 will deter entry. Under these conditions, we say that entry is "blockaded"—a firm could maximize current profit without attracting new entrants.

To summarize, limit pricing is possible if the minimum of the average total cost curve of the existing firms lies below that of potential entrants. The question then becomes why one might expect average costs to be lower for existing firms than for new entrants. While there are several alternative explanations, including such things as the ownership of raw materials or possession of the best locations, a more general explanation is the existence of substantial economies of scale. Suppose, as is illustrated in Figure 19.4, that there do exist substantial economies of scale. We might expect that the existing, established firms have used these economies of scale to their advantage and are

[2]In this discussion we will limit our attention to the case in which there exist established firms operating with the optimal plant size and potential entrants that would use much smaller plants. Thus, we will ignore the impact of the output of the potential entrants on market price.

Figure 19.3
Limit pricing

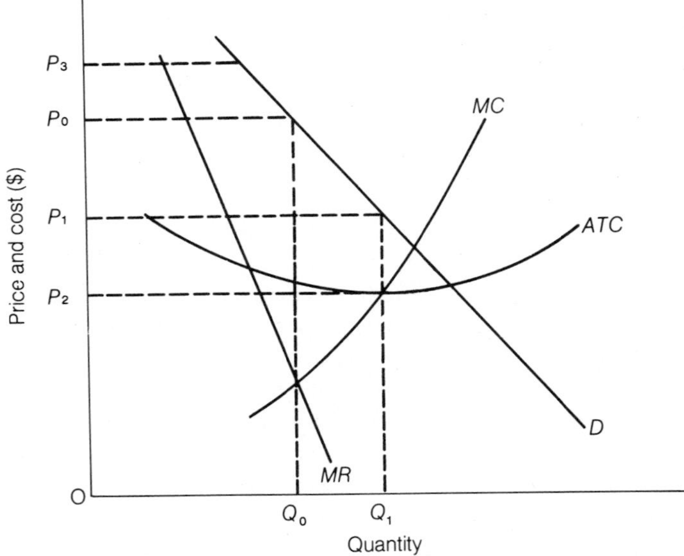

using relatively large plants as is shown by the location of their average total cost curve. If new firms enter with relatively small plants, their average total cost curves will be above those of the existing firms. Therefore, limit pricing would be possible for the existing firms.

Of course, it might be possible for new firms to enter with plants of the larger size. But these potential entrepreneurs may well recognize that demand conditions are such that the additional output of the new large firms would drive down price so far that both old and new firms would make losses. They might enter anyway and ''fight it out'' for the market, but in any case a lower limit price would, to some extent, deter entry. It follows then that increasing returns to scale may provide an explanation of the ability of firms to limit price.

Some complications

We have seen that limit pricing is a strategy in which firms abandon the traditional $MR = MC$ pricing rule in favor of a pricing rule that discourages or eliminates the entry of new competitors. In such a situation, the existing firm or firms forgo maximum profit in the current period in favor of the maintenance of a higher stream of future profits. The decision whether or not to limit price is based on the present value of the two streams of future profits. In order for the existing firm or firms to be able to limit price, it is necessary that the minimum average total cost for the existing firms be less than that for the potential entrants. Such a situation is possible if there exist substantial economies of scale.

Figure 19.4
Requirement for limit pricing

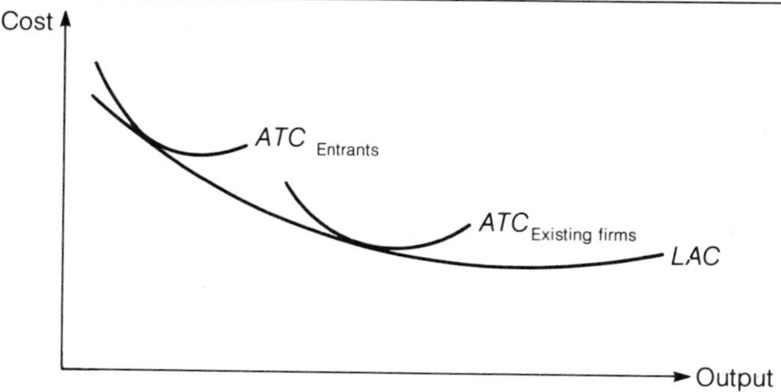

In our discussion and example of entry-limit pricing we have presented the simplest possible case. In reality, many complications can arise. For example, since the entry of new firms into a market takes time, a monopolist may choose a strategy of allowing gradual entry over a long period of time and can act as the price leader over this period. It retains its dominant position and earns profits, though not monopoly profits, as new firms enter and become established. After a substantial period of time it could lose its dominant position, if enough entry occurs. But this strategy could lead to a higher present value than would be the case under either limit pricing or monopoly pricing with full entry.

Or another mixed strategy would be to keep enough unused excess capacity to discourage entry while still charging the monopoly price. Potential rivals note this excess capacity, knowing that if they did enter, the established firm could lower its price to the limit price and cause them to make losses. But, carrying this unused capacity costs money and cuts into the profits being earned at the monopoly price. This would have to be taken into consideration when comparing present values under the different strategies. The cost of the extra capacity would have to be included in the present value of the profit stream.

19.4 PRESENT VALUE AND COST MINIMIZATION

Thus far in our discussion of present value and decision making over time we have concentrated on discounting streams of income. But the same type of analysis applies when costs are spread over several time periods. The most important topic in this area involves decisions about capital investments made to increase profits—the subject of the next chapter. For now, let's consider a firm's expenditure forced by a governmental regulation and look at cost minimization over time via an example.

APPLICATION

Minimizing the cost of regulation

The Environmental Protection Agency is charged with regulating the amount of pollutants that firms can emit into the environment. The EPA can force firms to cease polluting beyond some acceptable level or it can impose fines upon polluting firms. The Hardrock Mining Co. operates a metal refining plant—a smelter—near a small city. In the process of refining the ore, the smelter is emitting sulphur dioxide (SO_2) into the air at the rate of 10 parts per million (molecules). The EPA regulation states that the firm will be fined \$50,000 a year for every part per million in excess of five parts per million. The chief executive officer of Hardrock Mining asks his engineering department to investigate the problem and propose some solutions.

In their report, the engineering department notes that the firm will have an entirely new plant in 10 years; so the solution to the present problem will be short run. They report that there are two possible solutions. The first is to put in a new air purification process, which will reduce the sulphur dioxide below five parts after it is installed. The cost will be \$1,250,000, payable now. The second solution is to install scrubbers—that is, modify the present plant and equipment. This will reduce pollution to eight parts the first two years, and to seven parts thereafter. This will cost \$200,000 at the end of the first year and \$200,000 at the end of the second. Of course, the firm would have to pay a fine each year.

The CEO adds a third alternative by noting that the firm could do nothing and pay the fine. The fine would be \$250,000 a year, since five parts of sulphur dioxide above the maximum would be emitted each year.

The problem clearly involves present values. For this firm, the relevant rate of interest is eight percent. With the first option, installing the new equipment will cost \$1,250,000; but, since SO_2 pollution will be below five parts per million throughout the period, no fines will be paid. So the present value of the cost of using the first strategy is simply

$$PV_1 = \$1,250,000$$

Strategy two consists of installing some equipment to reduce pollution, but not below five parts. Since pollution is reduced to eight parts in the first two periods and to seven for the remainder, the firm must pay a fine of $(8 - 5) \times$ \$50,000 = \$150,000 the first two years and $(7 - 5) \times$ \$50,000 = \$100,000 the last eight years. It pays capital costs of \$200,000 at the end of each of the first two years. The present value of the cost of the second strategy is therefore

$$PV_2 = \sum_{t=1}^{2} \frac{\$200,000}{(1 + .08)^t} + \sum_{t=1}^{2} \frac{\$150,000}{(1 + .08)^t} + \sum_{t=3}^{10} \frac{\$100,000}{(1 + .08)^t} = \$1,116,824$$

Finally, the firm can pay a fine of $(10 - 5) \times \$50,000 = \$250,000$ a year. The present value of the cost of the third strategy is

$$PV_3 = \sum_{t=1}^{10} \frac{\$250,000}{(1 + .08)^t} = \$1,677,519$$

Clearly, strategy two leads to the lowest present value of cost for the firm. It is interesting that, for this strategy, the sum of all costs—the purchase of capital equipment and paying the fines—is $1,500,000, which is greater than the cost of new capital that would eliminate all fines. But the present value is lower. The reason is that the cost of the new air purification process equipment is all payable in the present period whereas much of the cost of the second strategy is deferred and therefore discounted.

19.5 SUMMARY

This chapter has introduced the time dimension into decision making. The basic point is that income or expenditure now is valued more than the same income or expenditure in future periods. The reason for the difference is the existence of a rate of interest. Income now can be invested at that rate of interest and more income can be received in the future.

The future value of an asset is

$$FV = A(1 + r)^t$$

where A is the value of an asset now, r is the relevant rate of interest, and t is the number of periods into the future when the income will be received.

The present value of an asset is

$$PV = \frac{R}{(1 + r)^t}$$

where R is the revenue expected t periods in the future. This is the concept of discounting. Any revenue or cost expected in the future must be discounted when making decisions, because any revenue or cost in the future is worth less than that same revenue or cost now. When making decisions involving alternative streams of income and/or costs, the present values of the alternatives must be compared.

TECHNICAL PROBLEMS

1. Calculate the future value of $1,000:
   a. In one year with an interest rate of 8 percent.
   b. In one year with an interest rate of 15 percent.
   c. In three years with an interest rate of 8 percent.
   d. In three years with an interest rate of 15 percent.

2. Calculate the present value of $1,000:
   a. To be received in one year, with an interest rate of 8 percent.
   b. To be received in one year, with an interest rate of 15 percent.
   c. To be received in three years, with an interest rate of 8 percent.
   d. To be received in three years, with an interest rate of 15 percent.
3. If the prevailing rate of interest is 12 percent, what is the present value of the following income stream (where all payments are made at year end)?

Year	*Income*
1	$10,000
2	15,000
3	20,000
4	10,000

4. What determines the maximum someone would be willing to pay for an income-generating asset?
5. In what sense would it be valid to say that a monopoly firm can only earn a normal profit?
6. Look again at out Application dealing with Zephyr Products' decision about whether or not to limit price. Reevaluate this decision
   a. Using a 10 percent interest rate.
   b. Using a 20 percent interest rate.
   c. Using the original 12 percent interest rate but assuming that entry would be somewhat slower, i.e., profits in year 2 would be $60,000 rather than $50,000 if entry is permitted.
7. Under what conditions would a firm be *able* to limit price?
8. Look again at our Application dealing with Hardrock Mining Co. Suppose the EPA lowers the maximum permissible SO_2 omissions from five to three parts per million. (The fine remains at $50,000 per year for every part per million in excess of the maximum.) Reevaluate Hardrock's decision.

ANALYTICAL PROBLEMS

1. During the "energy crisis" *Consumer Reports* evaluated refrigerators and made the point that "by choosing one that's thrifty with electricity, you may save almost $400 over the appliance's lifetime." This $400 figure was arrived at by summing monthly savings in electricity of $2.20 over the 15-year lifetime of a refrigerator. What's the problem with this calculation? How would you go about determining how much more you would pay for the "thrifty" refrigerator?
2. How much does it cost a firm to keep funds in a checking account rather than money market or savings accounts? Why do firms keep any money in checking accounts? How would the manager determine the optimal amount to keep in checking accounts?

3. Taxicabs in New York City are licensed—in order to operate a taxicab, you must have a "medallion." And, there are no new licenses available. If you want a medallion, you have to buy it from someone who owns one.

   If you were to purchase a N.Y.C. taxicab company, what is it you are purchasing? How would you calculate the value of the taxicab company? Under what conditions might this acquisition yield an economic profit?

   What would happen to the value of the taxicab company if N.Y.C. were to eliminate the licensing requirement? How would the present owner of medallions react if New York City were to consider such a policy?

4. What types of firms would you expect to be able to use limit pricing? What types either could not or would not use this strategy? Provide some examples of industries in which you might expect limit pricing and some for which limit pricing would not be expected.

5. Suppose there is some finite amount of a depletable natural resource. As the resource is extracted and becomes scarcer, what would you expect to happen to the price of the resource? If the price of the resource is rising at a faster rate than the relevant rate of interest, what would you expect to happen to the rate of extraction and hence to the change in the price of the resource? If the price of the resource is rising at a slower rate than the relevant rate of interest, what would you expect to happen to the rate of extraction and the rate of change of the price of the resource? Explain both answers. On average what would you expect the rate of change of the resource price to be?

6. Use your answer to the preceding question to answer this one. Since 1900 the yearly change in the price of 14 depletable natural resources has exceeded the AAA corporate bond rate in only 34 percent of the years. Based on these facts, would you deduce that firms have extracted our natural resources at too rapid or too slow a rate? Explain.

20

Theory of investment

One of the most important decisions managers must make concerns investment. The investment decision involves how much to invest, what capital should be purchased, how to finance the investment, and so forth.

We should note that when we speak of investment by a firm, we generally do not mean investment in stocks and bonds (although the theory to be developed can be applied to the purchase of such financial instruments). Rather, investment is simply an addition to the firm's stock of resources, generally involving the purchase of capital equipment or land.

Throughout most of this book we have treated factors of production such as capital within single-period models. And this approach is appropriate for a large amount of managerial decision making. But, since investment decisions are based upon expected *streams* of returns and costs, they involve multiperiod analysis. As you know from Chapter 19, when we use multiperiod analysis, the concepts of discounting and present value become crucial. Nonetheless, the basic theory is rather simple. As is the case for single-period managerial decisions, the investment decision is based on marginal analysis—marginal benefits and marginal costs.

We should note that this chapter is relatively brief, not because investment theory is unimportant but because the theory as set forth here is relatively straightforward and simple. This is not to say that the topics of investment and capital budgeting cannot be extended greatly beyond our coverage here. Indeed these topics form the core of entire courses. In order to do justice to an extension, we would be forced to expand this book far beyond its scope. Our purpose is simply to make you aware of the fundamentals of investment theory and how this theory is used in managerial decision making.

20.1 DEMAND FOR INVESTMENT

Any investment decision is made to obtain a stream of net income or profits. Obviously, a profit-maximizing firm wants any new capital purchased to have a flow of returns, the present value of which is greater than, or at least equal to, the (present) cost of the capital. Since a machine or another piece of capital equipment yields services for more than one period, the value of services for future periods must be discounted. Therefore, the present value of an additional unit of capital to a firm and the cost of that unit are the key variables in the investment decision-making process. The present value of the expected stream of income from a piece of capital equipment depends on several variables such as the market rate of interest, the price of goods produced, the expected lifetime and rate of depreciation of the capital, the flow of services (or capital productivity), the prices of the inputs employed, and so forth. Notwithstanding the number of variables involved, the basic decision process is not particularly complex.

Net present value approach

At any given time, firms have available various investment opportunities, which can be ranked as to desirability. The firm may purchase capital goods either by selling debt instruments or by reducing its own money balances, i.e., using internal funds. Note that if firms use internal funds to finance investments, the cost of the investment to the firm does not differ from the situation in which it borrows funds. The opportunity cost of funds raised internally must be the relevant market rate of interest. The firm may borrow or lend at this rate; and its borrowing or lending will not affect that rate. While a firm may be restricted in its borrowing by its overall net worth, we will assume for now that this restriction is not a relevant barrier.

Thus a firm evaluates all potential investments in terms of the net present value of each investment, defined as follows.

■ **Definition.** The net present value of an investment is the present value of the stream of net returns (revenues less costs) from the investment minus the current cost (or the present value of the cost) of making the investment.

Without capital (or time) limitations, the firm would undertake all potential investments with a positive present value. To see this, let's go to an example.

APPLICATION

An investment decision

A firm is contemplating purchasing a piece of machinery for \$60,000. The machine would be used for 10 years and would be expected to add \$10,000 a year in net revenue (revenue less variable cost) over the 10 years. At the end of the 10 years it is expected that the machine will have a scrap value of \$8,000. If the rate of interest is 8 percent, should the firm purchase the machine? The net present value of the machine is

$$NPV = \sum_{t=1}^{10} \frac{\$10,000}{(1.08)^t} + \frac{\$8,000}{(1.08)^{10}} - \$60,000 = \$10,806$$

Clearly purchasing the machine will add to the value of the firm, so the machine should be purchased—if there is no limitation on capital.

But if the interest rate is 13 percent (rather than 8 percent) the net present value of the machine becomes

$$NPV = \sum_{t=1}^{10} \frac{\$10,000}{(1.13)^t} + \frac{\$8,000}{(1.13)^{10}} - \$60,000 = -\$3,379$$

At this higher rate of interest, the machine will lower the value of the firm and therefore should not be purchased.

Thus we see that the rate of interest can make a great deal of difference when deciding whether or not to undertake a particular investment. Investments that may be profitable at one rate of interest may have a negative net present value at a higher rate.

In the preceding example, we assumed that the firm simply paid for the capital at the beginning of the first period, perhaps out of retained earnings. But, the analysis is not changed at all if the firm borrows to purchase the capital. The crucial value is still the present value of the stream of payments.

Suppose the firm in the preceding application were to borrow to purchase the machinery and is obligated to pay off the debt in three equal, annual payments. If the rate of interest is 8 percent, the payments would be \$23,282. In making its investment decision, the firm uses the present value of the stream of payments, which is

$$PV = \sum_{t=1}^{3} \frac{\$23,282}{(1 + .08)^t} = \$60,000$$

In order to purchase the machine the firm must pay back \$69,846 because of the interest charged. But, in making its decision, the firm uses the discounted amount—$60,000—rather than the $69,846 as the cost of capital, because the payments are spread into the future.

Internal rate of return

So far, we have established that, to increase its value, a firm should undertake those available investments for which the net present value is positive, so long as the capital funds available are not limited. But, we really didn't establish the firm's demand for investment in this discussion. To get at this demand function, let us introduce a new concept, the internal rate of return.

■ **Definition.** The internal rate of return from a particular investment is the discount rate that makes the net present value of an investment zero.

For example, suppose an investment costing $48,000, is expected to yield a net return (profit) of $20,000 a year for three years. To find the discount rate that makes the net present value zero, set

$$NPV = \sum_{t=1}^{3} \frac{\$20,000}{(1 + r)^t} - \$48,000 = 0$$

Solving for r, internal rate of return for this investment is approximately 0.12 (12 percent).

At a rate of interest above 12 percent, the net present value of this investment would be negative. For example, if the interest rate is 15 percent the net present value is

$$NPV = \sum_{t=1}^{3} \frac{\$20,000}{(1 + .15)^t} - \$48,000 = -\$2,336$$

Since net present value is negative, the firm would not undertake the investment. At interest rates below 12 percent the net present value would be positive; e.g., if the interest rate is 8 percent, the net present value is

$$NPV = \sum_{t=1}^{3} \frac{\$20,000}{(1 + .08)^t} - \$48,000 = \$3,543$$

and the firm should undertake the investment.

Clearly, the decision whether or not to undertake a particular investment project depends on the interest rate the firm faces. If the interest rate is above the internal rate of return for the project, the firm would be better off buying bonds yielding this higher rate rather than undertaking the investment. If, on the other hand, the interest rate is below the internal rate of return, the investment project would be more profitable than purchasing bonds.

■ **Relation.** When the rate of interest is above (below) the internal rate of return of a particular investment, a bond yielding that rate of interest is superior (inferior) to the investment.

Within this framework, we can think of the rate of interest as the opportunity cost of making a particular capital investment. The forgone interest is the cost of using funds to purchase capital equipment rather than purchasing bonds yielding the prevailing rate of interest.

Using the concept of the internal rate of return from an investment, we can derive the firm's demand for investment during a particular period. Assume that a firm is faced with several investment opportunities, which can be ranked according to their internal rates of return. Figure 20.1 shows the set of opportunities facing a hypothetical firm. As the figure shows, four investment opportunities are available to the firm during this time period.

The first and most profitable investment involves a capital expenditure of K_1 dollars. This investment project has an internal rate of return of r_1. The second most profitable investment project costs K_1K_2 dollars. The internal rate of return on this investment is r_2. The other two available investment projects involve the expenditures of K_2K_3 and K_3K_4, with internal rates of return of r_3 and r_4.

We should note that the internal rates of return plotted on the vertical axis are the rates on each *additional* unit of investment, not the average rate on all investment. For example, r_2 is the internal rate of return for investment proj-

Figure 20.1
Alternative investment opportunities

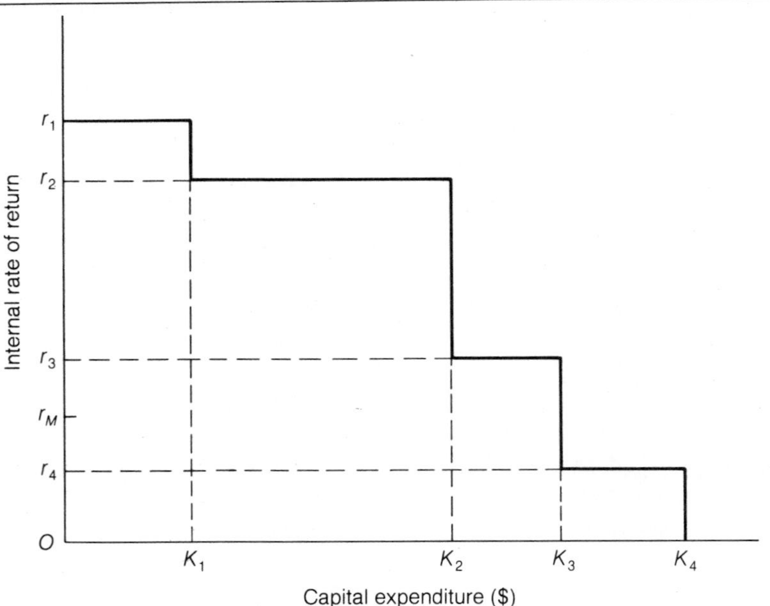

ect two, i.e., for *increasing* capital expenditure from K_1 to K_2. It is not the average internal rate of the total expenditure of K_2 dollars.

If capital acquisition is not a problem (the firm has no expenditure constraint), the number of investment projects the firm will undertake depends upon the market rate of interest. Suppose the market rate of interest is r_M in Figure 20.1. The firm would undertake the three investments with an internal rate of return above r_M, because the firm could earn a greater return from the investment projects than could be made by purchasing bonds at the market rate of interest. The firm would not undertake the last investment of K_3K_4 dollars, because a greater rate of return could be made in interest-bearing bonds.

Thus we have established the following principle:

■ **Principle.** A firm can rank potential investments according to their internal rates of return—the discount rate that would make the net present value of the investment zero. If investment funds are not limited, the firm should undertake those investments for which the internal rate of return is greater than the relevant rate of interest.

APPLICATION

Evaluation of investment projects

Argonaut Enterprises had available four potential investment projects that would all begin in 1986. The characteristics of these projects are summarized in the table below.

Project:	A	B	C	D
Capital cost:	$123,000	$89,200	$56,600	$55,800
Net income*:				
1986	30,000	50,000	20,000	40,000
1987	30,000	50,000	20,000	20,000
1988	30,000	0	20,000	10,000
1989	30,000	0	20,000	0
Scrap or resale value at end of 1989:	50,000	0	10,000	0

*All income is received at year end.

The question facing the management of Argonaut Enterprises was which—if any—of the projects should be undertaken. Using 15 percent as the relevant market interest rate, the net present values for the four investment projects as of January 1, 1986 were calculated. These values were

Project:	A	B	C	D
NPV:	−\$8,800	−\$7,900	\$6,200	\$700

Therefore, on the basis of the net present values, only Projects C and D would be undertaken.

This decision did not "sit very well" with the vice president for operations, for whom Project A was a particular favorite. He argued that the interest rate used in the calculation of the net present values was too high. In response, the board of directors had the staff calculate the internal rates of return for each of the projects. These values were

Project:	A	B	C	D
IRR:	12%	8%	20%	16%

From these values, the management could see that Project A would be profitable only if the relevant market interest rate was below 12 percent. For interest rates in excess of 12 percent, only Projects C and D should be undertaken.

If the firm has only four investment projects available, the firm's demand function for investment looks something like Figure 20.1. However, most (if not all) firms have a wide variety of projects available. As you should be able to see, as more potential projects are available, the "stair-step" demand function gets closer to a smooth—continuous—demand function. If we assume that the investment projects are divisible, we can talk about the internal rate of return associated with an additional dollar expenditure on capital and we can draw a continuous demand for investment function as in Figure 20.2.

This figure shows the internal rate of return for additional (marginal) investment. Capital investment in the relevant time period is plotted along the horizontal axis; the internal rate of return on the marginal investment and the interest rate are plotted along the vertical axis.

Suppose the market rate of interest is r_0. Every additional unit of investment from zero to K_0 has an internal rate of return greater than r_0. From our previous discussion, if the internal rate of return exceeds the rate of interest, the investment is profitable and should be undertaken (if there is no limit on the amount of capital that can be raised by the firm). Any additional investment beyond K_0 dollars has an internal rate of return below the rate of interest and therefore should not be undertaken. Thus with an interest rate of r_0 the firm would invest K_0.

By exactly the same type of reasoning, if the rate of interest if r_1, the firm should invest K_1 dollars. Likewise, at every other rate of interest the downsloping curve, showing the internal rate of return on each marginal investment, provides the optimal amount that the firm should invest at that interest rate. Thus, this downward-sloping curve is the firm's demand for investment.

Figure 20.2
Demand for investment

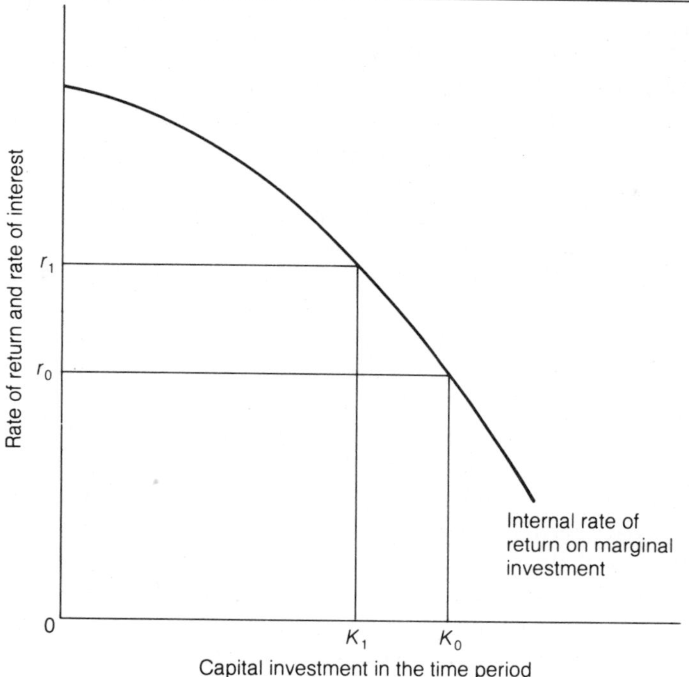

■ **Principle.** The internal rate of return for additional units of investment is the firm's demand for investment in a given time period. The firm should increase investment until the internal rate of return on the last unit of investment is equal to the rate of interest.

Before moving on we should mention several points. First, the relevant rate of return used in determining investment is the *after-tax* return. If, for example, the tax rate increases, we would expect to see a decrease in the demand for investment; less investment would be forthcoming at each rate of interest. Second, if the curve showing the internal rate of return intersects the vertical axis below the market rate of interest, no investment would be forthcoming during the time period, because the internal rate of return would be less than the market rate of interest for every potential investment. Finally, when deriving a firm's demand for investment we have held constant such factors as the prices of inputs and technology.

Shifts in the demand for investment

As is the case for any demand curve, if one of the factors we held constant when deriving the demand for investment changes, the demand-for-investment curve will shift. For example, an increase in the rate of taxation would decrease the after-tax stream of net returns and would therefore cause the internal rate of return to fall; thus the entire demand curve would decrease. In this case, less investment would be undertaken at each rate of interest.

On the other hand, technological change (which lowers the cost of production) would increase the demand for investment. Technological change allows the firm to produce a given output with less input usage. Thus when the production cost falls, the discounted stream of net returns must rise and the internal rates of return for investments rise—the demand curve shifts to the right. This means investments become more profitable; and at any given rate of interest more investment is desired.

Changes in input prices would also shift the demand for investment. A net increase in input prices would decrease the net present value of an investment at any given rate of interest and would therefore decrease the demand for investment. A net decrease in input prices would lower costs and increase the demand for investment.

Finally, we should note that we have taken a rather simplistic, though analytically useful, view of the potential investment opportunities of firms. For analytical purposes, we have simply assumed that the investment opportunities have been there for the taking and the firm somehow knows the present values of the various net income streams. Actually, the capital budgeting decision is a rather complex process, often involving several divisions of the firm. Ideas concerning future investments must be generated. Possible projects may originate in, say, the engineering department. But the various projects may be evaluated by the financial, marketing, and planning departments, in addition to top management. Nonetheless, if a project is to be undertaken, it must meet the criteria discussed here if it is to be profitable. In other words, the investment process is more complex than that discussed here, but the theoretical principles still hold.

Beyond the quantitative decisions we have outlined we should note that the basic feelings of optimism or pessimism will have an effect on investment demand. No one can know the exact stream of returns that will be forthcoming many years into the future. Predictions about the future state of the economy must enter into investment decisions. Things like the results of elections or changes in Federal Reserve policy can affect the demand for investment. Anything that makes managers more optimistic about future business conditions will increase investment demand. Conversely, if managers become more pessimistic, investment demand will decline. Unfortunately, these feelings of optimism and pessimism cannot be quantified.

20.2 CAPITAL RATIONING

Thus far we have discussed the firm's investment decisions under the assumption of no limit to capital funding—no credit limitations. Clearly, there may well be cases of capital limits or of mutually exclusive capital projects. Such cases involve capital rationing.

A theoretical analysis of the problem of funding limitations or credit restrictions is relatively simple. Suppose the firm is unable to borrow enough funds to finance all of the investment opportunities for which the internal rate of return exceeds the interest rate. (Or possibly, the board of directors puts a limit upon the amount of internal financing that can be used for capital investment.)

In such cases the task of the managerial decision makers is to allocate the limited funding to the investment opportunities with the highest internal rates of return or with the highest net present values. Obviously, in such cases, some investments with a positive net present value will have to be forgone. But, when the investments with the highest return are undertaken the firm is maximizing its return, subject to the constraint of the limited capital funding.

Normally, when there are alternative investment projects, the one with the highest net present value also has the highest internal rate of return. In such cases, there is no conflict between the two investment decision rules. But conflicts can arise when investment projects are mutually exclusive. For example, two projects may both have internal rates of return above the rate of interest but both cannot be carried out because of credit limitations. Or, the projects may be mutually exclusive because of technological considerations. Possibly the firm wants to build an additional plant and two sites are available. Since it would not wish to build two plants it must choose one project over the other. To illustrate this situation, let's look at an example.

APPLICATION

A choice between investment projects

A firm must make a choice between two investment projects. Project A costs $550,000 and Project B costs $628,000. The time horizon is four years and the net (undiscounted) streams of returns for the two projects are given in the following table.

	Net returns	
Year	*Project A*	*Project B*
1	$ 100,000	$ 400,000
2	100,000	200,000
3	400,000	200,000
4	400,000	200,000
	$1,000,000	$1,000,000

The firm computed the internal rates of return (the discount rate that makes the present value of Project A equal to $550,000 and that of Project B equal to $628,000). The internal rate of return for Project A was approximately 22 percent and the internal rate of return for B was approximately 25 percent. Thus at any rate of interest below 22 percent each project would have a positive net present value and would therefore be a profitable investment. But, only one project will be chosen. Should the firm simply choose the one with the higher internal rate of return—Project B? Not necessarily. It depends upon what the actual rate of interest is.

Suppose the interest rate is 12 percent. The present value of stream A is, in this case, $708,000; that of stream B is $786,000. Given the relative capital costs, the net present value of each project is $158,000, and the firm would be indifferent between the two.

Suppose the interest rate is below 12 percent, say, 6 percent. The net present value of Project A is $286,000 at this rate, and that of B is $254,000. Thus at 6 percent, and at any other rate below 12 percent, the net present value of Project A is higher and should be chosen above Project B.

At a rate of interest above 12 percent the net present value of Project B is greater. For example, at an interest rate of 18 percent, the net present value of A is $56,000 and that of B is $80,000. In this case B should be chosen.

As you can see, when the firm must choose between investment projects, the relevant market rate of interest determines which present value is higher. This, in turn, determines which project should be chosen when the two are mutually exclusive. This decision criterion holds even if one project has a higher internal rate of return.

It could of course be the case that one project has a higher net present value at all relevant interest rates and therefore has a higher internal rate of return. In such cases there is no conflict. But, in cases such as the one in the preceding Application, the net present values must be compared at the prevailing interest rate, and the project with the higher value should be chosen.

20.3 ADDITIONAL COMPLICATIONS

To this point, we have carried out the analysis under the assumption that there is one relevant rate of interest. But we know that there may be a spectrum of interest rates depending upon several factors. Let us mention a few of these factors that influence the relevant market interest rate.

First, of course, the interest rates available to firms differ according to the degree of riskiness, as perceived by the lending institutions. Not only do firms differ as to their riskiness as borrowers but also different projects undertaken by the same firm may be financed at different rates of interest because of perceived differences in the risk associated with the projects. Thus, a firm may assign different interest rates to different investment opportunities.

Interest rates also differ according to the maturities of the loans. Typically, though not always, long-term rates are higher than short-term rates. In the event that lenders expect inflation to increase in future, they may be willing to lend long-term only at rates higher than short-term. Thus, the length of the period of financing the investment determines to some extent the rate at which the firm can borrow.

This mention of inflation brings us to the difference between *real* and *nominal* rates of interest. The nominal rate is the rate actually charged. The real rate is the interest rate net of inflation. If a firm borrows for a year at a nominal interest rate of 12 percent and the rate of inflation is 6 percent that year, the real rate of interest is 6 percent. The firm pays back the loan with dollars that are worth less at the end of the year than at the beginning.

Interest rates can differ because of differing administrative costs associated with the loans. It is frequently the case that large loans cost proportionally less to administer and are therefore made at lower rates of interest. But, comparing large loans with small loans sometimes involves differences in risk; so, differences in the rate of interest can reflect both forces.

In our analysis we have assumed that a firm can lend (purchase a bond) at the same rate of interest at which it can borrow investment funds. This of course may not be the case. Nonetheless, the basic analysis is not changed; the firm compares the return it can obtain by lending with the income stream that can be obtained from various investment projects.

Another slight complication arises when the firm is considering capital projects but has the choice of purchasing the capital or leasing it. While this choice complicates the decision-making process, the basic analysis remains unchanged. The firm still compares the present values of the streams of income under the two conditions. An example should clarify this point.

APPLICATION

Purchase or lease?

A small but growing firm decides that it will require additional office space over the next 10 years. It limits itself to a 10-year time horizon because management believes that after 10 years the firm will be so large that it will again require new quarters. The firm has two options. It can purchase a suitable building for $1 million. The financial and marketing divisions have forecast that the building can be sold for $800,000 in 10 years when the firm is ready to expand. Alternatively, the firm can lease an equivalent building for 10 years at a fixed contract of $100,000 per year.

In making its decision the firm must compare the present values of the two cost streams. For simplicity assume that the rent is payable at the end of each year. If the interest rate is 10 percent, the present value of the cost of purchasing the building and then selling it in ten years is

$$PV = \$1{,}000{,}000 - \frac{\$800{,}000}{(1 + .10)^{10}} = \$691{,}565$$

The present value of the stream of rental payments is

$$PV = \sum_{t=1}^{10} \frac{\$100,000}{(1 + .10)^t} = \$614,457$$

Clearly the firm would be better off renting its building rather than purchasing it. With a different rate of interest the conclusion could easily be reversed.

One final point is worth noting before we end our discussion of investment theory. Throughout this chapter we have discussed investment within the context of purchasing capital equipment. But there are other types of investment decisions made by firms, and such decisions should be made using the same type of evaluation as used for capital purchases.

One example of investment in nonphysical capital is expenditures on research and development (R&D). Firms undertake R&D projects for many reasons: to find new uses or markets for the products, to develop new products, to reduce the cost of production, and so forth. Such an expenditure is similar to the purchase of physical capital. The firm bears expenditures now in the hope of increasing its net income in the future. Thus it must choose R&D projects based upon the present value of the costs and the present value of the enhanced future stream of income. In the absence of funding limitations, the firm would undertake those projects for which the expected net present value is positive. Alternatively, it could rank projects according to the internal rate of return, choosing those that have an internal rate of return greater than the rate of interest.

Certain types of advertising expenditures are similar to R&D expenditure. Advertising during early periods could have little payoff in the present; but such campaigns may be carried out in the expectation of a future stream of payoffs. Campaigns to establish a new product are examples of this type of expenditure. The costs are in the present, and the payoff is in the future. The net present value rule should be used to evaluate these types of advertising expense.

Expenditures on human capital are another example of nonphysical capital investment. Examples include on-the-job training for workers and executive training courses for management. Again, since the costs come early and the returns later, expenditure on increasing the human capital of employees must be evaluated according to net present value.

20.4 SUMMARY

Any expenditure that generates a future stream of net income can be treated as an investment. When deciding whether to undertake an investment, the firm should estimate the net present value—the present value of the future stream of net returns less the present cost of the investment. In a given period, the firm should undertake those investments that have a positive net present value at the relevant rate of interest. If capital funding limitations are placed on the firm, the firm should carry out those investments with the highest net present value up to the point of the expenditure limit.

The internal rate of return is the discount rate that makes the net present value from a given investment equal to zero. If the firm can rank potential investments according to the internal rate of return, from highest to lowest, this schedule is the firm's demand for investment. If there are no credit limitations, the firm should carry out investment until the internal rate of return equals the relevant rate of interest.

■ **Principle.** The firm can rank all potential investment opportunities according to each investment's internal rate of return—the discount rate that makes the net present value (the present value of the net receipts less the present value of the cost of the investment) equal to zero. The firm should carry out all investments for which the internal rate of return exceeds the interest rate, so long as there is no limit on capital funding. If capital funding is limited, the investments with the highest net present values should be carried out up to the amount of available funding.

Firms use the same criteria in evaluating projects other than the purchase of physical capital, if these projects involve net returns in future periods. Examples of such projects are the decision to buy or lease, research and development, certain types of advertising, and investment in human capital.

TECHNICAL PROBLEMS

In Problems 1 through 4, use the data presented in the Application dealing with Argonaut Enterprises.

1. Sketch Argonaut's "investment demand function." (Use Figure 20.1 as a guide.)
2. If it was felt that the relevant interest rate should be 10 percent, which projects would be undertaken? To check your answer, calculate the net present values for the projects, using 10 percent as the interest rate.
3. The vice president for operations came back to the board of directors with another argument: He believes that the resale value for Project A was underestimated and that the resale value should be $70,000 rather than $50,000. If this is true, should this project be undertaken, using 15 percent as the relevant interest rate? Use the net present value of the project to support your answer.
4. It turns out that Project B also has a supporter. The director of new-product development argues that the capital outlay necessary for Project B is $86,800 rather than $89,200. If this is true, what would be the internal

rate of return for Project B? Would this project be undertaken, using 15 percent as the relevant market interest rate?

5. What will be the impact on the firm's investment demand function and the optimal level of investment of the following changes?
   a. A decrease in the tax rate.
   b. An increase in the market interest rate.
   c. An increase in the price of the electrical power used to operate the capital equipment.
6. If the firm's investment decision is constrained by funding (or credit) limitations, how should it determine which projects to fund?
7. In Chapter 3, we proposed a general rule for constrained optimization. Does your answer to Problem 6 conform to this general rule? Explain why or why not.
8. What factors determine the interest rate that should be used by the firm as the "relevant" rate in making its investment decision?
9. Return to our Application entitled "Purchase or Lease?". What would be the firm's decision if the relevant interest rate is 8 percent? What would be the firm's decision if the relevant interest rate is 15 percent?

ANALYTICAL PROBLEMS

1. What factors would go into a firm's decision to finance an investment via borrowing or using internal funds?
2. In general, when would the concepts of *NPV* and *IRR* yield different decisions about which investment projects to undertake?
3. Why would we expect firms that produce capital equipment, e.g., producers of metal-working machines, to lobby Congress for changes in the tax laws—e.g., asking for more rapid depreciation?
4. At the time we were completing this revision (March 1984), concern about the size of the federal deficit was being voiced by almost everyone. How might a very large federal deficit impact on private investment—investment by firms and individuals?
5. The tools we have developed for the investment decision can also be used in the firm's inventory decision. Why is this so? How would a firm go about deciding on the optimal inventory level?
6. The fact that you are attending a college or university indicates that you have made an investment decision. What kind of investment decision is this? What factors did you (at least implicitly) evaluate when making this decision? In what way would the decision to go to graduate school differ?

Statistical tables

STUDENT'S t-DISTRIBUTION

Following is a table that provides the critical values of the t-distribution for three levels of confidence—90 percent, 95 percent, and 99 percent. It should be noted that these values are based on a two-tailed test for significance. These are, for example, tests to determine if an estimated coefficient is significantly *different* from zero (or one). For a discussion of one-tailed hypothesis tests, a topic not covered in this text, the reader is referred to R. J. Wonnacott and T. H. Wonnacott, *Econometrics*, 2d ed. (New York: John Wiley & Sons, 1979).

To illustrate the use of this table, let us refer to an application presented in Chapter 4. In this example, 30 observations were used to estimate three coefficients, a, b, and c. Therefore, there are $30 - 3 = 27$ degrees of freedom. Then, the critical t-value for a 95 percent confidence level can be obtained from the table as 2.052. If a higher confidence level is required, the researcher can use the 99 percent confidence level column to obtain a critical value of 2.771. Conversely, if a lower confidence level is acceptable, the researcher can use the 90 percent confidence level column to obtain a critical value of 1.703.

Critical T-values

Degrees of freedom	Confidence level 90%	95%	99%
1	6.314	12.706	63.657
2	2.920	4.303	9.925
3	2.353	3.182	5.841
4	2.132	2.776	4.604
5	2.015	2.571	4.032
6	1.943	2.447	3.707
7	1.895	2.365	3.499
8	1.860	2.306	3.355
9	1.833	2.262	3.250
10	1.812	2.228	3.169
11	1.796	2.201	3.106
12	1.782	2.179	3.055
13	1.771	2.160	3.012
14	1.761	2.145	2.977
15	1.753	2.131	2.947
16	1.746	2.120	2.921
17	1.740	2.110	2.898
18	1.734	2.101	2.878
19	1.729	2.093	2.861
20	1.725	2.086	2.845
21	1.721	2.080	2.831
22	1.717	2.074	2.819
23	1.714	2.069	2.807
24	1.711	2.064	2.797
25	1.708	2.060	2.787
26	1.706	2.056	2.779
27	1.703	2.052	2.771
28	1.701	2.048	2.763
29	1.699	2.045	2.756
30	1.697	2.042	2.750
40	1.684	2.021	2.704
60	1.671	2.000	2.660
120	1.658	1.980	2.617
∞	1.645	1.960	2.576

Source: Adapted with permission from R. J. Wonnacott and T. H. Wonnacott, *Econometrics*, 2d. ed. (New York: John Wiley & Sons, 1979).

THE *F*-DISTRIBUTION

Presented below is a table that provides the critical values of the F-distribution at both 95 percent and 99 percent confidence levels. To illustrate the manner in which this table is used, we return to an application presented in Chapter 4. Again 30 observations were employed to estimate three coefficients—that is, $n = 30$ and $k = 3$. The appropriate F-statistic has $k - 1$ degrees of freedom for the numerator and $n - k$ degrees of freedom for the denominator. Thus, in the example, there are 2 and 27 degrees of freedom. From the table the critical F-value corresponding to a 95 percent confidence level is 3.35. If a 99 percent confidence level is desired, the critical value is 5.49.

Critical F-values

Note: The values corresponding to a 95 percent confidence level are printed in roman type and the values corresponding to a 99 percent confidence level are printed in bold face type.

Degrees of freedom for denominator $(n-k)$	*Degrees of freedom for the numerator* $(k-1)$																		
	1	*2*	*3*	*4*	*5*	*6*	*7*	*8*	*9*	*10*	*11*	*12*	*14*	*16*	*20*	*24*	*30*	*40*	*50*	∞
1 . . .	161	200	216	225	230	234	237	239	241	242	243	244	245	246	248	249	250	251	252	254
	4052	**4999**	**5403**	**5625**	**5764**	**5859**	**5928**	**5981**	**6022**	**6056**	**6082**	**6106**	**6142**	**6169**	**6208**	**6234**	**6258**	**6286**	**6302**	**6366**
2 . . .	18.51	19.00	19.16	19.25	19.30	19.33	19.36	19.37	19.38	19.39	19.40	19.41	19.42	19.43	19.44	19.45	19.46	19.47	19.47	19.50
	98.49	**99.01**	**99.17**	**99.25**	**99.30**	**99.33**	**99.34**	**99.36**	**99.38**	**99.40**	**99.41**	**99.42**	**99.43**	**99.44**	**99.45**	**99.46**	**99.47**	**99.48**	**99.48**	**99.50**
3 . . .	10.13	9.55	9.28	9.12	9.01	8.94	8.88	8.84	8.81	8.78	8.76	8.74	8.71	8.69	8.66	8.64	8.62	8.60	8.58	8.53
	34.12	**30.81**	**29.46**	**28.71**	**28.24**	**27.91**	**27.67**	**27.49**	**27.34**	**27.23**	**27.13**	**27.05**	**26.92**	**26.83**	**26.69**	**26.60**	**26.50**	**26.41**	**26.30**	**26.12**
4 . . .	7.71	6.94	6.59	6.39	6.26	6.16	6.09	6.04	6.00	5.96	5.93	5.91	5.87	5.84	5.80	5.77	5.74	5.71	5.70	5.63
	21.20	**18.00**	**16.69**	**15.98**	**15.52**	**15.21**	**14.98**	**14.80**	**14.66**	**14.54**	**14.45**	**14.37**	**14.24**	**14.15**	**14.02**	**13.93**	**13.83**	**13.74**	**13.69**	**13.46**
5 . . .	6.61	5.79	5.41	5.19	5.05	4.95	4.88	4.82	4.78	4.74	4.70	4.68	4.64	4.60	4.56	4.53	4.50	4.46	4.44	4.36
	16.26	**13.27**	**12.06**	**11.39**	**10.97**	**10.67**	**10.45**	**10.27**	**10.15**	**10.05**	**9.96**	**9.89**	**9.77**	**9.68**	**9.55**	**9.47**	**9.38**	**9.29**	**9.24**	**9.02**
6 . . .	5.99	5.14	4.76	4.53	4.39	4.28	4.21	4.15	4.10	4.06	4.03	4.00	3.96	3.92	3.87	3.84	3.81	3.77	3.75	3.67
	13.74	**10.92**	**9.78**	**9.15**	**8.75**	**8.47**	**8.26**	**8.10**	**7.98**	**7.87**	**7.79**	**7.72**	**7.60**	**7.52**	**7.39**	**7.31**	**7.23**	**7.14**	**7.09**	**6.88**
7 . . .	5.59	4.74	4.35	4.12	3.97	3.87	3.79	3.73	3.68	3.63	3.60	3.57	3.52	3.49	3.44	3.41	3.38	3.34	3.32	3.23
	12.25	**9.55**	**8.45**	**7.85**	**7.46**	**7.19**	**7.00**	**6.84**	**6.71**	**6.62**	**6.54**	**6.47**	**6.35**	**6.27**	**6.15**	**6.07**	**5.98**	**5.90**	**5.85**	**5.65**
8 . . .	5.32	4.46	4.07	3.84	3.69	3.58	3.50	3.44	3.39	3.34	3.31	3.28	3.23	3.20	3.15	3.12	3.08	3.05	3.03	2.93
	11.26	**8.65**	**7.59**	**7.01**	**6.63**	**6.37**	**6.19**	**6.03**	**5.91**	**5.82**	**5.74**	**5.67**	**5.56**	**5.48**	**5.36**	**5.28**	**5.20**	**5.11**	**5.06**	**4.86**
9 . . .	5.12	4.26	3.86	3.63	3.48	3.37	3.29	3.23	3.18	3.13	3.10	3.07	3.02	2.98	2.93	2.90	2.86	2.82	2.80	2.71
	10.56	**8.02**	**6.99**	**6.42**	**6.06**	**5.80**	**5.62**	**5.47**	**5.35**	**5.26**	**5.18**	**5.11**	**5.00**	**4.92**	**4.80**	**4.73**	**4.64**	**4.56**	**4.51**	**4.31**
10 . . .	4.96	4.10	3.71	3.48	3.33	3.22	3.14	3.07	3.02	2.97	2.94	2.91	2.86	2.82	2.77	2.74	2.70	2.67	2.64	2.54
	10.04	**7.56**	**6.55**	**5.99**	**5.64**	**5.39**	**5.21**	**5.06**	**4.95**	**4.85**	**4.78**	**4.71**	**4.60**	**4.52**	**4.41**	**4.33**	**4.25**	**4.17**	**4.12**	**3.91**
11 . . .	4.84	3.98	3.59	3.36	3.20	3.09	3.01	2.95	2.90	2.86	2.82	2.79	2.74	2.70	2.65	2.61	2.57	2.53	2.50	2.40
	9.65	**7.20**	**6.22**	**5.67**	**5.32**	**5.07**	**4.88**	**4.74**	**4.63**	**4.54**	**4.46**	**4.40**	**4.29**	**4.21**	**4.10**	**4.02**	**3.94**	**3.86**	**3.80**	**3.60**
12 . . .	4.75	3.89	3.49	3.26	3.11	3.00	2.92	2.85	2.80	2.76	2.72	2.69	2.64	2.60	2.54	2.50	2.46	2.42	2.40	2.30
	9.33	**6.93**	**5.95**	**5.41**	**5.06**	**4.82**	**4.65**	**4.50**	**4.39**	**4.30**	**4.22**	**4.16**	**4.05**	**3.98**	**3.86**	**3.78**	**3.70**	**3.61**	**3.56**	**3.36**

Critical F-values (*continued*)

Degrees of freedom for denominator $(n-k)$	*Degrees of freedom for the numerator* $(k-1)$																		
	1	2	3	*4*	5	6	7	*8*	9	*10*	*11*	*12*	*14*	*16*	*20*	*24*	*30*	*40*	*50*	∞
13 . . .	4.67	3.80	3.41	3.18	3.02	2.92	2.84	2.77	2.72	2.67	2.63	2.60	2.55	2.51	2.46	2.42	2.38	2.34	2.32	2.21
	9.07	**6.70**	**5.74**	**5.20**	**4.86**	**4.62**	**4.44**	**4.30**	**4.19**	**4.10**	**4.02**	**3.96**	**3.85**	**3.78**	**3.67**	**3.59**	**3.51**	**3.42**	**3.37**	**3.16**
14 . . .	4.60	3.74	3.34	3.11	2.96	2.85	2.77	2.70	2.65	2.60	2.56	2.53	2.48	2.44	2.39	2.35	2.31	2.27	2.24	2.13
	8.86	**6.51**	**5.56**	**5.03**	**4.69**	**4.46**	**4.28**	**4.14**	**4.03**	**3.94**	**3.86**	**3.80**	**3.70**	**3.62**	**3.51**	**3.43**	**3.34**	**3.26**	**3.26**	**3.00**
15 . . .	4.54	3.68	3.29	3.06	2.90	2.79	2.70	2.64	2.59	2.55	2.51	2.48	2.43	2.39	2.33	2.29	2.25	2.21	2.18	2.07
	8.68	**6.36**	**5.42**	**4.89**	**4.56**	**4.32**	**4.14**	**4.00**	**3.89**	**3.80**	**3.73**	**3.67**	**3.56**	**3.48**	**3.36**	**3.29**	**3.20**	**3.12**	**3.07**	**2.87**
16 . . .	4.49	3.63	3.24	3.01	2.85	2.74	2.66	2.59	2.54	2.49	2.45	2.42	2.37	2.33	2.28	2.24	2.20	2.16	2.13	2.01
	8.53	**6.23**	**5.29**	**4.77**	**4.44**	**4.20**	**4.03**	**3.89**	**3.78**	**3.69**	**3.61**	**3.55**	**3.45**	**3.37**	**3.25**	**3.18**	**3.10**	**3.01**	**2.96**	**2.75**
17 . . .	4.45	3.59	3.20	2.96	2.81	2.70	2.62	2.55	2.50	2.45	2.41	2.38	2.33	2.29	2.23	2.19	2.15	2.11	2.08	1.96
	8.40	**6.11**	**5.18**	**4.67**	**4.34**	**4.10**	**3.93**	**3.79**	**3.68**	**3.59**	**3.52**	**3.45**	**3.35**	**3.27**	**3.16**	**3.08**	**3.00**	**2.92**	**2.86**	**2.65**
18 . . .	4.41	3.55	3.16	2.93	2.77	2.66	2.58	2.51	2.46	2.41	2.37	2.34	2.29	2.25	2.19	2.15	2.11	2.07	2.04	1.92
	8.28	**6.01**	**5.09**	**4.58**	**4.25**	**4.01**	**3.85**	**3.71**	**3.60**	**3.51**	**3.44**	**3.37**	**3.27**	**3.19**	**3.07**	**3.00**	**2.91**	**2.83**	**2.78**	**2.57**
19 . . .	4.38	3.52	3.13	2.90	2.74	2.63	2.55	2.48	2.43	2.38	2.34	2.31	2.26	2.21	2.15	2.11	2.07	2.02	2.00	1.88
	8.18	**5.93**	**5.01**	**4.50**	**4.17**	**3.94**	**3.77**	**3.63**	**3.52**	**3.43**	**3.36**	**3.30**	**3.19**	**3.12**	**3.00**	**2.92**	**2.84**	**2.76**	**2.70**	**2.49**
20 . . .	4.35	3.49	3.10	2.87	2.71	2.60	2.52	2.45	2.40	2.35	2.31	2.28	2.23	2.18	2.12	2.08	2.04	1.99	1.96	1.84
	8.10	**5.85**	**4.94**	**4.43**	**4.10**	**3.87**	**3.71**	**3.56**	**3.45**	**3.37**	**3.30**	**3.23**	**3.13**	**3.05**	**2.94**	**2.86**	**2.77**	**2.69**	**2.63**	**2.42**
21 . . .	4.32	3.47	3.07	2.84	2.68	2.57	2.49	2.42	2.37	2.32	2.28	2.25	2.20	2.15	2.09	2.05	2.00	1.96	1.93	1.81
	8.02	**5.78**	**4.87**	**4.37**	**4.04**	**3.81**	**3.65**	**3.51**	**3.40**	**3.31**	**3.24**	**3.17**	**3.07**	**2.99**	**2.88**	**2.80**	**2.72**	**2.63**	**2.58**	**2.36**
22 . . .	4.30	3.44	3.05	2.82	2.66	2.55	2.47	2.40	2.35	2.30	2.26	2.23	2.18	2.13	2.07	2.03	1.98	1.93	1.91	1.78
	7.94	**5.72**	**4.82**	**4.41**	**3.99**	**3.76**	**3.59**	**3.45**	**3.35**	**3.26**	**3.18**	**3.12**	**3.02**	**2.94**	**2.83**	**2.75**	**2.67**	**2.58**	**2.53**	**2.31**
23 . . .	4.28	3.42	3.03	2.80	2.64	2.53	2.45	2.38	2.32	2.28	2.24	2.20	2.14	2.10	2.04	2.00	1.96	1.91	1.88	1.76
	7.88	**5.66**	**4.76**	**4.26**	**3.94**	**3.71**	**3.54**	**3.41**	**3.30**	**3.21**	**3.14**	**3.07**	**2.97**	**2.89**	**2.78**	**2.70**	**2.62**	**2.53**	**2.48**	**2.26**
24 . . .	4.26	3.40	3.01	2.78	2.62	2.51	2.43	2.36	2.30	2.26	2.22	2.18	2.13	2.09	2.02	1.98	1.94	1.89	1.86	1.73
	7.82	**5.61**	**4.72**	**4.22**	**3.90**	**3.67**	**3.50**	**3.36**	**3.25**	**3.17**	**3.09**	**3.03**	**2.93**	**2.85**	**2.74**	**2.66**	**2.58**	**2.49**	**2.44**	**2.21**
25 . . .	4.24	3.38	2.99	2.76	2.60	2.49	2.41	2.34	2.28	2.24	2.20	2.16	2.11	2.06	2.00	1.96	1.92	1.87	1.84	1.71
	7.77	**5.57**	**4.68**	**4.18**	**3.86**	**3.63**	**3.46**	**3.32**	**3.21**	**3.13**	**3.05**	**2.99**	**2.89**	**2.81**	**2.70**	**2.62**	**2.54**	**2.45**	**2.40**	**2.17**

26 . . .	4.22 **7.72**	3.37 **5.53**	2.89 **4.64**	2.74 **4.14**	2.59 **3.82**	2.47 **3.59**	2.39 **3.42**	2.32 **3.29**	2.27 **3.17**	2.22 **3.09**	2.18 **3.02**	2.15 **2.96**	2.10 **2.86**	2.05 **2.77**	1.99 **2.66**	1.95 **2.58**	1.90 **2.50**	1.85 **2.41**	1.82 **2.36**	1.69 **2.13**
27 . . .	4.21 **7.68**	3.35 **5.49**	2.96 **4.60**	2.73 **4.11**	2.57 **3.79**	2.46 **3.56**	2.37 **3.39**	2.30 **3.26**	2.25 **3.14**	2.20 **3.06**	2.16 **2.98**	2.13 **2.93**	2.08 **2.83**	2.03 **2.74**	1.97 **2.63**	1.93 **2.55**	1.88 **2.47**	1.84 **2.38**	1.80 **2.33**	1.67 **2.10**
28 . . .	4.20 **7.64**	3.34 **5.45**	2.95 **4.57**	2.71 **4.07**	2.56 **3.76**	2.44 **3.53**	2.36 **3.36**	2.29 **3.23**	3.24 **3.11**	2.19 **3.03**	2.15 **2.95**	2.12 **2.90**	2.06 **2.80**	2.02 **2.71**	1.96 **2.60**	1.91 **2.52**	1.87 **2.44**	1.81 **2.35**	1.78 **2.30**	1.65 **2.06**
29 . . .	4.18 **7.60**	3.33 **5.52**	2.93 **4.54**	2.70 **4.04**	2.54 **3.73**	2.43 **3.50**	2.35 **3.33**	2.28 **3.20**	2.22 **3.08**	2.18 **3.00**	2.14 **2.92**	2.10 **2.87**	2.05 **2.77**	2.00 **2.68**	1.94 **2.57**	1.90 **2.49**	1.85 **2.41**	1.80 **2.32**	1.77 **2.27**	1.64 **2.03**
30 . . .	4.17 **7.56**	3.32 **5.39**	2.92 **4.51**	2.69 **4.02**	2.53 **3.70**	2.43 **3.47**	2.34 **3.30**	2.27 **3.17**	2.21 **3.06**	2.16 **2.98**	2.12 **2.90**	2.09 **2.84**	2.04 **2.74**	1.99 **2.66**	1.93 **2.55**	1.89 **2.47**	1.84 **2.38**	1.79 **2.29**	1.76 **2.24**	1.62 **2.01**
32 . . .	4.15 **7.50**	3.30 **5.34**	2.90 **4.46**	2.67 **3.97**	2.51 **3.66**	2.40 **3.42**	2.32 **3.25**	2.25 **3.12**	2.19 **3.01**	2.14 **2.94**	2.10 **2.86**	2.07 **2.80**	2.02 **2.70**	1.97 **2.62**	1.91 **2.51**	1.86 **2.42**	1.82 **2.34**	1.76 **2.25**	1.74 **2.20**	1.59 **1.96**
34 . . .	4.13 **7.44**	3.28 **5.29**	2.88 **4.42**	2.65 **3.93**	2.49 **3.61**	2.38 **3.38**	2.30 **3.21**	2.23 **3.08**	2.17 **2.97**	2.12 **2.89**	2.08 **2.82**	2.05 **2.76**	2.00 **2.66**	1.95 **2.58**	1.80 **2.47**	1.84 **2.38**	1.80 **2.30**	1.74 **2.21**	1.71 **2.15**	1.57 **1.91**
36 . . .	4.11 **7.39**	3.26 **5.25**	3.86 **4.38**	2.63 **3.89**	2.48 **3.58**	2.36 **3.35**	2.28 **3.18**	2.21 **3.04**	2.15 **2.94**	2.10 **2.86**	2.06 **2.78**	2.03 **2.72**	1.89 **2.62**	1.93 **2.54**	1.87 **2.43**	1.82 **2.35**	1.78 **2.26**	1.72 **2.17**	1.69 **2.12**	1.55 **1.87**
38 . . .	4.10 **7.35**	3.25 **5.21**	2.85 **4.34**	2.62 **3.86**	2.46 **3.54**	2.35 **3.32**	2.26 **3.15**	2.19 **3.02**	2.14 **2.91**	2.09 **2.82**	2.05 **2.75**	2.02 **2.69**	1.96 **2.59**	1.92 **2.51**	1.85 **2.40**	1.80 **2.32**	1.76 **2.22**	1.71 **2.14**	1.67 **2.08**	1.53 **1.84**
40 . . .	4.08 **7.31**	3.23 **5.18**	2.84 **4.31**	2.61 **3.83**	2.45 **3.51**	2.34 **3.29**	2.25 **3.12**	2.18 **2.99**	2.12 **2.88**	2.08 **2.80**	2.04 **2.73**	2.00 **2.66**	1.95 **2.56**	1.90 **2.49**	1.84 **2.37**	1.79 **2.29**	1.74 **2.20**	1.69 **2.11**	1.66 **2.05**	1.51 **1.81**
42 . . .	4.07 **7.27**	3.22 **5.15**	2.83 **4.29**	2.59 **3.80**	2.44 **3.49**	2.32 **3.26**	2.24 **3.10**	2.17 **2.96**	2.11 **2.86**	2.06 **2.77**	2.02 **2.70**	1.99 **2.64**	1.94 **2.54**	1.89 **2.46**	1.82 **2.35**	1.78 **2.26**	1.73 **2.17**	1.68 **2.08**	1.64 **2.02**	1.49 **1.78**
44 . . .	4.06 **7.24**	3.21 **5.12**	2.82 **4.26**	2.58 **3.78**	2.43 **3.46**	2.31 **3.24**	2.23 **3.07**	2.16 **2.94**	2.10 **2.84**	2.05 **2.75**	2.01 **2.68**	1.98 **2.62**	1.92 **2.52**	1.88 **2.44**	1.81 **2.32**	1.76 **2.24**	1.72 **2.15**	1.66 **2.06**	1.63 **2.00**	1.48 **1.75**
46 . . .	4.05 **7.21**	3.20 **5.10**	2.81 **4.24**	2.57 **3.76**	2.42 **3.44**	2.30 **3.22**	2.22 **3.05**	2.14 **2.92**	2.09 **2.82**	2.04 **2.73**	2.00 **2.66**	1.97 **2.60**	1.91 **2.50**	1.87 **2.42**	1.80 **2.30**	1.75 **2.22**	1.71 **2.13**	1.65 **2.04**	1.62 **1.98**	1.46 **2.72**
48 . . .	4.04 **7.19**	3.19 **5.08**	2.80 **4.22**	2.56 **3.74**	2.41 **3.42**	2.30 **3.20**	2.21 **3.04**	2.14 **2.90**	2.08 **2.80**	2.03 **2.71**	1.99 **2.64**	1.96 **2.58**	1.90 **2.43**	1.86 **2.40**	1.79 **2.28**	1.74 **2.20**	1.70 **2.11**	1.64 **2.02**	1.61 **1.96**	1.45 **1.70**
50 . . .	4.03 **7.17**	3.18 **5.06**	2.79 **4.20**	2.56 **3.72**	2.40 **3.41**	2.29 **3.18**	2.20 **3.02**	2.13 **2.88**	2.07 **2.78**	2.20 **2.70**	1.98 **2.62**	1.95 **2.56**	1.90 **2.46**	1.85 **2.39**	1.78 **2.26**	1.74 **2.18**	1.69 **2.10**	1.63 **2.00**	1.60 **1.94**	1.44 **1.68**
55 . . .	4.02 **7.12**	3.17 **5.01**	2.78 **4.16**	2.54 **3.68**	2.38 **3.37**	2.27 **3.15**	2.18 **2.98**	2.11 **2.85**	2.05 **2.75**	2.00 **2.66**	1.97 **2.59**	1.93 **2.53**	1.88 **2.43**	1.83 **2.35**	1.76 **2.23**	1.72 **2.15**	1.67 **2.06**	1.61 **1.96**	1.58 **1.90**	1.41 **1.64**

Critical F-values *(concluded)*

Degrees of freedom for denominator $(n-k)$	*Degrees of freedom for the numerator* $(k-1)$																			
	1	2	3	*4*	5	6	*7*	8	9	*10*	*11*	*12*	*14*	*16*	*20*	*24*	*30*	*40*	*50*	∞
60 . . .	4.00	3.15	2.76	2.52	2.37	2.25	2.17	2.10	2.04	1.99	1.95	1.92	1.86	1.81	1.75	1.70	1.65	1.59	1.56	1.39
	7.08	**4.98**	**4.13**	**3.65**	**3.34**	**3.12**	**2.95**	**2.82**	**2.72**	**2.63**	**2.56**	**2.50**	**2.40**	**2.32**	**2.20**	**2.12**	**2.03**	**1.93**	**1.87**	**1.60**
65 . . .	3.99	3.14	2.75	2.51	2.36	2.24	2.15	2.08	2.02	1.98	1.94	1.90	1.85	1.80	1.73	1.68	1.63	1.57	1.54	1.37
	7.04	**4.95**	**4.10**	**3.62**	**3.31**	**3.09**	**2.93**	**2.79**	**2.70**	**2.61**	**2.54**	**2.47**	**2.37**	**2.30**	**2.18**	**2.09**	**2.00**	**1.90**	**1.84**	**1.56**
70 . . .	3.98	3.13	2.74	2.50	2.35	2.32	2.14	2.07	2.01	1.97	1.93	1.80	1.84	1.79	1.72	1.67	1.62	1.56	1.53	1.35
	7.01	**4.92**	**4.08**	**3.60**	**3.29**	**3.07**	**2.91**	**2.77**	**2.67**	**2.59**	**2.51**	**2.45**	**2.35**	**2.28**	**2.15**	**2.07**	**1.98**	**1.88**	**1.82**	**1.53**
80 . . .	3.96	3.11	2.72	2.48	2.33	2.21	2.12	2.05	1.99	1.95	1.91	1.88	1.82	1.77	1.70	1.65	1.60	1.54	1.51	1.32
	6.95	**4.88**	**4.04**	**3.56**	**3.25**	**3.04**	**2.87**	**2.74**	**2.64**	**2.55**	**2.48**	**2.41**	**2.32**	**2.24**	**2.11**	**2.03**	**1.94**	**1.84**	**1.78**	**1.49**
100 . . .	3.94	3.09	2.70	2.46	2.30	2.19	2.10	2.03	1.97	1.92	1.88	1.85	1.79	1.75	1.68	1.63	1.57	1.51	1.48	1.28
	6.90	**4.82**	**3.98**	**3.51**	**3.20**	**2.99**	**2.82**	**2.69**	**2.59**	**2.51**	**2.43**	**2.36**	**2.26**	**2.19**	**2.06**	**1.98**	**1.89**	**1.79**	**1.73**	**1.43**
125 . . .	3.92	3.07	2.68	2.44	2.29	2.17	2.08	2.01	1.95	1.90	1.86	1.83	1.77	1.72	1.65	1.60	1.55	1.49	1.45	1.25
	6.84	**4.78**	**3.94**	**3.47**	**3.17**	**2.95**	**2.79**	**2.65**	**2.56**	**2.47**	**2.40**	**2.33**	**2.23**	**2.15**	**2.03**	**1.94**	**1.85**	**1.75**	**1.68**	**1.37**
150 . . .	3.91	3.06	2.67	2.43	2.27	2.16	2.07	2.00	1.94	1.89	1.85	1.82	1.76	1.71	1.64	1.59	1.54	1.47	1.44	1.22
	6.81	**4.75**	**3.91**	**3.44**	**3.13**	**2.92**	**2.76**	**2.62**	**2.53**	**2.44**	**2.37**	**2.30**	**2.20**	**2.12**	**2.00**	**1.91**	**1.83**	**1.72**	**1.66**	**1.33**
200 . . .	3.89	3.04	2.65	2.41	2.26	2.14	2.05	1.98	1.92	1.87	1.83	1.80	1.74	1.69	1.62	1.57	1.52	1.45	1.42	1.19
	6.76	**4.71**	**3.88**	**3.41**	**3.11**	**2.90**	**2.73**	**2.60**	**2.50**	**2.41**	**2.34**	**2.28**	**1.17**	**2.09**	**1.97**	**1.88**	**1.79**	**1.69**	**1.62**	**1.28**
400 . . .	3.86	3.02	2.62	2.39	2.23	2.12	2.03	1.96	1.90	1.85	1.81	1.78	1.72	1.67	1.60	1.54	1.49	1.42	1.38	1.13
	6.70	**4.66**	**3.83**	**3.36**	**3.06**	**2.85**	**2.69**	**2.55**	**2.46**	**2.37**	**2.29**	**2.23**	**2.12**	**2.04**	**1.92**	**1.84**	**1.74**	**1.64**	**1.57**	**1.19**
1000 . . .	3.85	3.00	2.61	2.38	2.22	2.10	2.02	1.95	1.89	1.84	1.80	1.76	1.70	1.65	1.58	1.53	1.47	1.41	1.36	1.08
	6.66	**4.62**	**3.80**	**3.34**	**3.04**	**2.82**	**2.66**	**2.53**	**2.43**	**2.34**	**2.26**	**2.20**	**2.09**	**2.01**	**1.89**	**1.81**	**1.71**	**1.61**	**1.54**	**1.11**
∞ . . .	3.84	2.99	2.60	2.37	2.21	2.09	2.01	1.94	1.88	1.83	1.79	1.75	1.69	1.64	1.57	1.52	1.46	1.40	1.35	1.00
	6.64	**4.60**	**3.78**	**3.32**	**3.02**	**2.80**	**2.64**	**2.51**	**2.41**	**2.32**	**2.24**	**2.18**	**2.07**	**1.99**	**1.87**	**1.79**	**1.69**	**1.59**	**1.52**	**1.00**

Source: Adapted with permission from R. J. Wonnacott and T. H. Wonnacott, *Econometrics*, 1st ed. (New York: John Wiley & Sons, Inc., 1970).

Index

D

This book has been set Linotron 202 in 10 and 9 point Times Roman, leaded 2 points. Part numbers and chapter titles are 18 point Times Roman. Part titles and chapter numbers are 24 point Times Roman. The size of the type page is 30 by 47 picas.